9th International Conference on Engineering, Project, and Production Management (EPPM2018)

MATEC Web of Conferences Volume 312 (2020)

Cape Town, South Africa
24-26 September 2018

Editors:

Lukasz Nazarko
John-Paris Pantouvakis
Bo Terje Kalsaas
Chien-Ho Ko

ISBN: 978-1-7138-0887-9

Printed from e-media with permission by:

Curran Associates, Inc.
57 Morehouse Lane
Red Hook, NY 12571

Some format issues inherent in the e-media version may also appear in this print version.

For additional information, please contact EDP Sciences – Web of Conferences at the address below.

EDP Sciences – Web of Conferences
17, Avenue du Hoggar
Parc d'Activité de Courtabœuf
BP 112
F-91944 Les Ulis Cedex A
France

Phone: +33 (0) 1 69 18 75 75
Fax: +33 (0) 1 69 28 84 91

contact-edps@webofconferences.org

Additional copies of this publication are available from:

Curran Associates, Inc.
57 Morehouse Lane
Red Hook, NY 12571 USA
Phone: 845-758-0400
Fax: 845-758-2633
Email: curran@proceedings.com
Web: www.proceedings.com

TABLE OF CONTENTS

THEORIES AND APPLICATIONS OF ENGINEERING MANAGEMENT

THEORIES AND APPLICATIONS OF PROJECT MANAGEMENT

THEORIES AND APPLICATIONS OF PRODUCTION MANAGEMENT

INTEGRATION OF ENGINEERING MANAGEMENT AND PROJECT MANAGEMENT

Statement of Peer review

In submitting conference proceedings to *Web of Conferences*, the editors of the proceedings certify to the Publisher that

1. They adhere to its **Policy on Publishing Integrity** in order to safeguard good scientific practice in publishing.
2. All articles have been subjected to peer review administered by the proceedings editors.
3. Reviews have been conducted by expert referees, who have been requested to provide unbiased and constructive comments aimed, whenever possible, at improving the work.
4. Proceedings editors have taken all reasonable steps to ensure the quality of the materials they publish and their decision to accept or reject a paper for publication has been based only on the merits of the work and the relevance to the journal.

9th International Conference on Engineering, Project, and Production Management (EPPM2018)
24 – 26 September 2018, Cape Town, South Africa

Proceedings editor(s):
Lukasz Nazarko, John-Paris Pantouvakis, Bo Terje Kalsaas, Chien-Ho Ko

Date and editors' signatures

22 March 2020

17, avenue du Hoggar - PA de Courtabœuf – BP 112 - 91944 Les Ulis Cedex A (France)
Tél. : 33 (0)1 69 18 75 75 - Fax : 33(0)1 69 07 45 17 – www.edpsciences.org

MATEC Web of Conferences **312**, 00001 (2020) https://doi.org/10.1051/matecconf/202031200001
EPPM2018

Editorial

Lukasz Nazarko[1], *Chien-Ho* Ko[2], *Bo Terje* Kalsaas[3], and *John-Paris* Pantouvakis[4]

[1] Białystok University of Technology, Poland
[2] College of Architecture, Arts and Humanity, Clemson University, USA
[3] University of Agder, Norway
[4] National Technical University of Athens, Greece

The 9th International Conference on Engineering, Project, and Production Management (EPPM2018) constitutes another step in establishing EPPM conferences as globally recognised fora where researchers and practitioners meet to discuss current phenomena, emerging trends, and future directions in engineering, project and production management. The conference was hosted by the Department of Construction Management, Nelson Mandela University, and the Department of Built Environment, Central University of Technology in Cape Town, South Africa from 24 to 26 September 2018.

The proceedings of this year's conference include 43 papers that have been carefully selected through a rigorous double-blind review process. These papers address theories and applications of engineering management, project management, and production management as well as the integration of these areas. The papers present a wide range of approaches and methodologies adopted to answer research questions that emerge in the fields covered by the conference. The topics reflect the transformation of engineering and management that is taking place under the umbrella of Industry 4.0. The authors are aware of an increasingly intimate relation of products and services, blending of the real and virtual and the growing complexity of stakeholder interactions in engineering and business projects. The conference participants tackled critical problems in engineering, manufacturing, logistics and technology management related to innovation, performance, productivity, maintenance, quality, risk, safety, sustainability, skills, and competences.

All the papers in the conference proceedings were double-blind reviewed by members of the International Scientific Committee. This process entailed detailed reading of the papers, reporting of comments to authors, modification of papers by authors, and re- evaluation of the revised papers. Manuscripts were checked for plagiarism, proofread, and professionally edited to ensure quality of the contents. The role of the Scientific Chairs was to ensure that the final accepted papers incorporated the reviewers' comments. Of the 168 abstracts originally received, 43 papers were finally accepted at the conference, representing an acceptance rate of 25%.

In recognition of an outstanding contribution to science, the Best Paper Award recognises a paper of exceptional quality. At the initial stage, nine contributions were selected based on the suggestions from the International Scientific Committee members who reviewed all papers submitted to the conference. Thereafter, the Best Paper Final Review Selection Panel headed by Dr Kassim Gidado evaluated the selected papers in terms of their contribution to the body of knowledge, quality of argument, and quality of presentation. As a result, the paper entitled *An investigation of Mixed Reality Technology for Onsite Construction Assembly* by Salman Azhar and Austin DeValle from Auburn University, USA was chosen for the EPPM2018 Best Paper Award.

Sincere appreciation is due to all authors, members of the International Scientific Committee, Keynote Speakers and the Organizing Committee for their great effort. We would also like to express our deep gratitude to the editorial support team (Ewa Chodakowska, Justyna Kozłowska, Julia Siderska, Krzysztof Stepaniuk, Dariusz Surel, Danuta Szpilko, Katarzyna Szum, and Tomasz Trochimczuk), Ms Leandra Jordaan, the conference website administrator, and Mrs Mariana Botes, the conference secretary. It is their contribution that makes this conference an important event that strengthens the interdisciplinary links between engineering and management.

Organisers

Conference Chairs

John Smallwood, Nelson Mandela University, South Africa

Fidelis Emuze, Central University of Technology, Free State, South Africa

Scientific Chairs

Lukasz Nazarko, Bialystok University of Technology, Poland

Bo Terje Kalsaas, University of Agder at Grimstad, Norway

John-Paris Pantouvakis, National Technical University of Athens, Greece

Organising Chairs

Fidelis Emuze, Central University of Technology, Free State, South Africa

Chien-Ho Ko, National Pingtung University of Science and Technology, Taiwan

EPPM-Academy Head

Michael Oladokun, Central University of Technology, South Africa

EPPM-Industry Minister

John Smallwood, Nelson Mandela University, South Africa

Organising Committee

Mariana Botes, Nelson Mandela University, South Africa

Fidelis Emuze, Central University of Technology, South Africa

Leandra Jordaan, Central University of Technology, South Africa

Michael Oladokun, Central University of Technology, South Africa

EPPM-Association President

Kriengsak Panuwatwanich, Thammasat University, Thailand

International Scientific Committee

Keynotes

Jeremy Gibberd

Smarter and More Sustainable Built Environments in a Changing World

Pierre Voges

Special Purpose Vehicles as a Model for Competitive Economic Development in South African Cities

Keith Cattell

The psychological well-being of construction professionals

Austin DeValle and Salman Azhar

An Investigation of Mixed Reality Technology for On-site Construction Assembly

MATEC Web of Conferences **312**, 01001 (2020) https://doi.org/10.1051/matecconf/202031201001
EPPM2018

Assessing the performance of Polish Regional Funds for Environmental Protection and Water Management using DEA model

Joanicjusz Nazarko[1*], and *Ewa* Chodakowska[1]

[1]Bialystok University of Technology, Faculty of Engineering Management, Wiejska 45A, 15-351 Bialystok, Poland

Abstract. The public sector is under growing pressure to increase its efficiency. Expectations from the political authorities, local communities, stakeholders and media towards the public-sector entities are high. Modern management methods must be introduced to meet them. Data Envelopment Analysis (DEA) is an important method used in comparative studies of public sector efficiency. Voivodeship Funds for Environmental Protection and Water Management (VFEPWMs) are public entities that financially support actions aimed at environmental protection and water management. Their task is to acquire and redistribute financial resources to support projects related to environmental protection. VFEPWMs face the challenge of increasing the use of available funds and the efficiency of their use. The paper presents the use of DEA method — which is as a modern engineering management tool — to evaluate the VFEPWMs performance. In the DEA performance analysis of VFEPWM, it is assumed that each unit may be characterised by their input resources, effects, environmental variables and transformation processes that transform resources into effects. VFEPWMs have better performance if they transform resources into desirable effects (actions) more efficiently. The results of the conducted analysis allow comparing the performance of particular VFEPWMs, to identify model units and to develop benchmarking graphs. The analysis is performed not only to assess the current level of VFEPWM performance but also to acquire information allowing to remove inefficiency.

1 Introduction

In many countries various public services and public goods like infrastructure [1], education [2] or environmental protection [3] are carried out by specialised government agencies. Public expenditure plays a critical role in ensuring the desired quality level of the natural environment [4-6]. Voivodeship Funds for Environmental Protection and Water Management in Poland (VFEPWMs) have been set up to support the area of public tasks, which is the financial support for environmental protection and water management. They collect but also redistribute funds to projects that aim to protect the environment.

---

* Corresponding author: j.nazarko@pb.edu.pl

Apart from 16 VFEPWMs, Poland also has the National Fund for Environmental Protection and Water Management (NFEPWM). Among other things, their mission is effective and efficient support for environmental activities, and the challenge resulting from their strategies: increasing the use of available financial resources as well as the efficiency of the use.

In addition, the dynamics of changes in the operational environment of organisations force the funds to adapt flexibly to changes and challenges related to EU policies and its financial instruments [4]. Therefore, it seems necessary to take an example from other sectors of the economy [7-8] and to assess the performance of the VFEPWMs, to look for benchmarks characterised by relatively higher efficiency in relation to others, and to search for good practices that can be applied.

VFEPWMs and NFEPWM are institutions financing environmental protection. They are not focused on achieving financial profit, but on maximising the ecological effect. In such cases, the use of typical profitability ratios would be inappropriate. This paper responds to the need to demonstrate and test an effective method of the VFEPWMs performance assessment. It also aims at indicating possibilities of the improvement of the effectiveness of public money expenditures on environmental protection.

The analysis was performed using the Data Envelopment Analysis (DEA) method. The DEA has been a recognised and popular method of analysing efficiency in various areas of economy and administration as well as the non-profit sector [9-11]. The world literature on the DEA method has been extensive and is constantly growing. More than 10 000 DEA articles have been published until the end of 2017, including both the application and innovative DEA models. Many publications have been published regarding, among others, the assessment of the performance of banks, education institution, and energy sector units. Eco-efficiency is also the subject of many considerations by DEA. Among others, the evaluation was given to countries (12-13) and technologies [14-16]. The analysis of the rich scientific literature suggests that DEA is a robust tool for the efficiency analysis of the public administration units. The legitimacy and the utility of DEA application to such problems is a grounded scientific opinion [17-18].

The article attempts to answer the question about the performance of Polish Regional Funds for Environmental Protection and Water Management. Authors evaluated changes in efficiency during 2011–2015. The presented dynamic analyses give a general idea of the financial resources that are administered in relation to their redistribution in 16 VFEPWMs over time. NFEPWM operates on a much larger scale, carrying out as many tasks as all voivodship funds together. At the same time, there are no other adequate entities for benchmarking. The analysis of the performance of the Polish Regional Funds was developed on the basis of their financial statements.

2 Methods and data consideration

Data Envelopment Analysis (DEA), introduced by Charnes *et al.* (1978) [19], is a powerful method for measuring the relative efficiency of a set of homogeneous decision-making units (DMUs). DEA has proved to be a useful tool for assessing the performance of various organisations and systems. The DEA assumes that each unit may be characterised by their input resources, effects, environmental variables and processes that transform resources into effects. The DEA evaluates systems with multiple inputs and outputs and provides a synthetic indicator that considers the strengths of each analysed unit (Fig. 1).

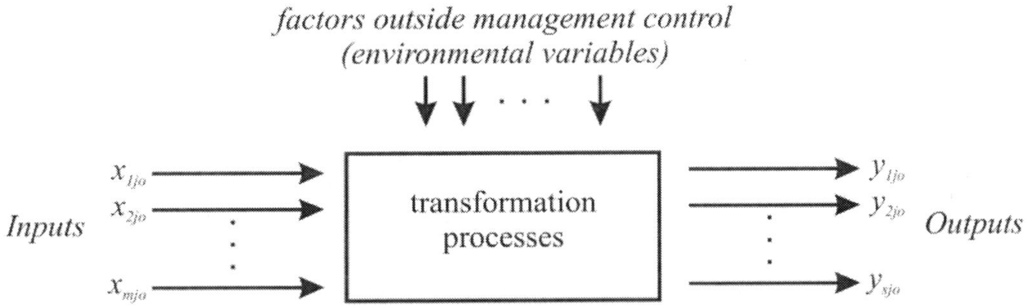

Fig. 1. Concept of DEA input-output assessment.

Mathematically, the idea of DEA for n DMUs, m different inputs and s different outputs: x_{ij}, y_{rj} where j=1, 2, …, j_O, …, n; i=1, 2, …, m; r=1, 2, … s can be written in the form of equations (1). The standard variable return to scale input-oriented radial DEA model (BCC-I DEA) for evaluating the efficiency of DMU_{jo} is [20]:

$$min\ \theta_{jo} \tag{1}$$
$$\sum_{j=1}^{n} \lambda_j x_{ij} \leq \theta_{jo} x_{ijo}, \forall i$$
$$\sum_{j=1}^{n} \lambda_j y_{rj} \geq y_{rjo}, \forall r$$
$$\sum_{j=1}^{n} \lambda_j = 1,$$
$$j = 1, \ldots, n,$$

where:

$X_j = (x_{1j}, x_{2j}, x_{3j}, \ldots, x_{mj})$ — input vector,

$Y_j = (y_{1j}, y_{2j}, y_{3j}, \ldots, y_{sj})$ — output vector,

λ_j — vector of weights specifying the intensity of the use of reference objects' technologies in optimal j-th DMU's technology.

Considering the potential variables for the VFEPWMs' assessment, the operational specificity of the funds should be considered. Revenues and outlays of the funds are determined by legal regulations. Revenues of funds may include money from the state budget, the European Union budget and other foreign sources. In addition, the funds may receive income from issuing their own bonds and take out loans and borrowings. The revenues of all funds can be used only for purposes related to environmental protection. Environmental financing may take the form of interest-bearing loans, subsidies, including subsidies for interest on bank loans, partial repayment of bank loans, interest subsidies or redemption prices for bonds or subsidies for dismantling end-of-life vehicles.

As a basis for building a synthetic efficiency indicator using the DEA method, variables controlled by the funds were selected. Interest income and the sum of loans and subsidy financing were used as outputs (effects), operating costs — as inputs, and revenue from fees and penalties —as an independent variable affecting the functioning of the fund. The input-oriented model was chosen because it was assumed that operating costs should be minimised in the existing financing system. Table 1 presents a summary of the characteristics of the considered variables; Table 2 gives the correlation coefficients between variables.

Table 1. Variable statistics 2011–2015, [PLN]

	Mean	Min	Max	Std. err.
Operating expenses X_1	8 644 752	4 125 016	16 673 333	3 647 270
Interest income Y_1,	15 016 582	2 447 673	41 289 166	10 307 955
Total financing Y_2	152 746 257	18 835 909	493 728 292	104 927 149
Revenue from fees and penalties Z_1	38 318 964	5 102 928	132 490 672	30 018 183

Table 2. Correlation coefficients between variables in 2011–2015

	X_1	Y_1	Y_2
Z_1	0.791	0.830	0.804
X_1		0.772	0.817

Next, the analysis of the relationship between variables must be underlined. A high correlation of variables can be noted. Operating costs are highly correlated with the total funding (Pearson's correlation coefficient is over 0.8) and revenue from fees and penalties is highly correlated with interest income and the sum of financing.

Considering the above, the final model was accommodated with the value of the total financing in relation to revenues from fees and penalties, the value of interest income in relation to revenues from fees and penalties as output variables (effects), and, on the side of input (resources), operating costs in relation to revenues from fees and penalties. The strength of the linear relationship between the selected variables is illustrated in Table 3. The DMU_{jo} model scheme is shown in Fig. 2.

Table 3. Correlation coefficients between variables 2011–2015

	Y_1/Z_1	Y_2/Z_1
X_1/Z_1	0.409	0.582
Y_1/Z_1		0.680

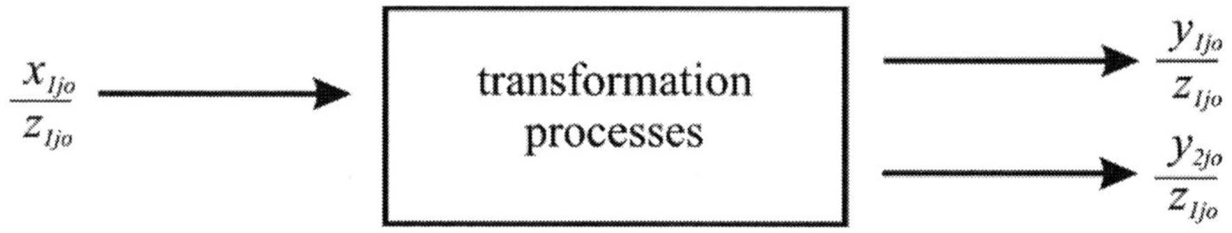

Fig. 2. DEA model for assessing the performance of Polish Regional Funds for Environmental Protection and Water Management

Since data includes ratio variables, the non-linear corrected model suggested in [21] in the presence of input-ratios and/or output-ratios with modified convexity assumption was adopted. Altered input-oriented DEA BCC model with input-ratio and output-ratio for VFEPWMs' is:

$$min\ \theta_{jo} \tag{2}$$

$$\sum_{j=1}^{n} \lambda_j x_{1j} - \theta_{jo} \frac{x_{1jo}}{z_{1jo}} \sum_{j=1}^{n} \lambda_j z_{1j} \leq 0,$$

$$\sum_{j=1}^{n} \lambda_j y_{rj} - \frac{y_{rjo}}{z_{1jo}} \sum_{j=1}^{n} \lambda_j z_{1j} \geq 0, \forall r$$

$$\sum_{j=1}^{n} \lambda_j = 1,$$

$$j = 1. \ldots . n.$$

It can be pointed out that due to the data assumptions there are no significant differences in the final results between the model (1) and (2) but only in the technologies benchmarks. The changes in productivity over time were measured using the productivity index developed by Malmquist (1953) [22] as a quantitative index of the use of inputs and first combined with the DEA [23]. Its construction is based on a comparison of the relation of inputs and outputs in time periods t and $t + 1$. Productivity changes over time in Malmquist Index (MI) can be decomposed into changes in efficiency and technology. The relative overall technical efficiency change (catch-up) for DMU*jo* is defined as:

$$TEC = \frac{D^{t+1}(x^{t+1}, y^{t+1})}{D^t(x^t, y^t)} \tag{3}$$

The frontier change between t and $t + 1$ is calculated as follows:

$$TC = \left[\frac{D^t(x^t,y^t)}{D^{t+1}(x^t,y^t)} \times \frac{D^t(x^{t+1},y^{t+1})}{D^{t+1}(x^{t+1},y^{t+1})}\right]^{1/2} \quad (4)$$

The overall MI is calculated by multiplying the overall efficiency change and technology change at periods t and $t + 1$:

$$MI^{t+1} = TEC \times TC = \left[\frac{D^t(x^{t+1},y^{t+1})}{D^t(x^t,y^t)} \times \frac{D^{t+1}(x^{t+1},y^{t+1})}{D^{t+1}(x^t,y^t)}\right]^{1/2} \quad (5)$$

where:

$D^t(x^t,y^t)$ — the efficiency of a unit transforming input x into outputs y in period t,

$D^{t+1}(x^{t+1},y^{t+1})$ — the efficiency of a unit transforming input x into outputs y in period $t+1$,

$D^{t+1}(x^t,y^t)$ — the efficiency of a unit in period t in relation to the frontier in period $t+1$,

$D^t(x^{t+1},y^{t+1})$ — the efficiency of a unit in period $t+1$ in relation to the frontier in period t.

The interpretation of MI is as follows: MI > 1 means an increase in productivity, progress; MI < 1 decrease in productivity, regress; and MPI = 1 no change in productivity at time $t+1$ in comparison with t.

Assessing the performance of VFEPWMs' completes with the benchmarks indication.

3 Results and discussions

The assessment of Polish regional funds for environmental protection and water management using DEA model is presented in Table 4 and illustrated in Fig. 3. Calculations were carried out with the use of a Microsoft Excel spreadsheet designed by the authors.

Table 4. Efficiency of VFEPWMs in 2011–2015 DEA BCC-I

Voivodeship Code	2011	2012	2013	2014	2015
V1	56.90%	68.30%	100.00%	100.00%	100.00%
V2	59.70%	74.10%	79.50%	91.20%	74.10%
V3	50.40%	59.60%	57.40%	90.20%	64.00%
V4	33.60%	36.20%	49.90%	40.20%	44.40%
V5	79.10%	88.20%	79.70%	78.80%	97.50%
V6	100.00%	100.00%	100.00%	100.00%	100.00%
V7	68.10%	60.10%	61.80%	60.40%	74.50%
V8	100.00%	100.00%	74.80%	100.00%	64.60%
V9	39.00%	43.10%	47.10%	44.80%	45.50%
V10	100.00%	29.70%	29.70%	26.70%	30.70%
V11	61.60%	64.70%	81.80%	58.30%	82.70%
V12	100.00%	100.00%	100.00%	100.00%	100.00%
V13	57.50%	61.20%	65.30%	63.40%	66.00%
V14	41.50%	22.80%	37.40%	25.30%	38.60%
V15	52.50%	56.10%	62.70%	56.50%	69.80%
V16	48.60%	50.80%	46.30%	55.90%	46.00%

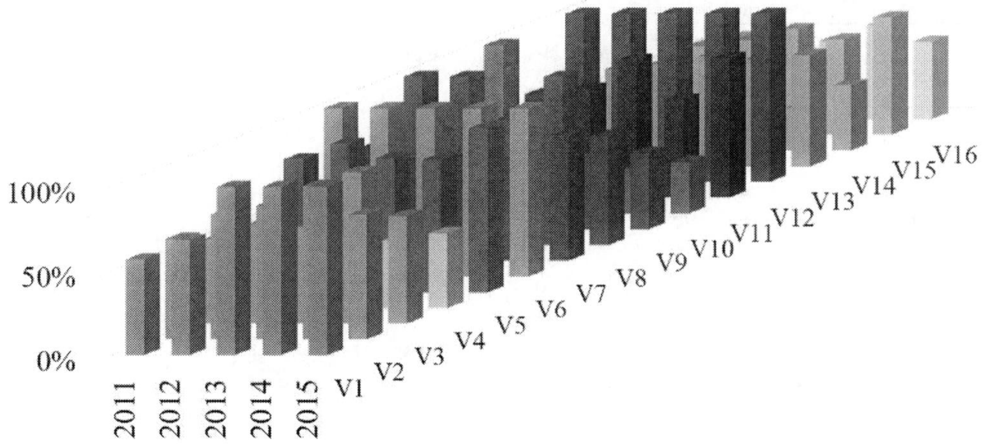

Fig. 3. Efficiency of 16 VFEPWMs' during 2011–2015

Evaluation of funds using the BCC-I DEA model considering operational costs, interest income and the sum of financing has emerged leaders, which in 2015 are funds in the voivodships V1, V6 and V12. Too high operating costs in relation to revenue and the total funding are observed in funds in V10 and V14 but also in V4, V9 and V16.

Perhaps, it would be worth reconsidering the idea of different financing of inefficient funds, which have been characterised by the lowest revenues from fees and penalties. An important argument in favour of "equalling" the level of voivodeship fund revenues is the higher quality of the natural environment, a higher percentage of naturally valuable areas in the area of "poor" funds. Supporting municipal investments as well as co-financing projects in the field of biodiversity and landscape protection, resulting from the need to maintain high environmental standards, exceeds the limited resources available to these funds. Meanwhile, the return of funds to individual provincial funds is directly proportional to payments made of environmental fees and penalties, whose amount depends on the region's economic development.

Malmquist index indicates that the leader in terms of change in the efficiency is V1. In the analysed period, funds decreased only in V16 and V13. The number of funds that recorded an increase in efficiency is ten out of sixteen regional funds in 2015 and eight in 2014. Particularly positive is the fact that the increase was noted in the funds with the lowest efficiency, i.e. in V4, V10 and V14.

Table 4. Malmquist Index, technical efficiency change and the frontier change of VFEPWMs in 2011–2015

	MI				TEC				TC			
Voivodeship Code	2012	2013	2014	2015	2012	2013	2014	2015	2012	2013	2014	2015
V1	1.060	1.055	0.999	1.144	1.200	1.465	1.000	1.000	0.883	0.720	0.999	1.144
V2	1.009	0.894	1.136	0.794	1.242	1.072	1.147	0.813	0.813	0.834	0.991	0.977
V3	1.027	0.907	1.636	0.674	1.183	0.962	1.572	0.710	0.867	0.942	1.041	0.950
V4	0.980	1.391	0.688	1.111	1.077	1.377	0.806	1.104	0.909	1.011	0.853	1.006
V5	1.025	0.704	1.189	1.063	1.115	0.905	0.988	1.238	0.920	0.778	1.204	0.859
V6	0.929	0.779	1.041	1.049	1.000	1.000	1.000	1.000	0.929	0.779	1.041	1.049
V7	0.808	0.887	1.240	1.087	0.883	1.027	0.977	1.234	0.915	0.863	1.268	0.881
V8	1.096	0.814	1.053	0.673	1.000	0.748	1.337	0.646	1.096	1.088	0.788	1.043
V9	0.963	1.141	0.736	1.010	1.104	1.093	0.953	1.014	0.873	1.044	0.773	0.996
V10	0.289	1.439	0.654	1.023	0.297	1.002	0.900	1.146	0.973	1.436	0.726	0.892
V11	0.938	0.943	0.882	1.357	1.051	1.263	0.712	1.420	0.893	0.746	1.238	0.956
V12	0.795	0.675	1.294	0.874	1.000	1.000	1.000	1.000	0.795	0.675	1.294	0.874
V13	0.977	0.918	0.914	0.889	1.064	1.068	0.970	1.041	0.918	0.860	0.942	0.853
V14	0.547	1.873	0.532	1.465	0.550	1.639	0.676	1.527	0.994	1.143	0.786	0.959
V15	0.937	0.954	1.151	1.083	1.069	1.118	0.901	1.235	0.877	0.854	1.277	0.877
V16	0.941	0.973	0.876	0.690	1.044	0.913	1.207	0.822	0.901	1.066	0.726	0.839

Another advantage of DEA method is the possibility of using its results in the benchmarking analysis. Benchmarking analysis allows to identify best practices in the fully efficient units and to point at measures which would lead to the performance improvement in the inefficient units. Benchmarking graph created on the basis of data from Table 6 is presented in Fig. 4.

Table 6. Benchmarks for inefficient funds in 2015

Voivodeship Code	λ_j			Benchmarks (code)		
V1	1			1		
V2	0.428	0.572		1	12	
V3	0.453	0.547		6	12	
V4	0.743	0.257		1	12	
V5	0.173	0.827		1	12	
V6	1			6		
V7	0.113	0.887		1	12	
V8	0.142	0.804	0.054	1	6	12
V9	0.335	0.379	0.286	1	6	12
V10	0.349	0.651		1	6	
V11	0.623	0.377		1	12	
V12	1			12		
V13	0.601	0.399		6	12	
V14	0.820	0.180		1	12	
V15	0.171	0.829		1	12	
V16	0.900	0.100		6	12	

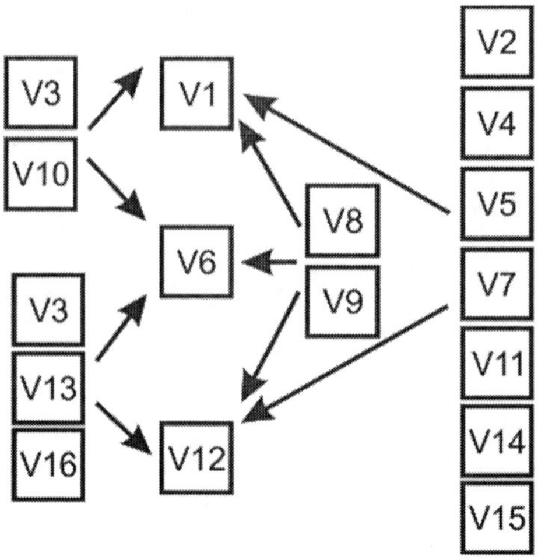

Fig. 4. Benchmark graph of 16 VFEPWMs in 2015

On the basis of the benchmarking graph fully efficient units may be identified. Their technology is a model for inefficient funds. Funds V1 and V12 draw special attention as they are, together, benchmarks for most of the other inefficient VFEPWMs.

4 Conclusions

Efficiency benchmarking plays a key role in policy analysis worldwide, given the limited resources available. Efficiency improvement is often regarded as one of the most important goals of many social and economic policies and reforms. The article presents the assessment of the performance of Polish regional funds for environmental protection and water management. The scale of financing operations of the funds can be described by the total funding allocated for the environment protection projects. In the analysed period of 2011-2015, VFEPWMs' redistributed PLN 23 511 603 204 to projects related to environmental protection. Their operating costs amounted to PLN 1 254 044 150.

The DEA performance analysis of VFEPWM allowed to compare the performance of particular funds and to indicate the ones that perform better and transform resources into desirable effects more efficiently. The noted differences could serve as an argument for government policy changes on the functioning of the funds and financing, but above all should become an inspiration to limit the operating costs of VFEPWMs.

Obtained results point at considerable possibilities of increasing the efficiency of public funds utilisation by the majority of VFEPWMs. Benchmarking graph developed on the basis of DEA analysis reveals that units V1, V6 and V12 may be treated as reference units and that their practices should be a basis for improving the performance of the remaining funds.

The analysis of VFEPWMs performance presented in this paper was solely based on the financial results of particular units. Environmental effects such as reduction of greenhouse gases emission, an increase of energy consumption from renewable energy sources or improved quality of water and air were not taken into consideration. Further research on VFEPWMs effectiveness should also include that dimension.

References

1. J. Nazarko, P. Radziszewski, K. Dębkowska, J. Ejdys, A. Gudanowska, K. Halicka, J. Kilon, A. Kononiuk, K. Kowalski, J. Król, L. Nazarko, M. Sarnowski, T. Vilutiene, Foresight Study of Road Pavement Technologies, *Procedia Engineering*, **122**, 129-136 (2015)
2. F. van Vught, U. Brandenburg, N. Burquel, D. Carr, G. Federkeil, J. A. dos Santos Rafael, J. Sadlak, J. Urban, P. Wells, D. Westerheijden, J. Nazarko, K. Kuzmicz, A practical guide. Benchmarking in European Higher Education, ESMU, Brussels (2008)
3. The Directory of Environmental Organizations and Environmental Government Agencies in Europe. United States Environmental Directories, [online] https://earthdirectory.net/europe#Agencies [11.07.2018]
4. F. Cucchiella, I. D'Adamo, M. Gastaldi, S. C. L. Koh, P. Rosa, A comparison of environmental and energetic performance of European countries: A sustainability index, Renewable and Sustainable Energy Reviews, **78**, 401-413 (2017)
5. G. E. Halkos, P. A. Paizanos, The effect of government expenditure on the environment: An empirical investigation, Ecological Economics, **91**, 48-56 (2013)
6. R. López, G. I. Galinato, A. Islam, Fiscal spending and the environment: Theory and empirics, Journal of Environmental Economics and Management, **62(2)**, 180-198 (2011)
7. J. Nazarko, Regionalny foresight gospodarczy. Scenariusze rozwoju innowacyjności mazowieckich przedsiębiorstw, ZPWiM, Warszawa (2013)
8. K. Dziekoński, O. H. M. F. Ibrahim, A-M. Mahamadu, P. Manu, Framework of performance measurement practices in construction companies in Egypt, Engineering Management in Production and Services, **10(2)**, 7-14 (2018)
9. E. Chodakowska, J. Nazarko, Network DEA Models for Evaluating Couriers and Messengers, *Procedia Engineering*, **182**, 106-111 (2017)
10. A. Emrouznejad, G. Yang, A survey and analysis of the first 40 years of scholarly literature in DEA: 1978-2016, Socio-Economic Planning Sciences, **61**, 4-8 (2018)
11. K. Halicka, Main Concepts of Technology Analysis in the Light of the Literature on the Subject, *Procedia Engineering*, **182**, 291-298 (2017)
12. E. Chodakowska, J. Nazarko, Environmental DEA method for assessing productivity of European countries, Technological and Economic Development of Economy, **23(4)**, 589-607 (2017)
13. J. Nazarko, E. Chodakowska, Labour efficiency in construction industry in Europe based on frontier methods: data envelopment analysis and stochastic frontier analysis, Journal of Civil Engineering and Management, **23(6)**, 787-795 (2017)
14. A. Shabani, R. F. Saen, S. M. R. Torabipour, A new data envelopment analysis (DEA) model to select eco-efficient technologies in the presence of undesirable outputs, Clean Technologies and Environmental Policy, **16(3)**, 513-525 (2014)
15. D. S. Kwon, J. H. Cho, S. Y. Sohn, Comparison of technology efficiency for CO2 emissions reduction among European countries based on DEA with decomposed factors, Journal of Cleaner Production, **151**, 109-120 (2017)
16. K. Halicka, The reference methodology of prospective analysis of technology in production engineering. In: S. Şahin (ed.) *8th International Conference on*

Engineering, Project, and Product Management (EPPM 2017). Proceedings Lecture Notes in Mechanical Engineering, Springer, Cham, 99-107 Springer (2018)

17. H. Ahn, M. Afsharian, A. Emrouznejad, R. Banker, Recent developments on the use of DEA in the public sector, Socio-Economic Planning Sciences, **61**, 1-3 (2018)
18. A. Mardani, D. Streimikiene, T. Balezentis, M. Z. M. Saman, K. M. Nor, S. M. Khoshnava, Data Envelopment Analysis in Energy and Environmental Economics: An Overview of the State-of-the-Art and Recent Development Trends, Energies, **11(8)** (2018)
19. A. Charnes, W.W. Cooper, E. Rhodes, Measuring the efficiency of decision-making units, European Journal of Operational Research, **2(6)**, 429-444 (1978)
20. W. W. Cooper, L. M. Seiford, K. Tone, *Data Envelopment Analysis. A Comprehensive Text with Models. Applications. References and DEA-Solver Software. Second Edition*, Springer (2007)
21. A. Emrouznejad, G. R. Amin, DEA models for ratio data: Convexity consideration, Applied Mathematical Modelling **33(1)**, 486-498 (2009)
22. S. Malmquist, Index Numbers and Indifference Surfaces, Trabajos de Estadística, **4(2)**, 209-242 (1953)
23. R. Färe, S. Grosskopf, B. Lindgren, P. Roos, Productivity Changes in Swedish Pharamacies 1980-1989: A Non-Parametric Malmquist Approach, Journal of Productivity Analysis, **3(1/2)**, 85-101 (1992)

A Comparative Study on New Product Development Projects: Supplier-client Partnerships in Manufacturing Industry

Vuyo T. Hashe[1*]

[1] Department of Mechanical and Industrial Engineering Technology, University of Johannesburg, South Africa

Abstract. This paper was to investigate, explore and gain an understanding of the factors that enable and support supplier-client collaboration in New Product Development Projects (NPDP) within the South African manufacturing industry. This study was based on two case studies where two NPDP within South African on two different firms were studied. The predominant focus of this report studied the supplier involvement and relationship factors, supplier selection factors, and cultural environment and collaboration factors. The main data used was collected via interviews and internal company documents. The collected data was then analyzed and the outcome provided insight into the factors and relationship between these factors. This study noted that firms can enter into collaboration to accelerate the product development process. This includes enhancing the ability of the firm to respond to key customer needs. Firms can make use of the collaboration advantage where they see a market opportunity where their teams have less to no expertise and skills required to capture the opportunity. In addition, research and development costs stand to be reduced significantly, where the collaboration partner is chosen effectively. This study concludes by seeing it as beneficial to firms to collaborate with their suppliers under proper management.

Keywords: buyer, product development, supplier

1 Introduction

Collaborations with suppliers in NPDP involves the amalgamation of the buyers and suppliers. Research and development resources together with the expertise and capabilities of each party are synchronized, to allow a strategic integration where both parties establish a solid foundation for an effective working relationship [1]. The buying firm's new product competitiveness is the one that provides support on the supplier's resources. As such, to create internal organization's modest advantage through supplier-client collaboration in NPDP

* Corresponding author: vhashe@uj.ac.za

requires that the client's firm build up a sustain appropriate practices and processes to enable the selection of the suppliers possessing matching competencies in NPDP [1].

According to Dimancescu and Dwenger [2], many world-class manufacturers have learned to involve suppliers early in the product development process. They understand that leveraging the parent firm's competencies with those of specialized suppliers is one of the keys to building competitive advantage and adding to the agility of the enterprise. The Japanese set out early in the 1950s to build supplier networks, and a growing number of Western-style supplier associations are reaping the benefits. For example, electronics firms in and around Silicon Valley have pioneered a regional supplier agglomeration [2].

Literature from different industries indicates benefits from supplier-client collaboration in generic product development to be significant. Birou and Fawcett [3] and Laura and E [4] argued that there is still an argument between researchers and no conclusions can be reached yet. They assert that buyers can benefit from involving suppliers early in the development process. The benefits include effective and efficient support in areas where it comes to time-to-market of new products. In addition, product quality can be improved with savings on development cost and the overall product cost. Supplier-client collaboration is reported as beneficial to the buying firm [4, 5]. The buying firm stands to gain new competencies with shared risks, quick market penetration and time-to-market shortened, and resources conservation is likely to be seen.

According to Takeishi [6] companies that go on partnerships in NPDP with their suppliers do so in order to gain access to the supplier's technology. The partnership agreements are most likely to include shared responsibilities and risk for design and development patents.

2 Literature reviews

There are multiple aspects to the requirements of successful collaboration. The literature identifies these to be divided into three sections. The first section covers supplier involvement and relationship factors. This area covers the factors that are supportive of collaborative efforts and the impact of these relationships. The second section covers the supplier selection factors, these are necessary before deciding to enter into an agreement to collaborate. Ensuring that the right partner is selected is vital and this is supported by the literature. The third section covers the cultural environment and collaboration. The understanding of the culture of an organization and country could affect collaboration and it is important to understand it. Collaboration is often referred to as strategic partnerships between supplier and client. Literature covers collaboration (or partnership) under various names and in this paper, the author investigated to understand the environmental and driving factors.

2.1 Earlier research

2.1.1 The 1980s

The first research said to have focused specifically on supplier involvement in NPDP was the study by Takeuchi and Nonaka [6] in 1986. This research contribution was based on Japanese companies looking at the same set of seven case studies. They looked at dedicated suppliers describing their commitment to supplier networks. They also went on to explain the superior performance by suppliers in NPDP.

2.1.2 The 1990s

A few more studies followed in the 1990s with the findings in the automotive industry analyzing the involvement of supplier in NPD. As the process goes on approaching the middle of the 1990s, research saw a move away from the automotive industry. A study by Bonaccorsi and Lipparini [8] appeared in the form of a case study at a food processing and packaging company in Italy where Bonaccorsi and Lipparini [8] saw benefits in the partnership. Eisenhardt and Tabrizi [9] published one non-automotive study which became one of the first non-automotive studies indicating that if technological uncertainty is obvious then fewer suppliers in the partnership is critical.

Hartley and colleagues [10] in their study concluded that collaboration involving product design engineers and engineering managers in assembly industries can add value if managed effectively

2.1.3 The 2000s

In NPDP where supplier selection and assessment was one element recommended dominates the literature [11]. However, a recent review by Johnsen [12] shows conflicting results with regards to technological uncertainty in supplier involvement in NPDP. Supplier-client partnerships research at the beginning and during the year 2000 has further looked at the need to establish relationships and adaptation especial in conditions where there is technological uncertainty [11]. This implies that firms should be careful when selecting suppliers to New Product Development projects where there are technological uncertainties.

3 Methodology

This paper was prepared to investigate and understand the phenomenon of supplier involvement in NPDP with the intention of gaining access to their technology. The available literature in the supply chain regarding this subject, in general, have compiled with less written about criteria for supplier involvement and relationship factors, supplier selection, and cultural environment and collaboration in NPDP. The methodology followed in this paper is as suggested by [13]. Melander [13] attest that a case study is a phenomenon and is recommended for the study of a complex unit with multiple variables especially in trying to understand a phenomenon. The logical approach to this work is presented in Fig 1.

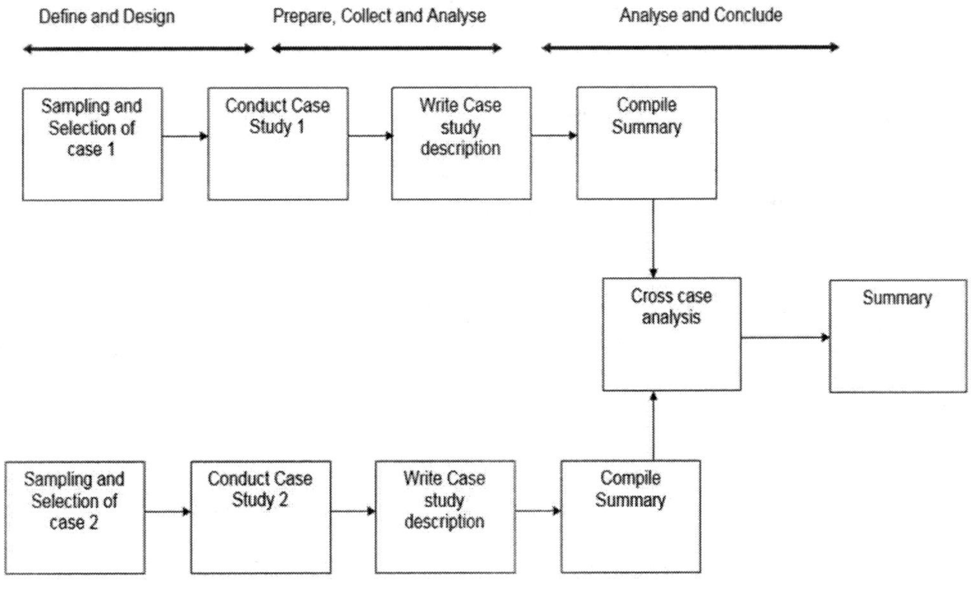

Fig. 1 Research Design (Modified from [13])

4 Case Studies

Both cases studied in this paper were surveying studies and both were initiated at the end phase of two separate NPDP. The end phase is the phase during which the projects were being finalized. This work started with a single case and thereafter one more case study was added. According to [14] a single case study would have been enough where the context is purely for understanding and has been properly selected.

Table 1 presents an overview of the two case studies. Both these case studies are conducted at different organisations, located in different areas within the Gauteng Province in South Africa. The two case studies have similarities with regards to company culture and location. Moreover, both cases involve a product that is important to the firm, as well as the inclusion of technology that is new to the firm and is delivered by an external supplier.

Table 1. Case study description

	Case 1	**Case 2**
Product	Pumps	Filters
NPD duration	2 years	1 year
Industry	Mining, water and municipal	Automotive, mining, construction
Technology	Pump	Filter
Technology uncertainty	High	Low
Degree of innovation	High	Low
No of supplier involved	Two	one

4.1 Data Collection

Data collection was conducted by the form of interviews, internal and external documents, brochures, company web pages, factory visits, and technical documents. The most consistent and relevant data were obtained from interviews. The interviews focused mainly on individuals involved in the NPDP. An interview guide with interview questions and the main topics for discussion was prepared. Additional follow-up questions were also noted. The interviews in this study were conducted in group interviews during NPDP meetings and also with face-to-face. One-on-ones were conducted in order to gain an individual's views assuming that some individuals may not be comfortable in speaking their views freely. Table 2 presents the interview overviews.

The questionnaire is aimed at collecting information on the factors that would lead to the formation of collaborative relationships in organizations and focused on three areas. The interview questions were developed based on literature review and were asked from the participants during interviews. The idea was to ask the respondents the questions and rate their answers to determine the negative as well as positive aspects. The three areas are cultural and demographic factors, the extent of collaboration, decision factors (supplier selection) for engaging with other organizations.

Table 2. interview overviews

Case	No. of interviews	Team members	Interview duration	Time period
Case 1	6	Design Engineer, Project Manager, Draughtsman, Foundry Engineer, Quality Engineer, Foundry Technician	10 hours	4 months
Case 2	3	Product Manager, Engineering Manager, Sales Engineer, Buying Manager, Sales Representative	12 hours	6 months

4.2 Data analysis

The collected data was analyzed, hence the data was organized, divided and categorized. Eisenhardt [15] pointed out that cross-case analysis is preferable when studying case studies, however, the researcher should be well familiar with each case. For this purpose, the matrix for comparison was identified and presented in Table 3. This matrix focused on the similarities and differences of both organisations in partnership.

Table 3. Matrix for comparison

Purchasing's Involvement	Case 1	Case 2
Similarities	Buying firm has a Purchasing department	Buying firm has a Purchasing department
	No participation in the technology selection	No participation in the technology selection
	No member from the Purchasing department in the project team	No member from the Purchasing department in the project team
Differences	Purchaser did not have prior knowledge of the supplier	Purchaser had prior knowledge of the supplier
	No participation in the supplier selection	Participation in the supplier selection

4.3 Results

The total number of people interviewed was 47, some were interviewed in groups and others on one-on-one as indicated in table 2. Below results are as per questions answered by each correspondent. For this paper, only the key questions answers are shown.

4.3.1 Demographic and Cultural Factors

A number of years in operation: Both companies have been in existence since the 1800s and their suppliers with an average 40 years in operation and an average 12.5 years dealing with each other. A number of employees in the organization: Both companies are in the employment of over 30 000 people worldwide and their suppliers are at an average of 5 000 employees each. Expenditure on suppliers and sales revenue: Both companies reflected that they have spent 18% on average of their turnover on suppliers. The physical distance between supplier and client: The average distance between the main supplier and the customer 230 km for both cases

Table 4. Frequency of communication

Very high	21.2%
High	49.1%
Neutral	5.6%
Low	19.7%
Very low	4.4%
Total	100%

Table 4 presents the results obtained regarding the frequency of communication between partners.

4.3.2 Collaboration Factors

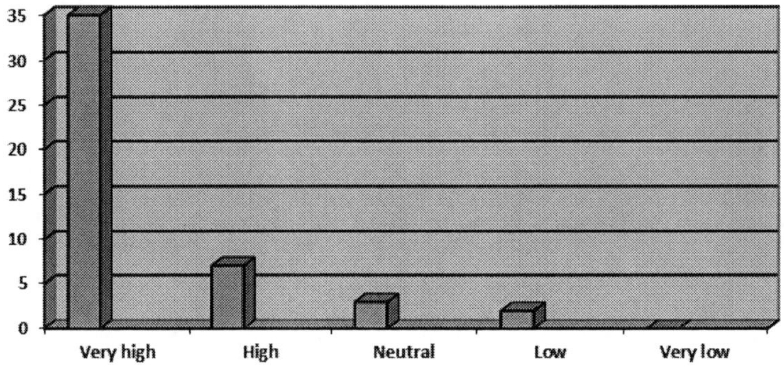

Fig. 1 In your view was collaboration successful?

The 74.47% indicates that most correspondents viewed collaboration as it was successful.

Table 1. Supplier Involvement in the early planning stages

Very high	7.2%
High	34.5%
Neutral	14.7
Low	26.4%
Very low	17.2
Total	100%

The results to this question indicate a proportion of almost equal high and low involvement in the planning stages of the business

Table 6. Joint problem solving – the extent of joint problem solving

Very high	17.2%
High	48.3%
Neutral	29.4%
Low	15.4%
Very low	5.1%
Total	100%

4.3.3 Supplier Selection Factors

Table 7. Supplier design and manufacturing capabilities

Very important	40.2%
Important	35.8%
Neutral	12%
Low important	12%
Not Important	0.0%
Total	100%

Supplier design and manufacturing capabilities appeared (Table 7) to be one of the factors used for strategic fit used by the two organizations.

Table 8. History on development costs, speed and competitiveness

Very important	53%
Important	42%
Neutral	5%
Low important	0.0%
Not Important	0.0%
Total	100%

Table 8 indicates that all parties in partnership understood the importance of competitiveness in the industry.

Table 9 shows that an overwhelming majority of respondents felt that collaboration had a positive impact on the product development partnership.

Table 2. Overall demographic, cultural factors and collaboration factors results (combined)

Collaboration Factors in General	% Agree (strongly)	%Disagree (strongly)
Product development process more efficient	85	6
An effective and efficient way to better respond to customer needs	68	4
Quick reaction to market opportunities	69	4
Low levels of commitment from one of the parties cause conflict and frustration	64	14
Product risks becoming more specified to a single customer's needs rather to a broader target market	58	15
Possible further partnerships for the future after current partnership expired	35	24

Risk of possible competition on the same product or similar product/service	36	34
Risk of losing proprietary information/ leaking	29	27
Partnership easy to manage	7	65
The process often stalls and cause to the long development process	4	70
Costing is viewed too high in partnerships	4	89

5 Findings and discussion

This paper was conducted to furthermore contribute to the field by providing an additional study where supplier selection is viewed from the perspective of both the buying firm and the supplying firm. It has been realized from this study that supplier selection criteria are divided into three areas:

- Basic criteria - what the firm considers to be the minimum number of criteria met for a firm to be considered as a future collaborator in NPD.
- Product criteria - those that evaluate the technology or product of the supplying firm
- Firm criteria - includes a number of criteria that assess the supplier according to its management and organization technology.

The basic criteria ensure that the supplying firm fulfils the minimum criteria for collaboration partners. The product criteria evaluate the product and the firm's technical expertise within the chosen technology. Lastly, the supplying firm's characteristics are assessed.

Results show that the majority of the interviewed individuals felt that the supplier-client partnership yielded a positive impact and enhanced the process efficiency [12, 16, 17].

Respondents noted that the partnership often focuses too much detail to a point where the product becomes too specific to one customer rather than to a whole targeted market. The issue of organizational culture has an effect on successful collaboration proved to be correct. Participants noted that the culture of an organization is vital towards the strategic fit of a supplier within a buying organization. Trust, communication and commitment are seen as the basic requirements towards collaborative culture and ease towards fitting in of two organization. This is to ensure that what is said to be confidential stays confidential.

6 Conclusion

The South African manufacturing industry is currently faced with challenges that include low economic growth and shortage of skills in order to compete effectively in the global markets. Companies have to constantly look at ways to which they can cut down of unnecessary spending, non-value adding operations, staff and other means to reduce their operating costs. To tap into the new technology, the South African manufacturing companies need to focus their attention on attracting the technologically frenzy suppliers into strategic partnerships. To do this, it is essential for companies to investigate so to understand the pros and cons that come with such partnerships. The supplier-client partnership goes beyond the transactions in an attempt to collaborate. Firms have to be aware of and understand the importance of the factors associated with supplier-client collaboration.

Studies on NPDP are reported to have been largely done in the developed countries within the technology-intensive industries. The key contribution of this paper is that it shows that companies are faced with challenging and pressured economic landscape. If companies in South Africa need to invest in supplier-client partnerships, they need to be aware of the factors associated with collaborations and not only the transaction and contracts.

This paper also shares a light regarding the dynamics of collaboration within the South African context. Managers across the manufacturing industry would need to fully understand the complexities and the importance of various factors in ensuring successful suppler-client partnerships. About 75% of the correspondents participated in this study view collaboration as beneficial to their organizations. Participants also indicated an accelerated product development process where customer requirements are fully attended. The gap in expertise and skills between the parties in the partnership was addressed better with effective leadership in place. The overall research and development costs decreased and the development time reduced significantly. Lack of commitment from one of the partners causes delays and frustration and penalties needed to be set out for defaulters

Reference

1. J.H. Dyer, H. Singh, The Relational View: Cooperative Strategy and Sources of Interorganizational Competitive Advantage, *The Academy of Management Review* **23**:660-679 (1998)
2. D. Dimancescu, K. Dwenger, *World-class New Product Development: Benchmarking Best Practices of Agile Manufacturers*, AMACOM (1996)
3. L.M. Birou, S.E. Fawcett, Supplier Involvement in Integrated Product development: A comparison of US and European Practices, *International Journal of Physical Distribution and Logistics Management* **24**(5):4-14 (1994)
4. B. Laura, F.S. E., Supplier Involvement in Integrated Product Development: A Comparison of US and European Practices, *International Journal of Physical Distribution & Logistics Management* **24**:4-14 (1994)
5. P. Shum, G. Lin, A world class new product development best practices model, *International Journal of Production Research* **45**:1609-1629 (2007)
6. A. Takeishi, Knowledge Partitioning in the Interfirm Division of Labor: The Case of Automotive Product Development, *Organization Science* **13**:321-338 (2002)
7. H. Takeuchi, I. Nonaka, The New New Product Development Game, *Harvard Business Review* **64** (1986)
8. A. Bonaccorsi, A. Lipparini, Strategic partnerships in new product development: An Italian case study, *Journal of Product Innovation Management* **11**:134-145 (1994)
9. Eisenhardt, K. M. & Tabrizi, B. N. 1995. Accelerating Adaptive Processes: Product Innovation in the Global Computer Industry. *Administrative Science Quarterly* **40**:84-110.
10. J.L. Hartley, B.J. Zirger, R.R. Kamath, Managing the buyer-supplier interface for on-time performance in product development, *Journal of Operations Management* **15**:57-70 (1997)
11. G.L. Ragatz, R.B. Handfield, T.V. Scannell, Success Factors for Integrating Suppliers into New Product Development, *Journal of Product Innovation Management* **14**:190-202 (1997)
12. T.E. Johnsen, Supplier involvement in new product development and innovation: Taking stock and looking to the future, *Journal of Purchasing and Supply Management,* **15**:187-197 (2009)

13. L. Melander, *Supplier Involvement in New Product Development under Technological Uncertainty*, Doctoral thesis, comprehensive summary, Linköping University Electronic Press, 1568 (2014)
14. A. Dubois, L.E. Gadde, Systematic combining: An abductive approach to case research, *Journal of Business Research* **55**:553-560 (2002)
15. K.M. Eisenhardt, Building Theories from Case Study Research, *The Academy of Management Review* **14**:532-550 (1989)
16. K. Peterson, R. Handfield, G. Ragatz, Supplier integration into new product development: coordinating product, process and supply chain design, *Journal of Operations Management* **23**(3-4):371-388 (2005)
17. M. Hoegl, S.M. Wagner, Buyer-supplier collaboration in product development projects, *Journal of Management* **31**(4):530-548 (2005)

Current Situation and Development of Green Building Rating System in Myanmar

May Lwin[1], and *Kriengsak* Panuwatwanich[1*]

[1]School of Civil Engineering and Technology, Sirindhorn International Institute of Technology, Thammasat University, Pathum Thani, Thailand

Abstract. Since 2016 Myanmar has undergone political and economic reforms. A movement to develop the country with economic growth is a significant matter for the country. In Myanmar, the construction sector is a main driving force for the country's economy in terms of investments and job opportunities of citizens. Electricity used for the construction industry leads to the insufficient energy output of the country. Moreover, waste and pollution are inevitable as a result of Myanmar's economic growth. Green building development in Myanmar is in its initial stage but currently lacks governmental, or voluntary support to devise appropriate rules and regulations for green construction. In particular, the lack of awareness among developers, stakeholders, architects, engineers, contractors, employees and the public about green building has worsened the development progress. This paper reveals why green building development is needed in Myanmar and provides an overview of the current level of green growth in Myanmar. In addition, this paper compares widely used seven existing environmental assessment tools around the world – LEED, BREEAM, Green Mark, Green Star, Three Star – Chinese Green Building Label-3, CASBEE, and HQE as references for the development of green building rating tool with the view to identify aspects that are compatible with the local conditions of Myanmar.

Keywords: Myanmar, green building development, rating system, public awareness

1 Introduction

Myanmar is located in South East Asia and starts to transform from an isolated economy to a middle-income country. Myanmar is also a member of the United Nations and ASEAN as a country that craves development by opening the door for investments. Total country area is 677,000 Square kilometers which are covered by mountain ranges, rivers, and forests. Myanmar has over 60 million people and 135 ethnic groups [1].

* Corresponding author: kriengsak@siit.tu.ac.th

Myanmar experiences a rapid population increase and urbanization problem especially in Yangon, the largest city in the country. High rise buildings, luxury residences, condominiums, and affordable housing are booming in Yangon and the government aims to build 1 million homes for public requirements by 2030. Hence, foreign and local investors are encouraged to subsidize infrastructure such as housing, bridges, roads, and industrial zones with the aim of sustainable development and high quality. Myanmar is a place with abundant natural resources such as water, land, and minerals and a worthwhile place for foreign investments. However, new construction and infrastructures entail to be fueled by electricity, and energy demand is a current crisis for Myanmar which has no adequate energy output for the whole country. Clean and cost-effective energy is also a special need for residents. What is more, waste and pollution from forthcoming factories and buildings are other factors to consider for environmental protection. The government has not set standards and specifications to define a green building. Hence, it is difficult to recognize what constitutes a green building design and construction among engineers and architects in the construction industry [2]. Moreover, companies and government organizations have no experts for modern technology and less awareness about the role of engineers for environmental sustainability. Traditional construction method impacts on environment and society. Besides, city planning is a preferential issue which needs to be considered, for residential building construction due to waste management and drainage systems are not systematic in Myanmar at present [3]. Thus, green building design including energy efficiency, water efficiency, pollution reduction and indoor environmental quality is required for the construction industry.

Green building is a widely adopted construction technique around the world to build a sustainable city. It is also a method that can minimize natural resources depletion for building consumption, pollution from construction materials, environmental degradation, and increase the wellbeing of the occupants [4]. Moreover, the assessment tool, a green building standard for the whole cycle of a building, which recognizes whether a building meets green building objectives, is the first step in the implementation of green building practice in all countries. Besides, if there is awareness for green building, customer demand will rise and companies will be more interested in green construction that leads to green building development. Hence, public awareness about green buildings and certification systems that will be suitable for local conditions are needed at the initial stage of sustainable development in Myanmar.

2 Factors Affecting Requirements of Green Buildings in Myanmar

2.1 Insufficient Current Energy Supply and Uncertainty for Future Energy Potential

For Myanmar, as a developing country, inadequate energy supply is a major problem for modifying all kinds of sectors for economic development. The highest amount of electricity generation is a demand for future infrastructure development in Myanmar [5]. According to National Electrification Plan (NEP) by the World Bank and United Nations, energy production targets are at 50% by 2020, 75% by 2025 and 100% by 2030 including renewable energy, 1/5 of total energy generation [5]. Although Myanmar has been going forward since 2016 by the policy of the new government for the energy sector, there is still an energy crisis and uncertainty for the future. While one-third of the country has access to energy supply, most areas of the country have not been connected to the national grid lines. Some rural areas use off-grid solar power and power generated by diesel [5]. Myanmar has the lowest rate of electricity generation around the world with 160 kWh per capita consumption a year in 2014 and increases 263 kWh in 2015/2016 which is 1/10 of UK consumption [5]. The current installed capacity of the whole country is 4,422 MW in 2014 which is lower than Asian countries – 32,600 MW in Thailand and 26,300 MW in Vietnam [6]. In 2015-2016, 5,029 MW has been produced by the mixed-use energy system [2]. According to the Asia Development Bank, energy demand increases 15% yearly and it will be doubled by 2020. Hydropower is applied mostly for electricity generation in Myanmar, but it is not possible to rely solely on it for the long term. Although coal is planned to be used for filling the gap of the Myanmar energy sector, local people are against the coal plant projects for the detrimental effect of green-house gas emissions. Myanmar is a country that possesses solar and wind power potential for renewable energy because of the geographical conditions of the country. However, energy generation potential is on an uncertain pathway with the lack of clear master plan and investments within the country.

2.2 Limited Water Supply and Inadequate Waste Water Treatment

Water resources sustainability is essential for all people around the world. In Myanmar, there are enormous sources for water usage but some areas are distant from resources and water supply connection system. In the largest city, Yangon, 135 million gallons of freshwater are supplied from Yangon City Development Committee every day and occupants consume over 200 million gallons a day. Thus, most people in extended urban areas depend on natural lakes, rivers, and tube wells [7]. Newly constructed high rise buildings in Yangon rely on 30 million gallons of water from tube wells daily because the current water supply of Yangon is unable to support water sufficiently. The more underground usage of water, the more dangerous the stability of buildings and some buildings constructed on soft soil are at risk of settlement in some townships [7]. Yangon, surrounded by the sea, will encounter saltwater intrusion if groundwater from tube wells is extracted too much. Saltwater intrusion will occur from the base when the freshwater at the upper layer is depleted. Yangon would not become a smart and sustainable city if groundwater sources face risky conditions. Hence, Myanmar needs to apply water resources effectively in the construction industry.

The rapid increase in population also leads to deterioration of the wastewater management system of the city. Wastewater from households and factories runs off to streams, lakes, and the river can be hazardous to the original water resource. According to Myanmar's conventional sewage system in cities, black water is stored in septic tanks and water is permeable into the soil after many years. Greywater from household flows to the surface drains without proper individual treatment and wastewater flooding can be occurred by blocking trash in the drain in the rainy season before reaching to main pipelines [8]. There are not enough treatment plants that connect to the main pipelines to discharge treated water to rivers. Moreover, waste from factories and other areas run to the streams and rivers directly without prior treatment [9]. This is the main reason affecting the health of residents from hazardous water sources. JICA has a plan for an upgraded system to link all waste lines and treatment plants from new areas of Yangon in greater Yangon project 2040. Consequently, water conservation and systematic wastewater treatment system, as part of the green building design is a necessity for the construction sector in Myanmar.

2.3 Carbon dioxide Emissions and Climate Change

Nowadays, climate change is a global issue and Myanmar cannot be separated from other countries that suffer from global warming, even though a vast amount of CO2 is not emitted as much as other industrialized countries. As a country moving forward for development, economic growth and environmental conservation need consideration in parallel. Approximately, 500 billion tons of CO2 have been released by burning fuel, gas, and oil from rapid population growth, increasing urbanization and the industrial revolution, and about half of emissions have been tracked in the atmosphere [10]. For Myanmar which has plans to put into the effort of energy necessity, this is an anxious issue for the future [3]. With economic development, energy consumption and greenhouse gas emission are great environmental challenges that will impact the prospects of a country [10]. Ancha Srinivasa, a principal climate change specialist at ADB remarks that Myanmar acquires to take an action of carbon reduction for climate change control when new investments are performed [11]. The massive amount of Green House Gas (GHG) emissions around the world can be a succeeding problem for vulnerable people to climate change from the lower part of Myanmar [11]. In the central region of Myanmar, drought, scarcity of water, and crop depletion can be in trouble with the livelihood of rural people. Rising sea level that results from soaring ocean temperature is the base of cyclone for people in coastal line and almost 140,000 of Myanmar residents were killed by cyclone Nargis in 2008 [11]. According to Myanmar's National Adaptation Programme of Action (NAPA) to climate change of 2012, it is predicted that the average temperature will rise from 0.8 to 1.4°C in 2050. By comparison of the economic sector, building energy consumption is about 35% of the total and CO2 emission from buildings is almost 30% of the total as well in both developed and developing countries [10]. Hence, renewable energy technology should be applied in building performance to reduce energy consumption, and it will also help control the emission of CO2 and climate change adaptation [10].

2.4 Solid Waste Management and Construction Industry

In Yangon, environmental deterioration and health problems are mostly affected by the inadequate solid waste management system, like many cities in developing countries [12]. Households and industries produce around 1690 tons of waste daily and waste is collected by manpower and garbage truck supported by Yangon City Development Committee (YCDC). There are six waste disposal landfill sites in Yangon and one of them can generate electricity from biogas [8]. YCDC has not set planning for equipment and needs investment to improve solid waste service [12]. In the whole country, 5,616 tons of rubbish is produced daily and it is expected that waste increases 21,012 tons per day, 0.85 kg/capita/day by 2025. Waste recycled volume and the number of the recycled industry has not yet been defined [9]. With the lack of measures to reduce the use of plastic bags and dumping biodegradable and non-biodegradable waste separately, systematic garbage dumping is not still practiced in Myanmar [12]. Moreover, the limitation of landfill sites within the city boundary has become considerable fact in correspondence with population growth [9]. Fifty percent of trash from the landfill site comes from buildings and households. Construction materials derive from different kinds of resources, and the reduction of construction waste is also a fact that needs to be examined. Regarding green building rating systems, waste management is one of the criteria and municipal waste collection will be effective if an individual waste management technique is utilized in buildings [13].

3 Green Buildings Movement in Myanmar

3.1 Green Building Committee – Building Engineering Institute Myanmar

Building Engineering Institute (BEI) was successfully established by the Myanmar Engineering Society (MES) and the Committee for Quality Control of High-Rise Building Construction Project (CQHP) on 23rd November 2014 in Yangon. Six committees are co-founded under BEI, including (1) Architecture, (2) Structure, (3) Geotechnical,

(4) MEP (M&E), (5) Construction, Quality Control & Safety, and (6) Green Building. Objectives of this organization are to promote the building sector and technology and to enhance the welfare of society by linking all stakeholders from related engineering fields, to cooperate institutional organizations, industries, and the government, to complete codes, rules and regulations and references, and to contribute seminar, training, and conference for technical improvement [14].

3.2 Green Building Chapter in Myanmar National Building Code

The initial stage of Green Building Certification System of Myanmar has been introduced by representatives from the Green Building Committee, BEI as section 2.12 ARCHITECTURE FOR ENERGY EFFICIENCY AND GREEN in the Myanmar National Building Code 2016, which is the guideline for Myanmar Construction Industry. The purpose of this section is to provide green building criteria and basic requirements for energy-efficient building design in Myanmar. This chapter includes green building criteria of Myanmar, namely, "Energy" for saving energy usage in buildings, using low embodied energy materials, considering air circulation and natural lighting in building design, and utilizing renewable energy, "Water" to harvest rainwater, recycle greywater, and manage wastewater for water efficiency and water resources conservation, "Human Comfort and Health" to maintain the indoor temperature in the comfort zone for occupants, provide adequate lighting and good quality of air for occupants' health, and "Environmental Impact" including carbon emission reduction, enhancing greenery to reduce urban heat island effect, decreasing pollution, and landfill waste. This code is proposed for new construction, extension and retrofitting of commercial building types (excluding religious buildings, low-cost housings, and the public buildings by the government or other non-government organizations) of more than 100,000 sq. ft area within Yangon and other places similar to Yangon. It also demonstrates environmental sustainability standards by referencing International Green Construction Code (version 2) and green building design guide by Building and Construction Authority, Singapore. The specified building types must act in accordance with these standards. This code will develop unceasingly for the design and construction of green buildings in Myanmar in such a way that it creates building's performance of resource efficiency, occupants' wellbeing, and environmental reputation. In addition, climate change in Yangon is considered in this code to mitigate global warming. Green building engineering and technology which is appropriate to geographical conditions, climatic background and construction market of Myanmar is a requirement to carry on this proposed code for green building development in Myanmar [15].

3.3 Green Building Construction in Myanmar

According to the Myanmar Times article on 1st of May 2017, U Ye Htun Aung, managing director of Team 6 engineering solution and control Company, remarks that although the government has not set rules and regulations for green building, there are some buildings in Myanmar which are qualified under the certification of Green Mark, Building Construction Authority - Singapore. Sedona Hotel's new portion, Inya Wing has complied with Green Mark's certification requirements to specify as a green building and Junction City shopping mall is attempting to achieve green certification from BCA, Singapore, especially for the hotel tower, office tower, and shopping mall phase 1 [2]. Ten hotels in Myanmar have been selected to confer ASEAN green hotel award which is honored to hotels in the ASEAN region annually. This prize has been awarded for resorts and hotels which meet the requirements of Green ASEAN hotel standard including 11 criteria at the ASEAN Tourism Forum 2018 observed in Chiang Mai, Thailand [16].

4 Comparison of Seven Green Building Rating Tools

Green building rating tools have been introduced since environmental conservation reaches at the center of global concern [17]. In recent years, green building rating tools have been applied to promote the sustainability of the built environment [18]. Rating tools can be defined as standards to assess the building performance that corresponds with a set of assessment criteria [17]. Moreover, these can be used as a technology to promote the quality of building in the construction industry [19]. This paper considers seven widely recognized green building rating systems namely LEED (Leadership in Energy and Environmental Design, United States), BREEAM (BRE Environmental Assessment Method, United Kingdom), BCA Green Mark (Singapore), Green Star (Australia), Three Star – Chinese Green Building Label-3, CASBEE (Comprehensive Assessment System for Built Environment Efficiency, Japan), and HQE (High-Quality Environmental Standard, France).

4.1 Overview of Assessment Tools

4.1.1 Leadership in Energy and Environmental Design (LEED)

LEED was established by the US Green Building Council (USGBC) and Green Building Certification Institute (GBCI) in the year 2000. LEED is a type of non-profit organization and has eight criteria for assessment such as location and transportation, sustainable sites, water efficiency, energy and atmosphere, materials and resources, indoor environmental quality, innovation, and regional priority. The certification level is defined as four stages - Platinum (80-100 points), Gold (60-79 points), Silver (50-59 points), and Certified (40-49 points). LEED is applied for building design and construction, interior design and construction, building operations and maintenance, homes, and neighborhood development (plan and build project) of commercial buildings, schools, healthcare, and single and multifamily homes [20,21].

4.1.2 BRE Environmental Assessment Method (BREEAM)

BREEAM was founded by the UK Government, Building Research Establishment and BRE Trust in 1990 and stands as a non-profit organization. There are ten green building criteria in BREEAM – management, transport, land use and ecology, water, energy, materials, health and wellbeing, innovation, waste and pollution. The score level is classified as Outstanding ≥ 85+, Excellent ≥ 70, Very Good ≥ 55, Good ≥ 45, Pass ≥ 30, and Unclassified < 30. Office, retail, industrial, data centers, education, healthcare, residential, mixed-use, other buildings, and courts and prisons are certified by BREEAM [20; 22].

4.1.3 Green Star

The Green Star was launched in Australia by Green Building Council Australia (GBCA) in 2003 and it is a type of non-profit organization. Green star divides criteria as nine categories – management, transport, land use and ecology, water, energy, material, indoor environment quality, innovation, and emissions. The point scale is defined as Assessed/Zero Star (less than 10%), Minimum Practice/One Star (10%-19%), Average Practice/Two Star (20%-29%), Good Practice/Three Star (30%-44%), Australian Best Practice/Four Star (45%-

59%), Australian Excellence/Five Star (60%-74%), and World Leadership/Six Star (75%+). Green Star is responsible for communities and precincts, design and construction of new buildings, major refurbishments, new interior fit-outs, public buildings, and sustainable building operations [20, 23].

4.1.4 Three Star, Chinese Green Building Label-3

Three-star, introduced by Ministry of Housing and Urban-Rural Development (MOHURD) in China in 2006, includes seven main criteria namely operational management, land saving, and outdoor environment, water-saving and water resources utilization, energy-saving and utilization, materials saving and materials resources utilization, indoor environmental quality, and preferences. Three-star is applicable for public and residential buildings. The score level is based on 3-Star (80), 2-Star (60), and 1-Star (50) for green building certification [20].

4.1.5 Comprehensive Assessment System for Built Environment Efficiency (CASBEE)

CASBEE is developed by Japan's Ministry of Land, Infrastructure, Transport, and Tourism (MLIT), and Institute for Built Environment and Energy Conservation (IBEC) in 2001. CASBEE covers all residential and non- residential buildings. The assessment criteria are divided into two main categories – Q (built environment quality) which consists of quality of service, outdoor environment on-site, and indoor environment, and L (Build load) which consists of resources and materials, energy, and off-site environment. The point system is designed by the result of BEE (building environmental efficiency) from Q for building performance divided by L for environmental impact. The certification levels of CASBEE depending on BEE are Superior: S (BEE $\geq$ 3.0 and Q $\geq$ 50), Very good: A (BEE $\geq$ 1.5), Good: B+ (BEE $\geq$ 1), Slightly poor: B- (BEE $\geq$ 0.5), and Poor: C (BEE<0.5) [20, 24].

4.1.6 High-Quality Environmental Standard (HQE)

HQE is a green building rating tool in France and it was initiated by HQE Association for France Scheme, and supported by Cerway for International Scheme in 2012. HQE is a type of non-profit organization and is based on eight criteria for certification such as maintenance, site, water, energy, components, indoor environmental quality, waste, and worksite. HQE enables residential, non-residential, and detached houses. Credit awards for buildings are HQE PASS (between 1 and 4 stars), HQE GOOD (between 5 and 8 stars), HQE VERY GOOD (between 9 and 11 stars), HQE EXCELLENT (12 stars and more with at least 3 stars for "energy" category) [20, 25].

4.2 Similarities and Differences between Criteria and Categories

By comparison of the above seven existing rating systems, BREEAM, the first certification system, proposed rating categories in 1990, which have been adopted by other rating systems using various alternative terminology. For example, 'Land Use and Ecology' in BREEAM is referred to as 'Sustainable Sites' in LEED, 'Climatic Responsive Design' in Green Mark, 'Land Saving and Outdoor Environment' in Three Star, 'Outdoor Environment on Site' in CASBEE and 'Site' in HQE. Similarly, 'Indoor Environmental Quality' from most tools can be seen in BREEAM and Green Mark in different names such as 'Health and Wellbeing' and 'Smart and Health Building'.

LEED provides 8 categories including 'Location and Transportation', 'Sustainable sites', 'Water Efficiency', 'Energy and Atmosphere', 'Materials and Resources', 'Indoor Environmental Quality', and 'Regional Priority' for green building assessment process in which 'Regional Priority' criteria is only standardized for LEED and not in other remaining 6 rating systems. BREEAM, Green Star, Three Star, CASBEE, and HQE evaluate for advancing the management procedure in all phases of the project with the green building objectives whereas LEED and Green Mark are lack of consideration of the 'Management' category in their standards. 'Innovation' is an applicable category in LEED, BREEAM, and Green Star while 'Pollution' in BREEAM and Green Star, and 'Waste' in BREEAM and HQE are prioritized for considering the contamination. Five common criteria which are inserted as the basic need of every certification system in all selected 7 green building rating tools are as follows.

- Land Use and Ecology
- Water
- Energy
- Materials
- Indoor Environmental Quality

Other different categories that are included in only some rating tools among the considered seven tools are as follows.

- Management
- Transportation
- Innovation
- Waste
- Pollution
- Regional Priority
- Advanced Green Effort

4.3 Comparison of Points and Credits

Almost all rating tools, except CASBEE which is emerged from Japan, designate score level upon criteria by percentage or points to determine the building with green standards. In the CASBEE scoring system, Building Environmental Efficiency (BEE) is an assessment specification which is attained from Build Environment Quality, Q (performance of a building) is divided by Built Load, L (Building's adverse impact on the environment). A building is deliberated more sustainable when the slope is steeper in the graph with a higher value of Q and lower value of L. Among the nominated seven rating tools compared in Table 1, 'Management' is assigned as one criterion in BREEAM, Green Star, Three Star, and HQE with the intention of promoting management system of the whole project performance as design, construction, and maintenance in accordance with objectives of green buildings. LEED from the United States favors 'Energy' by means of reducing energy usage and applying renewable energy in a building for mitigating greenhouse gas emissions in the environment, as the main criteria with 30% of the total score. Likewise, BREEAM, Green Star, and Three Star chose 'Energy' as the most effective category with a score of 20%, 20%, and 18% respectively. It is noticeable that 'Indoor Environmental Quality' criteria (improving occupants' health and comfort living) in HQE has the highest weighting of 43%. 'Climatic Responsive Design'(building and environment design for climate resilience, the purpose of site selection, and preservation of existing green space and natural characteristics) is the focus of Green Mark as represented by the score weighting of 25%.

Despite other rating systems defines 'Land Use and Ecology', Green Mark names 'Climatic Responsive Design' as climate change action is also considered in this criterion. 'Transport' (reducing carbon footprint from vehicles near the site) is stated as 15% in LEED, 8% in BREEAM and 9% in Green Star whereas 'Waste' and 'Pollution' are described 6% and 9% in BREEAM and, 2% and 6% in HQE respectively. To sum up, 'Energy' is the most powerful criteria except HQE and Green Mark. 'Materials' (choosing green products for preventing natural resources depletion and minimizing environmental impact with less embodied energy) and 'Water' (water efficiency and wastewater management) are vital elements after 'Energy' and 'Indoor Environmental Quality'.

Table 1. Points Percentage of Selected Green Building Rating Systems

Criteria	LEED	BREEAM	Green Mark	Green Star	Three Star	HQE
Energy	30%	20%	18%	20%	18%	14%
Indoor Environmental Quality	15%	14%	18%	15%	17%	43%
Materials	12%	9%	13%	13%	16%	8%
Water	10%	6%	9%	11%	17%	8%
Land Use and Ecology	9%	7%	25%	5%	17%	13%
Transport	15%	8%		9%		
Management		14%		13%	15%	6%
Innovation	5%	7%		9%		
Waste		6%	3%			2%
Pollution		9%		5%		6%
Regional Priority	4%					
Advanced Green Efforts			14%			

(Note: CASBEE is excluded due to having different assessment method from other systems)

5 Developing a Green Building Rating System for Myanmar: Future Work

Green building rating tools are widely used not only in developed countries but also in various ASEAN countries to assess the environmental performance of a building. Myanmar has taken an initial step to execute its own rating system as a developing country in order to move forward. Based on the comparison of the Green Building Rating systems, it can be seen that the similar criteria that have been adopted across all the systems fall in the areas of Energy, Indoor Environmental Quality, Materials, Water, and Land Use and Ecology. These areas are in line with the existing criteria proposed by Myanmar's Green Building Committee, including "Energy", "Water", "Human Comfort and Health", and "Environmental Impact". Even though it is easy to adopt rating systems from one country to another, one thing needed to be considered is that they are suitable or not with the local climate, economy, technology advancement, construction market, and geographical conditions. Therefore, this study aims to investigate in the future the Junction City, Yangon and Sedona Hotel, Inya Win which are certified as green buildings by Green Mark, Singapore, as case studies. The collection of engineering drawings and documents about these buildings and site observations will be carried out as the first step, and followed by questionnaires and interviews of representative persons (e.g. architects, civil engineers, M&E engineers, managers, and developers) who participated in these projects during design, and construction period. Questionnaires are divided into three parts; firstly, technical questions from site observation to architects and engineers which will be beneficial to technical requirements of Myanmar's green building rating system implementation. The future study will also examine the adoption of Myanmar's technical sustainability standards from Singapore, as reflected in the Myanmar National Building Code 2016. For the second component, challenges, and difficulties while attempting to achieve a green mark certificate from BCA, Singapore will be examined in order to assist the assessment process of developing Myanmar's rating system. Finally, interviews for the market condition of green materials and products in Myanmar, and how much degree of knowledge and experience about green building objectives and standards the experts have, will be conducted for the case of awareness about green buildings in Myanmar. The desired outcomes will support partly Green Building Committee – BEI (Myanmar) to adopt some technical standards from Green Mark, Singapore and to improve green building chapter in MNBC 2016 for the development of Myanmar's green building rating system.

6 Conclusions and Recommendation

By consideration of green building requirements and the current green movement in Myanmar, the certification system is fundamental to regulate the green building practice. Besides, rating tools can provide awareness for green environment and sustainable development. As a responsibility of the government, the environmentally friendly building design to reduce greenhouse gas emissions and the waste pollution should be taken into consideration in public housing projects that will be implemented for the increased population. To be successful in green building development, understanding about the green building objectives and unity of key players from all related fields are required. Hence, it is time to share relevant information and knowledge about sustainable building practices between professionals and the government for public awareness. Moreover, the comparison of seven green building rating systems demonstrates that energy efficiency is the most common criterion with the highest score points for assessment, followed by the aspects of Land Use and Ecology, Water, Materials and Indoor Environmental Quality. Although these common criteria have been, to some extent, considered in the current Myanmar National Building Code, the study concluded that to further develop a green building rating system for Myanmar, the remaining criteria should be considered with respect to the conditions that are domestic to the country, basing on the experience gained from the construction of buildings that have already been certified as green. Further understanding of the challenges and opportunities observed through these buildings will be the aim of future research.

References

1. U.T. Aung, Country analysis paper on 3R practice in Myanmar, Fourth Regional 3R Forum in Asia, Hanoi, Vietnam (2013)
2. Y.T. Tin, Construction sector going green, The Myanmar Times (2007), https://www.mmtimes.com/opinion/25803-construction-sector-going-green.html
3. MCEA presentation, Fulfilling Myanmar's affordable housing requirement: implementation plans and status, Myanmar infrastructure summit (2018)
4. S. Milad, The investigation of the barriers in developing green building in Malaysia, *Modern Applied Science* 7(2): 1913-1852 (2013)
5. Oxford Business Group, *The Report: Myanmar* (2017), https://oxfordbusinessgroup.com
6. R. Vakulchuk et al., *Myanmar's attractiveness for investment in the energy sector, a comparative international perspective*, Myanmar Institute of Strategic and International Studies (2017)
7. Y.L. Zay, Underground water demand could weaken buildings, The Myanmar Times (2015), https://www.mmtimes.com/business/16248-underground-water-demand-could-weaken-buildings.html.
8. *Burma – Environmental Technology* (2017), https://www.export.gov/ article?id=Burma-Environmental-Technology.
9. P.J.D. Gamaralalage, M. Hengesbaugh, O. May Tin Hlaing, *Quick study on waste management in Myanmar, current situation and key challenges*, Institute for Global Environmental Strategies (2016)
10. A. Mardiana, S.B. Riffat, Building energy consumption and carbon dioxide emissions: threat to climate change, *Journal of Earth Science & Climatic Change, **S3:001*** (2015)
11. A. Fatima, Climate change is undermining sustainable development in Myanmar. Here is what can be done about it, https://www.devex.com/news/climate-change-is-undermining-sustainable-development-in-myanmar-here-is-what-can-be-done-about-it-89885
12. L.L.A. Mya, *Improving solid waste management in urban Myanmar – A study from Yango*, Summary of EEPSEA Research Report No. 2016-SRG7 (2016)
13. N. Mahesh, K.P. Dhananjay, Solid waste management in green building (2016)
14. Development of Building Engineering Institute (BEI), Myanmar Engineering Society presentation, 1 November 2014, (2014)
15. GBC-BEI Myanmar, Myanmar National Building Code 2016: Part two – architecture and urban design, section 2.12 architecture for energy efficiency and green (2016)
16. L.M. Shwe, 10 Myanmar hotels win ASEAN tourism awards, Myanmar Business Today **6(4)** (2018), https://www.mmbiztoday.com/articles/10-myanmar-hotels-win-asean-tourism-awards.
17. L. Abdullah, N. Jumadi, R. Sabu, H. Arshad, F.F. Mohd Fawzy, Assessment criteria on sustainable rating tools used in Asian countries, *Jurnal Teknologi* (2015)
18. E.C. Mpakati-Gama, S.C. Wamuziri, B. Sloan, Green building challenges: evaluating the operation of adopted building assessment tools – case study, *Procs 28th Annual ARCOM Conference, 3-5 September 2012, Edinburgh, UK*: 1257-1267 (2012)
19. Z.M. Darus, N.A. Hashim, E. Salleh, L.C. Haw, A.K.A. Rashid, S.N.A. Manan, Development of rating system for sustainable building in Malaysia, *WSEAS Transactions on Environment and Development* **5(3)** (2009)
20. *A Review of Seven Regional and International Green Building Certification System, Final Draft.* Winrock International Institute for Agricultural Development, Hanoi (2014)
21. *LEED v4 for BD+C: new construction and major renovation, project checklist* (2018), https://new.usgbc.org/.

22. *BREEAM international new construction 2016 technical manual* (2016), https://www.breeam.com/.
23. *Green Star- design & as built scorecard V1.2 update 1/07/2017*, Green Building Council Australia (2017), https://new.gbca.org.au/
24. *CASBEE for new construction (2010 Edition), score sheet* (2010), http://www.ibec.or.jp/CASBEE/english/.
25. *HQE assessment scheme, evaluation tool EBR* (2014), http://www.behqe.com/

Identifying Critical Success Factors through Interactive Management

Nien-Tsu Tuan[1*]

[1]Department of Construction Economics and Management, University of Cape Town, South Africa

Abstract. Since its inception, the Critical Success Factor (CSF) concept has been increasingly adopted by industries to achieve business goals. However, the conventional approaches used for identifying critical success factors are underpinned by the mechanism paradigm. The mechanism paradigm doesn't take the interlaced relationships between system elements into account. Neither does it promote interaction between the relevant stakeholders. This paper proposes a systemic approach called Interactive Management (IM) to complement conventional ideas in determining the critical success factors. The Interactive Management process embraces the relevant stakeholders to collectively identify the critical success factors through four phases: generating critical success factors, clarifying the generated critical success factors, structuring a systemic digraph showing the interlaced relationships between the critical success factors, and identifying the real critical success factors in the systemic digraph. An example is provided to demonstrate how the Interactive Management methodology can be used to identify the real critical success factors.

Keywords: critical success factors, interactive management, systemic approaches

1 Introduction

Since its inception, the Critical Success Factor (CSF) idea has been gaining ground in the identification of competitive strategy for organizations. It has been used for establishing business strategies in various industries, e.g. R&D projects [1], automobile industry [2], and mobile learning [3]. However, the frequently used techniques for exploring CSFs are dominated by the thinking that sees human as subjects, treats systems elements as independent parts, or narrows down the scope of the investigation to a desirable level. These techniques can be exemplified by means of interviews, Likert Scale questionnaire surveys, or statistical correlation analysis. Different from the commonly adopted techniques, this paper uses an example to demonstrate how the Interactive Management methodology [4] can be employed to identify and prioritize CSFs. Interactive Management (IM) is a systemic approach echoing soft systems thinking. It enhances learning and interchanging perceptions

* Corresponding author: nien-tsu.tuan@uct.ac.za

among the relevant stakeholders through a disciplined process: generation of ideas, clarification of generated ideas, structuring the generated ideas, and interpretation of structured ideas. The output of the IM process is a digraph depicting the relationship between the system's elements. The following discussion will demonstrate how to use IM to structure a CSF model. Prior to the demonstration, this paper explains the concept of CSF and the techniques frequently used to identify the CSFs.

2 Critical Success Factors

The CSF concept was first put forward by Daniel [5]. It means the key areas that must be exceptionally well done for an organization to be successful. This idea was then popularized by Rockart [6], using CSF method to identify the key areas where things must be done right for different companies, such as Microwave Associates, an oil company, and a store-furnishing manufacturer. In some ways, one of the objectives of the CSF method is to reduce the variety of decision making impinging on top executives/general managers. They are frequently furnished with an enormous amount of unrelated information. The CSF method aims to provide executives with critical information derived from the identified critical areas requiring attention. With the attenuated variety of information derived from the critical areas, the executives can manage their organizations in an efficient and effective fashion.

Since its emergence, the CSF concept has been used in different areas. For example, Pinto and Slevin [7] used it to identify the critical factors in successful project implementation. They identified ten factors promoting project success. The ten factors range from the factor sweeping across all activities in various projects, like the factor 'communication', to the factor focusing on a specific project stage, such as the factor 'project schedule/plan'. Mahmood et al. [8] explored the critical success factors in research projects at universities in Pakistan. They concluded eleven critical success factors for research projects, such as project safety, team members' relationship, and transparency. Apparently, the eleven critical success factors identified by them for research projects are not identical to the ten critical success factors of generic projects identified by Pinto and Slevin [6]. In addition to exploring the project management arena, the CSF idea leaves visible traces in other issues as well. Cochrane [3] investigated the critical success factors in transforming pedagogy towards mobile learning. Luthra et al. [2] probed into the critical success factors for achieving sustainability in the automobile industry. Sahney [9] studied the critical success factors for E-business. For Sahney, the critical success factors refer to the design characteristics of meeting customers' requirements. The CSF concept has profoundly influenced the strategic planning in different industries.

There are some criticisms of the CSF idea. Cooper [10] summarizes various criticisms from the extant literature. For example, due to the limitation on short-term memory, managers might reduce CSFs to a manageable number. There may be other CSFs not taken into account. Focusing on a measurable factor is another problem: the focus on measurable factors could lead to the ignorance of unmeasurable 'soft' factors. Another concern is about the dynamic environment: the dynamic environment requires that the critical success factors identified for an organization should be frequently revisited to ensure their relevance to the organizational objectives. However, the criticisms didn't hamper the CSF idea that carves out its own line in different research domains through different techniques. The common approaches used to identify CSFs are briefly reviewed in the next part.

3 A Review of Commonly Used Approaches to the Identification of Critical Success Factors

Using a literature review to generate a list of CSFs is a predominant method [1, 2, 11, 12]. The collated CSFs from the literature may then be used to develop an instrument for surveys. The human subjects rate the CSFs predetermined by the researchers. The score received by each critical success, factor reveals how the predetermined CSFs are ranked by the subjects. The structured relationship between the CSFs appears to be 'more important'. This relationship is aimed at determining whether a critical success factor is more important than another critical success factor. But the spokesperson for CSF [6] urges researchers to note that the CSFs of each industry is characterized by the very nature of the industry itself. When zooming into organizational levels, the CSFs are amenable to change over time due to the change of an organization's situation. The idea of identifying invariant CSFs through literature to sweep across all industries and organizations is questionable.

Interviews are frequently used techniques in qualitative research. They are used for identifying CSFs as well [6-8, 13]. In general, the interview procedures require researchers to transcribe the interview, code and categorize the data and discover the pattern of meaning from the coding and categorization. To defend that the coding and categorization are not biased towards a coder's subjectivity, Cohen's Kappa or other measures might be introduced into the procedures to defend the reliability of the data analysis. Overall, the findings should reflect trustworthiness, such as credibility, transferability, and dependability. In general, the output from the interview is a list of CSFs, without describing the relationship between the identified CSFs. Different from other interview outputs, Pinto and Slevin [7] argue that the CSFs in project implementation discovered by them display 'precedent to' relationship. For instance, the success factor 'project mission' is precedent to the success factor 'top management support'. In brief, an interview is a qualitative approach assuming that the summation of individual's perceptions is equal to the whole. The researchers' subjectivity influences the analysis of data to some degree. The problems of using an interview include lack of interaction among the human subjects and dismissing interrelationships between system elements. Even if member checking is used to justify the validity of findings, there is no guarantee that each participant understands why others uphold different views. The frequency count used to determine the most frequently mentioned factors by the participants doesn't promote consensus among them due to the lack of interaction.

Statistical analysis is another frequently used technique in a quantitative study. It has also been used to investigate the relationship between CSFs and other variables. For example, Dvira et al. [14] used the multivariate method to investigate the relationship between the CSFs of the defence projects and critical management variables. They mention that the multivariate method has proved to be useful in reducing the dimensionality of variables space. This idea is employed to identify the CSFs in their research as well. The CSFs were reduced from four success dimensions to two dimensions. This approach manifests the idea of 'narrowing down'. It is the idea of reducing the variables in question to a manageable level or matching a researcher's interest. However, the spokesperson of CSF adopted 'interview' to identify CSFs [6]. It implies that determining CSFs is a subjective business. Therefore, reducing the dimension of interest by the researcher alone doesn't deal with the subjectivity among the participants. The statistical analysis hints that reaching consensus among different views is subordinate to discovering invariant principles through statistics.

The reviewed methods that have been used for identifying CSFs are not exhaustive. There are other approaches used for identifying CSFs as well, such as Analytic Hierarchy Process [15]. In general, the reviewed methods are characterized by lack of interaction, reduction of problem space, seeing the identified CSFs invariant in time, or paying no heed of the interrelationships between system elements. Human is seen as subjects in most of the frequently used methods. Therefore the commonly adopted approaches do not enhance learning or dwell on the systemic relationship between system elements. Warfield devised Interactive Management (IM) methodology [16], a methodology aligned with soft systems thinking. IM can be used to structure the systemic relationship between CSFs in an interactive way. The next part explains how to use IM to identify CSFs and structure the interrelationships between the identified CSFs.

4 Identifying CSFs through Interactive Management

In its early development stage, IM was called Interpretive Structural Modelling [16]. Warfield and Cárdenas [4] elaborated Interpretive Structural Modelling and called the new methodology Interactive Management. IM has been used to study various problems. For example, Nthunya et al. [17] used IM to explore the major factors causing basic education problems in Lesotho. Tuan [18] applied IM to explore the aggravating relationship between the factors leading to the AIDS epidemic in South Africa. The earlier version of IM, i.e. Interpretive Structural Modelling, was also used to investigate CSFs [9, 19, 20]. However, these works need to be augmented by incorporating the vital features of IM into the inquiry. For example, given the democratic nature of IM [21], the facilitator of an IM workshop needs to justify that the constituency of the participants is representative. Furthermore, the interrelationship between the CSFs to be structured is a major objective of IM inquiry. The interrelationship 'helps to achieve' is more adequate than 'leads to' because the 'helps to achieve' relationship can manifest the CSFs that have higher leverage to promote other CSFs. These structured interrelations can reveal the relative importance of the identified CSFs. The following discussion demonstrates how the major IM phases can be used to identify CSFs.

The first step of IM is to identify the relevant stakeholders who will be the participants of the IM workshop. The constituency of the participants should be justifiable, e.g. identifying the relevant stakeholders through the questions proposed by Manson and Mitroff [22]. The questions range from 'who is affected by the strategy' to 'who has an interest in it. It is noteworthy that the ideal number of participants in the IM workshop is between six to twelve participants [4]. The ideal number of participants shouldn't be seen as a sample size. The participants of an IM workshop can be seen as the representatives of a committee. It is not sensible to claim that the 'sample size' of a 'committee' is too small or too big. The major concern about the committee is whether it is representative and knowledgeable. Assume that a company intends to identify the CSFs for the business that they operate. The company has identified six participants who are willing to attend the IM workshop. Besides, the constituency of the six participants is legitimate.

The second step is to generate CSFs. Each participant carries out the silent generation of CSFs based on their own perceptions. The reason for generating CSFs silently is to avoid a power situation entering into the inquiry process. When each participant completes the generation of CSFs, the facilitator may start to collate the generated ideas for entering the next phase.

The third step is to clarify the generated CSFs. As people might use the same words to express different ideas or use different words to express the same idea, the clarification phase promotes the shared understanding of the generated ideas between the participants. This phase requires the participants to collectively review all of the generated ideas through the assistance of a facilitator. Therefore a properly equipped venue is needed for the group to collectively review the generated CSFs. In the process of reviewing the generated CSFs, the participants might decide to merge certain CSFs into one, delete certain CSFs, or rephrase the CSFs whose meanings are unclear. Assume that the participants of the scenario case have collectively generated and clarified eight CSFs, shown in Table 1. The list of CSFs in Table

1 is only used for demonstration purpose. In the real world, more CSFs could be generated for modelling.

Table 1. Example of Identified Critical Success Factors

Serial Number	Critical Success Factors
1	a skilful team
2	resources / financial support
3	top management support
4	recognition of project team
5	absence of red tape
6	sharing high-quality information
7	customer support
8	establishment of clear measurement of success

The third step is to structure a model/digraph showing the interrelationship between the identified CSFs. The digraph is structured by the group through answering a series of contextual questions examining whether the relationship exists between a pair of systems' elements. To determine the relative importance of CSFs, the contextual question 'Does the achievement of critical success factor A significantly helps to achieve the critical success factor B' may be used to build the model. The wording 'significantly' can help the group to avoid linking two CSFs when the intensity of the relationship between them is weak. The 'achievement of A helps to achieve B' means that attaining factor A has the power to promote factor B. If success factor A has the power to promote success factor B, success factor A should be given focus from a strategic point of view. It is noteworthy that the relationship in the model must be transitive. The 'helps to achieve' relation is transitive. If success factor A helps to achieve success factor B and success factor B helps to achieve success factor C, then it is plausible to infer that success factor A helps to achieve success factor C. The use of 'lead to' in the contextual question is questionable. The phrase 'lead to' has been used for both pleasant and unpleasant situations. This phrase might give rise to confusion in the modelling process because, in addition to the 'help to achieve' relationship, 'inhibiting' relationship might exist between the CSFs as well. Therefore, it is not adequate to use 'lead to' for the contextual question due to the possibility of causing semantic confusion.

When the group answer the series of contextual questions, a binary matrix is gradually completed. If the group decides that the relationship exists between the two posed elements, '1' is entered into the cell associated with the two elements in the binary matrix. If not, '0' is entered into the cell. Once the binary matrix is completed, a digraph can be extracted. Warfield [16] explains the process of extracting the digraph. But it is not in the scope of this paper. Currently, there is software capable of carrying out the modelling process and extracting the digraph, such as Concept Star. The software provides the options for modelling loops in the system. Assume that the group carried out extensive debate and answered all questions required to complete the binary matrix. The digraph extracted from the binary matrix is shown in Figure 1.

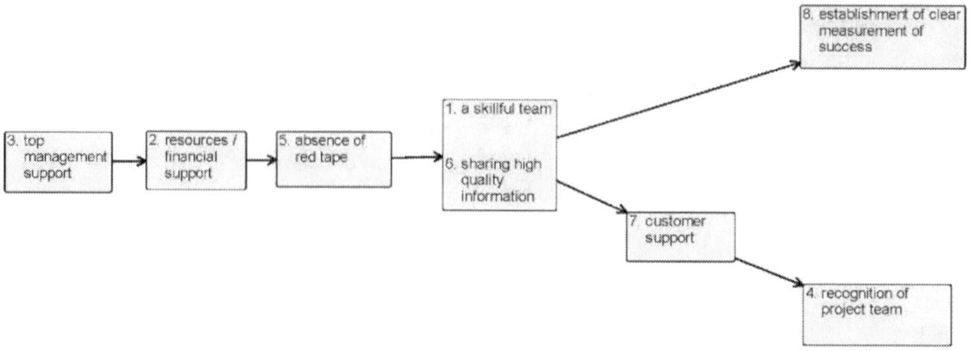

Fig. 1. An Example of 'Help to Achieve' Relationship between Critical Success Factors

The fourth step is to interpret the model built by the group. The facilitator of an IM workshop should be knowledgeable about IM and be able to carry out the interpretation of the structured model. In Figure 1, all of the arrows mean 'significantly helps to achieve'. For example, the leftmost element is critical success factor 3 'top management support'. The second stage element is critical success factor 2 'resources/financial support'. The arrow linking the two elements means that the achievement of critical success factor 'top management support' significantly helps to achieve the critical success 'resources/financial support'. The figure shows that the leftmost element 'top management support' can generate the greatest leverage because it significantly helps to achieve all of the critical success factors lying to its right. Therefore, critical success factor 3 'top management support' should be given priority from a strategic point of view. The second important element is the critical success factor lying in the second stage: critical success factor 2 'resources / financial support'. This factor has significant power to achieve other critical success factors. As for the two rightmost elements (establishment of clear measurement of success & recognition of project team), they have no power to achieve other critical success factors. Therefore, they shouldn't be given priority. Furthermore, Figure 1 shows a loop existing between two CSFs. The loop exists in the fourth stage box comprising two system elements: factor 1 (a skilful team) and factor 6 (sharing high-quality information). This box means that the achievement of 'a skilful team' significantly helps to achieve 'sharing high-quality information' and the achievement of 'sharing high-quality information' significantly helps to achieve 'a skilful team'. The loop reveals the systemic nature of CSFs which is a component leading to complexity.

The model structured in Figure 1 is not aimed at establishing universal laws. The IM methodology emphasizes learning and consensus. Through the IM process, the participants learn why others view the problems in different ways. The interactive process of building a model enhances the consensus among the relevant stakeholders. Because the environment and perceptions might change over time, the built model serves as the starting point for iterative learning.

5 Conclusions

This paper demonstrates how IM can be used for identifying/prioritizing CSFs. The output of the IM process is a digraph depicting the holistic relationship between the identified CSFs. This output is not visible in the methods frequently used for identifying CSFs in the surveyed literature, such as interview, questionnaire survey, and statistical analysis. In order to pick out the CSFs that can generate the greatest leverage, this paper proposes to use the contextual relationship 'help to achieve' for modelling. The model constructed in Figure 1 demonstrates the ripple effect of 'help to achieve' between the identified CSFs. In addition to the 'help to achieve' relationship, the foregoing paragraphs argue that 'inhibiting' relationship might exist between the CSFs as well. For example, assuming 'firmly adhering to the scope of work' and 'customer support' are both critical success factors. The success factor 'firmly adhering to the scope of work' might inhibit 'customer support'. 'Firmly adhering to the scope of work' implies the rejection of all customers' requests for the change in the scope of work, including minor variations. It is unlikely to obtain support from customers if their requests for minor changes are completely rejected. The IM can be further used to structure the 'inhibiting' relationship between CSFs to broaden the spectrum of appreciating CSFs. However, IM is a methodology anchored in soft systems thinking. Its inquiry process is to pursue learning and consensus among the stakeholders, rather than eternal laws.

References

1. N. DS, S. Thomas, Success factors of public funded R&D projects, *Current science* **108**(3):357-363 (2015)
2. S. Luthra, D. Garg, A. Haleem, Critical success factors of green supply chain management for achieving sustainability in Indian automobile industry, *Production planning & control* **26**(5):339-362 (2015)
3. T.D. Cochrane, Critical success factors for transforming pedagogy with mobile web 2.0, *British journal of educational technology* **45**(1):65-82 (2014)
4. J.N. Warfield, A.R. Cárdenas, *A handbook of interactive management*. Ames: Iowa State University Press (1994)
5. D.R. Daniel, Management information crisis. *Havard business review* **39**(5):111-121 (1961)
6. J.F. Rockart, Chief executives define their own data needs, *Havard business review* **57**(2):81-93 (1979)
7. J.K. Pinto, D.P. Slevin, Critical factors in successful project implementation, *IEEE transactions on engineering management* **34**(1):22-27 (1987)
8. A. Mahmood, F. Asghar, B. Naoreen, "Success factors on research projects at university" an exploratory study, *Procedia social and behavioral sciences* **116**:2779-2783 (2014)
9. S. Sahney, Critical success factors in online retail - an application of quality function deployment and interpretive structural modeling, *International journal of business information* **3**(1):144-163 (2008)
10. V.A. Cooper, The critical success factors method: a review and practical example, *International conference on information resource* (2008)
11. D. Baccarini, *Critical success factors for projects*, ANZAM Conference, Western Australia, (2003)
12. A. Shenhar, O. Levy, D. Dvir, Mapping the dimensions of project success, *Project management journal* **28**(2):5-13 (1997)
13. M.H. Shah, F.A. Siddiqui, Organisational critical success factors in adoption of e-banking at the Woolwich bank, *International journal of information management* **26**(6):442-456 (2006)
14. D. Dvira, S. Lipovetskya, A. Shenharb, A. Tishlerc, In search of project classification: a non-universal approach to project success factors, *Research policy* **27**(9):915-935 (1998)
15. D.K.H. Chua, Y.C. Kog, P.K. Loh, Critical success factors for different project objectives, *Journal of construction engineering and management* **125**(3):142-150 (1999)
16. J.N. Warfield, *Social systems: planning, policy and complexity*, New York: Wiley (1976)

17. M. Nthunya, N.T. Tuan, C. Shaw, I. Jay, A systemic exploration of Lesotho© basic education through Interactive Management, *Systemic practice and action research* **30**(3):257-276 (2017)
18. N.T. Tuan, A systemic inquiry into the AIDS epidemic in the Western Cape of South Africa through Interactive Management, *Systemic practice and action research* **31**(4):421-435 (2018)
19. S. Tripathy, S. Sahu, P.K. Ray, Interpretive structural modelling for critical success factors of R&D performance in Indian manufacturing firms, *Journal of modelling in management* **8**(2):212-240 (2013)
20. D.K. Yadav, A. Barve, Analysis of critical success factors of humanitarian supply chain: an application of Interpretive Structural Modeling, *International journal of disaster risk reduction* **12**:213-225 (2015)
21. G. C. Alexander, Interactive management: an emancipatory methodology, *Systemic practice and action research* **15**(2):111-122 (2002)
22. M.C. Jackson, *Systems thinking: creative holism for managers*, Chichester: Wiley (2003)

Predicting the length of a post-accident absence in construction with boosted decision trees

Anna Krawczyńska-Piechna[1]*

[1]Warsaw University of Technology, Faculty of Civil Engineering, Mechanics and Petrochemistry, 17 Łukasiewicza St., Płock, Poland

Abstract. Work safety control and analysis of accidents during construction performance are one of the most important issues of construction management. The paper focuses on post-accident absence as an element of occupational safety management. Somehow, the length of the post-accident absence can be treated as an indicator of building performance safety. The paper attempts to answer the question of whether it is possible to use boosted classifier ensembles to predict the post-accident absence length using a small set of historical observations, and which classification algorithm is the most promising to solve the prediction problem. It also proves that there is a dependence between the length of the post-accident absence and the cause of the accident or working conditions The choice of boosted algorithms is not accidental. Thanks to the use of aggregation methods it is possible to build classifiers that predict precisely and do not require any initial data treatment, which simplifies the prediction process significantly. The model of the prediction problem has been clarified. To identify the most promising classifier ensemble the prediction accuracy measures of selected classification algorithms were analyzed. The data used to build models was gathered on national (Polish) construction sites.

Keywords: classifier ensembles, post-accident absence, boosting

1 Introduction

An accident at work is defined in ESAW (European Statistics on Accidents at Work) methodology as a discrete occurrence during work which leads to physical or mental harm. Fatal accidents at work are those that lead to the death of the victim within one year, while non-fatal accidents at work collected within ESAW [1, 2] are those that imply at least four full calendar days of absence from work. For many years, in a majority of EU Member States, the highest incidence of accidents has been reported for persons employed in construction. In addition, for decades, more than half of all absence days registered are concentrated in only

* Corresponding author: Anna.Krawczynska@pw.edu.pl

three sectors of economic activity: manufacturing, construction and wholesale and retail trade. According to ILO [3] report, averagely, every 10 minutes one construction worker bears death during his work. This puts the construction industry at the head of the most hazardous professions basically due to the high variability of working conditions.

Accident statistics are being gathered and analyzed in all countries – in Poland by GUS (Main Statistical Office), in Europe by Eurostat, worldwide by ILO. However, collecting accidents' statistics itself is not the essence of the problem; it is identifying cause-and-effect relationships, the most common accidents' scenarios, factors affecting the severity of accidents, and occupational groups burdened with the highest risk of an accident. In Poland, such studies were conducted by Hoła's team, who developed computer knowledge database and a mathematical model of an accident event development in the construction industry [4, 5]. In turn, Drozd [6, 7] analyzed the costs of accidents and the length of a post-accident absence. A study on the above-mentioned papers and global research carried out by Saiful, Razwanul and Tarek [8], Mistikoglu et al. [9], Chua and Goh [10], or Chan, Leung and Liu [11] indicate that there is a strong need to build models of advisory systems supporting H&S management in its various aspects. Such systems should be effective, easy to use, and predict precisely with the historical data.

The paper matches up with work safety modelling problems. It attempts to answer the question whether it is possible to use boosted decision trees (a selected type of classifier ensembles) to predict the post-accident absence length using historical observations, and which algorithm is the most promising to apply in the prediction problem.

1.1 Why the post-accident absence and classifier ensembles?

The paper focuses on post-accident absence as an element of occupational safety management. According to Drozd [6], the length of the post-accident absence can be treated as an indicator of building performance safety. It is strongly affected by the working experience of the injured and the size of the company. In Polish conditions, the absence decreases with the increasing size of the company, which proves that larger construction companies pay more attention to works safety.

To solve the prediction problem classifier ensembles are suggested. In contrast to other prediction methods, classifier ensembles consist in building different models of the same phenomenon and then combining their judgments [12, 13]. The multi-model supervised learning in statistical data analysis has been used successfully in picture recognition, medical and biological sciences, customer segmentation, business modelling, etc. However, it is still less popular in project and construction planning, which is a pity, because aggregation algorithms, especially those based on decision trees or random forests, as Koronacki and Ćwik [14] claim, are thought to be the most effective classifiers. They do not require any initial data treatment, pre-processing, or analysis, which simplifies the prediction process significantly. They can also be used in case of missing data, what happens when collecting information on the construction site.

2 Mathematical model of the prediction problem

To predict the length of the post-accidence absence let's consider set U containing N observations which are different accidents at work. Each observation is described by a vector of attributes $[x_{i1}, x_{i2}, \ldots, x_{iL}, y_i]$. There are two kinds of attributes: predictors (called the input data) $X_1, \ldots, X_L$ and one target attribute Y (called the output data). Variables $x_{i1}, x_{i2}, \ldots, x_{iL}$, y_i describe attributes' values for the observation i ($i = 1,2,\ldots N$). The value of the target attribute is a class label. Therefore, set U can be defined as (1):

$$\left[x_i, y_i\right]_{N\times(L+1)} = \begin{bmatrix} \overset{X_1}{x_{11}} & \cdots & \overset{X_L}{x_{1L}} & \overset{Y}{y_1} \\ x_{21} & \cdots & x_{2L} & y_2 \\ \cdots & \cdots & \cdots & \cdots \\ x_{N1} & \cdots & x_{NL} & y_N \end{bmatrix}. \qquad (1)$$

Predictors are the circumstances of the accident. They are usually recorded to the accident report, and these are: the size of the company (the level of employment), work experience of the injured, type of work performed by the injured just before the accident, source of the accident, mechanization of works performed by the injured just before the accident. The target attribute is the length of the post-accident absence. The goal of the classification problem is to construct, using the historical data, a mathematical model that predicts the class of the unlabeled examples. This means that the dependence between the length of post-accident absence Y and accident's circumstances $\boldsymbol{X}=[X_1,\ldots, X_L]$ is being sought.

Classification can be done using a single classifier or a classifier ensemble, where a variety of classifiers (either different types of classifiers or different instantiations of the same classifier) are pooled before a final decision is made. Intuitively and mathematically, classifier ensembles provide an extra degree of freedom in the classical variance tradeoff, allowing solutions that would be difficult or impossible to reach with a single classifier [15]. There are several methods of combining classifiers: bagging (bootstrap aggregation), boosting, stacking, etc. In the present paper boosting technique is being analyzed. In this technique, learners are learned sequentially with early learners fitting simple models to the data. The training set used for each member of the series is chosen based on the performance of the earlier classifier in the series [16]. Observations wrongly classified by a single classifier receive a higher weight in order to be chosen to the next training set, so the algorithm is 'forced' to learn using them. The final classifier arises as a result of weighted component voting.

To build prediction models the data collected on 87 different construction sites in Poland and presented by Drozd [6] was used. The information about accidents was obtained from the statistical accident reports made after each accident. The observed predictors and the range of their historical values are collected in Table 1.

Table 1. Predictors and their historical values.

Predictor's name	Type of predictor's value	Observed predictors' values
company size (the level of employment)	numeric (number of company's employees)	from 4 to 241
experience of the injured workers	Numeric (number of years of work in construction)	from 1 to 16
type of work performed by the injured just before the accident	binary	1 in case of work at heights, 0 in other cases
the source of the accident	binary	1 – if the accident was caused by the worker himself (worker's psycho-physical state or improper behaviour, incl. not using protective equipment),

		0 – if the accident was caused by inappropriate workplace organisation and improper protection of the workplace
the state of mechanization of works performed by the injured just before the accident	binary	1 – if work was performed with equipment being moved or with a machine in motion, 0 – in other cases

In the examined data collection the target value (the length of the post-accident absence) varied between 2 and 29 days, while its mean value was 24.4 days and the standard deviation was 5.9 days. It should be mentioned here that, in Poland, if you are absent from work for more than 30 days, you are directed to repeat detailed medical examinations before returning to work. Therefore, for minor injuries, 29 or 30 days are usually the highest values. The problem that is being discussed and proposed methodology of its solution is of a discriminatory type. Therefore, the length of absence was divided into 6 separate classes (intervals): 0-5 days, 6-10 days, 11-15 days, 16-20 days, 21-25 days and 26-30 days.

3 The experiment

To answer the question of whether it is possible to use boosted decision trees to predict the post-accident absence length, and what is the prediction accuracy, two aggregation algorithms were examined: AdaBoost.M1 and Logit Boost. Five different classifiers were tested:

- Decision Stump – a weak, one-node decision tree,
- random tree classifier – a class for constructing a tree that considers randomly chosen attributes at each node and performs no pruning,
- J48 tree – a class for generating an unpruned or a pruned C4.5 decision tree,
- LMT tree – a classifier for building logistic model trees, which are classification trees with logistic regression functions at the leaves; the algorithm can deal with binary and multi-class target variables, numeric and nominal attributes and missing values;
- REPT tree – a fast decision tree learner, which builds a decision tree using information gain and prunes it using reduced-error pruning (with backfitting).

To obtain training sets it was acted in two ways: 70% dataset split and cross-validation with a different number of folds (incl. leave-one-out cross-validation) were performed. The maximum number of iterations was set to 100 and no resampling was allowed. All the calculations were performed in WEKA 3.8. environment.

The best predicting algorithms are gathered in Table 2. The prediction accuracy is a percentage of correctly classified instances, while MAE stands for a mean absolute error.

Table 2. Comparison of the prediction accuracy obtained with different ensembles.

Classifier	Max. prediction accuracy of a single classifier	Aggregation algorithm	Max. prediction accuracy of a classifier ensemble	MAE
Decision Stump	58,6%	AdaBoost.M1	65,3%	0,23
		LogitBoost	77,0%	0,08
LMT	74,7%	AdaBoost.M1	75,8%	0,11
J48	72,4%	AdaBoost.M1	77,0%	0,08
Random tree	73,6%	LogitBoost	77,0%	0,08
REPT tree	69,0%	AdaBoost.M1	79,3%	0,12
		LogitBoost	79,3%	0,16

4 Discussion and conclusions

Accuracy measures for different ensembles and models built in Weka indicate that, whatever the loss function is, logit (LogiBoost algorithm) or exponential (AdaBoost.M1), classifier ensembles, as expected, provide better prediction accuracy than a single decision tree. The best improvement is observed for the weak Decision Stump classifier. Better prediction (at 81,6%) was obtained only with Random Committee aggregation algorithm and Random Tree classifier being aggregated, which was a result of supplementary calculations. Similar prediction accuracies, ca. 75-80%, were achieved within Random Forest method and for different bagging ensembles. It means that the value of ca. 80% accuracy is a ceiling value for the data being analyzed, whatever the aggregation method is. It's not bad but it's not excellent either. Moreover, when analyzing the confusion matrix and detailed accuracy measures, such as the F-measure and PRC Area, see Fig. 1, it was noted that the prediction accuracy for classes 0-5 and 6-10 is very low, regardless of the aggregation algorithm. Then, in the course of further research and in order to build a reliable decision model it is necessary to expand the knowledge database with observations for which the post-accident absence varies between 0 and 10 days.

```
Classifier output
Number of performed iterations: 100


Time taken to build model: 0.84 seconds

=== Stratified cross-validation ===
=== Summary ===

Correctly Classified Instances          67               77.0115 %
Incorrectly Classified Instances        20               22.9885 %
Kappa statistic                          0.6205
Mean absolute error                      0.075
Root mean squared error                  0.2698
Relative absolute error                 35.3778 %
Root relative squared error             83.5934 %
Total Number of Instances               87

=== Detailed Accuracy By Class ===

                 TP Rate  FP Rate  Precision  Recall   F-Measure  MCC      ROC Area  PRC Area  Class
                 0,867    0,190    0,830      0,867    0,848      0,678    0,849     0,806     26-30
                 0,571    0,013    0,800      0,571    0,667      0,653    0,930     0,538     16-20
                 0,000    0,012    0,000      0,000    0,000      -0,017   0,782     0,276     0-5
                 0,714    0,153    0,690      0,714    0,702      0,557    0,798     0,709     21-25
                 1,000    0,012    0,800      1,000    0,889      0,889    1,000     1,000     11-15
                 0,000    0,000    0,000      0,000    0,000      0,000    0,849     0,071     6-10
Weighted Avg.    0,770    0,149    0,752      0,770    0,759      0,623    0,845     0,742

=== Confusion Matrix ===

  a  b  c  d  e  f   <-- classified as
 39  0  0  6  0  0 |  a = 26-30
  1  4  0  2  0  0 |  b = 16-20
  0  1  0  0  1  0 |  c = 0-5
  7  0  1 20  0  0 |  d = 21-25
  0  0  0  0  4  0 |  e = 11-15
  0  0  0  1  0  0 |  f = 6-10
```

Fig. 1. Classifier output for LogitBoost algorithm and Random Tree as a base classifier – an extract from Weka application window view.

The research proved that there is a strong dependence between the length of the post-accident absence and selected accident's circumstances. It also proved that classifier ensembles based on boosting algorithms are a valuable tool to support the prediction of the length of the post-accident absence, even if the set of historical data used to learn the classifier is relatively small or there is data missing. The most time-effective algorithms: boosted J48 decision tree and Decision Stump will be analyzed in further research.

Reference

1. European Statistics on Accident at Work (ESAW), *Summary methodology. Eurostat Methodologies and Working Papers* (Publications Office of the European Union, Luxembourg, 2013)
2. European Statistics on Accident at Work (ESAW), Accidents at work statistics (2016), http://ec.europa.eu/eurostat/statistics-explained/index.php?title=Accidents_at_work_statistics
3. International Labor Organization (ILO), A Vision for Sustainable Prevention, XX World Congress on Safety and Health at Work, Global Forum for Prevention, 24-27 August 2014, Frankfurt, Germany (2014)
4. B. Hoła, M. Szóstak, Analysis of the State of the Accident Rate in the Construction Industry in European Union Countries, Arch. Civ. Eng. **61(4)**, 13-34 (2015)
5. M. Szóstak, *Modelling of the development of an accident situation in the construction industry*, PhD Thesis (Wroclaw University of Technology, Wroclaw, 2017)
6. W. Drozd, *Regression analysis of accident absenteeism and variables describing working conditions* (Cracow University of Technology Publishing, Cracow, 2015)
7. W. Drozd, Analysis of Cost Regression and Post-Accident Absence, AIP Conference Proceedings **1863(1)**, 230004 (2017)
8. M. Saiful, I. Razwanul, M. Tarek, Safety Practices and Causes of Fatality in Building Construction Projects: A Case Study for Bangladesh, Jordan J. Civ. Eng. **11 (2)**, 267-278 (2017)
9. G. Mistikoglu, I.H. Gerek, E. Erdis, P.E. Mumtaz Usmen, H. Cakan, E.E. Kazan, Decision tree analysis of construction fall accidents involving roofers, Expert Syst. Appl. **42(4)**, 2256-2263 (2015)
10. D.H.K. Chua, Y.M. Goh, Incident Causation Model for Improving Feedback of Safety Knowledge, J. Constr. Eng. Manag. **130(4)**, 542-551 (2004)
11. I.Y.S. Chan, M.Y. Leung, A.M.M. Liu, Occupational health management system: A study of expatriate construction professionals, Accid. Anal. Prev. **93**, 280-290 (2016)
12. M. Walesiak, E. Gatnar, *Data analysis in R* (in Polish) (PWN, Warsaw, 2009)
13. E. Gatnar, *Multi-model approach in discrimination and regression* (in Polish) (PWN, Warsaw, 2009)
14. J. Koronacki, J. Ćwik, *Statistical learning systems* (in Polish) (Akademicka Oficyna Wydawnicza Exit, Warsaw, 2008)
15. N.C. Oza, K. Tumer, Classifier ensembles: Select real-world applications, Inform. Fusion, **9(1)**, 4-20 (2008)
16. D. Opitz, R. Maclin, Popular Ensemble Methods: An Empirical Study, Int. J. Artif. Intell. Res. **11(2)**, 267-278 (1999)

Rough Sets and DEA — a hybrid model for technology assessment

Ewa Chodakowska[1*], and *Joanicjusz* Nazarko[1]

[1] Bialystok University of Technology, Faculty of Engineering Management, Wiejska 45A, 15-351 Bialystok, Poland

Abstract. Technology management in complex ecosystems requires advanced technology assessment tools. Data Envelopment Analysis (DEA) is a powerful tool for a multi-criteria comparative performance assessment of different objects (Decision Making Unit — DMU) in the same class. However, the DEA method is capable of adequately differentiating DMUs only when the number of analysed criteria is a few times less than the number of DMUs. Application of DEA in technology assessment requires prior data redundancy reduction due to the multiplicity of technology assessment criteria. The literature suggests various approaches to limiting the cardinality of the criteria sets for the performance analysis using the DEA method. One of the popular approaches is to create synthetic criteria by means of the Principle Component Analysis (PCA). This paper, in turn, proposes a sophisticated rough sets concept. Due to the nature of technology analysis, namely, a small number of objects and many criteria with linguistic values, the proposed approach based on the concept of rough sets seems to be appropriate.

1 Introduction

The primary goal of technology assessment is to identify technologies that can generate the highest economic and/or social benefits to prioritise future investments. Technology assessment is a prospective activity that allows selecting the research and innovation projects which may translate into faster development of regions. At the enterprise level, proper management of technologies is the basis for building a long-term competitive advantage, determining the ability to sustain development. The importance of the problem of proper prioritization of technology means that different approaches, methods and tools are being developed in the area of technology assessment [1-3].

The discussion on the portfolio of methods with the potential to be used in technology assessment is the subject of many publications: [4-7]. One of the most popular typologies presented Popper (2008) [8] who proposed a typology of 33 foresight methods: quantitative, qualitative, mixed, and exploratory or normative. Cagnin *et al.* (2013) [9] suggest combining methods traditionally classified as quantitative with qualitative due to the fact that qualitative may ensure greater involvement of potential stakeholders, while the quantitative higher objectivity of the assessment. Triangulation understood as the integration of various types

* Corresponding author: e.chodakowska@pb.edu.pl

of information and techniques is indicated as an approach with higher value in use for decision-makers. However, the review of foresight projects shows the domination of quality methods (see: [10, 8, 10-11]). In the implemented foresight projects, one of the most frequently used methods was the Delphi method [12-14].

Data Envelopment Analysis (DEA) is a powerful tool for a multi-criteria comparative performance assessment of different objects (Decision Making Unit — DMU), and it is widely used for enterprises, non-profit organisations and systems' evaluation. A few published applications also indicate its legitimacy and suitability for technology assessment. However, DEA is still underused for technology management. Among the published works, significant numbers concern the assessment of technology considering the need for sustainable development, utilising the advantage of DEA to include information on undesirable effects of technology development. For example, Kwon *et al.* (2017) [15] assessed European countries regarding green-energy technology using a two-stage DEA evaluating energy generation with regards to C02. Environmental performance of European countries was also of the object interest in Chodakowska and Nazarko (2017) work [16].

Sueyoshi and Goto (2014) [17] examined the corporate sustainability of the Japanese industrial sector. Fan *et al.* (2015) [18] assessed the potential efficiency of twenty CO2 utilisation technologies in China. Shabani and Saen (2014) [19] analysed eco-efficient technologies of cooling towers in a power plant. Liu *et al.* (2013) [20] considered eco-efficiency of water systems in 31 provinces, regions, and municipalities in China.

There are also works on technology analysis by DEA, which consider non-ecological criteria. Lee *et al.* (2013) [21] used fuzzy AHP and DEA to prioritise R&D resources in energy technologies to establish the strategy against high oil prices. Lee *et al.* (2008) [22] set R&D priorities in technology foresight context. Yu and Lee (2013) [23] presented combining scores calculation using DEA and AHP for clustering similar technologies established based on required input resources to select promising emerging nanotechnology.

Numerous works are available demonstrating new approaches or models of DEA in the context of technology analysis. Amin and Emrouznejad (2013) [24] proposed a new non-iterative DEA on the dataset of robot selection from [25]. Earlier, using the same data set, Alinezhad *et al.* (2011) [26] proposed input-oriented DEA CCR multiple-criteria decision-making (MCDM) model. The dataset from [27] used Saen (2009) [28] to demonstrate an assurance region-nondiscretionary factor-imprecise DEA (AR-NF-IDEA) models for technology analysis.

In the technology analysis, it is necessary to consider many stakeholders and many aspects of the assessment. The criteria taken into account in the analysis of technologies always result from the context of the assessment and are implied by the subject and field of analysis. The challenge of the data aggregation stage is to reach a consensus on the weights of individual criteria or areas that will balance different opinions, values, needs. Klincewicz and Manikowski (2013) [29] developed a set of 184 detailed evaluation criteria, divided into 12 thematic groups: innovation, competitiveness, strategy, organisation–supplier experience, the importance of technology for the organisation–supplier, marketing, technology applications, technical aspects, production technologies, patent protection, social and ethical aspects, and ecology. In the situation of a specific assessment, considering the purpose of the research task, the characteristic of criteria appropriate to the analysed technologies can be selected from the set, e.g. only economic, technological, ecological and social. Nevertheless, the set of criteria is usually quite large (for example, Technology Foresight in the Czech Republic: 35 criteria in 6 fields [30], NT FOR Podlaskie 2020: 21 criteria [31]).

The DEA method is capable of adequately differentiating DMUs only when the number of analysed criteria is a few times less than the number of DMUs. Application of DEA in technology assessment requires a prior data redundancy reduction due to the multiplicity of technology assessment criteria and, sometimes, subtle differences between them. Many approaches have been developed to reduce the number of evaluation criteria in the DEA framework. A popular choice is to create synthetic criteria using the Principle Component Analysis (PCA) [32-33]. Rough sets are primarily used for the induction of decision rules. Revett (2008) [34] discovered decision rules that predict the features influencing the outcomes measured clinically in a patient dataset. Yang and Wu (2009) [35] used the rough sets theory to induce decision rules to set significant symptoms of diseases on the basis of data from a Taiwanese otolaryngology clinic. The analysis of data and setting rules is often preceded by a cardinal reduction of attributes. Dimitras *et al.* (1999) [36] used a rough set to reduce and discriminate between enterprises to predict business failure. Both methods, i.e. PCA and rough sets, can be combined for the simplification of systems by the elimination of attributes whose values have no influence on decisions or do not distinguish objects. An algorithm for feature selection using PCA and rough sets in facial pattern recognition and mammogram experiments was proposed by Swiniarski and Skowron (2003) [37].

The contribution of this article is a proposition of a concept of rough sets to reduce the number of criteria in the context of technology analysis by DEA [38].

2 Methods

The rough set theory introduced by Pawlak (1982) [39] is founded on the assumption that each object is associated with some information, i.e. attributes. An object characterised by the same values of attributes is indiscernible (similar) given the available information [40].

Let $IS = \{U, A\}$ be an information system, where U is non-empty, finite set of objects called the universe, and A — a non-empty finite set of attributes. With every subset of attributes $B \subseteq A$, the indiscernibility relations are defined as:

$$IND(B) = \{(x, x') \epsilon U^2 : \Lambda_{a \in B}\, a(x) = a(x')\} \quad (1)$$

Objects x, x' satisfying relations $IND(B)$ are indiscernible by attributes from B. The partition of U generated by $IND(B)$ is denoted as $U/IND(B)$.

An attribute $a \in B \subseteq A$ is dispensable in B if $IND(B) = IND(B - \{a\})$, otherwise, a is indispensable in B. The minimal subset $B \subseteq A$, such that $IND(B) = IND(A)$, is called a reduct of A. The set of all reducts of A is denoted as $RED(A)$. The intersection of reducts of A is referred to as a core of $B \subseteq A$: $CORE(B) = \cap\, RED(A)$. In other words, the reduct must be an independent set of attributes and must be able to distinguish between objects.

The idea of core and reducts illustrates the definition-based algorithm of discovery in Fig 1.

Input:
Information system $IS = \{U, A\}$
Set of attributes $B \subseteq A: B = \{a_1, a_2, \ldots, a_n\}$
Output:
$CORE(B)$
$RED(B)$
Method:
begin
$CORE(B) = \{\}$
Compute $U/IND(B)$
for each $a_i \in B$
  if $U/IND(B) \,!= U/IND(B - \{a_i\})$ **then** $CORE(B) = CORE(B) \cup \{a_i\}$
  //a_i is indispensable

if $U/IND(B) == U/IND(CORE(B))$ **then** RED(B)=CORE(B) **return**
//retains distinguishability
else
for each $B_i \subseteq B$
if $CORE(B) \subseteq B_i$ **then**
begin
independent=true
for each $a_i \in B_i$
if $U/IND(B_i) == U/IND(B_i - \{a_i\})$ **then** independent=false
if independent and $U/IND(B) == U/IND(B_i)$ **then**
$RED(B) = RED(B) \cup B_i$
end
end

Fig. 1. Definition-based algorithm for the core and reducts

Due to the computational complexity of the definition-based algorithm given above, it is suggested to use the indiscernibility matrix *M(IS)* of the information system: $M(IS) = [c_{ij}]_{nxn}$, where $c_{ij} = \{a \in A: a(x_i) \neq a(x_j), \text{for } i,j = 1,2,\ldots,n\}$. $CORE(B) = \{a \in A: c_{ij} = \{a\} \text{ for } 1 \leq i,j \leq n\}$, consist of the attributes that are single in the matrix. $RED(B)$ is the minimum subset of attributes and has a non-empty intersection with each non-empty element of the matrix *M(IS)*. The problem of finding a minimum or nearly minimum reducts is one of the main problems of the rough set theory. There are many propositions of reduct generations algorithms, both exact and approximate.

The selection of a satisfactory set of attributes from the obtained $RED(B)$ should consider two criteria [36]: the reduct should contain as few attributes as possible, and the reduct should not miss the attributes judged by the decision-makers as the most significant.

The idea of attribute reduction using indiscernibility relations is an interesting proposition of preparing data for prioritising technology. Firstly, a typical task of technology assessment is a selection from a few technologies characterised by a dozen criteria. Attribute reduction methods based on a correlation matrix/covariance (like PCA) is not statistically valid. Secondly, technology assessment is usually done by linguistic descriptions on the scale. The answers are encoded, however, performing arithmetic operations on encoded values is associated with the appearance of the problem of an unintentional change in the relationship between answers.

DEA, originally proposed by Charnes *et al.* (1978) [41], evaluates technologies regarding potential effects/benefits (referred to as outputs in the DEA nomenclature) in relation to expenditure of implementation/development costs (inputs) based on a weighted sum of outputs to inputs. The weights are optimally selected for each unit being assessed to maximise its score using linear programming algorithms. The final score ranges from 0 to 100%.

Considering the most appropriate DEA model among many possibilities and extensions, authors believe that the fuzzy DEA model is worth noting due to the aforementioned need to code linguistic responses. In addition, despite the limitation of the number of criteria using the rough set theory, the number of analysis objects in the technology assessment task will often not be significantly larger than the number of criteria. The result will be in a large subset of effective objects. Therefore, it will be reasonable to use a super-efficiency (SE) model proposed by Andersen and Petersen (1993) [42] to differentiate efficiency units (final efficiency score can exceed 100%).

In summary, to evaluate the technology based on the proposed rough sets concept SE fuzzy DEA model is proposed:

$$min\,\theta_{jo} \tag{2}$$
$$\sum_{j=1,j\neq jo}^{n} \lambda_j \tilde{x}_{ij} \leq \theta_{jo} \tilde{x}_{ijo}, \forall_i$$
$$\sum_{j=1,j\neq jo}^{n} \lambda_j \tilde{y}_{rj} \geq \tilde{y}_{rjo}, \forall_r$$
$$\lambda_j \geq 0, j = 1, \dots, n$$

where:

θ_{jo} — efficiency score of unit j_O,

λ_j — the vector of weighs,

$\tilde{x}_{ij} = \left(x_{ij}^{l}, x_{ij}^{m}, x_{ij}^{u}\right)$ — triangular fuzzy input,

$\tilde{y}_{rj} = \left(y_{rj}^{l}, y_{rj}^{m}, y_{rj}^{u}\right)$ — triangular fuzzy output,

m — the number of fuzzy inputs,

s — the number of fuzzy outputs,

n — the number of DMUs.

And the concept of the α-cut was applied and two models which give upper and lower bounds and triangular fuzzy numbers as proposed by Azadeh and Alem (2010) [43]:

$$min\left(\theta_{jo}\right)_{\alpha}^{U} \tag{3}$$
$$\sum_{j=1,j\neq jo}^{n} \lambda_j\left(\alpha x_{ij}^{m} + (1-\alpha)x_{ij}^{u}\right) \leq \theta_{jo}\left(\alpha x_{ijo}^{m} + (1-\alpha)x_{ijo}^{l}\right)$$
$$\sum_{j=1,j\neq jo}^{n} \lambda_j\left(\alpha y_{rj}^{m} + (1-\alpha)y_{rj}^{l}\right) \geq \left(\alpha y_{rjo}^{m} + (1-\alpha)y_{rjo}^{l}\right)$$
$$\forall\, r, i, \lambda_j \geq 0, j = 1, \dots, n$$
$$min\left(\theta_{jo}\right)_{\alpha}^{L}$$
$$\sum_{j=1,j\neq jo}^{n} \lambda_j\left(\alpha x_{ij}^{m} + (1-\alpha)x_{ij}^{l}\right) \leq \theta_{jo}\left(\alpha x_{ijo}^{m} + (1-\alpha)x_{ijo}^{u}\right)$$
$$\sum_{j=1,j\neq jo}^{n} \lambda_j\left(\alpha y_{rj}^{m} + (1-\alpha)y_{rj}^{u}\right) \geq \left(\alpha y_{rjo}^{m} + (1-\alpha)y_{rjo}^{u}\right)$$
$$\forall\, r, i, \lambda_j \geq 0, j = 1, \dots, n$$

Both the DEA model and the fuzzy membership function have been chosen arbitrarily among many possibilities based on a subjective assessment of the simplicity of the solution.

The used hybrid rough sets, i.e. the fuzzy SE DEA model, for technology assessment scheme consist of a few stages as illustrated in Fig. 2

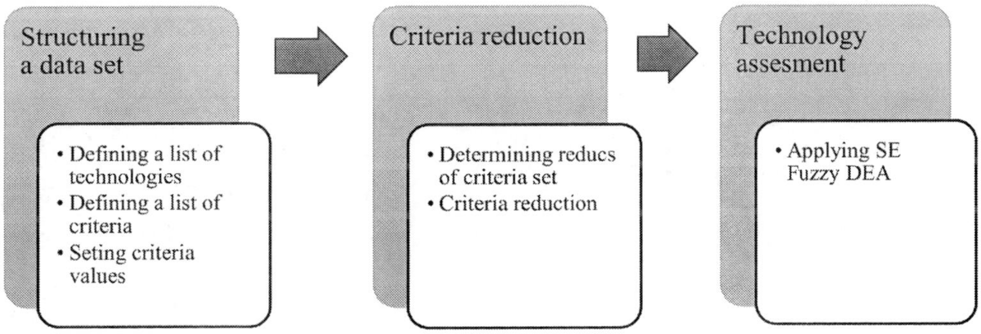

Fig. 2. Scheme of the hybrid rough SE fuzzy DEA model for the technology analysis

The first stage for the structuring of a dataset consists of the identification of available alternative technologies, defining criteria and setting criteria values. The data are collected through interviews with experts. Then obtained dataset is treated as IS and the number of criteria is limited to the use of the rough set rules. The DEA on reduced data allows prioritising technologies.

3 Results and discussions

To illustrate the concept of the rough and fuzzy DEA method, the assumptions for four hypothetical technologies were made. Twelve variables were adopted: six input (resource) and six output (benefits) criteria with a range of values from a set of linguistic terms, respectively: three variants for inputs and two for outputs transcoded into fuzzy numbers. Tables 1 and 2 respectively present that linguistic terms code and random values. Linguistic values represent the answer from the questionnaire determining the cost/resource needed (weak, moderate, strong) and the importance/future positive effect (yes/no).

Table 1. Linguistic terms and appropriated fuzzy numbers

	Linguistic value	Fuzzy numbers		Code
Input	Weakly	(0, 2, 4)	(0, 0.2, 0.4)	0
	Moderately	(3, 5, 7)	(0.3, 0.5 ,0.7)	1
	Strongly	(6, 8, 1)	(0.6, 0.8, 1)	2
Output	Yes	(0, 3, 6)	(0, 0.3, 0.6)	0
	No	(4, 7, 10)	(0.4, 0.7, 1)	1

Table 2. Technology criteria values

	Input						Output					
	i_1	i_2	i_3	i_4	i_5	i_6	o_1	o_2	o_3	o_4	o_5	o_6
T1	1	0	0	1	2	0	0	0	0	0	1	1
T2	1	0	0	1	0	0	1	0	1	0	1	1
T3	2	1	2	2	0	0	1	1	1	0	1	1
T4	0	0	0	0	1	0	0	0	1	0	1	1

Considering the input *IS*, the set of attributes $B = \{i_1, i_2, \dots, i_6\}$ and the set of technologies $U/IND(B) = \{T1, T2, T3, T4\}$, using the algorithm from Fig. 1: $CORE(B) = \{i_5\}$ and $RED(B) = \{i_1, i_5\}, \{i_2, i_5\}, \{i_3, i_5\}, \{i_4, i_5\}$. Analogously for the output IS, $B = \{o_1, o_2, \dots, o_6\}$, $U/IND(B) = \{T1, T2, T3, T4\}$, $CORE(B) = \{o_1, o_2, o_3\}$, $RED(B) = \{o_1, o_2, o_3\}$. Under the assumption of α=0.5, the results of fuzzy SE-DEA for each $RED(B)$ are given in Tables 3 and 4.

Table 3. Upper and lower bounds of efficiency — values

	$\{i_1, i_5\}$ $\{o_1, o_2, o_3\}$		$\{i_2, i_5\}$ $\{o_1, o_2, o_3\}$		$\{i_3, i_5\}$ $\{o_1, o_2, o_3\}$		$\{i_4, i_5\}$. $\{o_1, o_2, o_3\}$	
DMU	Lower	Upper	Lower	Upper	Lower	Upper	Lower	Upper
T1	31.6%	61.4%	33.3%	163.6%	33.3%	245.5%	31.6%	61.4%
T2	93.3%	300.0%	109.0%	600.0%	145.7%	900.0%	93.3%	300.0%
T3	78.7%	1000.0%	63.0%	1000.0%	63.0%	1000.0%	78.7%	1000.0%
T4	133.3%	600.0%	33.3%	300.0%	33.3%	300.0%	133.3%	600.0%

Table 4. Upper and lower bounds of efficiency – statistics

DMU	Average	Lower average	Upper average	Min	Max
T1	82.7%	32.4%	133.0%	31.6%	245.5%
T2	317.7%	110.3%	525.0%	93.3%	900.0%
T3	535.4%	70.8%	1000.0%	63.0%	1000.0%
T4	266.6%	83.30%	450.0%	33.3%	600.0%

Four different proposals of reducts differentiating the input set were obtained. The most adequate subset must be found. It would be reasonable to use expert knowledge. In the presented example, the high dispersion of results indicates a significant uncertainty of the assessment. Considering the average, the best technology is T3; however, due to the large range of the best and worst assessments, technology T2 should also be considered

4 Conclusions

Technology assessment is often based on a large dataset with vague and imprecise data due to the lack of information or human subjective judgment. This paper built a two-stage hybrid rough SE fuzzy DEA model for the technology analysis.

The concept of the rough set theory has been proved to be a useful tool for the analysis of information tables describing a set of objects by multi-valued attributes and has been applied in many applications, mainly in machine-learning expert systems. The rough set theory can be successfully used to reduce the number of dimension criteria and to remove some duplicate, correlated information in complex technology assessment systems. The numerical experiments provided that the hybrid approach integrating DEA and rough set algorithms are a possible solution for the technology analysis task. In the example, the set of 12 criteria was reduced to 5. Using SE fuzzy DEA the range of score for each technology was obtained. One of the most popular fuzzy DEA models was employed to show the limiting of the cardinality of the criteria sets by rough sets concept. Other fuzzy approaches and DEA models can be tested to check the stability of solutions.

In future works, the recommendations and suggestion for reduct selection in DEA context should be developed. In addition, to increase confidence in the results, it is worth comparing and assessing the consistency of results from the proposed approach and other proposition of limitation criteria set. It is also worth mentioning the possibility of combining the PCA method and the rough set concept for the reduction of attributes in the DEA framework.

References

1. A. Kononiuk, A. Gudanowska, (eds), *Kierunki rozwoju nanotechnologii w województwie podlaskim. Mapy. Marszruty. Trendy*, Oficyna Wydawnicza Politechniki Białostockiej, Białystok (2013)
2. J. Nazarko, *Regionalny foresight gospodarczy. Scenariusze rozwoju innowacyjności mazowieckich przedsiębiorstw*, ZPWiM, Warszawa (2013)
3. L. Nazarko, Future-Oriented Technology Assessment, *Procedia Engineering*, **182**, 504-509 (2017)
4. A. L. Porter, Technology Assessment, Impact Assessment, **13(2)**, 135-151 (1995)
5. M. Aaltonen, Evaluation and organization of Futures Research Methodology –V 3.0 [online] http://www.millennium-project.org/millennium/FRM-eval.pdf [11.07.2018] (2009)
6. A. Magruk, Innovative classification of technology foresight methods, Technological and Economic Development of Economy, **17(4)**, 700-715 (2011)
7. K. Halicka, Innovative classification of methods of the Future-oriented Technology Analysis, Technological and Economic Development of Economy, **22(4)**, 574-597, (2016)
8. R. Popper, How are foresight methods selected?, Foresight, **10(6)**, 62-89 (2008)

9. C. Cagnin, A. Havas, O. Saritas, Future-oriented technology analysis: Its potential to address disruptive transformations, Technological Forecasting & Social Change, **80(3)**, 379-385 (2013)
10. A. Kononiuk, A. Sacio-Szymańska, J. Gáspár, How do companies envisage the future? Functional foresight approaches, Engineering Management in Production and Services, **9(4)**, 21-33 (2017)
11. N. Li, K. Chen, M. Kou, Technology foresight in China: Academic studies, governmental practices and policy applications, Technological Forecasting and Social Change, **119**, 246-255 (2017)
12. L. Proskuryakova, Energy technology foresight in emerging economies, Technological Forecasting and Social Change, **119**, 205-210 (2017)
13. B. Förster, Technology foresight for sustainable production in the German automotive supplier industry, Technological Forecasting and Social Change, **92**, 237-248 (2015)
14. M. Choi, H.-L. Choi, H. Yang, Procedural characteristics of the 4th Korean technology foresight, Foresight, **16(3)**, 198-209 (2014)
15. D. S. Kwon, J. H. Cho, S. Y. Sohn, Comparison of technology efficiency for CO_2 emissions reduction among European countries based on DEA with decomposed factors, Journal of Cleaner Production, **151**, 109-120 (2017)
16. E. Chodakowska, J. Nazarko, Environmental DEA Method for Assessing Productivity of European Countries, Technological and Economic Development of Economy, **23(4)**, 589-607 (2017)
17. T. Sueyoshi, M. Goto, Environmental assessment for corporate sustainability by resource utilization and technology innovation: DEA radial measurement on Japanese industrial sectors, Energy Economics, **46**, 295-307 (2014)
18. J.-L. Fan, X. Zhang, J. Zhang, S. Peng, Efficiency evaluation of CO_2 utilization technologies in China: A super-efficiency DEA analysis based on expert survey, Journal of CO_2 Utilization, **11**, 54-62 (2015)
19. A. Shabani, R. F. Saen, A new data envelopment analysis (DEA) model to select eco-efficient technologies in the presence of undesirable outputs, Clean Technologies and Environmental Policy, **16(3)**, 513-525 (2014)
20. Y. Liu., C. Sun, S. Xu, Eco-Efficiency Assessment of Water Systems in China, Water Resource Management, **27(14)**, 4927-4939 (2013)
21. S. K. Lee, G. Mogi, K. S. Hui, A fuzzy analytic hierarchy process (AHP)/data envelopment analysis (DEA) hybrid model for efficiently allocating energy R&D resources: In the case of energy technologies against high oil prices, Renewable and Sustainable Energy Reviews, **21**, 347-355 (2013)
22. H. Lee, C. Lee, H. Seol, Y. Park, On the R&D priority setting in technology foresight: a DEA and ANP approach, International Journal of Innovation and Technology Management, **5(2)**, 201-219 (2008)
23. P. Yu, J. H. Lee, A hybrid approach using two-level SOM and combined AHP rating and AHP/DEA-AR method for selecting optimal promising emerging technology, Expert System with Applications, **40**, 300-314 (2013)
24. G. R. Amin, A. Emrouznejad, A new DEA model for technology selection in the presence of ordinal data, International Journal of Advanced Manufacturing Technology, **65**, 1567-1572 (2013)

25. E. E. Karsak, S. S. Ahiska, Practical common weight multicriteria decision-making approach with an improved discriminating power for technology selection, International Journal of Production Research, **43(8)**, 1537-1554 (2005)
26. A. Alinezhad, A. Makui, R. Kiani Mavi, M. Zohrehbandian, An MCDM-DEA approach for technology selection, Journal of Industrial Engineering International, **7(12)**, 32-38 (2011)
27. M. Khouja, The use of data envelopment analysis for technology selection, Computers & Industrial Engineering, **28(1)**, 123-132 (1995)
28. R. F. Saen, Technology selection in the presence of imprecise data. weight restrictions. and nondiscretionary factors, The International Journal of Advanced Manufacturing Technology, **41(7-8)**, 827-838 (2009)
29. K. Klincewicz, A. Manikowski, *Ocena. rankingowanie i selekcja technologii*, Wydawnictwo Naukowe Wydziału Zarządzania Uniwersytetu Warszawskiego, Warszawa (2013)
30. K. Klusacek, Selection of research priorities – method of critical technologies, Technology Centre of the CAS, [online] (2003) https://www.tc.cz/files/istec_publications/unido-course-critical-technologies-1029-1.pdf [13.07.2018]
31. J. Nazarko, A. Magruk (eds), *Kluczowe Nanotechnologie w gospodarce Podlasia*, Oficyna Wydawnicza Politechniki Białostockiej, Białystok (2013)
32. N. Adler, B. Golany, Evaluation of deregulated airline networks using data envelopment analysis combined with principal component analysis with an application to Western Europe, European Journal of Operational Research, **132(2)**, 260-273 (2001)
33. N. Adler, B. Golany, Including Principal Component Weights to improve discrimination in Data Envelopment Analysis, Journal of the Operational Research Society, **53(9)**, 985-991 (2002)
34. K. Revett, Diagnostic Feature Analysis of a Dobutamine Stress Echocardiography Dataset Using Rough Sets, In: J. F. Peters, A. Skowron, H. Rybiński, eds, *Transactions on Rough Sets IX*, Springer, 318-327 (2008)
35. H.-H. Yang, Ch.-L. Wu, Rough sets to help medical diagnosis – Evidence from a Taiwan's clinic, Expert Systems with Applications, **36**, 9293-9298 (2009)
36. A. I. Dimitras, R. Slowinski, R. Susmaga, C. Zopounidis, Business failure prediction using rough sets, European Journal of Operational Research, **114**, 263-280 (1999)
37. R. W. Swiniarski, A. Skowron, Rough set methods in feature selection and recognition, Pattern Recognition Letters, **24(6)**, 833-849 (2003)
38. E. Chodakowska, Rough and Fuzzy DEA in the Process of Prospective Technology Analysis, In: A. Emrouznejad, and E. Thanassoulis (eds), *Data Envelopment Analysis and Performance Measurement: Recent Developments: Proceedings of the DEA40: International Conference of Data Envelopment Analysis*, April 2018, Aston Business School, Birmingham, UK (2018)
39. Z. Pawlak, Rough sets, International Journal of Information and Computer Science, **11**, 344-356 (1982)
40. Z. Pawlak, A. Skowron, Rudiments of rough sets, Information Sciences, **177**, 3-27 (2007)
41. A. Charnes, W. W. Cooper, E. Rhodes, Measuring the efficiency of decision-making units, European Journal of Operational Research, **2(6)**, 429-444 (1978)

42. P. Andersen, N. C. Petersen, A procedure for ranking efficient units in data envelopment analysis, Management Science, **39(10)**, 1261-1264 (1993)
43. A. Azadeh, S. M. Alem, A flexible deterministic. stochastic and fuzzy Data Envelopment Analysis approach for supply chain risk and vendor selection problem: Simulation analysis, Expert Systems with Applications, **37(12)**, 7438-7448 (2010)

New Strategy for Enhancing Engineering Practical Teaching through the Development of Infrastructure Learning Hub (ILH)

Hesham S. Ahmad[1*], *Wejdan* Abu-Elhaija[1] *and Yousef* Qandoos[1]
[1]Al-Zaytoonah University of Jordan, Faculty of Engineering and Technology,
P.O. Box: 130 Amman 11733, Jordan

Abstract. Site visits to construction projects are considered essential to help engineering students understand many of the topics included in the study courses. Site visits are also important in helping engineering students gain more knowledge about common procedures and materials used during the life-cycle of construction projects, and thus better prepare the undergraduate students for the real work after graduation. However, site visits for undergraduate student groups may include safety risks, in addition to the fact that trainees need to spend a considerably extended period of time for learning during the long life-cycle of construction projects. The aim of this study is to propose a project of a learning centre for engineering students that provides a safe and easy-to-reach site while allowing faster learning of engineering practices. The proposed project is its planning phase and is named Infrastructure Learning Hub (ILH). A questionnaire survey was conducted with 108 under-graduate students from the Faculty of Engineering and Technology at Al-Zaytoonah University of Jordan (ZUJ). The questionnaire aims at revealing the evaluation of the engineering students about the training and site visits system currently applied in the University. Also, the questionnaire seeks the engineering students' opinions about the importance of the proposed ILH and their preferable type for the project. The results of the questionnaires showed high importance for the implementation of the ILH project, and to have better coordination and scheduling for site visits with construction projects and organizations. This study intends to pinpoint the courses which require more practical emphasis in order to improve learning outcomes. The results can be very important for other engineering faculties to enhance the learning process and gain competitive advantages.

Keywords: construction, engineering students, learning, project, safety

* Corresponding author: h.ahmad@zuj.edu.jo

1 Introduction

Site visits to construction projects are essential for undergraduate engineering students to help them to become more familiar with the work environment, and to make them more ready for real work after graduation. Training on construction projects is not only important on the final stages of the engineering study, but it is important from the early stages to improve students' learning and understanding of the different engineering courses and subjects. A trainee needs to wait a full life-cycle of a construction project to go through all the different stages of a project, which is not possible during the limited time period specified for engineering training (about 8 weeks in ZUJ).

In the literature, some projects, especially lab-scale and computerized models, were designed and implemented for the teaching and training of students in specific engineering topics. Some studies have developed models to test the behaviour of different materials when subjected to forces, such as earthquake and wind effects. Other studies have used software programs to build virtual models for teaching students such as Building Information Modeling (BIM) and Revit software [1].

The aim of this research project is to propose a learning and training tool for engineering students to become more familiar with the different stages, tools, procedures and materials of construction projects, in a relatively high level of safety and less time and effort for learning compared with the common training process during the life-cycle of construction projects. Practical engineering exercises can be performed to improve students' understanding of various engineering topics and accelerate learning.

This study recommends designing and developing a construction project model to provide an effective learning tool for many of the engineering courses such as survey, construction materials, engineering drawings, quantity survey, infrastructure networks, concrete design, construction project management, electrical and mechanical systems design etc.

2 Engineering Training Program and Site Visits

The engineering training is a compulsory requirement for the engineering students in all the universities in Jordan. The main aim of the engineering training program is to train the engineering students to practice and apply the knowledge gained during the stages of their study to qualify them for the future career they desire in their speciality of study. The duration of the engineering training is normally 8 weeks, and a student can start training after finishing 3 years of the 5 years of the required engineering study. Normally, a list of qualified companies is approved by the engineering faculty, and the trainees are tested and evaluated by the training companies and by the college training supervisors. Random visits by the supervisors are conducted to ensure the commitment of the trainees.

Normally, site visits during the study semesters are non-compulsory and depend on the availability of projects which are easy to reach and access, and also depend on the motivation of the lecturers. In most of the engineering colleges, site visits are not included in the study plans or course outlines. Sometimes, one or two scientific trips are conducted during the semester which is open to interested students from different stages and enrolled in a different course. These trips either conducted during working days that contradict with the time of classes or during non-working days where many students seem to lack the motivation to attend these trips.

The aim of this study is to apply a project that motivates site visits for engineering students, whether these visits are organized by courses' lecturers or in the shape of students' individual visits.

3 Infrastructure Learning Hub (ILH)

Infrastructure Learning Hub (ILH) is a project proposed to be applied in and sponsored by Al-Zaytoonah University of Jordan. The project will be designed to enhance the engineering training and site visits effectiveness for the students of the different department in the Faculty of Engineering and technology including Civil and Infrastructure Engineering, Electrical Engineering, Mechanical Engineering, Technology of Alternative Energy and Architecture. The project can also attract sponsoring from an interested organization and can provide services to people and organizations from outside the university. In the questionnaire survey of this study, the respondents were asked to choose their preferable shape of the project from the following alternatives:

1. Three-dimensional Virtual Reality (VR) technology to model a construction project, and allow users to go through the different items in the project and investigate its related work methods, tools, materials, tests, etc.
2. An interactive software program that can be accessed through the internet and provide information about construction stages, materials, tools, tests, etc.
3. A mobile application that allows users to go through a construction project and to retrieve useful information about work procedures, tools, materials, tests, etc.
4. Small size models that describe different parts of the construction project and present related information.
5. Real size building, supported by written information and monitors, that the learner can walk through and investigate the different construction stages and related materials, tools, tests, etc.
6. Real size building, supported by an electronic mobile application, that the learner can walk through to identify the different construction stages and items, and the different tools and materials used for the execution of these items. The mobile application provides detailed information for the existing items and materials as needed.

4 Literature Review

A study by Gharehbaghi and McManus [2] has identified important skills and abilities that learners should gain to manage construction projects effectively. The study introduced objectives which are important for construction managers such as the ability to set achievable and effective goals, monitor, and control the project, and ensure delivering work successfully within the constraints of time and budget. To achieve these objectives, construction managers should possess professional skills such as time management, resource management, budgeting, and risk management. According to the study, a successful manager must also know how to give the right task to the correct person, how to involve the client in the stages of the construction project and know the closeout procedure of the project.

Two studies by Cline [3, 4] has identified and discussed teaching strategies of construction project management in higher education. In the first study, Cline [3] has determined key competencies needed by construction project managers. It was found that the five most important skills for effective project management are leadership, construction management, professional and ethical judgement and plan reading.

In the second study by Cline [4], qualitative interview method was conducted with ten current faculty members of U.S. construction management colleges to determine which teaching strategy is the most often used when teaching construction management students.

The teaching strategies used in this study have been developed in the previous study by Pratt [5] who developed a conceptual framework of teaching in higher education. Pratt's study developed five different perspectives on teaching, including Social Reform, Nurturing, Transmission, Apprenticeship and Developmental Perspectives. The results of Cline's study showed that the developmental (i.e. "Teaching must be planned and conducted from the learner's point of view" [5]), and transmission (i.e. "The 'stand and deliver' approach requires the teacher to accurately put forth to the student the content to be delivered" [5]) perspectives were the most commonly used perspectives in teaching. Although the transmission perspective was found to be the most commonly used by the interviewees, they all believed that transmission teaching could be the least effective of all perspectives.

Accreditation standards and criteria for construction education programs were developed by the American Council for Construction Education [6]. These standards emphasize that effective construction management curricula should be responsive to evolving construction knowledge, technologies, and management trends.

5 Related Existing Practices

A study by Magoha [7] has discussed the methods and tools existing at the time of conducting the study to enhance the effectiveness of the training of engineers and technologists. According to the author, the development of new technologies has encouraged the achievement of new engineering training concepts. The study has recommended interactive methods to make engineering teaching and learning more interesting. The study has proposed effective instructional methods for training engineers and technologists, including the computer as an engineering design tool, virtual reality, multimedia (a combination of audio and visual materials), teaching and learning with the internet (e-learning), web-based engineering experiments and modular engineering teaching equipment. The author argued that the effectiveness of the teaching or learning methods to be used depends on the objectives of learning, group size, local constraints, students' abilities, teacher/student preferences, type and level of learning, and availability of time and facilities.

6 Study Objectives

Site visit of construction projects is normally an important practice used to improve understanding of engineering students to many of the topics in the engineering courses. In these visits, students can only see a few stages of the construction processes. To see most of the construction stages, trainees need to spend a long time during the project life-cycle. Also, the site visits can be associated with a high level of safety risk for the large groups of students.

This project aims at proposing a model of a construction project. This model can help to show variable stages, procedures, tools and materials of construction projects effectively with a high level of safety for students' groups. Various exercises and procedures can be applied in this project and many engineering related information can be introduced to help accelerate learning and improve understanding of different engineering topics. Also, the project will provide practical training that makes students more familiar with projects and more ready for work after graduation.

A questionnaire survey was conducted to evaluate the existing procedures and systems followed for engineering training and site visits. Also, the questionnaire assesses the expected usefulness and effectiveness of the proposed project (ILH) in the opinion of the engineering students. It is expected that this project will help educators in the teaching process, and will help students to learn better, faster and safer.

The proposed project (ILH), if applied successfully, can provide competitive advantages for engineering graduates in the engineering industry. The project can improve knowledge and skills for the engineering students to make them more ready for the work after graduation. Also, it will help students to better understand different engineering topics during the different engineering courses.

7 Questionnaire Survey

7.1 Questionnaire Objectives

The main aim of the questionnaire survey is to investigate and evaluate the opinions of engineering students about the engineering training and site visiting procedures currently used in the Faculty of Engineering and Technology in ZUJ, and the opportunity to develop these procedures by proposing a project (ILH) for engineering learning development. The questionnaire is composed of three main sections.

The first section asks respondents to provide their information such as speciality and stage of the study. The second section is dedicated to investigating the opinions of respondents about the effectiveness and sufficiency of the existing engineering training and site visit procedures. This section also includes an open-ended question that asks respondents to provide briefly, according to their opinions, a list of the most important constraints that negatively affect the effective implementation of site visits to construction projects.

Finally, the third section seeks the students' evaluation of the importance of a proposed project (ILH) that should be easy for students to reach and should enhance learning during their engineering study and also to enhance qualification for engineering career after graduation. This section also asks the respondents to select from different alternatives their preferable type for this project, and optionally to provide their additional ideas and suggestions.

7.2 Sample Analysis (Section 1)

From a population of about 1,000 students enrolling in the Faculty of Engineering and Technology, 165 students were contacted that represent about 16.5% of the population. This percentage is greater than the recommended percentage in previous studies [8]. The questionnaire was distributed electronically to students in courses which are normally enrolled by fourth and fifth-year civil engineering students. This student-level of the study was chosen to ensure that the questionnaire respondents have a high level of awareness about the subject of engineering training and site visits.

With a response rate of about 68.5%, 113 students have completed the survey. Five poor responses were rejected, to makes the total number of accepted questionnaires for the analysis equals 108 responses. Most of the accepted respondents (about 95%) are studying civil engineering, and only 5% are studying mechanical and architectural engineering. Also, the majority of the accepted respondents are undergraduate students in the 4th year (60%) and 5th year (33%). The rest of the respondents are graduates (3%), and students in the 3rd year (3%) and 2nd year (1%).

7.3 Evaluation of Existing Procedures (Section 2)

The results of the second section of the questionnaire evaluate the existing adopted training program and assess the importance of site visits during the enrollment in the engineering courses. The results indicated that only about 54% of the respondents are agreeing and strongly agreeing that the training program adopted in the study plan is adequate for providing the knowledge and skills required for effective starting of their career after graduation. Also, only about 50% of the questionnaire respondents feel that the existing training program adequately support the learning and understanding process required during the enrollment in engineering courses.

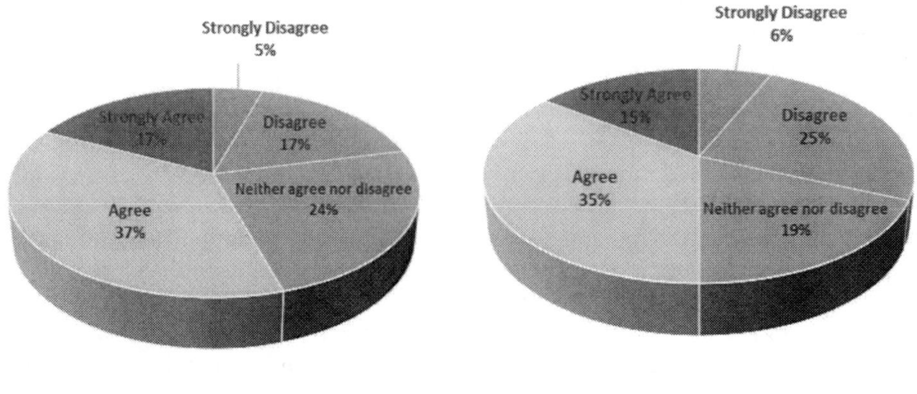

Existing training program is adequate for giving the knowledge and skills required for work after graduation.

Existing training program is adequate for giving the learning and understanding required during course enrollment.

Fig. 1. Adopted Training Program Adequacy for Professional Qualification and Study Learning

Furthermore, the results showed that 98% of the respondents agree and strongly agree that site visits during the enrollment in engineering courses are needed and important for the effective learning and understanding of engineering courses. Only 26% of the respondents feel that the site visits conducted during their enrollment in the engineering courses are adequate for the effective learning and understanding of the course contents.

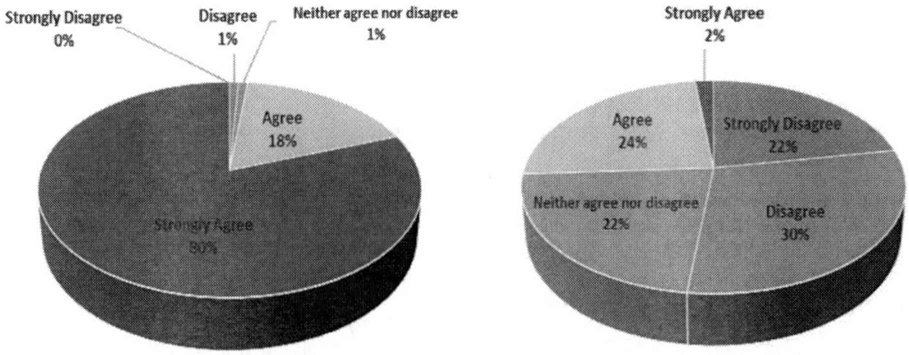

Site visits are needed and important during enrollment in courses for learning and understanding of courses.

Site visits conducted during enrollment in courses are adequate for learning and understanding of courses.

Fig. 2. Importance and Adequacy of Site Visits during Enrollment in Courses

The last question in the second section is an open-ended optional question that asks respondents to briefly list the most important constraints, which in their opinion cause lack of effective site visits during their enrollment in the engineering study. This question was completed by 67 respondents, resulted in 136 points categorized and listed in Table 1. The written constraints by respondents resulted in 28 sub-constraints categorized into five main groups of constraints.

As shown in Table 1, the constraints related to time are the most constraints written repeatedly in the respondents' answers, followed by the constraints related to coordination, and then awareness. Factors such as Time pressure for students during the study semester, time conflict between the course classes and site visits, lack of coordination between the department and engineering organizations, and difficulty of transportation to sites are the most constraining factors discussed by the respondents. Furthermore, factors such as lack of students' awareness and motivation for the importance of engineering site visits, and not including the site visits in course plans and descriptions, are moderately discussed in the responses.

Table 1. Constraints of Site Visits during Enrollment in Courses

Main Constraints		Sub-Constraints	Number of Responses
1. Awareness	1.1.	Student lack awareness and/or interest	7
	1.2.	Student lack of motivation	6
	1.3.	Lecturers lack awareness and/or interest	5
	1.4.	Management lack of awareness and/or interest	4
	1.5.	Projects' managers are unwilling to allow site visitors	3
	1.6.	Difficulty for students to connect the theoretical knowledge with its application in the field	1
	1.7.	Students unawareness of the work terms in projects	1
	1.8.	Site engineers are unwilling to give information	2
		Total=	**29**
2. Coordination	2.1.	Lack of coordination with organizations and projects	15
	2.2.	Difficulty of organizing large number of students	4
	2.3.	Lack of cooperation from students	1
	2.4.	Site visits not included in course plan or syllabus	7
	2.5.	Lack of clear definition and objectives for a site visit	1
	2.6.	Lack of available skilled people to provide information and take responsibility during visit	5
	2.7.	Difficulty of getting management approvals	4
	2.8.	Poor planning beforehand	2
	2.9.	Lack of coordination between students and Instructors	1
		Total=	**40**
3. Time	3.1.	Time pressure for students during semester	17
	3.2.	Time conflict between classes and site visits	15
	3.3.	Need for multiple visits to see variable stages	5
	3.4.	Time pressure for lecturers during semester	3
	3.5.	Time pressure for engineers in projects	1
		Total=	**41**
4. Safety	4.1.	Lack of project safety awareness for students	5
	4.2.	Lack of safety tools	1
	4.3.	Low safety level inside project sites	2
		Total=	**8**

5.	Location	5.1.	Unavailability and difficulty of transportation	10
		5.2.	Cost of transportation	4
		5.3.	Lack of projects inside or near the University	4
			Total=	**18**
			Total of all responses=	**136**

7.4 Importance and Types of the Proposed Project (ILH) (Section 3)

In the third part of the questionnaire, a project (ILH) was proposed as a model that can provide students with important practical information normally learned from engineering site visits and engineering training. The project is supposed to provide a safe site that is easy to reach. One of the expected objectives of this project is to represent variable types of works with its different details and materials for the different items and stages during the construction project life-cycle. This part of the questionnaire survey is dedicated to evaluating the importance of the proposed project and the preferred type for it according to the opinions of engineering students.

The first question in the third section asked the respondents to evaluate the importance of the proposed project (ILH) for students to gain knowledge and skills required for effective starting of specialized engineering jobs. The second section investigates the evaluation of respondents for the importance of the proposed project (ILH) to gain effective learning and understanding during enrolled courses. The results of the two questions, as shown in Figure 4, indicate the high importance of the project (ILH) in the opinions of the engineering students.

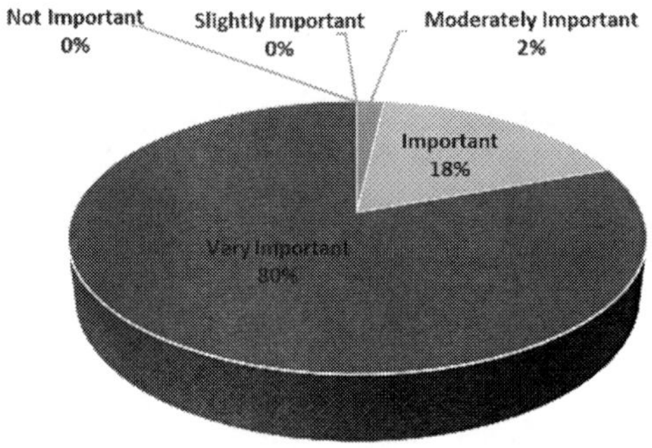

Importance of developing an engineering project (ILH) that helps supporting knowledge and skills required to work effectively after graduation.

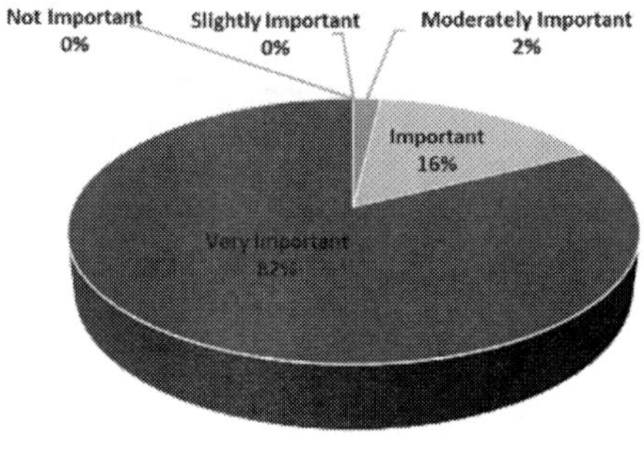

Importance of developing an engineering project (ILH) that helps providing effective learning and understanding in the enrolled courses.

Fig. 3. Importance of ILH for the Engineering Students

Finally, the third question in the third section seeks the preferences of the respondent engineering students for a number of suggested types or forms of the proposed project. The respondents were permitted to choose more than one answer if they have a similar preference for several alternatives. Also, the respondents were asked to ignore the financial factor when they make their selection. Adding other suggested solutions were also enabled for the respondents.

The results, as shown in Figure 5, showed that the most preferable type of the proposed project in the opinions of the questionnaire respondents is to develop a real-size building, supported by electronic application, the learner can walk through it to identify the different construction stages and items, and the different tools and materials used for the execution of these items, accompanied with a mobile application that provides detailed information for items and materials when needed. The second preferable type of the project, as shown in Figure 5, is applying three-dimensional virtual reality technologies to model a construction project, and allow users to go through the different items in the project and investigate its related work methods, tools, materials, tests, etc.

The respondents provided additional comments to their answers such as: "Models that describe the different tests required during the execution of projects can be added to the project", "I suggest to coordinate scheduled and well-organized visits with the help of interested construction organizations to go to a list of projects during important stages of the projects", "I suggest developing a real-size building with every section of the building supporting a specific course", "The building should show the details required to enhance the awareness and understand of the subjects of engineering design", and "This project should be supported with the various materials, tools and modern equipment used in construction projects".

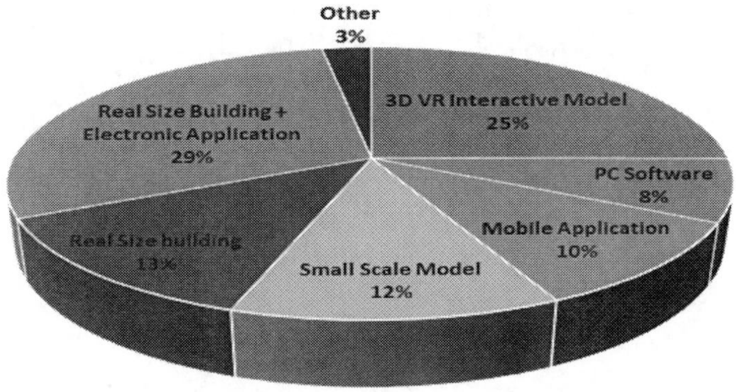

Fig. 4. Types for a Proposed Project for Engineering Learning Selected by Respondents

8 Conclusion

This study has highlighted a proposed project for developing a construction project model named Infrastructure Learning Hub (ILH) dedicated to providing a safe and effective place for students to practice engineering training and site visits. The project should be designed to provide information on the different stages and items of construction projects combined with the needed procedures, tools, equipment, materials and tests. A questionnaire survey was conducted (with a total of 108 accepted responses) to evaluate the existing training system and site visits for engineering students according to their opinions.

Furthermore, the proposed project was introduced to engineering students, and then the students were asked to evaluate the importance of the project and to decide their preferable shape for it. Most of the respondents to the questionnaire are students in the Civil Engineering Department in the 4th and 5th year (final year) of their study.

The conclusion of this study can be summarized as follows:

- About half (50-54%) of the respondents have not agreed that the existing training program is adequate to gain the required knowledge and skill needed for effective learning and understanding the different engineering courses and to effectively start their career after graduation.
- Most of the respondents (98%) have agreed and strongly agreed that site visits to construction projects during their enrollment in engineering courses are needed and important for effective engineering learning and understanding.

- Only, about a quarter of the respondents (26%) have agreed that the site visits conducted during their engineering study are adequate for the effective learning and understanding of engineering courses.
- Investigating the constraints, which cause lack of effective site visits during the engineering study, has shown that the constraints related to time pressure and lack of coordination among management, lecturers, construction organizations, and project staff, are the most critical constraints.
- The results for evaluating the importance of the proposed ILH project for learning showed that most of the respondents (98%) see this project as important and very important for effective learning and understanding during the enrollment in courses, and for gaining the knowledge and skills required for the effective start of their career in engineering.
- Different types were proposed for the learning project (ILH). The most selected type from the alternatives was a real-size building supported by electronic application where the learner can walk through to identify the different construction stages and items, and the different tools and materials used for the execution of these items, supported with a mobile application that provides detailed information for items and materials when needed. The second preferable type of the project is applying three-dimensional virtual reality technology to model a construction project and allow the user to go through the different items in the project and investigate its related work methods, tools, materials, tests, etc.

The results of this study are significant for gaining more effective planning for education and training methods and improving the effectiveness of future engineers in the construction industry. This project is still in its early stages that include analysis of end-users opinions and needs. Future stages will contain deeper planning and details of the project design, implementation and operation

References

1. A. Nejat, M.M. Darwish, T. Ghebrab, *BIM Teaching Strategy for Construction Engineering Students*, ASEE Annual Conference and Exposition, San Antonio, Texas (2012)
2. K. Gharehbaghi, K. McManus, Effective construction management, *Leadership and Management in Engineering*, 3(1): 54-55 (2003)
3. R.C. Cline, *Teaching key competencies of effective construction project managers to adults in higher education*, Thesis (PhD), University of Idaho, Moscow, Idaho (2008)
4. R.C. Cline, *Effective Construction Management Teaching Strategies*, 118th ASEE Annual Conference and Exposition, June 26-29, 2011, Vancouver, BC, Canada (2011)
5. D., Pratt, *Five perspectives on teaching in adult and higher education*, Krieger Publishing Company, Malabar, Florida (1998)
6. American Council for Construction Education – ACCE, *Standards and criteria for accreditation of postsecondary construction education degree programs*, Document 103 (2004)
7. P.W. Magoha, Effective methods and tools for training engineers and technologists: regional trends, *World Transactions on Engineering and Technology Education*, 1(2): 209-216 (2002)
8. M. Al-Hmadani, A. Al-Jadri, A. Qandaleje, A. Bani-Hani, Abu-Zenh, *Scientific research methods – fundamentals of scientific research. First edition*, Amman, Jordan (2006)

MATEC Web of Conferences **312**, 02002 (2020) https://doi.org/10.1051/matecconf/202031202002
EPPM2018

Attributes That Determine the Building Information Modelling Capability Maturity of Quantity Surveying Practice

Abdul-Majeed Mahamadu[1*], *Lamine* Mahdjoubi[1], *Patrick* Manu[2], and *Clinton* Aigbavboa[3]

[1]University of the West of England, Frenchay Campus, Bristol, BS16 1QY, United Kingdom
[2]University of Manchester, The School of Mechanical, Aerospace & Civil Engineering, Manchester M13 9PL, United Kingdom
[3]University of Johannesburg, The Faculty of Engineering and the Built Environment, Johannesburg, South Africa

Abstract. With more than 80% of all construction projects overrunning their budget, there is a need for more efficient management of the estimated 10% of Gross Domestic Product (GDP) that is expended annually on construction across the world. It has been proposed that better information and data management through Building Information Modelling (BIM) will lead to cost savings and greater predictability. Notwithstanding the role of quantity surveyors (QS) in modelling and managing construction cost, they remain among the least capable of assimilating BIM into their existing traditional processes. Despite the increasing need for BIM capability assessments for projects, there remains, no tool specifically developed for assessing QS firm's BIM utilisation capacity or performance. As a result, it is unclear the attributes that indicate BIM capability of QS firms as well as QS practices on projects. This study sought to address this through a review of BIM capability assessment frameworks in order to ascertain their suitability for QS practices. An expert focus group discussion was then used to identify peculiar attributes suitable for QS BIM capability assessment as a precursor to the development of a comprehensive model of QS BIM capability maturity. Findings reveal that most QS BIM capability attributes relate to processes including criteria for effective information definition and data management such that they are consistent with QS measurement standards. The BIM competence of staff also emerged as one of the key attributes highlighting the need for QSs to improve their knowledge, skills and experience in the application of BIM amidst current low levels of adoption. The proposed attributes would assist the development of performance and maturity indicators that would help QS firms better understand their own capability as well as the requirements for delivering costing services through BIM on projects.

Keywords: costing, information modelling, quantity surveying, projects, competence, maturity

* Corresponding author: abdul.mahamadu@uwe.ac.uk

1 Introduction

The majority (circa 80%) of construction projects overrun their budget [1, 2], thereby making it imperative for more efficient management of financial resources expended annually for the delivery of construction. Global initiatives on IT adoption for construction envisage significant cost savings from the implementation of novel digitally driven processes. For instance in the UK Government hopes to achieve up to 33% cost savings through the digitisation of processes with Building Information Modelling (BIM) [3]. Notwithstanding the role of Quantity Surveyors (QS) in modelling and managing construction cost, they remain among the least capable of assimilating BIM into their existing traditional processes: only a meagre 10% of the mostly SME QS firms are reported to be using digitised BIM-based practices[4]. Despite the increasing need for BIM capability assessments for projects, there remains, no tool specifically developed for assessing QS firm's BIM utilisation capacity or performance. Emerging tools and frameworks have been designed for organisations with high design responsibility (such as architects) rather than for QS who directly manage and control spending on projects [5-12].

The aim of this study is, therefore, to develop a BIM capability assessment framework specifically for QS BIM utilisation, benchmarking and performance. This will aid the development of a set of metrics for evaluating the ability of QSs to deliver services through BIM as well as serve as an evaluation tool to aid alignment of QS BIM implementation with performance expectations. In this article, the attributes that determine a QS organisation's BIM capability is explored as a precursor for the development of a comprehensive capability maturity model.

2 Quantity Surveying Practice and the Use of BIM and Related Technologies

The major role of QSs in construction projects is costing and managing cost-related activities, this requires expertise in the measurement of quantities of building elements with procedures such as quantity take-off (QTO), cost modelling as well as other contract administration and commercial management functions. The traditional approaches to QS rely on traditional paper-based tools [13, 14]. The potential of BIM to create efficient working approach among construction professionals has however been proven by the wide adoption of 3D BIM by architects and engineers in optimising design visualization and evaluation of design choices [15]. Building contractors have also adopted 4D BIM for construction planning and scheduling but the adoption of 5D (use of BIM for costing and commercial applications) is relatively low [4]. According to Ustinovičius et al. [16], 5D BIM is a critical element of building lifecycle management through precise cost estimation as well as the elimination of human-related errors. Furthermore, Reizgevicius et al. [17] have highlighted the importance of QS practices such as life cycle costing and reliable cost analysis of different construction scenarios in the attainment of sustainability through BIM use.

The Industry Foundation Classes (IFC) has increased the opportunities for QSs to collaborate with all other industry professionals through the facilitation of open data formats for the transfer of information across various applications [4]. BIM offers a faster and effective approach to generate relevant data for QS functions in order to develop cost estimates through automated extraction of quantities from building models, it also enables parametric links for automatic updates of quantities when design changes occur [18]. The efficiency of delivering cost-effective projects has been greatly influenced by innovative technology thus critical processes such as cost planning, cost control, cost estimating and analysis can now be achieved more effectively using BIM application and platforms (i.e. 5D BIM) [4, 14]. There are more opportunities offered by innovative technology towards improving the efficiency of project costing and QS practice overall. Most QS functions can, therefore, be more easily achieved with the application of digital technology and data analytics [4, 15].

Ashworth and Hogg [19] predicted the expansion of QS practices to cover automated measurement, environmental and sustainability analysis, facilities management, legal services, investment advice and quality management through the adoption of digital technology. Although there is a perceived threat to the QS profession with the prospect of replacing people with technology, the opportunities ahead are more than the threats [15]. Aside from the expanding opportunities in the scope of QS practice, there is an important role for QSs in the BIM development market. The skills required to drive such 5D BIM is however enormous and QS practice requires some capacity building [14, 20].

3 Organisational Capability and the Implementation of BIM

Capability Maturity Models (CMM) have been adopted for the assessment of the quality of organisational processes within software firms since the late 1970s [21]. Some of the most popular models include the quality management maturity grid by Crosby [22] and the CMM by Carnegie Mellon Software Engineering Institute (SEI) [21]. According to Eadie et al. [23], maturity models are characterised by structured elements representing key process areas as well as capability stages for progressing in these process areas. Thus, a maturity model aids the identification of critical process areas responsible for a firm's performance or capability in delivering a particular function [22]. They are popularly used in performance management to provide guidance on steps towards improving performance in key organisational process areas. Similarly, with the emergence of BIM, the maturity modelling concept has been adopted to model BIM capability [7, 12, 24]. Succar et al. [25] defined BIM maturity as "*the quality, repeatability and degree of excellence within a BIM capability*". According to Succar [24], BIM maturity is primarily used to benchmark performance improvement milestones during BIM implementation or use. The notable BIM capability maturity frameworks and toolsets include the Capability Maturity Model (CMM) by the National Institute of Building Science [7]; the Indiana University BIM proficiency matrix [26]; the BIM capability framework by Succar [24]; the BIM owners' competency framework by Giel and Issa [12]; the BIM Quickscan [6]; the BIM readiness frameworks by Gu and London [27]; BIM pre-qualification and selection framework [28] and ARUP's project maturity assessor [29]. The major limitation of these frameworks relative to QSs is, however, the fact that none of them has been specifically developed for QSs. Some generically apply to construction organisations [7, 8, 24, 28] while others apply to project scenarios [26, 29]. Giel and Issa's [12] model focussed on clients while all of the other frameworks do not specifically target particular disciplines however most suited for originations with design responsibility [28]. Some other frameworks have been developed for the assessment of the product (i.e. BIM model) maturity [11].

While these emerging standards, frameworks and tools have provided the basis for the identification of appropriate BIM capability criteria, none of them specifically address peculiar needs of QSs and QS practices. The only model with criteria for assessment cost-related BIM modelling process is the ARUP model [29]. However, this model pertains to BIM model maturity for projects rather than a QS organisation's maturity. Furthermore, it relies on a generic set of criteria that are used for assessing other disciplines such as Architecture, Mechanical and Electrical, thus, the criteria are not specific to QS. From the review of the state-of-the-art, it is clear that no BIM capability assessment tool exists for QSs, neither is it clear if the generic capability attributes proposed in existing frameworks are suitable for QS processes and organisations.

4 The Identification of Key Attributes for a BIM Capability Maturity Model for Quantity Surveying

The development of capability maturity models requires the identification of key attributes often referred to as key process areas (KPA) which represent the primary areas of performance in an organisation or system [5, 21, 23]. These capability attributes (KPA's) are distinct clusters of related activities, competencies and resources that are required for the attainment of goals [21]. The conventional notion of KPAs is that they must include processes, people and personnel, policy, systems and resources required to perform functions effectively and efficiently [24, 28]. This study, therefore, explored the attributes required for assessing a QS organisation's capability to deliver BIM as a precursor for developing a comprehensive capability and performance benchmarking framework based on capability maturity modelling principles.

5 Methodology

A focus group discussion (FGD) involving experts in the application of BIM for QS was used to identify a list of attributes that denote QS organisations ability to use BIM. This process allowed experts to propose criteria as well as review generic criteria derived from a review of the literature and existing BIM capability frameworks. The FGD further aided the exploration of expert views on the potential of BIM for transforming QS practices as well as review the current capacity and capability issues in the industry. A total of seven experts were engaged in the FGD. The FGD participants comprised mainly of QSs, BIM Managers, BIM Consultants and a QS software developer. All participants had a vast experience in the application of digital technologies for construction as well as QS practice in general. They were recruited from reputable organisations with departments or projects responsible for the digitisation of QS functions. High level of expertise was a criterion for selecting participants and was also in order to meet the requirements for selecting participants when using expert group methods for data collection [30]. The following criteria were specifically relied on in selecting participants: senior professional or academic in BIM and QS; a minimum of five years of industry experience; and possession of professional QS or BIM qualifications. The background information of FGD participants is presented in Table 1. FGDs normally involves a small group of participants to ensure effective management of the data collection by the researchers [31]. Focus group methods are the preferred approach for interrogation of the phenomenon to high levels of detail and depth while reducing interviewer-domination [31, 32]. FDGs have been previously used for the identification of capability attributes in the development of capability maturity models [33]. The FGD was adopted to allow the participants to draw from each other's expertise and experience regarding QS BIM capability in order to enrichen the discussions.

Table 1. Background of FGD Participants.

ID	Role/Position	Experience in Construction	Experience in Digital Construction	Qualification
1	BIM Manager	20	7	BSc
2	Director - QS Software Development (*MICE)	40	12	BSc
3	Associate Director - QS and Commercial Management (*MRICS)	15	5	BSc
4	Construction Manager	10	2	MSc
5	Digital Construction Consultant	16	15	BSc

6	Associate Director - QS and Commercial Management (*MRICS)	14	3	BSc
7	Academic and Professional QS (*MRICS)	30	10	MSc

***Notes**: BSc = Bachelors Degree; MSc = Masters Degree; MRICS = Member, Royal Institution of Chartered Surveyors; MICE = Member, Institution of Civil Engineering

6 Findings and Discussions

The QS BIM capability attributes derived from the FGD is presented in Table 2. In total 18 key capability attributes were proposed. Some of the attributes proposed are similar to proposed attributes in BIM capability and maturity frameworks but uniquely differ given its focus on the QS practice. The criteria that are similar to previously proposed BIM capability are: Staff competence; Organisations experience; Organisation's qualifications; Hardware; Software; Network capacity; Leadership; Policy; and Roles and responsibilities [10, 24, 28]. The criteria peculiar to QS BIM use include: Scope of QS services rendered digitally; Commercial and cost data security; Commercial data security; Cost model progression specification; Cost data exchange protocols; and 5D BIM execution planning.

Table 2. Summary of Quantity Surveying BIM capability attributes.

No.	QS BIM Capability Attributes	Key process area (KPA) category			
		People	Policy	Technology	Process
1	Staff Competence Skills, knowledge, experience and expertise among staff. Professional and academic qualifications relevant to 5D BIM and digital technology application.	X			
2	Organisations experience Historical/previous use of 5D BIM and digital technologies within the organisation and on projects.	X			
3	Organisations qualifications and certification Formal certifications indicating BIM capability, maturity, competence, standards and use of protocols.	X			X
4	Scope of QS services rendered digitally Delivery of core costing and QS functions through BIM, advanced digital technologies and data analytics.				X
5	Hardware Hardware to support 5D BIM, data capture, storage, analytics and advanced visualisation.			X	
6	Software Software to support 5D BIM, data capture, storage, analytics and advanced visualisation.			X	
7	Network capacity Adequate and secure network infrastructure to support 5D BIM through centralised or cloud-based interoperable data exchange.			X	
8	Workflow management Process maturity within the organisation for object-based, model-based or network-based integration of cost services into BIM (5D).				X

9	Commercial and cost data security Protocols, infrastructure and services that ensure commercial data privacy, protection and integrity.				X
10	Cost model progression specification Model progression specifications for 5D BIM modelling within the team and for specifying to other project consultants.				X
11	Cost data exchange protocols Protocols that ensure interoperable use of information from other consultants for 5D BIM (i.e. Data naming conventions and model element breakdown structures that conform or are mapped unto the classifications in QS and measurement standards such as NRM, ICMS, SMM)				X
12	Quality assurance Availability and use of quality assurance protocols and tools to ensure data integrity, accuracy and conformance in 5D/BIM models and outputs.			X	X
13	5D BIM execution planning Project-based execution planning and protocols for strategic implementing 5D BIM.				X
14	Roles and responsibilities Availability of specific BIM roles within the organisational hierarchy	X			
15	Leadership Availability of executive sponsorship, champions and dedicated implementation committees for 5D BIM implementation		X		
16	Policy Clear statement of purpose and objectives for BIM use within the organisation as well as the level of importance placed on digitisation within broader company vision, mission or policies.		X		
17	Research and development Directed work and resources for innovation and improvement of products and processes for 5D BIM		X		X
18	Digital culture Demonstrated culture of preference for technology-oriented processes in organisation or willingness to use innovative technologies for QS functions.	X			
	Related KPA frequency	5	3	4	9

Note: 5D BIM as used in the description of attributes refers to all applications of BIM to costing and quantity surveying functions.

Abbreviations: CPD Continuous Professional Development; ICMS- International Construction Measurement Standards; NRM- New Rules of Measurement; QS- Quantity Surveying/Surveyor; and SMM- Standard Method of Measurement.

Based on the categorisation of BIM maturity elements by Succar et al. [25], the attributes were reclassified into four distinct categories. The classification of attributes was as follows: technology, process, people and policy. The technology category describes specific abilities related to physical artefacts including software, hardware and data or networks. The process category is used to describe activities, workflows, services, procedures for delivering BIM. The people category describes knowledge skills and competence possessed within an organisation or by individuals for the delivery of BIM objectives. Finally, the policy dimension describes the guidance and principles of action adopted for the attainment of BIM implementation goals.

The majority of attributes (n=9) were ‘process’ related though unsurprising and supports the primary definition of BIM which emphasizes its process laden nature [5]. Capability maturity models are also premised on a philosophy that process improvement is responsible for the attainment of objectives in digital technology use [21]. A significant amount of the process criteria were related to the management of information and data exchange. This finding brings into focus the role of interoperability in the effective delivery of QS functions through BIM [4]. While the IFC has increased the opportunities for QSs to collaborate with other disciplines, there remains a need for protocols to facilitate the process and organisational interoperability [4]. The attributes proposed thus highlight the need for capacities in the definition and classification of data such that they are consistent with QS and measurement standards such as Standard Method of Measurement (SMM), International Construction Measurement Standards (ICMS) and the New Rules of Measurement (NRM). The majority of proposed QS BIM capability attributes align with a systems and hard technology deterministic view of BIM capability [28]. The category with the second-highest number of attributes (n=5) was the 'people' category with emphasis on competence and experience of individuals and the organisation as a whole in delivering QS related services through BIM. According to Succar et al. [9], the ability to adopt BIM-related processes is dependent on proficiency among staff, as well as its aggregated effect on the entire organisation through collective learning as well as the distribution of roles and responsibilities. Existing BIM frameworks and toolsets [5, 6, 8-10, 12] have similarly recognised people-centric competency measures as influential determinants of BIM capability. The concern is, however, the low level of QS BIM adoption which will invariably delay the process of developing a critical mass of QSs experienced in the use of BIM-related process and technology.

The findings reveal critical QS BIM capability attributes as well as dominant categories of attributes. The dominance of particular types of the QS BIM capability attributes does not, however, indicate their importance thus there is a need for further research to determine the relative importance of criteria.

7 Conclusion

The use of BIM within QS practice is becoming more necessary as a result of high levels of BIM use and diffusion across other segments of the construction industry. Despite the potential of BIM, however, QSs continue to lag behind in adoption as a result of capability issues among other reasons. A review of studies reveals that the majority of emerging tools and frameworks have been developed for organisations with high design responsibility (such as architects) rather than for QSs who directly manage and control spending on projects. Consequently, there are serious limitations regarding the suitability of criteria in existing BIM capability and maturity frameworks for use in QS scenarios. This study thus sought to address this by proposing QS specific BIM capability attributes. Findings reveal that most QS BIM capability relates to 'process' including criteria for effective information definition and data management such that they are consistent with QS and measurement standards. The proposed QS BIM capability attributes highlight the key process areas for the development of performance and maturity indicators that would assist QS firms to better understand capability issues as well as BIM implementation priorities. A limitation of this study is the lack of prioritisation of attributes to determine which is the most important. The subsequent phase of this study will, however, address this and prioritise these attributes as well as identify definitions of maturity levels for each. This study relied only on expert judgement, thus future studies could adopt longitudinal, ethnographic approach or case studies to explore further, the attributes identified in the current study as well their relative importance in practice.

References

1. B. Flyvbjerg, M.K.S. Holm S.L. Buhl, What Causes Cost Overrun in Transport Infrastructure Projects? Transp. Rev. **24(1)**, 3-18 (2004)
2. D.D. Ahiaga-Dagbui, S.D. Smith, Rethinking construction cost overruns: cognition, learning and estimation JFMPC **19(1)**, 38-54 (2014)
3. BIS, Industrial Strategy: Government and Industry in Partnership: Construction 2025, Report number: URN BIS/13/955 (Department for Business, Innovation and Skills, London, 2013)
4. RICS, Can Building Information Modelling (BIM) Support the New Rules Of Measurement (NRM1) (Royal Institution of Chartered Surveyors (RICS), London, 2014)
5. B. Succar, Building Information Modelling Framework: A Research and Delivery Foundation for Industry Stakeholders. Automat. Constr. **18(3)**, 357-375 (2009)
6. L. van Berlo, T. Dikkmans, H. Hendriks, D. Spekkink, W. Pel, *Benchmark of BIM Performance in the Netherlands*, in Proceedings 29th International Conference CIB W78 2012, 17-19 October 2012, Beirut, Lebanon (2012)
7. NIBS, National Building Information Modeling Standard - Version 2.0-Chapter 5.2 Minimum BIM (2012)
8. CIC - Computer Integrated Construction, *BIM Planning Guide for Facility Owners: Computer Integrated Construction* (Pennsylvania State University, Pennsylvania, 2013)
9. B. Succar, W. Sher, A. Williams, An Integrated Approach to BIM Competency Assessment, Acquisition and Application, Automat. Constr. **35**, 174-189 (2013)
10. C. Kam, D. Senaratna, B. McKinney, Y. Xiao, M. Song, The VDC Scorecard: Formulation and Validation. Stanford University: Center for Integrated Facility Engineering (CIFE), CIFE Working Paper WP135 (2014)
11. J. Du, R. Liu, R. Issa, BIM Cloud Score: Benchmarking BIM Performance, J. Constr. Eng. Manag. **140(11)**, 04014054-64 (2014)
12. B. Giel, R. Issa Framework for Evaluating the BIM Competencies of Building Owners, Comp. Civ. Build. Eng., ASCE, 552-559 (2014)
13. D. Mitchell, *5D BIM: Creating cost certainty and better buildings* (RICS Cobra, Las Vegas, Nevada, 2012)
14. N.A.A. Ismail, R. Drogemuller, S. Beazley, R. Owen, *A Review of BIM Capabilities for Quantity Surveying Practice*, in Proceedings of the 4th International Building Control Conference (IBCC), 7th -8th March 2016, Kuala Lumpur, Malaysia (2016)
15. S. Wu, G. Wood, K. Ginige, S.W. Jong, A technical review of BIM based cost estimating in UK quantity surveying practice, standards and tools, ITcon **19**, 534-562 (2014)
16. L. Ustinovičius, R. Rasiulis, L. Nazarko, T. Vilutienė, M. Reizgevicius, Innovative research projects in the field of Building Lifecycle Management, Procedia Engineering, **122**, 166-171 (2015)
17. M. Reizgevicius, L. Ustinovičius, D. Cibulskiene, V. Kutut, L. Nazarko, Promoting Sustainability through Investment in Building Information Modeling (BIM) Technologies: A Design Company Perspective, Sustainability **10(3)**, 1-22 (2018)

18. O.A. Olatunji Views on building information modelling, procurement and contract management, Proceedings of the Institution of Civil Engineers - Management, Procurement and Law **167(3)**, 117-126 (2014)
19. A. Ashworth, K. Hogg, *Willis's practice and procedure for quantity surveyor*, 12th ed. (Blackwell Publishing Ltd., Oxford, 2007)
20. W. Sher, S. Sheratt, A. Williams, R. Gameson, Heading into new virtual environments: what skills do design team members need? J. Inf. Tech. Cons. **14**, 17-29 (2009)
21. M. Paulk, B. Curtis, M. Chrissis, C. Weber, *The Capability Maturity Model for Software* (Software Engineering Institute, Carnegie Mellon University,1993)
22. P.B. Crosby, *Quality is Free: The Art of Making Quality Certain* (New American Library, New York, 1979)
23. R. Eadie, S. Perera, G. Heaney, Key Process Area Mapping in the Production of an E-capability Maturity Model for UK Construction Organisations, JFMPC **16(3)**, 197-210 (2011)
24. Succar, B. Building Information Modelling Maturity Matrix. Handbook of Research on Building Information Modeling and Construction Informatics: Concepts and Technologies, IGI, 65-103 (2010)
25. B. Succar, W. Sher, A. Williams, Measuring BIM Performance: Five metrics. Architect. Eng. Des. Manag. **8(2)**, 120-142 (2012)
26. IU, *Building Information Modeling (BIM) Guidelines and Standards for Architects, Engineers, and Contractors* (Indiana University, USA, 2009)
27. N. Gu, K. London, Understanding and facilitating BIM adoption in the AEC industry, Automat. Constr. **19(8)**, 988-999 (2010)
28. A.M. Mahamadu, L. Mahdjoubi, C. Booth, Critical BIM Qualification Criteria for Construction Pre-Qualification and Selection, Architect. Eng. Des. Manag. **13(5)**, 326-343 (2017a)
29. A. Azzouz, P. Hill, Hunting for perfection: How Arup measures BIM maturity on projects worldwide, Cons. Res. Innov. **8(2)**, 49-54 (2017)
30. M. Hallowell, J. Gambatese, Qualitative Research: Application of the Delphi Method to CEM Research, J. Constr. Eng. Manag. **136(1)**, 99-107 (2010)
31. D.E. Polkinghorne, *Phenomenological research methods*, in Existential-phenomenological perspectives in psychology, 41-60 (Springer, 1989)
32. J.W. Creswell, *Qualitative Inquiry and Research Design: Choosing among Five Approaches,* 3rd ed. (Sage Publications, London, 2013).
33. A.M. Mahamadu, P. Manu, A. Poghosyan, L. Mahdjoubi, A. Gibb, M. Behm, *Organisational attributes that determine design for occupational safety and health capability*, in Submitted to CRIOCM 2017 22nd International Conference on Advancement of Construction Management and Real Estate, 20-23 November 2017, Swinburne University of Technology, Australia (2017b)

Composite Criticality in Machinery Fleet Management of Construction Projects

John-Paris Pantouvakis[1*], and *Alexander* Maravas[1]

[1] Centre for Construction Innovation, Department of Construction Engineering and Management, Faculty of Civil Engineering, National Technical University of Athens, Greece

Abstract. During construction operations, fleet management aims at maximizing the uptime and efficiency of construction machinery while also minimizing the cost of ownership through lifecycle planning and management. In the deterministic approach, the theory suggests that one type of machinery is considered to be critical. However, taking into account the real circumstances under which projects are performed with issues such as machine reliability, worker performance, and/or errors in estimating the scope of work, it is evident that there are significant limitations to the existing approach. Hence, to address this issue, uncertainty in fleet productivity is modelled with fuzzy set theory. In this context, the notion of composite criticality under which the productivity of a fleet depends on more than one type of machinery because of the fluctuations of the individual productivities is introduced. To this purpose, a simple case study is presented to illustrate this concept. It is concluded that this approach leads to a better understanding of the estimation of activity duration and cost estimation which in turn means better project scheduling and financial planning.

Keywords: construction management, fleet management, fuzzy systems, financial planning, uncertainty management.

1 Introduction

In construction operations project managers are faced with the task of completing activities under multiple constraints while ensuring the optimal use of available machinery. In this context, construction equipment fleet management involves a variety of functions including machine maintenance, safety audits, GPS tracking, optimal fleet composition, cost tracking, fuel consumption monitoring and operator training. In ensuring efficiency, a primary goal is to maximize machinery uptime and reduce idle times by ensuring continuous flow and usage of machinery in all project activities. Similarly, managers seek to minimize rental or ownership costs by mobilizing the optimal number of necessary machinery.

* Corresponding author: jpp@central.ntua.gr

Productivity estimation remains a difficult task to be performed at the pre-construction stage [1]. For many years the deterministic approach has dominated the methodological approach to the estimations of machine productivity and consequently fleet composition. In construction operations, productivity theory and performance handbooks provide an excellent base for estimating the productivity of construction equipment. Thereafter, in determining fleet composition, the primary assumption is that in a group of machines the productivity of the machinery with the lowest productivity will determine the total production capability. However, productivity rates differ between projects because of the varying environments, characteristics, and level of management implementation [2]. Also, taking into account issues such as productivity, machine reliability, worker performance, and/or errors in estimating the scope of work, it is evident that there are significant limitations to the existing approach. Finally, the study of a fleet of machinery in which there is uncertainty in the productivity of its individual components poses a significant challenge.

The purpose of this paper is to apply a fuzzy set theory to examine issues of uncertainty and imprecision in machinery fleet composition. Initially, uncertainty is examined on the productivity of individual machines. Thereafter, the notion of composite criticality is introduced, under which the productivity of a fleet of machines depends on more than one type of machinery because of the fluctuations of the individual productivities. The concept is exemplified in an earthworks project. Finally, the conclusions and possibilities for future research are presented.

2 Literature Review

2.1 Performance Handbooks

Performance handbooks, provided by the manufacturers of construction machinery have assisted project managers in estimating productivity and optimizing fleet composition. The Caterpillar Performance Handbook [3] includes productivity estimations and guidelines for a variety of equipment such as tractors, graders, loaders, excavators, backhoe loaders, forest machines, pipelayers, scrapers, trucks, landfill compactors, pavers and asphalt pavers. The Performance Handbook serves as an aid which, when coupled with experience can assist in estimating true machine performance and optimizing fleet composition. Similarly, the Specifications and Applications Handbook [4] has extensive guidelines on productivity estimation. Overall, performance handbooks combined with productivity theory as in Peurifoy [5] and Nunally [6] provide an excellent basis for productivity analysis.

2.2 Match Factor

In earthworks activities, Douglas [7] published a formula based on the ratio of loader productivity to truck productivity that can be used to determine the optimal number of trucks to balance shovel output. Morgan and Peterson [8] introduced the concept of the match factor which is very useful in providing a measure of the productivity of a fleet and quite similar to the Douglas ratio. A match factor of 1 represents a balance point where trucks are arriving at the loader at the same time they are being served. If the ratio exceeds 1, the trucks are arriving faster than they are being served and a queue is formed. If the ratio is below 1, the loaders are serving faster than the trucks arriving [9]. In theory, a match factor of 1 is an indication of a maximized productivity level.

2.3 Fuzzy Set Theory

Fuzzy Set Theory is used to describe and quantify uncertainty and imprecision in data and functional relationships. A fuzzy subset A of a universe of discourse U is characterized by a membership function μ_A: U→ [0, 1] which associates with each element x of U a number $\mu_A(x)$ in the interval [0, 1] which represents the grade of membership of x in A. In fuzzy set theory, the triangular membership function which is defined by three numbers a,b,c is frequently utilized. As such, a triangular fuzzy number $\widetilde{x} = \langle a,b,c \rangle$ has the following membership function:

$$\mu_A(x) = \begin{cases} 0, & x < a \\ (x-a)/(b-a), & a \le x \le b \\ (c-x)/(c-b), & b \le x \le c \\ 0, & x > c \end{cases} \tag{1}$$

The rules that determine the operations of addition, subtraction, multiplication and division of fuzzy numbers are called fuzzy arithmetic [10].

The min ($\wedge$) and max ($\vee$) operators are useful in finding the maximum or minimum of two membership functions [10].

$$\mu_{A(\wedge)B}(z) = \bigvee_{z=x\wedge y} (\mu_A(x) \wedge \mu_B(y)) \tag{2}$$

$$\mu_{A(\vee)B}(z) = \bigvee_{z=x\vee y} (\mu_A(x) \vee \mu_B(y)) \tag{3}$$

As such the union and the intersection of two fuzzy sets are determined as:

$$\mu_{A\cup B}(x) = \mu_A(x) \vee \mu_B(x) = \max\{\mu_A(x), \mu_B(x)\} \tag{4}$$

$$\mu_{A\cap B}(x) = \mu_A(x) \wedge \mu_B(x) = \min\{\mu_A(x), \mu_B(x)\} \tag{5}$$

In describing linguistic variables defined by fuzzy sets, Zadeh [11] proposed that they can be characterized either by atomic terms (words which always occur together) or composite terms that contain one or more atomic terms. Furthermore, he defined formula for calculating composite truth variables based on the min operator. As such, the interpretation of a composite of two fuzzy sets (such as μ_A and μ_B) is based on the fuzzy min operator [12]. In applying fuzzy set theory in project scheduling, McCahon and Lee [13] explained the difference between the comparison method and the composite method in studying two fuzzy variables. The former compares fuzzy numbers based on metrics and considers one as being larger than the other, while the latter forms a new fuzzy number from pieces of the component fuzzy numbers. In this paper, the composite of two fuzzy sets refers to creating a new fuzzy set from parts of the component fuzzy sets.

3 Productivity Analysis Model

The purpose of the model is to utilize fuzzy set theory to represent uncertainty in the estimation of machinery productivity and the process of fleet composition based on Performance Handbooks and traditional productivity theory. Additionally, a fuzzy version of the well-established match factor is presented.

3.1 Machine Productivity

In the case of a construction project that involves earthworks, the fuzzy productivity of a single excavator can be calculated with the formula [14]:

$$\tilde{Q}_{ex} = \frac{60 \cdot V_e \cdot \tilde{f}}{\tilde{t}_s} \cdot \tilde{\eta}_{ex} \tag{6}$$

where $\tilde{Q}_{ex}$: the fuzzy production rate of an excavator in m³/h, 60: a conversion factor, V_e : the crisp bucket capacity in m³, $\tilde{f}$: the fuzzy bucket fill factor, $\tilde{t}_s$: the excavator cycle time in the min and $\tilde{\eta}_{ex}$: the operational efficiency.

Similarly, the fuzzy productivity of a truck can be calculated by the formula [15]:

$$\tilde{Q}_{tr} = \frac{60 \cdot \tilde{V}_{trans}}{\tilde{t}_{tr}} \cdot \tilde{\eta}_{tr} \tag{7}$$

where $\tilde{Q}_{tr}$: the fuzzy production rate of a truck in m³/h, $\tilde{V}_{trans}$: the fuzzy volume of the material to be transferred in m³, $\tilde{t}_{tr}$: the fuzzy cycle time of the truck in the min and $\tilde{\eta}_{tr}$: the operational efficiency.

Additionally, the fuzzy cycle time of the truck is given by the formula:

$$\tilde{t}_{tr} = \tilde{t}_{mov} + \tilde{t}_{du} + \tilde{t}_{re} + \tilde{t}_{man} + \tilde{t}_{load} \tag{8}$$

where $\tilde{t}_{mov}$: the fuzzy time for moving to the dump area in min, $\tilde{t}_{du}$: the fuzzy time for dumping in min, $\tilde{t}_{re}$: the fuzzy time for returning to the load area in min, $\tilde{t}_{man}$: the fuzzy time for maneuvering in the min and $\tilde{t}_{load}$: the fuzzy time for loading in min.

Finally, the total required fuzzy production rate of a worksite can be calculated as:

$$\tilde{Q}_{ws} = \frac{\tilde{V} \cdot \tilde{\varepsilon}}{t \cdot \tilde{\eta}} \tag{9}$$

where $\tilde{Q}_{ws}$: the fuzzy productivity of the worksite in m³/h, $\tilde{V}$: the volume of earthworks in m³, $\tilde{\varepsilon}$: the fuzzy swell factor, t: the contractual completion time in hrs and $\tilde{\eta}$: the operational efficiency.

3.2 Fleet Composition and Productivity Analysis

After estimating the uncertainty in trucks and excavators, fleet composition requires to find the optimal combination of these two types of construction equipment in order to meet project constraints. A deterministic analysis would state that in the case that the excavators are critical it be acceptable for the trucks to form queues. Similarly, if the trucks are critical, then the excavators will have periods that they are not able to load the trucks. If we apply fuzzy set theory to traditional fleet composition we have the following equations [15]:

Excavators are Critical

$$n_{ex} = \mathrm{int}((\tilde{Q}_{ws} / \tilde{Q}_{ex} + 1)) \quad (10)$$

$$\tilde{Q}_{fleet} = \tilde{Q}_{EX} = n_{ex} \cdot \tilde{Q}_{ex} \quad (11)$$

$$n_{tr} = \mathrm{int}((\tilde{Q}_{fleet} / \tilde{Q}_{tr} + 1)) \quad (12)$$

$$\tilde{Q}_{TR} = n_{tr} \cdot \tilde{Q}_{tr} \quad (13)$$

Trucks are critical

$$n_{tr} = \mathrm{int}((\tilde{Q}_{ws} / \tilde{Q}_{tr} + 1)) \quad (14)$$

$$\tilde{Q}_{fleet} = \tilde{Q}_{TR} = n_{tr} \cdot \tilde{Q}_{tr} \quad (15)$$

$$n_{ex} = \mathrm{int}((\tilde{Q}_{fleet} / \tilde{Q}_{ex} + 1)) \quad (16)$$

$$\tilde{Q}_{EX} = n_{ex} \cdot \tilde{Q}_{ex} \quad (17)$$

where $\tilde{Q}_{EX}$: the fuzzy productivity of all excavators in the fleet, $\tilde{Q}_{ex}$: the fuzzy productivity of a single excavator, $\tilde{Q}_{TR}$: the fuzzy productivity of all trucks in the fleet, $\tilde{Q}_{tr}$: the fuzzy productivity of a single truck, $\tilde{Q}_{ws}$: the required productivity of the worksite, $\tilde{Q}_{fleet}$: the fuzzy productivity of the fleet of excavators and trucks, n_{tr} : the number of trucks, n_{ex} : the number of excavators, *int*: the integers in a fuzzy set.

Applying equations 10-17 along with the underlying assumption that one type of machines is always critical yields values for n_{ex}, n_{tr}, $\tilde{Q}_{EX}$ and $\tilde{Q}_{TR}$. Similarly, $\tilde{Q}_{fleet}$ should be the minimum of the membership functions $\mu_{EX}(x)$ of the excavator productivity ($\tilde{Q}_{EX}$) and $\mu_{TR}(y)$ of the truck productivity ($\tilde{Q}_{TR}$). Thus, applying the minimum operator [15]:

$$\tilde{Q}_{fleet} = \mu_{EX(\wedge)TR}(z) = \bigvee_{z = x \wedge y} (\mu_{QEX}(x) \wedge \mu_{QTR}(y)) \quad (18)$$

In applying this formula, the membership function of the fleet productivity is not necessarily a triangular fuzzy number but in some cases a composite function that is derived from the membership function of the productivities of two or more type of machinery. In this context, the notion of composite criticality is defined as the situation in which the productivity of a fleet depends on more than one types of machinery because of the fluctuations and uncertainties of the individual productivities. Hence, the composite of two fuzzy productivity sets, form a new fuzzy set (from parts of the component fuzzy sets) that defines the criticality of the fleet.

In direct accordance with the deterministic analysis, the fuzzy match factor ($\widetilde{MF}$) is a measure for comparing the productivity of two types of machines. In the case of an earthworks project involving excavators and trucks it can be calculated as:

$$\widetilde{MF} = \tilde{Q}_{EX} / \tilde{Q}_{TR} \quad (19)$$

Furthermore, the analysis of the fleet productivity $\widetilde{Q}_{fleet}$ is much more intuitive with the fuzzy agreement index. Hence, the Agreement Index of the fleet (AI_{fleet}) is $AI(\widetilde{Q}_{EX}, \widetilde{Q}_{TR})$ of $\widetilde{Q}_{EX}$ in relation to $\widetilde{Q}_{TR}$ and is calculated as follows:

$$AI_{fleet} = AI(\widetilde{Q}_{EX}, \widetilde{Q}_{TR}) = (area\widetilde{Q}_{EX} \cap \widetilde{Q}_{TR})/(area\widetilde{Q}_{TR}) \tag{20}$$

4 Example

4.1 Excavator and Truck Productivity

Consider an excavator manufactured by Caterpillar with a bucket capacity of 3 m^3, a bucket fill factor of ⟨0.81, 0.83, 0.84⟩, a cycle time of ⟨0.51, 0.52, 0.54⟩ min and operational efficiency of ⟨0.78, 0.80, 0.81⟩. As shown in Table 1, the direct application of eq. 6 yields a fuzzy productivity estimate of $\widetilde{Q}_{ex}$ = ⟨210, 230, 240⟩ m^3/h. Similarly, for a Caterpillar truck, using the fuzzified parameters of productivity from the Performance Handbook, where the volume of transferred material is ⟨17.8, 18.0, 18.2⟩ m^3, the cycle time is ⟨17.5, 18, 18.5⟩ min and the operational efficiency is ⟨0.69, 0.75, 0.81⟩ then the fuzzy truck production rate will be ⟨40, 45, 50⟩ m^3/h (Table 2). The cycle time estimate is calculated by applying a 3% uncertainty to the respective crisp times i.e.

$$t_{tr} = t_{mov} + t_{du} + t_{re} + t_{man} + t_{load} = 8+1+4+1+4 = 18 \text{ min}$$

and $\widetilde{t}_{tr}$ =⟨17.5, 18.0, 18.5⟩ min.

Because of the non-linearity of fuzzy arithmetic, the value of the excavator and truck productivity is an approximation of a triangular fuzzy number.

Finally, if the volume of the earthworks is ⟨97000, 100000, 103000⟩ m^3, the swell factor is $\widetilde{\varepsilon}$ = ⟨1.55, 1.60, 1.65⟩, the operational efficiency is ⟨0.72, 0.75, 0.78⟩, the contractual completion time is 6*20*8=960 hrs (6 months), then the required productivity of the site is:

$$\widetilde{Q}_{ws} = \frac{\langle 97000, 100000, 103000\rangle \cdot \langle 1.55, 1.60, 1{,}65\rangle}{960 \cdot \langle 0.72, 0.75, 0.78\rangle} = \langle 200, 222, 245\rangle \text{ m}^3/\text{h}.$$

Table 1. Fuzzy Productivity of a Caterpillar Excavator

Parameter	Values
bucket capacity (m^3)	3
fill factor	⟨0.81, 0.83, 0.84⟩
cycle time (min)	⟨0.51, 0.52, 0.54⟩
operational efficiency	⟨0.78, 0.80, 0.81⟩
excavator production rate (m^3/h) $\widetilde{Q}_{ex}$	⟨210, 230, 240⟩

Table 2. Fuzzy Productivity of a Caterpillar Truck

Parameter	Values
volume of transferred material (m^3)	⟨17.8, 18.0, 18.2⟩
cycle time of truck (min)	⟨17.5, 18.0, 18.5⟩
operational efficiency	⟨0.69, 0.75, 0.81⟩
fuzzy truck production rate (m^3/h) $\widetilde{Q}_{tr}$	⟨40, 45, 50⟩

4.2 Fleet Productivity

Consider a fleet of excavators and trucks that have to complete an earthworks project. In applying uncertainty analysis, as shown above, it is possible to define the individual productivity rates with fuzzy numbers, i.e. $\widetilde{Q}_{ex} = \langle 210, 230, 240 \rangle$ m^3/h and $\widetilde{Q}_{tr} = \langle 40, 45, 50 \rangle$ m^3/h. Furthermore, the fuzzy productivity of a homogeneous group of 5 similar trucks is $\widetilde{Q}_{TR} = 5 \cdot \widetilde{Q}_{tr} = \langle 200, 225, 250 \rangle$ m^3/h. Understandably, as the number of trucks increases, so does the spread of the cumulative uncertainty of the group.

Table 3 shows the fleet productivity for some different compositions. In the issue of determining the critical machine, in case A that we have 1 excavator and 4 trucks and since $\widetilde{Q}_{TR}$ is definitely smaller than $\widetilde{Q}_{EX}$ it is evident that $\widetilde{Q}_{fleet} = \widetilde{Q}_{TR}$ meaning that the trucks are always critical (Figure 1). Similarly, in the case of C, if there are 6 trucks and 1 excavator, then the excavator is always critical. However, in the case of B, the combination of 1 excavator and 5 trucks leads to an instance of composite criticality. Overall, in Figure 1, in cases A and C, one type of machinery is definitely critical but there is also a waste of extra production capability since the total production is constrained by the lowest resource. In the case of B, there is a better matching and balancing of the two types of machines even though it is not possible to determine which one is critical because of a situation of composite criticality.

Table 3. The productivity of a Fleet of Trucks and Excavators

	$\widetilde{Q}fleet$ (m³/h)	$\widetilde{Q}_{TR}$ (m³/h)	$\widetilde{Q}_{EX}$ (m³/h)	n_{tr}	n_{ex}	Criticality
A	⟨160, 180, 220⟩	⟨160, 180, 200⟩	⟨210, 230, 240⟩	4	1	trucks
B	composite	⟨200, 225, 250⟩	⟨210, 230, 240⟩	5	1	composite
C	⟨210, 230, 240⟩	⟨240, 270, 300⟩	⟨210, 230, 240⟩	6	1	excavator

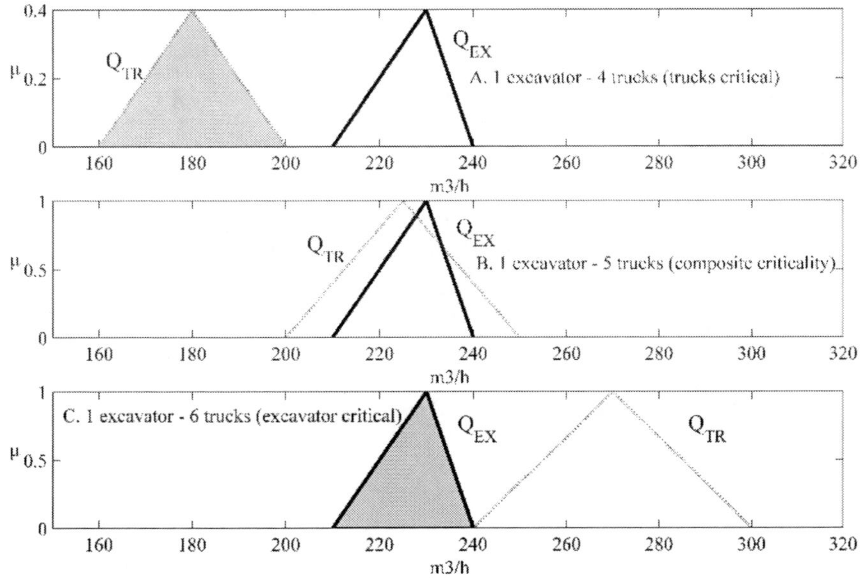

Fig. 1. Criticality in Different Fleet Compositions

Figure 2 helps us understand and interpret the situation of composite criticality. The single excavator has productivity of $\widetilde{Q}_{EX}$=⟨210, 230, 240⟩ m³/h and the 5 trucks have $\widetilde{Q}_{TR}$ = ⟨200, 225, 250⟩ m³/h. The resulting productivity of the fleet is depicted by the shaded area which is not a triangular fuzzy number. In the region of low risk (possibility level of 1 to that of 0.66) the trucks are critical since they have lower productivity. In the region of higher risk (possibility level of 0.66 to that of 0) the excavator is more likely to be critical because it has lower productivity. Physically, this means that for this particular combination in some cases the trucks are arriving at the loader faster than they are being served or the loaders are serving faster than the trucks arriving. Hence, contrary to deterministic analysis, no one type of machinery is definitely critical.

The agreement index for this fleet composition is:

$$AI_{fleet} = AI(\widetilde{Q}_{EX}, \widetilde{Q}_{TR}) = (area\widetilde{Q}_{EX} \cap \widetilde{Q}_{TR})/(area\widetilde{Q}_{TR}) = 21.65/25 = 0.86$$

which can be interpreted as a relatively high degree of matching and balancing of the two types of machinery.

Figure 3 shows a graph of the fuzzy Match Factor which is calculated as:

$$\widetilde{MF} = \frac{\widetilde{Q}_{EX}}{\widetilde{Q}_{TR}} = \frac{\langle 210, 230, 240 \rangle}{\langle 200, 225, 250 \rangle} = \langle 0.84, 1.02, 1.20 \rangle$$

The value of the match factor shows that there is a high level of matching that is very close to the ideal value of 1. Additionally, the match factor has a considerable spread of about +/- 18%. Overall, in the presence of uncertainty, there are situations of composite criticality under which the productivity of the excavators is lower than that of the trucks and vice versa. The agreement index and the fuzzy match factor help in quantifying the degree of machinery matching.

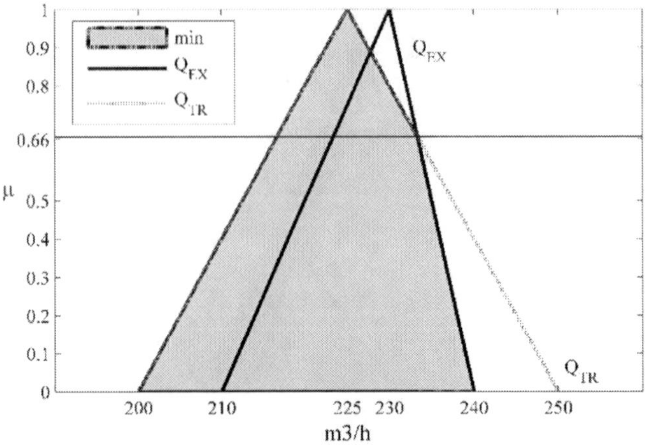

Fig. 2. Composite Criticality between Trucks and an Excavator

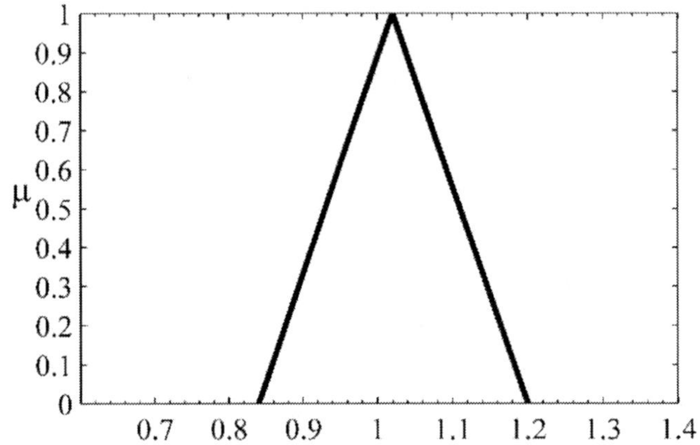

Fig. 3. Fuzzy Match Factor

5 Discussion and Conclusions

At the level of individual machines, this paper shows how the fuzzy productivity of excavators and trucks can be estimated based on fuzzifying parameters such as the bucket fill factor, the cycle time and the operational efficiency. Thereafter, a methodology is presented in order to find the optimal composition of a fleet of machines that have uncertain production rates. In the process, the paper has challenged the well established deterministic assumption, that in a fleet of construction machines one type is definitely critical. On the contrary, if productivities are characterized by fuzzy numbers, in some cases it is difficult to determine which machine is critical because of composite criticality.

In the presence of uncertainty, a fuzzy match factor with a value near 1 and a small spread is an indication of a maximized production level. However, such a match factor, besides high efficiency, may also imply a situation of composite criticality because of the interference and overlapping of fuzziness. Similarly, a fleet Agreement Index close to 1 indicates optimal matching. In this particular example, composite criticality means that in some cases the trucks are arriving at the loader faster than they are being served and in others, the loaders are serving faster than the trucks arriving. Overall, when dealing with two different types of machinery in a fleet, it is usually required that their productivities are similar in order to reduce "waste" and idle times. The situation of composite criticality may actually be more efficient than having definite criticality.

While this paper has used an approach of applying fuzzy set theory to well-established methodologies in Performance Handbooks and traditional productivity theory equations, there may be potential in applying concepts presented in this paper to a fuzzy expert system regarding fleet management. Fuzzy expert systems, which can be useful in estimating productivity, are based on many fuzzy if-then rules that relate the input factors to the output factors. As illustrated by Fayek and Oduba [16] and Zhang et al. [17] to this extent a) system inputs would have to be defined b) linguistic descriptions of the inputs and numerical scales would have to be set c) the outputs would have to be defined and d) a detailed set of rules relating the inputs to the outputs would have to be presented.

Finally, additional future research can be directed into studying fuzzy costs along with fuzzy productivities. Thus, extensive search and optimization algorithms can be applied in determining the optimal composition and operation of construction fleets in the presence of uncertainty. Also, field testing of this theoretical model in an actual project may assist in verifying the concept. Overall, the proposed methodology can lead to a better understanding of productivity estimation, which in turn means better project scheduling and financial planning.

References

1. J.P. Pantouvakis, Data Analysis and Design of Construction Productivity Efficiency Multipliers, *In*: Şahin S. (ed.) *8th International Conference on Engineering, Project, and Product Management (EPPM 2017. Lecture Notes in Mechanical Engineering*. Cham: Springer, 119-128 (2018)
2. H. Park, Conceptual framework of construction productivity estimation, *KSCE Journal of Civil Engineering* **10**(5):311–317 (2006)
3. Caterpillar, *Caterpillar Performance Handbook (Edition 46)*, Illinois: Caterpillar Inc (2016)
4. Komatsu, *Specifications and application handbook (Edition 31)*, Japan: Komatsu (2013)
5. R.L. Peurifoy, C.J. Schexnayder, A. Shapira, R. Schmitt, *Construction Planning, Equipment and Methods (8th Edition)*, USA: McGraw Hill (2010)
6. S.W. Nunally, *Construction methods and management*, Upper Saddle River: Prentice Hall (2007)
7. J. Douglas, Prediction of shovel-truck production: a reconciliation of computer and conventional estimates, *Technical Report no. 37*, Department of Civil Engineering, Stanford University (1964)
8. W. Morgan, L. Peterson, Determining shovel-truck productivity, *Mining Engineering* 76 – 80 (1968)
9. C.N. Burt, L. Caccetta, Match factor for heterogeneous truck and loader fleets, *International Journal of Mining, Reclamation and Environment* **21**(4):262-270 (2007)
10. Kaufman, M.M. Gupta, *Introduction to fuzzy arithmetic*, Amsterdam: North Holland (1985)
11. L.A. Zadeh, The Concept of a Linguistic Variable and its Application to Approximate Reasoning – II, *Information Sciences* **8**:301-357 (1975)
12. T.J. Ross, *Fuzzy Logic with Engineering Applications (2nd Edition)*, Chichester-West Sussex, England: Wiley (2004)
13. C.S. McCahon, E.S. Lee, Project Network Analysis with Fuzzy Activity Times, *Computers and Mathematics with Applications* **15**(10):829-838 (1988)
14. Maravas, J.P. Pantouvakis, A Process for the Estimation of the Duration of Activities in Fuzzy Project Scheduling, *In*: Ayyub B.M. (ed.), *Vulnerability, Uncertainty and Risk*

/ Analysis, Modeling and Management - Proceedings of the first International Conference on Vulnerability and Risk Analysis and Management (ICVRAM 2011) and the fifth International Symposium on Uncertainty Modeling and Analysis (ISUMA 2011) 11-13, Maryland. USA: ASCE, 62-69 (2011)
15. Maravas, *Scheduling and Financial Planning of Projects and Portfolios with Fuzzy Constraints*, Thesis (PhD), National Technical University of Athens, Athens (2016)
16. A.R. Fayek, A. Oduba, Predicting industrial construction labor productivity using fuzzy expert systems, *Journal of Construction Engineering and Management* **131**(8):938-941 (2005)
17. H. Zhang, C.M. Tam, J.J. Shi, Application of fuzzy logic to simulation for construction operations, *Journal of Computing in Civil Engineering* **17**(1):38-45 (2003)

Container depot location problem in the frame of the Polish part of the New Silk Road

Katarzyna Anna Kuźmicz[1*], and *Erwin* Pesch[2]

[1]Faculty of Engineering Management, Bialystok University of Technology, Bialystok, Poland
[2]Department of Management Information Science, University of Siegen, Siegen, Germany

Abstract. The Chinese project One Belt One Road, in Europe often referred to as the New Silk Road, triggers infrastructural investments enabling seamless transportation of goods on the Eurasian route. Since most of these goods are transported in containers, the optimal location of inland container depots, where containers wait for future repositioning after they had been emptied at the importers, is an interesting problem. In this paper conditions determining the optimal location of inland container depots in the Polish part of the NSR are analysed. They include proximity of container transhipment terminals located on the Polish stretch of the NSR, structure of highway network enabling distribution of containers by trucks to other destinations, as well as green aspects mainly referring to avoidance of city congestion caused by trucks transporting containers.

Keywords: container depots, empty containers, intermodal transportation, location problem, New Silk RoadPage layout

1 Introduction

The Chinese Initiative One Belt One Road (OBOR), also referred to as the New Silk Road (NSR) embraces the development of rail (One Belt) and maritime (21st century Silk Road) transportation corridors linking Europe with China. It can be considered as an important factor triggering changes in Eurasian intermodal transportation. For some kinds of cargo, rail option may become attractive because of the significantly shorter lead time in comparison to maritime transportation. Although the price remains much higher, for those goods for which time of transportation is important rail becomes a good alternative. It could be attractive for example for food producers like meat and dairy products but it has to be taken into consideration that currently these goods are banned from transportation through Russia. Some producers of computers and RTV equipment like HP and Samsung have already shifted their transportation on the Eurasian route to rail taking benefit from the shorter lead time and higher flexibility of inventory supplementation.

Since trade imbalance between China and Europe remains high, an important problem of containers arriving loaded from China and returning empty persists. In the past years, the

* Corresponding author: k.kuzmicz@pb.edu.pl

trade imbalance between China and the EU amounted to EUR 176 billion [1]. China has been the largest partner for EU imports, and the second-largest partner for EU exports, e.g. in 2017. Among EU states The Netherlands has been the largest importer from China and Germany the largest exporter to China. Poland imported from China goods summing up to 16 322 mln Euro, which accounts for a share of 27,8 % of Polish import from countries outside the EU. Polish export to China sums up to 2062 mln Euro, which stands for 5% of the Chinese share in Polish export to countries outside the EU. The majority of goods exchanged between Poland and China consists of machines, other manufactured goods and chemicals (similarly like in the case of goods exchanged between the EU and China – Figure 1).

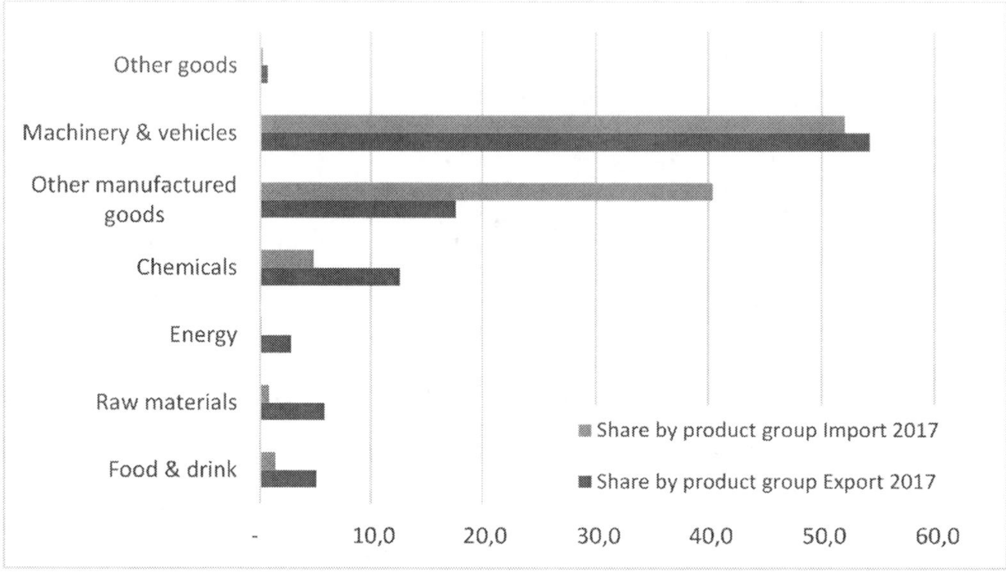

Fig. 1 EU exports to and imports from China by product group 2017 (EUR billion)
Source: Eurostat [1]

As China's export to Poland is very small its role on the NSR is more of a transit country to Germany and further to Western Europe. However enhanced by the new transport possibilities offered by the NSR initiative, intensive efforts of Polish exporters to enter the Chinese market and play an active part in the NSR are made. The dynamics of the Polish-Chinese trade exchange is promising. In 2017 the total turnover of trade exchange between Poland and China increased by 20% and Polish export to China rose by 18% [2].

In 2016, 1075 000 tonnes of goods were exported from Poland to China by rail and 1421 000 tonnes were imported by rail from China to Poland [3]. The intermodal connections between Poland and China are growing, according to PKP Cargo, the Polish Railway company, they comprise 18% of all intermodal connections of Poland [4]. Currently, train services on the route China-Poland are performed every day and most of the loads contain industrial machines and bulk. Taking the Chinese demand into account, the export of Polish food, cosmetics, chemicals, paper and wood can be intensified.

Due to its geographical location, Poland can serve as an important hub facilitating distribution of goods in Europe. Since freight on the Eurasian route is mainly transported in containers, container depots, enabling storage of empty containers as well as their repair, maintenance and cleaning, might importantly influence freight traffic in this region.

In this paper, the criteria for choosing the location of a container depot in Poland is discussed. In this process, the structure of the highway network enabling distribution of containers by trucks to other destinations, as well as green aspects mainly referring to avoiding city congestion caused by trucks transporting containers are taken into consideration.

The remainder of this paper is constructed as follows: first, the role of a container depot in a container transportation chain is underlined and location criteria, introduced in the literature, are presented. Later the infrastructural situation in Poland in the light of the NSR corridor is described and a recommendation of a depot location is formulated.

2 Depot location problem

Since the container storage capacity of ports and rail terminals is limited and it is often impossible to extend the storage area due to the neighbourhood constraints, container depots are established in the proximity of the terminals. Container depots can be defined as large facilities located in the vicinity of seaports or rail transhipment terminals embracing different zones in which different activities are performed, e.g. the reparation, cleaning and storage of empty containers [5]. In container depots leased or carrier owned containers are handled, custody of containers between shippers is transferred and storing containers that are currently surplus is performed. Container depots serve as a supply point for empty containers and servicing/repairing containers under contract [6]. Transporting empty containers back to their origin or owner/leasing party is more expensive than keeping them hinterland in a depot where they wait for repositioning. The cost and space required for transportation of a full or empty container are similar but empty containers do not generate profit.

Inland container depots are an essential element of container transportation chains. Location of a depot should be chosen in the proximity of an array of importers and exporters using containers. Importers, after unloading cargo from containers, send them either back to the port/rail terminal, or directly to the exporters (in the frame of the so-called street turns) or they transport them to container depots where they wait for future demand [7]. Inland container depots can also support rail container terminals and ports as storage places reducing congestion at their sites and reducing costs of transportation of empty containers to the rail terminals/ports. A role of a container depot in the container transportation chain is illustrated in Figure 2.

With the predicted rise of intermodal transportation on the NSR, the increase in capacity of container storage space is inevitable. When the inventory capacity limit is outperformed, the stack height is increased, often from standard height of 3-4 containers up to 8 [8]. Such storage areas spoil the landscape and negatively influence the prices of land [9, 10]. Another important aspect is the increased traffic around container storage places causing an increase of CO_2 emissions, noise, congestion and risk of accidents. Therefore the location of a depot should be distant from residential areas.

Truck delivering or pickup of containers at the depots should be well managed in order to avoid congestion and unnecessary waiting times. Time intervals of service should be established and they can be priced differently in order to equally spread the truck arrivals over the planning horizon [11, 12].

As storage space is rare and costly and the number of empty containers that need to be stored might accumulate to a substantial amount, decisions are necessary where to locate empty container inventory. This requires high-quality forecasting methods in order to foresee the amount of inbound and outbound empty containers.

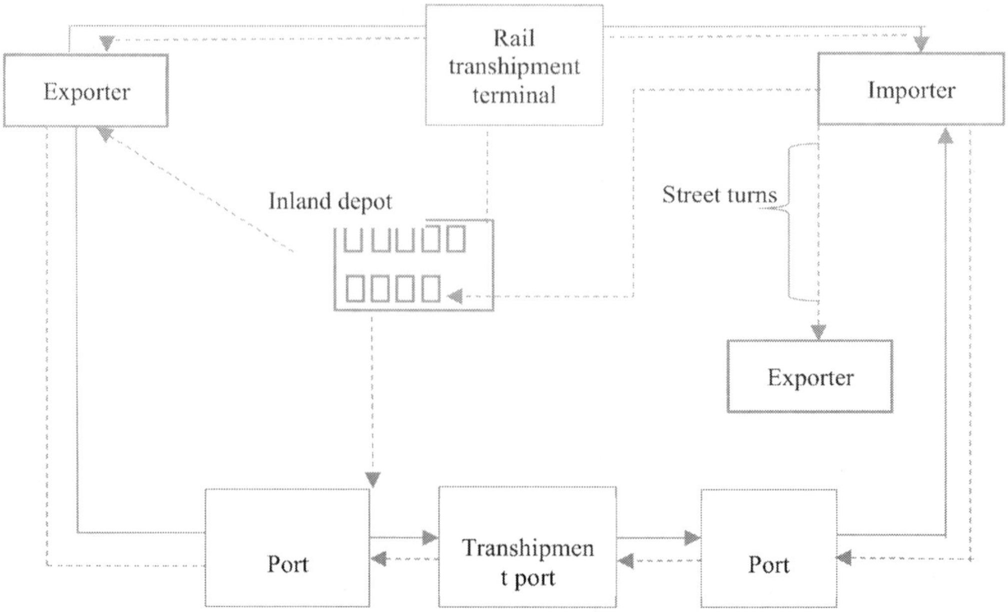

Fig. 2 Container depot role in container transport chain

Insufficient planning of retrieving containers causes reshuffling. It means unnecessary movements of containers which occurs when among any two containers positioned (not necessarily directly) on top of each other the bottom container need to be retrieved earlier [7]. As a consequence, the top container has to be removed before the bottom container becomes accessible. Reshuffling causes cost and energy consumption and should be avoided as much as possible. Methods for optimally stacking and retrieving containers to/from storage yard blocks have been described in Kovalyov et al. [13] and Nossack et al. [14].

The main objective in determining the optimal location of a depot is cost reduction of transporting containers. Palacio et al. [5] propose a multiobjective approach based on the multicommodity capacitated location problem with balancing requirements aiming not only to minimize costs but also to minimize the environmental impact caused by the setting up and maintenance of container depots and by the transport operations inside and in the proximity of the depots. They consider the capacity of the depots as a fuzzy constraint and they use a fuzzy optimization approach to address the problem. They go a step further in their study of 2018 [15] where they design a container depot logistic network minimizing the cost of the whole system, the environmental impact of transport and the environmental impact of establishing and operating of depots with the use of a three-objective, fuzzy optimisation model. They extend the model of Gendron et al. [16, 17] by adding two objective functions and considering one more kind of nodes.

Demand and supply of containers are difficult to forecast. Therefore some authors tried to model the location problem in empty container repositioning under uncertainty. Mittal et al. [8] generate scenarios to solve the optimal location of a container depot problem and formulate a two-stage stochastic program with recourse. They address it as a strategic empty container relocation problem as it requires decisions about facility location in the transportation network. They consider the fixed cost of building new depots and transportation cost of repositioning of empty containers. By this means their model solution can recommend the opening of a depot with a higher fixed cost of opening because of the benefit of lower transportation costs. Another group of costs included in the model are costs concerning environmental impact.

3 Infrastructural conditions in Poland

Container depots in Poland in the frame of the NSR should serve as supporting storage places for container terminals with limited capacity. They should be located in proximity to the container terminals receiving (empty) containers from the EU for freight transport to Asia or closer destinations or receiving loaded containers from China for redistribution within the EU. Depots should be close to importers and exporters using containers and they should be located with good access to the highways to enable convenient distribution of containers. Therefore the access to road and rail transport network should be taken into account. In Figure 3a and 3b, both networks are presented with the border crossings indication in case of the rail network presented in Figure 3b.

Figure 3a. Roads and highways in Poland
Source: A map by Sliwers derivative works of Historia budowy autostrad i dróg ekspresowych.gif,
CC BY 3.0 Licence,
File: DocelowyUkladDrog.svg, Wikipedia [18]

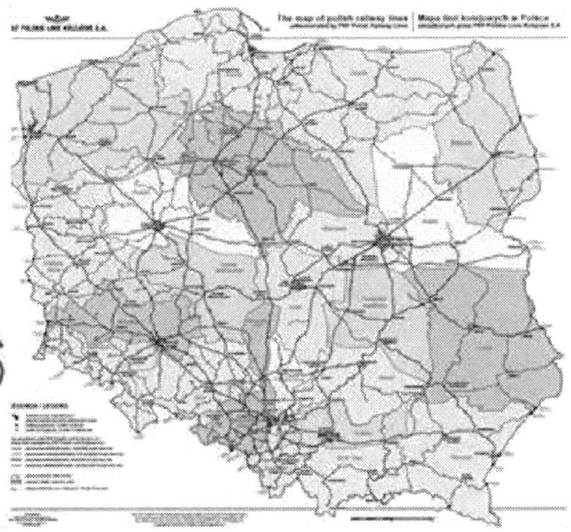

Figure 3b. Railway network in Poland
Source: PKP Polskie Linie Kolejowe S.A., www.plk-sa.pl [19]

Both densities of roads and railways are much higher in the Western and Southern-Western part of the country. Container depots are needed to support the container terminals located on the NSR and link them to highways.

In Poland, inland container terminals have a smaller share in transhipments than sea terminals. Terminals located in the central part of Poland in Warsaw, Pruszkow, Lodz and Kutno have 11% of share in the annual potential of TEU transhipment in Poland. Another important region is Gorny Slask, where terminals Slawkow, Gliwice, Dabrowa Gornicza have 13% of the annual transhipment [20]. There is a big discrepancy in a terminal location with the majority located in the central and western part of the country (Figure 4).

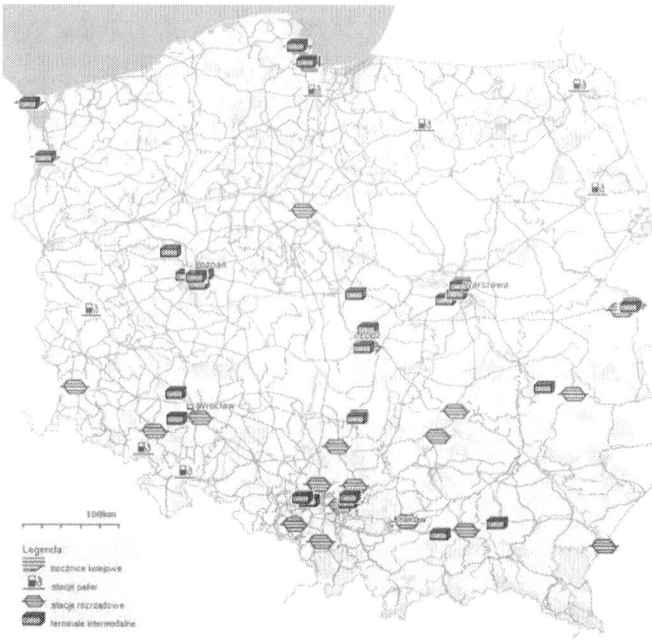

Fig. 4 Container terminals location in Poland
Source: Urząd Transportu Kolejowego; Internet ART s.c. K. Ozimek-Litwin, J. Litwin, M. Baszczak [21]

The terminals with the biggest transhipment potential are Polzug HUB Terminal Poznan, PCC Intermodal – Terminal PCC Kutno, Polzug Terminal Dąbrowa Górnicza, Euroterminal Slawkow and PKP Cargo Centrum Logistyczne Malaszewicze. The last two are crucial border crossings receiving trains with containers from Eastern countries including China.

The main route of the NSR part in Poland leads through Malaszewicze transhipment terminal (at the border crossing with Belarus), which requires a shift from broad to standard track width. The trains to/from China also go through Warsaw and Lodz. Lodz serves as the main logistics hub on the Polish stretch of the NSR, 25% of trains China-Poland is served there [22]. As a consequence of the political instability in Ukraine, the flow of trains from/to China goes through Belarus, Russia and Kazakhstan. By the shift of train transport from Ukraine to Belarus container terminal Slawkow, which formerly received trains from the East coming through Ukraine, lost its significance on the NSR and Malaszewicze took over this role in this region. Since most of the trains coming from China go through Malaszewicze, the insufficient capacity of this terminal (14 pairs of trains per day [22] cause a capacity bottleneck so that further trains need to wait in Belarus or even Kazachstan. In 2017, Malaszewicze received 2200 trains from China with 40 containers each. Over the last years, it was a significant rise from 17 trains yearly in 2011. According to experts predictions, in 2030 the trains from China will bring to Poland 1 billion TEU, which will be five times more than in 2017. The increase of container transport is supported by the Chinese subsidy to each container reaching 3000-5000 of US $ [23].

The insufficient capacity of Malaszewicze triggered searching of the Chinese side for other border crossings on the North-Eastern border of Poland. The trials have been performed in Kuznica Bialostocka and Siemianowka. Furthermore, the modernisation works of the tracks on the route Malaszewisze-Warsaw will contribute to congestion and will result in moving some of the trains to the North-East. Therefore the development of intermodal infrastructure including the establishment of a container depot in the North-Eastern region is important to meet the future demand. A depot located near Kuznica Bialostocka or Siemionowka terminals at the North-Eastern border crossings and close to the roads to provide convenient transport to local industry (importers and exporters) and further to the North and Central Poland could serve well supporting the container transport in this region. Since in the Northern-Eastern region of Poland many dairy products, machines and mechanical parts producers are located, they seem to have the potential to increase export to China and therefore increase their demand for containers.

Another desired location for a container depot would be a proximity of Lodz as a central hub on the NSR and a place well connected to the industry. There are plans to extend the terminal in the city but it will have a harmful impact on the city in terms of congestion and detrimental emissions. Therefore locating a container depot in some distance from Lodz and good connection to the highways, so that containers can be further distributed by trucks to containers users, is advisable.

4 Conclusions

The location of container depots might be a result of competing regions for market share [24] were not the only location but also price decisions, i.e., the incorporation of price competition into competitive location models, has an important relevance. As a result, there might not exist any price equilibria or the multiple local equilibria in prices can be found. Different price sensitivity levels of customers may actually affect optimal locations of depots. Kress and Pesch [25] provide first insights into the performance of heuristic algorithms for these location problems.

Acknowledgements

This study was supported by Bialystok University of Technology (S/WZ/1/2014).

Reference

1. Eurostat, China-EU - international trade in goods statistics (2018), Available from: http://ec.europa.eu/eurostat/statistics-explained/index.php?title=China-EU_-_international_trade_in_goods_statistics#Manufactured_goods_dominate_trade_with_China [Accessed on 17.05.2018]
2. M. Kalwasinski, Eksport z Polski do Chin najwyższy w historii, Bankier.pl. Available from: https://www.bankier.pl/wiadomosc/Eksport-z-Polski-do-Chin-najwyzszy-w-historii-7568470.html [Accessed on 14.06.2018]
3. Statistics Poland, Transport activity results in 2016 (2017), Available from: http://stat.gov.pl/en/topics/transport-and-communications/transport/transport-activity-results-in-2016,6,12.html. [Accessed on 16.06.2018]
4. R. Kolejowy (2018), Available from: http://www.rynek-kolejowy.pl/wiadomosci/nowy-jedwabny-szlak-infrastruktura-nie-nadaza-za-przewozami-87005.html [Accessed on 17.05.2018]
5. A. Palacio, B. Adenso-Díaz, S. Lozano, A fuzzy approach to the location of depots for returned maritime containers, *7th IFAC Conference on Manufacturing Modelling, Management and Control International Federation of Automatic Control*, Saint Petersburg, Russia (2013)
6. M. Rahimi, A. Asef-Vaziri, R. Harrison, Integrating Inland Ports into the Intermodal Goods Movement System for Ports of Los Angeles and Long Beach, Report No. 07-01 (2011)

7. K.A. Kuzmicz, E. Pesch, Approaches to empty container repositioning problems in the context of Eurasian intermodal transportation, *Omega – the International Journal of Management Science*, in press (2018)
8. N. Mittal, M. Boile, A. Baveja, S. Theofanis, Determining optimal inland-empty-container depot locations under stochastic demand, *Research in Transportation Economics* **42**:50-60 (2013)
9. N. Perez-Rodriguez, J. Holguin-Veras, The Accumulation of Empty Containers in Urban Areas: Policy Implications from a Stochastic Formulation, *Networks and Spatial Economics* **14**:379–408 (2014)
10. M. Ramphul, V. Ramesh, V.C. Jaunky, The impact of foldable/collapsible containers on empty container management: a case study at Port Luis, *International Journal of Management and Applied Sciences* **3**:32-39 (2017)
11. K.A. Kuzmicz, E. Pesch, Prerequisites for the modelling of empty container supply chains, *Engineering Management in Production and Services* **9**:28-36 (2017)
12. M. Jarocka, U Ryciuk, Pricing in the railway transport, The 9th International Scientific Conference "Business and Management 2016": Conference Proceedings, Vilnius Gediminas Technical University (2016)
13. M.Y. Kovalyov, E. Pesch, A. Ryzhikov, A note on scheduling container storage operations of two non-passing stacking cranes, *Networks* **71**:271–280 (2018)
14. Y. Nossack, D. Briskorn, E. Pesch, Container dispatching and conflict-free yard crane routing in an automated container terminal, *Transportation Science*, in press (2018)
15. A. Palacio, B. Adenso-Díaz, S. Lozano, A decision making model to design a sustainable container depot logistic network: the case of the port of Valencia, *Transport* **33**:119-130 (2018)
16. B. Gendron, J.Y. Potvin, P. Soriano, A tabu search with slope scaling for the multicommodity capacitated location problem with balancing requirements, *Annals of Operations Research* **122**:193-217 (2003a)
17. B. Gendron, J.Y. Potvin, P. Soriano, A parallel hybrid heuristic for the multicommodity capacitated location problem with balancing requirements, *Parallel Computing* **29**: 591-606 (2003b)
18. Wikipedia, Highways and roads in Poland (2018), Available from: https://pl.wikipedia.org/wiki/Autostrady_i_drogi_ekspresowe_w_Polsce, [Accessed on 04.06.2018]
19. PKP Polskie Linie Kolejowe, A map of Polish railways (2018), Available from: https://www.plk-sa.pl/biuro-prasowe/mapy/ [Accessed on 01.07.2018]
20. M. Jacyna, D. Pyza, R. Jachimowski, *Transport Intermodalny – Projektowanie Terminali Przeładunkowych*, Wydawnictwo Naukowe PWN, Warszawa (2017)
21. U.T. Kolejowego, Internet ART s.c. K. Ozimek-Litwin, J. Litwin, M. Baszczak, A map of intermodal terminals in Poland (2014), Available from: https://utk.gov.pl/pl/aktualnosci/4164,Mapa-obiektow-infrastruktury-uslugowej-i-bocznic-kolejowych.html [Accessed on 01.07.2018]
22. J. Jakobowski, K. Poplawski, M. Kaczmarski, The Silk Rail Road The EU-China rail connections: background, actors, interests, Centre for Eastern Studies, OSW Studies 72 (2018), Available from: https://www.osw.waw.pl/sites/default/files/studies_72_silk-railroad_net.pdf [Accessed on 09.06.2018]
23. Rzeczpospolita, Wojna o obsługę Chińczyków [Fighting for servicing the Chinese] **114**:11054 18 Mai, A24 (2018)
24. D. Kress, E. Pesch, (r|p)-centroid problems on networks with vertex and edge demand, *Computers and Operations Research* **39**:2954–2967 (2012)
25. D. Kress, E. Pesch, Competitive location and pricing on networks with random utilities, *Networks and Spatial Economics* **16**:837–863 (2016)

MATEC Web of Conferences **312**, 02005 (2020) https://doi.org/10.1051/matecconf/202031202005
EPPM2018

Container truck transportation routing as a Mixed Fleet Heterogeneous Dial-a-Ride Problem

Mohamed Amine Masmoudi[1], *Katarzyna Anna* Kuzmicz[2*], *Erwin* Pesch[3], *Emrah* Demir[4] and *Manar* Hosny[5]

[1]Geneva School of Business Administration, University of Applied Sciences Western Switzerland (HES-SO) 1227 Carouge, Switzerland

[2]International China and Central-Eastern Europe Institute of Logistics and Service Science, Faculty of Engineering Management, Bialystok University of Technology, ul. Wiejska 45 A, 15-351 Bialystok, Poland

[3]Department of Management Information Science, University of Siegen, Hölderlinstraße 3, D-57068 Siegen, Germany, E-mail: erwin.pesch@uni-siegen.de and Centre for Advanced Studies in Management, HHL Leipzig Graduate School of Management, Jahnallee 59, 04109 Leipzig, Germany

[4]Panalpina Centre for Manufacturing and Logistics Research, Cardiff Business School, Cardiff University, Cardiff CF10 3EU, UK

[5]Computer Science Department, College of Computer and Information Sciences (CCIS), King Saud University (KSU), Riyadh, Saudi Arabi

Abstract. In this paper, a new variant of the Heterogeneous Dial-a-Ride Problem (HDARP) is innovatively applied to a routing problem of trucks picking up and delivering full and empty containers in the logistic chain, including container depots, importers demanding full containers and exporters requesting empty containers. On the route different types of trucks pick-up and deliver full and empty 20- and 40-foot containers. We consider trucks that are operated by alternative fuel, as well as the need for refuelling of trucks in any alternative fuel station to eliminate the risk of running out of fuel during its route. The objective of the paper is to contribute to the optimization of container truck transport routing with multiple pick-ups and deliveries by providing a mathematical programming model aiming at minimizing the transportation cost as well as the negative environmental impacts.

Keywords: dial-a-ride problem, full and empty containers, green vehicle routing, intermodal transportation

* Corresponding author: k.kuzmicz@pb.edu.pl

1 Introduction

Container transportation on long distances is performed by sea and rail. On short distances between ports, transhipment terminals, container depots, exporters' and importers' containers are transported by trucks. The Organisation for Economic Cooperation and Development - OECD (54 member countries) predicted global trade-related freight and emissions to quadruple by 2050. As the majority of goods are transported in containers, the container traffic on the road will rise significantly. Therefore a problem of optimal routing of trucks, transporting containers, especially with consideration of environmental issues is worth attention.

In container truck transportation the following three basic types of service can be differentiated [1, 2]:

- an order request from an importer for moving a full container from an origin terminal to a given location, where the cargo is unloaded from the container, and then to move the empty container to its destination;
- an order request from an exporter to move an empty container from an origin terminal or a depot to a given location, where some freight is loaded into the container, and then to move the full container to its destination, mostly a terminal;
- a request of transporting an empty container from a given container terminal to an empty container depot, or vice versa.

For each order, hard time windows may be present at each of the visited locations.

After a pickup request for an emptied container has been conducted, an empty container is released at the destination location (where the cargo was unloaded) and is either transported to a depot or to the origin location of a delivery request for an empty container. Thus, each pickup request has to be followed by a delivery request/depot. Similarly, each delivery request requires an empty container at the origin location and either receives an empty container from a depot or a pickup request, i.e., a pickup request/depot has to precede a delivery request. This empty container assignment problem is solved in the first phase of the method by Nossack and Pesch[1,2] by constructing pickup and delivery pairings such that each pickup and delivery request is paired exactly once and each pairing is feasible related to the time windows.

An excellent survey on the fundamental problem of empty container repositioning in intermodal transport supply chains, embracing trade route between Asia and China in particular, can be found in Kuzmicz and Pesch [3].

Trucks can transport one or two containers. The maximum weight of a loaded module (truck-trailer) is restricted by national law depending on the type of road used for transportation. It is estimated that transportation of two heavy containers, despite the heavy pressure on the road, is more environmentally friendly than transporting each container separately, and can contribute to CO_2 emission reduction even by 35% considering the amount of CO_2 to the amount of load transported [4]. Consequently, it also contributes to lower fuel consumption.

In the DARP it is assumed that Conventional Vehicles (CVs) are used to serve the customers. In classical routing problems, it is usually assumed that Conventional Vehicles (CVs) are used to serve the requests. Furthermore, it is normally assumed that CVs have unlimited fuel tank capacity; thus, there is no need for the vehicle to refuel during its service route to customers. However, CVs are one of the main contributors to emissions, such as greenhouse gases (GHGs) and air pollutants. In fact, the European Environment Agency (EEA) has estimated that transportation is responsible for approximately 22% of GHG emissions in 2012. To overcome the environmental challenges as well as the limited energy resource concerns, the transport industry looks for solutions that make use of Alternative Fuel Vehicles (AFVs) (i.e., alternative fuel trucks), such as biodiesel or ethanol operated vehicles.

It is obvious that AFVs can help in reducing GHGs emissions compared to CVs that use gasoline or diesel [5]. In this regard, AFVs have started to gain attention in the last few years, due to their benefits in the field of transportation routing (see, e.g., [5, 6, 7]. Thus, this has inspired us to consider the use of AFVs in the current work within the context of the container routing problem.

The routing of container transportation service is exemplified in the Figure1.

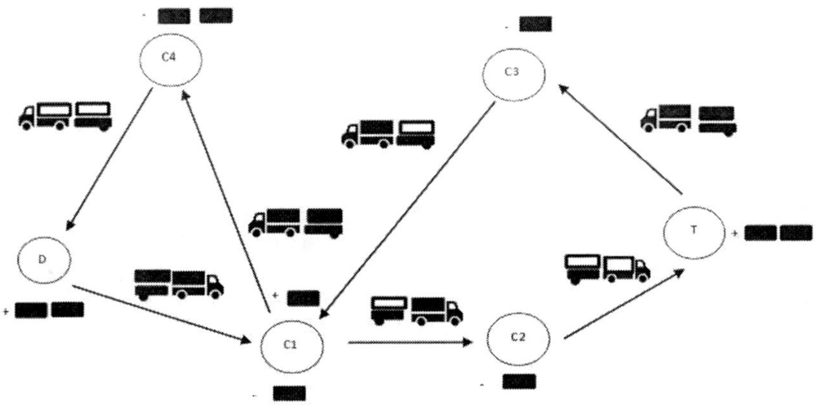

Figure 1. Container truck transportation routing

In the exemplified case a truck picks up two loaded containers at a terminal at a depot or a terminal D and visits client C1 where one container is emptied. Later it continues with one full and one empty container. At client C2 the remaining full container is emptied and the truck continues with two empty containers to container terminal T. At container terminal T two empty containers are left and two full containers are picked up. The next stop is at client C3 where one container is emptied. Later the truck visits once more client C1 where the empty container is filled. With two full containers, it goes to client C4 where the two full containers are emptied. The truck finishes its route at depot D with two empty containers. Note that a '+' and a '-' next to a node of the network indicates whether loaded containers are picked up or dropped off, respectively.

Different models can be used for container truck routing. Here a Dial-a-Ride Problem (DARP) has been applied. Typically applications serve to optimize transportation of elder and/or disabled people with reduced mobility but also in shared taxi services [8] or courier services [9] with multiple pick-up and delivery.

The contribution of this paper includes mathematical modelling of the aforementioned truck routing problem as a heterogeneous dial-a-ride problem with a mixed fleet and refuelling of vehicles.

The remainder of the paper is the following. First, the general idea and standard application of a DARP is presented, later a problem description of HDARP applied to routing of a container pick-up and delivery in the logistic chain of container depots, terminals, exporters and importers are described. Then a mathematical model is proposed followed by a short description of computational experiments.

2 The heterogenous dial-a ride-problem

The DARP involves designing vehicle routes and schedules for different users who specify pick-up and delivery requests between origins and destinations under a number of constraints, typically concerning trip duration, time windows, and vehicle capacity. It is a generalisation of a number of vehicle routing problems such as the Pick-up and Delivery

Vehicle Routing Problem (PDVRP) and the Vehicle Routing Problem with Time Windows (VRPTW) [10]. The specificity of this problem relies on variable vehicle capacity. There is a static and dynamic version of DARP based on schedules fully planned in advance, and with consideration of requests incoming on the day of the service. However, in reality, it is difficult to imagine a pure static or pure dynamic situation because most of the requests would be scheduled in advance but some requests for moving a container could be placed on the day of the service.

DARP with Heterogeneous users and/or alternative fuel vehicles called HDARP [11] is a generalization of the DARP, but it has not been extensively studied in the literature. The first time a formal definition of the HDARP was introduced by [11]. The authors consider two types of conventional fuel vehicles and four different resources (i.e., staff seat, patient seat, stretcher, and wheelchair). They propose a Branch-and-Cut (B&C) and Variable Neighborhood Search (VNS) algorithms and solved 36 instances with up to four vehicles and 48 requests. In a related study [12] introduce a variant of the HDARP, in which the requirements like lunch break constraints are considered. In Braekers et al. [13], multiple depots of heterogeneous vehicles and users are considered to reduce the total routing costs. The authors propose a B&C and a Deterministic Annealing metaheuristic to solve instances containing 2-8 vehicles and 16-96 requests. More recently, Masmoudi et al. [14] apply a hybrid Genetic Algorithm (GA) to the standard HDARP. The proposed algorithm was tested on small and medium benchmark instances for the HDARP with up to 8 vehicles and 96 requests proposed by Parragh [11] and Braekers et al. [13]. To best of our knowledge, the hybrid GA provides the best-known results on these instances so far and outperforms current state-of-the-art algorithms for the standard DARP and HDARP. In another study, Masmoudi et al. [15] augment the multi depots and coffee break concepts on the standard HDARP. They propose hybrid methods based on nature-inspired algorithms and tested them on both newly generated instances and on the benchmark Multi-Depot HDARP instances of Braekers et al. [13]. Recently, Braekers and Kovacs [16], extend the single period HDARP to a Multi-Period DARP and consider a limited number of drivers to serve each user over a predefined number of days.

For other variants of (H)DARP applied to real concepts the interested readers are referred to surveys on the DARP by Cordeau and Laporte [10] and Molenbruch et al. [17].

Container transportation is performed by a mixed fleet of different types of vehicles. We assume usage of trucks carrying 20-foot containers and tractors with semi-trailers carrying one 40-foot container or two 20-foot containers or one 20-foot and one 40-foot container (see Figure 2).

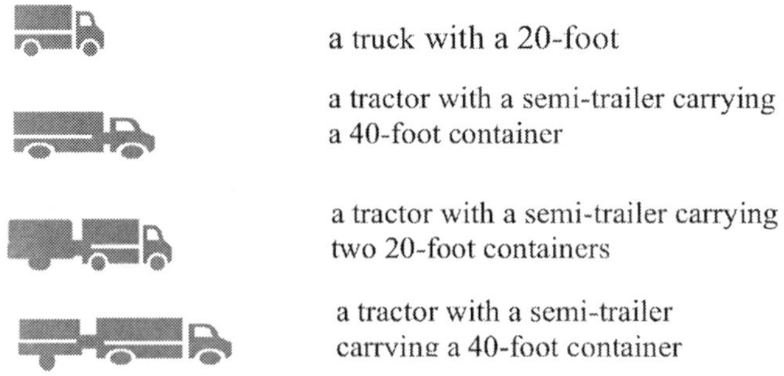

Figure 2. Trucks and tractors with semi-trailers carrying containers

Fuel consumption is dependent on this construction of the transportation module and on the weight of the containers and whether they are transported full or empty.

Consolidating containers and limiting the number of trucks leads generally to lowering the fuel consumption needed for the transportation task.

Due to the limited driving ranges of the AFVs (around 120 miles) because of their limited tank capacity [5], these types of vehicles need to be refuelled from Alternative Fueling Stations (AFSs). In fact, in the context of the DARP, not taking the refuelling requirements beforehand in planning the service route may cause service disruption due to a shortage in fuel, and possible violation of the problem constraints, such as the visiting time windows and/or the maximum ride time of drivers. Such violations can largely lead to the dissatisfaction of customers, which impacts the overall service quality and breaks one of the main conditions of the DARP. Therefore, effective transportation planning should take into consideration the visits of users as well as visits to AFSs, since the need to refuel the tank is frequently encountered during the customary working day, especially when travelling long distances [5].

Another realistic assumption in routing problems is the use of an appropriate fuel consumption function based on several factors, such as vehicle speed and load (e.g., [18, 19, 20, 21]).

3 The green vehicle routing problem

Sanguinetti et al. [22] indicate six classes of eco-driving actions, driving, cabin comfort, trip planning, load management, fuelling, and maintenance.

The Green Vehicle Routing Problem (GVRP) with consideration of the alternative fuel tank capacity limitation is an extension of the VRP that has received increasing attention recently. Erdoğan and Miller-Hooks [5] were the first authors that introduced the GVRP, where refuelling stops are incorporated. The authors proposed a mixed-integer linear model to minimize the travel distance and developed two efficient heuristics and tested them on instances with up to 500 users. Other studies on GVRP with refuelling can be found on Felipe et al. [23] and Adler and Mirchandani [6]. An in-depth investigation of GVRP is developed by Lin et al. [24].

The incorporation of real fuel consumption and emission in the context of the green vehicle routing (GVR) has been widely studied in the recent literature, where these factors play an important role in routing models, taking into account fuel costs and vehicles' emissions (see, e.g., Bektaş and Laporte [18]; Demir et al. [19] and Goeke and Schneider, [25]; Franceschetti et al. [26]; and Androutsopoulos and Zografos [27]. Demir et al. [21], [28]) performed a thorough study of the energy consumption of related routing problems.

Although the concept of heterogeneous vehicles and/or users have been already studied within the context of (H)DARP, what distinguishes our study is that we consider a mixed fleet of trucks that differs in their capacity.

4 Problem definition and model formulation

The Container Mixed Fleet Heterogeneous Dial-a-Ride Problem (CMF-HDARP) can be formally described as follows. Consider a graph $G = (V, A)$ with node set V and arc set $= \{(i,j): i,j \in V, i \neq j$, where V is further partitioned into subsets; $N = \{1, \ldots, 2n\}$ corresponds to n users requesting a transport service. In other words, a user can be identified with an ordered pair of nodes (i,j), $i \neq j$, where i is the pick-up location of a loaded container and j or, for convenience $n + i$, is the predefined drop-off/delivery location. Alternatively, we say container i is picked up at location i and delivered to its destination n+i. If the container is empty, one of the two locations might be a result of the optimization.

Let $P = \{1, \ldots, n\}$ and $D = \{n+1, \ldots, 2n\}$ be the not necessarily disjoint subsets of nodes corresponding to pick-up and delivery locations, respectively. Moreover, $F = \{2n + 1, \ldots, 2n + f\}$ defines the set of Alternative Fuel Stations (AFSs). Nodes 0 and $2n + 1 + f$ correspond to the origin and destination depots, respectively. Thus, we get $V = N \cup F \cup \{0, 2n + 1 + f\}$. There is a non-negative travel cost c_{ij}, depending on travel speed v_{ij} and transportation time t_{ij} associated with each arc (i, j) from set A. We assume the speed to be constant over an arc (i, j) as done in Goeke and Schneider [25], and the number of stops that can be made for refuelling is unlimited. When refuelling takes place, it is assumed that the tank is refilled to its maximum capacity. The time windows to visiting any refuelling node are set as $[0, T]$, where T is the length of the planning horizon. Moreover, a mixed fleet of heterogeneous vehicles $K = \{k_1, \ldots, k_k\}$ composed of trucks and tractors with semi-trailers is available to transport all containers.

We note that in the mathematical model there is a difference between visits to users' nodes and visits to AFSs nodes/depot, where user nodes must be visited exactly once, while AFS nodes may be visited more than once or not visited at all. Also, the depot must be visited at the start and end of the tour, and can also be considered as an AFS node. Moreover, in order to allow some vertices to be visited more than once, while others are visited exactly once, we augment a set of dummy vertices f' on the graph G, such that $F' = \{2n + f + 1, \ldots, 2n + f + f'\}$ (see, e.g., Erdoğan and Miller-Hooks [5]; Goeke and Schneider [25]. Each of these nodes represents a potential visit to an AFS or depot. Thus, the graph $G' = (V', A')$ will consist of $V' = V \cup F'$.

Each truck has a capacity $Q^{r,k}$ that gives the amount of resource r available on each vehicle k, where each type of resource is dedicated to: the full 20-foot container $Q^{0,k}$, full 40-foot container $Q^{1,k}$, empty 20-foot container $Q^{2,k}$ and empty 40-foot container $Q^{3,k}$. Each vehicle type contains a fuel tank capacity H^k, which is consumed and reduced at a fuel rate FR_{ij} on each travelled arc (i,j). Each pick-up location i is associated with a demand requirement of transport space $-2 \le q_i^r \le 2$ for each resource r, and a time window $[T_i^-, T_i^+]$, where T_i^- and T_i^+ represent the earliest and latest visiting time, respectively, of this location. A positive value q_i^r indicates that there is a request for an empty truck position suitable to capture a container at location i. A negative demand value means, a container is dropped from the truck and the position becomes available for a pick-up of another container either at the same location or at a subsequent one on the route. A value of zero either indicates that there is no container demand or supply at location i or the number of containers of the same type (resource) dropped and picked at this location is the same. A maximum container transportation time L_{max} is considered as a service promise for maximum waiting time. In addition, a service time s_i is imposed when visiting each node ($\forall\, i \in N$), and a refuelling time s_f is considered when visiting a recharging station node ($\forall\, f \in F'$).

As studied in Demir et al. [19], for the fuel consumption rate of the vehicles, the constant fuel rate FR_{ij} required on each arc (i, j) can be calculated as a function of the mechanical power and a couple of other parameters.

In summary, the CMF-HDARP consists of determining a set of routes to satisfy the users' demands while minimizing the total routing costs. A solution must have the following conditions: *i*) the pick-up node must be visited before the corresponding delivery node, *ii*) the total demand for the route must not exceed the capacity of each resource of the vehicle, *iii*) each node must be served within its time window; if a vehicle arrives early, it must wait until the beginning of the service, *iv*) the maximum transportation time of each container must be respected, *v*) the pick-up and delivery nodes of each container must be visited by the same vehicle, *vi*) each vehicle must be refuelled at any AFS node if the remaining tank fuel level is not enough to visit any node $i \in V$, and *vii*) each route should start and end at the same depot and the route has a maximum duration of T_{max}.

Now we present the integer programming formulation for the CMF-HDARP, which is based on Cordeau [29] and inspired by the formulations of the HDARP of Parragh [11] and the GVRP with the refuelling of Erdoğan and Miller-Hook [5]. The CMF-HDARP can be formulated as follows: Binary variable x_{ij}^k is equal to 1 if vehicle k travels from node i to j and 0 otherwise. Variable Q_i^{rk} indicates the load of resource r on vehicle k immediately after visiting node i. Continuous variable B_i^k represents the time that the vehicle k begins its service at node i. Moreover, continuous variable l_i^k represents the transportation time of loaded container (from location) $i \in P$ on vehicle k. Continuous variable z_i^k represents the remaining fuel level in the tank upon arrival to node i with vehicle k. It is noted that z_i^k is set to H^k at each visit to any alternative fuel station node $f \in F'$.

$$\text{Minimize} \sum_{k \in K} \sum_{i \in V'} \sum_{j \in V'} c_{ij} x_{ij}^k \qquad (1)$$

Subject to

$$\sum_{k \in K} \sum_{j \in N} x_{ij}^k = 1 \qquad \forall i \in P \qquad (2)$$

$$\sum_{k \in K} \sum_{j \in N} x_{ji}^k = 1 \qquad \forall i \in D \qquad (3)$$

$$\sum_{j \in N} x_{ij}^k = \sum_{j \in N} x_{j,n+i}^k \qquad \forall k \in K, \forall i \in P \qquad (4)$$

$$\sum_{j \in V'} x_{0j}^k = 1 \qquad \forall k \in K \qquad (5)$$

$$\sum_{i \in V'} x_{i,2n+1+f'}^k = 1 \qquad \forall k \in K \qquad (6)$$

$$\sum_{j \in V'} x_{ji}^k = \sum_{j \in V'} x_{ij}^k \qquad \forall k \in K, \forall i \in V' \qquad (7)$$

$$Q_j^{rk} \geq (q_j^r + Q_i^{rk}) x_{ij}^k \qquad \forall k \in K, \forall (i,j) \in A, r \in \{0,1,2,3\} \qquad (8)$$

$$0 \leq Q_i^{rk} \leq Q^{rk} \qquad \forall k \in K, \forall i \in N, r \in \{0,1,2,3\} \qquad (9)$$

$$Q_0^{rk} = 0 \qquad \forall k \in K, r \in \{0,1,2,3\} \qquad (10)$$

$$l_i^k = B_{n+i}^k - (B_i^k + s_i) \qquad \forall k \in K, \forall i \in P \qquad (11)$$

$$t_{i,n+i} \leq l_i^k \leq L_{\max} \qquad \forall k \in K, \forall i \in P \qquad (12)$$

$$B_j^k \geq (B_i^k + s_i + t_{ij}) x_{ij}^k \qquad \forall k \in K, \forall (i,j) \in A' \qquad (13)$$

$$T_i^- \leq B_i^k \leq T_i^+ \qquad \forall k \in K, \forall i \in V' \qquad (14)$$

$$B_{2n+1+f'}^k - B_0^k \leq T_{\max} \qquad \forall k \in K, \forall f \in F' \qquad (15)$$

$$z_j^k - z_i^k + M_{ij} x_{ij}^k + (M_{ij} - FR_{ij} c_{ij} - FR_{ij} c_{ji}) x_{ji}^k \leq M_{ij} - FR_{ij} c_{ij} \qquad \forall i,j \in N, i \neq j, \forall k \in K \qquad (16)$$

$$z_j^k = H^k \qquad \forall j \in F', \forall k \in K \qquad (17)$$

$$z_j^k \geq \min\{FR_{ij} c_{j0}, FR_{ij}(c_{jf'} + c_{f0})\} \qquad \forall j \in V, \forall f \in F', \forall k \in K \qquad (18)$$

$$x_{ij}^k \in \{0,1\} \qquad \forall k \in K, \forall (i,j) \in A' \qquad (19)$$

The objective function (1) minimizes the total routing costs assuming that the travel costs are proportional to the travelled distance. Constraints (2)-(4) guarantee that each pick-up and delivery location is served by a vehicle. Constraints (5)-(6) ensure that each vehicle k starts at the origin depot and ends at the corresponding destination depot, while constraints (7) satisfy flow conservation. Constraints (8) and (9) enforce the consistency with respect to vehicle capacity constraints. Constraints (10) ensure that the load variable on the depot is set to zero, which means that the vehicles leave the depot with empty load. This can be adjusted to values one or two if empty containers are picked there. Constraints (11) define the ride time of each container transported from i to $n+1$ in each route, which is bounded by constraints (12). These constraints also impose the precedence relation between the pick-up and delivery nodes of a user. Constraints (13) define the beginning of service at each node and the consistency of the time variables. Constraints (14) impose time windows compliance. Constraints (15) ensure that the time duration of the route for each vehicle is limited by T_{max}. Constraints (16) impose that the fuel level is reduced based on the distance travelled between nodes i and j and the fuel consumption rate, where M_{ij} is a constant applied to each arc (i,j) $\forall\, i,j \in A'$. Constraints (17) guarantee that the fuel level is reset to its maximum H^k after visiting each recharging station node. Constraints (18) guarantee that the remaining tank fuel level of the vehicle is enough to return to the initial depot or to reach a fuel station from any user location. Finally, constraints (19) guarantee that the decision variables are binary.

Conclusions

The problem is certainly NP-hard as dial-a-ride problems are NP-hard. However, it is a challenge to see how far a standard solver can get in solving instances of these problems. Initial implementation in CPLEX is intended which then will be enriched by a decomposition. Earlier experiments let us hope that competitive results for smaller to medium-sized problems can be achieved within an hour of run time.

Container truck transportation routing with several pick-up and delivery with optimizing transportation cost, fuel consumption and pollution emission is a topical problem requiring further investigation. In this paper, a new and more realistic version is proposed and its application to container truck transportation can be perceived as innovative. We considered a mixed fleet of vehicles (Alternative Fuel Vehicles) composed of both alternative fuel trucks and tractors with semi-trailers subject to constraints of capacity of transporting 20-foot and 40-foot full or empty containers including refuelling of vehicles.

Our model is limited in that respect that the vehicles will be refuelled in each visit to the station.

In a centralized decision process, as mentioned above, a global optimum maximizes a kind of social welfare while different transport requests do not equally contribute to the emissions and pollution. As a consequence, the clients wish to participate in the development of a fair solution and fair pricing strategy. Therefore the transport company might develop a mechanism (a game) so that all clients can reach a satisfying solution, see Kress et al. [30, 31]. In the ideal case, the mechanism encourages the clients (or players) to provide truthful information in any negotiation process with the transport company or competitor and to discourage selfish behaviour. A mechanism is needed where selfish behaviour does not provide any advantage in comparison to truth-telling. Moreover, the clients have insight and understand the functions of the mechanism. In equilibrium, no client would like to change its position in the transport sequence and the transport company would focus on those equilibria that maximize social welfare. For details, see Kovalyov and Pesch [32]. Fast and efficient methods need to be developed in order to find an equilibrium as this might be a strongly NP-hard problem or good approximations of equilibrium are to be found.

Acknowledgements

This study was supported by Bialystok University of Technology (S/WZ/1/2014).

References

1. J. Nossack, E. Pesch, A truck scheduling problem arising in intermodal container transportation, *European Journal of Operational Research* **230**: 666–680 (2013a)
2. J. Nossack, E. Pesch, *Planning and scheduling in intermodal transport, Manufacturing Modelling, Management and Control 2013* in The Proceedings of the IFAC International Conference, St Petersburg, Russia (2013) (2013b)
3. K.A. Kuzmicz, E. Pesch, Approaches to empty container repositioning problems in the context of Eurasian intermodal transportation, *Omega - The Int. Journal of Management Science*, in press. (2018)
4. 40ton.net, https://40ton.net/dwa-ciezkie-kontenery-20-stopowe-w-ramach-az-74-tonowego-zestawu-jak-najbardziej-moga-miec-sens
5. S. Erdoğan, E. Miller-Hooks, A green vehicle routing problem, *Transportation Research Part E: Logistics and Transportation Review* **48**: 100-114 (2012)
6. J.D. Adler, P.B. Mirchandani, The vehicle scheduling problem for fleets with alternative-fuel vehicles, *Transportation Science* **51**: 441-456 (2016)
7. Ç. Koç, I. Karaoglan, The green vehicle routing problem: A heuristic based exact solution approach, *Applied Soft Computing* **39**, 154-164 (2016)
8. D.O. Santos, E.C. Xavier, Taxi and Ride Sharing: A Dynamic Dial-a-Ride Problem with Money as an Incentive, *Expert Systems with Applications* **42**: 6728–6737 (2015) 8
9. Hunsaker, M.V.P. Savelsbergh, Efficient feasibility testing for dial-a-ride problems, *Operations Research Letters* **30**: 169-173 (2012)
10. J.-F. Cordeau, G. Laporte. The dial-a ride problem: models and algorithms, *Annals of Operations Research* **153**: 29-46 (2007)
11. S.N. Parragh, Introducing heterogeneous users and vehicles into models and algorithms for the dial-a-ride problem. *Transportation Research Part C: Emerging Technologies* **19**: 912-930 (2011)
12. S.N. Parragh, J.F. Cordeau, K. F., Doerner, R. F., Hartl, Models and algorithms for the heterogeneous dial-a-ride problem with driver-related constraints, *OR Spectrum* **34**, 593-633 (2012)
13. K. Braekers. A. Caris, G.K. Janssens, Exact and meta-heuristic approach for a general heterogeneous dial-a-ride problem with multiple depots, *Transportation Research Part B: Methodological* **67**: 166–186 (2014)
14. M.A. Masmoudi, K. Braekers, M. Masmoudi, A. Dammak, A hybrid genetic algorithm for the heterogeneous dial-a-ride problem, *Computers & Operations Research* **81**: 1-13 (2017)
15. M.A. Masmoudi, M. Hosny, K. Braekers, A. Dammak, Three effective metaheuristics to solve the multi-depot multi-trip heterogeneous dial-a-ride problem, *Transportation Research Part E: Logistics and Transportation Review* **96**: 60-80 (2016)
16. K. Braekers, A. Kovacs, A multi-period dial-a-ride problem with driver consistency. A multi-period dial-a-ride problem with driver consistency, *Transportation Research Part B: Methodological* **94**: 355-377 (2016)
17. Y. Molenbruch, K. Braekers, A. Caris, Typology and literature review for dial-a-ride problems, *Annals of Operations Research* **259**: 295-325 (2017)
18. T. Bektas, G. Laporte, The pollution-routing problem. *Transportation Research Part B: Methodological* **45**: 1232-1250 (2011)

19. E. Demir, T. Bektas, G. Laporte, An adaptive large neighborhood search heuristic for the pollution-routing problem, *European Journal of Operational Research* **223**: 346–359 (2012)
20. E. Demir, T. Bektas, G. Laporte, The bi-objective pollution-routing problem. *European Journal of Operational Research*, **232**: 464-478 (2014a)
21. E. Demir, T. Bektas, G. Laporte, A review of recent research on green road freight transportation. *European Journal of Operational Research* **237**: 775–793 (2014b)
22. A. Sanguinetti, K. Kurani, J. Davies, The many reasons your mileage may vary: Toward a unifying typology of eco-driving behaviours, *Transportation Research Part D: Transport and Environment* **52** (Part A), 73–84 (2017)
23. Á. Felipe, M.T. Ortuño, G. Righini, G. Tirado, A heuristic approach for the green vehicle routing problem with multiple technologies and partial recharges. *Transportation Research Part E: Logistics and Transportation Review* **71**: 111-128 (2014)
24. C. Lin, K.L. Choy, G.T.S. Ho, S.H. Chung, H.Y. Lam, Survey of Green Vehicle Routing Problem: Past and future trends, *Expert Systems with Applications* **41**: 1118–1138 (2014)
25. D. Goeke, M. Schneider, Routing a mixed fleet of electric and conventional vehicles, *European Journal of Operational Research* **245**, 81-99 (2015)
26. A. Franceschetti, E. Demir, D. Honhon, T. Van Woensel, G. Laporte, M. Stobbe, A metaheuristic for the time-dependent pollution-routing problem, *European Journal of Operational Research* **259(3)**: 972-991 (2017)
27. K.N. Androutsopoulos, K.G. Zografos, An integrated modelling approach for the bicriterion vehicle routing and scheduling problem with environmental considerations, *Transportation Research Part C: Emerging Technologies* **82**:180-209 (2017)
28. E. Demir, Y. Huang, S. Scholts, T. Van Woensel, A selected review on the negative externalities of the freight transportation: Modeling and pricing, *Transportation Research Part E: Logistics and Transportation Review* **77**: 95-114 (2015)
29. J.-F. Cordeau, A branch-and-cut algorithm for the dial-a-ride problem. *Operations Research* **54**: 573–586 (2016)
30. D. Kress, S. Meiswinkel, E. Pesch, Mechanism design for machine scheduling problems, *OR Spectrum* **40**: 583–611 (2018a)
31. D. Kress, S. Meiswinkel E. Pesch, Incentive compatible mechanisms for machine scheduling problems with job agents, *Discrete Applied Mathematics* **242**: 89-101 (2018b)
32. M.Y. Kovalyov, E. Pesch, A game mechanism for single machine sequencing with zero risk, *Omega - The Int. Journal of Management Science* **44**, 104-110 (2014)

Evaluation of an OBCE Conversion Contract in a Large-scale Oil and Gas Project

Ruveyda Komurlu[1], and *Akin* Er[2*]

[1]Department of Architecture, Kocaeli University, Kocaeli, Turkey
[2]TUPRAS General Management, Kocaeli, Turkey

Abstract. Billion-dollar investments are quite common in oil and gas industry and owners generally prefer engineering, procurement, construction (EPC) contracts since they would like to minimize their risks and guarantee the most consistent project cost and shortest timeline scheme. Considering the size of contracts, owners are unsurprisingly seeking an ideal tender awarding method to avoid deviation from project schedule or budget and get the maximum benefit for them. They may prefer to award the EPC contract directly (i), have a front-end engineering design (FEED) study done first and award the EPC contract afterwards (ii), or set up a convertible contract and convert it to EPC after an open book cost estimate (OBCE) process (iii). It is a question of concern which option for large-scale oil and gas projects is the most favourable. As a case study, outcomes of a project which was administrated with a conversion type of contract will be reviewed in detail, and a number of principles based on lessons learned will be listed. Thus, the authors aim to provide a verifying approach for the interpretation of EPC conversion type contract management based on analysis of the distinguishing features of large-scale oil and gas projects.

Keywords: convertible contracts, FEED study, EPC contracts, OBCE (open book cost estimate), oil and gas projects.

1 Introduction

Oil and gas companies should invest in several projects every year. This is inevitable for them as there are so many forcing factors like new environmental regulations, operational requirements, modernization, renovation, profitability, etc. Some of these projects cost more than billion-dollars. Considering the negative consequences of mistakes that could be made during the investment period of such projects, owners are unsurprisingly investigating for the correct contract strategy which fits well with their project objectives.

In general, contract strategy refers to organizational and contractual policies which are selected for the execution of a specific project [1]. It is one of the key parameters which has significant effects on the project. Risk allocations of project actors, namely owner, contractor

* Corresponding author: akin.er@tupras.com.tr

and vendor, are tightly linked to that decision given by the owner at the beginning of the project. Tendering process, responsibilities, interfaces between phases, management policies are all evolved around that decision which certainly means that contract strategy has also an important impact on the project schedule and the budget [2].

This article will primarily focus on contract strategies which could be followed during a project. After making an overview of the characteristics of large scale projects in oil and gas, EPC lump sum type contracts will be reviewed individually. Different methods of EPC contract will be discussed. Finally, an implementation of a conversion type EPC contract will be evaluated as support for theoretical conclusions. By this way, it is aimed at an approach to verify the interpretation of EPC conversion type contract management will be provided.

2 Overview of Contract Strategies

2.1 Main Components of Contract Strategy

Contract strategy shapes the management decisions of all parties in the project. It basically depends on three main components namely project delivery method, contract price arrangement and contract clauses [3].

2.1.1 Project Delivery Method

Project delivery method determines the sharing of responsibilities of each project phase between the parties of the contract. There are four types of project delivery methods [3]:

- Design - Bid - Build (Traditional)
- Design-Build or EPC
- Construction Management (CM)
- Relational contracting models

Design - Bid - Build, Design-Build and Construction Management methods are compared in Table 1.

Table 1. Comparison of Project Delivery Methods

	Design - Bid – Build	**Design-Build or EPC**	**Construction Management (CM)**
Basic characteristics	- Separate design and construction contracts - Bidding is after the design is completed	- A single contract that consists of engineering, procurement and construction - Enables to overlap project phases	- A designated contractor performs construction management on behalf of the owner
Advantages	- Project scope and procedures are well defined before construction - Changes during design development have no significant cost impact	- Transfer risk to the contractor - The shortest path for the project duration - Project cost is determined at an early stage	- Enables the owner to set up a smaller organization
Disadvantages	- The owner takes the coordination and risk - The longest path for the project duration - Project cost is not definite at the beginning	- Owner's control is limited - Requires more qualified and expensive contractors	- Additional cost due to CM - Decisions can be more in favour of counterparties compared to the owner's direct involvement

The relational contracting model also offers a contract to represent a relationship between the parties. However, unlike the other three models, it introduces a degree of flexibility into the contract on the basis of understanding the other party's objectives [4]. By this way, all project participants intend to work as one integrated team in the project from the design stage until completion [5]. Alliance, IPD (Integrated Project Delivery) and project partnering contracts could be listed in this group.

2.1.2 Contract Price Arrangements

Provision of the contract price is another component of the contract strategy. It could be classified into three main categories in view of some studies [2, 6] about the subject.

- Price Based Contracts
- Cost-Based Contracts
- Guaranteed Maximum Price Contracts

Price Based Contracts, Cost-Based Contracts and Guaranteed Maximum Price Contracts are compared in Table 2.

Table 2. Comparison of Contract Price Arrangements

	Price Based Contracts	**Cost Based Contracts**	**Guaranteed Maximum Price Contracts**
Basic characteristics	- Prices are agreed in the contract - Costs are unknown by the owner - Preferred when scope or design are well defined	- The contractor is reimbursed for all costs plus fee - Costs are known by the owner - Preferred when scope or design is not mature	- Combination of price and cost-based contracts - The contractor is reimbursed up to a maximum fixed amount
Types	- Unit Price (Admeasurement) - Fixed Price (Lump sum)	- Cost-plus ratio of cost - Cost-plus fixed fee - Cost-plus incentive fee	
Payment Types	- Unit Price – time intervals - Fixed Price – time intervals or achieved milestones	- Time intervals	- Time intervals
Advantages / Disadvantages	- Unit Price – Total price is not known since it is related to actual quantities - Fixed Price – Total price is known, risks are transferred to the contractor	- More flexible - Risks are on the owner	- Shared risks

2.1.3 Contract Clauses

Contract clauses principally adjust general responsibilities of parties during the execution of the project. The main body of contracts usually describes basic matters of the project like parties, reference documents, scope, price, time for completion, bonus and penalties.

A general and special condition of contracts typically explains definitions, guarantees and liabilities, risk distributions and details of work execution. Owners should define contract clauses considering their contract strategy.

2.2 Parameters Designated Contract Strategy

Although some projects have almost the same scopes, it should be recognized that each project is unique since it has its own conditions, constraints or opportunities. Thus, taking into account some key factors, owners should determine the contract strategy specifically for each project. Those key factors could be listed as follows [7]:

- Risk allocation between owner and contractor
- Type, location and size of the project
- Division of responsibilities between parties
- Interfaces between project phases
- Market situation
- Splitting of works and services between concerned parties
- Project time constraints
- Owner's existing organization and resources

Legal regulations, qualifications of potential contractors, availability of specific construction equipment and payment method [8] could be also added to the listed factors above. Hence, owners should evaluate their resources, objectives and project characteristics before deciding their contract strategy.

3 Characteristics of Large-Scale Oil and Gas Projects

3.1 Project Development Stages

A large-scale oil and gas project should pass various stages (Figure 1) which begin with idea generation and ends with an operational start-up. The first four stages express the maturity of the project, whereas the last two are the implementation of the project. The end of the first four stages are called decision gates where project cost estimates should be updated and investment feasibilities should be reassessed.

Maturity of Project				**Implementation of Project**	
Idea Generation	**Conceptual Design**	**Basic Engineering**	**FEED**	**Project Execution**	**Commissioning & Start-up**
	Pre-feasibility	Feasibility	Part of Detailed Engineering	• Detailed Engineering • Procurement • Construction	
GATES					

Fig. 1. Project Stages

3.2 Fast Track Execution

Project execution stage consists of three main phases i.e. detailed engineering, procurement and construction. Each phase requires several months to be completed. Hence, the project duration of those projects lasts much more than many other construction projects. However, owners want to put their projects into operation quickly because they want the return of their considerable investments as soon as possible. To shorten the duration of the execution period such phases should be overlapped. Therefore, large-scale oil and gas projects are fast track projects. However, this approach also brings the risks of revision and rework.

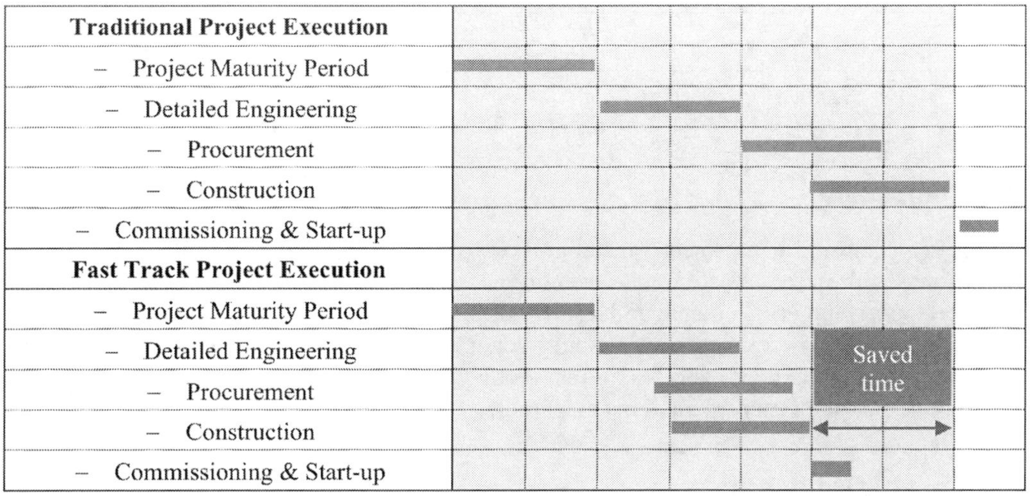

Fig. 2. Fast Track Project Execution

3.3 Estimation Range of CAPEX

Accuracy of CAPEX is another important point in those projects. It directly affects the financial parameters of the investment (e.g. net present value, internal rate of return) and has a significant role at the investment decision. Thus, owners would like to know CAPEX with a certain degree of accuracy before the commencement of the project execution. However, due to the aforementioned facts, the accuracy of the project cost is a question mark for decision-makers. AACE 18R-97 [9] recommends five estimate classes and corresponding accuracy ranges regarding the maturity level of project deliverables.

Table 3. AACE Cost Estimate Classification [9]

AACE Recommended Practice - 18R-97				Corresponding Project Stage
Estimate Class	Maturity Level of Deliverables	Expected Accuracy Range		
Class 5	0% To 2%	L:	-20% to -50%	Conceptual Design
		H:	+30% to +100%	
Class 4	1% To 15%	L:	-15% to -30%	Basic Design or Early Stage of FEED
		H:	+20% to +50%	
Class 3	10% To 40%	L:	-10% to -20%	FEED
		H:	+10% to +30%	
Class 2	30% To 75%	L:	-5% to -15%	Final Stage of FEED or Project Execution
		H:	+5% to +20%	
Class 1	65% To 100%	L:	-3% to -10%	Project Execution
		H:	+3% to +15%	

3.4 Complexity

Large-scale oil and gas projects are complex projects since they are multi-discipline and multi-phase projects. Fast track execution creates interfaces between phases due to overlapping and brings management difficulties like other types of projects carried out in this way. Multiple contractors, financing scheme, etc. are some other factors that may increase the complexity. Owner's contract strategy determines the degree of complexity and the required level of management organization.

3.5 Cost of Design Changes

Several key design decisions are given by the owners during project development. However, the cost of change could be significantly high in large-scale oil and gas projects. The relative cost of making a design change in the various phases of such a project has been stated in Table 4 [10].

Table 4. Relative Cost of Making a Design Change

Phase	Impact	Relative Cost (USD)
Process Design Package Basic Engineering	tens of engineering hours	Thousands
Detailed Engineering	hundreds of engineering hours	tens of thousands
Sourcing	thousands of engineering hours	hundreds of thousands
Construction	engineering, construction time, equipment	Millions
Post-Start-up	engineering, equipment, installation	millions to tens of millions

4 EPC Contracting Methodologies

Considering the characteristics of large-scale oil and gas projects, EPC lump-sum contracting appears as the most advantageous strategy for the owners. Because it ensures to owners not the least but the most reliable budget and minimum risk. Fast track execution enables to complete the project in the shortest duration. Owners could manage the project with a smaller organization compared to alternative strategies. On the other hand, some disadvantages of the strategy could be mentioned such as maximum contingency in the contract price and less involvement of the owner in the detailed design. Nevertheless, considering benefits of the aforesaid advantages, owners widely prefer EPC lump sum for the execution period of their projects.

It is possible to follow different methodologies while awarding an EPC contract. Owners may prefer to award the EPC contract directly (i), have a front-end engineering design (FEED) study done first and award the EPC contract afterwards (ii), or set up a convertible contract and convert it to EPC after an open book cost estimate process (iii). Last two methodologies have been developed to minimize the disadvantages of EPC contracting in the course of time.

In case of a direct EPC contracting, the owner defines the project frame and assigns a contractor to follow all engineering, procurement and construction activities of it. The role of the owner is mainly limited to project controls and contract management. The contractor bears the risks and responsibilities. Therefore, the contract price includes maximum contingency. If the project frame was not clearly defined in the bidding document, possible design changes might result in significant change orders. However, the project duration will be the minimum.

In order to minimize aforesaid drawbacks, owners may prefer to have a FEED contract first and award the EPC contract afterwards. By this way, design development will reach a reasonable level of maturity before EPC contracting. Project cost could be estimated more precisely since long lead items become ready for purchase orders and quantities could be reckoned pretty close to exact figures. Cost deviation is inversely proportional to the level of information. However, this methodology requires two awarding periods both for FEED and EPC. In the second awarding, if the EPC contractor is selected different than the FEED contractor, that will create a discontinuity in the detailed engineering. In this case, some owners may request from the EPC contractor to process existing detailed engineering document once again which results in additional time and money.

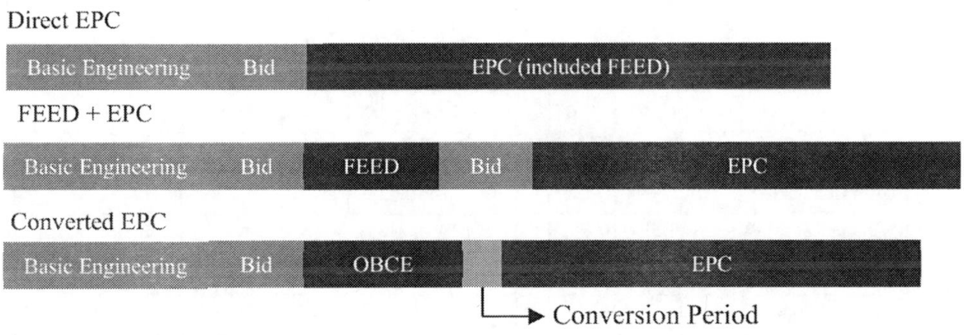

Fig. 3. EPC Contracting Methodologies

Convertible contracts prevent the discontinuity of FEED plus EPC contracts. In this method, the owner and the contractor agree on a two-stage contract. In the first stage, detailed design is advanced up to a certain level where project cost could be calculated reasonably accurate. Cost estimation study should be transparent and traceable for the owner. The process is called as OBCE (open book cost estimate). In this stage, the contractor could be paid in any price adjustment structure. Later on, the contract is converted into EPC lump sum following the conversion method previously defined in it. By this way, all project costs, contingency amount and the contractor's profit are all known by the owner. Moreover, the contractor could proceed to the second stage immediately and uninterruptedly after the conversion. As the final outcome of the above comparison, it can be concluded that convertible contracts solve most of the concerns of a project.

5 Implementation of an OBCE Conversion Contract

Resid Upgrading Project has been executed in TUPRAS Izmit Refinery-Turkey. It is a typical sample of large-scale oil and gas projects which consist of civil works, steelworks, piping, equipment erection, electrical works, instrumentation etc., thus require coordination of various sub-contractors for the success of the project [11]. The total cost of the project is 2.7 billion dollars including financial expenditures. Basic engineering of the main three units was completed prior to the bidding stage. EPC package was including basic engineering of smaller units and detailed engineering, procurement, construction of the complete project. Owner's preference was direct EPC awarding methodology in the previous large-scale projects. However, considering the size of the package and level of information for bidders, it was anticipated that the contingency amount in the tenders could be extremely high. Thus, an OBCE conversion contract has been implemented in the project.

Timeline of the project is shown in Figure 4. The project was divided into two stages namely OBCE Period and Project Execution Period (EPC). There is a two months conversion period between two stages, in which OBCE calculations were rechecked and an EPC contract was put into final form. However, an extra four months have been spent to finalize for financial agreements due to creditors involvement that was not forecasted at the initial planning. The two stages, i.e. OBCE and EPC, were clearly defined in the contract. The contract gave the right to TUPRAS not to continue the project after the OBCE stage. By this way, the last decision gate was kept in the contract.

Contract price adjustment was set on a fixed price for both the OBCE and the EPC stages. The total project cost has been separated into five categories; detailed engineering, itemized materials (equipment), bulk material, construction and ancillary costs (transportation, customs, insurance, training services, etc.). A lump sum price was agreed for detailed engineering considering the OBCE and the EPC stages separately. For other categories, contractor's fee and allowance ratios were agreed in the contract which was necessary for the conversion.

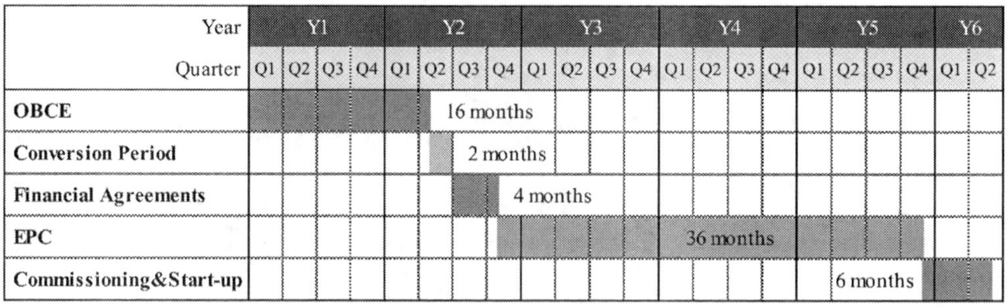

Fig. 4. Timeline of Resid Upgrading Project

Contractor's fee corresponds to the profit overestimated cost and they are proposed by the contractor for each cost category during the bid. However, allowance ratios are defined by TUPRAS in the bidding document to cover some potential costs of the contractor which could not be foreseen during the OBCE studies. Allowance ratio was between 3% and 5% in this project, and was defined to cover items listed below:

– Increments in quantities that may occur due to detailed design development after the conversion,

- Small design changes due to construction requirements at the site,
- Consumables that could not be included in quantities,
- Wastes due to the nature of manufacturing or construction activities,
- Normal levels of rework due to construction errors, bad welds, and incorrect installations,
- Lost, damaged or broken materials.

Itemized materials correspond to equipment which is defined in the basic engineering design packages. Those equipment were grouped in order to define purchase order packages according to their types and properties. The contractor collected a minimum of three bids for each PO packages from the vendors which were listed by TUPRAS in the contract. Bids were transparently opened and evaluated with the participation of both parties and that procedure has been applied to 98% equipment during the OBCE. Moreover, for long-lead items, vendors were called to face to face meetings, and after technical and commercial negotiations, awarded bids were decided. TUPRAS sent letters of intent to awarded vendors on behalf of the contractor and fixed the price for the project's execution period. Regarding bulk material, bids were requested in the unit price base. The total cost has been calculated according to the bill of quantities taking into account the detailed engineering document developed until the end of OBCE studies.

Construction cost was also studied in the unit price base. The project was divided into seven construction packages. Bill of quantities of each package has been calculated according to the developed detailed engineering document. Awarding stage has been conducted with the participation of both parties. Also, final negotiations have been done in this category and subcontractors were agreed for each construction package prior to the conversion.

Ancillary costs were determined in several ways. The method of collecting bids was preferred upmost. If it is not possible to use such a method, in-house data of both parties and rule of thumbs were used.

A complete file including all OBCE studies has been issued at the beginning of conversion period. All data have been reviewed again together by both parties. Total lump sum price of the project has been calculated as shown in Table 5. Finally, opportunities which could decrease the total price were discussed by the management of the parties and the lump sum EPC price was determined.

Table 5. Simple Illustration of Lump Sum Conversion Calculation

COST CATEGORIES	OBCE	Allowance	Fee	Converted Cost
Detailed Engineering	-	-	-	CC1 = Lump sum price
Itemized Materials	C2	a_2%	F_2%	CC2 = C2 x (1+ a_2%+ F_2%)
Bulk Material	C3	a_3%	F_3%	CC3 = C3 x (1+ a_3%+ F_3%)
Construction	C4	a_4%	F_4%	CC4 = C4 x (1+ a_4%+ F_4%)
Ancillary Costs	C5	a_5%	F_5%	CC5 = C5 x (1+ a_5%+ F_5%)
				SUM = Total Project Price

Regarding the EPC stage, the project was completed on time and on budget. This is one of the results of good preparation and planning conducted during the OBCE period. Commissioning & start-up periods were also accomplished successfully. However, an extra four months have been spent before the commencement of EPC to finalize the financial agreement which is not generally forecasted in such kind of projects at the beginning. This should be noted as a learning outcome from the project.

6 Conclusions

EPC convertible contracts enable the owner to optimize the combination of some important project parameters such as initial cost, change order ratio, duration of the project and management organization. Therefore, it becomes a preferred contracting method for large-scale oil and gas projects in recent decades. This method could be utilized in other sectors with similar characteristics and constraints, such as mining, IT etc., where the cost of large-scale projects could not be estimated efficiently at the bidding stage.

Successful implementation has been applied in TUPRAS Izmit Refinery Resid Upgrading Project. Regarding the lessons learned from that project key principles for future use are advised as below:

- OBCE studies should be done in a transparent manner with the participation of the owner and the contractor.
- The owner should define the procedure clearly which should be followed during OBCE studies and conversion calculation in the bidding document.
- The owner should have a compact but experienced project team. Commercial evaluations should be done regarding the recent development of engineering studies and technical evaluations. Thus, an OBCE coordinator should be assigned to synchronize both commercial and technical groups.
- Vendor list should be included in the contract by the owner. If the contractor proposes a new vendor, it must be up to the owner's consent.
- Engineering should reach a certain level of progress before the conversion for a clear scope definition and reasonable accuracy of quantity calculation. That progress figure is suggested as 50% to 60% [12].

However, regarding the Resid Upgrading Project, engineering progress of 40% to 45% seems reasonable for the conversion. The figures below show the engineering progress of the project at the time of the conversion:

Engineering Services:	
Detailed Engineering	*43,21%*
Procurement Services	*61,29%*
Home-Office Construction Services	*70,00%*
Weighted Progress of Eng. Services	45,30%

- Final negotiations with vendors and subcontractors should be done after the purchase order packages reach a certain level maturity.
- The total cost of categories should be reported periodically during OBCE studies. By this way, the content of the final OBCE report could be established prior to the conversion period with the consent of both parties which may help to shorten the conversion process significantly.

It is hoped that these findings may be applied in other similar projects regardless of the industry, and it helps improve the efficiency of EPC contracts.

References

1. E. Ebeltagi, Construction project management. Lecture Notes, Mansoura University, Department of Structural Engineering, Egypt (2009)
2. D. Bower, *Management of procurement* (Thomas Telford, London, 2003)

3. M. Moazzami, R. Deghan, G. Jergeas, J. Ruwanpura, A theoretical framework to enhance the conversion process in convertible contracts, *International Journal of Construction Engineering and Management* **4**(6), 248-262 (2015)
4. N. Faisol, A.R.J. Dainty, A.D.F. Price, The concept of ©elational contracting©as a tool for understanding inter-organizational relationships in construction, *Procs 21st Annual Association of Researchers in Construction Management Conference, Vol. 2:* 1075–1084 (2005)
5. Y. Salamah, *Alliance contracting models in construction projects: leadership and management*, Master Thesis, Metropolia University of Applied Science, Helsinki, Finland (2017)
6. E.R. Fisk, W.D. Reynolds, *Construction project administration* (Pearson Education, New Jersey, 2014)
7. C. Schramm, A. Meissner, G. Weidinger, Contracting Strategies in the oil and gas industry, *3R International, Special Edition*, **1/2010**: 33-36 (2009)
8. M. Ducros, G. Fernet, *Project management guide* (Editions Technip, Paris, 2010)
9. AACE International Recommended Practice No.18R-97, *Cost estimate classification system – as applied in engineering, procurement and construction for the process industry* (2006), https://web.aacei.org/resources/publications/recommended-practices
10. M. Fenton, K. Armstrong, J. Huebsch, Convertible lump sum EPS contracting model – how to get the plant you need now and still enjoy in 20 years?, *Procedia Engineering* **138**: 206–219 (2016)
11. A. Er,, R. Komurlu, Importance of Planning in Refinery Projects and Recommendations for Successful Planning, *Journal of Architecture and Life*, **2**(2): 253-264 (2017)
12. M. Moazzami, J. Ruwanpura, G. Jergeas, Conversion method for applying convertible contracts in oil and gas project, *Procs 4th Construction Specialty Conference, Montréal, Canada* (2013)

Improving Formwork Using Lean Tools

Chien-Ho Ko[1]*, and *Jiun-De* Kuo[2]

[1]College of Architecture, Arts and Humanity, Clemson University, USA
[2]Department of Civil Engineering, National Pingtung University of Science and Technology, Taiwan

Abstract. Materials for modules and payments for your workers are some of the main expenses for the concrete structures with stiffness. In view of this, module construction is one of the essential factors if the project succeeds or not. Traditional module construction that is involved in those activities without adding values results in wastes. This study aimed at adopting a compact method to reduce waste in the module works. The compact module construction model is developed to achieve this goal. Andon of this model is made use of build a spot assurance system. Labours can be assisted immediately in case of any issues are raised. Besides Andon, module processes are introduced to the Kanban system to decrease mold stock and fulfil the flow of process behind ceaseless work. There was one real case discussed to verify if the proposed module applies to all. Application findings indicate that the developed method is able to conduct mandatory banishment in the module flow of the process and add value in the operation.

Keywords: Kanban system, compact, module, Andon.

1 Introduction

Module operations depend on teamwork substantially. However, elder workers may deteriorate productivity. This worker structural problem directly impacts deliverables in the project and performance, as well as cost [1, 2]. For the purposes of improving the aforementioned problems, scholars have suggested other materials, including paper, fabric, fibre, Fiber-Reinforced Plastic (FRP), metal, compound, and composite materials to substitute wooden molds [3-6].

Lean manufacturing is a management rationale utilized by firms to improve flow in recent years. The construction industry introduced the compact production concept named Lean Construction since the '90s [7]. A variety of studies proved that compact construction may be able to replenish the construction industry with another kind of philosophy in the management [7-10]. Lean construction could make a breakthrough in the limit of traditional construction costs and time in the trade [11]. The purpose of this research was to apply a compact manufacturing mode to eliminate waste in module engineering. This paper started with the introduction of background in the study hereof, wherein production waste, Kanban,

* Corresponding author: eppm.journal@gmail.com

and Andon were illustrated, followed by the practice of module construction and development of a compact module construction process. At last, we validated the applicability of the suggested approach through Case Study herein and also finalized conclusions and direction for any researches in the future.

2 Background

2.1 Kanban

Kanban means a signboard, billboard, bulletin board, and card generally in the Japanese language [12]. Kanban originates from a stamping line of production at the Toyota manufacturing site [13]. The post-supplementary production pursued by a stamping production line is considered as a production signal if we view it from the perspective of consumptive material. Decreased inventory of the storage site supports it directly; here come three types of Kanban at Toyota Production System as follows [14]:

Kanban for production

It is a tool used at the interval between the storage site containing finished products and the production line. It plays the role of triggering the production in a post-supplementary production system.

Kanban for Material Pick-up

This kind of Kanban is used by workers to take the required parts from the storage yard and record any item with its respective number of parts to be collected.

Mark and management Kanbans

This Kanban is a board placed on the facility, which is to be differentiated by two kinds. One of them enables to display of information to everyone and the other one focuses on displaying administrative figures.

2.2 Andon

Andon originates from a kind of loom that was originated from Sakichi Toyoda. It stops and the alarm lamp lights up when the device detects the broken yarns. Toyota Motor is conducted with quality control with this concept. There is an error sensor installed on production equipment, and it stops automatically when the sensor detects a fault. Toyota Motor also authorizes workers to press the button or pull the Andon Cord to stop the production line when they find a problem or need help to solve problems. Nowadays such an alarm system means a signal-based help [12].

3 Module Process for Operation

Module operational process shall consist of a total of 10 steps as follows, that is: 1) planning and designing, 2) shop drawing & preparation, 3) material preparation, 4) mold machining, 5) setting out, 6) module assembly, 7) inspection, 8) monitoring and remedy of concrete pouring, 9) stripping and 10) re-supporting module, please refer to Figure 1 [15]. Contractors design module system and subcontractors prepare for shop drawings and materials according to the module system. Module subcontractors also will consult for mold inventory and hardware fittings, with which reordering any materials from material vendors as per request in case of shortage. Molds are positioned prior to assembly. The module subcontractor has to review if they are set to correct for the machining process, followed by assembly. Modules are assembled with third parties, i.e. piping, rebar, and wiring. During pouring concrete into the mold, module subcontractors shall assign a module engineer to avoid a collapse of the module and take care of emergent explosion, if any. Molds are stripped based on codes for recycled use in the next one or next project or storage yard.

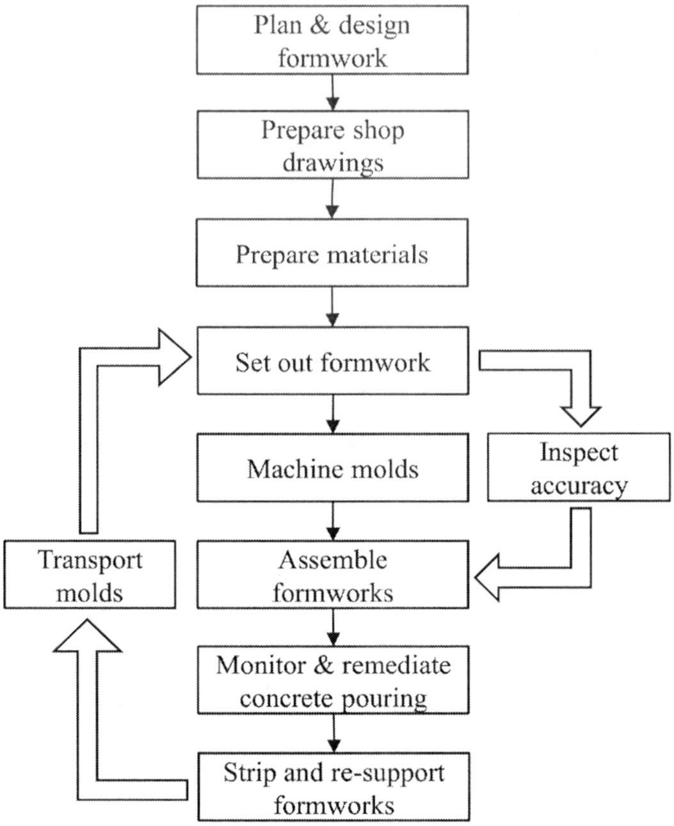

Fig 1. Module Flow of Process [16]

Any defects occurred to the module system would mostly lead to collapse or deformation, thereby causing unsuccessful result during pouring concrete in case of none of the remedies taken by field workers. The main reason could be attributed to the disputed quality assurance (QA) process, which resulted in wasteful defective products. Such issues require services with extra expenditure incurred with follow-up procedures, time, energy and waste.

4 Lean Module

The module system is built from the design done by the general contractor. Insofar it has seldom emphasis on the quality it is built, or any improvement of quality based on nature, thereby leading to a versified level of quality. A module system with poor performance may bulge, even falling apart. In addition, the random piled up molds in the piling field which extends duration in the search and further procedures [17]. We used Andon and Kanban systems to establish a compact module construction model in the troubleshooting. Andon is primarily utilized in the settings of performance assurance sentiment, while the Kanban system enables to reduce material stock. For the framework of the compact module construction model, please refer to Figure 2.

Toyota Mode adds significance to the setting of the performance assurance culture, among of which, the production line will not restart until solutions are given [18]. Amid a compact working module, Andon system is used to help module workers stop works and ask for help in the occurrence of problems. During establishing this culture, module workers are educated that support is constantly available and no one will be fined in case of any issue, with which no worry is needed; improvement of performance forms a culture of cooperation and Andon tool is to develop a quality management system that emphasizes QA process primarily, which also helps engaged partners (i.e. general contractor, module subcontractor, third parties) identify and give solutions. However, the burden of pressure rises up in case of any suspension, i.e. delivery and extra costs thereof; in this case, the entire team shall identify solutions accordingly, or it causes excessive waste. Another reason is that we made use of the Andon tool to have effective control over further issues. Module subcontractors, in general, considered workers as the parties whom they shall attribute any errors or mistakes, while only improper system, flow and methods are traced for any mistakes in the compact construction module. Teammates make efforts in formulating a more effective system, instead of defending themselves.

Kanban system is used to alternate ways of oral confirmation of orders, which responds to customer requests and reduces the potential amount of waste from the materials in the storage yard and used as a base for communication to give solutions among superintendents, module foreman and workers. The flow of module construction is thereby created to control progress.

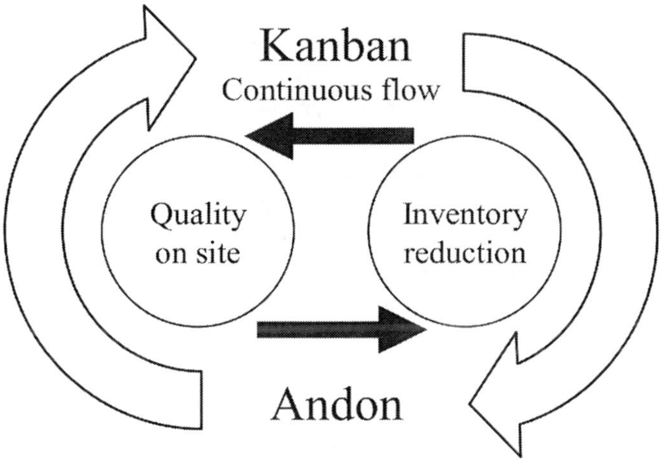

Fig 2 Lean Module Schema [19]

5 Case Study

We used a real case to make an illustration of the feasibility of the proposed compact construction module. The cased building, situated in Pingtung of Taiwan, has a basement with four stories, which accounts for 2185.3 square meters; module construction on the 2nd floor was taken as the subject in the case, which accounts for 1646 square meters. Wooden molds and supports, steel tubes and shaped steel were utilized in the construction, among of which, it also has scaffold, steel bar, electromechanical, and concrete engineering works; please refer to Table 1 for total hours module workers spend in the construction.

Table 1: Module Construction Hours by Workers

Activity	Workers[1]	Total hours[2]
Set out	0.5	4
Prepare storage yard	2	16
Assemble and machine mold	140.5	1124
Strip mold	26.5	212
Arrange mold	14.25	114
Transport mold	35	282

[1]1 worker = 1 worker has 8 hours of work.
[2]total hours = Workers * 8 hours.

For module assembly and machined process, movements including measure, pull, cut, pass, nail, and mend add value while walk, search, and wait for waste. Transportation of mold generates value; however, the on-hold moments are wastes. Appropriate layout of the site reduces movements without incremental value, such as by foot, wait while assembling and machining, as well as transporting module, hence, efficiency shall be improved.

Elimination of movements without incremental value like by foot, search and wait in assembling, machining and transportation of modules may decline a total of 570.24 worker-hours (i.e. 71.28 workers), while the proposed method may reduce 437.28 worker-hours waste (54.66 workers) in assembling and machining modules. Productivity increases from 11.72 to 19.18 square meters per daily worker, while it increases from 46.7 to 88.35 square meters per daily worker during transporting molds. Please refer to Figure 3 for the comparative results before/after improvement.

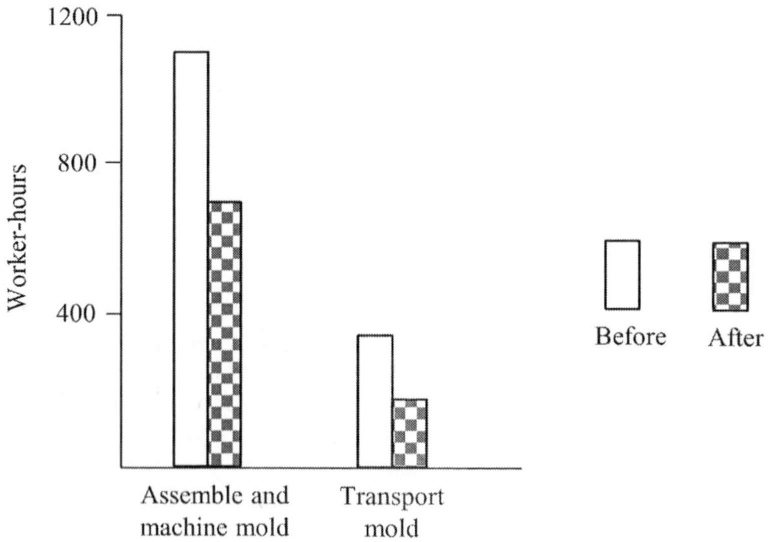

Fig. 3. Worker-Hours Improvement

Teamwork coming from the general contractor, module subcontractor and third parties involving the project forms a kind of free-of-plan culture leads to wasteful on-hold time among subcontractors due to loss of coordination. The result in the analysis indicated that the flow of process consists of wasteful movement and the main reason is that module foreman has no plan of layout for the construction site beforehand, thereby generating waste of movements such as walk, search, and wait during assembling, machining, and transporting molds. Furthermore, the module foreman instructs workers orally that workers may have a loss of information regarding the production. Moreover, teams generally are in the shortage of conceptual on-site quality control that workers are not sure about the process well and all of these factors constitute wastes of defects.

6 Conclusions

Waste is generated from current practices in assembling, machining, and transporting molds. We used a compact way to establish a compact module construction model, which is a production system based on reduced waste and value-added customer. The signals transmitted by the Kanban system are followed to reduce mold inventory.

Improved module quality depends on the attitude of learning and improving as a whole. Andon tool and Kanban system may be used to eliminate non-adding-value waste; however, foreman and superintendent also shall take the resistance of reform into consideration when they perform the transformation. Education is required behind implementing the compact module construction model. Workers may resist the reform since managerial philosophy varies between compact module construction model and current practices.

Acknowledgements

This research was funded by the Ministry of Science and Technology, Taiwan with grant number MOST 103-2221-E-020-027-MY2. Thanks are also due to the case study's general contract and formwork subcontractor, for their generous assistance.

References

1. M. Sutherland, Formwork economics, *Concrete Engineering International*, **9**(4):18-19 (2005)
2. H.C. Chang, Productivity Analysis of Construction Formwork in Residential Buildings, *MS Thesis*, Department of Civil Engineering, National Taiwan University, Taiwan (in Chinese) (2007)
3. M. Arslan, O. Simsek, S. Subasi, Effects of formwork surface materials on concrete lateral pressure, *Construction and Building Materials* **19**(4):319-325 (2005)
4. D. Veenendaal, M. West, P. Block, History and overview of fabric formwork: Using fabrics for concrete casting, *Structural Concrete* **12**(3):164-177 (2011)
5. A.J. Spottiswoode, L.C. Bank, A. Shapira, Investigation of paperboard tubes as formwork for concrete bridge decks, *Construction and Building Materials* **30**:767-775 (2012)
6. R. Yip, C.S. Poon, Comparison of timber and metal formwork systems, *Proceedings of Institution of Civil Engineers: Waste and Resource Management* **161**(1):29-36 (2008)
7. L. Koskela, Application of the New Production Philosophy to Construction, Technical Report, Stanford University, USA (1992)
8. G. Ballard, The Last Planner System of Production Control, The University of Birmingham, *PhD Thesis*, UK (2000)

9. C.H. Ko, Y.C. Chen, Evaluating Production Time Buffer for Precast Fabrication, *Journal of Engineering, Project, and Production Management*, **2**(2):101-111 (2012)
10. C.H. Ko, Production control in precast fabrication: considering demand variability in production schedules, *Canadian Journal of Civil Engineering* **38**(2):191-199 (2011)
11. Best and de Valence (Editors), *Building in Value: Project Delivery*, John Wiley & Sons, New York (2000)
12. J.K. Liker, *The Toyota Way: 14 Management Principles from the World's Greatest Manufacturer*, McGraw Hill, New York (2003)
13. H.S. Li, C.C. Yang, Meticulously Discuss Toyota Production System, *Quality Monthly Journal* **45**(3):13-18 (2009) (in Chinese)
14. H.S. Li, C.C. Yang, Kanban in Toyota Production System, *Quality Monthly Journal* **45**(4):42-49 (2009) (in Chinese)
15. C.F. Shen, *Formwork Engineering: Economic, Design, Assembly, and Safety*, Shen, Taipei (1996) (in Chinese)
16. C.H. Ko, J.D. Kuo, Making Formwork Construction Lean, *Journal of Civil Engineering and Management* **21**(4):444-458 (2015)
17. Y.H. Peng, Consulting Service for Automation in Architectural Engineering, *Research Report*, Architecture and Building Research Institute, Ministry of the Interior, Taipei, Taiwan (1998) (in Chinese)
18. J.K. Liker, D. Meier, *The Toyota Way Fieldbook*, Mc Graw Hill, New York (2006)
19. C.H. Ko, J.D. Kuo, Lean Formwork, *Proceedings of the 24nd Annual Conference of the International Group for Lean Construction*, Chennai, India, 1283–1290 (2018)

Key Factors Influencing Multimodal Transportation of Natural Block Rubber in Thailand

Pimnapa Pongsayaporn[1*], *Thanwadee* Chinda[1], *Veeris* Ammarapala[1]

[1] School of Management Technology, Sirindhorn International Institute of Technology, Thammasat University, 131 Moo 5 Tiwanont Rd. Bangkadi, Muang, Pathumthani 12000 Thailand,

Abstract. Thailand is the world's largest natural rubbers exporter. The major type of natural rubbers exported is block rubber. Currently, the transportation of natural rubbers in Thailand depends mainly on truck mode because of the convenience and extensive network of roads. However, Thailand confronts road transportation limitations including maximum acceptable weight, traffic congestion and high fuel prices. Dealing with these problems, the multimodal connection from roads to container yards (CY) and ports is expected to decrease logistics cost, and increase various opportunities to trade with neighbouring countries. This paper, thus, aims at examining key factors influencing the use of multimodal transportation utilizing the exploratory factor analysis (EFA). The principal components analysis (PCA) method, together with the eigenvalue over 1, factor loading of 0.40, and varimax rotation method, extracted five key factors with a total of 20 associated attributes, which are the Multimodal Operation, Service Operation, Multimodal Service Provider, Market Consideration, and Road Constraints factors. The result also pinpoints the capacity of container yard (CY) or port, accessibility to container yard (CY) or port, documentation process, logistics cost, adequacy of a multimode service provider, and law enforcement on truck driving hours, as crucial attributes in planning for multimodal transportation. This paper can be used as a guideline for a feasibility study of multimodal transportation of natural block rubber in Thailand.

Keywords: factor analysis, key factors, logistics, multimodal transportation, natural block rubber

1 Introduction

Thailand is a major supplier of agricultural products in the world [1]. It is the world's leading exporter of natural rubbers, rice, and cassava [2]. In particular, Thailand is the largest producer and exporter of natural rubbers due to its tropical climate as well as effective and advanced cultivation methods [3]. Nearly 90% of Thailand's natural rubber production is for export and only 10% is used for domestic consumption [4]. The major type of natural rubbers

* Corresponding author: meiw.pimnapa@gmail.com

exported is block rubber. It takes more than one-third of the total amount and still increases with 4.5 % growth rate because they are mainly used in automobile tires manufacturing in China, which is the biggest importer of black rubber from Thailand [4].

Currently, the transportation of block rubber in Thailand depends mainly on truck mode because of the convenience and extensive network of roads. However, the logistics cost of road transportation is higher than rail and ship modes. Moreover, Thailand confronts road transportation limitations including maximum acceptable weight, traffic congestion and high fuel prices [5]. Dealing with these problems, the multimodal connection from roads to container yards (CY) and ports is expected to decrease logistics cost, and increase various opportunities to trade with neighbouring countries [6]. According to Muller [7], the multimodal transportation is the combination of two or more modes of movement of goods, such as road, rail, or sea under the control or ownership of one operator. It is also termed 'intermodal transportation', all of which function in exactly the same way [8].

In recent years, there are a number of initiatives of modal shifts proposed by the government. It realizes the importance of inland transportation connecting with the export gateways. Thus, it proposes the "Thailand's Transport Infrastructure Development Strategy 2015-2022" [9] to develop the efficient transportation network for being a regional hub. This plan aims to enhance the efficiency of multimodal transportation and reduce logistics cost. The plan includes two main parts; the double-track railway project for improving the transportation network and the development of ports to support the increasing amount of export products.

In general, block rubber has a low price and low value [5]. The most effective transportation mode for block rubber is the mode that can carry them in large volume [5] which is the characteristics of multimodal transportation. According to Tanachodrungsatis [10], multimodal transportation is suited with products that can be transported in a heavy bulk and products that have low value, the low selling price per unit, and not perishable. In this respect, the objective of this paper is to examine key factors influencing the use of multimodal transportation for block rubber transportation utilizing the exploratory factor analysis (EFA). It is expected that private companies and government could use the study results as a guideline for a feasibility study of multimodal transportation of block rubber in Thailand. The research steps are summarized, as shown in Figure 1.

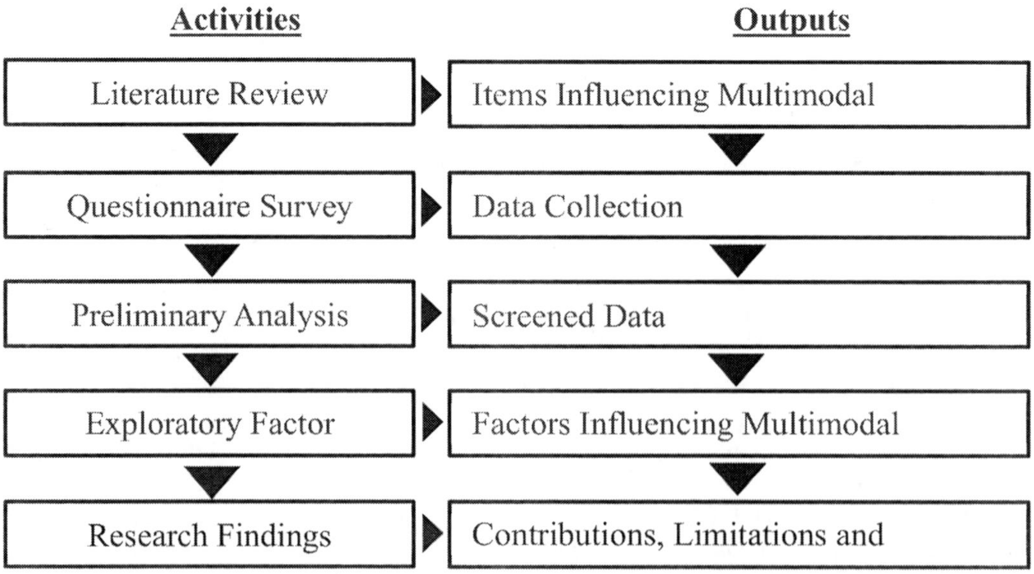

Fig. 1. Research Steps

2 Items Influencing Multimodal Transportation

A total of 20 items influencing multimodal transportation were extracted, with reference to the citation frequency in the recent multimodal transportation-related previous studies (see Table 1). These items were used in the questionnaire survey development to measure the opinions or experiences of respondents on each item.

Table 1. Items Influencing Multimodal Transportation

No.	Item	References
1	Government Policy	[11, 12]
2	Road Traffic Congestion	[8, 11]
3	Law Enforcement on Truck Driving Hours	[13, 14]
4	Road Accident	[14, 15]
5	Adequacy of Multimode Service Providers	[16, 17]
6	Company and Service Provider Relationship	[18, 19]
7	Punctuality	[16, 20]
8	Delivery Speed	[14, 21]
9	Accessibility of CY or Port	[13]
10	Capacity of CY or Port	[13]
11	Transshipment Equipment	[11]
12	Transhipment Cost	[8]
13	Tracking System	[19, 20]
14	Volume Flexibility	[14, 22]
15	Multimodal Equipment Design	[14, 20]
16	Logistics Cost	[13]
17	Green Image	[14, 15]
18	Market Competitiveness	[8]
19	Skilled Employee	[19]
20	Documentation Process	[13, 19]

3 Questionnaire Survey and Data Screening

3.1 Questionnaire Survey Development

To gain information from the rubber production companies and transportation service providers, a questionnaire was designed and distributed through face-to-face interviewing, mail, online survey and e-mail. In this study, the questionnaire survey was developed to extract factors influencing multimodal transportation of natural block rubber in Thailand utilizing EFA. The questionnaire survey comprised three parts. Part I considered the information of the respondent and company. Part II consisted of 20 statements related to items influencing multimodal transportation. A 5-point Likert scale was used to rate the level of agreement on each statement based on respondents' experience, from 1 = strongly disagree to 5 = strongly agree. An example of statements in Part II is presented in Table 2. Part III was the open-ended question requesting qualitative data regarding suggestion or comment about issues related to the multimodal transportation based on respondents' experience.

Table 2. Sample of Questionnaire Survey Questions

NO.	Statement	Level				
		1	2	3	4	5
1	Government policy supporting multimodal transportation					
2	Road traffic congestion					
3	Law enforcement on truck driving hours					
4	Accident occurrence during road transportation					
5	Adequacy of multimodal transportation service providers					
6	Good relationship between company and transportation service providers					

Note: Please indicate the level of your agreement on each statement based on your experience using the scale from 1 to 5, for which 1 = strongly disagree and 5 = strongly agree.

3.2 Survey Responses

A total of 1,411 questionnaires were distributed to medium and large rubber production companies and transportation service providers located in the north-eastern and the southern parts of Thailand. There were 159 returns of the questionnaire, representing an 11.27% response rate. In this respect, all 159 questionnaires were used for further analyses.

It was found that all respondents were in managerial or senior positions in their organizations, and the majority of the respondents (69%) has been working in rubber production industry or transportation service industry for at least 5 years. This implied that the respondents had strong practical experience and were competent enough in providing reliable responses. Moreover, most of the companies (60%) have been exporting their products through Laem Chabang port with partially using multimodal transportation. This implied the possibility of enhancing the use of multimodal transportation in their companies. In summary, these results prove the credential and suitability of the respondents in providing data for the analysis.

3.3 Preliminary Analysis

The collected data were then screened to confirm its level of confidence. The study applied two statistical methods, including the normality test and outlier test. The normality in distribution was tested by examining skewness and kurtosis before conducting an EFA [23]. Skewness measures asymmetry of a distribution of a variable. The skew value of a normal distribution is zero. A skewed variable is a variable whose mean is not in the centre of the distribution. Kurtosis, on the other hand, measures a peakedness of the distribution [24]. Garson [25] proposed a reference of substantial departure from normality as an absolute skew value > 2 and kurtosis value > 7. In this respect, the absolute values of skewness < 2 and kurtosis < 7 are acceptable. The results showed that the data of all 20 attributes were normally distributed, thus, increasing the confidence for factor analysis.

The 5% trimmed mean and standardized scores (z – scores) were used to detect outliers in this study. The 5% trimmed mean is a mean calculated by discarding a 5% of the lowest and the highest scores and then computing the mean of the remaining scores. If a difference between mean and 5% trimmed mean is not beyond the criteria of 0.20, it demonstrated an insignificant influence of any possible outliers within the data. The results showed that there was no outlier in the collected data. To confirm the use of 5% trimmed mean method, the influence and presence of outliers was assessed by standardized scores (z – scores) for each case. A case was considered to be a potential outlier if its absolute standardized residual was greater than 3.29 at $p < 0.01$, two-tailed test [26]. The results also showed the absence of outlier in this study. Therefore, it can be confirmed that the 159 sets of data were suitable for the EFA.

4 Exploratory Factor Analysis (EFA)

Before performing the EFA, the 20 items were categorized into three groups, which are 'operation', 'market', and 'road constraints' (see figure 2). Cronbach's alpha test was then performed as a measure of the reliability of each group [27]. According to De Vellis [28], a minimum of Cronbach's alpha value of 0.70 is considered to be reliable. The results showed that all groups had α values ranging from 0.81 to 0.83, thus confirming the reliability of all groups.

The Kaiser-Meyer-Olkin (KMO) and Bartlett's test of sphericity were then conducted to determine if the data was suitable for EFA, and to confirm that the data had patterned relationships [29] By theory, the minimum acceptable value of KMO is 0.60 [30] and Bartlett's Test of Sphericity should be significant ($p < 0.05$). KMO values of all three groups were 0.78, 0.77, and 0.71, respectively, and all of them were significant at $p < 0.05$. The results confirmed that all groups were suitable for applying the EFA method.

Group I Operation

1. Capacity of Container Yard (CY) or Port
2. Accessibility of Container Yard (CY) or Port
3. Delivery speed
4. Punctuality
5. Transshipment equipment
6. Government policy
7. Multimodal Equipment Design
8. Documentation Process
9. Skilled Employee
10. Tracking System
11. Volume Flexibility

Group II Market

12. Adequacy of Multimode Service Providers
13. Company and Service Provider Relationship
14. Green image
15. Logistics Cost
16. Market Competitiveness
17. Transshipment cost

Group III Road Constraints

18. Law Enforcement on Truck Driving Hours
19. Road Traffic Congestion
20. Road Accident

Fig. 2. Three Groups of 20 Items

Each group was then analyzed with the EFA method to determine how items are interrelated [31] and to reduce the number of items into a smaller number of factors [33]. In this study, a principal component analysis (PCA) extraction method together with the eigenvalue over 1, a cut-off factor loading of 0.40, and varimax rotation method were applied to examine the dimensionality of items in each group [33]. The EFA results classified 20 items into five key factors, accounting for the total variance for each group of 55.75%, 62.66%, and 72.55%, respectively (see table 3). All five key factors had α values ranging from 0.75 to 0.84, thus confirming the reliability of the five factors.

Table 3. EFA Results

Items	Group I		Group II		Group III
	Factor I	Factor II	Factor III	Factor IV	Factor V
Capacity of Container Yard (CY) or Port	0.82				
Accessibility of Container Yard (CY) or Port	0.82				
Delivery Speed	0.79				
Punctuality	0.75				
Transshipment Equipment	0.74				
Multimodal Equipment Design	0.49				
Government Policy	0.46				
Volume Flexibility	0.42				
Documentation Process		0.85			
Skilled Employee		0.81			
Tracking System		0.75			
Logistics Cost			0.84		
Green Image			0.82		
Market Competitiveness			0.81		
Transhipment Cost			0.63		
Adequacy of Multimode Service Providers				0.87	
Company and Service Provider Relationship				0.84	
Law Enforcement on Truck Driving Hours					0.87
Road Traffic Congestion					0.85
Road Accident					0.83

Note:
Factor I was named as ‘Multimodal Operation Factor’
Factor II was named as ‘Service Operation Factor’
Factor III was named as ‘Market Consideration Factor’
Factor IV was named as ‘Multimodal Service Provider Factor’
Factor V was named as ‘Road Constraints Factor’

5 Conclusion

Currently, natural rubber transportation in Thailand depends mainly on truck mode. The road transportation limitations include maximum acceptable weight, traffic congestion, high accident occurrence and high fuel prices. The implementation of multimodal transportation would help alleviate these problems and environmental effects. It also helps maximize the effectiveness of transportation because it can carry more quantity of goods while helping save energy and save logistics cost.

The study results revealed five key factors influencing the multimodal transportation of natural block rubber in Thailand, including Multimodal Operation, Service Operation, Multimodal Service Provider, Market Consideration, and Road Constraints factors. These factors can be used as a guideline for a feasibility study of multimodal transportation of natural block rubber in Thailand. The capacity of container yard (CY) or port, accessibility to container yard (CY) or port, documentation process, logistics cost, adequacy of the multimode service provider, and law enforcement on truck driving hours are found to be the most important variables for successful implementation of multimodal transportation.

The survey has been limited to a sample of rubber production companies and transportation service providers in north-eastern and the southern parts of Thailand because they are the growing area of the government plan and the heart of rubber plantation and production in Thailand, respectively. The results, however, provided a useful fundamental data in order to increase the use of multimodal transportation.

The 20 items were grouped to explain five latent factors which lead to a baseline model for further examination of interrelationships among them by using structural equation modelling.

References

1. P. Luathep, S. Jaensirisak, S. Saengpradab, The impact of transport infrastructure development on modal shift: case study of rubber goods in the southern Thailand, *KKU Engineering Journal*, 43: 225-227 (2016)
2. USDA, *Thailand Exporter Guide*, United States Department of Agriculture (2017)
3. BOI, *Thailand's Rubber Industry*, Bangkok: Thailand Board of Investment (2017)
4. CPD, *Direction of Thai Rubber Industry in the ASEAN (*in Thai), Bangkok: Cooperative Promotion Department (2015)
5. W. Timaboot, N. Suthikarnnarunai, Designing the Distribution Network in a Cassava Supply Chain in Thailand, *Marketing and Branding Research*, 4, 206-216 (2017)
6. B. Polyiam, The Study of Cost and Time of Rice Transportation: Export Route from Nakhonsawan (in Thai), *The 9th Logistics and Supply Chain Conference (ThaiVCML2009*), Thailand, 2009.
7. G. Muller, *Intermodal Freight Transportation (3rd ed.)*. Westport, Connecticut: Eno Transportation Foundation (1995)
8. M. SteadieSeifi, N.P. Dellaert, W. Nuijten, T. Van Woensel, R. Raouf, Multimodal Freight Transportation Planning: A Literature Review. *European Journal of Operational Research*, 233:1-15 (2013)
9. Thai government, *Thailand's Transport Infrastructure Development Strategy 2015-2022*, Bangkok: Thai government (2015)

10. K. Tanachodrungsatis, Efficiency and Effectiveness of Thai Rice Transportation Logistic: A Case Study Transportation Route from Nakornsawan Province to Foreign Countries, *Suthiparithat Journal*, 28: 309-342 (2014)
11. B.L. Choi, K.Y. Chung, K.D., Lee, The impact of policy measures on promoting the modal shift from road to rail, *Personal and Ubiquitous Computing*, 18: 1423–1429 (2014)
12. F. Corman, F. Viti, R.R. Negenborn, Equilibrium models in multimodal container transport systems, *Flexible Services and Manufacturing Journal*, 29:125–153 (2017)
13. D. Kritchanchai, W. Chanpuypetch, A Framework for Decision Support Systems in Logistics: A Case Study for Thailand Rubber Exports, *International Journal of Logistics and SCM Systems*, 3(1): 24-31 (2009)
14. M. Heljedal, *Factors Influencing the Choice between Road and Multimodal Transportation*, Thesis (Master), Linköping University, Sweden (2013)
15. E. Kreutzberger, C. Macharis, L. Vereecken, J. Woxenius, Is Intermodal Freight Transport More Environmentally Friendly Than All-Road Freight Transport? A Review, *NECTAR Conference No 7*, 13-15 June, 2003, Umeå, Sweden (2003)
16. T. Bektas, T.G. Crainic, *A Brief Overview of Intermodal Transportation*. Canada: Interuniversity Research Centre on Enterprise Networks, Logistics and Transportation (2007)
17. K. Roberts, Key Factors and Trends in Transportation Mode and Carrier Selection, *Pursuit - The Journal of Undergraduate Research at the University of Tennessee*, 4(1): 40-52 (2012)
18. A.C. Paixao-Casaca, P.B. Marlow, Logistics strategies for short sea shipping operating as part of multi-modal transport chain, *Maritime Policy and Management*, 36(l): 1-19 (2009)
19. T.L. Butta, M.B. Abegaz, Challenges in the operation of multimodal transport system: The case of Ethiopian shipping and logistics services enterprise, *International Journal of Applied Research*, 2(7): 927-932 (2016)
20. D.M. Islam, S. Ricci, B.L. Nelldal, How to make modal shift from road to rail possible in the European transport market, as aspired to in the EU Transport White Paper 2011, *European Transport Research Review*, 8(18): 1-14 (2016)
21. R. Danielis, E. Marcucci, Attribute Cut-Offs in Freight Service Selection. *Transportation Research Part E,* 43 (2007)
22. P. Arnold, P. Dominique, I. Thomas, Modelling a rail/road intermodal transportation system, *Transportation Research Part E*, 40: 255-270 (2003)
23. T. Yu, J.C. Richardson, An Exploratory Factor Analysis and Reliability Analysis of the Student Online Learning Readiness (SOLR) Instrument, *The Online Learning Journal (OLJ)*, 19(5), 120-141 (2015)
24. H.Y. Kim, Statistical notes for clinical researchers: assessing normal distribution (2) using skewness and kurtosis, Open lecture on statistics, Korea University College of Health (2013)
25. D. Garson, *Testing of assumptions* (2009), http://faculty.chass.ncsu.edu/garson/PA765/assumpt.htm.
26. B.G. Tabachnick, L.S. Fidell, *Using multivariate statistics (6th edition)*, Boston, MA: Pearson (2013)
27. M. Tavakol, R. Dennick, Post-examination analysis of objective tests, *Med Teach.*, 33: 447-458 (2011)

28. R. De Vellis, *Scale development: theory and applications: theory and application*, Thousand Okas, CA: Sage (2003)
29. A.G. Yong, S., Pearce, A Beginner's Guide to Factor Analysis: Focusing on Exploratory Factor Analysis, *Tutorials in Quantitative Methods for Psychology*, 9(2): 79-94, (2013)
30. B.G. Tabachnick, L.S. Fidell, *Using Multivariate Statistics. 5th ed.*, New York, NY, U.S.A: Pearson Education Inc (2007)
31. C.K.H. Hon, A.P.C Chan, M.C.H. Yam, Determining safety climate factors in the repair, maintenance, minor alteration, and addition sector of Hong Kong, *Journal of Construction Engineering and Management,* 139(5): 519-528 (2013)
32. J.F. Hair Jr., W.C. Black, B.J. Babin, R.E. Anderson, R.L. Tatham, *Multivariate data analysis, 7th Ed.,* Upper Saddle River, NJ: Prentice-Hall (2010)

Organisational Attributes that Determine Integrated Safety, Health and Environmental Management Capability

Millicent Asah-Kissiedu[1*], *Patrick* Manu[2], *Colin* Booth[1] and *Abdul-Majeed* Mahamadu[1]

[1]University of the West of England, Frenchay Campus, Bristol, BS16 1QY, United Kingdom
[2]University of Manchester, The School of Mechanical, Aerospace & Civil Engineering, Manchester M13 9PL, United Kingdom

Abstract. Implementing separate Environmental Management System (EMS) and Safety and Health Management System (SHMS) can be costly for organisations and hence the advent of integrated management systems. The effective implementation of integrated safety, health and environmental (SHE) management would require companies to have the appropriate organisational capability. Within the academic literature, it is unclear which organisational attributes are important for ascertaining integrated SHE management capability of construction companies. This study sought to address this through a comprehensive review of literature relating to SHE management in construction and SHE management systems and models. The study revealed that organisational attributes that could determine integrated SHE management capability include: senior management commitment to SHE; SHE risks management; SHE objectives and programs; staff competencies; resources for SHE implementation; SHE roles and responsibilities; SHE communications; SHE documentation and control measures; SHE emergency plans; SHE monitoring and performance measurement; and SHE auditing and management review to capture lessons learned. These attributes could enable construction companies and other key industry stakeholders to understand construction companies' capability to implement an integrated SHE management system.

Keywords: Organisational, Maturity, Capability, Safety, health and environment

1 Introduction

Despite the social and economic significance of the construction sector in any nation's economy, it has earned the unenviable rank of being one of the highest contributors to the work-related injury, accounting for not less than 30% of the work-related fatalities, injuries and illnesses globally [1], [2]. Additionally, the construction sector is one of the main sources of environmental pollution and responsible for the substantial exploitation and consumption of both natural and processed resources. For instance, in the USA the construction sector accounts for about 21% of all occupational deaths from injuries [3]. In Botswana, the sector

* Corresponding author: author@email.org

is also responsible for 55% of workplace accidents [4]. In addition to poor safety and health, the construction industry is also one of the largest industrial contributors to poor environmental sustainability. In the Organisation for Economic Co-operation and Development (OECD) countries, construction is responsible for about 25-40% of total energy use [5]. In the UK, the construction industry is responsible for 33% of all waste generated [6]. Certainly, there is an urgent need to improve safety, health and environment (SHE) management in the construction industry. To address the SHE problems in construction, many SHE management solutions and initiatives have emerged over the years. Amongst these initiatives have been the adoption and implementation of management systems particularly environmental management system (EMS) and safety and health management system (SHMS). The parallel implementation of such stand-alone systems within a company can, however, be costly [7], [8] and therefore having an integrated SHE management system is desirable.

More so in developing country context where financial resource commitment to health, safety and environmental issues is scant. The implementation of such an integrated management system would require companies to have the appropriate organisational capability. However, there is a lack of clarity within the academic literature, about what organisational attributes are important for ascertaining integrated SHE management capability of a construction company. This study, thus, through a review of the literature, investigates organisational attributes that determine a construction company's capability to implement an integrated SHE management. The next section presents a brief review of SHE management and capability maturity literature. Subsequently, the research method and findings are presented, followed by the discussions and concluding remarks.

2 Safety, Health and Environmental Management Capability in construction

Though considerable efforts have been made to address SHE problems in construction, the industry today is still characterised by accidents, injuries, fatalities, and negative environmental impacts. Over the last few decades, the construction industry has embraced management systems (MSs) particularly, EMS and SHMS based on management system standards as a systematic approach for controlling the key management functions of safety and environment [7]. Construction companies are therefore implementing such management systems, to effectively address SHE issues and their associated undesirable outcomes and also demonstrate and achieve sound SHE performance

The implementation of EMS and SHMS in the industry, though on a low scale have provided an effective way for organisations to reduce environmental incidents and civil liabilities, improved awareness of environmental impacts of their operations, increased the efficiency of operations by cutting waste, lessening injuries and fatalities and improving a company's productivity [9], [10]. However, the parallel implementation of independent systems in a construction organisation is bureaucratic, onerous and costly [7]. More so, in the developing country contexts where the implementation of MSs tend to be low due to limited funds, resources and expertise [6]. As a consequence, integrated management of SHE through a single system is desirable to control and manage the key SHE operations, resources and structure with maximum effectiveness and minimum bureaucracy [8].

The implementation of such a system by construction organisation, therefore require them to have the appropriate organisational capability in respect of SHE management. However, conspicuously missing in the body of academic SHE management literature is a thorough understanding of what constitutes SHE management capability of a construction company with the responsibility of improving SHE performance. In addition, no studies have sought to identify and categorise SHE management capability attributes to aid objective assessment of SHE management capability of construction companies.

3 Towards SHE management capability modelling in construction

Currently, one of the widely-accepted frameworks for assessing the maturity of organisations in the performance of its tasks and managing its organisational processes is the capability maturity model (CMM) and/or its extension, the capability maturity model integrated (CMMI) [11]; [12]. Increasingly CMM has become a tool, used to assess and improve organisational processes, systems, products, and competencies on the evolutionary path towards excellence and the attainment of desired outcomes [18]. The concept of CMM has been applied in the construction industry as a means of accessing capability in areas such as risk management [13], supply chain [14]) and BIM [15]. In the area of safety, health and environment, CMM frameworks have been developed to address safety culture [16], assess construction site safety management (AC2E performance matrix by Carillon Plc), and also for design in the offshore sector [17], [18]. However, no maturity model exists for assessing a construction company's capability to implement an integrated SHE management in construction. The first step in developing a CMM for SHE management is to identify and define the key attributes that will serve as the criteria in assessing capability to achieve the overall SHE goals of an organisation.

The application of CMM is reliant on the identification of key attributes referred to as key process areas (KPA) which represent performance indicators for benchmarking capability and process improvement areas across organisation and systems [11]. These capabilities attributes refer to a set of organisational processes, activities, practises, competencies and resources that are required or performed to reach some desired outcomes or achieve a set of goals [19]. They largely include processes, people, policy, and resources required to execute germane organisational functions. This study, therefore, explored the relevant attributes required for assessing construction organisations' SHE management capability as a precursor for developing an integrated SHE management CMM (SHEM-CMM).

4 Research Methodology

A comprehensive review of literature related to SHE management and not limited to construction was used to generate a list of SHE capability attributes. The literature comprised of safety and health, and environmental management guides and international standards, journal articles and texts covering SHE management systems/models as outlined in Table 1. The relevant literature related to maturity models on safety and health, and environmental management [16], [20], AC2E performance matrix by Carillon Plc and the design safety maturity models [17], [18] were also reviewed.

The literature analyses revealed that existing SHE management texts, guides, and international standards generally follow the Plan - Do- Check- Act (PDCA) management approach and thus, share common requirements which allow most of the elements to be integrated. As a result, in developing the list of organisational attributes for ascertaining SHE management capabilities, information from already established internationally recognised SHE management standards and published works were extracted, by comparing their components in order to determine key similarities and differences, thereby establishing the potential integrated SHE capability attributes. The literature sources and the SHE management components and practices are shown in table 1.

Table 1. SHE management literature sources

	Component /Practices	Environmental management system (EMS) standards and published works					Component /Practices	Safety and health management system (SHMS) standards, guidelines and published works								Component /Practices	Integrated management system (IMS) standards and published works		
		ISO (2015) [21]	EC (2008) [22]	BSI (2003) [23]	Responsible Care (2015) [24]	Chan (2011) [25]		HSE (2013) [26]	BSI (2007) [27]	ILO (2001) [28]	BSI (2012) [23]	IOSH (2015) [29]	AS/NZS (2001) [30]	Hughes and Ferret (2015) [31]			BSI (2012) [23]	Hamid et al. (2004) [32]	Re Bello et al. (2015) [33]
PLAN	SMC	✓	✓	✓	✓	✓	SMC	✓	✓	✓	✓	✓		✓	PLAN	Leadership and commitment	✓	✓	✓
	EMS-C	✓	✓	✓		✓	SHMS-C	✓	✓	✓	✓	✓	✓	✓		Implementation team		✓	✓
	PR	✓	✓	✓	✓		PR	✓	✓	✓	✓	✓	✓	✓		Baseline review		✓	✓
	EMS-B	✓	✓	✓			SH-B	✓	✓	✓	✓	✓	✓	✓		Identification of IMS Hazards, aspects and impacts identification	✓	✓	✓
	IEAI	✓	✓	✓	✓	✓	ISHH	✓	✓	✓	✓	✓	✓	✓		Risk assessment and identification of control measures	✓	✓	✓
	AEAI	✓	✓	✓	✓	✓	SHRA	✓	✓	✓	✓	✓	✓	✓		Legal and other requirements		✓	✓
	ICULR	✓	✓	✓	✓	✓	ICULR	✓	✓	✓	✓	✓	✓	✓		Integrated management policy	✓	✓	✓

	ENVPO	✓	✓	✓	✓	✓	SHPO	✓	✓	✓	✓	✓	✓	✓		Objectives and Targets of IMS	✓	✓	✓
	ENOT	✓	✓	✓	✓	✓	SHOT	✓	✓	✓	✓	✓	✓	✓		Management programmes of IMS		✓	✓
	ENVMP	✓	✓	✓		✓	SHMP	✓	✓	✓	✓	✓	✓	✓		Organisational roles and responsibilities	✓	✓	✓
DO	SRR	✓	✓	✓		✓	SRR	✓	✓	✓	✓	✓	✓	✓	DO	Resources	✓	✓	✓
	PAR	✓	✓	✓			PAR	✓	✓	✓	✓	✓	✓	✓		Communication	✓	✓	✓
	EINV	✓	✓	✓	✓	✓	EINV	✓	✓	✓	✓	✓	✓	✓		Participation and Consultation of Employees		✓	✓
	COENVI	✓	✓	✓	✓	✓	CSHI	✓	✓	✓	✓	✓	✓	✓		Training and awareness	✓	✓	✓
	EINV	✓	✓	✓	✓	✓	EINV	✓	✓	✓	✓	✓	✓	✓		Competence of employees	✓	✓	✓
	ITNT	✓	✓	✓	✓	✓	ITNT	✓	✓	✓	✓	✓	✓	✓		Documentation of the IMS	✓	✓	✓
	COE	✓	✓	✓	✓	✓	COE	✓	✓	✓	✓	✓	✓			Control of documents	✓	✓	✓
	EMSDO	✓	✓	✓	✓	✓	SHMSDO	✓	✓	✓	✓	✓	✓	✓		Operational Control	✓	✓	✓
	EMSDC	✓	✓	✓	✓	✓	SHMSDC	✓	✓	✓	✓	✓	✓	✓		Emergency preparedness and response plans and procedures		✓	✓
CHECK	OPC	✓	✓	✓	✓	✓	OPC	✓	✓	✓	✓	✓	✓	✓	CHECK	Performance monitoring and measurement	✓	✓	✓
	EPAR	✓	✓	✓	✓	✓	EPAR	✓	✓	✓	✓	✓	✓	✓		Evaluation of Compliance		✓	✓
	MAM	✓	✓	✓		✓	PMAM	✓	✓	✓	✓	✓		✓		Incidents investigation		✓	✓

	EOC	✓	✓	✓	✓	✓	EOC	✓	✓	✓	✓	✓		✓		Non-conformity and corrective actions	✓	✓	✓
	NCP	✓	✓	✓		✓	IIVES	✓	✓	✓	✓	✓		✓		Records Control		✓	✓
	RC	✓	✓	✓	✓	✓	NCP	✓	✓	✓	✓	✓		✓		Combined Internal Audits	✓	✓	✓
	EMSAUD	✓	✓	✓	✓	✓	RCM	✓	✓	✓	✓	✓		✓	ACT	Integrated Management review	✓	✓	✓
	TALL	✓	✓	✓	✓	✓	SHAUD	✓	✓	✓	✓	✓		✓		Continuous improvement and innovation	✓	✓	✓
ACT	MR	✓	✓	✓	✓	✓	TALL	✓	✓	✓	✓	✓	✓	✓					
	PER		✓				MR	✓	✓	✓	✓	✓	✓	✓					
	CERT	✓	✓	✓	✓		CERT	✓	✓	✓	✓	✓	✓	✓					
	SD	✓	✓	✓		✓	SD	✓	✓	✓	✓	✓	✓	✓					
	CI	✓	✓	✓		✓	CI	✓	✓	✓	✓	✓	✓	✓					

Notes: AEAI=Assessment of environmental aspects and impacts in order to select significant aspects; CERT= Certification; CI=Continuous improvement; COE =Competency of Employees; COENVI=Communication of environmental information to all employers; CSHI= =communication of safety and health information; EMSAUD = environmental management systems auditing ; EMS- B = EMS budgets ; EMS-C = EMS champion selection; EMSDC=EMS documentation control; EMSDO =EMS Documentation; EINV=Employees involvement; ENVPO =Environmental policy ; ENVMP=An environmental management program and an action plan ; ENOT = Environmental objectives and targets; EIOPM=Establishment and implementation of operational control measures; EOC= Evaluation of compliance with relevant laws and regulation; OPC = Operational control; EPAR=Emergency preparedness and response; ICULR= Identification, communication and updating all applicable legal and other requirements; IEAI = Identification of all environmental aspects and related impact; IIVES= incidents investigations; ISHHR = investigation of safety and health hazards and risks; ITPT=Identification of training needs and provision training programmes; MAM= Monitoring and measurement; MR = Management review; NCCPA=Nonconformance and corrective and preventive action; PAR= Provision and Allocation of Resources; PER = Publishing Environmental report; PMAM = Performance monitoring and measurements; PR= Preliminary review; RC= Records control; RCM = Records control and management; SD = Self-declaration of an EMS/SHMS adoption; SHAUD = SHMS Auditing; SH-B = safety and health budgeting; SHMP = safety and health management programme; SHMS-C = safety and health and management safety champion selection; SHMSDC=safety and health documentation control; SHMSDO=safety and health documentation; SHOT = Safety and Health objectives and targets; SHPO= safety and health policy; SHRA safety and health risks assessment SMC = Senior management commitment and leadership; SRR = Structure, roles and responsibilities; TALL=Taking action on lessons learned

5 Findings and discussions

The SHE capability attributes obtained from a review of the literature are shown in Table 2. The attributes include: Senior management commitment; SHE policy; Objectives and targets; SHE management programme; SHE risk management; Management of outsourced services; operational control; SHE emergency preparedness and response; SHE performance monitoring and measurement; SHE incidents investigation; SHE system auditing; Roles and responsibilities; Training; Employee involvement; Competence; Physical and financial resources; Communications; Documentation and control; Lessons and knowledge management. These, SHE capability attributes share similarities with the requirements of existing integrated management systems, the criteria proposed by Strutt *et al.* [18] for the development of an offshore design safety capability maturity model (DSCMM) and the health and safety maturity model (HSMM). A significant difference, however, is the reliance on 12 key safety processes areas and 6 key safety factors in comparison with the 27 capability attributes that emerged in this study.

Table 2 Summary of organisational capability attributes for SHE management

No.	Capability attributes	Description and examples of indicators of attributes	Related key process area category				
			Strategy	processes	People	Resources	Information
1	Senior management commitment	Senior management commitment to safety, health and environment (SHE) management	x				
2	SHE implementation team	SHE teams solely for the implementation of SHE management in the company			x		
3	Baseline review	A preliminary review of the company's current status of SHE management processes	x				
4	Hazards, environmental aspects and impacts identification	Systems, processes and procedures for SHE hazards and environmental aspects and impact identification		x			
5	SHE Risks assessment and identification of control measures	Systems, processes and procedures for SHE risks assessment and identification of control measures		x			
6	Legal and other requirements	Identification, having access to and analysing applicable legal and other					x

		requirements which apply to all activities					
7	SHE Policy	An integrated policy that serves as the foundation for a company's she development and implementation	x				
8	SHE objectives and targets	SHE objectives and targets for a company in line with SHE policy	x				
9	SHE Management programme	Company's action plans for achieving SHE objectives and targets	x				
10	SHE roles and responsibilities	Availability of dedicated SHE roles, and responsibilities within an organisational hierarchy			x		
11	SHE resources	Provision of physical and financial resources for SHE implementation				x	
12	SHE Training	Provision of suitable SHE training for personnel			x		
13	SHE Competence	The skills, knowledge and experience of personnel to undertake responsibilities and perform SHE activities			x		
14	Management of outsourced SHE services	Process or a mechanism for assessing the competence outsourced personnel, subcontractors and suppliers with regards to the management of SHE		x			
15	SHE Communication	Communication of relevant SHE information and requirements to personnel and other relevant stakeholders					x
16	Employee Involvement in SHE	Consultation and involvement of all employees at all			x		

		stages of SHE management		
17	SHE Documentation	Provision and maintenance of adequate SHE documentation and records		x
18	Control of SHE documents	Processes and procedures for ensuring that SHE documents are maintained, current and available to employees	x	
19	SHE Operational Control	Processes, procedures and measures for controlling SHE risks, to ensure SHE regulatory compliance in operational functions and to achieve the overall SHE objectives.	x	
20	SHE Emergency Preparedness and Response	Emergency procedures and measures to minimise the impact of uncontrolled events and unexpected incidents.	x	
21	SHE Performance Monitoring and Measurement	Systems, processes and procedures to monitor and measure SHE performance	x	
22	Evaluation of Compliance	Processes and procedures to monitor and access compliance with SHE regulations and other applicable requirements	x	
23	SHE Incidents Investigations	Processes and procedures for investigating the causes of SHE incidents.	x	
24	Non-conformance; corrective and preventive actions	Processes, procedures and systems for the identification and correction of problems and prevention of their recurrence.	x	

25	SHE Records Control	Processes and procedures for maintenance and management of records of SHE performance		x			x
26	SHE System Auditing	Processes and procedures to conduct SHE audit to assess compliance and SHE management system effectiveness.		x			
27	SHE Lessons Learned and Knowledge Management	Learning lessons from inspection, accident investigations audits etc. and acting on them.					x
		Related key processes area frequency	5	12	5	1	5

Following the work by Mahamadu *et al.,* [34] on the determination of Organisational attributes for the design for occupational safety and health capability (DfOSH) and the categorisation of attributes in capability modelling [11], the emergent SHE attributes were further reclassified. The reclassification adopted are: '*strategy*' for the organisation's vision and senior management commitment for SHE management; '*people*' for describing organisations human capital, their roles, responsibilities and involvement in SHE management; '*process*' for required organisation's procedures, processes and systems for SHE management; '*information*' for SHE related documents, data, lessons, records and their communication across an organisation, and '*resources*' for describing attributes related to the financial and physical resources necessary for effective SHE implementation. From Table 2, the majority of the SHE management capability attributes are either related to '*process*' followed by '*strategy*' '*people*' and then *information*. The resources category was associated with the least number. The high number of processes related criteria is unsurprising and supports the primary ethos of CMMI/CMM which is premised on a philosophy that key process improvement leads to sustained and repeatable attainment of goals. For construction companies to effectively manage SHE issues, there is a need for commitment, leadership and management (including all appropriate organisational processes), and competent personnel operating in an environment where people are engaged and trusted [26]. The process attributes are therefore recognised as an important aspect of SHE management capability, albeit the strategy, resources, systems, information and people that facilitate the processes also need full consideration. However, the prevalence of particular types of the integrated SHE attributes does not necessarily indicate their weight or importance and therefore, further research is required to determine the relative importance of the attributes.

6 Conclusions

The use of integrated SHE management systems could help construction organisations manage SHE challenges while reducing the cost of implementing separate or stand-alone management systems. In order to implement integrated SHE management systems successfully, there is a need for understanding what constitutes a construction company's capability to effectively manage SHE issues. The study explored the integrated SHE management capability attributes of construction companies as a precursor for identifying metrics for the development of a bespoke SHEM-CMM. This study, based on the review of literature, revealed 27 organisational attributes that could determine integrated SHE management capability. The findings highlight the prevalence of process and strategy capabilities attributes. The findings also acknowledge the role of people and information capability attributes. The study further highlights the prevalence of process, people and strategy capabilities attributes. Overall, the research findings could assist construction companies and other stakeholders (e.g. clients who appoint construction companies) to ascertain and understand the construction company's capability in effectively implementing integrated SHE management system. Moreover, it could aid the objective assessment of integrated SHE management capability maturity of construction firms and allow them to target efforts at addressing any areas of capability deficiency. Future work will involve refinement of the 27 attributes by the way of further integrating closely related attributes. Additionally, future work would ascertain the relative importance of the attributes and also define maturity levels and a scoring method for the assessment of integrated SHE management capability.

References

1. ILO. The Role of Worker Representation and Consultation in Managing Health and Safety in the Construction Industry. Geneva (2010)
2. Ministry of Manpower, *Workplace Safety and Health Report 2017 National Statistics. Ministry of Manpower* (2017), http://www.mom.gov.sg/~/media/mom/documents/safety-health/reports-stats/wsh-national-statistics/wsh-national-stats-2017.pdf?la=en
3. M. Hallowell, J. Gambatese, Construction Safety Risk Mitigation, *Journal of Construction Engineering and Management*, 1316-1323 (2009)
4. J.O. Mosanawe, Construction Safety and Occupational Safety and Health in Botswana. *African Newsletter on Occupational health and safety* **23(3)**, 66-67 (2013)
5. United Nations Environment Programme (UNEP) *Buildings and Climate Change: Status, Challenges and Opportunities*, United Nations Environment Programme (2007)
6. BRE, *Multi-residential, BREEAM Scheme Document., vSD 5064 (2)*, British Research Establishment Global Limited (2008)
7. A. Griffith, Integrated management systems: a single management system solution for project control? *Engineering Construction and Architectural Management* **7(3)**,. 232–240 (2008)
8. S.X. Zeng, J.J. Shi, G.X. Lou, A synergetic model for implementing an integrated management system: an empirical study in China, *Journal of Cleaner Production* **15(18)**, 1760–1767 (2008)
9. N. Darnall, Y. Kim, Which types of environmental management systems are related to greater environmental improvements? *Public Administration Review* **72 (3)**, 351- 365 (2012)
10. P. Fewings, *Construction project management – An integrated approach*, 2nd ed. Oxon: Routledge Publishing (2013)
11. M.C. Paulk, C. Chrissis, M.B. Weber,. Capability Maturity Model SM for Software version 1.1. *IEEE Software* **10(4)**, 18–27 (1993)
12. E.W.T. Ngai, D.C.K. Chau, J.K.L. Poon, C.K.M. To, Energy and utility management maturity model for sustainable manufacturing process. *International Journal of Production Economics* **146**, 453–464 (2013)

13. P.X.W. Zou, Y. Chen, T.Y. Chan, Understanding and Improving Your Risk Management Capability: Assessment Model for Construction Organisations, *Journal of Construction Engineering and Management* **136(8)**, 854–863 (2010)
14. K. Vaidyanathan, G. Howell, Construction supply chain maturity model – conceptual framework. P*roceedings of the International Group for Lean Construction, Lansing*, MI, USA, (2007)
15. T.L. McCuen, P. C. Suermann, M. J. Krogulecki, Evaluating Award-Winning BIM Projects Using the National Building Information Model Standard Capability Maturity Model, *Journal of Management in Engineering* **28(2)**, 224-240 (2012)
16. M. Fleming, *Safety Culture Maturity Model. Report 2000/049. Health and Safety Executive* (2001), Colegate, Norwich, http://www.hse.gov.uk/research/otopdf/2000/oto00049.pdf
17. J.V. Sharp, J.E. Strutt, J.E. Busby, E. Terry, *Measurement of organisational maturity in designing safe offshore installations*, Oslo: Offshore Marine and Arctic Engineering. (2002)
18. J.E. Strutt, J.V. Sharp, E. Terry, R. Miles, Capability maturity models for offshore organisational management, *Environment International* **32(8)**,1094-1105 (2006)
19. B. Curtis, W. Hefley, S. Miller, *People capability maturity model Pittsburgh: Pittsburgh Software Engineering Institute*. Carnegie Mellon University. (1995)
20. A.P.G. Filho, J.C.S. Andrade, M.M. de Oliveira Marinho, A safety culture maturity model for petrochemical companies in Brazil, *Safety Science* **48(5)**, 615–624 (2010)
21. *ISO 14001 - Environmental Management Systems – Requirements with guidance for use* (2015), International Standards Organisation. Geneva
22. *European Commission EMAS-Eco-Management and Audit Scheme Systematic Environmental Management Fact Sheet. 3rd ed.* (2008), *https://www.emas.de/fileadmin/user_upload/04_ueberemas/PDF-Dateien/Unterschiede_iso_en.pdf*
23. British Standard Institute, *PAS 99 - Specification of common management system requirements as a framework for integration*. London (2012)
24. *RC127- Responsible Care management systems guidance* (2015), 4th ed. London, https://www.nsf.org/newsroom_pdf/rc14001_transition-guide.pdf
25. E.S.W. Chan, Implementing Environmental Management Systems in Small- and Medium-Sized Hotels: Obstacles, *Journal of Hospitality & Tourism Research* **35(1)**, pp. 3–23 (2011)
26. HSE, *Managing for health and safety- HSG65* (2013), 3rd edition. Suffolk: HSE Books.
27. *British Standards Institution OHSAS 18001-Occupational health and safety management systems specification*, BSI (2007)
28. *Guidelines on occupational safety and health management systems*, ILO-OSH, Geneva (2001)
29. *Systems in focus Guidance on occupational safety and health management systems*, Institution of Occupational Safety and Health (2015), www.iosh.co.uk/systems
30. *Occupational health and safety management systems – general guidelines on principles, systems and supporting techniques (AS/NZS4804)*, Joint Standards Australia/Standards New Zealand Committee, Sydney, Australia (2001)
31. P. Hughes, E. Ferrett, *Introduction to Health and Safety in Construction*. 2nd edition. Oxford: Butterworth-Heinemann, (2007)

32. A.R.A. Hamid, Z.W. Wan, B. Singh, A.K.T.Y. Yusof, *Integration of Safety, Health, Environment and Quality (SHEQ) Management System in Construction: Review, Jurnal Kejuruteraan Awam* **16(1)**, 24–37, (2004)
33. M. Rebelo, G. Santos, R. Silva, Integration of Standardized Management Systems: A Dilemma? *Systems* **3(2)**, 45-59, (2015)
34. A.M. Mahamadu, P. Manu, A. Poghosyan, L. Mahdjoubi, A. Gibb, M. Behm, Organisational attributes that determine the design for occupational safety and health capability, *CRIOCM 2017, 20 - 23 November 2017, Melbourne, Australia*, 964-971. (2017)

Performance of Framework Contract Projects in South Africa

Calistus Ayegba[1*], and *David* Root[1]

[1]School of Construction Economics and Management, University of Witwatersrand, Johannesburg, 2000, South Africa

Abstract. There is increasing adoption of framework contracts (FC) for construction project delivery in South Africa, but it is not yet clear what the performance of the approach is in accomplishing client® expected outcomes of projects being delivered on time, within budget and to required quality and satisfaction. In this study, the performance of FC and the variables that influences the performance is investigated empirically. A qualitative research methodology was adopted for the study. Data were collected via semi-structured interviews with key informants of eight purposively selected client organizations employing FC in South Africa. From the findings, FC is indicated to have performed spectacularly in dealing with unnecessary cost overruns, time delays, and improvement in the quality of delivery. However, it was reported that the approach work best for repetitive works and when a client has the intention of a long-term programme of work. In which case, clients also have to take care to avoid complacency from the contractors. The results provide substantial evidence that FC can perform better than the conventional approaches to short-term relationships and contracts. The result of the study provides insights that can encourage construction stakeholders to appreciate and adopt FC as a viable alternative approach for construction project delivery.

Keywords: framework contracts, performance, performance variables, South Africa.

1 Introduction

The performance of projects is primarily measured using key indicators such as the cost, time, quality and satisfaction objectives. Therefore, projects which are delivered within cost and schedule; and to required quality and satisfaction are regarded to have performed successfully. Compared to the manufacturing and other industries, construction projects have a history of poor performance, as reports of construction projects failing to meet clients expected outcomes proliferate across the globe (for example see: Construction Sector Transparency Initiative's [1]; Baloyi and Bekker [2]; Flyvbjerg, Garbuio and Lovallo [3]).

* Corresponding author: 1174370@students.wits.ac.za

Laryea and Watermeyer [4] attributed the poor performance of construction projects to the development and adoption of inappropriate procurement strategies. Particularly as the traditional construction procurement strategy which is the most common and widely used procurement strategy in the construction industry has been found not to be flexible and responsive enough in handling the growing challenges of the construction industry [5-7]. Thus, indicating the need for developing and adopting appropriate construction procurement strategies for construction project delivery.

The underperformance of the traditional procurement strategy is attributed to the fragmentation, adversarial, arms-length and short-term relationships which characterised the procurement strategy [8, 9]. Therefore, a shift from the traditional procurement to procurement strategies that internalise collaboration and long-term relationships such as framework contracts are advocated and it is gaining adoption in the construction industry.

A framework contract which may also be referred to as "framework agreement" or "umbrella agreement" [8] is an agreement which is reached between two parties to cover a long-term collaborative arrangement, particularly where clients have a long-term program of work in mind and are looking to set up a process to govern the individual construction or supply packages that may be necessary during the term of the framework [10]. FC has increasingly gained adoption for construction project delivery in recent years. For example, a survey by the Royal Institute of Chartered Surveyors [11] In the United Kingdom (UK), reported an increase from 2.9% to 4.4% of construction projects by value were being procured using the approach in 2007 and 2010 respectively. Creamer [12] reported that the South African government is developing FC that can be adopted by municipalities for the procurement of key infrastructures. Also, the Municipal infrastructure support Agency (MISA) releases an expression of interest for FC that will cover across twenty regions in South Africa [13]. The increasing adoption of FC is attributed to the potentials of the approach in addressing the key failings of short-termism and fragmentation of the production team and processes of traditional contracting practices in response to the challenges of complexities and uncertainties in construction [14]. With the increasing adoption of FC in South Africa, the purpose of this study is, therefore, to investigate the performance of FC and identified the variables which could influence the performance of FC projects.

2 Literature Review

2.1 Framework Contracts in Practice

Framework contracts (FC) are increasingly being employed as a contracting strategy to deliver projects successfully in the construction industry. Sources of FC via Scopus in September 2016, using the search word "framework contracts" indicates publications on this topic from 17 countries, with the UK, Germany and Netherland dominating with 10, 5 and 4 publications respectively. FC is reported to be particularly used for high risk, high-value construction projects such as schools, hospitals, roads, and other significant capital expenditure [15].

A survey by the Royal Institute of Chartered Surveyors [11] reveals that 2.9% and 4.4% construction projects by value were procured in the UK in 2007 and 2010 respectively using FC. Similarly, of the 65 new universities projects awarded in South Africa from 2013 to 2016, available at the new university website (www.newuniversities.ac.za), 19 are within FC. Furthermore, in a study examining innovative procurement practices at Wits University by Laryea and Watermayer [4], the FC was explicitly indicated as one of the contracting strategy and procurement innovations adopted by the university in delivering capital projects that result within 6% control of budget over a period of 6 years.

In addition, the South African government is adopting FC which can also be embraced by the municipalities for the procurement of key infrastructures from 2016 [13]. The rationale for the adoption of FC by the South African government as reported was to achieve economy of scales, accelerate purchases, reduce the threat of procurement-related corruption, and ensure better prices, especially for under-resourced municipalities. Likewise, the municipal infrastructure support agency of South Africa expresses interest in March 2016 in pioneering FC for managing contractors across 20 regions in South Africa. The rationale is to reduce the scope of resources dedicated to procurement processes, so as to focus more resources on project implementation.

Several empirical studies have reported a range of benefits associated with the use of FC, which include a significant reduction in cost that would have been incurred in several separate tendering exercises [15]. Lam and Gale [17, 18] reported significant cost savings and contractors performance. Also, in a study examining the procurement of pumps via FC in the UK, Holden [19] reported a reduction of 90% in the number of suppliers used and 10-30% reduction in price. Balcik and Ak [20] in their study on supplier selection in relief organizations, demonstrated that the use of FC delivered a 28% increase in response capacity, 13% decrease in delivery delays and 7-14% cost reduction of relief supplies by the international federation of red cross and red crescent societies in 2012. From the foregoing, FC has shown to have clear benefits capable of adding value and significantly contribute to the achievement of project outcomes.

3 Research Method

Data on the performance of FC and the variables that influences the performance was elicited from the narrative experience of key informants of organizations that have employed FC in South Africa. This is typical to qualitative research methodology. This is typical to qualitative research methodology in which participants are allowed to provide data in the meanings of their own words will be informed from their point of view in line with the interpretivism philosophy [21].

Semi-structured interviews were conducted face to face with key informants of purposively selected organizations employing FC in South Africa. The Key informant interviews involve interviewing people, who are selected for their first-hand knowledge about a topic of interest and are likely to provide needed information, ideas, and insights on the topic of interest [22, 23]. Particularly, the interview questions focused on the key informant's assessment of the performance of FC in terms of cost, time and quality of delivery and the factors that influence the performances.

Sixteen key informants from eight organizations with different background and positions participated in the interviews. The organizations are thereafter coded using the pseudonyms A1 to A8. The key informants that took part in the study are of a diverse set of representatives with different positions and from a wide range of backgrounds and experience in construction procurement and FC. The data collected from the key informant interviews were analysed with the aid of the Nvivo 11 pro qualitative data analysis software for windows and following thematic qualitative data analysis methodology outlined by Miles et al. [24].

4 Findings and Discussions

The findings are presented in a case by case analysis using the matrix table following Miles et al. [24] guide with the aid of Nvivo 11 software. Using supporting direct quotes from the key informants, Table 1 shows the findings from the study on the performance of FC in South Africa. The findings are discussed below based on data presented in Table 1.

Table 1 Performance of Framework Contracts

Org I.D	Performance of Framework contracts
A1	- "It is worthwhile in terms of the spin-off benefits that you get." - "It saves cost definitely." - "It improves quality, and improves safety." - "Time is better managed as it determines the invite to the next work package." - "It promotes skills development."
A2	- "We proud that in the last 3-4 years we haven't gone over budget with FC." - "If you want to make sure that your cost is controlled then an FC over the years is the best way to go." - "It also provides a better speed of delivery and quality, that's the triangle."
A3	- "On cost, yes it does give you a more competitive cost value aspect of it." - "The benefits it's even more when you consider the time you spend with the tender process which is less and time always equals money." - "It does influence the quality of work." - "In general they definitely perform better because they know what you want and you know how they do their work."
A4	- "We have delivered with great success I'm still shattered by the outcomes and results, in Solplaaitjie, we put 7 hundred million worth of buildings in 14 months, the total cost paid by the client was 3% below the cost on average of the two projects. In Kimberly, 1% below the starting price adjusted for inflation and in Mpumalanga, we were 1% above." - "The Solplaaitjie buildings have been shortlisted in an international architectural competition. Quality was therefore not compromised.
A5	- "Definitely cost wise the approach serves better than a normal contract." - "It assists in terms of it saves time especially for procurement processes that can take forever, with the possibility of a change that can bring forth a cost implication." - "It does support to deliver the project on time compared to the normal contract. Without having to return the budget money for a fiscal year." - "I wouldn't say quality wise it is better, because you've got measures."
A6	- "It assists and typically reduces the procurement period." - "Provides technical capacity for rural municipalities."
A7	- "It saves you time to go to the market." - "It's better for labour development." - "So under any circumstances, it makes 110% sense to have an FC because it safeguards the interest of any company, more than anything else, it also ensures that we have an expedited resolution of the problem that we have."
A8	- "In terms of quality of delivery, I will say there is a benefit." - "You are able to reduce the time spent on the tender process."

4.1 Framework Contracts Performance Cost-wise

As shown in Table 1, virtually all the organizations indicated that FC performs well and better than normal contracts cost-wise. This is well illustrated by the responses from A2 and A4: "We are proud that in the last 3-4 years we haven't gone over budget with framework contracts. If you want to make sure that your cost is controlled then a framework contract over the years is the best way to go."A2

"We have delivered with great success I'm still shattered by the outcomes and results, in Solplaaitjie, we put 7 hundred million worth of buildings in 14 months, the total cost paid by the client was 3% below the cost on average of the two projects. In Kimberly, 1% below the starting price adjusted for inflation and in Mpumalanga, we were 1% above."-A4

In an African Construction and Totally Concrete conference in South Africa, one of the concerns was the cost escalations and overruns of construction projects in South Africa and according to Cokayne [25] one of the delegates indicated that the cost of projects in South Africa escalates "by 400 percent, 500 percent and even more". Some other reports of cost escalations and overruns of construction projects in South Africa includes the Gautrain projects in which there were cost overruns from R7 billion to R25.4 billion, the soccer city stadium project in Johannesburg with cost overruns from R 1.916 billion to R 3.7 billion and the Moses Mabida stadium Durban with cost overruns from R 1.6 billion to R 3.1 billion ([2]). Comparing these reports to the findings on the performance of FC cost-wise indicate that FC is very cost-effective.

The associated variables reported to have influenced the performance of FC cost-wise are as follows:

- "The benefit of working in the NEC is certainty about cost. It does place an obligation on the client to get their payment systems right. We've got one obligation and that is to pay on time. If we pay on time, then we can point fingers everywhere. But if we don't pay on time there's no way you can keep the contractor responsible." **A1**
- "It's because of all the good planning and hard work to make sure that all our tender qualifications and our bill of quantities are accurate." **A2**
- "Since you actually build a relationship it is also a lot more efficient and again impacting on price."A3
- "The whole thing about volume discount plays a big role in it." **A3**
- "We brought the contractor into a more prominent position than he could have ever been in under traditional methods and the contractor inputs contributed." **A4**
- "The sharing of pains and gains principles which provide incentives for doing well." **A4**

These responses imply that the relationship with contractors, the large scope of work, early involvement of contractors, the use of NEC form of contracts which ensures on-time payments and the incentives provided pain and gain sharing of cost are the variables that influenced the performance of FC cost-wise.

4.2 Framework Contracts Performance Time-wise

With regards to the time performance of FC, from Table 1, it can be seen that all the organizations indicate that FC performs well time-wise when used for construction project delivery. As A3 and A5 put it:

"The benefits are more when you consider the time you spend with the tender process which is less and time always equals money." **A3**

"It assists in terms of it saves time especially for procurement processes that can take forever, with the possibility of a change that can bring forth a cost implication.

It does support to deliver the project on time compared to the normal contract, without having to return the budget money for a fiscal year." **A5**

The variables that were suggested to have influenced the FC performance time-wise by the organisations include:

- "The early warning system provided by the NEC says that if there's an impact on time don't hide it because if you hide it you are on your own." **A1**
- "The repetition of work, you can ask us 99% of anything now and we can give you the rate because we've done it so many times." **A2**
- "The project is not sometimes delayed because they actually know exactly what they need to do due to the relationship you build, there is not time extension and no variation orders so that decreases all those possibilities of cost overruns." **A3**

- "The flexibility such that if an item is not in your contract, you can use the market-related cost of that item and multiply it by the profit and overheads that you have agreed and end of the story." **A4**
- "There's no procurement process, you're just placing an order once the framework contract is in place." **A6**
- "You can easily make an order for projects based on existing agreements, as opposed to when you will have to go through check technical capabilities again." **A8**

These findings are consistent with the findings from other studies on the benefits of FC discussed earlier under the related literature section.

4.3 Framework Contracts Performance Quality-wise

Table 1 shows that with regards to the quality of delivery, most of the organizations indicate that employing FC assists in improving the quality of their project delivery. To quote from the transcripts of the interviews:

"The Solplaaitjie buildings have been shortlisted in an international architectural competition. Quality was therefore not compromised. It is a quality building; there is no question about it."-**A4**

"In terms of quality of delivery, I will say there is a benefit."-**A8**

However, some of the organisation does not agree that it's the adoption of FC that improves the quality of their projects as illustrated by A5: "I wouldn't say quality wise it is better, because you've got measures."**A5**

Nevertheless, the variables that were indicated to have influenced the performance of FC quality-wise include:

- "Bad quality impacts on my ability to get an invite for the next work package." **A1**
- "Repetition also helps the subbies on more or less the same design."**A2**
- "If you got a good relationship it impacts everything else." **A3**
- "We took some of the savings and put it into the enhancement of quality that was improving things that you realised that we could've done."**A4**
- "Site and inspection meetings and quality control basically those entire things safeguard these three pillars of quality, cost and time." **A7**
- "Contractors tend to do the works to the best of their capability so as to maintain the long-term relationship and for us to always come back to them."**A8**

Therefore, the performance of FC quality-wise is a significant factor in maintaining long-term relationships with contractors and the familiarity of contractors by virtue of the long-term relationships and the repetitive jobs influences the performance of projects in terms of quality of delivery.

Other Performance of FC elicited from the organisations are that FC promotes skills development and better for labour development; and Since its same crop of people that you use it also enhance safety on site which is better than doing a new induction with a new person whom you are not sure understands you properly. Nevertheless, issues concerning contractor's becoming complacent as a result of the long-term relationships and concerns relating to "not spreading the sunshine" in using same contractors for several projects are some of the drawbacks reported in the adoption of FC.

5 Conclusions

The use of traditional approaches for construction project delivery is greater in practice but there is growing adoption of FC in South Africa. The findings from this study show that the FC strategy performs well with regards to cost, time quality, safety and skills development. This is in contrast to the reports of the poor performance of construction projects using other procurement methods particularly the traditional procurement strategy. The variables that influence the performances of FC from the findings are the good relationships build with contractors, the repetitive works, the pain and gain sharing practices, the use of NEC contracts and intensive tendering and selection process in selecting suitable contractors for FC. others are the flexibility provided, the early involvement of the contractors in the project and the prospect of placing an order for new projects based on existing agreements without having to go through a new procurement process when FC is in place.

The result of the study is useful in providing insights that can encourage construction stakeholders to appreciate and adopt FC as an alternative viable procurement strategy for construction project delivery.

Acknowledgements

The assistance of Mosetengwane Maredi, Nothando Moloi and Lebogang Mokgosi in data collection for this study is acknowledged.

Reference

1. Construction Sector Transparency Initiative, Report on baseline studies: International comparison (2011)
2. L. Baloyi, M. Bekker, Causes of construction cost and time overruns: The 2010 FIFA World Cup stadia in South Africa, Acta Structilia **18**:51–67 (2011)
3. B. Flyvbjerg, M. Garbuio, D. Lovallo, Delusion and deception in large infrastructure projects: two models for explaining and preventing executive disaster, California management review **51**: 170–194 (2009)
4. S. Laryea, R. Watermeyer, Innovative construction procurement at Wits University. *Proceedings of the ICE-Management, Procurement and Law* **167**: 220–231 (2014)
5. Ruparathna, R., Hewage, K. Review of contemporary construction procurement practices, *Journal of management in engineering* **31**:04014038 (2013)
6. M.L. Sinclair, Developing a Model for Effective Stakeholder Engagement Management, *Asia Pacific Public Relations Journal* **12** (2011a).
7. Chartered Institute of Building, A report exploring procurement in the construction Industry, Ascot: CIOB (2010), Available at: http://www.ciob.org/procurement
8. M. Suprapto, H.L. Bakker, H.G. Mooi, W. Moree, Sorting out the essence of owner–contractor collaboration in capital project delivery, *International Journal of Project Management* **33**:664–683 (2015)
9. P.E. Eriksson, M. Westerberg, Effects of cooperative procurement procedures on construction project performance: A conceptual framework. *International Journal of Project Management* **29**: 197–208 (2011)
10. Joint Contracts Tribunal (JCT), Framework Agreement, (2011) https://www.jctltd.co.uk/product/framework-agreement (Accessed 1 March 2017).
11. J. Glover, Framework agreements: practice and pitfalls, Fenwick Elliott (2008)
12. RICS, Contracts in Use: A Survey of Building Contracts in Use during 2007. London, RICS (2010)
13. T. Creamer, Municipal agency moves to pioneer framework contracts in water milieu, (2016), INTERNET.http://www.polity.org.za/article/municipalagency-moves-to-pioneer-framework contracts-in-water-milieu-2016-01-27 (accessed 27 August 2016).
14. T. Creamer, Govt aims to pioneer "framework contracts" for municipal goods and services in 2016, (2015), INTERNET.http://www.engineeringnews.co.za/article/govt-

aims-to-pioneer-framework-contracts-formunicipal-goods-and-services-in-2016-2015-10-05 (accessed 27 August 2016).

15. H. Cohen, JCT Framework Agreement: Same again? Try the 2007 vintage, Building, (2008), URL http://www.building.co.uk/jct-framework-agreement-same-again?-try-the-2007-vintage/3103405.article (accessed 1.3.17).
16. Construction Excellence, Why use a framework agreement? (2005). available at http://goo.gl/MdQAxQ (Accessed 19 January 2017).
17. R. Morledge, A. Smith, Building Procurement, Wiley-Blackwell, Oxford (2013)
18. T. Lam, K. Gale, Framework procurement for highways maintenance in the UK: can it offer value for money for public-sector clients? Structure and Infrastructure Engineering **11**: 695–706 (2015)
19. T. Lam, K. Gale, Highway maintenance: impact of framework agreements on contractor performance, *Engineering, Construction and Architectural Management* **21**: 336–347 (2014)
20. M.J. Holden, Procurement of pumps via framework agreements, *World Pumps* 34–37 (1995)
21. B. Balcik, D. Ak, Supplier selection for framework agreements in humanitarian relief, Production and Operations Management **23**:1028–1041 (2014)
22. M.N.K. Saunders, P. Lewis, A. Thornhill, Research methods for business students. 6th ed. Harlow, UK: Pearson Education (2012)
23. K. Kumar, Conducting key informant interviews in developing countries, Agency for International Development Washington DC, (1989)
24. M.B. Miles, A.M. Huberman, J. Saldaña, Qualitative data analysis: A methods sourcebook. SAGE Publications, Incorporated (2014).
25. R. Cokayne, Construction delegates call for end to cost overruns, (2016) Available at: https://www.iol.co.za/business-report/economy/construction-delegates-call-for-end-to-cost-overruns-2020126, [Accessed: 06 November 2017]

Relationship Investigation of Organizational Agility Characteristics and Portfolio Management Maturity

Nick Hadjinicolaou[1], *Jantanee* Dumrak[1*], *and Sherif* Mostafa[2]

[1]Global Project Management, Torrens University Australia, Australia
[2]Construction and Engineering Project Management, School of Engineering and Built Environment, Griffith University

Abstract. Today's organizations operate within rapid changes in economy and market conditions. Organizational agility (OA) provides organizations with the ability to adapt rapidly to internal and external changes productively and cost-effectively. Furthermore, the adaptive ability and real-time responsiveness of organizations are generally necessitated for projects and portfolios to reach maturity. While the characteristics of OA and portfolio management maturity (PfMM) have been studied in the existing literature, the relationships between these two variables have not been fully explored. This study employs canonical correlation analysis (CCA) not only to investigate relationships among the characteristics of OA and PfMM but also to present the status quo of the studied variables from Australian perspectives. The results of the analysis are graphically presented to identify the formation of each OA characteristics at different levels of PfMM. The research data was collected from 36 respondents in public and private Australian sectors. The research findings show diverse combinations of the OA characteristics constructed at different levels of PfMM. The results also identify specific OA characteristics that highly contribute to the highest level of PfMM. This allows organizations with limited resources to precisely concentrate on the characteristics that will improve performance and achieve PfMM.

Keywords: canonical correlation analysis, maturity, organizational agility, project management, project portfolio management

1 Introduction

The concepts of Organisational Agility (OA) and Portfolio Management Maturity (PfMM) have evolved around an organisations desire to improve performance and competitiveness. This has occurred as a result of pressures from digital disruption, merging of technology, greater customer needs and levels of customer satisfaction demanded. Market competition,

* Corresponding author: jantanee.d@gmail.com

legislative, political and economic pressures [1] have also played a role in the need for increased organizational agility. According to PMI [2] (p. 2), organizational agility is "the capability to quickly sense and adapt to external and internal changes to deliver relevant results in a productive and cost-effective manner". Agility accelerates organizational learning to meet the pace of rapid environmental change through flexibility in assembling resources, knowledge, processes and capabilities [3, 4]. It is believed that agility helps organisations to sustain their competitive advantage by increasing responsiveness in managing and making business decisions. However, the application and improvement in Portfolio Management Maturity (PfMM) demands more than commitments of new policies and procedures but rethinking in organisational structures, systems and management practices [5, 6]. In this research, characteristics of organisational agility are examined and the results of the analysis are graphically presented to identify the formation of each OA characteristics at different levels of PfMM. The research data was collected from 36 respondents in public and private Australian sectors. The research findings show diverse combinations of the OA characteristics constructed at different levels of PfMM. The results also identify specific OA characteristics that highly contribute to the highest level of PfMM. This allows organizations with limited resources to precisely concentrate on the characteristics that will improve performance and achieve PfMM.

2 Literature Review

2.1 Portfolio Management Maturity

According to PMI [7], Portfolio Management (PfM) aims to achieve strategic objectives through the centralised management of one or more portfolios. PfM has been referred as a means to deliver value to organisations with its abilities, at the long-term organisational level, in selecting the right projects, maximizing resource allocation, measuring and evaluating portfolio success, strategic alignment and balance, and value maximization of project/program investment [8-10]. Furthermore, strong strategic portfolio execution is required for maintaining organisational competitiveness [2, 7, 11]. To implement PfM successfully, a supportive environment with impacting factors in PfM implementation must be identified [8]. These may include, but not limited to, organization culture and structure, law limitations, government or industry standard, infrastructure, human resources, staff management, company task authorization system, market condition, commercial database and project management information systems. Any changes to these factors will affect the implementation of PfM positively or negatively. Nevertheless, changes are inevitable and require responsively adaptive management for PfM to remain effective.

As benefits of PfM, such as organizations become more flexible, impulsive, dynamic, innovative, creative, communicative, strategic oriented, efficient and motivated [12], have been increasingly realized, many organisations aim to maximize and sustain the PfM implementation by achieving the high level of PfM maturity (PfMM). PMI [13] identifies five categories of PfMM: ad hoc, getting started, structured and improving, established and optimized for continuous improvement (Figure 1).

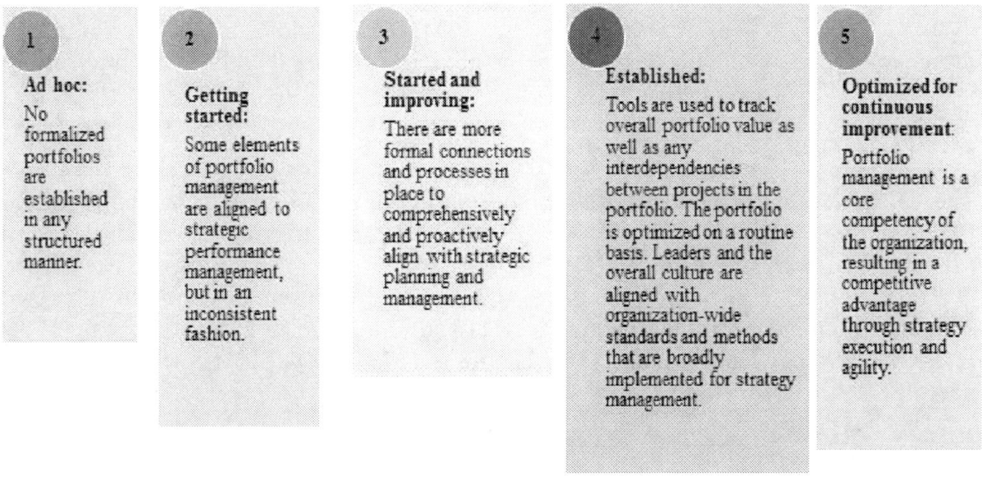

Fig. 1. Portfolio Management Maturity (Adapted from PMI [13], p5)

Young et al. [14] state that organisational governance, stakeholder management, management control, risk management, benefits management, portfolio, financial management and resource management are the key attributes to PfMM. In their study, PfMM was carefully examined using the Australian Federal Government as a case study. Their study shows that not only financial management and resource management were considered as the only key focused areas in PfMM, but also generic attributes of roles and responsibilities, experience, capability development, planning and estimating and scrutiny and review that are highly sensitive factors to PfMM. The results showed in [14] are aligned with a study by Pennypacker (2002 cited in [12] p. 241) that attaining PfMM relies on a set of knowledge, skills, tools, and techniques applied to a collection of projects in order to meet or exceed needs and expectations of an organization's investment strategy.

2.2 Linking Portfolio Maturity to Organisational Agility

As stated by PMI [15], the success of organisations depends on the ability to adapt quickly in response to changes to sustain competitive advantage. Organizational agility (OA) is the ability to responsively accommodate changes and implement required actions. Most important characteristics of OA as identified by PMI [15] include flexibility and adaptability, open communication, openness to change, empowered team members, experiential learning, rapid decision making, and a strong customer focus. Successful implementation of OA generally requires continuous communication, collaboration, engagement and support within organisations.

Martinsuo and Lehtonen [16] suggest that there is a link between PfM and organisational performance. PMI [7, 11] states that organisational resources are a primary input for PfM and strategic changes driven by the integration of organisational planning and business analysis enable the planned portfolios to support strategic objectives. Heising [17], on the other hand, views PfM as a strategic role that enables organizations to respond and adapt to changing environmental conditions by monitoring and altering the project portfolio. Killen and Hunt [9] discover connections between PfM and OA in supporting organisations with responsive decision making and resource allocation as well as building dynamic capability at the organisational level. It is also found that OA supports strategic flexibility by enabling organisations to anticipate, identify, develop and implement change and investment strategies that are aligned with strategic objectives. Nevertheless, it has been minimal research on how characteristics of OA interact with different levels of PfMM. This research, therefore, is to examine the interactions between the studied PfMM levels and characteristics of OA to gain more understanding and maximizing any positive impacts resulted from the interactions.

3 Research methodology

The categorical data were analysed from 36 PfM practitioners who aimed at improving PfMM through the application of OA. The collected data were coded to conduct a nonlinear canonical correlation analysis (NLCCA) or known as OVERALS. The purpose of OVERALS analysis is to examine the associations between two or more sets of categorical variables (nominal or ordinal scaling level) [18] to introduce an integrative analysis of non-linear relations between variables [19]. The formulation of OVERALS was conducted using the SPSS statistics software.

The data collected in this analysis were categorised into three sets containing 21 variables as inputs to perform OVERALS. The first data set was the categories of PfMM identified in the respondent's organisation. The second and the third data sets were OA characteristics which had been grouped into the process and people drivers in relation to the high agility focus stated by PMI [11]. These sets of data identified the views of respondents in the existing OA characteristics in organizations to support PfMM. The three data sets are demonstrated in Table 1.

Table 1. Variable Coding

Set	Variable	No of categories	Variable type	Category symbol
1. Portfolio Management Maturity (PfMM)	PfMM category	5	Nominal	PfMM
2. Organisational Agility Characteristics (People)	Flexible and adaptable	3	Ordinal	PP1
	Open communications	3	Ordinal	PP2
	Open to change	3	Ordinal	PP3
	Self-aware and honest	3	Ordinal	PP4
	Customer-orientated	3	Ordinal	PP5
	Focused on talent development	3	Ordinal	PP6
	Committed to agility	3	Ordinal	PP7
	Empowered team members	3	Ordinal	PP8
	Catalyst leadership	3	Ordinal	PP9
	Continuous learning from experience	3	Ordinal	PP10
3. Organisational Agility Characteristics (Process)	Transparency in decision making	3	Ordinal	PC1
	Rapid decision making	3	Ordinal	PC2
	Decentralized decision making	3	Ordinal	PC3

	Action-based	3	Ordinal	PC4
	Agility recognised as a team competence	3	Ordinal	PC5
	Effective methods of rapid knowledge transfer	3	Ordinal	PC6
	Clear guidelines for tailoring standardised processes to suit the size and type of project	3	Ordinal	PC7
	Effective environmental screening	3	Ordinal	PC8
	Appetite for risk	3	Ordinal	PC9
	Active Governance	3	Ordinal	PC10

The results obtained from OVERALS included the loss index, eigenvalues, fit index and component loading index. The component loadings were demonstrated within a two-dimensional graph for each plotted variable. The plot of centroids was generated to view categories under each variable.

4 Research findings

After the research data collection, individual respondents were carefully assessed on their experience in organisational agility through the use of filtering questions to ensure the validity of responses. Thirty-six out of 50 who had completed the research questionnaires were satisfied with the screening criteria. Descriptive statistics were employed to demonstrate the percentages of respondents according to their organisational roles. The percentage of each respondent category is shown in Figure 1 below. The major categories of respondents in this research were business managers (33%), project managers (17%) and corporate executives (14%) respectively.

OVERALS was performed on the collected data to identify and graphically present relationships between OA characteristics and PfMM as well as the relationship formed between categorial parameters used within the studied variables. OVERALS as demonstrated in Table 2 presented loss values, eigenvalues and fit values. The fit and loss values were used to confirm the degree of NLCCA solution to the optimally quantified data with respect to the association between sets [18]. Loss values indicated the percentage of variation in object scores that were not explained by the current model [20]. Whereas the average loss values of the two dimensions are 0.058 and 0.227 respectively, the average loss over sets is 0.285. This indicated the average loss or the difference between the perfect and the modelled relationship. The maximum fit value presented equals the number of dimensions and indicates that the relationship is perfect.

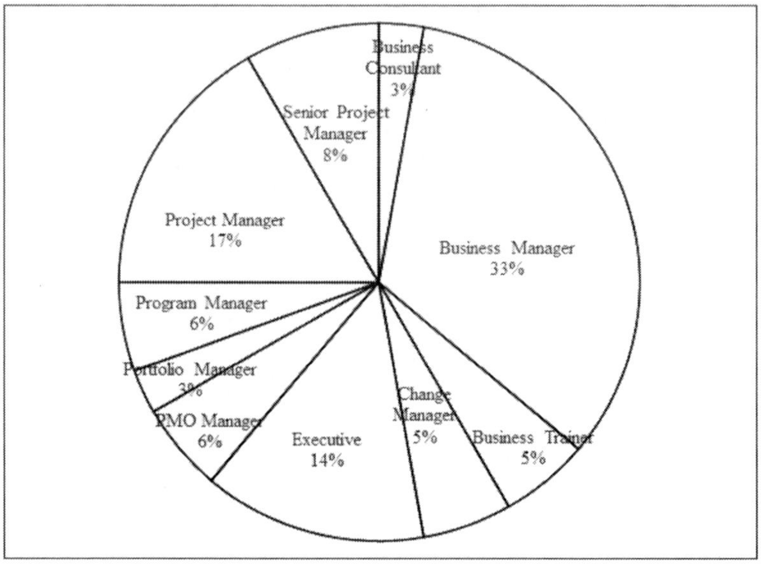

Fig. 2. Percentage of Respondents in Category

Table 2. OVERALS Summary of Analysis

		Dimension 1	Dimension 2	Sum
Loss	**Set 1**	.044	.233	.277
	Set 2	.031	.299	.330
	Set 3	.099	.149	.248
	Mean	.058	.227	.285
Eigenvalue		.942	.773	
Fit				1.715

The eigenvalue in each dimension was the result of 1 minus the average loss of the dimension. The result of eigenvalue shows not only how much relationship is presented in each dimension, but also the importance of the dimension. The value of eigenvalue can determine the percentage of actual fit of the dimension over the fit value in the "Sum" column, i.e. the actual fit among the sets of variables in the first and second dimensions are 0.942/1.715 = 0.549 and 0.773/1.715 = 0.451 respectively which are not necessarily high. The maximum potential relationship over sets associated to the current model can be calculated by dividing the fit value with the total dimensions. The analysis shows that the maximum potential relationship of the current model is 1.715/2 = 0.858. Canonical correlations (ρ) of more than two data sets per dimension were obtained from the given formula below:

$$\rho_d = ((K \text{ x } E_d) - 1)/(K\text{-}1)$$

Where *d* is the dimension number, *E* is the eigenvalue and *K* is the number of sets.

The correlations of the first and second dimensions were calculated as and 0.91 and 0.66 respectively. The correlation values suggest that the positively strong relationships between PfMM and OA characteristics were found within the studied groups both in Dimensions 1 and 2. As a result, it can be interpreted that the application of overall OA characteristics to support PfMM were significant to organisations at PfMM categories.

The examination of the weight load of variables is presented in Table 3. The variables with the highest contribution to the Dimension 1 were PP3 (0.604) and PC3 (0.282). The highest contribution to the Dimension 2 were PfMM category (0.843), PP9 (0.804), PP10 (0.716), PP5 (0.579), PC8 (0.565) and PC6 (0.400) respectively.

Table 3. The Weight Load of Variables

Set			Dimension	
			1	2
1	PfMM Category		0.100	**0.843**
2	PP1:	Flexible and adaptable	-0.280	-0.134
	PP2:	Open communications	-0.428	-0.047
	PP3:	Open to change	**0.604**	-0.181
	PP4:	Self-aware and honest	-0.469	-0.026
	PP5:	Customer orientated	-0.022	0.579
	PP6:	Focused on talent development	-0.093	-0.723
	PP7:	Committed to agility	-0.247	-0.004
	PP8:	Empowered team members	-0.470	-0.002
	PP9:	Catalyst leadership	0.068	**0.804**
	PP10:	Continuous learning from experience	0.053	**0.716**
3	PC1:	Transparency in decision making	-0.386	-0.211
	PC2:	Rapid decision making	-0.026	-0.101
	PC3:	Decentralized decision making	**0.282**	0.193
	PC4:	Action based	-0.516	0.107
	PC5:	Agility recognised as a team competence	-0.208	0.131
	PC6:	Effective methods of rapid knowledge transfer	-0.290	0.400
	PC7:	Clear guidelines for tailoring standardised processes to suit the size and type of project	0.103	-0.034
	PC8:	Effective environmental screening	0.019	**0.565**
	PC9:	Appetite for risk	-0.153	0.086
	PC10:	Active Governance	-0.253	-0.778

The component loading in Figure 3 below shows the plot of component loadings for the collected data. The component loadings presented are equivalent to the Pearson correlations between the quantified variables and the object scores. This means the distance from the origin to each variable point indicates the significance of that variable [18]. The line joining the origin and the coordinate of component loading is called the coordinate vector. The strength of association between the two studied variables can be determined from the angle between the coordinate vectors of the variables. The smaller the angle, the higher the strength of the association and vice versa.

As demonstrated in Figure 1, the variance of PP4, PP8, PP1, PfMM and PC10 were the most explained variables respectively as their vector lengths were the greatest among the studied variables. On the other hand, PP5, PP2, PP3, PC2 and PP7 were the least explained variables by NLCCA. From the angle between the coordinate vectors, it was found that PP4,

PP8, PP1, PC1, PC9, PP7, PP3, PP2 and PP5 formed a major cluster. On the other hand, PfMM and PC3, as well as PC8 and PP9, also aligned to form smaller clusters.

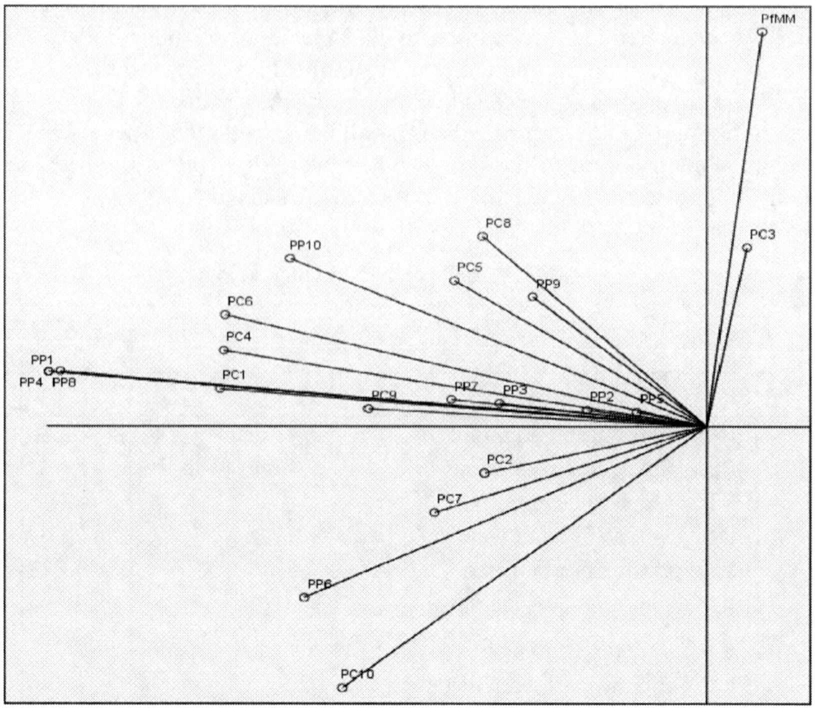

Fig 3. Component Loadings

It was observed in the Centroids plot (Figure 4) that most of the High degrees of OA characteristics, especially PP9, PC8 and PC5, aligned to form a significant cluster with the PfMM Categories 3 (Started and improving) and 4 (Established). On the other hand, the PfMM Category 1 (Ad hoc) formed a cluster with PC10.

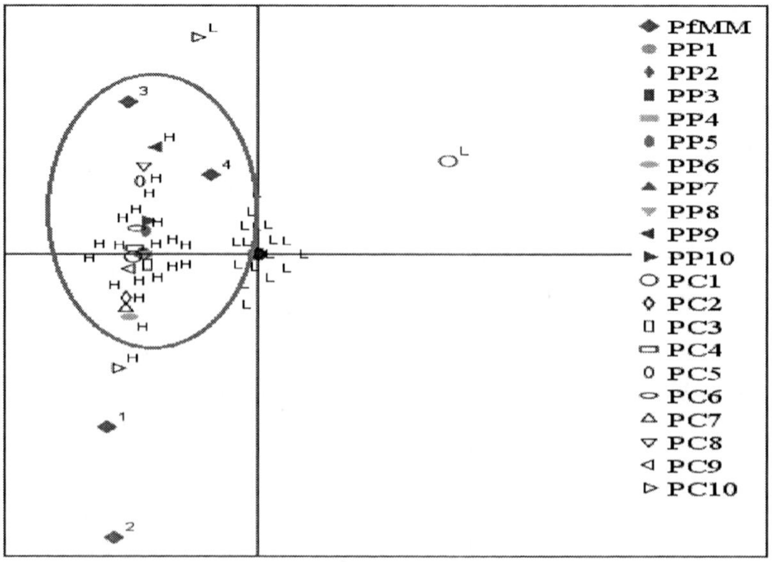

Fig. 4. The Centroids Plot

It was also found that the PfMM Category 5 (Optimized for continuous improvement) as well as the Medium degree variables of OA characteristics, regardless the significance of these variables, were plotted at a distance farther away from other PfMM Categories and the High degrees of OA characteristics variables (see Figure 5). The variables aligned themselves and formed different clusters indicating different sets of relationships without any PfMM Categories.

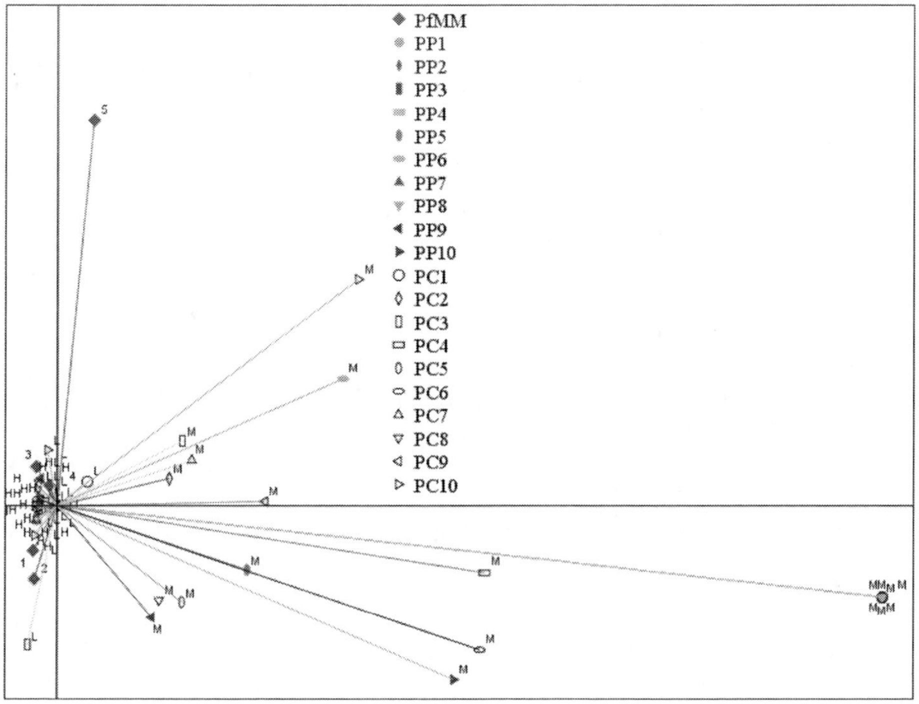

Fig. 5. The Centroid Plot of Distant Variables

5 Conclusion and Recommendations

The organizational agility and portfolio management maturity concepts have been developed to improve organizational performance and adapt to external pressures. Agility improves organizations to sustain their competitive advantage by increasing responsiveness in managing and making business decisions. Whereas, portfolio management maturity (PfMM) aims to deliver value to organizations with its abilities, at the long-term organizational level, in selecting the right projects, maximizing resource allocation, measuring and evaluating portfolio success, strategic alignment and balance, and value maximization of project/program investment. This research provides a significant examination of the relationships between the existing organizational agility (OA) characteristics and its support to PfMM. Three sets of data contacting 21 variables of PfMM and OA were carefully examined using canonical analysis. The results showed a significant positive strong correlation between PfMM and OA characteristics within the studied groups. The research also found various combinations of the OA characteristics constructed at different levels of PfMM, and there are specific OA characteristics that highly contribute to the highest level of PfMM. This allows organizations with limited resources to precisely concentrating on the implementation of PfM and on the characteristics that improve performance and achieve PfMM. This may require further research to be undertaken to identify these characteristics in different organization size and sectors. Furthermore, it is recommended to extend the investigation into differing environmental settings of OA and PfMM to generalise the research findings.

References

1. S. Drew, C. Coulson-Thomas, Transformation through teamwork: the path to the new organization?, *Team Performance Management: An International Journal* **3**(2):162-78 (1997)
2. PMI. *Pulse of the profession®: Achieving the greater agility-the people and process drivers that accelerate the j5t results*. Newtown Square, PA: PMI (2017c)
3. D.J. Wischnevsky, Change as the winds change: the impact of oganizational transformation on firm survival, *Organizational Analysis* **12**(4):361-377 (2004)
4. C. Yang, H. Liu, Boosting firm performance via enterprise agility and network structure, *Management Decision* **50**(6):1022-1044 (2012)
5. G. Hamel, Moon shots for management (reinventing management to make it more relevant to a volatile business environment), Harvard Business Review **87**(2):91-99 (2009)
6. N. Hadjinicolaou, J. Dumrak, S. Mostafa, Improving Project Success with Project Portfolio Management Practices, *In* S. Şahin, eds, *Proceedings of the 8th International Conference on Engineering, Project, and Product Management*, 20-22 September2017, Amman, Jordan: Springer International Publishing 57-66 (2018)
7. PMI. *The standard for portfolio management (4th ed.)*, Newtown Square, PA: Project Management Institute (2017a)
8. N. Guo, S. Yu, The necessity of project portfolio management in the construction industry of China mainland, *Applied Mechanics and Materials* 357-360:2238-2241 (2013)
9. C. Killen, R. Hunt, Robust project portfolio management: capability evolution and maturity, *International Journal of Managing Projects in Business* **6**(1):131-151 (2013)
10. M. Martinsuo, C. Killen, Value Management in Project Portfolios: Identifying and Assessing Strategic Value, *Project Management Journal* **45**(5):56–70 (2014)
11. PMI. *The drivers of agility: Engaging people and building processes to accelerate results*. Newtown Square, PA: Project Management Institute (2017b)
12. B. Madic, V. Trujic, I. Mihajlovic, African Project portfolio management implementation review, *Journal of Business Management* **5**(2):240-248 (2011)
13. PMI, *Winning through Project Portfolio Management: The Practitioner's Perspective*, Newtown Square, PA: Project Management Institute (2015a)
14. M. Young, R. Young, J.R. Zapata, Project, programme and portfolio maturity: A case study of Australian Federal Government, *International Journal of Managing Projects in Business* **7**(2):215-230 (2014)
15. PMI, *Capturing the value of project management through organizational agility*, Newtown Square, PA: Project Management Institute (2015b)
16. M. Martinsuo, P. Lehtonen, Role of single-project management in achieving portfolio management efficiency, *International Journal of Project Management* **25**:56–65 (2007)
17. W. Heising, The integration of ideation and project portfolio management-A key factor for sustainable success, *International Journal of Project Management* **30**(5):582-595 (2012)
18. Meulman J., Heiser, W. *IBM SPSS Categories 21*, USA: IBM Corporation (2012)

19. K.G. Frie, C. Janssen, Social inequality, lifestyles and health – a non-linear canonical correlation analysis based on the approach of Pierre Bourdieu, International *Journal of Public Health* **54**:213-221 (2009)
20. D. Garson, *Canonical correlation*. Asheboro, NC: Statistical Publishing Associates (2012)

Remanufacturing of electric vehicles: Challenges in production management

Achim Kampker[1], *Johannes* Triebs[2], *Ansgar* Hollah[1*], and *Andreas* Unruh[1]

[1]PEM of RWTH Aachen University, Templergraben 55, 52062 Aachen, Germany
[2]Chair of Production Engineering of E-Mobility Components, RWTH Aachen University, Templergraben 55, 52062 Aachen, Germany

Abstract. Due to the conceptual degrees of freedom in their product structure, electric vehicles offer high potential for remanufacturing-oriented product design. This potential is, however, not realized yet. Remanufacturing as one fundamental element of a circular economy is characterized by specific challenges caused by uncertain information about the condition and the timing of the returning product. By means of a case study within the remanufacturing industry, the effects of uncertainties on remanufacturing operations are examined and different approaches within the field of production management to meet these specific challenges are pointed out. Based on the result of the case study a production management framework outlining fields of action to deal with remanufacturing specific uncertainties is developed. In this context, the requirements for remanufacturing of electric vehicles are derived by analyzing similarities from other industry sectors. In conclusion, a solution approach for the implementation for electric vehicles is presented for strategic, tactical and operational procurement logistics and remanufacturing operations.

Keywords: remanufacturing, electric vehicles, production management

1 Introduction

1.1 Motivation

The concept of a circular economy aims to decouple economic growth from the use of finite resources and the associated negative effects on the environment [1]. Remanufacturing corresponds to the objective of the circular economy since it enables the recovery of product components for further use in order to extend the useful life of products or their components.

The global remanufacturing industry has reached a total size of approximately 110 billion USD per year and creates about 450,000 jobs worldwide [2]. The automotive industry accounts for two-thirds of the remanufacturing market volume, even though remanufacturing

* Corresponding author: a.hollah@pem.rwth-aachen.de

is currently limited to vehicle components [3]. In other sectors, remanufacturing is executed on the level of the final product and is a central element of the manufacturer's business models.

The growing market share of electric vehicles offers new opportunities to implement remanufacturing at the vehicle level for passenger cars and light commercial vehicles. While vehicles with a powertrain based on an internal combustion engine have a predefined product and functional structure, conceptual degrees of freedom can be used in the design of electric vehicles to implement remanufacturing-oriented product design [4]. Additionally, the components of an electric powertrain are characterized by lower complexity and fewer mechanical interfaces to each other.

Several definitions of remanufacturing exist with slightly different foci. All definitions have in common that remanufacturing is described as an industrial process in which cores are brought into a condition that meets at least the quality and functional requirements of a new product [2, 5, 6]. Cores can also be upgraded to enhance product functionality. Remanufacturing includes re-using, processing or replacing of single components of the returned cores in order to enable a further product life cycle [7].

The generic remanufacturing process begins with the delivery of the cores and storage [8]. After optional cleaning, the product is disassembled. Components, which are technically or economically unsuitable for remanufacturing due to their condition are sorted out. All other cores may need detailed defect diagnosis before the actual reprocessing of the disassembled parts takes place. In reassembly, the processed components are reassembled, if necessary in combination with new parts.

1.2 Problem Statement

Remanufacturing is characterized by additional challenges in comparison to linear value chain production. As discussed in the literature and proven by different studies, the uncertainty about the condition, quantity and timing of returning cores is elementary for these challenges [9]. Varying failure patterns caused by different usage behaviours and multiple external factors lead to the unpredictable timing of product failure and different remanufacturing needs. The more components a product contains, the greater the deviations in causes and times of core returns are.

The combination of a fluctuating number of available cores and varying core conditions results in unreliable forecasts about the availability of remanufacturable cores and spare parts as well as the required production capacity [10]. Moreover, remanufacturers often have to deal with an asymmetry between core returns and market demand since the availability of cores increases during the saturation and degeneration phases of a product's market cycle while demand decreases [11]. Furthermore, depending on the condition of the cores required remanufacturing processes and process times may vary in order to achieve the desired condition [12]. Therefore, it is hardly possible to schedule the process reliably before disassembly and inspection of the cores. Subsequent changes in process and material requirements planning can also occur if further defects are detected during the remanufacturing process that were not detected during quality inspection.

These challenges are dealt with in numerous publications and a variety of solutions is presented. Remanufacturing research to date is characterized by an isolated consideration of the individual problem areas [13]. Due to the high planning complexity of remanufacturing, approaches are necessary that deal with the specific challenges in an integrated framework. Accordingly, only limited theoretical conclusions can be drawn for the implementation of remanufacturing in electric vehicle production. Rather, it is promising to investigate the production management of remanufacturing operations in other industries with regard to the applicability of remanufacturing at the vehicle level. Therefore, the following research question occurs:

Which configuration options in product management for remanufacturing of electric vehicles can be derived from practice in order to meet uncertainty-related challenges?

2 Approach

In order to derive implications for the remanufacturing of electric vehicles, the industry practice is described and analyzed in five companies. The cases are derived in a three-step approach. First, publicly available information was examined in order to select suitable companies. Based on this, a comprehensive literature analysis was carried out with regard to the respective remanufacturing operations. Finally, experts from the production management department were interviewed using a standardized questionnaire.

The products examined in the study show a different level of complexity in order to consider a wide range of different approaches to solving the uncertainties discussed above. The products are becoming gradually more complex from brake callipers, starters, and generators, clutches, printers, combustion engines for heavy-duty trucks and construction machines to gas turbines. All companies, whose remanufacturing operations are examined in this study, are original equipment manufacturers (OEM) of the described products. This is important in order to ensure applicability to the production of electric vehicles since the complexity of remanufacturing products such as electric vehicles can only be controlled by its original manufacturer.

Firstly, as structuring means for the study, a framework is developed, depicting the fields of action for managing the production-related remanufacturing specific uncertainties. The fields of action are differentiated according to their *strategic, tactical* or *operational* character, depending on the planning horizon. Strategic tasks have a rough planning level and are typically carried out by the management for the long term. The tactical management level implements the planning requirements of the strategic level in the medium term and the operational level is responsible for detailed order management.

The management challenges described divide the fields of action associated with remanufacturing into two categories: *procurement logistics* and *remanufacturing operations*. One significant difference compared to conventional systems lies in procurement logistics, since remanufacturing is characterized by exogenous parts availability and therefore the coverage of dependent requirements cannot be completely controlled [12]. Additionally, depending on the core condition, the process steps to be carried out and the process times can vary considerably, which makes the planning of production operations complicated and requires an appropriate strategy.

3 Case study

3.1 Framework

Companies either purchase cores directly from the customer or access third-party service providers such as used parts dealers, scrap yards or core brokers. The multitude of supply sources increases the overall coordination effort and the complexity of procurement logistics. Since there is also a high degree of uncertainty regarding the return time of cores by the customer, close, cross-company cooperation with third-party service providers is necessary for supply chains that are directed backwards, as well as the active involvement of customers in the take-back process [14]. The configuration of the *closed-loop supply chain* represents the increased demands on cooperation with customers and third-party service providers and therefore represents the strategic management field of action of procurement logistics.

In a conventional forward supply chain, manufacturers sell their products directly to their customers or use retailers. Backward material flows typically only occur in connection with product returns, e.g. when the customer asserts warranty claims. In remanufacturing, more extensive requirements are placed on product take-back systems, as returned products are the raw material for production and thus indispensable for the value-adding process. Remanufacturing companies must create logistics systems that work efficiently despite the high number of material sources and the uncertainty regarding the availability of cores. The planning, implementation and control of efficient and cost-effective product flows from the end-user to the original manufacturer, with the purpose of generating added value by restoring the product, is called *reverse logistics* and is on the tactical level of procurement logistics [15].

The operational management task of procurement logistics is to ensure that a number of components tailored to the primary requirement are procured and made available for production. Remanufacturing differs from conventional logistics systems in terms of warehousing, procurement and distribution [16]. Therefore, a reliable forecast of how many reusable components will be available for remanufacturing and how many spare parts are needed cannot be precisely made. For these reasons, the *dependent requirements supply* needs to ensure the availability of cores to be remanufactured.

On the strategic management level of remanufacturing operations, the fundamental decision must be made for the question to what extent remanufacturing is in line with the corporate strategy. Numerous factors such as revenue potential, the consideration of marketing, the availability of specialists and legislative requirements can influence this decision [17]. Furthermore, a decision must be made about which products are technically and economically feasible for remanufacturing. In addition, a balance must be struck between the availability of cores and the market demand for reclaimed products. Therefore, at the strategic level, the *remanufacturing scope* is defined.

The design of efficient production processes is a success determining factor in the development of remanufacturing systems since both the costs and quality of the processed products as well as the performance of the system are influenced by the choice and design of the production processes [18]. Consequently, the tactical field of action for remanufacturing operations is defined as *production design*.

The operational level of remanufacturing operations is characterized by variable process times and production sequences due to the high inconsistency of the core condition, which is particularly challenging for *inhouse-production planning and control* [9]. Since not all cores have to undergo the same processes in order to be restored to a new condition, it is usually not possible to carry out precise process planning before certainty about the condition of the cores has been achieved. Processing times on the same workstation can also vary depending on the core's condition. Therefore, the scheduling of production processes is more complex than with conventional production systems.

	Procurement logistics	Remanufacturing operations
Strategic	Closed loop supply chain	Remanufacturing scope
Tactical	Reverse logistics	Production design
Operational	Dependent requirements supply	Inhouse-production planning & control

Fig. 1. Framework for production management of remanufacturing-related uncertainties

3.2 Case studies

3.2.1 Case 1: Remanufacturing of brake callipers, starters, and generators

The company in the first case is a multinational technology group with a strong focus on mechanical, mechatronic and electric automotive parts with activities in 60 countries. At the examined production site, remanufacturing of brake callipers, starters and generators is carried out for aftermarket activities. At the location, 300 employees remanufacture more than one million products yearly, handling over 3.000 different types of products.

The cores are taken back via three channels. The first channel is the repurchase from independent workshops. Via agents, the cores are picked up and delivered to one of the regional sorting centres from a network of twelve such stations in Europe where the cores are identified, pre-sorted and evaluated. If the cores meet predefined criteria such as completeness and absence of obvious material eruptions and cracks, the value of the core is credited to the customer. The second option is the direct repurchase from major customers. Contracted workshops are advised to store and forward cores of certain product types. These major customers purchase an agreed quantity of remanufactured products at a reduced price. Lastly, the option of purchasing cores from independent core brokers is used.

The remanufacturing process begins with sorting and inspecting the quality of the delivered cores. If testing and sorting have already taken place at one of the sorting centres before delivery, the cores are stored without checking. The storage time can vary depending on the product type from a few days up to several years. When an order is placed, a corresponding number of cores is removed from stock. Since it cannot be assumed that all components of each product type can be remanufactured due to condition variations, forecasts approximate how many cores of a certain product type are required to meet the existing primary requirement for each product type.

The cores are disassembled non-destructively into their individual components and forwarded to the subsequent processes. Obviously defective components as well as wearing parts and small parts such as screws are directly sorted out and replaced. Components, which in any case have a limited life, are also excluded from reuse. Various cleaning processes like degreasing with technical alcohol and subsequent irradiation with blasting media are carried out depending on the type of component and the degree of contamination. The reusability of the individual components is assessed manually after cleaning. Depending on the test results, mechanical processing is carried out according to a predefined process for each component family. The reassembly follows immediately without intermediate storage. Non-recoverable components are replaced either by equivalent components of the same batch or by new parts. In the last step, a test of the finished remanufactured product as well as packaging and handover to shipping takes place.

3.2.2 Case 2: Remanufacturing of heavy-duty vehicles clutches

The company is a global technology group for automotive systems with activities in 40 countries including a network of fifteen remanufacturing locations in Europe, Asia, North and South America, and Africa. At the analysed plant, 200 employees remanufacture more than 200,000 units per year of a broad variety of different clutches.

The cores are procured via three channels. The most important channel is the direct repurchase from major customers who deliver used parts several times a week and in return, they purchase a certain quantity of remanufactured products. The second take-back channel is the purchase of cores from core brokers. Either they receive an order to procure a defined number of a product type or cores are acquired from the existing stock of the respective core broker. Furthermore, cores are supplied directly by workshops. Workshops collect the used parts resulting from the repair of customer vehicles and sell them.

The delivered cores are stored and remanufacturing is only conducted, once a primary purchase order has been received. In the first process step, the cores are categorized according to the extent of defects. The categorized cores are disassembled, which requires controlled destruction of the rivets or welded joints. The separated products are first disassembled and then cleaned of dirt and corrosion by means of a shot-blasting cleaning process. Cleaned components are inspected for defects and, if necessary, sorted out and sent for recycling. Quality control also determines which mechanical treatment processes are necessary to restore the component in mint condition. During the abrasive cleaning process, any identification numbers applied to the surface are removed. The subsequent sorting of the components according to their type requires highly qualified employees who can draw conclusions about the product type on the basis of the component geometries.

The subsequent mechanical processing implements the processing measures defined during quality control as well as adjustments that are necessary due to technical product upgrades. The mechanical processing to be carried out depends on the type of component and the state of wear and includes separating processes such as the removal of burrs and face turning of end faces as well as joining production processes such as the bonding of wear plates. In the last step, the reprocessed components are reassembled and a final functional test is carried out. The cores can go through the entire process several times.

3.2.3 Case 3: Remanufacturing of heavy commercial vehicles combustion engines

One of the world's largest manufacturers of trucks, buses, construction machinery and industrial engines with production sites in 18 countries including remanufacturing sites in Europe, USA and China for transmissions, engines, turbochargers, and hydraulic pumps remanufactures 200 different variants of truck engines with a total volume of about 3.000 units per year for the European and Asian markets at the analysed production site.

Cores are supplied by an external core broker, who supplies the plant once every two weeks. The required number of cores is forecasted from historical data and the order is placed with the core broker without direct order reference. The delivered cores are stored and, as soon as free production capacity is available, fed into the remanufacturing process.

The remanufacturing process starts with the disassembly of the engine. No initial testing of the engine, but a continuous quality test of the engine components during the entire remanufacturing process is executed. Engine components that prove to be defective during dismantling or in subsequent remanufacturing steps are disposed of or recycled accordingly. Among others, surface crack inspections, 3D coordinate measurements and dynamic testing methods are carried out. During disassembly, the components are sorted according to quality and the cleaning process required. Afterwards, the component cleaning is carried out, which is subject to highly varying process times, as the components must be soaked for a long time before the actual, abrasive cleaning process can take place. Cleaned components are then mechanically processed. The processing steps required for processing vary depending on the component group and condition of the respective component.

One major challenge for production planning and control is that the setup and processing times can differ by up to fifteen times depending on the type and condition of the component. Likewise, the recovery rate varies substantially between 10 % and 100 % depending on the component group. Consequently, a very high stock for some components is unavoidable, while other components have to be purchased externally to meet demand.

The components of an individual engine are not reassembled to the same engine but are at first stored. If all components necessary for the fulfilment of an order are in stock, reassembly can take place, otherwise, missing components must first be purchased externally. Finally, the end of line test is carried out, during which the remanufactured engine must meet the same quality standards as a newly manufactured engine.

3.2.4 Case 4: Remanufacturing of printers

The company in case four is a US manufacturer of office equipment including tabletop printers, multifunction devices, commercial production printing systems and printer cartridges. The company operates remanufacturing plants in North and South America, Europe, Australia and Japan.

Used products are mainly taken back via two channels. In particular, commercially used production printing systems and multifunctional systems are replaced by new equipment under lease agreements after a contractually agreed timespan. The second channel is to take back the device directly from the end customer, for example through exchange campaigns, in which the customer is granted a discount on the new device when returning an old product.

The returned devices are centrally checked for optical defects as well as for noise and heat generation and vibrations. According to their condition, the cores are sent to different plants. Devices without any signs of wear are centrally stored and prepared for direct reuse while faultlessly working cores with light signs of wear are sent to remanufacturing plants. Non-reusable devices are recycled. The products are completely disassembled and the components are sorted by type. The components are then cleaned using a minimal-abrasive dry ice blasting process, which gently cleans the plastic, glass and precious metal components. Mechanical processing is not carried out. Only painting of the panel components is carried out. Component not suitable for reuse as well as wear parts like seals and bearings are replaced by a new component. Components for which technical upgrades exist are also replaced by the new components.

The tested and partially newly painted components are assembled in the next process step. New and remanufacturing products are assembled on the same line. For the assembly of new devices, no remanufactured components are used. Finally, the latest software is installed for all products and final function tests are carried out.

3.2.5 Case 5: Remanufacturing of constructions machine engines & gas turbines

A US manufacturer of mining machinery, diesel engines and industrial gas turbines and construction machinery remanufactures more than 6,000 of its products including engines, transmissions, hydraulic components and turbochargers at 17 production sites, employing over 4,000 people. In addition to processing its own product line, the company acts as a contract remanufacturer for third-party products and thus offers remanufacturing as a service. At the analysed remanufacturing plant diesel engines from construction machines, gas turbines and military equipment are remanufactured.

The company uses a deposit- or rebate-based take-back system in order to acquire cores. If a customer, or a licensed dealer, buys a remanufactured product, first, the same price as when buying an equivalent new product is paid. This price consists of the actual product price and a deposit for the return of the product. The deposit can be up to 50 % of the price paid and will be refunded to the customer or dealer as soon as the customer returns a similar type of product. If the cores meet all criteria like being complete, having no obvious cracks or break-outs and no independent repair measures have been carried out, the full deposit amount is refunded to the customer. Otherwise, the core will be rejected or the deposit will be repaid partially.

While the engines are returned directly from major customers or via contracted workshops in specifically provided transport boxes the gas turbines are transported to the plant by the customer. The single-item remanufacturing process is triggered by the arrival of a core and begins with an incoming quality check before disassembly. During disassembly, the components are sorted according to type and condition. The process steps are roughly defined for the respective components. The disassembled components lose their affiliation to the original product and are thus reused anonymously, so typically, components of many different products are used in a remanufacturing product. After cleaning and defect detection, all necessary mechanical processing steps are carried out, with the goal to not only restore the original condition but also upgrade the components to the current state of the art. Damaged components are treated with additive processes, to restore worn surfaces or repair microcracks. Ultimately defect components are replaced either by an equivalent remanufacturing part or by a new part. Finally, the engine or the gas turbine is assembled, the product is painted and a final function test is carried out.

3.3 Analysis

Based on the cases described, the following table summarizes the generic options currently available from the OEM remanufacturer to address specific reprocessing uncertainties. The management alternatives described within the six management tasks of the regulatory framework are often found in practice in combination.

Table 1. Generic production management options for remanufacturing-related uncertainties

	Procurement logistics	Remanufacturing operations
Strategic	*Closed-Loop Supply Chain* • Buyback from single customers • Independent core brokers • Long term customer relationships with major customers • Remanufacturing as a service • Contractually agreed repayment • Leasing	*Remanufacturing Scope* • Complete disassembly of cores • Processing of defect parts • Replacement of defect parts • Replacement limited to wear parts • Replacement of old parts with product upgrades
Tactical	*Reverse logistics* • Bulk deliveries from major customers or core brokers • Core collection via sorting centre network • Returns via network authorised dealers or workshops • Core pick-up as part of an integral part of the product-related services • Single item deliveries	*Production design* • Separate remanufacturing facilities • Shared production facility for remanufactured and new product • Flow shop • Job Shop • Fixed-site production • Segmented production
Operative	*Dependent requirements supply* • Make-to-Stock • Make-to-Order • Assembling products from cores and newly produced parts regardless of product history • Product assembly only from own remanufactured or new components • Upgrade of old product versions by (mechanical) processing	*In-house-production planning & control* • Batch production • One-piece flow • Predefined process sequence/times • Variable process sequence/times • Conventional production planning heuristics • Manual definition of remanufacturing requirements

4 Conclusion and outlook

Taking into account the technical, regulatory and market-related boundary conditions, the following management measures result within the six defined fields of action for the qualification of remanufacturing in electric vehicle production. In order to implement the proposed measures, however, further detailed investigations are necessary.

Securing the supply of cores in a *closed-loop supply chain* can be achieved through close customer loyalty by means of circular economy business models. A combination of different options is an appropriate solution depending on the targeted customer groups such as private customers or commercial fleet operators. When leasing vehicles, the OEM remains the owner of the vehicle and can set a defined return date for the vehicle in the contract. Furthermore, it is possible to establish a deposit system in which the purchase price is increased with a premium, which is paid back in addition to the buy-back price after the vehicle is returned. Additionally, an OEM can secure a right of repurchase against the reduction of the purchase price in the purchase agreement. Finally, it is possible to offer buy-back prices above market prices on the free used-car market in order to secure returns.

The automotive industry typically works with a network of authorised dealers, through whom the *reverse logistics* of vehicles can be organized. In the case of affiliated contract workshops, it is possible to carry out the (preliminary) assessment of the condition on-site and to calculate the profitability of the order depending on the condition of the vehicle. The advantage is that vehicles can be sorted out directly when remanufacturing is economically or technically unfeasible to avoid expensive transport to the remanufacturing site.

When remanufacturing electric vehicles, it must be ensured that the *dependent requirements* of remanufacturing orders are covered by components of the original vehicle or by new parts. Therefore, components that are removed and intended for further use are assembled into the same original vehicle. In order to be able to carry out product recalls and warranty measures due to technical problems, the traceability of vehicle parts and the identifiability of their technical design must be ensured in the automotive industry [19]. Recalls typically relate to vehicle production periods. If components from different production periods do not match the production date of the vehicle, the definitive assignment of components to vehicles can only be guaranteed by a very complex data management system. Due to the number of components in a vehicle and the fact that vehicles are subject to constant design changes during ongoing production, the effort required to trace the production and usage history for electric vehicles is disproportionate. In addition, remanufacturing practice shows that customer acceptance of remanufacturing increases significantly when the product returns with the same parts. Consequently, spare parts must be supplied from the series production.

The *remanufacturing scope* results from the product structure of electric vehicles, which consists of core elements that are durable under normal conditions of use and components that wear and age. Consequently, disassembling the entire product and testing all components is likely to involve process steps that do not add value if no additional reprocessing needs are identified. In order to implement efficient production, it is important to design a functioning mechanism for reliable identification of defects and wear.

Electric vehicles have a fixed disassembly sequence, which must be reflected in the *production design* in the form of a sequential order of the stations. Consequently, the stations have a fixed assignment of the disassembly tasks. However, to ensure that only the order-related remanufacturing scope is actually taken into account during disassembly, it must be ensured that only the required stations can be approached. In contrast to disassembly at the vehicle level, removed components such as powertrain, battery pack or axles are completely disassembled, cleaned, inspected, processed if necessary and reassembled in accordance with industrial standards. The configuration of the reassembly corresponds to the disassembly in order to enable the same job-related route flexibility. Capacities are designed because of the defect and wear probabilities based on historic values.

In-house production planning and control is characterized by decisions under uncertainty. Only complex data processing concepts are suitable to guarantee the required efficiency within the described production design. First, a reliable identification of defects must be ensured. Machine learning algorithms that can process a large amount of influence data and independently identify complex dependencies are suitable for such a classification task. This information must then be processed within the scheduling process. The aim of scheduling is to utilize production resources as efficiently as possible and at the same time to react robustly to deviations due to extended process times or additional process steps. Simple planning heuristics do not meet these requirements, which is why the use of genetic algorithms to optimize order processing is expedient for the complexity of this task. To ensure the productivity of the remanufacturing system, the profitability of the single orders must be reassessed if there is a major deviation from the initial planning.

References

1. Ministerium für Umwelt, Forsten und Verbraucherschutz, Ministerium für Wirtschaft, Verkehr, Landwirtschaft, *Kreislaufwirtschaftsland Rheinland-Pfalz,* Mainz, Germany (2008)
2. B. Walsh, R. Waugh, H. Symington, *Circular Economy Evidence Building Programme. Remanufacturing Study Full Report* (2015)
3. P. Barttel, *Triple Win: The social, economic and environmental case for remanufacturing,* London (2014)
4. P. Thomes, A. Kampker, D. Vallée, A. Schnettler, G. Kasperk. In A. Kampker, D. Vallée, A. Schnettler (eds.), *Elektromobilproduktion*, Berlin, Germany: Springer Vieweg, 5–58 (2014)
5. E. Sundin, *Product and process design for successful remanufacturing*, PhD Thesis, Linköping University, Linköping, Sweden (2004)
6. J. Kurilova-Palisaitiene, E. Sundin, B. Poksinska, Remanufacturing challenges and possible lean improvements, *Journal of Cleaner Production* **172**: 3225–3236 (2018)
7. A. Kampker, K. Kreisköther, A. Hollah, C. Lienemann, Electromobile Remanufacturing: Nutzenpotenziale für batterieelektrische Fahrzeuge, *5th Conference on Future Automotive Technology Focus Electromobility, 3-4 May 2016, Fürstenfeld, Germany* (2016)
8. Q. Ke, H. Zhang, L. Liu G., B. Li, Remanufacturing Engineering. Literature Overview and Future Research Needs. In J. Hesselbach, C. Herrmann (eds.), *Glocalized Solutions for Sustainability in Manufacturing,* Berlin, Heidelberg, Germany: Springer, 437-442 (2011)
9. R. Gagnon, S. Morgan, A Literature Review of Remanufacturing Production Planning and Control, *Annual Meeting of the Decision Sciences Institute*, *21-24 November 2015, Seattle, USA* (2015)
10. M.P. Brito, E.A. van der Laan, Inventory control with product returns. The impact of imperfect information, *European Journal of Operational Research* **194**(1): 85–101 (2009)
11. J. Jia, S.H. Xu, V.D.R. Guide, Addressing Supply-Demand Imbalance. Designing Efficient Remanufacturing Strategies, *Production and Operations Management* **25**(11): 1958–1967 (2016)

12. P. Lundmark, E. Sundin, M. Björkman, Industrial Challenges within the Remanufacturing System, *Proceedings of Swedish Production Symposium, 30 November 2009 - 3 December 2009, Gothenburg, Sweden:* 132–138 (2009)
13. M. Matsumoto, S. Yang, K. Martinsen, Y. Kainuma, Trends and research challenges in remanufacturing, *International Journal of Precision Engineering and Manufacturing-Green Technology* **3**(1): 129–142 (2016)
14. R. Frei, A. Bines, I. Lothian, L. Jack, Understanding reverse supply chains, *International Journal of Supply Chain and Operations Resilience* **2**(3): 246–266 (2016)
15. K. Hawks, What is Reverse Logistics?, *Reverse Logistics Magazine* **1**(1): 12-21 (2016)
16. M. Fleischmann, J.M. Bloemhof-Ruwaard, R. Dekker, E. van der Laan, J. A.E.E. van Nunen, L.N. van Wassenhove, Quantitative models for reverse logistics. A review, *European Journal of Operational Research* **103**(1): 1–17 (1997)
17. J. Chaowanapong, J. Jongwanich, W. Ijomah, Factors influencing a firm's decision to conduct remanufacturing. Evidence from the Thai automotive parts industry, *Production Planning & Control* **28**(14): 1139–1151 (2017)
18. Z. Jiang, Z. Fan, J.W. Sutherland, H. Zhang, X. Zhang, Development of an optimal method for remanufacturing process plan selection, *The International Journal of Advanced Manufacturing Technology* **72**(9-12): 1551–1558 (2014)
19. VDA, Vor- und Rückverfolgbarkeit von Fahrzeugteilen und Identifizierbarkeit ihrer technischen Ausführung. *VDA Empfehlungen,* 5005 (2005)

Strategic Risk Management among Small Enterprises in the Construction Industry

Tlangelani Baloyi[1*] and *Aghaegbuna* Ozumba[1]

[1]University of the Witwatersrand, 1 Jan Smuts Ave, Johannesburg 2000, South Africa

Abstract. The purpose of this study is to develop knowledge around the practice of risk-management by small enterprises in the construction sector. The study will discuss the shortfalls in practice, and possible risk-management strategies suggested. This research is a literature review based study. An integrative review of a purposive sample of literature was used to generate articles discussing SMMEs and their business challenges. The search narrowed down to risk management articles with a specific focus on strategic risk management. The significant limitation to the study is the theoretical nature at this stage. Findings, however, suggest that non-systematic risk management in business operations by small enterprises and lack of innovative strategies that accommodate for market competition, hinder their transition to medium enterprises. However, small enterprises that practice strategic risk management stand a better chance of transitioning into medium enterprises because of their better understanding of risks and resource organization.

Keywords: business, enterprise, risk, SMME, strategic risk management.

1 Introduction

Small, Medium and Microenterprises (SMMEs), are important in the economic progression of countries through job creation, and entrepreneurial innovation [1]. Such entities have an employment level of fewer than 250 employees. Small enterprises, in particular, have employees ranging from 5 -100 depending on their country and industry. Any enterprise's development greatly relies on its ability to efficiently manage its risks [2]. Risks will punitively affect an enterprise if adequate mitigation measures are not effectively structured [3]. A common method of managing an enterprise's threats is their risk management plan. Risk management is identified as an essential element in the running of businesses as it helps to yield the highest returns for an enterprise by minimizing unforeseen costs accruable from risks [4]. Strategic risk management, in particular, allows an enterprise to align its management practices to its long-term planning based on its organizational goals and objectives [5]. Risk management is therefore broad and interpreted differently according to the individual knowledge backgrounds. Nevertheless, the strategy chosen to deal with risks

* Corresponding author: 556926@students.wits.ac.za

should fulfil the generic aim of risk management [6]. However, Venturini and Verbano [7] assert that risk management strategies practised by small enterprises are likely to be less effective due to their reduced risk management abilities.

The business for small enterprises in construction occurs in the form of projects secured through bidding processes. The enterprise will bid as a contractor, subcontractor, consultant or special skills experts. The stated nature of business occasions occurs with varying risks [8]. The enterprise needs to develop strategies that enable it to best factor for such risks [9]. However, a manager, owner, or employee will recognize risks according to their cognition of threats [1]. The training and knowledge a manager has about risks, inform their risk management decisions [2]. Unfortunately, for most small enterprises, there is evidence of deficiency in strategic risk management, resulting in slow business development and transition to medium scale enterprises [9]. Consequently, the pertinent research question is: What hinders small enterprises in construction from the effective practice of strategic risk management in their business planning and operations?

Ekwere [4], states that small enterprises have more challenges in practising conventional risk management when compared to medium and large enterprises. They tend to emulate large enterprise practices instead of developing approaches that will match their risk appetite and risk handling capabilities. Thus only a few enterprises practice strategic risk management with proof that it develops the business of small enterprises [6]. Nevertheless, there is a scarcity of information about the general inadequacy of strategic risk management practice by small enterprises. In an emerging economy context such as South Africa, small enterprises are vulnerable to internal structural problems when compared to their counterparts in other developing countries [10]. They lack specialized services and products that they can introduce in the market, and as a result, have to compete with large enterprises to offer the same products and services [11]. The critical emphasis on small business survival and transition in South Africa is highlighted in the relevant literature such as [12] who assert that due to the 26.7% unemployment rate in the country, SMMEs need to create the majority of the needed jobs. This makes small-enterprise development highly critical in such contexts. In the absence of adequate information, there is a need to identify risk management practices gaps by small enterprises in the construction industry. There is also a need to articulate such findings towards suggesting feasible solutions that will assist in developing well adapted long-term strategies to mitigate their business risks. The current study aims to investigate existing risk management practices within the construction industry and assess the barriers hindering small enterprises from the conventional practice, with particular reference to the South African context as a possible setting for empirical data in subsequent stages. The methodology presented hereunder was used in an attempt to achieve the study aim.

2 Methodology

The study is at the preliminary stage of a broader research project. An integrative literature review approach of purposively sampled literature on SMMEs and their business challenges was used. The purposive sampling strategy was used to find articles discussing small enterprises and their development limitations. Articles and papers for the literature review were retrieved from the following databases: Emerald, Google Scholar, Science Direct, and Taylor & Francis. The following keywords were used for searching through databases: Challenges affecting SMMEs, business enterprise, business strategy, risks, risk management, risk management adoption, risk management in SMMEs, risk management in construction, strategic risk management, strategic risk management in small enterprises in construction, market niche, and market niches in construction.

The staged approach to the integrative literature review is as follows:

- A quick perusal of abstracts was conducted to assess the relevance and currency of the papers. The findings in the studied articles demonstrated poor risk management as a barrier to business development and effective running of small enterprises.
- Following the first step, a search for articles discussing how enterprises can effectively practice risk management was conducted.
- In order to relate findings to the construction industry, the literature on strategic risk management in construction was also reviewed.

The stated approach assured alignment to the broader focus of risk management and strategy. The two main knowledge areas were combined to get a more unobstructed view of the challenges around strategic risk management implementation in construction. An annotated literature review table with the following headings was used to summarize essential information from the reviewed papers: Full reference, research problem, consequences of the problem, methods, findings, theory, and relevance of the study. Following an analysis of the information extracted from the review template, available information was grouped under the given headings and resulting sub-headings. Results are presented hereunder.

3 Knowledge from Previous Studies

3.1 Risk

As much as there are various definitions of risk, the common defining attributes are uncertainty and the consequences the risk brings, either positive or negative, to any organizations' objectives [13]. Risk and uncertainty are often used interchangeably. However, they differ on the basis that an enterprise knows risk because its probability can be calculated; whereas, uncertainties cannot be predicted [14]. Risk classification is greatly affected by one's knowledge about risks. Essentially the concept of risk lies in a person's knowledge and valuation of risks, thereby making risk perception a strong factor for risk behaviour [15]. Common types of risk include credit risk, market risk, project risk, business risk, strategic risks, operational risks, reputational risks, liquidity risks, political risk, employee risk, enterprise risk and financial risk [16]. The current study focuses on business risks.

Business risk entails internal and external events of which their uncertainties need to be understood by an enterprise to effectively implement strategies that direct the business to achieve its goals and objectives while maximizing the value for shareholders [11]. Types of business risks include: strategic risk, reputational risk, compliance risk, reputational risk, financial risk and others [15]. Arguably with business risks comes the need for risk management.

3.2 Risk Management

According to Verbano and Venturini [7], risk management (RM) assists enterprises with reducing uncertainty and ensuring continuity in production and market trading whilst maximizing profits through costs reduction. There are various definitions of risk management, for which definitions, the authors have articulated the following origins:

- Risk management involves measuring risks through the use of a geometric mean and distributing it across a set of events that are dependent, to minimize it.

- Economic, monetary losses, damage to property, as a resulting from an inherent uncertainty related to the action taken.
- Regressive and unfavourable outcomes of an incident, which might hinder the success of operating, strategic and monetary goals of an enterprise.

Venturini and Verbano [7] also assert that RM should create value, consist of strategic planning, be systemic and structured, be transparent and inclusive, and be responsive to change, and account for human factors.

Conventional RM procedure explains that all risks need to be identified and known to determine their severity and management style [17]. The risks will then be analyzed and prioritized, to plan for mitigation strategies. An RM professional will need to monitor and evaluate the usefulness of the selected management strategies [18]. The RM process arguably needs to be systematic for efficiency. Mills [19] explains that the greater advantages of a systematic risk management approach include the ability to rank risks, identifying opportunities to improve project performance, and making informed decisions on mitigation plans. It also includes defining the roles of the enterprise and other stakeholders in risk-sharing and transfer. Types of risk management include: Enterprise RM, Operational RM, Currency RM, Financial RM, Market RM, Software RM, RM, Quantitative RM, Commodity RM, Bank RM, Project RM, Integrated RM, Technology RM, IT RM and Strategic RM [11]. The current study is focused on strategic risk management.

Enterprises need adequate RM principles to survive. The requirement can be achieved through long-term planning and strategic thinking [20]. An enterprise needs to identify its risk appetite to develop a hierarchy of strategies [21]. Mainardes et al. [6] highlight that the notion of strategy has been extensively used in the management field and describes anything formulated in a particular environment, to be the course of action in improving a specific aspect of a company based on its goals and objectives. Lechner and Gudmundsson [5] discovered that an enterprise's advancement depends on its entrepreneurial behaviour and the application of competitive strategies in its business planning. Mainardes et al. [6] emphasize however that it is futile to have strategies that will not work for the enterprise, thus it is crucial for new/young enterprises owners to have the capacity to develop and manage strategies that will enable the enterprise to factor out market challenges, reaching their objectives in the short, medium and long terms. The greater advantage brought by strategic risk management to an enterprise is its ability to increase the enterprise's value, especially for enterprises sensitive to market fluctuations [22].

3.2 Risk Management in Construction

Construction businesses face many risks due to in-built uncertainties related to construction projects [20]. Risk management is, therefore, an essential aspect of decision-making processes in construction enterprises [19]. As mostly observed in the industry, the risk is likely to be shifted to small contractors. Their poor long-term planning leaves them financially stranded in such cases [23]. Risk identification is a crucial step in decision making when an enterprise is uncertain about the probability of unforeseen risks [24]. Small contractors will thus need a reliable tool that measures the extent of the potential risk because a precise estimate of risk can be time-consuming [25]. Ranking of the importance of risks differs among developed and developing countries. For example, UK construction enterprises prioritize changes in the initial design, while their counterparts in Ghana prioritize delay in payment from the client [26]. The list of risks in construction includes: natural disasters, subcontractor and supplier issues, equipment damage and theft of tools, building material availability, poorly administered contracts, undefined scopes, drawings that are not complete, management of changes in orders, and poor risk management [27]. The different lines of business for contractors and consultants in construction dictate the prioritization of risks. Contractors will factor in weather, groundworks, contaminants, and construction methods. The hierarchy will differ for consultants. They consider poor communication among team members in a project and inflation when treating their risks [26].

Chileshe and Kikwasi [26] regarding the adaptation of risk assessment and management by SMMEs in Tanzania, present a discussion of the challenges to risk management as identified by other researchers around the globe. Interestingly, developed countries are not exempt from the barriers to the systematic practice of risk management. The table below depicts the findings:

Table 1. Risk Management Adoption for Construction Enterprises around the Globe

Country	Barriers
Hong Kong	Challenges in getting input estimates and their probability assessment; Time constraints; challenges in understanding risk management techniques; IT resources and managerial support.
Korea	The absence of awareness and expertise in risk management practices; Tangible risk-probability calculations.
US	Personal prejudices; traditional norms.
Ghana	Lack of experience; lack of facts and figures, coordination among stakeholders; accessibility of risk-management specialists; time limitations; lack of knowledge and expertise.
UK	Late start to projects; inexperienced employees; attitude towards risk; not robust enough and risk identification incompetency.
Singapore	Competition among SMME contractors; the complexity of analytical tools; lack of prospective benefits; budget deficiency; lack of government legislation; lack of knowledge; lack of trained professionals; lack of time; low-profit margin; and not economical.
Tanzania	Risk management awareness; coordination among project team members; risk management styles; effective use of tools and methods; enterprise strategic objectives; internal and external environment; less qualified risk professionals; client requirements and cooperative culture.

Source: Chileshe and Kikwasi [23]

As seen in the table, the critical challenges to adopting a conventional risk management approach are affected by the poor awareness of risk handling techniques, enterprise managers' lack of risk management, time constraints, inadequately trained risk personnel, and poor budget allocation for risk training and practice. If an enterprise fails to practice conventional risk management, there is little chance of integrating other risk management techniques. In summary, poor adoption RM still poses a great threat to the development of small enterprises.

4 Additional Findings in Literature

- Small and medium enterprises have challenges embracing risk analysis strategies that are qualitative-based due to their reduced knowledge and practice of risk management and lack of trained specialists to perform risk identification [20].
- Construction small enterprises fail to practice systematic risk management because of limited qualitative and quantitative data from previous projects that could enable them to establish a proper risk response strategy for their enterprise [17].

- Identified the top three critical success factors for company success by Turkish construction company managers/owners include: business management, financial conditions, and owner-manager characteristics [28].
- Developing an effective business strategy is critical for business stability when an enterprise is small and undeveloped [5].
- Small enterprises practising strategic risk management stand a better chance at survival if the principles are applied at an organizational level [21].

According to [29] there are options available to construction enterprises to the best factor for risks while maximizing profits and business growth. The following suggestions were made for contractors when designing their risk handling methods:

Table 2. Risk Mitigation Strategies for Construction Enterprises

Risk Response Strategy	Risk Handling Method
Risk avoidance	• Increase unit cost or overhead • Develop substitutes for risk events • Remove risk events by avoiding them
Risk transfer	• Use insurance • Subcontract work • Train and educate staff
Risk mitigation	• Develop a strategic staffing plan • Use proven construction materials and methods • Safeguard both workers and property • Provide best supplies (e.g., computers, equipment, etc.)
Risk-retention	• Prepare contingency planning • Accept profit losses

Source: [29]

5 Discussion

The success of enterprises relies essentially on the implementation of effective risk management. This assertion holds for small enterprises also. However, risk management practices by small enterprises do not seem to be in line with known/conventional approaches, despite given benefits. Essentially there is the case of non-systematic risk management in business operations by small enterprises. They also seem to lack innovative strategies and adequate sensitivity to market competition. Evidence from the literature suggests that small enterprises are currently in need of a holistic risk management approach. A possible solution for their competitiveness and growth is strategic risk management. Enterprises need to develop their risk integrity, and an efficient RM, to maximize organizational goals. In Falkner and Hiebl [2]'s study, a holistic risk management approach is suggested for small enterprises as a measure to bridge the gap between theoretical and practical risk management competencies. In an earlier study, owners and managers of small enterprises, are advised to be sensitive to business and managerial risks when planning and executing business strategies as part of RM [29]. However, there is currently limited research on how small construction enterprises practice risk management in their daily business activities and how this informs decision-making [3]. A notable recommendation to small enterprises as highlighted by Tshikhudo et al. [10] is the need to invest in risk management training programs. Mainardes et al. [6] support this recommendation and state that small enterprises receiving risk management education and training, better inform their business objectives and competitive strategies. It is also advised that small enterprises engage in business collaborations and ventures to maximize their performance, particularly in countries with unstable economies [30].

6 Conclusions

The purpose of this study was to understand risk-management practices by small businesses within the construction sector and the implications. This stage of the study is a literature review. There is, therefore, an opportunity to explore other relevant theories and bodies of knowledge, beyond the current study. Findings from this stage of the research can be summarized thus: Small enterprises that have adopted strategic risk management stand a better chance of survival due to their improved capacity for managing business risks. Furthermore, the emerging relationships of concepts explored in the study also highlight the need for emphasis on niche and aligned business risk strategies, as presented in Figure 1.

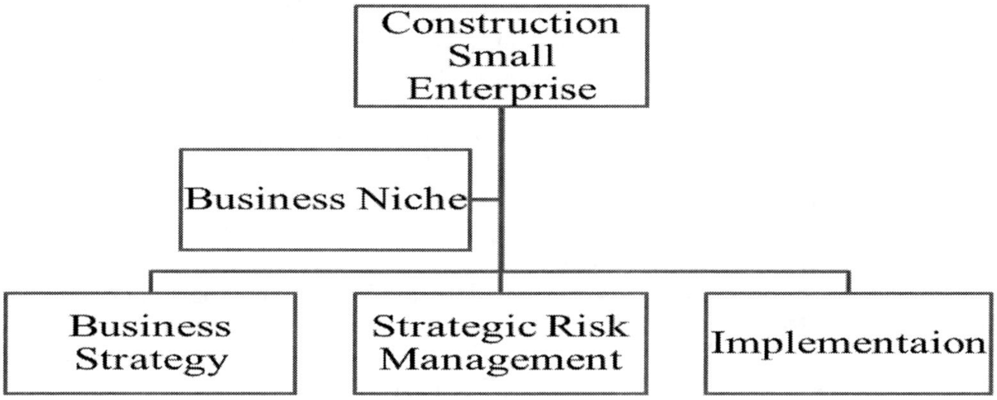

Fig. 1. The proposed relationship of concepts identified in the literature.

Figure 1 shows the emerging relationship of concepts explored in the current study. From Figure 1, small construction enterprises need to develop a specific market product to specialize in. They also need to establish business strategies that will optimize their profits. Since the construction industry is very competitive, it is important for the strategy developed to align with the principles of strategic risk management for an effective business transition.

The stated summation at this stage remains to be given specific cause and effect description. It is necessary to understand how business failure/non-transition to higher levels for small businesses, is inferred by the identified gaps. It is essential to provide the empirical basis for the identified gap and the nature of the impact, for further discussion. The dearth of relevant information in this regard is supported by [31] and [32], and the various suggestions by authors such as Tshikhudo et al. [10] and Kossyva et al. [30]. Future research should focus on empirical studies of challenges to the effective practice of risk management for small enterprises in construction. Such studies should emphasize strategic risk management.

Furthermore, the possible link between business synergies and improvement of strategic risk management practice among small enterprises should be explored. Figure 1 is proposed as the basis for developing a conceptual framework, in the next stages of this research. Regardless of the theoretical nature of the current study, it is very relevant to construction industry development because risk management is a major factor in business growth and competence. The current study has attempted to articulate knowledge on the practice of strategic risk management by small enterprises in construction, which constitutes a knowledge gap area. The current study has also proposed a conceptual relationship which can be utilized as a basis for developing a conceptual framework for empirical studies in the identified knowledge gap.

References

1. T. Mazzarol, D.N. Clark, S. Reboud, Strategy in action: Case studies of strategy, planning and innovation in Australian SMEs, *Small Enterprise Research* **21**(1):54–71 (2014)
2. E.M. Falkner, M.R.W. Hiebl, Risk management in SMEs: a systematic review of available evidence, *The Journal of Risk Finance* **16**(2):122–144 (2015)
3. S. Laryea, W. Hughes, Risk and Price in the Bidding Process of Contractors. Journal of Construction Engineering and Management **137**(4): 248–258 (2011)
4. N. Ekwere, Framework of effective risk management in small and medium enterprises (SMES): A literature review 23–28 (2016)
5. C. Lechner, S.V. Gudmundsson, Entrepreneurial orientation, firm strategy and small firm performance. *International Small Business Journal* **32**(1):36–60 (2014)
6. E.W. Mainardes, J. Ferreira, M.L. Raposo, Strategy and Strategic Management Concepts: Are They Recognised by Management Students? *E+M Ekonomie a Management* **17**(1):43–61 (2014)
7. C. Verbano, K. Venturini, Managing Risks in SMEs: A Literature Review and Research Agenda, *Journal of technology management & innovation* **8**(3):33–34 (2013)
8. Taroun, Towards a better modelling and assessment of construction risk: Insights from a literature review, *International Journal of Project Management* **32**(1):101–115 (2014)
9. M.P. Johnson, Sustainability Management and Small and Medium-Sized Enterprises: Managers' Awareness and Implementation of Innovative Tools: Sustainability Management Tools and SMEs, *Corporate Social Responsibility and Environmental Management* **22**(5):271–285 (2015)
10. L. Tshikhudo, C. Aigbavboa, W. Thwala, Critical Success Factors for the survival of small, medium and micro enterprise construction companies in the South Africa construction industry 5 (2015)
11. Y. Smit, A literature review of small and medium enterprises (SME) risk management practices in South Africa, *African Journal of Business Management* **6**(21) (2012)
12. J. Nonyana, P. Njuho, Modelling the length of time spent in an unemployment in an unemployment state in South Africa, South African Journal of Science **114**(11/12):1–7 (2018)
13. I.J. Dabari, S.Z. Saidin, A Theoretical Framework on the Level of Risk Management Implementation in the Nigerian Banking Sector: The Moderating Effect of Top Management Support, *Procedia - Social and Behavioral Sciences* **164**:627–634 (2014)
14. J.G. Vargas-Hernández, Modeling risk and innovation management, 14 (2011)
15. F. van Winsen, Y. de Mey, L. Lauwers, S. Van Passel, M. Vancauteren, E. Wauters, Determinants of risk behaviour: effects of perceived risks and risk attitude on farmer's adoption of risk management strategies, *Journal of Risk Research* **19**(1):56–78 2016
16. D. Griffin, *Types of Business Risk* (2018), Smallbusiness.chron.com. Available from: https://smallbusiness.chron.com/types-business-risk-99.html [Accessed 29 Jun. 2018].
17. A.F. Serpella, X. Ferrada, R. Howard, L. Rubio, Risk Management in Construction Projects: A Knowledge-based Approach, *Procedia - Social and Behavioral Sciences* **119**:653–662 (2014)
18. L. Williams, *Risk Management* 1-3 (2004)

19. Mills, A systematic approach to risk management for construction, *Structural Survey* **19**(5):245–252 (2001)
20. Y. Yoon, Z. Tamer, M. Hastak, Protocol to Enhance Profitability by Managing Risks in Construction Projects, *Journal of Management in Engineering* **31**(5):04014090 (2015)
21. C. Adendorff, G. Appels, B. Botha, Strategic management: An Eastern Cape construction SME case study, *Strategic management* 24 (2011)
22. S.W. Rawls, C.W. Smithson, Strategic risk management, *Journal of Applied Corporate Finance* **2**(4):6–18 (1990)
23. M. Hardie, Influences on innovation in small Australian construction businesses, *Journal of Small Business and Enterprise Development* **17**(3):387–402 (2010)
24. A.A.G. Hassanein, H.M.F. Affify, *Risk management for contractors: a case study of power station projects in Egypt* **12**(3): 165–179 (2007)
25. Jannadi, S. Almishari, Risk Assessment in Construction, *Journal of Construction Engineering and Management* **129**(5):492–495 (2003)
26. N. Chileshe, G.J. Kikwasi, Risk assessment and management practices (RAMP) within F. Racher, Over Promising, Under Delivery, Why Your Approach to Bidding Could Be Killing Your Business (2015) [Online] Available from: http://www.riskdecisions.com/risk-analysis-for-winning-bids/ [Accessed 16 October 2017].
27. the Tanzania construction industry: Implementation barriers and advocated solutions, *International Journal of Construction Management* **14**(4):239–254 (2014)
28. K. Jones, 4 Common Risk Factors on Construction Projects, *ConstructConnect.com.* [online] ConstructConnect.com. Available from: https://www.constructconnect.com/blog/operating-insights/4-common-risk-factors-on-construction-projects/ [Accessed 31 Jul. 2018]
29. G. Arslan, S. Kivrak, Critical Factors to Company Success in the Construction Industry **2**(9):4 (2008)
30. D. Berkeley, P.C. Humphreys, R.D. Thomas, Project risk action management, *Construction Management and Economics* **9**(1):3–17 (1991)
31. D. Kossyva, K. Sarri, N. Georgopoulos, Co-opetition: A business strategy for SMES in times of economic crisis 18 (2014)
32. N. Georgopoulos, D. Kossyva, K. Sarri, Co-epitition: A Business Strategy for SMEs in times of crisis, South-Eastern Europe Journal of Economics **1**: 89–90 (2014)

Success Factors for Effective Contractor-led Stakeholder Relationship Management: Perspectives from the Botswana Construction Industry

Marian Taimu[1*], *Bankole* Awuzie[2], and *Alfred* Ngowi[2]

[1] School of Business, Plot 50661, Fairgrounds, Gaborone, Botswana
[2] Central University of Technology, Private Bag X20539, Bloemfontein 9300, South Africa

Abstract. Stakeholder relationship management (SRM) remains critical to the attainment of successful project outcomes. This is particularly the case in the construction industry: an industry often described as considerably fragmented and project-based with a multiplicity of stakeholders with vested interests. Burgeoning incidences of project failure has been attributed to poor SRM. A lot of studies investigating stakeholder management exist, yet a paucity of studies looking into SRM has been noticed. Most of these studies have sought to investigate the phenomenon from a client perspective without taking cognizance of the contractor's role in SRM. Also, the tendency of these studies to overlook stakeholder dynamics as it concerns power, uncertainty, etc. during various stages of the project lifecycle is observed. These are the gaps which this study will seek to fill relying on the customer relationship model (CRM) theoretical lens. A multi-case study research design is proposed. Different contractor organizations were selected based on a set of predetermined criteria. A plethora of within-case interviews and document reviews will be utilized in eliciting data concerning the approach adopted by construction contractors for managing extant relationships with critical stakeholders. The data was analysed thematically. It is expected that success factors will result from the elicited narratives. The following success factors for effective management of stakeholder relationship management emerged from the interviews and documents: Communication, understanding of stakeholders, the different types of stakeholders and type of project, management, and interpersonal skills, collaboration, engagement, and conflict management. This artefact will be compared to different CRM models to identify probable success factors for engendering effective stakeholder relationship management. Furthermore, the study's findings will seek to contribute towards the development of a contractor-centric stakeholder relationship management framework for the Botswana construction industry.

Keywords: Botswana, Case studies, Construction, Customer Relationship Management, Stakeholder

* Corresponding author: mataimu@gmail.com

Introduction

Globally, construction industry clients have continued to grapple with increasing rates of dissatisfaction with project delivery outputs. The burgeoning rates of dissatisfaction have continued despite several interventions of industry stakeholders at different intervals and across geographical contexts. The largely fragmented and task-oriented nature of the industry, the fixation of inherent management techniques on the project delivery process instead of the functionality and utility of the project to the client as well as the opportunistic behaviour exhibited by project stakeholders have served, singularly or as a combination, to undermine the aspirations of industry clients, hence the dissatisfaction experienced. The scenario painted above is not peculiar to the developed world context but its predominance in the developing world context is troubling. This is particularly the case as countries in the latter require and are constantly commissioning new projects to meet their commitments to their citizenry in terms of improved welfare, productivity levels as well as national competitiveness. This aspiration has led to increased national borrowing and indebtedness, hence the need to ensure that projects deliver on their outline/original business cases. The debate on project management success and project success are yet inconclusive as both aspects are critical to engendering client satisfaction. Botswana happens to be one of such countries, classified as developing and in dire need for significant investments in infrastructure. As such, the onus falls on the local construction industry to provide the formwork for achieving this objective through efficient delivery of infrastructure and other ancillary services. The criticality of the industry to this venture cannot be overemphasized.

However, available evidence indicates that the Botswana construction industry has been unable to provide this support in a manner that is congruent with increasing levels of client satisfaction. Also, this shortcoming has negated the growth of the construction industry as clients are increasingly wary of inaugurating new projects, culminating in low receipts for the industry and indirectly impeding economic growth. In as much as certain studies have aligned themselves with previous studies which blame the nature of the construction industry and attitude of the stakeholders, particularly the client and the contractor, as constituting a hindrance to effective project delivery in Botswana, others have blamed the lack of skills and finance as failure factors bedevilling the industry. Furthermore, other studies have identified poor stakeholder management models or approaches applied by project teams as a salient failure factor [1-10].

Also, contracting organizations have been at the receiving end for the heightening levels of client dissatisfaction observed in the industry. This much is buttressed in a study by BIDP [11] wherein it was stated that: *"Delays are common to construction projects in Botswana and contractors have often been unfairly singled out as the main culprits even when the delay was of a much more complex problem involving several stakeholders"*. This implies that contractors and contracting organizations in construction have a salient role to play in engendering improved project delivery via effective management of relationships with stakeholders. It must be acknowledged that whilst all the points raised in the literature remain valid, the extant literature on the management of stakeholders appears to be fixated on a static and dogmatic approach to stakeholder relationship management. A cursory look at the industry and the plethora of contractual arrangements governing the relationships reveal the sub-optimal nature of such static and dogmatic approaches for obvious reasons. However, a paucity of studies seeking, both to challenge the inadequacy of extant models and explore nascent ways of managing stakeholder relationships by contracting organizations in the Botswana construction industry and elsewhere has been noticed. This observation makes this study imperative.

The construction industry is renowned for adopting processes for continuous improvement from other industrial sectors. Such innovative steps have culminated in new taxonomies like lean construction, servitization, etc. Taking a cue from such precursors, this study attempts to explore the utility of the extant customer relationship model (CRM) in bridging the gaps observed in the extant stakeholder management models. To do this effectively, this study will seek to explore the difference between stakeholder relationships and customer relationships and the management thereof. In furtherance to this, it is expected that elicitation of the success factors for optimal stakeholder relationship management by contractors will ensue following from a review of both approaches and the nature of construction project stakeholders. The problem statement of the study is to find the success factors for effective stakeholder relationship management in the context of Botswana's construction industry. The research question is what are the success factors for the effective management of stakeholder relationships for contractor firms in the Botswana construction industry? Based on the foregoing and seeming inability of the extant SRM models to cater effectively for the dynamics experienced by the contractors in the management of stakeholder relationships in construction projects, this study seeks to explore the utility of CRM models in catering to this gap.

2 Literature Review

2.1 Concept of Customer Relationship management

Oluseye [12] refers to the term relationship management as the process of managing the relationships between a firm and its internal and external publics. Since the inception of Customer Relationship Management (CRM) in the early 1990s, many attempts have been made to succinctly define the concept. One of the most comprehensive definitions cited by Buttle [13] is that 'CRM is an integrated approach to identifying, acquiring and retaining customers. Further to that Buttle [13] also defines CRM as the core business strategy that incorporates internal processes and functions, and external networks, to create and deliver value to targeted customers at a profit. Berndt and Tait [14] argue that the customer is jointly involved in adding value, thus more creative ideas are produced, and deeper relationships are built with them. Working with the customer and building relation through the project life cycle is an important aspect of project success.

2.1.1 CRM in the Construction Industry

Customer relationship management (CRM) is the all-inclusive process of building and maintaining profitable customer relationships in delivering superior value and satisfaction, dealing with acquiring, keeping and increasing consumers. Berndt and Tait [14] argue that the customer is jointly involved in adding value, thus more creative ideas are produced, and deeper relationships are built with them. CRM is a powerful concept to align the interests of a company and its customers [15]. CRM in the construction is mostly applied in the western world in comparison to Africa, Botswana. Stakeholder Relationship management in the construction industry is a relatively new phenomenon.

2.1.2 Construction Industry and Customer Relationship Management in Botswana

The construction industry in Botswana has had phenomenal growth, particularly in the last two decades. However, it has also experienced some problems and still faces numerous challenges, among them, human resource development, capacity development, and lack of competitiveness for citizen firms. According to Keaketswe [16], the construction industry has provided infrastructural support for the economy. Ssegawa-Kaggwa et al. [17] grouped the players in the construction industry into four categories mainly suppliers, regulators, clients, and facilitators.

2.1.3 CRM Models

There are numerous CRM models in existence CRM and these include Gartner's CRM Performance Scorecard [18], Forrester CRM Model [19], Conceptual Model (from [20]); The Strategic Model for CRM [21], The CRM Value Chain [13], the QCI Customer Management Model [22]. For this study, only three models will be discussed below.

The table below summaries a number of models that are found in customer relationship management. This IDIC model offers a simple way of relating with customers and it may be useful in construction, this is so because in construction there is always customisation of the end product to the customer's needs. The model identifies four actions that are needed to have a good relationship with the customer which are to identify the customer, differentiating the customer first by value and then secondly by need, interaction with the customer according to their needs and values and lastly to customise the final product to the specification of the customers' requirements. Strategy, Process, Technology, and People are the four types of groups by the Forrester CRM Model. The model is useful for kick-starting CRM programs for an organization that want to launch a CRM program [19]. This model will be able to help firms that find challenges in implementing the CRM. The Gartner's CRM Maturity model enables the firm to know where they are at the present and where they want to be over a period of time, what the requirement they will need to achieve that status of where they want to be [18].

2.2 Customer Relationship Models

Table 1. Summary of CRM models

CRM Models	Scholars	Relationship Management	Contractors use of model (Analysis)
CRM Value Chain	Buttle [13]	Analysis of customer	Contractor to provide supporting conditions
The QCI CRM	Hewson [22]	Variety of activities to acquire and retain customers	Contractors need of technology to manage relations
Gartner's Crm Performance Scoreboard	IDM [18]	Consideration of strategy, processes, technology and people	Help contractors that find it challenging to implement CRM
IDIC Model	Pepper and Rodgers [23]	Identify, Differentiate Interaction and Customize customer requirements	Contractors to customize the product to the customers© specifications.
The Strategic Model for Crm	Payne [21]	5 stages used to manage relations, Strategy process, Value creation, Multichannel integration, Performance assessment and information management	Contractors may tally the five stages with the project life cycle from inception to end user in order to manage relations
Conceptual Model	Desai [20]	Linking the relationship between dynamic	Contractors may be able to try the direct

		capability for CRM and competitive CRM performance	competences of the IT variables see if they make a change to CRM
Forrester Crm Model	Forrester [19]	4 classes to manage relations, Strategy, Process, Technology and People	Helps contractors that find challenges in implementing the CRM

2.3 Understanding the Dichotomy between Stakeholder and Customers

Construction project stakeholders would normally comprise of owners and users of facilities, project managers, employees, suppliers, visitors, suppliers, shareholder, subcontractors, banks, insurance companies, competitors, process and service providers, media, pressure groups, civic institutions, regional development agencies, the press, the natural environment, general public, community representatives, etc. Magliolo [24] eliminates the confusion between stakeholders and customers for projects as the customers have also been referred to as stakeholders. A customer can be described as any party that would be affected by a new product, including the main customers in the execution of the projects. Also, they may have both positive and negative implications on the project [24]. For this study, the customers include the above-mentioned stakeholders. The study will seek to view stakeholders like customers and the shareholders in the contracting firms. Relationships with the customer/s is key aspect in the business world and more so for the construction industry where there are projects with life cycles and different stakeholders at each stage. Future developments of the stakeholder theory should acknowledge that there is a lack of models to manage stakeholder relationships more efficiently [1]. Thus, the basis of this study will be underpinned by Customer Relationship Management (CRM) theoretical lenses as various models in CRM may be able to provide probable success. There is a range of definitions for CRM however for purposes of this study the following shall suffice, "CRM is a dynamic process of managing customers company relationships such that customers elect to continue mutually beneficial commercial exchange and are dissuade from participating in exchange that is not profitable".

2.4 Significance of Stakeholders

Weiss [25] defines a stake from stakeholder as a share or interest and the stakeholder being the individual with the stake. A contracting firm has many stakeholders who affect its operations and these contractors are in turn affected by the project. These consist of those which provide inputs (such as suppliers, society, financiers); regulatory bodies such the government; the community; owners (concerned with profits and survival of the firm or project); facilitators (e.g. employees, lawyers and financial advisers) and the customer who is the receiver of the final project. All these stakeholders need to have their concerns taken into consideration to avoid conflict that may hinder the progression and success of the project.

2.5 Stakeholder Relationship Management

Considering stakeholder management in the construction industry, the question of "Why does a project manager adopt a stakeholder management approach?" should be answered in advance [26]. Stakeholders being people the project manager will work with, must have their strategic and management processes to achieve success in the project. This may be achieved by managing relations with the stakeholders aiming for progression and success within the project. A construction project comprises of a series of complex activities. Bourne [2] observed that the project's success or failure was strongly influenced by both the expectations and perceptions of its stakeholders, and the capability and willingness of project managers to manage organizational politics. From previous studies, it can be found that stakeholder management is important in managing construction projects, and the reasons of managing stakeholders in construction projects include: Firstly, that the construction projects are complicated with many process and parties involved and secondly the relationships among stakeholders in construction projects are temporary [26]. Considering that the construction project is temporary and unique, relations with stakeholders need to be managed effectively to avoid conflicts that will lead to failure or abandonment of the project. Stakeholders are critical for a project's success thus it is of paramount importance to monitor them as they change positions during the life cycle of the project's progression [27].

Bourne [28] admits the importance of the processes supporting effective communication to the mission of building and maintaining healthy relationships with organizational stakeholders, through analysis of a case study – that of the construction and opening of Heathrow Terminal 5. The Heathrow T5 project was deemed to be one of the most successful projects because of innovative project management practices that focused on collaboration, cost £4.3bn.

Bourne [28] argues that for effective stakeholder relationship management the organization must be ready to absorb the new processes and practices further to that it must be fully developed, sensible and reliable and this defines maturity.

Six attributes have been identified as critical to the development of that a stakeholder relationship management model. They include: Standard Process, Centralized support Improvements in stakeholder relationship management a part of Key Performance Indicators, Organization-wide implementation, Developing Baseline and Proactive reporting on stakeholder relationship [28].

These attributes are used to determine the SRRM level form 1 to 5 with level 5 being the highest level. Level 5 shows that the organization can achieve all the five attributes within their projects.

3 Research Method

The study adopted a qualitative approach to investigates the phenomenon outlined previously. The case study strategy was deployed to develop an in-depth understanding of the phenomenon [29]. Three case studies where conveniently sampled from the building and construction works contractors. A total of 7 within the case- interviews were conducted. Relevant documents used by the contractors were availed for purposes of the report.

3.1 Background of Case Studies

Three privately owned contracting companies in the building category in Gaborone, Botswana were purposively selected. The cases were chosen based on their willingness to participate in the study. Convenience sampling was used. The cases were predetermined and selected on the basis of small, medium and large contracting firms based on grade. Case 1 is a small contracting firm, Case 2 a medium contracting firm and Case 3 a large contracting firm by grade. Recruitment calls were made to different contracting firms whose numbers were available on the integrated procurement management system-IPMS online Public Procurement and Asset Disposal Board (PPADB) website. The PPADB has the obligation to register contractors intending to bid for Central Government's procurement and asset disposal in respect of these three disciplines, works, supplies and services [30]. With the participant's consent, interviews were scheduled. Table 1: below summaries the characteristics of the three cases. Case numbers are used to protect the identity of the participating contracting firms and interviewees due to confidentiality reasons.

Table 2. Summary of the case study characteristics

Case	Grade	Projects	Position	Code
1	A	1	Owner	PM1A
1			Assistant Project Manager	PM1B
2	C	2	Contractor Manager	PM2A
2			Project Manager	PM2B
3	E	6	Project Manager	PM3A
3			Project Manager	PM3B
3			Construction Site Manager	PM3C

There are 10 types of ownership in contracting firms in Botswana ranging from 100% citizenship to 100% foreign, joint ventures and other types of ownership fall in between the two. Emphases are on empowering citizens in the construction industry. The contractor grades start from OC being the lowest grade A, B, C, D and E with E being the highest grade in accordance with their financial capability to fulfil the demands of the project.

Although the cases had contracts with different disciplines, the study focused on the Building and maintenance code underworks. Thou filed documents from previous projects were used, Case 1 2 and 3 had 1,2, and 6 projects respectively taking place at the time of the research.

3.2 Data Collection

Seven interviews of the Project Managers or similar position which had a role in managing the different stakeholders in their relevant projects within the contracting firm. A variety of semi-structured questions and in some cases unstructured were asked. Being a study that may be relatively new in the Botswana context a convenience sampling was used. These respondents were all permanent employees in the sampled constructing firms. Interviews were done in three months at the convenience of the participant.

During the interviews, notes were taken by the researcher and also recoding of the interviews was done through a voice recorder. Documents that were availed were those that were not confidential such as tender documents of past tenders and files for previous projects completed.

3.3 Data Analysis

Data were analyzed thematically relying on guidelines from Braun and Clarke [31]. The data from the three contractor cases were transcribed and to check for “accuracy” the researcher listened to the recordings on the voice recorder. The notes from the interviews and the documents from the contractors were read and re-read to obtain an appropriate level of detail for the study. The data that was generated from the transcription phase led to the coding phase which was comprehensive and thorough. The codes showed data that was relevant to the research question. There were repeated patterns of checking with the original data and the themes that were emerging. Thematic maps helped the research to draw themes from the codes, the maps helped to see links and visualize relationships between the themes [31].

The next stage of analysis of the data was interpreted and provided an organized story about the data and topic.

4 Discussion of Findings

4.1 Presentation of findings

The following success factors for effective management of stakeholder relationship management emerged from the interviews and documents: Communication, Understanding of changing dynamics of stakeholders, the stakeholders, and type of project, management skills, collaboration, engagement, and conflict management.

Table 3. Narration of respondents

Theme	Case	Quotes	Interviewee Source
Communication	1	*Communication is very important, …….customer wants to save time and costs*"	PM1A
Understanding of the changing dynamics of stakeholders	2	The *general public, clients, ………general stakeholders, and we have a generally positive relationship with them but at times things do get out of shape during the project.*	PM2B
Identification of stakeholder/type of project	1	*"The government projects are currently the best type ……… the private clients usually present problems when it comes to payment.*"	PM1B
Collaboration	3	*Sometimes we take a long time asking for drawings from government departments".*	PM3B
Management support	2	*"We do not have any theoretical model that we follow".*	PM2A
Interpersonal Skills	3	"*We have a special position….who takes care of all documentation, we always have meetings with our customers and final decisions are done by management".*	PM3A
Engagement	3	*"We always hold a meeting for us to maintain good practices when it comes to stakeholder management, they become committed and work with us".*	PM3C
Conflict Management	1	*"When we are building for private clients, it is always best we avoid building for family and friends."*	PM1A
Supporting environment	3	*" The industry has a long way to go, it has great potential. There is a need for more support from government departments".*	PM3B

The table above gives a narration of the respondents from the interviews conducted. Bourne [28] defines communication as the primary tool for stakeholder relationships. Factors that can influence the effectiveness of communication and can include the relationship between the sender and the receiver, personal preferences, and cultural differences. Communication came out as one of the themes that are key when building or maintaining relationships with stakeholders. This theme emerged in all the data provided by the participants. There was an emphasis to be on the same understanding of the various issues that come up in the project. Communication is important both internally and externally in the contracting firm. Internally for the processes and progression of the project with the contracting firm and externally to monitor the environment. The above quotes on the table support that it is important to have effective communication plans with the various stakeholders during the life cycle of the project.

4.2 Understanding the changing dynamics of stakeholders during the different stages of the project.

Chinyio [27] states that for each project to avoid any negative effects, there is a need to monitor the stakeholders and their stakes and respond to their dynamism. Being able to identify all the possible stakeholders that are within the confinements of the project was found to be important. All the cases were supportive that it is at the beginning of the project that stakeholders should be prioritized for the project to succeed. Another highlight was the fact that stakeholder priority and responsibility changes at different stages of the project life cycle as their power, interest, and urgency differed across the progression of the projects [27].

4.3 Identification of stakeholders and the type of project

The type of project that the contractor will be working on, will involve a different community of stakeholders and will also call for a different strategy to manage the relations. Also, the procurement method affects the project whether it is designed and build or traditional there are different stakeholders involved and these should be identified as per project. In comparison to the IDIC model, this finding aligns with the steps of the model.

4.4 Management Support and Interpersonal skills

Involvement by management from a strategic level and all other employees in the firm. Having an alignment of the stakeholder's interests with the requirements for the project to succeed. With the guidance of management relations within the progress of the project can be checked consistently and monitored throughout the project. Thacker [32] within the context of construction projects who pointed out that "Stakeholders make or break a project, and often Project Managers do not spend the time to **effectively manage the stakeholder relationship** – to the project's disadvantage. To be successful, Project Managers need to learn how to leverage the stakeholder relationship and how to balance their competing needs". Even thou interviewees had no knowledge of CRM and SRM from a theoretical perspective, certain practices and showed that they had ways of managing relations from a practical point of view. When inquired they had any documented CRM or SRM strategies. Case 2 replied, "*We do not have any theoretical model that we follow*." Management can also keep a database of all the relations they had with different projects as a reference to improve bad relations or maintain good relations in the coming projects.

4.5 Engagement

Including all or representatives of the stakeholders that would have been identified as those that would possibly have an influence that may affect relations within the project. Engaging the stakeholders in hearing their viewpoints and making them see their contribution to the success of the project.

4.6 Conflict management

Conflicts are unavoidable in situations where there are different stakeholders with different interests or stakes that need to be met. If left unmanaged conflicts can harm the relations with various stakeholder and this consequently may affect the value of the firm. Gibson [33] supports this aspect by concluding that stakeholders have the power to be either a benefit or a threat to the organization.

4.7 Collaboration

Karlsen et. al [34] assert that collaboration is the best alternative for the stakeholders who have a high potential to affect the project, these stakeholders need to be closely worked with and always kept satisfied. Working together in the industry with all stakeholders with a common goal of progression and project success. In some instances, the contractors have a difficult time with certain government departments, policies and legal frameworks that delay the progression of their projects thus damaging relations with affected stakeholders.

4.8 Supporting environment for the industry

There was a different perception of the industry in Botswana from the three cases, mainly possibly because they are all in different grades and see the industry from the lenses of the grade they are in. Having a baseline that supports the industry for the country as a whole was found to be key. With a supportive business environment and probably a construction body such as the Construction Industry Development Board (CIBD), the contractors may be able to effectively manage their stakeholders. Ssegawa-Kaggwa-Kaggwa [35] supports this theme by stating that one of the reasons behind Botswana's inadequate capacity is the ineffective structure and organization of the construction industry characterized by constraints such as unavailability, insufficient or inappropriate use of resources, functions, and institutions.

5 Conclusions

This paper had success factors that emerged from the themes of the three case studies in the construction industry of Botswana. This highlights that the industry is currently fragmented and there is a need for all affected stakeholders to participate in creating good relations for the success of the projects. Some of the factors are well-known in literature as having relevance to the management of stakeholder relationships such as communication. The firms all agreed that managing relations with stakeholders is important Case 1 and 2 did not have any framework that provides guidelines for effective management of stakeholders they just take each case as it comes. Usually, the front office is the one that is first to meet or communicate with the different stakeholders. Case 3 had a more formal structure that deals with stakeholder's relationships and has an assigned person. Awareness of any formal models for SRM and CRM models was limited to none in all cases. It is recommended that the Industry is made aware of such models and adopt those that are applicable for their specific projects. Further studies in different regions in Botswana on SRM in the construction industry is encouraged, it is expected that future research would show more knowledge and insight into this study.

Reference

1. R.E. Freeman, Strategic Management: A stakeholder Approach (Pittman Publishing Company, Boston, 1984)
2. L. Bourne, and D. H.T. Walker, *Visualising and mapping stakeholder influence*, Management Decision, **43(5)**: 649–660 (2005)
3. T. Donaldson, and L.E. Preston, *The stakeholder theory of the corporation: Concepts, evidence, and implications*, The Academy of Management Review **20(1)**, 65-91 (1995)
4. A.L. Friedman, and S. Miles, *Developing Stakeholder Theory*, Journal of Management Studies **39**: 1-21 (2002)

5. R. Phillips, R., Stakeholder Theory and Organizational Ethics (Berrett-Koehler, San Francisco CA, 2003)
6. D.I. Cleland, *Project Stakeholder Management,* Project Management Journal **17(4)**: 36-44 (1986)
7. J. Yang, Q.P. Shen, L. Bourne, M.F. Ho, and X.L. Xue, *A typology of operational approaches for stakeholder analysis and engagement: findings from Hong Kong and Australia*, Constr. Manag. Econ. **29(2)**: 145–162 (2011)
8. J. Frooman, *Stakeholder influence strategies* The Academy of Management Review 24(2): 191–205 (1999)
9. J. Nasi, Understanding Stakeholder Thinking (LSR-Julkaisut Oy, Helsinki, 1995)
10. T.J. Rowley, *Moving BEYOND Dyadic Ties: A Network of Stakeholder Influences*, Academy of Management Review **22(4)**: 887-910 (1997)
11. BIDP, Botswana Institute of Development Professionals, *Delays, Disruptions and Suspensions in Construction contracts*, http://bidp.bw/?q=node/13 (2015)
12. O.O. Oluseye, B.T. Tairat, and J.T. Emmanuel, *Customer Relationship Management Approach and Student Satisfaction*, Higher Education Marketing 6(3): 49-62 (2014)
13. F. Buttle, Customer relationship management: Concepts and technologies (Elsevier Butterworth-Heinemann, Burlington MA, 2009)
14. A. Berndt, and M. Tait, Relationship Marketing and Customer Relationship Management, 3rd Edition (Juta Academic, 2014)
15. W. Boulding, R. Staelin, M. Ehret, and W.J. Johnston, *A Customer Relationship Management Roadmap: What is Known, Potential Pitfalls, and Where to Go*, Journal of Marketing **69(4)**: 155–166 (2005)
16. K. Keaketswe Botswana Press Agency,(BOPA) http://www.dailynews.gov.bw/mobile/news-details.php?nid=24042&flag=5 (2015)
17. J. Ssegawa-Kaggwa, A.B. Ngowi, and K. Ntshwene, *Using a Situation Analysis to Identify the Construction Industry Deficiencies in Botswana*, Journal of Construction in Developing Countries **18(1)**:1–18 (2013)
18. IDM, Institute of Direct Marketing, The IDM Guide to CRM Mastery (2002)
19. Forrester Research, Forrester's Best Practices Framework for CRM (2007)
20. D. Desai, S. Sahu, and P.K. Sinha, Role of dynamic capability and information technology in customer relationship management: A study of Indian companies, Vikalpa **32(4)**: 45-62 (207)
21. A. Payne, and P. Frow, *Customer relationship management: from strategy to implementation*, Journal of Marketing Management **22(1-2)**: 135-168 (2006)
22. Hewson Group, CRM in the public sector, http://www.hewson.co.uk (2002)
23. D. Pepper, and M. Rodgers, Managing Customer Relationships: A Strategic Framework (Jon Wiley &Sons,Inc,, Hoboken NJ, 2004)
24. J.M. Magliolo, The guerilla principle - winning tactícts for Global Project Managers, 1st Edition (Juta and Company, 2008)
25. J.W. Weiss, Business Ethics - A stakeholder and Issues Management Approach, 4th Edition (Mason Thomson Higher Education, 2006)
26. J. Yang, Q. Shen, and M. Ho, *An overview of previous studies in stakeholder management and its implications for the construction industry*, Journal of Facilities Management **7(2)**: 159-175 (2009)
27. E.A. Chinyio, and P. Olomolaiye, *Construction stakeholder management* (Wiley-Blackwell, Oxford, England, 2010)
28. L. Bourne, Stakeholder Relationship Management: A Maturity Model for Organisational Implementation (Routledge, 2009)
29. R.K. Yin, Case study research, Design and methods, 4th Edition (Sage, 2009)

30. PPADB, Public Procurement Asset Development Board, http://www.ppadb.co.bw/ (2016)
31. V. Braun, and V. Clarke, *Using thematic analysis in psychology*, Qualitative Research in Psychology **3(2)**: 77–101 (2006)
32. A. Thacker, The relationship manager (CreateSpace Independent Publishing Platform, 2017)
33. K. Gibson, *The moral basis of stakeholder theory*, Journal of Business Ethics **26(3)** :245-257 (2000)
34. .J.T Karlsen, K. Græe, and M.J. Massaoud, *Building Trust in Project – Stakeholder Relationships*, Baltic Management Journal **3(1)**:7-23 (2008)
35. J. Ssegawa-Kaggwa, *Construction industry's contribution towards Botswana's vision 2016*, 15th Annual ARCOM Conference, Liverpool, 15-17 September 1999

Sustainability in Project Management Practice

Aghaegbuna *Ozumba*[1*], Tasmiyah *Chothia* [1], Zanoxolo *Booi*[1] and Nikiwe *Madonsela* [1]

[1]University of the Witwatersrand, 1 Jan Smuts Ave, Johannesburg 2000, South Africa

Abstract. The study focused on the application of sustainability in project management, with reference to attendant difficulties experienced, which affect the goal of achieving sustainability outcomes in project management. As such the study explored the nature and occurrence of challenges to the integration of sustainability principles with PM practice. A review of purposively sampled literature was complemented with fieldwork, which involved an online questionnaire with eighty-nine participants, to collect qualitative data, using South Africa as context. The major limitation was the purposive use of professional project managers as a sample population. The findings reveal that project managers experience significant challenges when implementing sustainability in their practice. While confirming deductions from the literature review, findings suggest that the most significant challenge may be the lack of information among participants and other stakeholders. One major implication is that other identified difficulties may be traceable to the same lack of knowledge in the subject area. Identified consequences include delayed projects and complete abandonment of the sustainability principles in projects. The integration of sustainability principles with project management practice is a growing niche area of project management knowledge. The study contributes a unique exploration of nature and occurrence, and dynamics of attendant challenges, through a comparison of experience and perception. The comparison has highlighted the differences between the experience and perception of project managers, with reference to the application of sustainability principles.

Keywords: challenges, knowledge, practice, project management, sustainability

1 Introduction

The research interest here is the apparent challenge faced by project managers in practising sustainable construction. Essentially the challenges faced when incorporating the relevant sustainability principles in project management (PM) practice. Sustainability is the general principle of a balanced approach to development which considers the three-fold perspective of the environment, people, and the economy [1]. The increasing global sensitivity towards sustainability has resulted in the effort by industries to research and establish effective

* Corresponding author: Obinna.Ozumba@wits.ac.za

methods to incorporate the relevant principles in their processes [2]. The built environment is a major contributor to economy and employment, which also has a profound negative impact on the people, and the biophysical environment. In view of the implications, the construction industry has made efforts to incorporate sustainability into design, procurement, and construction processes [3]. The growing interest in applying sustainability in construction projects has been reported in the literature such as Kivilä et al. [4]. There is also evidence in the literature, of the growing discourse and efforts in the application of sustainability to construction project management such as Yu et al. [5], Doskočil and Lacko [6] and Zavadskas et al. [7]. Since construction runs by projects, it follows that relevant sustainability principles would have to be integrated with project management practice, to achieve the aim. According to Bocchini et al. [8], this is a means to positively introduce sustainability in construction projects. Marcelino-Sádabaa et al. [2] had proposed PM as a largely unexploited vehicle for the achievement of sustainability.

2 Sustainability and Project Management

By nature, sustainability is focused on the long-term view of any situation, seeking to integrate the social, environmental and economic aspects of a project. Conversely, PM is focused on the project duration, seeking to achieve the desired time, cost and quality specifications of the project. However, according to Silvius et al. [9] the application of sustainability in PM considers the whole life-cycle of the project. It is also suspected that the integration of economic, environmental and social aspects in the management of projects may occasion changes in the project management profession. Project managers (PMs) are said to be concerned that such integration will affect project management practices and project managers' competencies [10]. In addition, Silvius, et al. [9] notes that the failure of PM standards to address sustainability in terms of competency makes it difficult to apply sustainability in projects. Misopoulos et al. [11] with a focus on the manufacturing industry highlights the lack of holistic approaches which do not factor in the systemic and institutional issues. Kivilä et al. [4] further support the need for a holistic approach to achieve sustainable project goals. It has also been reported that while there is more focus on sustainability in projects by PMs, there is a gap between what they perceive as important and the practical application [12].

From the multi-dimensional systemic view of sustainability, the need should be to achieve environmental, economic and social sustainability from project outcomes. As such, there is a need to integrate sustainability in all its ramifications, into the functions, roles, and responsibilities of project managers. However, attempts at achieving such integration in many countries have been known to face challenges [3]. It has been said that sustainability dimensions/principles are difficult to incorporate into construction programmes and projects. However, there is insufficient information in the area of challenges, especially empirical studies. Marcelino-Sádaba et al. [2] highlight the scarcity of relevant information. Silvius et al. [28] acknowledge the growing momentum in research around sustainability in project management. The authors also highlight the need for more empirical research. Yu et al. [5] also highlight the lack of project-level focus in the design of evaluation systems for sustainability in projects. Marcelino-Sádaba et al. [2] further assert that more progress has been made in the environmental focus of relevant research, than the social aspect, which would be the domain for PM. Generally, extant literature, for the most part, is focused on issues such as analysing key aspects of sustainability projects [6]; introduction of management systems [13]; PM commitment to sustainability [14]; sustainability assessment [7]; Project sustainability performance [15]; technology, Materials, risk, and cost [7]; Design [7, 16, 17]; Critical success factors [18]; stakeholders, organisational goals [19]; and innovation diffusion [18, 20]. Most existing studies do not present a concise picture of the nature and occurrence of challenges, for better classifications and articulation of the dynamics, with regards to PM practice, and from the experiences and perceptions of PMs. Thus the pertinent research question is:

What is the nature and occurrence of challenges to the integration of sustainability principles with PM practice? Based on the foregoing, it would be necessary to understand the factors which threaten the integration of sustainability principles with PM practice, especially from the views of PMs. The research aim can then be stated as: To determine the nature and occurrence of challenges to the integration of sustainability principles with PM practice, the dynamics if any, in relation to PM practice, from the views of PMs. The current study attempts to explore this gap area, starting with a review of extant literature, which is complemented with the analysis of field data.

2.1 Challenges to Project Managers' application of Sustainability Principles

A review of relevant literature on the topic was conducted. The following categories were derived from literature review findings: Planning-related challenges, project-related challenges, client-related challenges, project team-related challenges, labour-related challenges, and external challenges. For the purpose of this paper, this section summarises findings on challenges faced by project managers when applying sustainability principles in project management, citing key references. They are described in more detail, hereunder, using key literature sources for the above-mentioned challenges.

Planning-related challenges

Individual Challenges identified under this heading from extant literature are: Adoption of different contract forms of project delivery; the design, orientation and structure of the building; planning of different construction sequence; planning of different construction technique; lengthy approval process for new green technologies within the organization; longer time required during the pre-construction process; and difficulty in comprehending the green specifications in the contract details. It is noteworthy that challenges identified under this heading relate more to the organisational environment.

Project-related challenges

Challenges identified under this heading from extant literature are: Difficulty in approving payment disbursement to suppliers and subcontractors; difficulty in assessing the progress of completion in green construction; difficulty in the selection of subcontractors in providing green construction service; more time is required to implement green construction practices onsite; and more alteration and variation with the design during the construction process.

Client-related challenges

Challenges identified under this heading from extant literature are: Specific budget specification of the green project; the objective of the building project; required date of completion; the level of risk the client is willing to take on green technologies; the client uses a lot of time in making a decision; and a special request from client pertaining to specified green technologies to be used.

Project team-related challenges

Challenges identified under this heading from extant literature are: Conflict with the architect over the type of material to be used; lack of communication and interest among project team members; frequent meetings with green specialists; green consultant delay in providing information; conflict of interest between consultant and project manager; specific performance required for green building projects; material and equipment -related challenges; high cost in green material and equipment; uncertainty with green material and equipment; availability of green material and equipment; decision on different green material and equipment; imported green material or equipment.

Labour -related challenges

Challenges identified under this heading from extant literature are: Resistance to change from their traditional practices; lack of the technical skill regarding green technologies and techniques; workers' unaware of the correct methods and procedures.

External challenges

Challenges identified under this heading from extant literature are: Government policy; the lengthy body of standards' approval process for new technologies; and unforeseen circumstances in a green project [9, 10, 21, 22-26].

Considering the categories and individual challenges, it is noteworthy that while some challenges are grouped under external and labour-related, the PM and client role players, seem to have the most influence. Essentially, most of the threats to the application of sustainability in PM are related to planning, the project, the project team, and the client. There is an appreciable effort in the existing literature to explore project managers and client on the topic of integrating sustainability with PM. Most authors have focused generally on the diffusion of sustainability principles in PM practice. Other authors have looked at the compatibility of principles from sustainability and PM, and standards and competency issues. Thus, while some explorations of the specific perspective on project managers' experiences have begun, there is still an appreciable gap in this area. In addition, there seems to be a dearth of information regarding such issues, in writings that are specifically focused on emerging economies/developing countries of the world. Few authors have looked at the specific perspective of project managers experiences, within developing country contexts. This perspective is pertinent as developing countries are known to be facing strains from the demands for development and construction, and constrained economies, with the emergent need for higher sustainability in projects.

Martens and Carvello [12], note that PM is already inherent in construction projects. As such the incorporation of sustainability will generate difficulties due to conflicts of objectives, and knowledge gaps. It is therefore arguable that the achievement of sustainability in projects constitutes additional responsibility for PMs generally. It is further argued that the situation would be even more so for PMs in developing countries such as South Africa.

In the context of South Africa, there are some landmark events which highlight efforts to improve sustainability in construction. There are legislations such as the SANS 204 [27], which provides guidelines for energy efficiency in buildings. There is the green building council of South Africa which currently advocates sustainable construction through their green building rating system. There is also an increase in research, however, there is still a knowledge gap in the specific aspect of project managers' application of sustainability in their practice.

Hence the current study attempts to establish an additional understanding of the dynamics, by specifically comparing experiences with perceptions, and exploring other constructs such as the consequences. The comparison of experiences and perceptions of PMs provide insight into the influence of identified challenges in terms of their impact, and the response of PMs to their occurrence and perceived existence. The research design presented hereunder was purposed to collect primary data for the current study.

3 Research Design for the study

This research starts from a positivist view, based on available information on the topic. However, the specific focus required an exploratory/inductive reasoning approach to finally collect and analyse qualitative data. Filed work questions were formulated based on literature review findings. A cross-sectional survey strategy was used through an online questionnaire, sent to a sample of construction and project managers. The participants were registered with the South African Council for Project and Construction Management Professions (SACPCMP). Participants were invited through the council's official mailing system, while completed responses were only accessible to the authors. A semi-structured questionnaire with a combination of closed and open-ended questions was designed through the Qualtrics online survey system. Responses were retrieved in September 2016. Issues of validity and reliability were addressed by analysing and testing the instruments and assessing the response magnitude (130), and completeness of responses. Ethical issues adhered to include anonymity, confidentiality, informed consent, and voluntary participation.

3.1 Findings

A total of (130) responses were received. About (32%), 41 responses were incomplete and therefore discarded, leaving (89) usable responses. Project managers with experience in sustainable construction projects numbered 55 (62%) out of the 89 responses, while those without experience in sustainable construction made up the remaining (38%) 34 responses. This diversity provided rich data as participants were asked to provide answers according to what they have experienced (for those who had experience with sustainable construction) and what they perceive to be experienced (for those who have only experienced conventional projects). Other constructs were explored in the study. However, for the purpose of this paper, 'challenges' are presented, from the results of preliminary qualitative analysis, aimed at achieving a description.

General Ranking of Challenges Experienced and Perceived

Respondents indicated and ranked challenges according to their experience and perception respectively. Table 1 summarizes and ranks the results according to the challenges (perceived and experienced) by project and construction managers.

Table 1. Challenges Experience and Perceived

Ranks	Experienced Challenges	Perceived Challenges
1	Meeting the objectives within the defined budget.	Increased costs of materials and equipment.
2	Increased costs of materials and equipment.	Meeting the objectives within the defined budget.
3	Meeting the objectives within the defined time.	Increased level of risk involved.

4	Incorporation of new technologies.	More alterations and variations with the design.
5	Communication between stakeholders.	Meeting the objectives within the defined time.
6	Selection of subcontractors in providing green construction service.	Communication between stakeholders.
7	Increased level of risk involved.	Planning of different construction technique.
8	Specific performance required for green building projects.	Comprehending specifications with the contract.
9	Planning of different construction technique.	Selection of subcontractors in providing green construction service.
10	More alterations and variations with the design.	Specific performance required for green building projects
11	Availability and uncertainty of the materials and the equipment.	Incorporation of new technologies.
12	Conflicts with project team members.	Meeting the objectives within the defined quality.
13	Increased involvement of project team members.	Availability and uncertainty of the materials and the equipment.
14	Incorporation of standards, regulations and legislation.	Conflicts with project team members.
15	Meeting the objectives within the defined quality.	Increased involvement of project team members.
16	Comprehending specifications with the contract.	Incorporation of standards, regulations and legislation.
17	Green consultant delay in providing information.	Adoption of different contract forms for project delivery.
18	Adoption of different contract forms for project delivery.	Green consultant delay in providing information.

All challenges identified from the literature were indicated by the two respondent groups. The inexperienced respondent group saw 'increased costs of materials and equipment', as the top-ranking challenge, followed by 'meeting the objectives within the defined budget', and the 'increased level of risk involved'. Experienced respondents viewed the 'achievement of objectives within defined budget', as top ranking, followed by increased costs of materials and equipment, meeting the objectives within the defined time, and the incorporation of new technologies.

Challenges according to Project Stages

Considering project lifecycle phases, respondents' indications (perceived/experienced) sit generally between the design development (stage 3) and construction and contract administration (stage 5). Stage 5 also seems to have the most number of challenges. Experienced participants indicated a ranking order of stages 5, 3, 4, etc. In contrast, inexperienced participants perceive the order of stages 5, 4, 3, etc. This ranking is according to the prevalence of challenges at respective project stages. See Table 2.

Table 2. Challenges Experience and Perceived

Stages	Ranks	Challenges Experienced in projects	Challenges Perceived as occurring in projects
Stage 1 - Project initiation and briefing	1	Communication between stakeholders.	Communication between stakeholders.
	2	Increased involvement of project team members.	Increased involvement of project team members.
	3	Meeting the objectives within the defined quality.	Green consultant delay in providing information.
Stage 2 - Concept and viability	1	Communication between stakeholders.	Communication between stakeholders.
	2	Green consultant delay in providing information.	Conflicts with project team members.
	3	Increased involvement of project team members.	Incorporation of standards, regulations and legislation.
Stage 3 - Design development	1	Green consultant delay in providing information.	Incorporation of standards, regulations and legislation.
	2	Communication between stakeholders.	Green consultant delay in providing information.
	3	Incorporation of standards, regulations and legislation.	Increased involvement of project team members.
Stage 4 - Tender documentation and procurement	1	Selection of subcontractors in providing green construction service.	Comprehending specifications with the contract.
	2	Comprehending specifications with the contract.	Adoption of different contract forms for project delivery.
	3	Adoption of different contract forms for project delivery.	Selection of subcontractors in providing green construction service.
Stage 5 - Construction and contract administration	1	Meeting the objectives within the defined time.	Meeting the objectives within the defined time.
	2	More alterations and variations with the design.	Meeting the objectives within the defined quality.
	3	Increased costs of materials and equipment.	Increased costs of materials and equipment.
Stage 6 - Project closeout	1	Increased involvement of project team members.	Communication between stakeholders.
	2	Incorporation of standards, regulations and legislation.	Meeting the objectives within the defined quality.
	3	Communication between stakeholders.	Meeting the objectives within the defined time.

Prevalence of Identified Challenges

With regards to prevalence according to the rate of occurrence, the following key was used (seldom, moderate and often). Experienced respondents indicated most of the challenges as often occurring, while inexperienced respondents perceived a moderate rate of occurrence for most challenges. Both groups indicated differently in terms of ranking of prevalence, though they agree on the top-ranked "Meeting the objectives within the defined budget". See Table 3.

Table 3. Frequency of Challenges Experience and Perceived

Ranking	Experienced Challenges	Perceived Challenges
1	Meeting the objectives within the defined budget.	Meeting the objectives within the defined time.
2	More alterations and variations with the design.	Green consultant delay in providing information.
3	Communication between stakeholders.	Incorporation of standards, regulations and legislation.
4	Increased costs of materials and equipment.	Increased costs of materials and equipment.
5	Increased level of risk involved.	Comprehending specifications with the contract.
6	Meeting the objectives within the defined time.	Meeting the objectives within the defined budget.
7	Comprehending specifications with the contract.	More alterations and variations with the design.
8	Selection of subcontractors in providing green construction service.	Communication between stakeholders.
9	Increased involvement of project team members.	Specific performance required for green building projects.
10	Incorporation of standards, regulations and legislation.	Selection of subcontractors in providing green construction service.
11	Conflicts with project team members.	Increased involvement of project team members.
12	Meeting the objectives within the defined quality.	Availability and uncertainty of the materials and the equipment.
13	Incorporation of new technologies.	Meeting the objectives within the defined quality.
14	Specific performance required for green building projects.	Increased level of risk involved.
15	Planning of different construction technique.	Planning of different construction technique.
16	Adoption of different contract forms for project delivery.	Incorporation of new technologies.
17	Availability and uncertainty of the materials and the equipment.	Conflicts with project team members.
18	Green consultant delay in providing information.	Adoption of different contract forms for project delivery.

Significance of Identified Challenges

Following the five categories derived from analysis of literature review findings, participants were asked to rate their relative significance. The questionnaires were given in a five-point Likert type scale (from [5] - extremely challenging, to [1] - not challenging at all). According to experienced participants, the challenges range from moderately challenging to extremely challenging. See Figure 1.

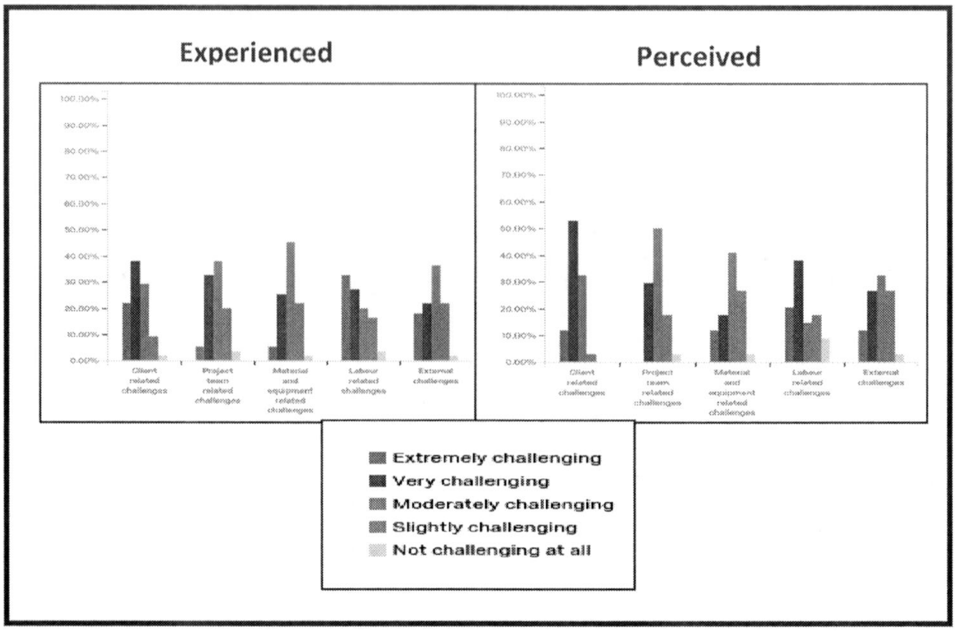

Figure 1. Comparison of the significance of identified Challenges

Labour-related challenges were ranked as the most significant factors. Client related challenges were very challenging. The rest were moderately challenging. Inexperienced respondents perceived a shorter spectrum, which ranged between moderately challenging and very challenging. They also highlighted client and labour related challenges as being very challenging. Project team challenges, material and equipment related challenges, and external challenges were perceived as being moderately challenging.

3.2 Discussion

Firstly, from the results presented thus far, there is a suggestion of strong correspondence with literature review findings. Secondly results of analysis highlight labour issues as top-ranking amongst the extremely challenging factors. However, among researchers, the economic factors remain the most critical and the main challenge when integrating sustainability into construction project management. The survey result, however, suggests that major costs result mostly from a lack of knowledge about sustainability principles and their application. Thirdly there seems to be a lack of knowledge and experience among stakeholders within sustainable projects. This knowledge gap seems to manifest as incompetence by project managers which contributes to difficulties encountered. Another major source of difficulties is poor implementation of processes and financial feasibility of sustainable projects, which could be indirectly linked to knowledge-related issues. Consequently, there are project delays, cost increases, quality compromises and poor working relationships. Poor implementation of the process is arguably traceable to a lack of knowledge among project managers and other stakeholders.

In addition, one of the major challenges to South African construction industry growth is the high cost of construction materials. However, regarding sustainable construction, Akadiri [26] asserts the existence of misperceptions about the costs of sustainable materials. The same notions were noted in the current study. From other evidence gathered during the study, it was deduced that poor perceptions of sustainable project management, and inadequate understanding of the full spectrum of associated costs, constitute a major part of the knowledge-related issues. Gaps in the demonstrated understanding of important issues around the application of sustainability by project managers were also suggested in Martens and Carvalho [12]. Without clear evaluation systems for sustainability at the project level, as noted by Yu et al. [5], there is very little check and balances that highlight the knowledge-related gaps. Also, Marly et al. [17] emphasised the knowledge gap between ecological/sustainable design and project management, in the area of product development. The need for Project management guidelines was also highlighted. These assertions point more at knowledge-related factors.

About (83%) of respondents agreed that project and construction managers need specified skills and knowledge beyond the PMBoK to effectively deliver sustainability goals in projects. Most respondents also see the integration of sustainability and PM as 'the comparison of the incomparable', which speaks to the conflicts of principles highlighted in Silvius and Schipper's [10]. Such conflicts would also emanate from organisational factors, which manifest as institutional and systemic challenges, as suggested by Misopoulos et al. [11]. Some respondents specifically highlight these conflicts and demonstrate discomfort in relation to the question. They also hint at the natural reaction of generating a coping mechanism when there is a perceived lack of capacity or difficulty:

Conflicting specifications and goals. At best difficult to achieve financial and project goals with sustainability. You have to mix the negatives with the positives and be content with what you get.

There is a moderate level of alignment between experienced and perceived difficulties, from the survey result. However, there are some less subtle misalignments, of which the seven most significant relate to quality, risks involved in projects, contracts, materials and equipment, and incorporation of new technologies and design variations. There are also clear misalignments with then two groups of responses, in timing the occurrence of some challenges. Such clear misalignments suggest knowledge gaps ultimately. This will occasion inadequacy in current approaches because the full spectrum of relevant issues may not be factored into PM planning and execution. The need for a holistic approach to sustainability in project management was highlighted in Silvius et al. [28]; Kivilä et al. [4].

In the context of South Africa, the existing preferential procurement environment acts as a challenge to industry growth because it forces stakeholder selection based on factors other than quality and competence. In the context of sustainable construction, this situation would increase the risk of failure and therefore act as a major deterrent towards the integration of sustainability principles. Some respondents in the current study identified certain factors as external and beyond the immediate environment of PMs and stakeholders. In response to the question of the consequences of applying sustainability to PM, some respondents answered:

Taxpayer will be held responsible in case of failure! As well BEE policies occur into the failure of the project (qualifications are not existent).

We end up with projects with long term environmental impacts.

The said BEE policies refer to preferential procurement policies aimed at empowering local companies that are owned by people of African descent. From the responses, it is evident that in the case of failure; people who had no contribution and sometimes even knowledge of such projects happen to be the ones held responsible. The use of an exclamation indicates an emotion that is related to the question. It could also hint at a point of frustration. The second response highlights the inevitable negative consequences, which become long term negative influence on the environment. Preferential procurement has been strongly linked to the failure of such projects, which again suggests issues of knowledge and competence.

4 Conclusions

The current study explored the difficulties experienced by project managers when sustainability principles are applied in PM. The effect of this integration on the dual goals of achieving sustainability and project success within the South African construction industry was explored. Purposively selected literature was used for secondary data while an online survey strategy was used for primary data. While various constructs were explored in the survey, the focus of the current paper is challenging. Although the analysis was conducted at various levels, only results of the descriptive analysis were presented in the current paper.

Limitations in the study relate to purposive sampling, nature of survey response, and completeness of responses. Though over (30%) of the (130) retrieved responses were discarded, the remaining (89) complete responses amounted to an appreciable numerical strength, which allowed for rich comparison between two groups of data. In addition, the agreement of the results with extant literature sampled globally lends a measure of strength to the results in terms of generalisability beyond South Africa, at least to similar developing country contexts. Following the findings from data analysis and the subsequent discussion of the findings with extant literature, the guiding research question stated earlier can be addressed hereunder.

With regards to the nature and occurrence of challenges, there is a strong similarity with extant literature. The overarching deduction at this stage is a strong suggestion that the challenges may be largely traceable to gaps in knowledge among project managers and other project stakeholders. It is however in the indicated patterns of occurrence that various dynamics are highlighted. Such differences relate more to the unique nature of the analysis in the current paper. The uniqueness refers to the comparison of experience with perception, of the respondents. While the respondents generally agree on the existence of all challenges explored, there are clear areas of disagreement for seven of the identified challenges. Further on the dynamics, the occurrence of challenges differed by views of respondent groups, project stages, and prevalence. Similarly, the extent of consequences from the challenges ranged from delayed projects to complete abandonment of the sustainability principles. Furthermore, there is an appreciable level of discomfort/concern with the notion of integrating sustainability with PM, among respondents generally. Moreover, the differences between the views of experienced and inexperienced PMs with regard to sustainable construction ranged between subtle and strong. The function of knowledge in the outcomes derived from the current paper is highly suggested.

Arguably the current study brings a unique perspective to the growing area of research, which is sustainability in project management. While there is limited information on the challenges of integrating sustainability in PM practice, there is even more scarcity of literature exploring dynamics related to experiences and perceptions of PMs. The uniqueness refers to the comparison of experience-based assessment with views based on people's perception of the probable nature and occurrence of the relevant challenges. Thus, a stronger basis has been achieved, for future extrapolations, analysis and articulation of findings from future studies. Essentially the current study contributes new material, with a focus on threats to the integration of sustainability in project management practice, as opposed to most studies which focus more on diffusion generally. The current study also brings new insights to the study area by highlighting the emerging dynamics in actual experiences/observations vs. perceptions of nature and occurrence thereof.

Appreciable conjectures have been drawn at this stage of the study. There is however a need to further explore the highlights and the seeming patterns. Such future studies will provide further insight into the dynamics of the factors that influenced the experiences and perceptions of participants. It would also be beneficial to attempt at drawing a stronger demarcation between the assessment of observed/actual occurrence of challenges, and the perceptions, even for respondents with experience in sustainable construction projects. While some of the challenges are most probably linked to contextual factors in South Africa, the appreciable agreement with extant literature sampled globally expands the generalisability beyond South Africa. It also demands the continuance of the study to higher levels of generalisability.

In furtherance of the current study, the following are suggested: A widening of the sample to a regional level, more detailed qualitative analysis with the use of relevant software packages, and the derivation of propositions, or hypotheses in future studies.

References

1. World Commission on Environment and Development, Our Common Future. Great Britain: Oxford University Press (1987), Available at: www.un-documents.net/our-common-future.pdf. [Accessed: 17 April 2016]
2. S. Marcelino-Sádabaa, L.F. González-Jaenb, A. Pérez-Ezcurdiaa, Using project management as a way to sustainability: From a comprehensive review, *Journal of Cleaner Production* **99**:1-16 (2015)
3. F. Tessema, K. Taipale, J. Bethge, Sustainable Buildings and Construction in Africa, (2009), Available from: http://www.scp-centre.org/fileadmin/content/files/6_Resources/1_Publications_pdfs/28_Tessema_Taipale_Bethge__2009__Sustainable_Building_and_Construction_in_Africa_en.pdf. [Accessed: 17 April 2016]
4. J. Kivilä, M. Martinsuo, L. Vuorinen, Sustainable project management through project control in infrastructure projects, *International Journal of Project Management* **35**(6):1167-1183 (2017)
5. W. Yu, S. Cheng, W. Ho, Y. Chang, Measuring the Sustainability of Construction Projects throughout Their Lifecycle: A Taiwan Lesson, *Sustainability* **10**(6):2027 (2018)
6. R. Doskočil, B. Lacko, Risk Management and Knowledge Management as Critical Success Factors of Sustainability Projects, *Sustainability* **10**(5):1438 (2018)
7. E.K. Zavadskas, J. Šaparauskas, J. Antucheviciene, Sustainability in Construction Engineering, *Sustainability* **10**(7):2236 (2018)
8. P. Bocchini, D.M. Frangopol, T. Ummenhofer, T. Zinke, Resilience and sustainability of civil infrastructure: toward a unified approach, *Journal of Infrastructure Systems*, **20**(2) (2014)

9. A.J. Silvius, J. Van der Brink, A. Kohler, *The Impact of sustainability on project management,* in H. Linger, J. Owen (Eds), The Project as a Social System. Asia-Pacific Perspectives on Project Management (Monash University Publishing, 2012)
10. A.J. Silvius, P.J Schipper, Sustainability in Project Management Competencies: Analysing the competence gap of project managers (2014), Available at: http://file.scirp.org/pdf/JHRSS_2014060310032620.pdf . [Accessed 19 May 2016].
11. F. Misopoulos, R. Michaelides, M.A. Salehuddin, V. Manthou, Z. Michaelides, Addressing Organisational Pressures as Drivers towards Sustainability in Manufacturing Projects and Project Management Methodologies, *Sustainability* **10**(6):2098 (2018)
12. L.M. Martens, M.M. Carvalho, The challenge of introducing sustainability into project management function: multiple-case studies, *Journal of Cleaner Production* **117**(20):29-40 (2016)
13. S. Martínez-Perales, I. Ortiz-Marcos, J.J. Ruiz, F.J. Lázaro, Using Certification as a Tool to Develop Sustainability in Project Management, *Sustainability* **10**(5):1408 (2018)
14. G. Clinning, C. Marnewick, Incorporating sustainability into IT project management, *South African Computer Journal* **29**(1) (2017)
15. L. Shen, V.W.Y. Tam, L. Gan, K. Ye, Z. Zhao, Improving Sustainability Performance for Public-Private-Partnership (PPP) Projects, *Sustainability* **8**(3):289 (2016)
16. F. Ali, C. Boks, N. Bey, Design for Sustainability and Project Management Literature – A Review, Procedia CIRP **48**:28-33 (2016)
17. F.B. Marly, M. de Carvalho, E. de Senzi Zancul, Ecodesign in project management: a missing link for the integration of sustainability in product development? *Journal of Cleaner Production* **80**(1):106-118 (2014)
18. S. Banihashemi, M.R. Hosseini, H. Golizadeh, S. Sankaran, Critical success factors (CSFs) for integration of sustainability into construction project management practices in developing countries, *International Journal of Project Management* **35**(6):1103-1119 (2017)
19. M.A. Sánchez, Integrating sustainability issues into project management, *Journal of Cleaner Production* **96**(1):319-330 (2015)
20. L. Larsson, J. Larsson, Sustainable Development in Project-Based Industries–Supporting the Realization of Explorative Innovation, *Sustainability* **10**(3):683 (2018)
21. E. Kaatz, D. Root, P. Bowen, Broadening project participation through a modified building sustainability assessment, *Building Research & Information* **33**(5):441-454 (2005)
22. B.G. Hwang, W.J. Ng, Project management knowledge and skills for green construction: Overcoming challenges, *International Journal of Project Management* (2013)
23. B.G. Hwang, W.J. Ng, *Are Project Managers Ready for Green Construction? Challenges, Knowledge Areas, and Skills*, in CIB World Building Congress, Queensland, Australia, 1-12 (2013)
24. B.G. Hwang, J.S. Tan, Green building project management: Obstacles and solutions for sustainable development, *Sustainable development* 335-349 (2012)
25. B.G. Hwang, W.J. Ng, Project management knowledge and skills for green construction; Overcoming challenges. *International Journal of Project Management* (2012)

26. P.E. Akadiri, Understanding barriers affecting the selection of sustainable materials in building projects. *Journal of Building Engineering* 4:86-93 (2015)
27. The South African Bureau of Standards (n.d.) Giving you the quality edge, Available at: https://www.sabs.co.za/About-SABS/index.asp [Accessed: 7 June 2018]
28. A.J.G. Silvius, M. Kampinga, S. Paniagua, H. Mooi, Considering sustainability in project management decision making: An investigation using Q-methodology, *International Journal of Project Management* **35**(6):1133-1150 (2017)

TALK Capability of Biomimicry for Disruptive and Sustainable Output in the Construction Industry

Olusegun Aanuoluwapo Oguntona[1*], and *Clinton* Ohis Aigbavboa[1]

[1]Sustainable Human Settlement and Construction Research Centre, Faculty of Engineering and the Built Environment, University of Johannesburg, South Africa

Abstract. Several sustainability trends have evolved and proliferated for greening the processes and activities of the construction industry (CI). Striking among the trends is biomimicry, a novel and nature-inspired approach that seeks a sustainable solution to human challenges by emulating time-tested patterns and strategies in nature. This study sets out to evaluate biomimicry potentials for sustainable outputs in the construction industry. An extant review of the literature was conducted on nature-inspired approaches for sustainable and innovative solutions. Findings revealed technology readiness, awareness, leadership competence, and knowledge (TALK) as critical areas where biomimicry will offer a unique step-by-step path to disruptive outcomes and potentially aid the greening agenda of the construction industry.

Keywords: biomimicry, built environment, innovations, nature, sustainability

1 Introduction

Globally, the construction industry (CI) is a major sector that aid economic stability and growth, especially in developing nations. Critical infrastructures such as roads, energy production, transmission and distribution plants, rails, bridges, and educational, commercial, residential and industrial buildings among many others are direct beneficial impacts of the CI [1]. Humanity has significantly benefitted from the provision of these infrastructures which has, in turn, contributed significantly to urbanisation and the economic growth of nations, especially the developing ones [2, 3]. Generally, it is of the belief that there is a causal link between the CI and economic growth in developing and developed countries with a focus on infrastructural developments and industrialisation. In New Zealand, the industry is recognised as one of the most significant sectors of the nation's economy, accounting for 8 per cent of the total employment [4], while accounting for another 8 per cent of the total workforce in Malaysia [5]. In developed countries of the world, the CI contribute

* Corresponding author: architectoguntona12@gmail.com

significantly to the gross domestic product (GDP) and employs a notable portion of the population. Therefore, the CI is not only an indispensable fraction of the modernisation process; its adoption in developing countries as a strategy for employment creation due to its labour-intensive nature [6], attest to its global importance.

Virtually all the products of the CI, have a prolonged impact on the human environment and the ecosystem due to their continuous emission of a significant amount of pollution [7]. The use of plants and equipment to achieve project objectives is also on the increase [8], as their exhausts and emissions during operation is another contributor to the pollution of the environment. A report by the United States Environmental Protection Agency (USEPA) revealed that the indoor air levels of many pollutants may be 2.5 times and occasionally more than 100 times higher than outdoor levels [1]. These pollutant concentrations are those within buildings and emanate from backing materials, finishes, paints, and other components. Also, literature has identified that the atmospheric release of greenhouse gases (GHGs) and other emissions caused by construction activities, remains a significant contributor to ozone layers depletion, global warming and climate change. For instance, 50 per cent of the carbon emissions in the UK is traceable to the CI [9], while in China, 1260 million tons of carbon emissions associated with energy use in buildings was reached in 2008 [10]. In addition to air, water and land pollution, the CI generates a significant amount of waste from the manufacturing process and use of construction materials. As reported by Azis et al. [2], an assessment of material waste generated was carried out on a construction project in the Netherlands. The findings revealed that the quantity of materials wasted on the site is relatively high and equals to 9 per cent by weight of the purchased materials originally [2]. The sustainability issue is therefore imperative to curtail the adverse environmental impact of the CI.

Numerous interpretations of sustainability have emanated since the Brundtland definition. However, it is common knowledge and globally accepted that sustainability must encompass at least, three dimensions which are the social, economic, and environmental pillars [11]. Sustainability entails the balanced utilisation of the natural resources in a way that they do not reach the state of deterioration, attenuation and a non-renewable state and can be passed on to the coming generation [12]. According to Kibert [13], three forces propel the shift towards sustainability. Firstly, the pressures experienced by increased demand placed on natural resources, resulting in the paucity and high materials cost. Secondly, the massive and escalated destruction of the natural ecosystems and biodiversity, modification of biogeochemical cycles, a significant increase in consumption rate and population size, all resulting in the threat of global warming, depletion of marine life, deforestation, and desertification, amongst others. Thirdly, the transformation movement coupled with the various approaches adopted in agriculture, tourism, medicine, manufacturing, and other sectors, towards greening their activities and processes. These have, however, led to the growing recognition and importance of embracing and implementing the tenets of sustainability in the CI [14].

Throughout literature, terms such as 'sustainable construction' (SC), 'green', 'environmental-friendly', and 'high-performance' are interchangeably utilised [2, 13, 15], to describe the creation and responsible management of a healthy built environment based on efficient resource use and ecological principles [16, 17]. Sustainable construction (SC) aims to maximise the potential benefits accrued to the economy and society at large by the reduction or elimination of environmental challenges associated with construction processes and activities, and the built environment [1]. Other aims can be inferred from the principles of SC as presented by different authors. An international construction research organisation, the Conseil International du Bâtiment (CIB), proffered seven principles as guidelines for the integration of SC to aid the decision-making process during the entire lifecycle of a building. According to Kibert [13], the principles are: a reduction in resource consumption (reduce);

reuse of resources (reuse); use of resources with recyclable attributes (recycle); protection of the natural environment (nature); toxics elimination (toxics); application of life-cycle costing methodology (economics); and focus on quality (quality). These principles are applied when carrying out a sustainability assessment of the elements and other resources required for construction [18]. Not only do these principles apply across the lifecycle of construction (planning to deconstruction), they are also applicable to the resources (materials, land, ecosystem, water, and energy) required for creating and operating the built environment throughout its lifecycle.

Terms such as the Natural Step, ecological rucksack, ecological footprint, biophilia, ecological economics, Factor 4 and Factor 10, eco-efficiency, and biomimicry among many others have emerged and are utilised in describing the all-embracing philosophy and scientific concepts that apply to a conscious transference towards the sustainability paradigm [13]. Outstanding among these sustainability trends is biomimicry. As a relatively new field of study, biomimicry encourages the teaming up of biologists with designers and professionals from various fields (industrial design, medical science, material science, architecture, and interior design) to study and emulate the procedures and strategies operational in nature for sustainable solutions to the challenges facing the human or built environment. This paper, therefore, evaluates and presents the potentials of biomimicry for sustainable and innovative solutions in the CI. A literature review of related studies on biomimicry and novel sustainable solutions borne out of its adoption and implementation was done and presented. Presented in the final section of the paper is an overview of the issues discussed in the paper alongside the conclusions drawn and recommendations proffered.

2 Overview of Biomimicry

Historically, humanity has been dependent on the natural world to meet their shelter, and food needs and generally for survival. Due to human observation of nature and natural phenomenon, there are native innovations and developments in the areas of weapons and defence mechanisms; processes related to manufacturing; shelter architectures; agriculture and food production; and medical and pharmaceutical sciences [19]. As a result of its more than 3.8 billion years of existence, nature has become an exceptional blueprint for innovative solutions that encompasses efficiency, resource utilisation, collaboration, and longevity [20]. The application of nature-inspired knowledge to meet human needs is therefore not a contemporary practice, whereas, the term describing it is relatively new.

The concept of 'biomimicry' was widely circulated and popularised through the book *Biomimicry: Innovation Inspired by Nature*. The book was published in 1997 and authored by Janine M. Benyus (referred to as biomimicry founder), a biologist and co-founder of the Biomimicry Guild [21]. However, throughout literature, multiple terms are used to describe this practice of emulating and learning from the natural world to solve human challenges. As affirmed by Aziz and El Sheriff [22], the terms 'biomimetics' and 'biomimetics' fundamentally shares the same meaning, noting that other terminologies like bioinspiration, bionics, nature-inspired design, bioanalogous design, biomimesis, biognosis, and bio-inspired design are often used interchangeably with biomimicry and biomimetics [23-25].

Also, the term biomimicry came from the amalgamation of the Greek words *bios* (life) and *mīmēsis* (imitation), which literally means the 'imitation of life' or 'life imitation' [19, 26]. It is described as the study and emulation of natural forms, systems, strategies, processes, operations and elements with the potential to resolve human complexities and issues in a sustainable manner [27]. Biomimicry entails proffering design solutions with sustainable attributes through the study and conscious emulation of forms, processes, and ecosystems in nature [28].

3 Biomimicry Potentials for Sustainable Solutions

Biomimicry keeps attaining immense importance as a global and popular sustainability trend in planning for eco-friendly developments typified by its capability to trigger unconventional innovations and breakthroughs (25, 29). It is also understood by many as a branch of biological science going by the term. However, the scientific knowledge encapsulated by biomimicry only aids the ingenuity of learning about and from nature [30]. It heralds a shift from human's exploitative era of extracting from nature to mastering the attributes that support its evolution and survival over the years [31]. While biomimicry can be employed specifically as a method of improving the eco-friendliness of what is existing [29], it can also be used in developing sustainable innovations and technologies as well [32]. Biomimicry potentials for sustainable innovations and outputs in the CI are, therefore, presented in the areas of *technology readiness*, *awareness*, *leadership competence*, and *knowledge* (TALK).

3.1 Technology Readiness

Biomimicry proponents believe that the CI needs to examine the exceptionally successful 3.8 billion years of research and development (R+D) lab that the earth operates. Here, about 10-30 million organisms have mastered and perfected doing everything human intend to accomplish, without causing environmental pollution, or mortgaging the fortune of future generations [33]. Owing to these strategies employed by nature to evolve and sustain itself over the years, innovations, ideas, and solutions inspired by nature are now believed to be the panacea to the challenges facing humanity.

Biomimicry has now taken the frontline of technological and scientific research because of its potential to propel new ideas for the invention of sustainable solutions and technologies [34]. Also, the study and application of biomimicry have been observed in a broad range of fields such as material research, aerodynamics, communications, architecture, transportation, human safety, products design, and mechanics [35, 36]. Many researchers have investigated bio-inspired (biomimetic) materials and technologies in the construction and built environment (C&BE). Based on their application, the materials and technologies are found to have advantageous attributes such as low weight and reduced manufacturing costs compared to traditional ones [37]. Other researchers seek new pathways to achieve novel construction materials and technologies with sustainable properties in line with the biomimicry paradigm, thus leading to the revelation of more remarkable characteristics such as self-repairing, self-organising, self-cleaning, self-healing amongst others [38]. Bio-inspired adhesives and coatings, self-cleaning finishes, biotechconcrete, and energy conversion and conservation technologies are few of the numerous successes recorded with the application of biomimicry. Table 1 shows a few of the existing biomimetic technologies and materials that can be applied and utilised in the CI.

Table 1. Biomimetic materials and technologies applicable in the construction industry.

Product	Source of Inspiration	Function
Eco-Cement	Sea Snail	Neutral and strength-enhancing carbon-sequestering cement
Self-repairing Concrete	Pipevine, human skin, cells, vertebrates bone	Self-repairing concrete that increases the durability of structures and reduces life-cycle cost
Lotusan® Paint	Morpho butterfly, sacred lotus	Automatic self-cleaning coat after the mere rinse of a rain shower
Lotus Clay Roofing Tiles	Morpho butterfly, sacred lotus	Self-cleaning clay roof tiles/coverings
Dye-Sensitised Solar Cells and Panels	Cooke's koki'o (photosynthesis)	Low-cost and efficiently produced electricity by artificial photosynthesis
ORNILUX Insulated Glass	Orb-web spider	The insulated architectural glass that prevents bird collisions
Biolytix® System	Soil ecosystem	Waste treatment and water filtering system
Eco-Machine	Forests	Wastewater treatment system that purifies water without chemicals
Purebond	Blue mussels	Formaldehyde-free wood glue
I2™ Modular Carpet	Forest floor	Individually replaceable and recyclable carpet tiles

Source: [46].

3.2 Awareness

It is imperative to be aware of the principles underlying the application of biomimicry, to maximise the potential benefits accrued to its adoption and implementation of in the CI. For biomimicry to attain its overall target of sustainable and innovative solutions, Goss [21] advocated that asking the following questions is pertinent: Does the design integrate cycles? Does it heal after a disturbance? Is the design locally attuned and responsive? Is it informed by local inhabitants of all species? Is it resourceful and connected to local feedback loops? Does the design integrate cycles? Does it adapt to seasons, reuse materials, and maintain itself through turnover? Does the design leverage its interdependence in the system? Is the design resilient? Can it withstand disturbance while maintaining function? Does it fit form to function? Does the design optimise rather than maximise? Does it reuse materials or use recycled materials? Does the design use benign manufacturing? Is the reaction done at standard pressure and temperature? Does it enhance the system's capacity to support life long-term? Is its success based on whether it contributes to the continuity of life?

These questions are deductions from the basic principles underpinning the concept of biomimicry, also referred to as nature principles. According to Benyus [20], these are the canon of laws, principles and strategies divined from nature's notebooks. They are abstracted biological systems and strategies, some of which are self-explanatory and obvious, and can be found in most of the organisms, enabling life to successfully regenerates itself [39]. They are also the creative common tools and checklists which aids the sustainability evaluation of biomimetic designs, materials, technologies and application [40]. Resonating in the book *Biomimicry: Innovation Inspired by Nature* authored by Benyus [20], nature principles are:

- Nature taps the power of limits.
- Nature curbs excesses from within.
- Nature demands local expertise.
- Nature banks on diversity.
- Nature rewards cooperation.
- Nature recycles everything.
- Nature fits form to function.
- Nature uses only the energy it needs.
- Nature runs on sunlight.

3.3 Leadership Competence

With nature as the underlying concept of biomimicry, the proponents lead the advocacy that human should relate to nature as a *model*, *measure*, and *mentor*. Based on this ideology, designers, professionals, and other stakeholders will be equipped with the requisite capacity to apply biomimicry to increase the sustainability of existing creations and to produce novel designs, materials, technologies and inventions with sustainable attributes. With nature as a *model*, inspiration is drawn from nature's forms, strategies and systems to tackle challenges in a sustainable manner [27]. Seeing nature as a *measure*, human innovations, designs and solutions will be evaluated for sustainability against standards exhibited in nature through their over 3.8 billion years of evolution [41]. With nature as a *mentor*, a purposive and deliberate human intent to learn from and develop a joint correlation with the natural world is employed, backed by the responsiveness that nature is an integral part of the human environment. These three herald a contemporary way of perceiving and evaluating the natural world thereby introducing an era based on what we can study, learn and emulate from it [31].

3.4 Knowledge

Two primary approaches exist in the application of biomimicry for sustainable interventions and innovative solutions to human challenges. They are the *problem-based approach* and the *solution-based approach*. These approaches are the dimensions through which knowledge is transferred in biomimicry application for sustainable and innovative outputs that are genuinely biomimetic [42]. Biomimicry proponents believed that these approaches would aid the steps towards transiting the built environment to a sustainable and resilient state [43, 44], as it helps proffer solutions to identified challenges and the creation of novel materials and technologies. Also, the approaches offer unique step-by-step paths under the larger umbrella of biomimicry [45]. The sole aim of these approaches is to proffer methodologies through which biomimicry can be integrated into different professions to arrive at a sustainable, efficient and effective solution.

The problem-based approach entails drawing inspiration from nature for solutions by first defining the problems and then pairing such problems with organisms in nature that have resolved similar problems. This approach endeavour to find a sustainable solution to an identified problem. Aquaporin membrane technology and Watreco Vortex Generator are examples of breakthroughs recorded with the application of this approach as a result of water treatment and purification issues. On the other hand, the solution-based approach involves identifying an attribute, behaviour and function in an organism or ecosystem and then translating it into design solutions or innovation [29]. This approach is at the forefront of providing amazing and sustainable inventions and innovations. An example under this approach is the Mercedes-Benz bionic car which was inspired by the shape of the boxfish which controls water movement around its body to influence stability and manoeuvrability [46, 47].

4 Conclusion and Recommendations

The natural world has been existing for around 3.8 billion years with models that manufacture without heat, beat, and treat; ecosystems powered by sunlight and create design solutions rather than waste. As observed and discovered, the activities, processes, strategies, and systems displayed in nature are found to be sustainable, effective, efficient and aesthetically pleasing too. These, among other attributes, has made biomimicry to be outstanding among the sustainability trends applied in the CI and other sectors.

Biomimicry has already instituted the realisation of some appropriate and exceptional innovations in different sectors and specific areas of global interest such as energy engineering and waste re-use, where multiple-scale efficiency improvements are much needed. Examples include the noiseless Shinkansen Bullet Train (inspired by the splashless water entry of kingfishers and silent flight of owls), the smart-windows and walls called RavenBrick (inspired by passive pigmentation in cephalopods and many species of lizards), wind energy harvesting Vibro-Wind without turbine (inspired by the movement of leaves in windy condition), and Green infrastructure stormwater control (inspired by the filtering mechanism provided by the vegetation in an ecosystem) amongst others.

Also, the Biomimicry Guild, now named Biomimicry 3.8, which is the world-leading bio-inspired consultancy organisation co-founded by Janine M. Benyus, has collaborated with major multinational companies and corporations to apply the knowledge of biomimicry (nature-inspired strategies) in creating sustainable and innovative solutions. Few of these corporations include Nike, Procter and Gamble (P&G), Interface (carpet company), Boeing, Colgate-Palmolive, Coca-Cola Company, Hewlett-Packard, HOK architects, Kohler, and Shell. It is therefore pertinent to ensure the holistic application of biomimicry to arrive at a sustainable outcome which is the sole target of this new field. Also, a multidisciplinary collaboration among designers, engineers, architects and other stakeholders should be encouraged if numerous sustainable and disruptive innovations are to be birthed to militate the adverse environmental impacts of the CI.

References

1. A. Pearce, Y.H. Ahn, *Sustainable buildings and infrastructure: paths to the future* (Routledge, 2012)
2. A.A.A. Azis, A.H. Memon, I.A. Rahman, S. Nagapan, Q.B.A.I Latif, *Challenges faced by construction industry in accomplishing sustainability goals*, ISBEIA, 2012 IEEE Symposium, 630-634 (2012)
3. L. Shi, K. Ye, W. Lu, X. Hu, Improving the competence of construction management consultants to underpin sustainable construction in China, Habitat Int. **41**, 236-242 (2014)
4. M. Noktehdan, M. Shahbazpour, S. Wilkinson, Driving innovative thinking in the New Zealand construction industry, Buildings **5(2)**, 297-309 (2015)
5. R. Rostami, H. Lamit, S.M. Khoshnava, R. Rostami, Industrialization and sustainable construction A case study of Malaysia, Asian J. Microbiol. Biotechnol. Environ. Sci. **15(2)**, 433-440 (2013)

6. R. Ramsaran, R. Hosein, Growth, employment and the construction industry in Trinidad and Tobago, Constr. Manag. Econ. **24(5)**, 465-474 (2006)
7. N. Wang, The role of the construction industry in China©sustainable urban development, Habitat Int., **44**, 442-450 (2014)
8. G.I. Idoro, *Sustainability of mechanisation in the Nigerian construction industry*, J. Civ. Eng. Manag. **18(1)**, 91-105 (2012)
9. P. Akadiri Oluwole, O. Fadiya Olaniran, Empirical analysis of the determinants of environmentally sustainable practices in the UK construction industry, Constr. Innov., **13(4)**, 352-373 (2013)
10. R.C. Diamond, Q. Ye, W. Feng, T. Yan, H. Mao, Y. Li, Y. Guo, J. Wang, Sustainable building in China — A green leap forward?, Buildings **3(3)**, 639-658 (2013)
11. A. Cotgrave, M. Riley (Eds.), *Total sustainability in the built environment* (Palgrave Macmillan, 2012)
12. M. Yılmaz, A. Bakış, Sustainability in construction sector, Procedia Soc. Behav. Sci. **195**, 2253-2262 (2015)
13. C.J. Kibert, *Sustainable construction: Green building design and delivery,* 3rd ed. (John Wiley & Sons, Hoboken, 2013)
14. R.J. Plank, *Sustainable Construction - A UK Perspective*. Structures Congress 2005: Metropolis and Beyond, 1-7 (2005)
15. H. Zabihi, F. Habib, Sustainability in building and construction: Revising definitions and concepts, IJESE **2(4)**, 570 (2012)
16. Y. Tan, L. Shen, H. Yao, Sustainable construction practice and contractors' competitiveness: A preliminary study, Habitat Int. **35(2)**, 225-230 (2011)
17. M.A. Marhani, H. Adnan, F. Ismail, OHSAS 18001: A pilot study of towards sustainable construction in Malaysia, Procedia Soc. Behav. Sci. **85**, 51-60 (2013)
18. S. Al Sanad, Awareness, drivers, actions, and barriers of sustainable construction in Kuwait, Procedia Eng. **118**, 969-983 (2015)
19. L.E. Murr, Biomimetics and biologically inspired materials, in *Handbook of Materials Structures, Properties, Processing and Performance*. (Springer International Publishing, 2015)
20. J.M. Benyus, *Biomimicry: Innovation inspired by nature* (William Morrow & Company, New York, 1997)
21. J. Goss, *Biomimicry: Looking to nature for design solutions* (Corcoran College of Art and Design, ProQuest Dissertations Publishing, 2009)
22. M.S. Aziz, A.Y. El Sherif, *Biomimicry as an approach for bio-inspired structure with the aid of computation*. Alex. Eng. J., **55(1)**, 707-714 (2015)
23. J.F. Vincent, O.A. Bogatyreva, N.R. Bogatyrev, A. Bowyer, A.K. Pahl, Biomimetics: Its practice and theory, J. R. Soc. Med. **3(9)**, 471-482 (2006)
24. L. Shu, K. Ueda, I. Chiu, H. Cheong, *Biologically inspired design*, CIRP Ann. Manuf. Techn. **60(2)**, 673-693 (2011)
25. A. Gamage, R. Hyde, A model based on biomimicry to enhance ecologically sustainable design, Architect. Sci. Rev. **55(3)**, 224-235 (2012)
26. P.O. Arnarson, *Biomimicry: New Technology*. Reykjavík University (2011), http://olafurandri.com/nyti/papers2011/Biomimicry%20-%20P%C3%A9tur%20%C3%96rn%20Arnarson.pdf

27. N.N. El Din, A. Abdou, I.A. El Gawad, Biomimetic potentials for building envelope adaptation in Egypt, Procedia Environ. Sci. **34**, 375-386 (2016)
28. A. Singh, N. Nayyar, Biomimicry-an alternative solution to sustainable buildings, IJCEE, **2(14)**, 96-101 (2015)
29. M.P. Zari, Biomimetic approaches to architectural design for increased sustainability, (SB07 Auckland, New Zealand, 2007)
30. A. Marshall, *Biomimicry, Encyclopedia of Corporate Social Responsibility* (Springer Berlin Heidelberg, 2013)
31. J.M. Benyus, *A biomimicry primer* (The Biomimicry Institute and the Biomimicry Guild, 2011)
32. C. Okuyucu, Biomimicry based on material science: The inspiring art from nature (review article), Matter **2(1),** 49-53 (2015)
33. Strategic Direction, Nature®inspiration: Solving sustainability challenges, Innovation **24(9)**, 33-35 (2008)
34. M. Zhang, Z. Gu, M. Bosch, Z. Perry, H. Zhou, Biomimicry in metal-organic materials, Coord. Chem. Rev. **293**, 327-356 (2015)
35. I. De Pauw, P. Kandachar, E. Karana, D. Peck, R. Wever, *Nature inspired design: Strategies towards sustainability*, Knowledge Collaboration & Learning for Sustainable Innovation: 14th European Roundtable on Sustainable Consumption and Production (ERSCP) conference and the 6th Environmental Management for Sustainable Universities (EMSU) conference, Delft, The Netherlands, October 25-29, Delft University of Technology; The Hague University of Applied Sciences; TNO (2010)
36. F. Al Amin, H. Taleb, *Biomimicry approach to achieving thermal comfort in a hot climate*, Proceedings of SBE16 Dubai 2016, Dubai, United Arab Emirates (2016)
37. M.F.A. Yazdi, R. Zakaria, M. Mustaffar, M.Z. Abd. Majid, R.M. Zin, M. Ismail, K. Yahya, *Bio-composite materials potential in enhancing sustainable construction*, Desalin. Water Treat. **52(19-21)**, 3631-3636 (2014)
38. M. Mirkhalaf, D. Zhu, F. Barthelat, A. Lakhtakia, R. Martín-Palma, Biomimetic hard materials, in A. Lakhtakia, R.J. Martín-Palma (Eds.), *Engineered Biomimicry*, 59-79 (Elsevier, Waltham, 2013)
39. J. Polit, C. David, *Regreening nature: Turning negative externalities into opportunities*, Master®thesis (Delft University of Technology, Delft, 2014)
40. E. Kennedy, D. Fecheyr-Lippens, B. Hsiung, P.H. Niewiarowski, M. Kolodziej, Biomimicry: A path to sustainable innovation, Des. Issues **31(3)**, 66-73 (2015)
41. A. Pronk, M. Blacha, A. Bots, *Nature's experiences for building technology*, in Proceedings of the 6th International seminar of the international association for shell and spatial structures (IASS) working group (2008)
42. J. Pandremenos, E. Vasiliadis, G. Chryssolouris, Design architectures in biology, Procedia CIRP **3**, 448-452 (2012)
43. W. McDonough, M. Braungart, *Cradle to cradle: Remaking the way we make things* (MacMillan, 2010)
44. R.M.A. El-Zeiny, Biomimicry as a problem-solving methodology in interior architecture, Procedia Soc. Behav. Sci. **50**, 502-512 (2012)
45. P.H. Niewiarowski, D. Paige, Proceedings of the First Annual Biomimicry in Higher Education Webinar, The Biomimicry Institute (2011), https://biomimicry.org/shop/proceedings-higher-ed-webinar-2012/

46. Ask Nature, Strategy, The Biomimicry Institute (2018) https://asknature.org/strategy/body-shape-influences-stability-and-maneuverability/#.W4F8LegzbIU
47. Ask Nature, Inspired Ideas, The Biomimicry Institute (2018), https://asknature.org/?s=&page=0&hFR%5Bpost_type_label%5D%5B0%5D=Inspired%20Ideas&is_v=1#.WxRD3EiFPIU

Technical enablers of human errors and violations in construction

Fidelis Emuze[1*], and *Lesiba* Mollo[1]

[1]Department of Built Environment, Central University of Technology, Bloemfontein, Republic of South Africa

Abstract. The performance of public sector projects in developing countries such as South Africa is an on-going concern in a region where injuries and fatalities are almost a daily occurrence in the industry. This reported study assessed the human errors and violations consistently encountered on public sector projects. The feedback from the survey research reinforced the notion that technical matters such as poor planning or the lack of it significantly erode safety system capacities on construction sites. The technical problems are aided by latent conditions such as design errors and negligence. The issues highlighted imply that public sector projects tend to fail to achieve the required conditions of satisfaction by clients. In other words, the reduction of human errors and violations as safety concerns should look beyond the set-up of construction site operations and people in the front line of construction.

Keywords: Accident, Construction, Human error, Human violations

1 Introduction

There are numerous challenges that construction organisations are struggling to eliminate. One of such problems is the high rate of accidents and incidents related to human errors and violations [1]. This study sought responses to a question that asked, 'what is the cause of human errors and violations in construction' using the construction site context. According to Reason [2], human error may include a deviation of some path, either from an intended course of action, from a planned of effort towards the desired goal, and from the appropriate behaviour at work. Violations are a type of mistakes, which happens when individuals fail to follow the instruction or decide to make their own rules when undertaking an activity [3]. In essence, violations are a deliberate act that often happens due to conscious decisions and actions of individuals in the workplace.

The outcomes of human errors are evident in social contexts, and their prevention could be addressed with a motivational process, and organisational remedies [3]. The notion by Lopez et al. [3] that errors manifest and evolve within a social context explains why

* Corresponding author: mfemuze@cut.ac.za

Reason [2] contends that regardless of a skill level, experience or training of people, mistakes and violations often find expressions in workplaces. In addition, deprived organisational deficiency in a workplace is a major source of human errors that contribute to accident causality [1].

To address the dilemma of this study, one needs to understand the causes of human error in construction. According to Dekker [4], there are two views of human errors: the old view and the new view. In the former, 'human error is a cause of accidents' and in the new view 'human error is a symptom of trouble deeper inside a system'. These two views might sound similar, but they are common in that when investigating human errors, you must understand why individuals did what they did (i.e. examining accident or system failure) and not to judge decision-making of the individuals [4].

2 Literature Review

Human failure is in two ways, the person approach and system approach [5]. The person approach focuses on either the mistake, error, slips or lapse of individuals by blaming them for forgetfulness, inattention, and moral weakness. The system approach focuses on the condition under which individuals work and tries to build defences to avert the error and mitigate their effects [5]. Human error is described as a systematically connected frame of individual tools, for example, tasks and operating environment [6]. Progress on the safety of individuals at the job site comes from understanding and influencing system connections [7]. One significant consequence of human errors is the manifestation of accidents.

2.1 Accidents and latent failures

An accident is an unforeseen event that results in a disagreeable consequence, which is linked to human activities instead of natural phenomena [1]. They are the central issue of safety management in any manual and mechanical industry, and the construction industry is no exception [8]. The reason is that the construction industry accounts for a high number of occupational fatal and nonfatal injuries because of accidents [9]. According to Albert et al. [9], collisions may be influenced by the underlying conditions from errors and violations. To address human mistakes and abuses, Reason et al. [10] used a model for illustrating the interventional mechanisms. The 'Swiss Cheese' accident causation model designed by Reason with the purpose to prevent accidents by defences that disallow risks and hazards that can cause loss (see Figure 1). The 'Swiss Cheese' model is divided into two groups namely, hard defence group that are automatic alarming system and the soft defence group which are depended upon the personnel and procedures of required performance [11].

As indicated in Figure 1, each slice of cheese has holes in it, and the gaps between the cheeses are in continues motion, moving from culture and leadership (staff shortage) to clinical support (poor team communication). The holes in the cheese slices represent individual weaknesses in individual parts of the system and are continually varying in size and position in all slices. The gaps arise from unsafe acts and latent failure, permitting "a trajectory of accident opportunity", so that a hazard passes through holes in all of the defences, leading to an accident [10]. Therefore, the latent failure shown in the holes in the cheese slices refer to events, activities, or conditions that deviate from expectations, and cause adverse consequences of organisational significance [12].

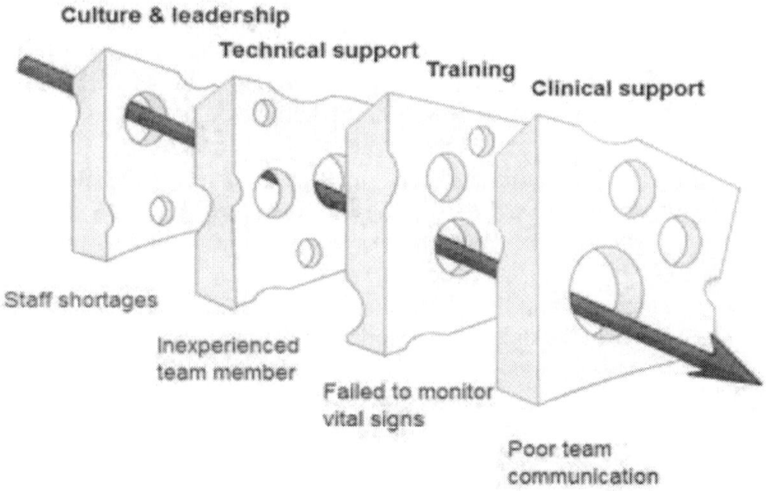

Fig. 1. Reason's 'Swiss Cheese' Model (Source: [10])

Therefore, latent failures could be deduced from an accident caused by the decisions and actions of construction professionals not directly involved in the frontline of physical site work. The failures are typically found in the safety system of a project [10]. Mostly, latent failings happen when there is a lack of supervision or inadequate understanding of the standard work procedure. Practitioners and researchers have argued that the causes of project failure could be traced to latent failure [8]. Latent failures are found in the work system as they merge with natural human tendencies and results in human error and violation of the event [13].

According to Salmon et al. [6], latent failures are inevitable human errors and are always present on construction sites. Most of the time, the latent failures are unforeseen, and they tend to be hidden and trigger at a later stage of the project causing accidents which either result in injuries or fatalities [14]. According to Ellison ([13] citing [2]), latent failure could be caused by limited resources supplied by management. There are numbers of factors causing latent failure in the industry include ineffective training, poor design of plant and equipment, inadequate supervision, ineffective communication, insufficient resources, and uncertainties in roles and responsibility [2]. These factors are technical enablers of latent failures in safety defence systems.

3 Research Methodology

This study aims to identify the causes of human errors and violations in construction. The focus of the reported research is poor safety practice on construction sites. To achieve this goal, an inductive research approach explained by Maxwell [15] was conducted. The reason for using an inductive research approach was to understand the problem through the lived experiences of practitioners. The primary data were synthesised with the reviewed literature in the subject areas. Notable sources include Reason [10], Reason [2] and Dekker [4]. The data of this study was collected using in-depth interview technique with a semi-structured protocol as the instrument. The interviews were conducted on a construction site with several contractors. Some interviewees were provided with the protocol before the sessions through emails to ensure comprehension of the issues.

The interviewees were the member of the contractors working from different construction organisations specialising in the building and civil engineering projects. The primary data were collected from three major municipalities in the Eastern Cape Province of South Africa.

In effect, contractors in three towns, which include Buffalo City Metropolitan Municipality, Ndlambe Local Municipality, and Nelson Mandela Bay Metropolitan Municipality, took part in the study. The selection of the contractors was purposive as explained by Maxwell [15] and the database of each municipality was used to identify contractors who have been appointed by the city to deliver their projects.

The interview sessions were between 15 to 30 minutes in duration. The interviewees who preferred questionnaire to be emailed to them took two to five days to respond to the emails sent to them. In total six (6) construction professionals were interviewed personally, and twenty (20) construction professionals responded to the questionnaire through email communication. In total 45 construction professionals were approached, and only six agreed to be interviewed, and thirty-nine (39) professionals were sent emails, and only twenty (20) responded to the email (see Table 1). The data were analysed using the human error and violations themes.

Table 1. The interview Sample.

Participants	Male	Female	Percentage (%)
Construction managers	4	2	23.1
Site engineers	3	1	15.4
Foreman	4	1	19.2
Quantity surveyors	2	3	19.0
Artisans (skilled workers)	6		23.1
Total	**19**	**7**	**100.0**

4 Research Findings and Discussion

4.1 The impact of an organisational system that produces the human error

Majority of the interviewees responded that they are using a different method to prevent human mistakes on sites and that the order they are using is determined by the scope and nature of the project. It is reported that a safety system is supposed to be designed according to the risk assessment plan, risk management plan, and quality control plan of projects. They further explained that project specifications are very significant as it often helps them to understand the details of the project design concerning hazardous activities. The responses of the interviewees appear to resonate with the importance of a safety system explained by Albert et al. [9] who opined that the fundamental goal of an effective safety system is to help organisations to eliminate or reduce safety risk before work begins on a construction site.

Majority of the respondents explained that they use toolbox talk to analyse the risks in an activity that they were about to undertake on a daily basis. For example, a foreman explained that they had designed a risk assessment checklist to highlight and identify actions that are dangerous and to help them to provide the right safety protective clothes for the task they are undertaking. An interviewee explained that he fails to understand why the construction industry is still experiencing a high rate of accidents despite the introduction of safety regulations to eliminate accidents and promote safety culture on sites.

It is reported that safety guidelines and safety warning boards are very significant to warn and remind the workers about hazardous and dangerous activity on sites. A construction manager and site engineer had a similar response about a safety signboard, which they argued should be designed using the home language of the area they are working on, instead of using the English language because local workers may not be fluent the English language. According to McAleenan and McAleenan [16], a site safety warning sign informs the workers that they are about to enter a 'dangerous site'. Furthermore, several authors regarding the famous saying that a language is a universal medium of communication corroborate a statement of a construction manager and a site engineer about the importance of language.

4.2 Accidents on construction sites

There are various factors causing accidents on construction sites, and such elements are linked to workers' decisions, actions and behaviours. Some interviewees argued that productivity is the leading cause of accidents. They explained that management always prioritises productivity more than the safety and well-being of workers. They contend that workers work under extreme working conditions and when they are tired, they tend to lose concentration to the extent that they would succumb to the temptation to take shortcuts, which end up causing accidents. This explanation is linked to a system approach as described by Reason [10].

Most of the interviewees responded that accidents had become a standard practice in their line of work. A health and safety manager states that to start and finish a project without experiencing a minor or major injury is a significant achievement, which deserves a celebration. Accidents in the construction industry is a substantial concern as explained by Albert et al. [9] who presented statistics that argued that in the United State of America (USA), construction workers are more likely to be killed or injured more than workers in other industries.

Furthermore, it is reported that failure by the employers and employees to follow and respect the organisational safety regulations, designed risk assessment tool and failure to set safety prevention measure will always contribute towards accidents on sites. A construction manager explained that most of the accidents they had experienced in their projects are the results of an error made either by the supervisor or foreman while workers are busy on an activity. This statement of a construction manager is surprising because often a member of the management always blames the workers for accidents, but in this case, both management and the workers are accused of error, which leads to accidents. The reason why human error is blamed on the employers and employees is explained by Dekker [4] with the so-called 'bad apple theory'. In this theory, Dekker [4] suggests that disastrous outcome are preventable if somebody had paid a bit more attention at the job site.

4.3 The impact of the human violation on construction sites

Majority of the interviewees responded that the leading causes of violation on a project site are workers. Furthermore, they explained that often workers fail to concentrate while undertaking an activity, especially if a supervisor is not present. It is clear from the start that violation on-site is blamed on the workers as Holden [7] states that the blame on people continues because it is both a fundamental psychological tendency as well as an industry-standard that remain strong in the human activity industry. In addition, it represents the person approach as explained by Reason [10] in the literature.

Furthermore, the interviewees expressed that workers are careless, and this is a significant problem, which organisation are struggling to handle. A foreman gave an example to support this statement that they had an incident where a worker had stepped on a nail while not wearing safety boots. Instead, the worker was wearing sneaker shoes because he complained that the safety boots make his feet to have a grump. This statement raises questions about organisational safety regulations. A foreman as a leader is not supposed to allow a worker to disrespect the organisational safety rule, and when an incident happened, he cannot blame the worker while he is the one who allowed this situation to occur under his watch. Furthermore, Reason [10] explained that often individuals may forget to be afraid at the workplace or that a nail might hurt his feet while wearing sneaker shoes, but the culture of a high-reliability organisation provides them with both the reminders and the tools to help them remember.

One of the interviewee, working on a road construction project responded that fatigue of the workers causes a human violation. He explained that the majority of their workers are the relatively young adults who do not rest because during the week they come to work, and on weekends, they go to parties. This explains why they often experience fatigue in construction work that is difficult and complex. Fatigue should therefore not pervade a worksite, which requires high energy and strength of the workers. He further explained that they have a breathalyser test to check the worker if they are trunk or not especially on the first Monday of the month. Some interviewees further explained that lack of payment causes a violation. They suggest that often the Government Department fail to pay them on time and because of this result, they fail to pay their skilled workers on time, and often they resign, and the organisations end up promoting unskilled workers to carry out activities that require skilled workers to do.

5 Conclusions

Worldwide, construction work is recognised as hazardous and accident-prone. While other sources exist, accidents in construction are linked to human errors and violations [2,3]. Furthermore, it is reported in the literature that infringements are a type of errors or mistake, which happens when workers fail to follow instructions. In effect, contractors should pay closer attention to site operations to identify and eliminate factors causing human errors. It was discovered that most of the interviewees are aware of the impact of human errors and violations. The interviewees cited ways in which human errors and violations could be reduced. The use of a safety signboard to warn the workers and visitors about hazardous activities serves as an intervention in this context. In conclusion, this study is recommending that training workshop should be introduced to individuals to teach them how to identify and eliminate human errors and violations in the construction

Acknowledgement

The first author has drawn on treatises produced by his students in 2017. The authors gratefully recognise the following students; Luyolo Sigudla, Lubabalo Mabentsela, Bonisile Xashe, Genevieve Coetzee, Amava Ndinisa, and Keletso Letosu.

Reference

1. E. Hollnagel, Barriers and Accident Prevention. Ashgate Publishing Limited, Aldershot, (2004)
2. J. Reason, Human Errors and Models Management. Cambridge: TECNATOM (2011)
3. R. Lopez, E. Peter, D. Love, D.J. Edwards, Design error classification, causation in construction engineering, *Journal of Performance of Constructed Facilities*, **24**(2) (2014)
4. S. Dekker, *Field Guide to Understand 'Human Error'*, Ashgate Publishing Ltd (2014)
5. J. Reason, Human error: models and management, *BMJ* **320**: 768-770 (2000)
6. P.M. Salmon, M. Cornelissen, M.J. Trotter, Systems-based accident analysis methods: a comparison of AcciMap, HFACS and STAMP, *Safety Science* **50**(4): 206-220 (2012)
7. R.J. Holden, People or systems? To blame is human. The fix is to engineer, *National Primary Care (PMC)* **54**(12) (2009)

8. P. Promsorn, P. Soponsaulrat, C.A. Adulyamukosol, P. Kaiyarit, T. Chinda, Identifying root causes of construction accidents: non-human error factors, *Journal of communication and instrument* **2**(1): 4 (2015)
9. Albert, M.R. Hallowell, B.M. Kleiner, Emerging strategies for construction safety & health hazard recognition, *Journal of Safety, Health & Environmental Research* **10**(2) (2014)
10. J. Reason, The Human Contribution: Unsafe Acts, Accidents and Heroic Recoveries. New York, USA: Routledge (2008)
11. S.S. Hosseinian, Z.J. Torghabeh, Major theories of construction accident causation models, *International journal of advanced in engineering* **4**(2) (2012)
12. R. Ramanujam, P.S. Goodman, Latent errors and adverse organizational consequences: a conceptualization, *Journal of Organizational Behavior* **24**: 815-836 (2003)
13. M. Ellison, Construction law made easy, CmCKomodo (2014)
14. S. Kum, B. Sahin, A root analysis for Arctic Marine Accidents from 1993 to 2013, *Safety Science* **74** (2015)
15. J.A. Maxwell, Qualitative Research Design: An Interactive Approach. (3rd ed.), California, USA, Sage Publications (2013)
16. McAleenan, P. McAleenan, Critical Theory: Understanding the Impact Languages has on Workers Safety and Health, *Proceedings of Institution of Civil Engineers: Management, Procurement and Law*, **170**(MP2): 52-58 (2017)

The contribution of Project Team Personal Competence to Sustainable Outcomes in Development Projects

, *Jantanee* Dumrak[1*], *Sherif* Mostafa[2], and *Nick* Hadjinicolaou[1]

[1]Global Project Management, Torrens University Australia, Australia
[2]Construction and Engineering Project Management, School of Engineering and Built Environment, Griffith University

Abstract. Projects are undertaken to serve the particular purposes of organizations. Many projects focus on having monetary benefits, but some projects are non-profit oriented and funded by international or national non-governmental organizations (NGOs) or donors to serve the development of communities. These funded projects are usually established in many disciplines including health, environment, economics, education, social and human rights in countries where the welfare of the population is deficient. From perspectives of project teams and sponsors, having a project-oriented approach allows more project control over their available resources and expected outcomes, especially long-term or sustainable outcomes. In this study, the term 'sustainable outcomes' refers to project activities and their outcomes that survive after the termination of external funding. Sustainable outcomes are derived from the maintenance of benefits generated from an initial project, the continuation of project activities within a new organization, and the maintenance of benefits realization. The sustainable outcomes are impacted by abilities to carry out both on-going and long-term implementation. Therefore, it is important to ensure that personal competence in development projects contribute to sustainable outcomes. This study employs a correlation coefficient analyses to identify personal competence of project team members that contribute to achieving sustainable outcomes. Seventy-five respondents from development projects participated in the questionnaire survey. The research findings show that each of the sustainable outcome domain required different combinations of personal competence attributes.

Keywords: development projects, project management, personal competence, sustainable outcomes

1 Introduction

According to Bossert [1], sustainable outcomes within health development projects can be defined as any project that has expanded its funding yet the flow of benefits can be maintained for at least three years after the life of the project. According to Glasier et al. [2],

* Corresponding author: jantanee.d@gmail.com

it is undeniable that many factors such as socio-cultural, political, economic and educational factors have direct impacts on the longevity of projects. These factors could make any health development projects and programs difficult to accomplish and maintain. The implementation of health improvement requires significant amounts of time, as well as other resources. Most development aspects are highly associated with a population's behavioural change and life cycle which are generally influenced by at least one of the factors mentioned above. Moreover, in some developing countries cultures such as those in Asia, the Middle East, and Africa, health issues are considered to be extremely personal, gender-related, and culturally sensitive issues.

In order to attain sustainable outcomes in health development projects, the barriers to desired outcomes must be mitigated. Many aspects related to sustainable outcomes have been discussed. One of the concerning aspects is to improve skills and personal competence of project officers [3]. To investigate personal competence in relation to sustainable outcomes of health development projects, this paper is structured into four sections. The next section is the literature review.

2 Literature Review

2.1 Personal Competence

Competency is defined as "*an important trait of professionalism*" [4]. Crawford [5, 6] spots a significant relationship between project management competence and organisational performance as well as the core elements of competences including knowledge, skills, attitudes and behaviours that lead to superior performance. The study is conducted on the ground that "*if people who manage and work on projects are competent, they will perform effectively and that this will lead to successful projects and successful organisations*"[6].

According to PMI [7], *Project Manager Competency Development (PMCD) Framework* is applied to direct individuals and organisations towards professional development in project management. The framework is designed incompatibility with the Guide to Project Management Body of Knowledge (PMBOK® Guide). Project management competence according to the PMCD Framework consists of three dimensions including knowledge, performance and personal competences. While knowledge competence focuses on project management credentials, performance and personal capability place their significance on technical and human performance skills as well as competent actions and behaviours in delivering and managing projects.

From the dimensions of competency, it can be said that an individual can be fully competent when he/she is able to integrate all three dimensions and deliver project performance that meets organisational expectations. The framework explains further that an individual competency assessment can be conducted by examining the level of knowledge and understanding of project management, ability to manage a project successfully, and the core personality characteristics that one is expected to possess in order to lead a project. The knowledge and performance competence exist in people-oriented professions, i.e. the selected project practitioners in this research, which can be explicitly presented within task descriptions and performance dashboards. Therefore, this paper only focuses on personal competence, an implicit dimension which is not commonly documented within projects.

2.2 Sustainable Outcomes and Significance in Development Projects

The term "sustainable outcomes" has been increasingly discussed among managers of development programs and projects. In development studies, terminologies including "sustainability" or "benefit sustainability" or "sustained benefits" or "sustainable benefits" have been used interchangeably to express sustainable outcomes. Benefits of sustainable outcomes can be seen from the study of Swidler and Watkins [8] that having sustainable outcomes, not only benefits from the optimization of project investment into the nation's population but also gains in knowledge and skills transfer in long-term perspectives. The concept of sustainable outcomes also includes the continuation of program activities within a new organization, the maintenance of initiatives by building community capacity, the maintenance of benefits generated from an initial program and the maintenance of program services for ongoing operations after the termination of funding and assistance from a donor [9, 10]. Funding termination profoundly impacts on development projects especially when problems remain unsolved and require long-term implementation. With the concepts and application of sustainable outcomes, this could be one of the best solutions to ensure that the benefits and health interventions can be maintained [11-13]. Many research works have attempted to identify the impact of lacking sustainable outcomes to benefits and activities in development projects and programs when the major sponsoring agencies stop their funding [1, 8, 9, 14]. Most of these studies found that benefits are generally discontinued after funding termination.

3 Research Method

Descriptive statistics employed in this data analysis presented project management background of 75 project practitioners who participated in the questionnaire survey (see Figure 1). The majority of the respondents had project experience of three years (51.61%) and worked between 1-3 projects (79.03%) at the time the survey was conducted. The respondents who experienced project works for more than three years but less than five years were reported to be 27.42%. Only 9.68% of this respondent group in this survey that delivered 4-5 projects during these years of experience. The respondents who had more seven years of project experience were counted to be 19.36% with different numbers of projects undertaken. Only 6.45% of these practitioners delivered 8 projects and over.

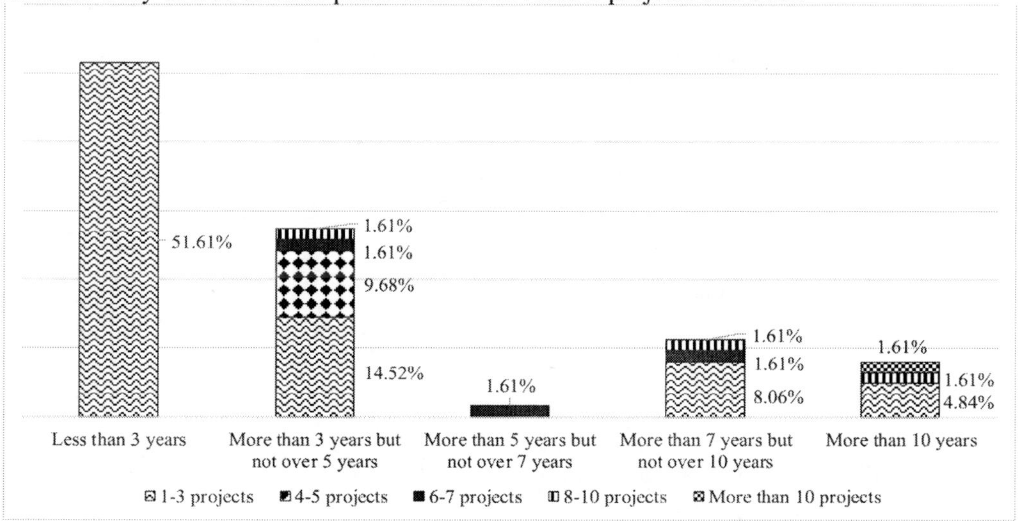

Fig. 4. Project Experience and Numbers of Projects Involved

The results of data analysis conducted using Spearman's Rho in Table 2 below show the directional relationships between attributes of personal competence and studied domains of sustainable outcomes. It was found that each of the sustainable outcome domain required different combinations of personal competence attributes.

At the sustainable outcome orientation where benefits realisation and knowledge are focused, all attributes, except Teamwork and Coordination, were chosen by the respondents as required attributes in this domain. According to the result, Task Organization (r = .390, $p < 0.001$) contains the strongest relationship to sustainable outcome orientation, followed by Self-confidence and Flexibility (r = .385, $p < 0.001$ and r = .380, $p < 0.001$), respectively. In the domain of sustainable outcome capability building, not all attributes were related to this domain. The personal competence areas mostly associated with the sustainable outcome capacity building were Cognitive Ability and Effectiveness. Teamwork and Coordination has the strongest relationship (r = .438, $p < 0.001$), followed by Assertiveness (r = .352, $p < 0.001$). The last domain of sustainable outcome examination was sustainable outcome delivery. In this domain, it was found that the personal competence attributes associated with this domain were lesser than others, especially Leading which has none of the attributes significantly associated with sustainable outcome delivery. Amongst the associated attributes to this domain, Information Seeking forms the strongest relationship (r = .391, $p < 0.001$), followed by Flexibility (r = .334, $p < 0.001$) and Self-motivation (r = .333, $p < 0.001$).

Table 2. Spearman's Rho (r) Correlations between Personal Competence Attributes and Sustainable Outcome Domains

Personal competence	Attribute	Sustainable outcome orientation	Sustainable outcome capability building	Sustainable outcome delivery
Communication	Interpersonal Understanding	.359**	-	-
	Information Seeking	**.326****	-	**.391****
	Stakeholder Oriented	.276*	**.357****	.267*
Leading	Team Leading	.302*	-	-
	Relationship Building	.296*	-	-
	Developing Others	.263*	.318*	-
	Impact and Influencing	.254*	-	-
Managing	Teamwork and Coordination	-	**.438****	-
	Task Organization	**.390****	-	.285*
Cognitive Ability	Analytical Thinking	.253*	.310*	-
	Critical Thinking	.259*	**.345****	-
	Self-motivation	**.340****	.312*	**.333****
	Self-confidence	**.385****	**.349****	.269*
Effectiveness	Initiative	.254*	.329**	-
	Flexibility	**.380****	.290*	**.334****
	Assertive	.282*	**.352****	-
Professionalism	Commitment	-	-	-
	Organizational Awareness	.296*	**.344****	.291*
	Achievement Orientation	.257*	-	-

**. *Correlation is significant at the 0.01 level (2-tailed).*
*. *Correlation is significant at the 0.05 level (2-tailed).*

Kruskal-Wallis Test was conducted across the studied sustainable outcome dimensions. The statistical significance (Asymp. Sig.) presented in Table 3. Any tested data where $p > 0.05$ indicates that all respondents from different grouping agreed to the same level of the studied variables.

Table 3. Kruskal Wallis Test

Personal competence	Attribute	Sustainable outcome orientation	Sustainable outcome capability building	Sustainable outcome delivery
		Asymp. Sig.	Asymp. Sig.	Asymp. Sig.
Communication	Interpersonal understanding	**0.012**	0.358	**0.078**
	Information seeking	**0.043**	0.315	**0.020**
	Stakeholder orientation	**0.025**	0.748	0.129
Leading	Team leading	0.092	0.413	0.426
	Relationship building	0.120	0.374	0.387
	Developing others	0.198	0.115	0.368
	Impact and influence	0.109	0.308	0.082
Managing	Teamwork and coordination	0.494	0.391	0.641
	Task organization	**0.019**	0.288	0.131
Cognitive ability	Analytical thinking	0.124	0.291	0.269
	Critical thinking	0.229	0.620	0.306
	Self-motivation	**0.040**	0.083	0.053
	Self-confidence	**0.019**	0.055	0.126
Effectiveness	Initiative	**0.085**	0.335	0.117
	Flexibility	**0.029**	0.186	0.063
	Assertive	0.150	0.741	0.228
Professionalism	Commitment	0.509	**0.050**	0.194
	Organizational awareness	**0.087**	0.282	0.114
	Achievement orientation	0.139	0.845	0.199

According to the results shown in Table 3, most attributes across sustainable outcome dimensions demonstrate that the respondents agreed with the correlation results presented in Table 2. A main personal competence category with the sustainable outcome orientation respondents had a different agreement on the attributes was Communication. It is evident from Table 3 that the personal communications attributes had strong significance with the sustainable outcome orientation and delivery of projects. The cognitive ability and effectiveness characteristics showed the only significant positive relationship with the suitable outcomes dimension. Whereas two of the professionalism attributes (org. awareness and commitment) demonstrated a significant association with the sustainable orientation and capability building dimensions.

4 Conclusions

This study examined the correlation between the project managers personal competencies with suitable outcomes in health development projects. The study utilised a list of 19 attributes within the six main areas of personal competence that has been defined in the Project Manager Competency Development (PMCD) framework. According to the data analysis and research findings, the study found that each of the sustainable outcome domain required different combinations of personal competence attributes. The sustainable outcome orientation is positively correlated with the communication, managing and cognitive ability competencies. The correlation analyses discovered that the personal competence areas essentially associated with the sustainable outcome orientation. The attributes of task organisation, self-motivation and confidence, flexibility and information seeking have the most robust relationship. Moreover, the domain of sustainable outcome delivery demonstrated strong associated with few attributes including information seeking, and flexibility. To validate this research results, more dimensions of project sustainable outcomes are recommended for further investigation with the PMCD framework.

References

1. T.J. Bossert, Can they get along without us? Sustainability of donor-supported health projects in Central America and Africa, *Social Science & Medicine* **30**:1015-1023 (1990)
2. Glasier, A.M. Gülmezoglu, G.P. Schmid, C.G. Moreno, P.F.A. Van Look, Sexual and reproductive health: a matter of life and death, *The Lancet* **368**(9547):1595-1607 (2006)
3. Government of the Republic of Guinea, *Project name Guinea-Population and Reproductive Health Project*, Ministry of Plan, Guinea (1998)
4. P.W.G. Morris, L. Crawford, D. Hodgson, M.M. Shepherd, J. Thomas, Exploring the role of formal bodies of knowledge in defining a profession - The case of project management, *International Journal of Project Management* **24**(8):710-721 (2006)
5. L. Crawford, *A global approach to project management competence*, AIPM National Conference, Gold Coast, Australia (1997)
6. L.H., Crawford, *Project Management for Strategy Realisation*, 14th World Congress on Project Management, Ljubljana, Slovenia (1998)
7. PMI, *Project manager competency development framework*, PMI (2017)
8. A. Swidler, S.C. Watkins, Teach a man to fish: the sustainability doctrine and its social consequences, *World Development* **37**:1182-1196 (2009)
9. N. LaPelle, J. Zapka, J. Ockene, Sustainability of public health programs: the example of tobacco treatment services in Massachusetts, *American Journal of Public Health* **96**:1363–1369 (2006)
10. E.G. Sarriot, P.J. Winch, L.J. Ryan, J. Bowie, M. Kouletio, E. Swedberg, K. LeBan, J. Edison, R. Welch, M.C. Pacque, A methodological approach and framework for sustainability assessment in NGO-implemented primary health care programs, *International Journal of Health Planning and Management* **19**:23–41 (2004)
11. Tango International., *Sustainability of rural development projects: best practices and lessons learned by IFAD in Asia*, Rome: Tango International, Rome (2009)
12. M.A. Scheirer, G. Hartling, D. Hagerman, Defining sustainability outcomes of health programs: illustrations from an on-line survey, *Evaluation and Program Planning*, **31**: 335-346 (2008)

13. N.C. Edwards, S.M. Roelofs, Sustainability: The elusive dimension of international health projects, *Canadian Journal of Public Health* **97**:45-49 (2006)
14. D. Argaw, M. Fanthahun, Y. Berhane, Sustainability and factors affecting the success of community-based reproductive health programs in rural Northwest Ethiopia, *African Journal of Reproductive Health* **11**:70-79 (2007)
15. S.L. Jackson, *Research methods and statistics: A critical thinking approach*, Cengage Learning (2015)

A Study of the Impact of Project Managers' Power and Influence on their Organisation's Project Management Maturity

Virginia Shahida Ngonda[1*] and *Larry E.* Jowah[2]

[1]Department of Industrial and Systems Engineering, Cape Peninsula University of Technology, P.O. Box 1906, Bellville, South Africa
[2]Department of Management and Project Management, Cape Peninsula University of Technology, P.O. Box 1906, Bellville, South Africa

Abstract. Project managers are determinants of their organisations' project management maturity as their competence is one of the factors that affect their organisations' capability of an organisation to successfully execute projects. This capability of an organisation is reflected in its project management maturity. The study reported in this conference paper sought to investigate whether there is a correlation between South African project managers' power and influence on their organisation's project management maturity. This was done to determine if project managers have sufficient power to influence their organisation's project management maturity. The paper reports on a nation-wide survey that collected data from self-identified project managers. It received three hundred and six valid responses which were edited, coded, and analysed descriptively and inferentially. The study found weak positive correlations between project managers' power, project managers' technical expertise and their organisations' project management maturity. Thus, as project managers' power and technical expertise increase, it is likely that their organisation's project management maturity also increases. However, causation could not be established as it was not possible to establish the temporal order amongst the variables. The established correlations were too weak to be used for prediction.

Keywords: organisation, power, project management maturity, project management maturity model, project manager

1 Introduction

Formalised project management posts are a recent addition to South African organisations. In a 2013 study, Labuschagne et al. [1] claim that only 35% were senior enough to influence change in their organisations. This presents a challenge as by and large a project is a specialised undertaking which requires unique competencies from the project leader

* Corresponding author: ngondas@cput.ac.za

to meet the requirements of the iron triangle – the triple constraints of time, budget and scope [2]. In addition, a project requires an enabling environment. The larger the project, the more likely it is to be complex and interdisciplinary. Thus, involving the formation of interdisciplinary teams to participate in the creation of this unique structure. Projects are characterised by high failure rates, high risks, team conflicts, and many other unique problems.

The project execution process involves the ability to apply the requisite knowledge, appropriate skills, relevant tools and ideal techniques in the process of creating the project product [3]. The success of the project execution process is generally mandated to the project leader. Hence, the existence of is a common belief by senior executives that "picking the right project manager" is the answer for the success of the project execution [4]. However, this is one side of the equation as other functionaries (the project team and the project organisation) has a bearing on the effectiveness of project execution [5].

The parent organisation structures and practices may provide a framework that can aid or hinder project success [6]. The maturity of an organisation can be evaluated based on its ability to provide adequate support, manage the resources, and nurture the project management talent [7]. The ability of an organisation is to practice project management principles that permeate through the entire organisation demonstrates project management maturity [8]. Such an organisation provides structural support for the implementation of projects within itself at all levels.

The concept of project management maturity is used to provide an indication of an organization's capability to manage projects [9]. The more project management mature organisation is more likely to achieve higher overall project success, has less scope creep and less cost and schedule variation. Cooke-Davies and Arzymanow [7] concur with the above that higher maturity reduces variations in an organisation's project execution effectiveness. To measure project management maturity, various project management maturity models have been developed. The project management community uses many more project management maturity models. Grant and Pennypacker [10] report that there were more than 30 maturity models that were used with none receiving worldwide acceptance. Archibald and Archibald [11] report that by the end of the decade, 2006-2016, the number of project management maturity models had grown to hundreds, covering all types of industries.

The link between the project manager and the project organisation is often ignored in the literature on project management maturity. The study reported in this paper seeks to establish a relationship between project managers' attributes and their organisations' project management maturity. To achieve this, the study evaluated the existence of the statistical association, correlation or causation between the project managers' power, project managers' technical expertise, and project managers' project management experience and their organisations' project management maturity. If relationships amongst the parameters exits, then project managers cannot be ignored in initiatives which organisations embark on to improve their project management maturity.

2 Project management maturity models

The majority of (most) project management models measure project management maturity of a five-level ordinal scale following the structure of the first project management maturity model, Software Engineering Institute's Capability Maturity Model (SEI-CMM). SEI-CMM was developed for assessing the capability of an organisation's software development process [12]. SEI-CMM describes the key elements of an effective software development process. SEI-CMM can be used to evaluate an organisation's software development processes against standard criteria and allocate an organisation's maturity to one of its five levels of maturity.

The SEI used a US government grant to adapt the CMM for assessment of organisations' effectiveness in managing non-software projects [13]. The maturity levels for a generalised capability maturity model that was termed Capability Maturity Model Integration (SEI-CMMI) are described in Table 1.

Table 1. Maturity levels in the SEI-CMMI

Maturity Levels	Description
Level 5 (Optimising)	Continuous improvement using both quantitative and qualitative data generated from previous and current projects is practised. Innovation in both processes and project management tools is routine.
Level 4 (Managed)	Metrics are collected for both products and processes. All projects are carefully monitored and controlled.
Level 3 (Defined)	Standardisation and documenting of project process becomes the norm. The organisation develops its own way of managing projects. Each section/department manages projects in the same way.
Level 2 (Repeatable)	Project management processes are in place and track the triple constraints of each project: time, cost, and requirements. Lessons learned are used in the execution of similar projects. Project success can be repeated for similar projects.
Level 1 (Initial)	Project management process is ad hoc or even chaotic. The organisation does not provide support for the project manager. Success in projects depends on the competency and the effort of individual project managers. While organisations in this level can succeed in a project, success is not often repeatable.

Over the years, other project management models have been developed. Project management maturity models are divided into three broad categories: technical delivery process models, project management process models and organisational maturity models. SEI-CMM and other technical delivery process models focus on documenting project management processes and increasing the level of application on standardised project management processes within an organisation. Project management process models are an evolution of the technical delivery process models where they can apply the same concept of increased capability within the context of an organisation which practises project management based on a standard such as PMBOK or PRINCE2. PMS-PMMM is an example of such a model that integrates the capability structure of SEI-CMM. Organisational maturity models go beyond project management and review the entire organisation. They can be applied to organisations that are not project-orientated. Table 2 provides examples of the models and highlight their evolution.

Table 2. Key developments in the evolution of project management maturity models

Year	Model	Developer and application
1986	Capability Maturity Model (CMM)	Developed by Carnegie Mellon University Software Engineering Institute to access software development capability
2000	Kerzner Project Management Maturity Model (Kerzner-PMMM)	Developed by Harold Kerzner as a generic model that was meant to extend CMM into general project management
2002	Berkeley Project Management Process Maturity Model, $(PM)^2$	Developed by Young Kwak and William Ibbs as a generic model that the encompassed key project management knowledge areas and key processes that occur within the knowledge areas
2002	Project Management Maturity Model (PMS-PMMM)	Developed by PM Solutions as a generic model that is aligned with the PMBOK knowledge areas

2003	Organizational Project Management Maturity Model (OPM3)	Released by the PMI-USA as a generic organisation-wide model for project, programme, and portfolio management maturity assessment
2009	PRINCE2 Maturity Model (P2MM)	Developed by United Kingdom's Office of Government Commerce to support maturity assessments in organisations that are using PRINCE2

Project management maturity models are not silver bullets that solve project management capability challenges. Cooke-Davies [14] warns that project maturity models do not confer a competitive advantage to an organisation, but they are rather a valuable tool that can assist an organisation in its quest for project management excellence. Perhaps the value of the models can be appreciated when one considers anecdotal evidence of project success rates of organisations that have low maturity levels. In a Brazilian study, Prado, Oliveira and Romano [15] found that there is a direct positive relationship between project management maturity and project success. They found that as project maturity increased from 1 to 5, project success also increased from 38.7% to 81%. Conversely, as maturity decreased from 5 to 1, the project failure rate increased from 5% to 18.6%. Other researchers reported similar findings as well.

3 Relationship between project management maturity and the project manager

An organisation's project management maturity depends on the competency of its staff, particularly that of the project manager [4]. Competency is "the ability to mobilise, integrate and transfer knowledge, skills and resources to reach or surpass performance in work assignments adding economic and social value to the organisation" [16]. Although the competency of a project manager cannot be directly measured it can be inferred from personal attributes such as qualifications, experience, attitudes, and behaviours [4]. Project management associations have recognised the impact of project managers on project management success such that they have introduced frameworks for assessing and certifying PM competencies [16].

Chipulu, Neoh, Ojiako and Williams [17] investigated and mapped key project manager competencies from a study of project manager recruitment adverts from all over the world. They found that employers sought project management knowledge and expertise as evidence of project management qualifications, certifications, and years of project management experience. They also found that employers sought senior managerial experience that can provide strategic leadership as well as manage change. High emotional intelligence and understanding of professional ethics were also sought. Lastly, highly sought project managers are expected to be experts in risk management.

A project manager is defined as an individual who is responsible for managing a project [18]. It is not a title that makes one a project manager. Gray and Larson [18], correctly note that most people who manage projects do not carry a project manager title, suggesting that the function is unique given the unique nature of the projects themselves. Crawford [4] concurs and posits that their function goes beyond mere coordination of activities to implement a plan since they are liable for the success or failure of the project execution process.

Effective project managers are essentially leaders in that they too often do not have the formal authority [19]. However, Mersino [20] notes that like other managers, project managers are expected to be able to get work done. Mazibuko, Tait and Jowah [21] concur and assert that project leaders have a serious problem because they have an authority gap (no formal authority) and thus find themselves having to develop other competencies to enable them to overcome the authority gap and deliver on expectations. The issues of power and influence are very crucial as, according to Mersino [20], project managers achieve their objectives through the work done by other people whom the project manager has no functional authority over.

4 Research design

The study reported in this conference paper adopted a correlational survey methodology. The study used a questionnaire that based on concepts of Kerzner's Project Management Maturity Model and project managers' attributes that were developed by Cooke-Davies and Arzymanow [7] to collect data from self-identified South African project managers by their membership of a project management association. An invitation to participate in the study, with a link to the online questionnaire, was published in the selected association's newsletter that was sent to all their members. The invitation was sent out in January 2017 and by February 2017, three hundred and six completed responses were received.

The data was cleaned and edited for any errors and omissions that were identified, the questions were coded, and the information was captured onto a spreadsheet. After the preparation, analysis of the response data was conducted using a commercial statistical analysis package. The data was analysed¡¡ in two ways. First, data were analysed to provide means, percentage, and standard deviations of the variables. This data was then converted to illustrations in the form of tables, pie charts, histograms, and bar charts. Secondly, hypotheses testing was conducted using the Pearson Chi-Squire test of independence [22]. This analysis provided information on the basis on which generalisations may be made to the research findings.

5 Findings and discussion

The study found that in South Africa, the project management profession is relatively STEM orientated and comprise relatively older, more qualified, and more experienced practitioners. The respondents had media age 37.58 years, most worked in IT (59.1%) followed by construction and engineering (23.5%). Both are in STEM. In addition, most respondents had a postgraduate degree (73.5%), followed by those with a degree (18.6%) and lastly those with a diploma (7.8%). Lastly, it seems that project management in South Africa is a relatively male-dominated profession. This might reflect on the fact that STEM in South Africa is male-dominated.

The study showed that South African project management industry has slightly matured since the 2013 PMSA commissioned a study by Labuschagne et al. [1]. When compared with global trends, the perceived maturity of South African organisations is still very low, although, there are pockets of high maturity. 8.2% of the respondents' companies had achieved a perceived maturity of five. 42.2% of the organisations had a project management maturity of three. Most of the organisations were practising aspects of project management and had structures that would support a higher maturity than what they were currently at.

As shown in Table 3, a test of association using Spearman's rho and partial correlation test indicated that project managers' power and their organisation® project management maturity are not independent of each other. The association is significant. A correlation test revealed a weak positive relationship between the two. Thus, as project managers' power increases, it is likely that their organisation's project management maturity also increases. The study did attribute the organisation's improvement to the increase in project managers' power as the study would not establish the temporal order between the two. Similar tests for project management maturity and project managers' technical expertise also revealed that as project managers' technical expertise increases, it is likely that their organisation's project management maturity also increases. Like before, temporal order could not be established.

Table 3. Spearman's correlation for project managers' power, influence, project managers' project management experience, project managers' technical expertise and project management maturity

		Project managers' influence	Project managers' power	Project managers' technical expertise	Project managers' project management experience
Project managers' influence	Correlation Coefficient				
	Sig. (2-tailed)				
Project managers' power	Correlation Coefficient	.730**			
	Sig. (2-tailed)	0.000			
Project managers' technical expertise	Correlation Coefficient	.055	.126*		
	Sig. (2-tailed)	0.335	0.028		
Project managers' project management experience	Correlation Coefficient	.108	.083	.131*	
	Sig. (2-tailed)	0.059	0.150	0.022	
Project management maturity of organisation	Correlation Coefficient	.191**	.292**	-.137*	.113*
	Sig. (2-tailed)	0.001	0.000	0.016	0.049

The study found that although project management maturity and project managers' project management experience as indicated these are not independent of each other, their association was spurious as it was mediated by project managers' power (see Table 4). Similar findings were made about project managers' influence and their organisations' project management maturity. In this case, project managers' power was also the mediating variable. Partial correlation of project managers' technical expertise yielded a significance value of 0.000, which is below the 0.01 value that indicates significance. Thus, only project managers' power and technical expertise are correlated with project management maturity. Inspection of Table 3 shows that correlation between project managers' technical expertise and project management is only significant at the 0.05 level.

Table 4. Partial correlation of project managers' influence, technical expertise and project management experience, and project management maturity with project managers' power as the mediating variable

		Project managers' influence	**Project managers' technical expertise**	**Project managers' project management experience**
Project managers' influence	Correlation			
	Significance (2-tailed)			
Project managers' technical expertise	Correlation	-.054		
	Significance (2-tailed)	0.349		
Project managers' project management experience	Correlation	.087	.161	
	Significance (2-tailed)	.128	.005	
Project management maturity of organisation	Correlation	.027	.282**	.044
	Significance (2-tailed)	0.636	0.000	0.449

The study indicates that project managers, particularly the power that they have in their organisations, cannot be ignored in initiatives that organisations embark on to improve their project management maturity. It shows that an organisation's project managers' power and technical expertise have an influence on its project management maturity. Thus, to guarantee project management maturity, organisations should assist their project managers to develop their technical expertise. For example, organisations could assist their project managers to develop expert power, which is based on the individual's relevant experience and knowledge for the team to complete the task [23]. They could facilitate their project managers to achieve certification such as PMI-USA's PMP certification, a certification from the South African Council for Project and Construction Management Professions, or any other reputable body whose members are perceived to be project management experts. In addition, project managers can be granted connection power which is not related to someone's position in the organisation or team but rather tied to the connection to power players that an individual might have [24]. Having a visible executive sponsor might provide the required connection power. Facilitating access to power would assist in narrowing the authority gap of project managers by giving their sufficient authority. Their organisations would benefit from this as project managers would be able to implement the changes that are required for project management maturity improvement.

6 Conclusion

The study found that there are non-spurious relationships between project managers' power and their organisations' project management maturity and between project managers' technical expertise and their organisations' project management maturity. The study did not find statistical evidence supporting the existence of relationships between project managers' influence and their organisations' project management maturity, between project managers' project management experience and their organisations' project management maturity, and between project managers' technical expertise and their organisations' project management maturity. The findings of this study indicate that organisation s would benefit if they facilitated the project managers' efforts to narrow their authority gap through the acquisition of expert and connection power.

References

1. L. Labuschagne, C. Marnewick, M. Eloff, H. Steyn, P. Tobin, Project Management Maturity vs Project Outcomes in Africa (Project Management South Africa, Pretoria, 2013)
2. H. Kerzner, Project Management Best Practices: Achieving Global Excellence, 3rd ed., New Jersey, USA: Wiley (2014)
3. Project Management Institute, *A Guide to the Project Management Body of Knowledge (PMBOK Guide)*, 4th ed., Pennsylvania, USA: Project Management Institute (2008)
4. L. Crawford, Senior Management Perceptions of Project Management Competence, *International Journal of Project Management* **23**(1): 7–16 (2005)
5. J.M. Nicholas, H. Steyn, *Project Management for Engineering, Business and Technology*, 4th ed., London, UK: Routledge (2012)
6. Project Management Institute, *A Guide to the Project Management Body of Knowledge (PMBOK Guide)*, 5th ed., Pennsylvania, USA: Project Management Institute (2013)
7. T.J. Cooke-Davies, A. Arzymanow, The Maturity of Project Management in Different Industries: An Investigation into Variations between Project Management Models, *International Journal of Project Management* **21**(6): 471-478 (2003)
8. J. Farrokh, A.K. Mansur, Project Management Maturity Models and Organizational Project Management Maturity Model (OPM3): A Critical Morphological Evaluation, *Project Management* **2**(7): 23–33 (2013)
9. C.W. Ibbs, J.M. Reginato, Y.H. Kwak, Developing Project Management Capability: Benchmarking, Maturity, Modeling, Gap Analyses, and ROI Studies. In J.K. Pinto P.W.G. Morris (eds.), *The Wiley Guide to Managing Projects*, New Jersey, USA: Wiley, 1214–1233 (2004)
10. K.P. Grant, J.S. Pennypacker, Project Management Maturity: An Assessment of Project Management Capabilities among and between Selected Industries, *IEEE Transactions on Engineering Management* **53**(1): 59–68 (2006), http://ieeexplore.ieee.org/lpdocs/epic03/wrapper.htm?arnumber=1580894
11. R.D. Archibald, S.C. Archibald, *Leading and Managing Innovation: What Every Executive Team Must Know about Project, Program, and Portfolio Management*, 2nd ed., Boca Raton, USA: CRC (2016)
12. G.A. Kumta, M.D. Shah, Capability Maturity Model, *Delhi Business Review* **3**(1) (2002)
13. M. Paulk, *A Comparison of ISO 9001 and the Capability Maturity Model for Software*, Pittsburgh, USA: Carnegie Mellon University (1994)
14. T. Cooke-Davies, Project Management Maturity Models. In J.K. Pinto, P.W.G. Morris (eds.), *The Wiley Guide to Managing Projects*, New Jersey: USA: Wiley, 1234–1255 (2007)
15. D. Prado, W.A. de Oliveira, L.M. Romano, *Project Management Maturity Research Report 2014: "General Report" Part A: Indicators* (2015), http://www.maturityresearch.com/novosite/en/index.html
16. S.M. Takey, M.M. de Carvalho, Competency Mapping in Project Management: An Action Research Study in an Engineering Company, *International Journal of Project Management* **33**(4): 784–96 (2015)

17. M. Chipulu, J.G. Neoh, U. Ojiako, T. Williams, A Multidimensional Analysis of Project Manager Competences, *IEEE Transactions on Engineering Management* **60**(3): 506–17 (2013)
18. C.F. Gray, E.W. Larson, *Project Management: The Managerial Process*, 5th ed., New York, USA: McGraw-Hill/Irwin (2011)
19. T. Roeder, *Managing Project Stakeholders: Building a Foundation to Achieve Project Goals*, New Jersey, USA: Wiley (2013)
20. A. Mersino, *Emotional Intelligence for Project Managers*, 2nd ed., New York, USA: American Management Association (2013)
21. N.E. Mazibuko, M. Tait, L.E. Jowah, Critical Core Competencies Required for Effective Project Leadership in the Presence of the Authority Gap, *Journal of Contemporary Management* **12**: 313–35 (2015)
22. M. Saunders, P. Lewis, A. Thornhill, *Research Methods for Business Students*, 5th ed., Edinburgh, UK: Pearson (2009)
23. J. Schermerhorn, J.G. Hunt, R.N. Osborn, *Organizational Behaviour*, 7th ed., New York, USA: Wiley (2002)
24. Elearn Limited, Leadership and Management in Organisations, Oxford, USA: Elsevier (2007)

Approach to increase flexibility in automobile body shops through component-integrated fixture functions

Achim Kampker[1], *Johannes* Triebs[1], and *Jan Ole* Hansen[1*]

[1]RWTH Aachen, Chair of Production Engineering of E-Mobility Components, Campus Boulevard 30, Aachen, Germany

Abstract. Due to shorter product life-cycles, increasing product customization and the co-existence of electric and combustion engine vehicles, variant flexibility is gaining importance in the automobile production. The automobile body shop is characterized by inflexible, rigid fixture systems dedicated to meet the geometrical requirements of specific body parts. Changes in part geometry or dimension require the development of new fixture systems, thus increasing product variety results in higher fixture costs. This paper presents an approach for a fixtureless body shop based on component-integrated fixture-functions, increasing variant flexibility and reducing fixture costs. The approach is implemented using a body part assembly of an electric vehicle.

Keywords: automobile body shop, electric vehicles, fixtureless body shop, variant flexibility

1 Introduction

Automobile body shops are often rigid production systems with a high degree of automation for high production volumes. Due to its low flexibility and high investment costs in mid-digit million ranges [1], the body shop is particularly affected by increasing number of variants and shorter product life cycles. A significant part of the investment costs is caused by development and production of fixtures. According to Meichsner, variant-specific fixture costs can rise up to 40% of the total system costs in certain body shop stations [2]. Since fixtures are generally dedicated to meet the geometrical requirements of specific body parts, changes in part geometry or dimension, due to design changes between model years or due to integration of a new model to an existing production line, require the development and production of new fixtures. Consequently, the increasing product variety results in higher fixture costs.

Existing approaches in the body shop to flexibilize fixture are based mainly on the kinematisation of the fixture system whereby investment costs for kinematized fixture

* Corresponding author: j.hansen@pem.rwth-aachen.de

systems can surpass those of conventional fixtures by 50%. Further, flexibility gain of kinematized fixture systems is low due to limitations in adaptability and change time restrictions [3]. Therefore, research has increased efforts to replace fixture systems by an economic and flexibility increasing alternative technology. Feature-based fixturing approaches, enabling fixtureless body shop concepts by integrating fixture-functions within the body part through geometrical features, are expected to be advantageous in terms of investment costs savings and flexibility gain [4].

This paper describes a methodology to select and evaluate application-specific combinations of geometrical features and joining technologies suitable to replace conventional fixture systems. The approach is based on component-integrated fixture-functions, which have been implemented in a fixtureless body shop station for an electric vehicle body part assembly using the described methodology.

2 Practical approaches on fixture flexibilization

In order to be able to produce cost-efficiently despite high initial investments and declining variant-specific quantities, body shops must be able to produce several vehicle variants flexibly on a single body shop line. By making body shops more flexible, investments in high-grade automation can be allocated to a larger number of products to be manufactured and justified economically. While the potential for flexibility in industrial robots can be exploited, for example, by changing tools and programs, fixtures that are specially adapted to specific part geometries considerably limit flexibility in automobile body shops. In recent years, increased efforts have been made to make the fixtures in body shops more flexible. The approaches implemented nowadays are mainly based on the kinematization of the fixture system, whereby the motion may concern the complete fixture (fixture changing systems) or be present within the fixture (e.g. adaptive clamping techniques).

Depending on the size of the fixture, the required kinematics are performed by industrial robots, rotary tables and drums or gantry systems and linear units (see Fig. 1) [5]. Small, lightweight fixtures are often stored in a fixture magazine and are replaced by industrial robots. Medium and large fixtures are mounted on rotary tables or drums, which are rotated to the body construction line depending on the vehicle variant to be manufactured. Despite the high total weight of up to 17,000 kg for table/drum and payload, the fixture change takes place within the cycle times. Due to the high space requirement, rotary tables and drums are suitable for accommodating two to four fixture variants. Rotary drum systems are used, for example, in the side frame production of the Audi Q5 [6]. The largest and heaviest fixtures weighing up to 2,500 kg are used in the framing stations of body shops, in which the base assembly, side frame and roof of the body are brought together. The vertical fixtures are mounted on gantry systems and linear units for transport to the body shop line.

The use of fixture change systems is suitable for a limited number of part variants and allows only limited flexibility in body shops. If the part geometry is changed, the complete fixture must still be replaced or an additional changing system must be integrated. Disadvantages are not only the costs for design and production, but also the space required, the associated storage and logistics costs as well as the capital commitment.

Compared to fixture changing systems, flexible fixtures use adaptable function carriers, whereby the clamping and determining elements adapt to different part geometries. On the one hand, the function carriers can be mounted on movable elements, which adapt to shape and size variations of the parts within given dimensions. The moving elements are often operated automatically via a pneumatic drive. In addition to movable function carriers, the clamping elements can be made more flexible by means of shape-variable adjustments. The clamping elements adapt to the part geometry by means of force or form-fit control, whereby pin cushions are often used in body shops [7]. The application flexibility of flexible fixtures is limited to just a few centimeters due to the adjustment ranges of the elements, consequently limiting the number of part variants. Further, investment costs in flexible fixtures often surpass those for conventional fixture systems and quality issues are common due to frequent adjustments and the elasticity of the systems. Thus, neither fixture changing systems nor flexible fixtures are economic viable solutions to increase flexibility in future automobile body shops.

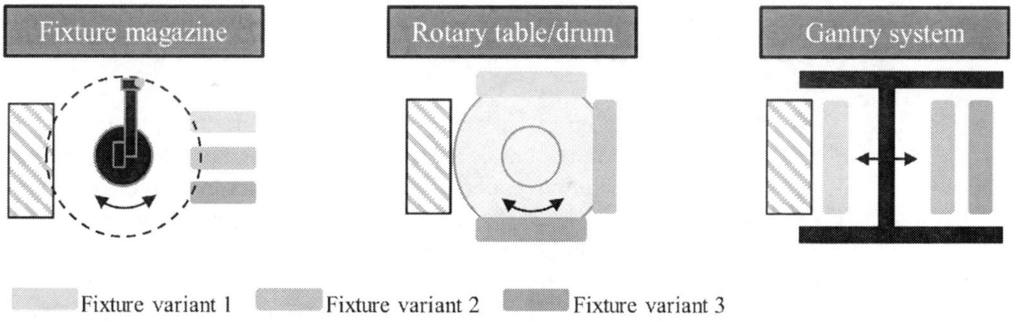

Fig. 1. Concepts for fixture changing systems in automobile body shops.

2.1 Literature review

As mentioned above, a concept to reduce fixture costs and increase flexibility in a fixtureless body shop consists of relocating fixture-functions into the parts to be joined. In this concept, the fixture functions are taken over by geometrical features integrated into the parts. Therefore, approaches discussed following are related to the research area of feature-based fixturing (FBF). Adams and Whitney define these so-called 'assembly features' as objects that restrict one or more degrees of freedom between two parts to be joined and fix this restriction [8]. Naing supplements this description with the note that features used must always be considered as pairs, since the degrees of freedom constraint by a feature always depend on the mate [9].

When considering FBF approaches for body shop applications, several evaluation criteria should be taken into account according to Schlather [10]. Firstly, since geometrical feature are being integrated into the body parts, approaches should be applicable in early phases of the product development to ensure appropriate part design. Further, geometrical features should be considered to replace fixture and their functionalities, specifically positioning, clamping and fixing of body parts. A logic relating fixture-functions to geometrical features taking body shop tolerances and part accuracies into consideration should be presented. Considering the processes in automobile body shops, commonly used joining technologies such as spot welding or gluing should be considered when selecting features for specific use applications. In the following main approaches applicable to automotive body shops are discussed and evaluated regarding the described criteria listed in Table 1.

Table 1. Criteria to evaluate FPF approaches for use in body shops.

Evaluation Criteria
Considers early phases of product development
Considers geometrical features to replace fixtures
Presents logic to relate geometrical features to fixtures-functions
Contemplates accuracy and tolerances in body shops
Considers joining technologies used in body shops
Describes feature selection process according to use-case

Koonmen developed a methodology called 'precision assembly technique' in 1994, which enables the assembly of components according to requirements from aircraft floor assemblies without fixtures. The technical concept is based on a combination of plug-in and mounting features. Together they can restrict a certain number of degrees of freedom before the joining operation. Further the author describes to what extent the entire assembly organization within a company would have to be adapted to the new concept and which extensive changes would be necessary for this [11]. The approach misses to describe the relation between fixture-functions and geometrical features. Further, neither accuracies and tolerances nor joining technologies utilized in body shops are considered.

In their approach to model assembly processes by pair characteristics, Chang and Perng focus on the development of capable feature-based part positioning mechanisms. To this end, characteristics and their characterizing properties (volumes, reference systems and interfaces) are described. Three types of combinations of features are outlined by the authors: fit-based, contact-based and orientation-based. Chang and Perng also examine the fastening of several superimposed parts and subdivide the assemblies into individual subassemblies [12]. Summarizing, the investigations focus less on descriptive or selection processes for geometrical features, but rather on the simplifications that can be achieved in the design phases for part positioning processes through the use of features.

Walczyk et al. developed a methodology for the fixture-free assembly of simple sheet metal parts for the aviation industry. The technical basis is tolerated alignment holes, which are drilled into the parts via CNC machines. At these alignment holes, the parts are connected to each other by temporary closures. On the basis of this part alignment and fixation, the parts are then finally joined at the points where the rivets or bolts are already positioned in the conventional case. Depending on the application, it may also make sense to use rivet or bolt holes already provided as alignment holes in order to avoid additional holes. To determine the optimum position and suitable tolerances of alignment holes, Walczyk et al. provide several indications, which refer in particular to the desired restriction of all degrees of freedom by the closures in interaction with the part geometry. The authors name so-called 'cleo clamps' as an exemplary temporary clamp lock, which expand after insertion into the holes and thus allow the parts to be centered and fixed. The clamps are removed after the joining process [13]. Nevertheless, no logic relating geometrical features to fixture-functions is given by the authors. Further, neither accuracies and tolerances nor joining technologies utilized in body shops are considered.

Naing applies the FBF principle in the developed 'integrated methodology for jigless assembly' to the assembly of parts from the aviation industry. Naing explicitly includes the design phase in the methodology in order to integrate fixture functions into parts. The approach is divided into two main parts. Firstly, the author represents a mapping of all influences affecting the feature selection process. The influences are reflected time, cost and quality dimensions. However, it is pointed out that the cost dimension is a priority aspect and is related to all other influences. In a second part the author describes in detail the feature selection process as part of the methodology. He differentiates between location, support, clamping and fastening features for use in assembly processes. Based on this distinction, the author describes the selection process for positioning features in detail using examples from the aviation industry. For the selection of other characteristic types, general notes are given as to which influences should be taken into account in the selection. A feature library with characteristics for all four features types is created within the work. The characteristics library should be comprehensive, but no claim to completeness is made [9]. For the utilization in body shop applications, the approach misses considering joining technologies as well as the accuracies and tolerances arising in these processes.

With their principle of 'integral attachment', Messler et al. developed an approach for the mechanical fastening and joining of components by means of integrated attachment features. A firm connection is made by means of elastic, plastic or combined elastic-plastic deformation of the fastening features. The aim of integrated fastening is to implement fastening processes without additional tools, such as closures or fixtures. The main fastening features examined are snap-fits, in which an elastic plug feature is inserted into a fixed recording feature. On this basis, Messler et al. differentiate between positioning features ('locating features') and fixing features ('locking features'). 'Extended features' or 'Attributes' can also perform other supporting functions, such as improving user-friendliness. The authors also developed a classification scheme for various representative geometries of features and used this as a basis for investigating the combinability of different feature forms. The identified characteristics are divided into 'latches' and 'catches'. A combination matrix ('matrix of locking pairs') makes it possible to determine whether the respective plug-in and recording features can be combined with each other. A methodology consisting of six steps has been developed to facilitate the selection of appropriate fastening features. In doing so, all influences with regard to functions, arrangement, manufacture and robustness of features are taken into account. The selection of different fastening concepts is based mainly on a cost-based performance assessment [14]. Since the approach was developed for utilization in assembly processes, joining technologies in body shops are not taken into account. Further, the authors miss presenting a description of the feature selection process which considers accuracies and part tolerances.

Schlather developed a four-step methodology for the feature-based, fixtureless assembly of sheet metal structures, which was to address and improve various weak points of these based on an analysis of existing approaches. At first, the authors investigated and structured those factors that influence the dimensional accuracy and absorption potential of clamping and joining forces of feature-based fixture approaches. Based on this study, an approach for integrating the fixture functions into the parts was then developed in which the influencing factors are taken into account when selecting features. In a first step, suitable characteristic pairs for this approach are identified. Then characteristic pairs and parts are modeled and simulated to determine their influence on dependent variables. The core of the methodology follows with a detailed analysis of the interactions between features, parts and variables dependent on assembly and joining technologies. Concrete design guidelines for further implementation are derived from this analysis [10]. Nevertheless, neither a logic relating geometrical features to feature-functions nor a use-case specific feature selection process are presented.

By using FBF approaches, the use of conventional fixtures can be almost completely dispensed, resulting in corresponding investment reduction and flexibility gain. Nevertheless, the application of FBF approaches to automotive body shops presents further challenges which can be summarized in following points:

- Further research is needed to determine to what extent feature-based approaches are suitable for meeting the requirements specified in body shops, in particular with regard to tolerances and accuracies,

- The influence of joining technologies relevant for automotive production on feature-based approaches has not yet been taken into account,
- There are no guidelines for designers in early development phases on how to select geometrical features for specific use cases taking the above points into account.

The points are to be supplemented by the lack of inclusion of methodological considerations in the design of the respective features. Thus, the identified research demand forms the central motivation of the approach presented following.

3 Approach to select geometrical features for fixtureless body shops

Since the approach is to be understood as part of an early stage development process, its procedure must be based on a theoretically founded design methodology. In this case, the Pahl/Beitz design methodology is used as a basis [15]. The proposed approach comprises a total of four steps (methods), each of which is used to develop an overall methodology using suitable tools. Each method of the overall methodology generates output variables at product and data level, taking into account the input variables at product and data level and the associated methods at method level (see Fig. 2). Basis for the methodology is a model of the considered system, in this case a product, and the associated framework (replacing fixture in body shop), which is used as an input variable and then further developed in the course of the methodology.

Therefore, the methodology is initially provided with a 'model of the framework' as a mapping of the application case with all data relevant to the methodology. By applying method I, these data is systematically mapped for further use in the methodology. In the following steps, internal data generated in the previous methods is used in addition to relevant external data supplied. All data systematized and generated in the methodology is systematically presented in the form of a 'product development sheet' and made available for further use in the development process.

The first step of the methodology takes up the model of the framework and prepares it for further analysis. An essential component of method I is to depict the considered joining points in the 'effector system' of the fixtures used in the production process. The effector system for fixtures was introduced by Trummer and Wiebach [16] and is used to systematically record and categorize the multitude of influences within fixture-related processes. The basic idea is that the considered joining points with integrated geometrical features take up the place of fixture within conventional body shop and must accordingly take into account all influences acting there. Therefore, the metal sheets to be joined in the body shop station are abstracted to their joining points. Joining points are described by means of the type of joint between the parts, in general parallel-joint or line-joint. Thus, the output of the method are the considered joining points in a transformed effort system for fixtures in the body shop.

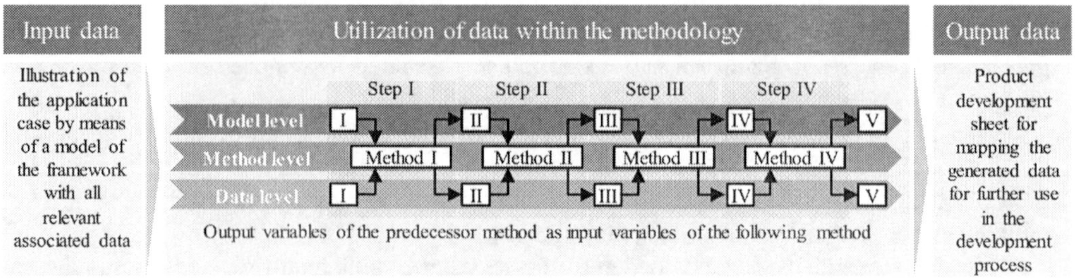

Fig. 2. Input-Output relations between methods and levels of the methodology.

The requirements for the joining point can be derived from this transformed effort system for step 2 of the methodology. These requirements are divided into requirements derived from fixture-functions and further original requirements that have to be considered for joining points. The derived requirements with their characteristics are presented in a morphological box. Since the features to be selected are to take over the functions of a fixture in conventional body shops, it must first be derived how the fixture functions can be recorded and which associated characteristics can occur. The identified requirements thus reflect the role of the fixtures in the original effort system or the role of the joining points in the transformed effort system.

The fixture-function positioning is represented in the methodology from the perspective of relative assembly time and centering. The relative assembly time takes into account the cycle times specified in production planning. On this basis, the portion of the cycle time available for the positioning of the metal sheets within the overall process is determined. Centering describes the location of the parts relative to each other. By centering the assembly through geometrical features integrated into the parts, tolerances and accuracies inherent by the features are considered. Production-related tolerances and accuracies of the features can be described by knowledge of their manufacturing processes. The fixture-functions clamping and fixing are represented by the number of degrees of freedom to be restricted per direction of movement before the joining process. Accordingly, three translatory and three rotational degrees of freedom must be taken into account, each of which must be restricted in none, only in positive, only in negative or in both coordinate directions. In most applications it is generally desirable to restrict all degrees of freedom. However, there are cases in which a fixing in one coordinate direction is explicitly not desired. This may be the case, for example, if thermal expansion due to joining processes follow and the degrees of freedom must remain unrestricted. The size and exact geometry as well as the number of features to be selected determine whether the parts remain safely in the determining position under the influence of the joining process. The three elements of fixing forces, magnitude, direction and point of application, are considered in this work.

The feature assignment and selection processes in steps 3 and 4 of the methodology require describing all possible eligible geometrical features, taking into consideration the constraints and degrees of freedom resulting from joining technologies. As shown in Fig. 3, the relation between part integrated geometrical features, joining processes as well as the joining point requirements derived in the second step of the methodology are therefore considered within multi-domain matrices (MDM). According to Maurer [17], an indefinite number of domains can be analyzed within MDM matrices, as matrix entries are themselves matrices.

Domains	Requirements	Geometrical features	Joining technologies
Requirements	-	MDM: requirements – geometrical features (step 3)	MDM: requirements – joining technologies (step 4)
Geometrical features	MDM: requirements – geometrical features (step 3)	-	MDM: geometrical features – joining technologies (step 4)
Joining technologies	MDM: requirements – joining technologies (step 4)	MDM: geometrical features – joining technologies (step 4)	-

Fig. 3. Requirements, features and joining technologies are related in multi-domain-matrices (MDM).

Feature assignment, as the third step in the methodology, describes the relation between the requirements derived in step 2 with all eligible geometrical features, depending on their degree of requirement fulfillment. For this purpose, an abstracted description of geometrical features is required in order to structure and classify the large amount of possible features. Feature characteristics differ, among others, in regard to their geometry, material and assembly process. The authors therefore propose to describe features by geometrical (e.g. ball), functional (e.g. undercut) and process related (e.g. fixing force) factors. Geometrical characteristics of the features are outlined by formulas, as e.g. volume or surface of a ball can easily be calculated. From the geometry of the feature, a functional characteristic is derived. The functional characteristic then defines a requirement fulfillment within the process of geometry setting between the parts to be joined. A feature with an undercut structure would, for example, constraint more degrees of freedom than an overlaying feature due to the fixing force it applies to the mate sheet (see Fig. 4). Therefore, it can occur that degrees of freedom are over-determined, which leads to constraints regarding certain feature-feature combinations.

For the final selection of geometrical features, the constraints and degrees of freedom resulting from the influence of joining technologies need to be considered. Certain combinations of geometrical feature and joining technology can meet requirements the feature alone would not meet. For example: if waterproofness is a joining point requirement and the pre-selected feature a hole or slot, which initially would not meet the requirement, the feature could be sealed by the joining technology in case of laser welding or gluing. Therefore, new degrees of freedom can be generated through the utilization of certain joining technologies. On the other hand, there are geometrical (e.g. unilateral accessibility), functional (e.g. heat input) or company related (e.g. joining guidelines) limitations towards the utilization of specific joining technology and feature combinations. All possible feature-joining technology combinations and their requirement fulfillment are outlined within the multi-domain-matrices used to describe the relations between these domains. Positive relations (additional degrees of freedom) are assigned accordingly, while negative relations (additional constraints) are disqualified within the matrix.

The eligible combinations result in a reduced selection of suitable features and joining technologies. From this selection, the feature amount and type is determined. Criteria for the final feature-joining technology combination selection comprise economic factors. Thus, the investment costs for conventional fixture systems have to be compared with the costs of feature integration, as well as costs for the respectively utilized joining technologies. Criteria regarding body quality and process stability are included in the requirements derived in the second step of the methodology and therefore being taken into account in steps 3 and 4.

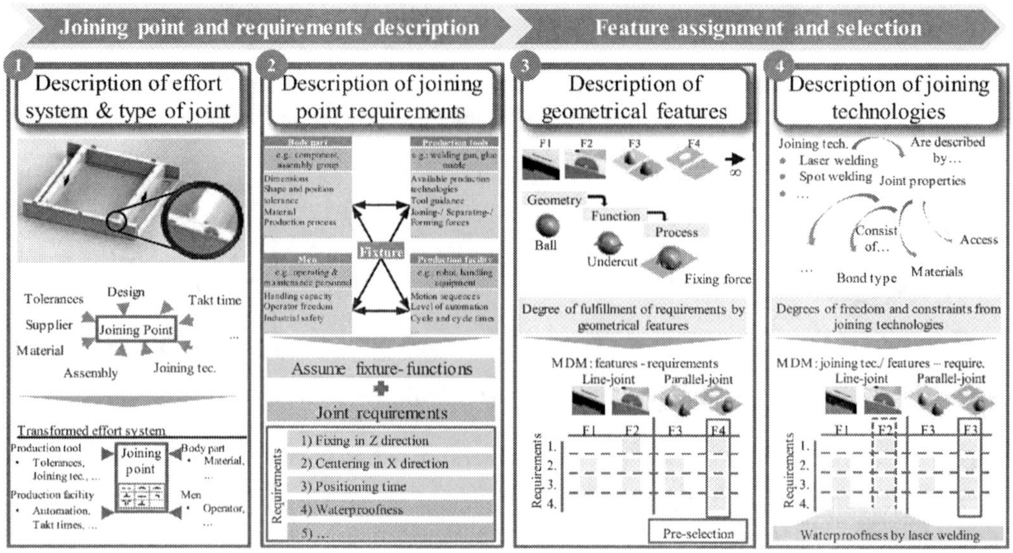

Fig. 4. Methodology to select geometrical features for a fixtureless body shop.

Implementation

The methodology to select geometrical features and joining technologies has been applied for a fixtureless body shop station of an electric vehicle body part. In the reference body station three body parts are joined, whereby the station contains several fixtures for part positioning and clamping as well as spot welding and transport robots for fixing and transportation of the assembly[†]. For this work the original body parts were redesigned incl. geometrical features for positioning and fixing based on the reference requirements regarding parts and processes. Further, joining technologies for the pre-selected features were analyzed and selected. Finally, two combinations of geometrical features and joining technologies fulfilled all requirements and were considered besides the use of conventional fixture systems. Both features show an undercut structure and therefore consider fixing of the parts. While one feature is joined using conventional spot welding, the other feature is combined with laser welding due to accessibility constraints.

All three scenarios (conventional fixtures, undercut feature-spot welding as well as undercut feature-laser welding) were afterwards analyzed in regard to their economic potential, taking into account investment costs for the fixture, costs for the production and part integration of the features, costs for joining as well as the cycle time. Overall cost reductions amounted to 18% and 31% respectively for feature-spot welding and feature-laser welding combinations in comparison to the conventional fixture system. Cycle time savings of up to 30% were also realized. Further, the fixtureless options increase flexibility, as otherwise the integration of an additional variant would have cost a mid-6-digit investment amount due to new fixtures and other adaptions necessary.

Conclusions and future work

In this paper, a methodology to select geometrical features and related joining technologies to realize a fixtureless body shop concept is outlined. The methodology is based on a four step approach to describe requirements and joining points as well as assign and select features and joining technologies. Ongoing research on the methodology comprises further detailing of the process steps and further practical realization on body shop station in larger scale. Generating more data in practical implementations will allow detailing the assessment of the methodologies´ advantage regarding investment cost reduction and flexibility gain.

References

1. S. Spieckermann, K. Gutenschwager, H. Heinzel, S. Voß, Simulation-Based Optimization in the Automotive Industry, Simulation **75(5)**, 276-286 (2000)
2. T. Meichsner, *Migrationskonzept für einen modell- und variantenflexiblen Automobilkarosseriebau*, PhD Thesis (Universität Hannover, Hannover, 2007)
3. T. Haunstetter, *Methoden des Data Mining in Anwendung an die Flexibilitätsattribute des automobilen Karosseriebaus zur strategischen Investitionsplanung*, PhD Thesis (Universität der Bundeswehr Hamburg, Hamburg, 2010)
4. J. Hansen, A. Kampker, J. Triebs, *Methodology for flexibility in the future automobile body shop: results of a comprehensive cross-industry study* (Presentation CIRP-CMS, Stockholm, 2018)

[†] All values and numbers have been adjusted or are being omitted as not to allow any conclusions to be drawn about the company regarded.

5. J. Abulawi, *Beherrschung der Komplexität von 3D-CAD-Modellen*, PhD Thesis (Universität der Bundeswehr Hamburg, Hamburg, 2012)
6. O. Schol, *Der neue Audi Q5: Entwicklung und Technik* (ATZ/MTZ-Typenbuch, Vieweg+Teubner, Verlag, 2009)
7. M. Franzkowiak, *Methodik zur Strukturierung von Vorrichtungssystemen in der Lohnfertigung*, PhD Thesis (Technische Universität München, München, 2013)
8. J. Adams, D. Whitney, Application of Screw Theory to Constraint Analysis of Mechnical Assemblies Joined by Features, J. Mech. Des. **123(1)**, 26-32 (2001)
9. S. Naing, *Feature Based Design for Jigless Assembly*, PhD Thesis (Cranfield University, Cranfield, 2004)
10. F. Schlather, F. Oefele, M. Zeah, Toward a feature-based approach for fixtureless build-up of sheet metal structures, J. Eng. Technol. Res. **5(4)**, 97-102 (2016)
11. P. Koonmen, *Implementing precision assembly techniques in the commercial aircraft industry*, Master Thesis (Massachusetts Institute of Technology, Massachusetts, 1994)
12. C.F. Chang, D.B. Perng, Assembly-part automatic positioning using high-level entities of mating features, Comput. Integr. Manuf. Syst. **10(3)**, 205-215 (1997)
13. D.F. Walczyk, V. Raju, R. Miller, *Fixtureless assembly of sheet metal parts for the aircraft industry*, in Proceedings of the Institution of Mechanical Engineers Part B Journal of Engineering Manufacture, **214(3)**, 173-182 (2000)
14. R. Messler, *Integral Mechanical Attachment* (Butterworth-Heinemann, Oxford, 2006)
15. J. Feldhusen, K.H. Grote, Der Produktentstehungsprozess (PEP). In J. Feldhusen, K.H. Grote (Eds.), *Pahl/Beitz Konstruktionslehre* (Springer Vieweg, Heidelberg, 2013)
16. A. Trummer, H. Wiebach, *Vorrichtungen in der Produktionstechnik* (Viewegs Fachbücher der Technik, Springer Fachmedien, Wiesbaden, 1994)
17. M. Maurer, *Structural Awareness in Complex Product Design*, PhD Thesis, (Technische Universität München, München, 2007)

Occupational Health (OH) Practices in South African Construction

John Smallwood[1*], and *Claire* Deacon[1]

[1] Nelson Mandela University, Department of Construction Management, PO Box 77000, Port Elizabeth, 6031, South Africa

Abstract. Health hazards in construction include: ergonomic stresses such as bending, lifting and repetitive movement and vibration; environmental stresses such as heat, sun, noise, poor illumination, and wet or damp work; skin and respiratory exposure to chemicals and dust, as well as mental stress among managers, supervisors, and workers. In South Africa, these may add to the health problems experienced by construction workers because of poor community health, substance abuse, and inadequate health services. A self-administered questionnaire survey was conducted among the professional category of construction health and safety (H&S) practitioners to determine OH issues in construction. Findings include: the extent to which OH aspects were identified by respondents on projects in 2017 indicates that construction entails exposure to a range of OH hazards and risk; the degree of OH knowledge and awareness is limited as opposed to extensive; the source of OH knowledge is informal; there is a need for OH to be embedded in tertiary built environment programmes, OH continuing professional development (CPD), and a construction industry OH standard, and OH practice notes.

Keywords: construction, health and safety, occupational diseases, OH, Worker health and wellbeing

1 Introduction

Ill health kills and ruins lives in the construction industry. A construction worker is at least 100 times more likely to die from a disease that has been caused or exacerbated from their work, than from a fatal accident [1-4]. Construction work itself is known as dirty, tough and hazardous, highly manual, and transient in nature. Further to the conditions, approximately 30% of workers are transient in nature [5].

NIOH [4] state that occupational or work-related diseases are caused by exposure to occupational hazards during a contract of employment. NIOH [4] further cites the construction industry as one of three industries with the highest rate of work-related injury risks. Hazards that workers are exposed to include chemical, biological, poor ergonomics,

* Corresponding author: john.smallwood@mandela.ac.za

and psychosocial hazards. Extended exposure to such risks results in occupational and work-related diseases [4].

The South African Constitution [6], as the over-arching legislation, enshrines several rights that could be linked to the rights of workers in the context of this paper. Section 24 states: "Everyone has a right to an environment that is not harmful to their health" [5].

The OH and Safety Act (OHSA) No. 85 of 1993 requires employers to comply with the rights of citizens as stated in the Constitution, as they relate to employees. Employers have a further responsibility as it relates to those directly affected by activities, and are expected to ensure that all equipment and substances designed for use are safe and without risk to health. While these duties apply to the working environment, in many cases, accommodation could be adjacent, within or close to the construction works Smallwood and Deacon [3, 5].

Given the aforementioned, a study was conducted to determine:

- The perceptions of CHSAs with respect to project OH;
- CHSAs' project OH related practices;
- The potential of interventions to contribute to an improvement in project OH, and
- CHSAs' source of construction OH knowledge.

2 Review of the Literature

2.1 Construction Health and Safety

While the focus is generally on the safety end of H&S, the management of OH risks is no different from that of safety. OH risks should be identified and managed using risk assessments, to take sensible and proportionate measures to control such risks. A range of OH and H&S specialists are generally involved in identifying and managing health risks [2].

According to Obiozo and Smallwood [7], the well-being and performance of construction workers is an issue at several structural levels. The physical state of the site directly affects health, and at the organisational level, overall performance, through the environment, H&S, and the traditional parameters of construction, namely cost, quality, and time. Construction activities could occur in isolated locations, or in the middle of heavy traffic. There could, furthermore, be up to 20 contractors on a single project, increasing the complexity of project management.

2.2 Practices and Responsibilities among Construction Health and Safety Professionals

Enabling legislation from the South African Council for the Project and Construction Management Professions (SACPCMP) has outlined the need for anyone practising in H&S in the construction industry to be registered in one of three categories. Such categories include the construction H&S Officer (CHSO), Manager (CHSM), and the professional category as agent (Pr CHSA). Each of the roles has different deliverables, with a clear scope of work. The Pr CHSA practices across all six stages of construction, and the CHSO and CHSM during stages four to six. The six stages of construction are:

1. Project initiation and briefing;
2. Concept and feasibility;
3. Design development;
4. Tender Documentation and procurement;
5. Construction documentation and management, and
6. Project Closeout [8].

Smallwood and Deacon [8] indicate that the role of the Pr CHSA decreases in efficacy the later their appointment. Most are only appointed during stages four or five, which limits the ability to ensure that H&S risks relative to design are identified and mitigated as far as possible.

2.3 Designing for Construction Health & Safety

Generally, in managing risks to workers the hierarchy of control is widely practised in industry. The hierarchy essentially attempts to find the earliest point of action to reduce risk. Elimination of the activity or process would be the highest level of action, however, if elimination is not an option, then to substitute is the next option. Engineering options such as encasing or exhaust systems, administration through safe working practices and finally allowing personal protective equipment (PPE) to be used [2, 3, 9].

In construction, the actions during stage 3 or design are the earliest opportunity to apply the hierarchy of control. There are several methods and processes that could be considered that do not only determine the risks to construction workers during construction (stage 5) but also the life cycle of the structure that could affect those working there. The Pr CHSA, if appointed at the earliest point (stage 1), can reduce risk at the earliest opportunity [3].

3 Occupational Health

OH is defined by the World Health Organization (WHO) as "the promotion and maintenance of the highest degree of physical, mental and social well-being of workers in all occupations by preventing departures from health, controlling risks and the adaptation of work to people to their jobs" [10, 11].

The lack of understanding of what OH is, the role and the benefits thereof are mostly misunderstood. During the construction of the Olympic Park in London, Park Health, who provided the OH services, described occupational damage as 'the slow accident', which illustrated the effects of exposure are slow-moving, but just as dramatic as an accident [2].

The benefits of OH related interventions at work are numerous: workers feel valued, motivated to keep fit to carry out their work, and their own health; an increase in life expectancy and quality of health; have a positive impact on attitudes and behaviour towards health risks and further provides an opportunity to coach workers regarding H&S risks at work [2].

3.1 Occupational Exposures

In most cases occupational disease and illness can be prevented, provided risks are identified, managed, and controlled. Managing the ill health effects of occupational exposure is not an instant fix, like placing a dressing on a cut to a finger. Occupational diseases manifest years following exposure, asbestos, for example, could take up to 40 years to present with an asbestos-related disease [2].

Construction workers are exposed to many forms of hazards that cause target organ damage that is considered as an occupational disease (OD). For example, crystalline silica, as dust, affects the respiratory system, mainly the lungs (the target organ), causing silicosis (an occupational disease). Exposure to asbestos also affects mainly the lungs, and causes severe damage and fibrosis of the lung tissue, and is diagnosed as asbestosis (Center to Protect Workers Rights (CPWR).

Different forms of work expose workers to risks. Fumes from welding and soldering; dust from cutting, drilling stone and various materials, gasses, and waste products. Several natural hazards are a further risk to which workers are exposed, such as biological hazards (legionella, zoonoses), temperatures and weather, spores, and sunlight [2].

3.2 Ergonomic Factors

Construction work is physically demanding, with workers required to adopt awkward body postures, while frequently required to manually handle materials and products during a workday. While it is important to train workers in ergonomic factors, training alone is not deemed effective without determining interventions to limit the effects of such work. Ergonomic interventions are better addressed during the design stages but should consider the life cycle of the project [12, 13].

3.3 Occupational Hygiene Monitoring

The monitoring of measuring the extent of exposure is the responsibility of the Occupational Hygienist. The Occupational Hygienist collects data to measure the extent of physical and chemical risks, which in turn is used to determine how risks are to be mitigated and managed, or measured for effectiveness following mitigation. An example includes conducting of noise, dust and chemical surveys against a set of strictly defined criteria that are set internationally [2].

3.4 Medical Surveillance

Medical surveillance is also termed health surveillance. However, the purpose is the same. Botha, Ross and Michell [14] cite Rogers, who defines medical surveillance as "the systematic and ongoing analysis, collection and evaluation of employee health data to identify specific instances of illness or health trends suggesting an adverse effect of illness or health trends suggesting an adverse effect of workplace exposures." The purpose of conducting medical surveillance, therefore, considers a variety of appropriate times to conduct surveillance. Most commonly, surveillance is done at pre-employment or pre-placement, periodically according to legislative requirements (such as when exposed to noise above 85dB(a)), and when exiting employment [2]. Botha et al. [14], and IOSH [2], state that surveillance is done to assess the workers' ability or fitness to work, relative to the risks they are likely to be exposed to or to determine previous exposure that could place them at risk. Generally, the greater the risk, the more frequent the surveillance.

4 Research

4.1 Research Method and Sample Stratum

A survey involving a questionnaire was sent to all SACPCMP registered Pr CHSAs throughout South Africa, per e-mail. Out of the 72 invited to participate, only 20 responses were returned, despite following up with the sample stratum, which equates to a response rate of 27.8%. Due to the low response rate, the findings are deemed to be indicative, but likely to be from the more committed practitioners. Respondents indicated that their experience since 2017 included the infrastructure sector (44.7%), the industrial sector (25.1%), commercial sector (13.7%), and the residential sector (9.6%).

4.2 Research Results

Table 1 indicates the importance of addressing OH during the six stages of projects in terms of percentage responses to a scale of 1 (not important) to 5 (very important), and a mean score (MS) ranging between 1.00 and 5.00. It is notable that all the MSs are above the midpoint of 3.00, which indicates that in general, the respondents perceive the addressing of OH during the six project stages to be important. The MSs of design development (stage 3), construction documentation and management (stage 5), and concept and feasibility (stage 2) are > 4.20 ≤ 5.00 – between more than important to very important / very important. Tender documentation and procurement (stage 4), project initiation and briefing (stage 1), and project closeout (stage 6) in turn fall within the range > 3.40 ≤ 4.20 – between important to more than important / more than important.

Table 1. The importance of addressing OH during the six stages of projects.

Stage	Response (%)						MS	Rank
	Un-sure	Not ……… 1	2	3	4	……… Very 5		
Design development	0.0	0.0	5.0	10.0	25.0	60.0	4.40	1
Construction documentation and management	0.0	5.0	0.0	5.0	30.0	60.0	4.40	2
Concept and feasibility	0.0	0.0	10.5	10.5	26.3	52.6	4.21	3
Tender documentation and procurement	0.0	0.0	10.0	10.0	40.0	40.0	4.10	4
Project initiation and briefing	0.0	5.3	5.3	21.1	26.3	42.1	3.95	5
Project close out	0.0	5.3	10.5	10.5	36.8	36.8	3.89	6

Table 2 indicates the extent to which OH aspects were identified by respondents on projects in 2017. All thirty aspects were identified by more than 50% of respondents, twenty-four (80%) by ≥ 75%, and nine (30%) by 90%. Manual tasks (100%) predominate, and was followed jointly (94.7%) by oils/petrol (hydrocarbons), paints, cement dust, concrete dust, labour-intensive work, noise, and vibration. These aspects were followed closely by heat (90%), jointly (89.5%) by solvents, mechanised methods (potential), and work pressure. In terms of the percentage of projects on which OH aspects were specified, the highest mean was relative to cement dust (75.8%), followed by concrete dust (72.8%), labour intensive work (71.9%), manual tasks (70.5%), oils/petrol (hydrocarbons) (66.7%), and block/brick dust (61.9%).

Table 2. The extent to which aspects were identified on projects in 2017.

Aspect	Response (%)			Percentage of projects		
	Unsure	Did not	Yes	Lowest	Highest	Mean
Manual tasks	0.0	0.0	100.0	10.0	100.0	70.5
Oils / Petrol (hydrocarbons)	0.0	5.3	94.7	2.0	100.0	66.7
Paints	0.0	5.3	94.7	15.0	100.0	58.7
Cement dust	0.0	5.3	94.7	10.0	100.0	75.8
Concrete dust	0.0	5.3	94.7	10.0	100.0	72.8
Labour intensive work	0.0	5.3	94.7	25.0	100.0	71.9
Noise	0.0	5.3	94.7	5.0	100.0	53.2
Vibration	0.0	5.3	94.7	5.0	100.0	46.5
Heat	0.0	10.0	90.0	5.0	100.0	52.9
Solvents	0.0	10.5	89.5	5.0	100.0	57.2

Mechanised methods (potential)	0.0	10.5	89.5	10.0	100.0	52.5
Work pressure	5.3	5.3	89.5	5.0	100.0	53.2
Bitumen	0.0	15.0	85.0	5.0	100.0	43.5
Fumes	0.0	15.8	84.2	5.0	100.0	48.8
Adhesives	0.0	15.8	84.2	5.0	100.0	44.3
Vapours	5.3	10.5	84.2	5.0	100.0	55.1
Epoxy-resins	0.0	16.7	83.3	10.0	100.0	30.0
Cold	0.0	16.7	83.3	5.0	100.0	41.9
Quartz / Silica dust	0.0	16.7	83.3	4.0	100.0	45.3
Asbestos dust	0.0	21.1	78.9	5.0	70.0	25.0
Block / Brick dust	0.0	21.1	78.9	10.0	100.0	61.9
Shift work	0.0	21.1	78.9	5.0	100.0	45.4
Illumination (Poor)	5.3	15.8	78.9	5.0	100.0	42.5
Insects	0.0	25.0	75.0	5.0	100.0	46.4
Waterproofing	0.0	26.3	73.7	10.0	100.0	34.6
Monotony	10.5	15.8	73.7	5.0	100.0	51.8
Stress	10.5	15.8	73.7	15.0	100.0	55.7
Unsociable hours	10.5	15.8	73.7	5.0	100.0	42.5
Viruses	0.0	42.1	57.9	5.0	100.0	35.1
Mineral wools	11.1	33.3	55.6	5.0	100.0	35.0

Table 3 indicates the extent to which environmental measurement was specified by respondents on projects in 2017. All environmental measurements were identified by more than 50% of respondents. Noise (85%) predominates, followed by air quality (ventilation), illumination, and dust (silica).

In terms of the percentage of projects on which environmental measurement was specified, the highest mean was relative to noise (55%), followed closely by dust (silica) (49%). The lowest was relative to air quality (ventilation) (0%), and the highest (100%) relative to all measurements.

Table 3. The extent to which environmental measurement was specified by respondents on projects in 2017.

Measurement	Response (%)			Percentage of projects		
	Unsure	No	Yes	Lowest	Highest	Mean
Noise	0.0	15.0	85.0	5.0	100.0	55.0
Air quality (ventilation)	0.0	31.6	68.4	0.0	100.0	33.4
Illumination	0.0	31.6	68.4	10.0	100.0	33.1
Dust (silica)	0.0	36.8	63.2	5.0	100.0	49.0

Table 4 indicates the extent to which OH related interventions were specified by respondents on projects in 2017. All OH related interventions were identified by more than 50% of respondents. Pre-employment medicals (85%) predominate, followed jointly (84%) by annual in-employment (periodic) medicals, and plant operator medicals.

Table 4. The extent to which OH related interventions were specified by respondents on projects in 2017.

Intervention	Response (%)			Percentage of projects		
	Unsure	No	Yes	Lowest	Highest	Mean
Pre-employment medicals	0.0	15.0	85.0	50.0	100.0	97.1
Annual in-employment (periodic) medicals	0.0	15.8	84.2	5.0	100.0	92.5
Plant operator medicals	0.0	15.8	84.2	25.0	100.0	92.2
Pre-employment audiometric tests	5.3	15.8	78.9	5.0	100.0	83.0

Contract specific (client required) medicals	0.0	21.1	78.9	15.0	100.0	89.0
Exit medicals medicals	0.0	36.8	63.2	60.0	100.0	96.7
Exit audiometric tests	0.0	38.9	61.1	5.0	100.0	91.4
Contract specific (self-initiated) medicals	0.0	47.4	52.6	10.0	100.0	63.0

Table 5 indicates the respondents' self-rating of their knowledge of various OH related aspects in terms of percentage responses to a scale of 1 (limited) to 5 (extensive), and an MS ranging between 1.00 and 5.00. It is notable that all the MSs are above the midpoint of 3.00, which indicates that in general, the respondents rate their knowledge of various OH related aspects as above average. It is notable that they rate their knowledge relative to all the OH related aspects as between average to more than average / more than average (MSs > 3.40 ≤ 4.20). It is notable that construction OH is ranked first (MS = 4.00), whereas 'designing for construction OH' is ranked last (MS = 3.50), as in the case of the latter, design development was ranked first in terms of the importance of addressing OH during the six stages of projects, and design development was ranked first in terms of the extent to which OH can be influenced during the six stages of projects.

Table 5. Respondents' self-rating of their knowledge of various OH related aspects.

Aspect	Unsure	Limited.....................				...Extensive	MS	Rank
		1	2	3	4	5		
Construction OH	0.0	0.0	5.3	15.8	52.6	26.3	4.00	1
Knowledge of appropriate protection equipment for categories of workers linked to risk	0.0	0.0	5.0	20.0	60.0	15.0	3.85	2
Identification of adequacy of certificate of fitness	0.0	0.0	5.0	25.0	50.0	20.0	3.85	3
Linking exposure to determining adequate identification of risks for the Annexure 3	0.0	0.0	10.0	20.0	55.0	15.0	3.75	4
Limitation or management of workers deemed limited or unfit for work	0.0	0.0	5.0	30.0	55.0	10.0	3.70	5
OH	0.0	0.0	15.8	21.1	52.6	10.5	3.58	6
Designing for construction OH	0.0	0.0	15.0	25.0	55.0	5.0	3.50	7

Respondents indicated that experience (20.2%) predominates in terms of the source of their knowledge of OH, followed by workshops (15.5%), tertiary education (14.9%), magazine articles (11.9%), and journal papers (10.7%). The remaining five sources were identified by less than 10% of respondents. Clearly, the source of knowledge of OH is informal as opposed to formal.

A total of 8.3% respondents indicated they had post-graduate qualifications, and 14.9% had tertiary education.

5 Conclusions

Although the number of respondents was limited, and therefore the findings can be deemed indicative, the respondents are above average in terms of their OH knowledge, which increases the reliability of the findings. However, the respondents' source of OH knowledge is more informal than formal, which leads to the conclusion that OH is not addressed to the extent that it should be in their formal education programmes.

The respondents perceive the addressing of OH during the six project stages as important, and therefore understand and appreciate the role of upstream interventions. The respondents further understand and appreciate that OH can be influenced during the six stages of the construction process.

The extent to which OH aspects were identified by respondents on projects in 2017 leads to the conclusion that construction entails exposure to a range of OH hazards and risk. It was noted that the respondents undertake a range of OH related interventions, including environmental measurement, medicals and tests, and OH related training.

Finally, it is concluded that OH is a multi-stakeholder issue.

6 Recommendations

Recommendations include, among others, that tertiary built environment education should address OH. Designing for construction OH should be introduced and more importantly, embedded in tertiary built environment education programmes, especially designer related, and a construction industry OH standard, OH practice notes, and CPD should be evolved to guide the sector.

Construction Project Managers and CHSAs must ensure that all stakeholders address OH, and that project H&S plans focus thereon. Employer associations must afford OH the requisite recognition in their industry H&S programmes, star grading process, and regional and national H&S competitions.

References

1. D. Snashall, *Hazards of Work*, in E. Snashall, D. Patel (Eds.), ABC of Occupational and Environmental Medicine, 3rd ed. (John Wiley and Sons, United Kingdom, 2012)
2. Institute of Occupational Safety and Health (IOSH), *OH risk management in construction. A guide to the key issues of OH provision* (IOSH, United Kingdom, 2016)
3. C.H. Deacon, *The Effect of the Integration of Design, Procurement, and Construction relative to Health and Safety*, PhD Thesis (Nelson Mandela Metropolitan University, South Africa, 2016)
4. National Institute of OH (NIOH), OEHS in the Construction Industry (2018), http://www.nioh.ac.za/?page=construction_industry&id=190
5. J.J. Smallwood, C.H. Deacon, *Construction Camps in Building and Civil Engineering Construction*, in Proceedings of the 2nd International Conference on Development and Investment in Infrastructure – Strategies for Africa. 16-18 September 2015, Livingstone, Zambia. University of Johannesburg, Johannesburg, South Africa, 201-223 (2015)
6. Republic of South Africa, *The Constitution of the Republic of South Africa* (Government Printer, Pretoria, 1996)
7. R.N. Obiozo, J.J. Smallwood, *Rethinking Construction: The Transformational Change Strategy of a Biophilic Construction Site Experience*, in E. Fidelis (Ed.), Conference Proceedings Second NMMU Construction Management Conference, 25-27 November, 2012, Port Elizabeth, South Africa. Nelson Mandela Metropolitan University, Port Elizabeth, South Africa, 121-130 (2012)
8. J.J. Smallwood, C.H. Deacon, *Construction Health and Safety Agents (CHSAs') contribution to health and safety in South Africa*, in Proceedings 7th West Africa Built Environment Research (WABER) Conference, 16-18 August 2017, University of Ghana, Accra, Ghana, 502-513 (2017)

9. R. McCaig, *Physical Agents*, in E. Snashall, D. Patel (Eds.), ABC of Occupational and Environmental Medicine, 3rd ed. (John Wiley and Sons, United Kingdom, 2012)
10. A. Adisesh, *Practising OH*, in E. Snashall, D. Patel (Eds.), ABC of Occupational and Environmental Medicine, 3rd ed. (John Wiley and Sons, United Kingdom, 2012)
11. L. Jansen van Rensburg, K. Michell, K., *Models of OH Service Delivery*, in K. Michelle (Ed.), A practical approach to OH Nursing (South African Society of OH Nursing Practitioners, Wilpro Printers, Johannesburg, 2011)
12. J.J. Smallwood, *Construction ergonomics: A support work manufacturer's perceptions and practices*, in Proceedings of International Commission of OH (ICOH): OH and Wellbeing: linking research to practice. Poster presentation. 29 April to 4 May 2018, ICOH, Dublin, Ireland (2018)
13. S. Visser, H.F. van der Molen, J.K. Sluiter, M.H.W. Frings-Dresen, The process evaluation of two alternative participatory ergonomics intervention strategies for construction companies (2018), https://www.tandfonline.com/doi/full/10.1080/00140139.2018.1454514
14. L. Botha, M. Ross, K. Michell, *Health Surveillance in OH*, in K. Michelle (Ed.), A practical approach to OH Nursing (South African Society of OH Nursing Practitioners, Wilpro Printers, Johannesburg, 2012)

An Approach for Integrating Mixed Reality into BIM for Early Stage Design Coordination

Abhinesh Prabhakaran[1], *Abdul-Majeed* Mahamadu[1*], *Lamine* Mahdjoubi[1], and *Patrick* Manu[2]

[1]University of the West of England, Frenchay Campus, Bristol, BS16 1QY, United Kingdom
[2]University of Manchester, The School of Mechanical, Aerospace & Civil Engineering, Manchester M13 9PL, United Kingdom

Abstract. Building Information Modelling (BIM) and its associated technologies have proved to be one of the most promising developments in the Architectural, Engineering and Construction (AEC) industry. Over the past few decades, the AEC sector has been restricted in its communication of design as a result of single interface methods based on 2D and 3D visualization of information. Thus, most issues with respect to construction are identified fairly late, resulting in costly changes. With the introduction of BIM, many other approaches to data visualization can be leveraged including Mixed Reality (MR) applications for the virtual representation of spaces and objects beyond 3D. MR offers a revolution in the virtual representation of objects and space through context awareness as well as the incorporation of information beyond 3D offering countless opportunities for more effective design visualization and coordination. Despite the capability of MR, however, few examples exist of its application to design coordination in the AEC. In addressing this gap this study proposes a novel methodology for the application of MR in design coordination as well as investigates the impact of introducing MR into BIM workflow with a focus on the identification and avoidance of clashes. A prototypical model of the MR design coordination is presented and discussed. Findings indicate that MR improves design productivity and quality but also highlights potential infrastructure issues inhibiting the mainstreaming of MR for design practice.

Keywords: virtual reality, design, productivity, quality, coordination

1 Introduction

Construction industries productivity index has always struggled to catch up with other industries. There is, therefore, an attendant need for the improvement of construction. According to Teicholz [1] and Gerbert et al. [2], construction industry productivity has stagnated for decades across the globe due to among other reasons, poor innovation and adaptation. The report "Reinventing Construction: A Route to Higher Productivity", released

* Corresponding author: abdul.mahamadu@uwe.ac.uk

in February 2017 reiterates the argument by suggesting that the productivity issues in the construction industry are due to lack of research development and innovation [3]. Kymmell [4] argues that an increase in the complexity of the construction as the main reason for this productivity lag. With such increases in complexity, the design has also become increasingly complex with multidisciplinary input that requires coordination. According to Maing and Vargas [5], despite the increasing complexity of design, productivity gains can be made through the adoption and application of digital innovations such as Building Information Modelling (BIM).

BIM has proved to be one of the most promising developments in the AEC industry [6]. NBS [7] defines BIM as the "*process for creating and managing information on a construction project across the project life cycle where the key output of this process is the digital description of every aspect of the built asset*". Bernstein et al. [8] have reiterated that the diffusion of BIM in the AEC industry has substantially increased in recent years, especially among contractors who are increasingly becoming responsible for coordinating design due to evolving procurement. BIM has the capability to leverage intelligent 3D models to design, construction, delivery, operations and facility management [9].

Indeed, having an accurate 3D modelling solution, upheld by well-defined data requirements are capable of delivering benefits at every stage of the design and construction process. The transition from a 2D documentation to 3D BIM modelling was a natural evolution which aided in improving team communication and coordination. Viewing the 3D BIM model through a 2D screen is very common, however, interacting with volumes of data behind the 2D is extremely beneficial [10]. Mixed Reality (MR) offers a revolution in the virtual representation of objects and space through context awareness as well as the incorporation of information beyond 3D offering countless opportunities for more effective design visualization and coordination. Despite the capability of MR, however, few examples exist of its application to design coordination in the AEC. In addressing this gap this study explores the following research questions: (1) How can MR be leveraged to support design coordination? (2) How effective is MR use in design coordination? The research thereof proposes a novel methodology for the application of MR in design coordination as well as investigates the impact of introducing MR into BIM workflow with a focus on the identification and avoidance of clashes. A prototypical model of the MR design coordination is presented and discussed.

2 Information Delivery and Design Coordination

The linear flow of information exists in the design communication between the designers, specialist consultants and on the other hand constructors. Shannon [11] explains this mode of communication through the theory of linear standard communication where a message is generated, encoded into a single transmittable in a desired medium and further decoded upon arrival at the receiver's end Barnes [12] points out that traditional means of communication in the construction was solely based on 2D paper plans which potentially created a risk of noises ineffective transmission of the information. In construction, the design is embraced as a collaborative activity by necessity due to the division of labour and expertise between organizations [13]. A consequence of the structure of the sector is that design activity involves the coordination of complex information exchanges in multi-disciplinary design teams. Coordination and communication challenges underlie difficulties in the integration of work activities of design teams. Communication is central to design collaboration and the coordination of design inputs [13].

Decision made during the design coordination could potentially affect many stakeholders including architects, engineering consultants, construction managers and facility maintenance organization. Coordination among stakeholders is critical to ensure that facility design meets the intended functionality, aesthetic and economic requirements of the owner [14]. Riley and Horman [15] point out that efficient Design coordination is key to reduce uncertainty in the production process in the construction project by decreasing disruption and reducing waste in the construction process. The relationship found on a case study project between the effort spent on design coordination and the resulting elimination in field conflicts revealed that projects A and B which carried out design coordination with 100% diligence and treated as a prerequisite for construction has zero or negligible field generated change orders whereas projects C and D have a considerable number of change orders [15].

The early stage of a design process is of particular importance for the quality of the final results as most of the building lifecycle characteristics and costs are already committed at this stage and the opportunity to influence the final design decreases rapidly as the cost of making the changes or correcting the design errors increases dramatically [16].

Mehrbod et al. [17] identified in their study that despite several advantages of BIM in design coordination, utilization of the 3D BIM models on a 2D screen during design coordination were ineffective as the navigation with the digital artefacts were often inefficient. The major challenge Mehrbod et al. [17] identified in information delivery 3D BIM models during design coordination was navigation in BIM environment on 2D screens which forced the participants to often revert to the 2D paper-based drawings for better understanding. CAD and virtual visualization could be regarded as complementary technologies in design visualization where such Interactive visualization tools are capable of playing a critical role in the effective information delivery during the design coordination phase of a project [14].

Woksepp [16] argues that a 3D system has an inherent limitation when it comes to conveying an understanding of the complex virtual environment. 3D CAD system is developed for a design specialist to create precise three-dimensional representations of the real object, while virtual immersive technology allows the user to display and interact with objects in the virtual world thereby enhancing the design coordination [16]. Recently, studies executed to identify the impact of 3D physical and virtual mock-ups in supporting the design coordination which revealed that physical mock-ups potentially can offer values for design coordination but they can be impractical to communicate design at every stage of the project and physical mock-up could incur cost, time and physical space requirements to set up [18]. On the other hand, virtual mockups are capable of delivering in-depth high-level detail of any system and their interfaces without the high-cost burden [19].

3 Immersive Technology Applications for Visualisation

Immersive technology is an integration of virtual content with the physical environment in such a way that enables the user to interact naturally with the amalgamated reality [20]. Virtual reality, augmented reality and mixed reality is the most commonly available immersive technology. Virtual reality is the utilization of computer technology to create a simulated environment where the user is completely immersed in the virtual world by simulating as many senses as possible [21]. Thus, the user becomes a part of the virtual or immersed world within its environment and whilst they are able to manipulate or interact with the object. On the other hand, augmented reality is capable of superimposing spatially contextual information over the user's view of the real world providing additional data while still permitting interaction with the real environment [22]. The inherent limitation of augmented reality as per Foundary [23] is that while augmented reality is capable of overlaying virtual object in a physical environment, the virtual content cannot be anchored to the real world. Thus the physical environment and the overlayed virtual object fail to interact which limits its application in the AEC sector especially where coordination relating to different trades are impossible. Mixed reality is a hybrid of augmented reality which is capable of overlaying synthetic content on the real world which can be anchored to and interacts with the physical world [23].

4 The Role of Mixed Reality

Mixed reality is capable of bridging the gap between virtual and physical world thus eliminating the inefficiency in the current workflow. As discussed earlier, interacting with the information-rich 3D model behind 2D screens are extremely limited where mixed reality tools are capable of bringing those 3D models out of the screen even on to real construction site, allowing the user to engage and interact with the design data more intuitively [10]. Mixed reality tools can potentially play a great role in the design coordination by allowing the stakeholders to visualise and explore the design in virtual 3D without the need for an expert to guide them and dictate the point of view [10]. Feiner et al. [24] investigated the possibility of using 3D Head-mounted displays (HMDs) in conjunction with mobile computing technology, creating a digital prototype which overlaid campus information on top of an unobstructed view of a university campus which was a first of its kind innovation in the construction industry. During the design phase, MR was used for information delivery by presenting relevant data points to the user without interpreting the normal workflow [25].

MR's potential as an onsite visualisation tool has also been well tested and studied where 3D building models were visualised on physical location [26, 27]. Further exploration of possibilities of using MR has been carried to augment BIM content enabling on-site viewing [28] documentation and monitoring of construction process [29] and to detect onsite miscoordination issues [30]. The possibilities of deploying MR for training purposes in construction are also well studied. Wang, Dunston and Skiniewski MR training system is a great example for the utilisation of MR for training construction workforce where they utilized it for training heavy construction equipment operation including cranes [31].

While the use of MR for onsite model visualisation and construction workforces training are well documented any efforts to utilize the enormous possibilities of MR in early design coordination has not been studied specifically. This paper examines the feasibility of integrating MR into early design coordination workflow for the purpose of better design communication between various stakeholders, thus reducing reworks, cost overruns, material wastage, thereby promoting lean construction.

5 Mixed Reality Application for Design Coordination

Mixed reality uses head-mounted devices to project virtual 3D objects into the user occupied physical environment [32]. For the purpose of this study, Microsoft HoloLens is used as the hardware to identify the possibilities of using Mixed reality in for design coordination. Microsoft HoloLens is a wearable, self-contained a holographic computer with advanced sensors that are capable of mapping the physical environment which allows the device to detect physical objects which is very important for coordination in any industry [10]. Emerging devices such as the Microsoft HoloLens is capable of encouraging two key approaches when it comes to collaborative design planning. Firstly, it allows multiple users to examine and coordinate same projected 3D design simultaneously from remote locations [32]. Secondly, the accurate convenience of the visibility of the physical space is an important factor that makes HoloLens projected mixed reality far better than virtual reality for collaboration and coordination of designs [32]. Various software such as Visualive3D, Trimble Connect, BIM Holoview, enables the interoperability between BIM modelling tool and the Hololens. For this study, Trimble Connect was used as the software platform for integrating a digital model of design (Autodesk Revit) into the MR environment (HoloLens).

6 Methodology

This work uses a mechanical plant room as a prototypical model to develop an understanding of the performance impacts observed using MR for design coordination. Plant room as chosen to implement the proposed system given its complexity in the design coordination process thus often leading to clashes and redesign in typical project scenarios. A qualitative approach was used for evaluating the effectiveness of the proposed system with six participants given the opportunity to visualize the model assembly using two different visualization approaches viz MR and traditional paper-based method. Out of the six participants, three had more than eight years of MEP design experience; two were facility managers with 11 years experience, responsible for mega facilities and one of the participants was a client representative who is responsible for ensuring client requirements are met as required. The following section presents a detailed discussion on the procedure adopted in developing, pushing the model for MR experience and evaluation of the system based on the participant's experience.

7 Description of Approach and System Architecture

To develop an approach for integrating MR into the early design phase, the 3D model developed using Autodesk Revit needed to be imported into an MR environment. Even though a number of devices could theoretically be used for this purpose, the researcher chooses to use a Microsoft Hololens, which is head-mounted display (HMD) device with see-through a screen which is capable of augmenting 3D virtual object on a physical environment. The MR capabilities of a Microsoft HoloLens include the ability to augment virtual objects by relying on spatial mapping to identify the physical surface which enables the consistent visualization of the model. The chosen HMD has an inbuilt Windows operating system which provides the virtue of hands-free operation without plugging into an external computer, which further enabled the participants to manoeuvre freely in space without jeopardizing the user's safety. Below, Fig. 1 demonstrates the process flow from model preparation to visualization using various software and hardware.

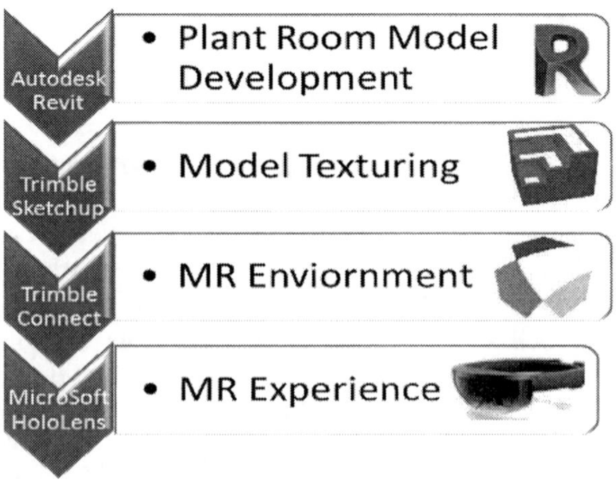

Fig. 1. MR Experience Development Workflow.

8 Development of MR Visualization Environment

To develop the chosen MR environment, the prototypical plant room model is developed using parametric software (Autodesk Revit). Due to the interoperability issues between the Revit native file format (.rvt) and the MR environment cloud-based software, Trimble Connect (requires .skp file format) is used to enhance data transfer of the plant room model developed using Revit and subsequently imported to Trimble Sketchup. Texture property loss during importing is restored using Trimble Sketchup. Further, the model is then uploaded to the Trimble Connect cloud-based platform to generate an MR environment on Microsoft HoloLens. Once the model is successfully imported into Trimble Connect, the model is opened by executing Trimble Connect on Microsoft HoloLens as shown in Fig. 2. The true scale (1:1) MR model is anchored to a physical space for the participants to visualize and walk freely to explore the model further in detail.

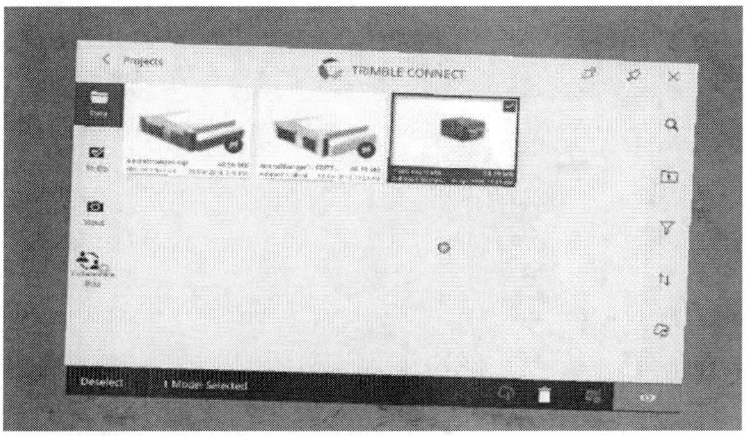

Fig. 2. Trimble Connect Interface.

9 Evaluation of System

All the participants were initially given the opportunity to visualize the paper-based drawing Fig. 4, followed by model visualization through the MR environment. Participants were provided with an opportunity to walk through the model to visualize every placement and installation details of the MEP equipment. Fig. 3 illustrates the full scale (1:1) first-person view of the plant room and equipment viewed through the Microsoft Hololens. Participants explored different options such as scaling down to view as a tabletop model, teleporting enabling walkthrough at smaller physical space, anchoring model at different orientation etc. through Trimble connect MR environment. All the participants were able to use the device with ease even without having previous experience using such devices.

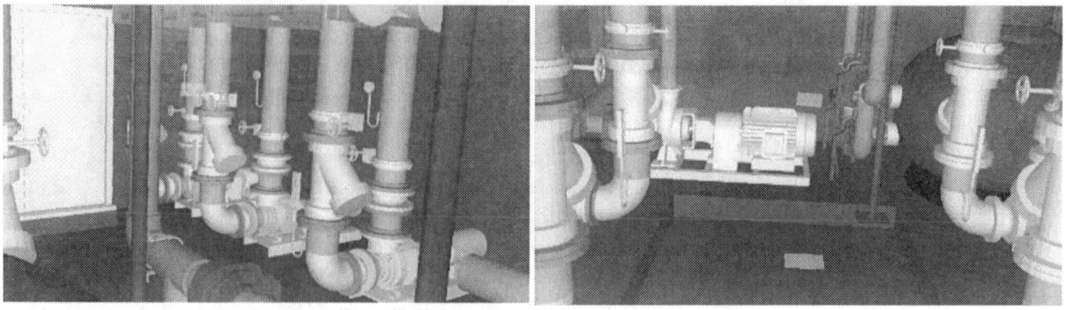

Fig. 3. First Person View of Prototypical Plant Room in MR Environment.

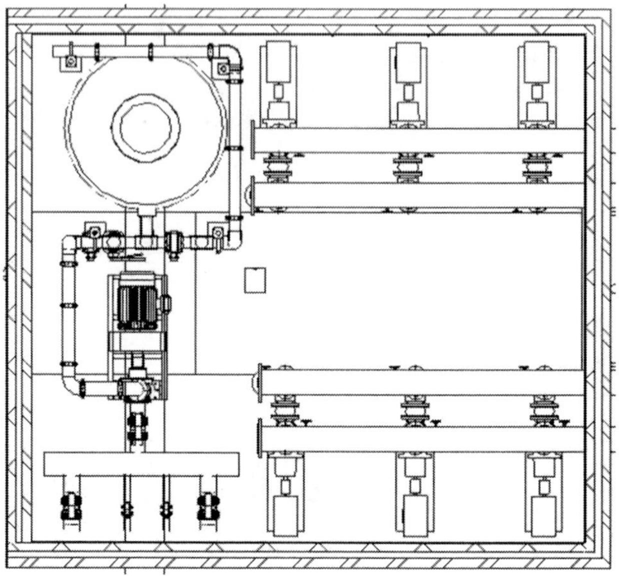

Fig. 4. Paper-Based Drawing of Plant Room.

Few of the participants reported a lack of model brightness as a limiting factor when used at well lite physical space. All the participants (100%), however strongly agreed that the use of immersive technology improved their appreciation of design information much better than traditional approaches. According to participants, the use of the proposed system in the early design coordination workflow can enhance the coordination process reducing the amount of time by up to 50-80%. This is exemplified by quote for evaluator below: *"we will take required actions to bring this kind of visualisation tools for all our projects at the earliest and this will be added as one of our requirement in our EIR (i.e. Employers Information Requirement) for all the projects" [Evaluator 1 – Client Representative].*

10 Discussion

The prototypical MR model anchored to physical space revealed that the placements and installation details of the equipment and piping were very easy to visualize and understand rather did on a paper-based drawing. The participants had no previous experience using MR devices and they could adapt and explore the model in the MR environment quickly. Walkthrough using MR model revealed all the maintenance accessibilities issues that may have arisen only during installation or mostly during the operation phase of the facility, that would have led to rework, cost overrun and time. Further visualization of the model in the

MR environment enabled the designers to understand the requirements of different stakeholders involved in the project, without putting many efforts. Also, it provided an opportunity for designers to try different installation methods and pipe routing which could reduce the cost at the same time keeping the health and safety of the installation and maintenance team in mind. However, few of the participants were concerned about the capability of using the device on well lite physical space due to the inherent brightness control limitations.

11 Conclusion and recommendations

In this paper, the authors propose a novel methodology for the application of MR in design coordination as well as investigates the impact of introducing MR into BIM workflow with a focus on the identification and avoidance of clashes. A prototypical model of the MR design coordination was presented and discussed. Findings indicate that MR improves design productivity and quality but also highlights potential infrastructure issues inhibiting the mainstreaming of MR for design practice. It is clear that integration of MR at the early design stage and active participation of all stakeholders in design coordination with the aid of MR devices can considerably reduce reworks, cost and time overruns at the same time enhancing the safety of the personals handling the task.

References

1. P. Teicholz, Labor-Productivity Declines in the Construction Industry: Causes and Remedies (a second look), AECbytes Viewpoint #67 **4(14)**, 1-11 (2014)
2. P. Gerbert, S. Castagnino, C. Rothballer, A. Renz, R. Filitz, *Digital in Engineering and Construction: The transformative Power of Building Information Modeling* (BCG-the Boston Consulting Group, 2016)
3. F. Barbosa, J. Woetzel, J. Mischke, M.J. Ribeirinho, M. Sridhar, M. Parsons, N. Bertram, S. Brown, *Reinventing Construction: A Route to Higher Productivity* (McKinsey Global Institute, 2017)
4. W. Kymmell, *Building Information Modeling: Planning and Managing Construction Projects with 4D CAD and Simulations* (McGraw-Hill, New York, London, 2008)
5. M. Maing, R. Vargas (Eds.) *Digital Fabrication Processes of Mass Customized Building Facades in Global Practice*, in Proceedings of the 17th Conference of the Iberoamerican Society of Digital Graphics-SIGraDi: Knowledge-Based Design, 12 January 2014 (Bulcher, 2013)
6. C. Eastman, P. Teicholz, R. Sacks, K. Liston, *BIM Handbook: A Guide to Building Information Modeling for Owners, Managers, Designers, Engineers and Contractors*, 2nd ed. (John Wiley & Sons, Hoboken, 2011)
7. NBS, What is Building Information Modelling (BIM)? (2016), https://www.thenbs.com/knowledge/what-is-building-information-modelling-bim
8. M.H. Bernstein, A.S. Jones, A.M. Russo, D. Laquidara-Carr, *Design and Construction Intelligence-SmartMarket Report* (McGraw Hill Construction, Bedford, 2013)
9. B. Hardin, D. McCool, *BIM and Construction Management: Proven Tools, Methods, and Workflows*, 2nd ed. (John Wiley & Sons, 2015)
10. Constructible, Mixed Reality for Architecture, Engineering, and Construction (2017), https://constructible.trimble.com/construction-industry/mixed-reality-for-architecture-engineering-and-construction

11. C.E. Shannon, A mathematical theory of communication, Mob. Comput. Commun. Rev. **5(1)**, 3-55 (2001)
12. M. Barnes, Construction project management, Int. J. Proj. Manag. **6(2)**, 69-79 (1988)
13. UK Research and Innovation, Co-Ordination and Communication in Construction Design Team Meetings (2018), http://gtr.ukri.org/projects?ref=EP/H025421/1
14. M. Tory, S. Staub-French (Eds.), Proceedings of the 2008 Workshop on Beyond Time and Errors: Novel evaluation Methods for Information Visualization (2008), http://citeseerx.ist.psu.edu/viewdoc/download?doi=10.1.1.546.6205&rep=rep1&type=pdf
15. D. Riley, M. Horman (Eds.), Proceedings of the 9th Annual Conference of the International Group for Lean Construction (IGLC-9), Singapore, 25-27 May 2001 (2001), https://pdfs.semanticscholar.org/37f2/56eb20f4961182b858609bf676f96e58519b.pdf
16. S. Woksepp, *Virtual Reality in Construction: Tools, Methods and Process*, PhD Thesis (Luleå tekniska universitet, Luleå, 2007), https://www.diva-portal.org/smash/get/diva2:999878/FULLTEXT01.pdf
17. S. Mehrbod, M. Tory, S. Staub-French, S. (Eds.) Interactions with BIM Tools in Design Coordination Meetings: 4th Construction Specialty Conference, 29 May 2013 Montréal, Québec (2017)
18. T.R.B. Taylor, G.B. Dadi, P.M. Goodrum, C.M. Carswell, Cognitive Workload Demands Using 2D and 3D Spatial Engineering Information Formats, J. Constr. Eng. Manag. **140(5)**, 4014001 (2014)
19. M. Maing, Physical Or Virtual? Effectiveness of Virtual Mockups of Building Envelope Systems (2017), https://c.ymcdn.com/sites/www.nibs.org/resource/resmgr/BEST/best3_maing.1.14.pdf
20. M. Rouse, Immersive Technology (2018), https://whatis.techtarget.com/definition/immersive-technology
21. B. Jackson, What is Virtual Reality? (2015), https://www.marxentlabs.com/what-is-virtual-reality/
22. D. Campbell, 6 Ways Virtual Reality Construction Technology can Save You Money Now (2015), https://connect.bim360.autodesk.com/virtual-reality-construction-technology-saves-money
23. Foundary, VR? AR? MR? Sorry, I'm Confused (2017), https://www.foundry.com/industries/virtual-reality/vr-mr-ar-confused
24. S. Feiner, B. MacIntyre, T. Höllerer, A. Webster, A touring machine: Prototyping 3D mobile augmented reality systems for exploring the urban environment, Personal Tech. **1(4)**, 208-217 (1997)
25. S. Côté, M. Beauvais, A. Girard-Vallée, R. Snyder (Eds.), A Live Augmented Reality Tool for Facilitating Interpretation of 2D Construction Drawings: International Conference on Augmented and Virtual Reality (2014), https://link.springer.com/chapter/10.1007%2F978-3-319-13969-2_32
26. P. Honkamaa, S. Siltanen, J. Jäppinen, C. Woodward, O. Korkalo (Eds.) Interactive Outdoor Mobile Augmentation using Markerless Tracking and GPS: Proc. Virtual Reality International Conference (VRIC) (Laval, France, 2007), http://virtual.vtt.fi/virtual/proj2/multimedia/media/publications/aronsite-vric2007.pdf

27. M. Kopsida, I. Brilakis (Eds.) *Markerless BIM Registration for Mobile Augmented Reality Based Inspection*, 16th International Conference on Computing in Civil and Building Engineering (ICCCBE2016), Osaka, Japan, 13 July 2016 (2016)
28. C. Woodward, M. Hakkarainen, O. Korkalo, T. Kantonen, M. Aittala, K. Rainio, K. Kähkönen (Eds.) *Mixed Reality for Mobile Construction Site Visualization and Communication*, in Proceedings 10th International Conference on Construction Applications of Virtual Reality (2010)
29. S. Zollmann, C. Hoppe, S. Kluckner, C. Poglitsch, H. Bischof, G. Reitmayr, Augmented reality for construction site monitoring and documentation, Proceedings of the IEEE **102(2)**, 137-154 (2014)
30. C. Park, D. Lee, O. Kwon, X. Wang, A framework for proactive construction defect management using BIM, augmented reality and ontology-based data collection template. Automat Constr. **33**, 61-71 (2013)
31. X. Wang, P.S. Dunston, M. Skiniewski (Eds.), *Mixed reality technology applications in construction equipment operator training*, in Proceedings of the 21st International Symposium on Automation and Robotics in Construction, USA, Citeseer (2004), http://www.irbnet.de/daten/iconda/CIB13601.pdf
32. A. Stocking, 4 Ways to Leverage Mixed Reality for Smarter Infrastructure Design (2018), https://www.autodesk.com/redshift/mixed-reality-for-infrastructure/

Development of a Dynamic Model of Quality Performance in Thai Construction Industry

Thanwadee Chinda[1*], *K.* Sittimak[2], *N.* Thalaengkij[2], *P.* Chaiyapong[2], *P.* Sornpasit[2], *W.* Ketnak[2]

[1]School of Management Technology, Sirindhorn International Institute of Technology, Thammasat University, 131 Tiwanont Rd. Bangkadi Muang Pathumthani 12000 Thailand, Email: thanwadee@siit.tu.ac.th

[2]School of Management Technology, Sirindhorn International Institute of Technology, Thammasat University, 131 Tiwanont Rd. Bangkadi Muang Pathumthani 12000 Thailand

Abstract Many quality performance tools are implemented in the construction industry to enhance the quality performance standard. This paper utilizes an ISO 9001 standard implementation to develop a dynamic model of construction quality performance in the Thai construction industry. The model consists of five sub-models, namely the Leadership, Plan, Do, Check, and Act sub-models. Five levels of performance maturity are also developed in this study to plan for long-term improvement. The simulation results reveal that a company takes seven years to proceed from level 1 to level 2 of maturity as it lacks experience and knowledge. With more experience, the company progresses through to higher maturity levels in a shorter period of time. The model achieves the perfect implementation score of 1,000 points at the end of year 23. This study results can be used to aid the construction industry in the effective planning for long-term quality improvement.

Keywords: construction industry, ISO 9001, Plan-Do-Check-Act Cycle, quality performance, system dynamics modelling

1 Introduction

The construction industry is dynamic in nature, and the concept of good performance in the construction industry is hard to define. Aspects of project quality are often overlooked in order to conform to the schedule and cost constraints. Many international quality standards, such as the ISO 9001 standard, Deming Cycle, and the balanced scorecard, are therefore developed as a foundation for quality management system [1]. The ISO 9001

* Corresponding author: thanwadee@siit.tu.ac.th

is an international standard that indicates requirements for a quality management system. It is used to demonstrate the ability of a company to consistently provide products and services that meet customer and regulatory requirements. It places a strong emphasis on product quality and continuous improvement [2]. In the South-East Asia region, the perception of ISO 9001 quality standard is good; however, there are several issues, such as a poor culture of continual improvement and lack of process approach utilization throughout the organization that are yet studied. Bubshait and Al-Atiq [3], for example, evaluated a contractor® quality assurance system in Saudi Arabia against the ISO 9000 standard. Pheng and Teo [4] examined the compatibility of the recently released ISO 9001: 2000 with OHSAS 18001: 1999 for the purpose of integration, and concluded that the newly introduced ISO 9001: 2000 standard serves as an opportune platform for construction firms to consider certification to OHSAS 18001: 1999 through an integration exercise.

Despite the above researches, there is a need to examine interactions among key factors affecting quality enhancement to effectively plan for construction quality improvement. Different maturity levels should also be developed so that the company can plan for construction improvement, and progress through to higher maturity levels in the long term. This paper, therefore, aims at developing a dynamic model of quality performance in the construction industry using an ISO 9001 standard. It is expected that a company can better understand causal relationships among key factors affecting construction quality, and plan for quality improvement in the long-term.

2 Key Factors affecting Quality Performance

2.1 Five Key Factors Affecting quality Performance

According to [5], the ISO 9001: 2015 can be generally classified into ten factors. Gonzalez [6], however, stated that the ISO 9001:2015 management system standard clauses can be overlaid with the Plan-Do-Check-Act (PDCA) Cycle to work in conjunction with each other. Paulova and Mlkva [7], on the other hand, mentioned that leadership is the key element in improving quality management. In this study, therefore, five key factors, including 1) Leadership, 2) Plan, 3) Do, 4) Check, and 5) Act factors are used for the dynamic model of quality performance development. They are associated with a total of 22 items extracted from a number of construction-related literature, such as Senaratne and Mayuran [8], Neyestani [9] and Shah and Pitroda [10]. They form a number of causal relationships, as shown in Figure 3. For instance, good management review leads to better and realistic quality policy and quality plan [11]. It could include the provision of proper training to enhance worker's skill. With a better skill, rework tends to reduce, and workers tend to assist each other to improve quality [12]. This, in turn, brings a better management review.

- Leadership factor: This factor consists of five associated items, namely management review, top-down communication, management commitment, resource allocation, and accountability [3, 10].
- Plan factor: This factor is associated with four items, namely quality policy, quality plan, reliable plan, and employee empowerment [13].
- Do factor: Five items are associated with this factor. They are documentation, quality awareness, rework, customer focus, and training [12, 8].
- Check factor: This factor consists of four items, including customer satisfaction, auditing, peer review, and competitiveness [14, 15].

- Act factor: this factor is associated with four items: continuous improvement, preventive action, innovative action, and prompt response [9; 14].

2.2 Importance Weights

2.2.1. Importance weight of key factors affecting quality performance

The more relationships an item has on the other items, the more important it is. To be able to assess a construction quality performance, and progress through to higher levels of maturity, each of the five key factors is assigned with its importance weight. In this study, a total weight of 1,000 points is assigned based on the relationships a factor has on the other factors (see Figure 1). Leadership, Plan, Do, Check, and Act factors have the importance weights of 230, 256, 179, 230, and 105 points, respectively.

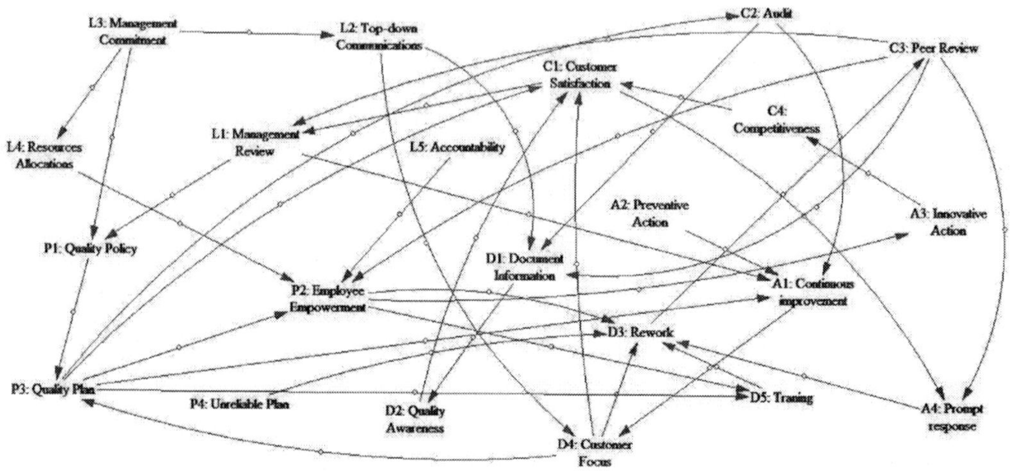

Fig. 1. Causal relationships of items affecting quality performance.

2.2.2. Importance weight of items affecting quality performance

The 22 items associated with five key factors also have different weight. This is based on the influences each item has on each other (see Figure 3). To explain, the "management commitment" item under the Leadership factor influences the other three items, namely the "top-down commitment", "quality policy", and "resource allocation" items. The "management review" item, on the other hand, has the influences on two items, which are the "quality policy" and "continuous improvement" items. The five items under the Leadership factor have a total of nine influences on the other items; this is converted to the importance weight of each item. For example, the "management commitment" item has the importance weight of 3/9 or 0.33 of a maximum of 230 points (i.e. 75.9 points) of the Leadership factor. The importance weight of each item is summarized in Table 1.

2.3 Influence Values among Key Factors Affecting Quality Performance

Influences among key factors affecting quality performance are achieved from the number of influences, represented by a number of flows a factor has on another factor. Each influence value is calculated and normalized based on the total influences a factor has on the other factors, as shown in Table 2. The importance weights and influence values among the five key factors are later used for the dynamic model development.

Table 1. Importance Weight of the 22 Items Associated with Five Key Factors

Factor	Item	Importance Weight	Maximum Score
Leadership	Management commitment	0.33	75.9
	Management review	0.22	50.6
	Top-down communication	0.22	50.6
	Accountability	0.12	27.6
	Resources allocation	0.11	25.3
Plan	Quality plan	0.50	128.0
	Employee empowerment	0.30	76.8
	Quality policy	0.10	25.6
	Unreliable plan	0.10	25.6
Do	Customer focus	0.44	79.0
	Document information	0.14	25.0
	Quality awareness	0.14	25.0
	Rework	0.14	25.0
	Training	0.14	25.0
Check	Peer review	0.44	101.2
	Customer satisfaction	0.23	52.9
	Auditing	0.22	50.6
	Competitiveness	0.11	25.3
Act	Continuous improvement	0.25	26.3
	Preventive action	0.25	26.3
	Innovative action	0.25	26.2
	Prompt response	0.25	26.2
Total score			1000

3 Quality Performance Maturity Level

The quality performance maturity level is developed in this study to assess the maturity level of construction quality performance. Each maturity level needs a score-range [16], for example, divided a total score of 1,000 points into five levels. Chinda [17], on the other hand, divided the 1,000 points into six safety maturity levels with the score-ranges. In this study, a total of 1000 points of quality performance are divided into five maturity levels based on the ISO 9001 and Plan-Do-Check-Act Cycle. Level 1 of maturity has the score-range from 0 – 230 points, following the implementation of the Leadership factor. Level 2 of maturity then has the score-range from 231 – 486 points, implying the implementation of the Leadership and Plan factors. Levels 3, 4 and 5 have score-ranges of 487 – 665, 666 – 895, and 896 – 1000 points, respectively.

Table 2. Influence Values among Five Key Factors

From	To				
	Leadership	Plan	Do	Check	Act
Leadership	-	0.51	0.33	-	0.16
Plan	-	-	0.50	0.25	0.25
Do	-	0.33	-	0.67	-
Check	0.25	0.13	0.37	-	0.25
Act	-	-	0.67	0.33	-

4 The Dynamic Model of Quality Performance

4.1 Leadership Factor Sub-model

Leadership factor sub-model is illustrated in Figure 2. It consists of five associated items. The score of each item increases based on its increasing rate and influences from the other factors (see Equation 1). The total score of the Leadership factor is then the summation of the five items' scores and the influential score from the Check factor (see Table 2), as shown in Equation 2.

*Management_review = IF (Item1_L+Item1_L*Increasing_R_LDS)≥LDS_item1*
THEN (LDS_item1-Item1_L) (1)
*ELSE Item1_L*Increasing_R_LDS*

Leadership score = Min (IF (HISTORY (Item1_L,count_y)
+HISTORY (item2_L,count_y)+ HISTORY (item3_L,count_y)
+HISTORY (item4_L,count_y) +HISTORY(item5_L,count_y))
=(Item1_L+item2_L+item3_L+item4_L+item5_L (2)
*+ (Check_to_others*Cor_C_to_LDS))*
THEN (ROUND (Item1_L+item2_L + item3_L+item4_L+item5_L))
ELSE ((Item1_L+item2_L+item3_L+ item4_L+item5_L), Max_LDS)

4.2 Plan Factor Sub-model

The total score of this factor is the summation of the four items' scores and the influential scores from the Leadership, Do, and Check factors (see Figure 3 and Table 2), as shown in Equation 3.

Plan score = Min (IF (HISTORY (Item1_P,count_y)
+HISTORY (item2_P,count_y)+HISTORY (item3_P,count_y)
+HISTORY (item4_P,count_y))
=(Item1_P+item2_P+item3_P+ item4_P
*+(LDS_to_others*Cor_LDS_to_P)* (3)
*+(Do_to_others*Cor_D_to_P)*
*+(Check_to_others*Cor_C_to_P))*
THEN (ROUND (Item1_P+item2_P+item3_P+item4_P))
ELSE ((Item1_P+item2_P+item3_P+item4_P), Max_Plan)

4.3 Do Factor Sub-model

The total score of this factor is the summation of the five items' scores and the influential scores from the other four factors (see Figure 4 and Table 2), as shown in Equation 4.

Do score = Min (IF (HISTORY (Item1_D,count_y)
+HISTORY (item2_D,count_y)+HISTORY (item3_D,count_y)
+HISTORY (item4_D,count_y)+HISTORY (item5_D,count_y))
= (Item1_D+item2_D+item3_D+item4_D+item5_D
*+(LDS_to_others*Cor_LDS_to_D)*
*+(Plan_to_others*Cor_Plan_to_D)* (4)
*+(Check_to_others*Cor_C_to_D)*
+(Act_to_others Cor_A_to_D))*

THEN (ROUND (Item1_D+item2_D+item3_D+ item4_D+item5_D))
ELSE ((Item1_D+item2_D+item3_D+item4_D+item5_D), Max_Do)

4.4 Check Factor Sub-model

The total score of this factor is the summation of the four items' scores and the influential scores from the Plan, Do, and Act factors (see Figure 5 and Table 2), see Equation 5.

Check score = Min (IF (HISTORY (Item1_C,count_y)
+HISTORY (item2_C,count_y)+HISTORY (item3_C,count_y)
+HISTORY (item4_C,count_y))
=(Item1_C+item2_C+item3_C+ item4_C
*+ (Plan_to_others*Cor_Plan_to_C)* (5)
*+(Do_to_others*Cor_D_to_C)*
*+ (Act_to_others*Cor_A_to_C))*
THEN (ROUND (Item1_C+item2_C+item3_C+ item4_C))
ELSE ((Item1_C+item2_C+item3_C+item4_C), Max_Check)

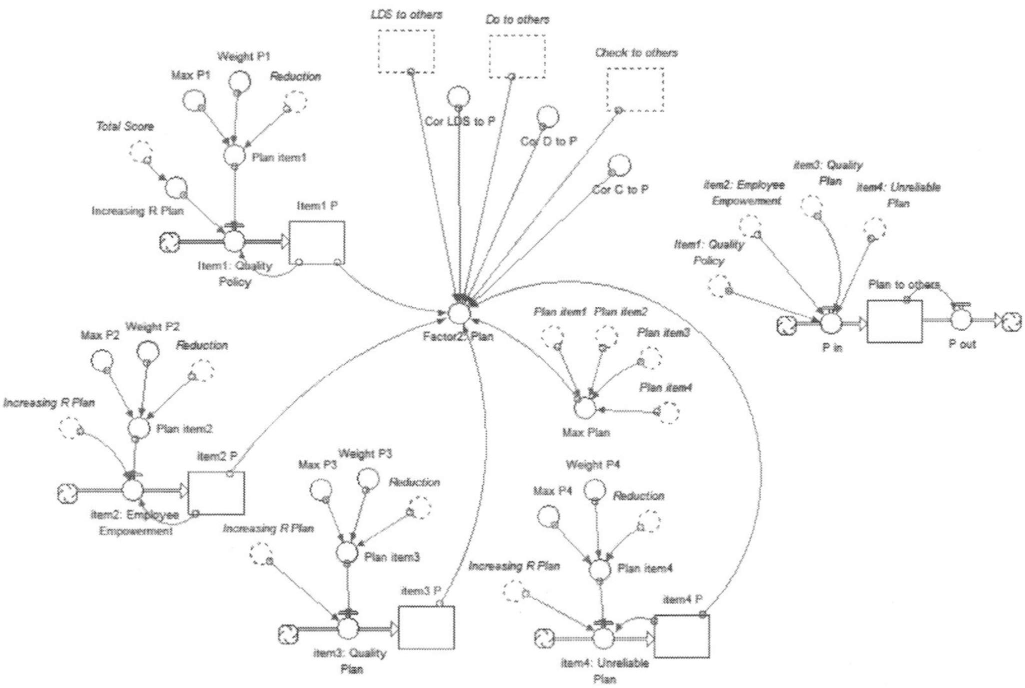

Fig. 2. Leadership Factor Sub-model.

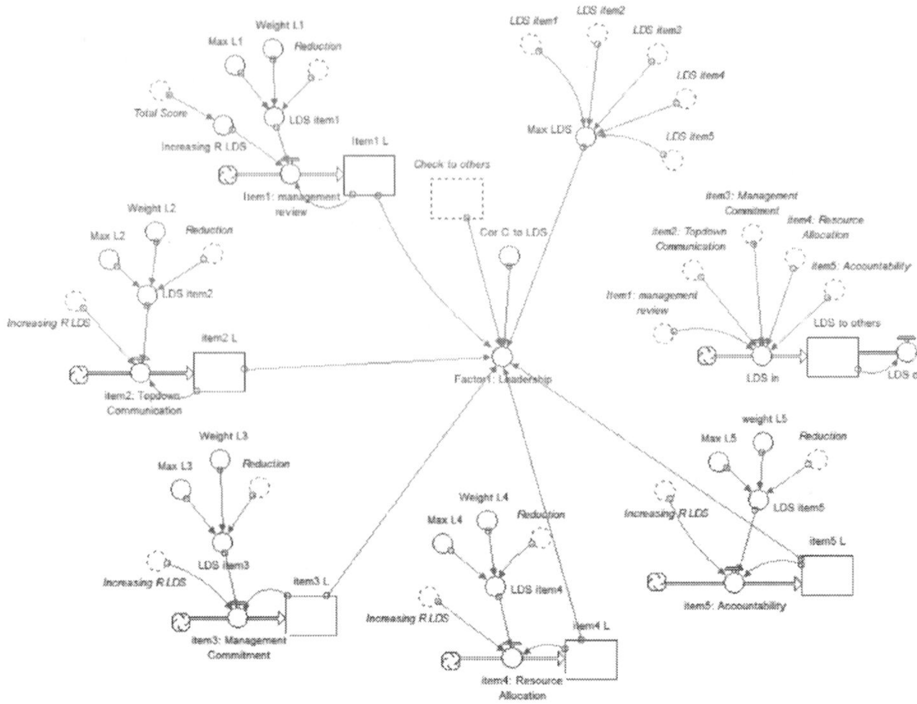

Fig. 3. Plan Factor Sub-model.

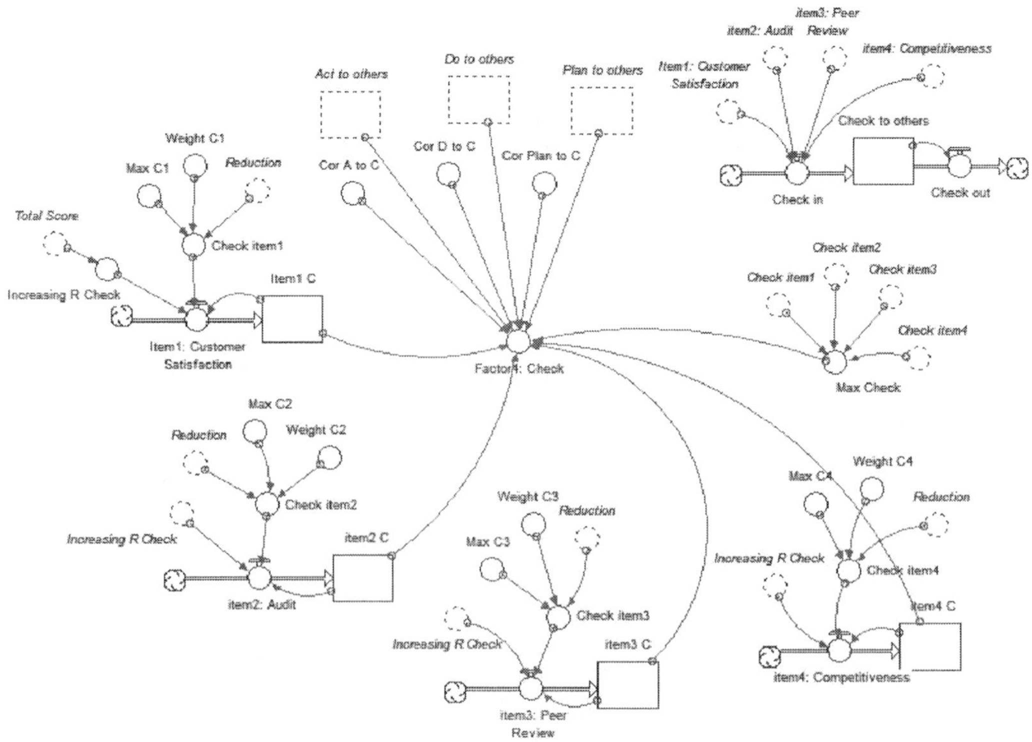

Fig. 4. Do Factor Sub-model.

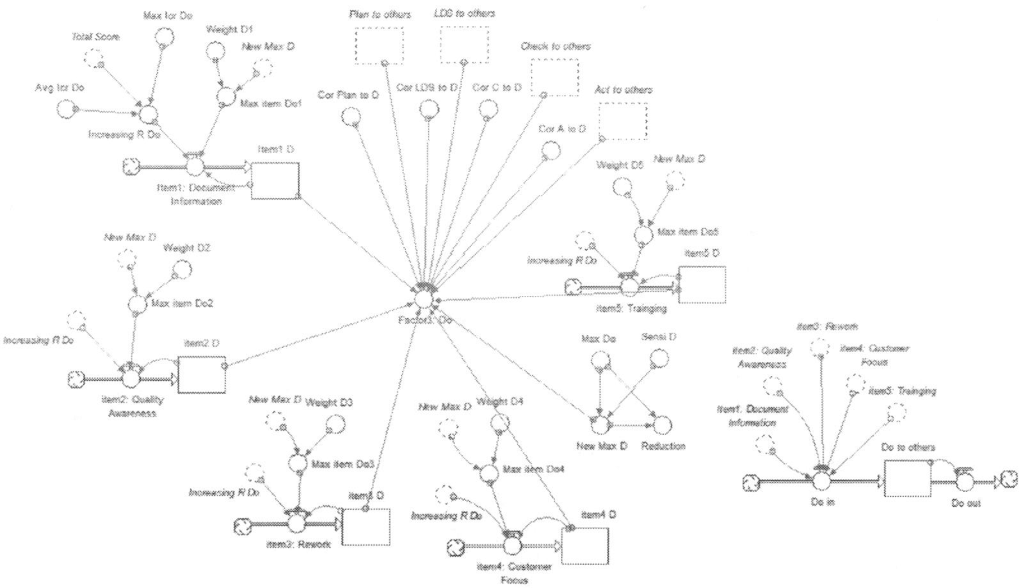

Fig. 5. Check Factor Sub-model.

4.5 Act Factor Sub-model

Act factor sub-model is illustrated in Figure 6. The total score of this factor is the summation of the four items' scores and the influential scores from the Leadership, Plan, and Check factors (see Table 2), as shown in Equation 6. Based on the five sub-models, the total score of quality performance and the quality performance maturity level are calculated, see Equations 7 and 8.

$$\begin{aligned} \textit{Act score} = \; & Min\ (IF\ (HISTORY\ (Item1\_A,count\_y) \\ & +HISTORY\ (item2\_A,count\_y)+HISTORY\ (item3\_A,count\_y) \\ & +HISTORY\ (item4\_A,count\_y)) \\ & =(Item1\_A+item2\_A+item3\_A+ item4\_A+(LDS\_to\_others*Cor\_LDS\_to\_A) \\ & +(Plan\_to\_others*Cor\_P\_to\_A) \\ & +(Check\_to\_others*Cor\_C\_to\_A)) \\ & THEN\ (ROUND\ (Item1\_A+item2\_A+item3\_A+item4\_A)) \\ & ELSE\ ((Item1\_A+item2\_A+item3\_A+item4\_A),\ Max\_Act) \end{aligned} \tag{6}$$

$$\begin{aligned} \textit{Total score} = \; & Leadership\ score+Plan\ score \\ & +\ Do\ score+Check\ score+Act\ score \end{aligned} \tag{7}$$

$$\begin{aligned} \textit{Maturity level} = \; & IF\ ((0 \leq Total\_Score)\ AND\ (Total\_Score \leq 230)) \\ & THEN\ (1)\ ELSE\ (IF\ ((230<Total\_Score)\ AND\ (Total\_Score \leq 486)) \\ & THEN\ (2)\ ELSE\ (IF\ ((486<Total\_Score)\ AND\ (Total\_Score \leq 665)) \\ & THEN\ (3)\ ELSE\ (IF\ ((665<Total\_Score)\ AND\ (Total\_Score \leq 895)) \\ & THEN\ (4)\ ELSE\ (IF\ ((895<Total\_Score)\ AND\ (Total\_Score \leq 1000) \\ & THEN\ (5)\ ELSE\ (0))))) \end{aligned} \tag{8}$$

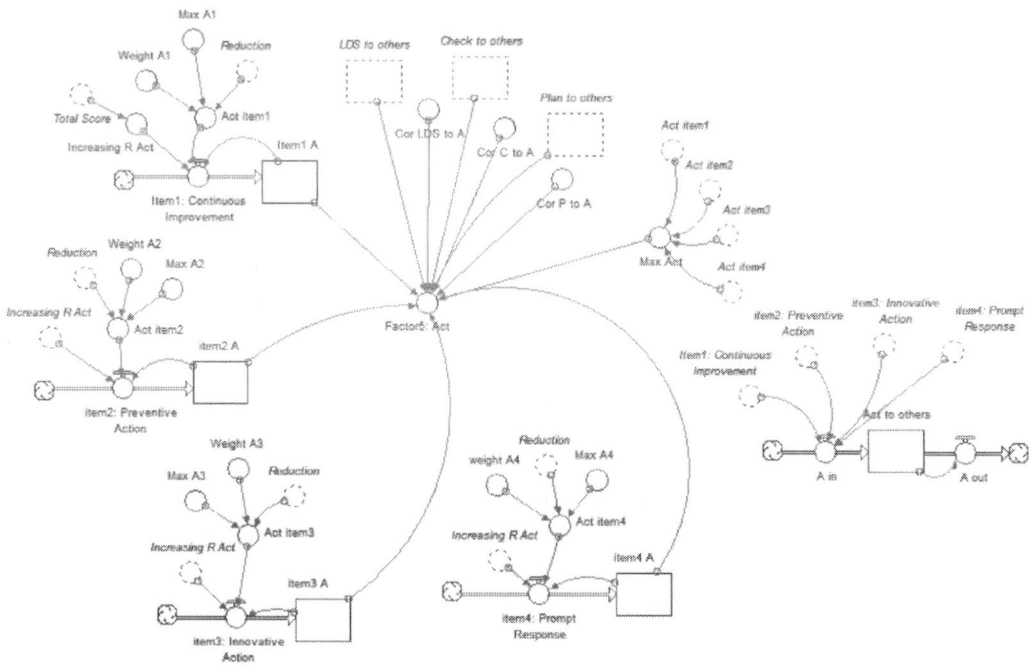

Fig. 6. Act Factor Sub-model.

5 Simulation Results

The dynamic model of construction quality performance is simulated, and the simulation results are as shown in Figure 7. The results show that it takes six years for the company to implement the quality improvement program, and progress from level 1 to level 2 of maturity. With more experiences, the company spends four years each to achieve levels 2 and 3 of quality maturity. With cooperation from management and workers, the company reaches level 5 of quality performance maturity at the end of year 20. The results also show that the company achieves a perfect score of 1,000 points in 23 years.

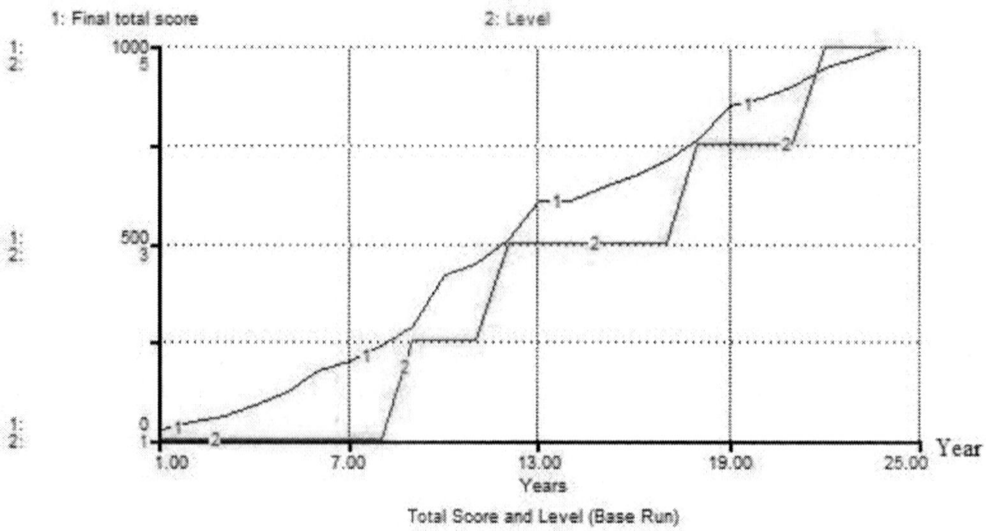

Fig. 9. Graphical Results of Total Score and Maturity Level.

6 Conclusions

With a growth in the country's economic, there is a need for Thai construction companies to achieve high-quality performance to gain competitive and conform to customer's requirement. This study utilizes the ISO 9001 and Plan-Do-Check-Act Cycle to develop a dynamic model of quality performance to examine the quality performance of the Thai construction industry in the long-term. The model consists of five sub-models, namely the Leadership, Plan, Do, Act, and Act sub-models. The simulation results reveal that the construction company struggles to progress to a higher level of maturity at the beginning years of quality improvement program implementation. This might be because of the lack of cooperation from management and working levels. With more management support and reliable quality policy, the company can achieve levels 3 and 4 in a shorter period of time. To progress through to level 5 of maturity, the continuous improvement plan must be executed. The results show that the company can achieve level 5 of quality performance maturity in 23 years. The dynamic model of quality performance developed in this study is based on the data gathered from construction-related literature. Primary data can be used to increase the accuracy of the model results. Moreover, each causal relationship is assumed to have equal importance. Further clarification could be performed using, for example, cross-impact analysis.

References

1. S.X. Zeng, P. Tian, J.J. Shi, *Implementing integration of ISO 9001 and ISO 14001 for construction*, Managerial auditing journal, 20(4), 394-407, (2005)
2. J. Nolan, *Would construction companies benefit fromISO9001?* [online]. Available from: https://advisera.com/9001academy/blog/2016/06/07/would-construction-companies-benefit-from-iso-9001/ (2016)
3. A.A. Bubshait, T.H. Al-Atiq, *ISO 9000 quality standards in construction*, Journal of management in engineering, 15(6), 41-46, (1999)
4. L.S. Pheng, J.A. Teo, *Implementing total quality management in construction through ISO 9001: 2000*. Architectural science review, 46(2), 159-165, (2003)
5. M. Chaudron, *ISO 9001:2015 Key changes in the world's most popular QMS standard* [online]. Available from: https://www.asqhouston.org (2016)
6. M. Gonzalez, *The ISO 9001:2015sStandard and the Plan-Do-Check-Act Cycle* [online]. Available from: https://www.qualitywbt.com/wp-content/uploads/The-ISO-9001-2015-Standard-and-the-PDCA-Cycle.pdf (2016)
7. I. Paulova, M. Mlkva, *Leadership – the key element in improving quality management*, Kvalita inovacia prosperita/Quality innovation prosperity, 15(1), 27-36, (2011)
8. S. Senaratne, J. Mayuran, *Documentation management based on ISO for construction industries in developing countries*, Journal of construction in developing countries, 20(2), 81–95, (2015)
9. B. Neyestani, *Effectiveness of quality management system (QMS) on construction projects,* Munich Personal RePEc Archive, Department of Civil Engineering, De La Salle University, Manila, Philippines, (2016)

10. H. Shah, J.R. Pitroda, *A critical literature review on quality management for infrastructure projects*, International journal of engineering research and development, 14(3), 18-21, (2018)

11. *Management review* [online]. Available from: https://www.iso-9001-checklist.co.uk/tutorial/5.6-management-review.htm, ISO 9001, (2008)

12. N.M. Cachadinha, *Implementing quality management systems in small and medium construction companies: a contribution to a road map for success,* Leadership and management in engineering, 9(1), 32-39, (2009)

13. M. Hammar, *Plan-Do-Check-Act in the ISO 9001 standard* [online]. Available from: https://advisera.com/9001academy/knowledgebase/plan-do-check-act-in-the-iso-9001-standard/ (2018)

14. B. Neyestani, *Impact of ISO 9001 certification on the projects' success of large-scale (AAA) construction firms in the Philippines.* International research journal of management, IT and social sciences *(IRJMIS)*, 3(11), 35-45, (2016)

15. N. Shaari, M.N. Abdullah, S.Z. Sheng, M.A.A. Lokman, *Quality management system in contractor organizations: an empirical study on costs and benefits of ISO 9001: 2008 implementation*. International journal of real estate studies, 11(5), 1-10, (2017)

16. *Self-assessment: guidelines for Companies*. European Foundation for Quality Management, Brussels, Belgium, EFQM, 1998

17. T. Chinda, *A safety assessment approach using safety enablers and results*, International journal of occupational safety and ergonomics, 3, 343-361, (2012)

Does proximity to tourist site affect the rental value of residential properties? Empirical evidence from Nigeria

Olalekan Oshodi[1*], *Oyewale* Oyedeji[1], and *Clinton* Aigbovboa[1]

[1]Sustainable Human Settlement and Construction Research Centre, Faculty of Engineering and the Built Environment, University of Johannesburg, South Africa

Abstract. The property market plays a vital role in the economy of any nation. The industry provides jobs, investment opportunities and constructed space for productive activities, among others. Several authors have developed predictive models for the rental value of residential properties. However, little is known about the impact of tourist site on the rental value of residential properties. This study seeks to examine the effect of tourist sites on the rental value of residential properties using an artificial intelligence technique. The predictive modelling approach was utilised in this study. It was found that proximity to tourist site and security are the most important factors influencing rental prices of residential properties. In addition, the developed Neural Network (NN) model could adequately predict the rental value of residential properties (93.75% were correctly predicted). The results of this study demonstrate that the NN model is a useful tool for forecasting of the rental value of properties. The findings of this study provide valuable information for policy makers, professionals in the built environment and property investors.

Keywords: Forecasting, modelling, neural network, rental value, residential property.

1 Introduction

Research in the real estate sector has evolved over the years. This situation has led to the development of several models for forecasting of rental values of residential properties. The process of assembling residential properties contributes to economic growth through employment generation, production in the manufacturing sector and business opportunities, among others [1, 2]. Also, foreclosures in the real estate market have been linked to the Global Financial Meltdown [3]. These shreds of evidence found in the literature show that the residential property market is an important segment of any economy. In the existing literature, the predictive models for this class of properties focused on countries such

* Corresponding author: os.oshodi@gmail.com

as Australia [4]; Dubai [5]; Hong Kong [6]; New Zealand [7]; Nigeria [8]; United Kingdom [9] and United States of America [10], among others.

The approach used for modelling and forecasting of the value of residential properties can be classified into two. First, modelling the relationship between economic variables and the value of residential properties [11]. Second, forecasts of the value of residential properties are generated based on attributes, such as the number of rooms [4, 7]. Despite the rapid development of residential market research, certain markets in developing countries (such as Nigeria) are under-researched. This has been attributed mainly to the lack of data [12]. Also, little is known about the impact of tourist sites on the rental value of residential properties.

The purpose of this study is to develop a predictive model for rental values of residential properties using the neural network. The goal of this study was achieved through two objectives: (i) model the relationship between the rental value of a residential property and its attributes and (ii) examine the impact of property attributes on rental value. The findings of this study provide an answer to the question 'does the tourist site affect the rental value of residential properties?". This is the main contribution of this study to the existing knowledge.

2 Literature Review

2.1 Property attributes

Research into residential property value forecasting has a long history. Some of the studies found in the literature include Abidoye and Chan [8] and Lam et al. [6], among others. Bond and Hopkins [7] found that proximity to high voltage overhead transmission lines does not affect the value of residential properties in New Zealand. Lam et al. [6] reported that the presence of a garden has a significant impact on the value of residential properties in Hong Kong. Other attributes affecting the value of residential properties include property location; a number of bedrooms; a number of toilets; a number of bathrooms; property type; a number of boy's quarters; number of parking space; age of property, number of floors and availability of sectors [6, 8, 10]. Information gleaned from the literature shows that a multiplicity of factors affect the value of residential properties.

2.2 Forecasting techniques used in previous research

A significant and growing body of studies has used modelling techniques for forecasting of the value of residential properties. In forecast oriented research, the process of model development can be divided into five distinct but iterative stages. First, relevant theories useful for prediction of the outcome variable are identified from the literature. Second, the theoretical constructs are operationalised into measurable constructs. Third, relevant data relating to the constructs are collected from reliable sources. Fourth, the collected data is divided into two groups (training data which is used for estimating the model and test data used for evaluating the predictive accuracy of the developed model). Finally, the model is calibrated, and the predictive performance of the model is calculated. The outcome of forecasting oriented research is useful in testing existing theories [13]. The theory upon which the model is developed is revised or discarded if the predictive accuracy of the developed model is low.

Based on a review of the literature, the techniques used for modelling and forecasting of the value of residential properties include analytical, regression (also referred to as hedonic), neural network and support vector machine, among others [4, 6, 8]. These techniques can be classified into two broad groups: linear and non-linear approaches. Comparative analysis of the predictive accuracy of different techniques has been used to evaluate the performance of the developed models. For example, Abidoye and Chan [14] found that the neural network model outperformed the regression model when applied to residential property value forecasting. Also, Nghiep and Al [10] reported that the predictive performance of the neural network model was better than that of the regression model when used for residential property value forecasting. Based on the findings of previous research, the neural network was used for forecasting of the rental value of residential property in this study.

3 Study Area

Recently, the Nigerian economy has been in a recession. This situation is primarily due to low revenue from crude oil sales. Previous research has shown that changes in crude oil prices have an impact on construction cost [15]. However, it must be noted that the effect of changes in crude oil prices on rental value is unknown. This could be attributed to the lack of quantitative data in developing countries, such as Nigeria [16]. Based on the foregoing, there have been government reforms aimed at improving the volume of internally generated revenue. Also, rent is one of the potential sources of revenue for private sector investors.

Nigeria is made up of 36 states and a federal capital territory – Abuja. According to Olaleye [17], the Nigerian property market can be classified into two groups: primary (characterised with high rental and capital values) and secondary markets (characterised with the low rental and capital values). Osun state is situated in the South-West region of Nigeria. A lot of tourist sites, which holds historical information about the Yoruba race, are located within Osun State. For example, the Osun Grove is a tourist site that attracts a large volume of tourists to Osun State [18]. Although the state contains predominantly single-family residential homes, there are some multi-unit houses and a small number of commercial properties.

4 Research Method

4.1 Data

Advancements in the field of artificial intelligence (AI) has been tremendous. This has led to the development of several techniques for modelling and forecasting. These techniques have been applied to problems in the different field of research, such as food processing [19], construction economics [20], structural mechanics [21] and structural health monitoring [22], among others. Hence, the NN, which is an AI modelling technique, was applied to rental value prediction in this research.

To achieve the first objective of this study, there is a need to collect data relating to the rental value of residential properties. To this end, transaction data were collected from real estate firms and property owners. This is because there is no centralised database for property transactions in Nigeria [8]. The collected data contained information about transaction details of properties located in Oshogbo, Osun State. The information relating to structural attributes for each property was collected. This is consistent with the approach used in previous studies [7, 8, 10]. In addition, spatial information relating to the proximity of each property to tourist site (i.e. Osun grove) was collected.

Information relating to 160 property rental transactions were retrieved, and this represents the data used for the study. The transaction data contains information on ten independent variables and one dependent variable (i.e. the rental value of the residential property). The variables in the final NN model are presented in Table 1.

Table 1. Variables used in the model.

Variable Name	Variable	Definition of variable
DFCS	Distance from cultural site	Classified into four groups (0-200m, 201-400m, 401-600m, 601-800m)
State	Age of building	Numeric values of 1, 2, 3, 4, …
Security	A perceived sense of security	Numeric values of 1, 2, 3, 4, …
Security.S	Presence of security operatives	1 if available and, 0 if not available
Interior	State of building's interior	Numeric values of 1, 2, 3, 4, …
Exterior	State of building's exterior	Numeric values of 1, 2, 3, 4, …
Dist.to.shopping	Proximity to the shopping centre	Numeric values of 1, 2, 3, 4, …
Water	Pipe-borne water	1 if available and, 0 if not available
Road	Road infrastructure	1 if available and, 0 if not available
Rooms	Number of rooms	Numeric values of 1, 2, 3, 4, …
Rent	Rental value (per annum in Naira)	Less than 50,000; 50,001-100,000; 100,001-150,000; over 150,001

4.2 Model Specification

In the current study, a three-layer feed-forward neural network (NN) model was applied to the forecasting of the rental value of residential properties. NN model is inspired by the human brain. The NN model is made up of interconnected neurons whose functioning is similar to the human brain. The neurons in the NN model is calibrated during the learning phase. The final forecast computed by the model is largely dependent on the initial weights of the neurons. To reduce the variations in the final forecast from the NN model due to randomisation, an ensemble of NNs was applied in the present study. The final predictions from each NN model were averaged [23]. The architecture of the NN model is 10-H-1. The input layer has 10 neurons (i.e. 10 independent variables). The number of nodes in the hidden layer (H) is the only parameter of the ANN model that was tuned using a grid search algorithm. The output layer (neuron) of the NN model is the rental value.

The predictive experiments were carried out using the R-programming [24] and minor package, which facilitates the application of artificial intelligence models (such as ANN) to real-world problems [25]. The process of developing predictive models entails two important phases: model estimation and model validation. The NN model was estimated by capturing the relationship between the 10 independent variables and rental value. To validate the model, the collected data were divided into two groups (i.e. training and test data set). Zhang et al. [26] mentioned that the ratio for training and test data set in previous studies include 90:10; 80:20 and 70:30, respectively. For this study, the collected data were randomly divided into two groups based on 70% and 30% (112 and 48).

5 Results and Discussion

5.1 Results

Artificial intelligence models are used to predict numerical values (regression) and groups (classification). In this study, the rental value of residential properties was grouped into four classes: (A) less than N 50,000; (B) N 50,001 - N 100,000; (C) N 100,001 - N 150,000; and (D) over N 150,001. For classification problems, the predictive performance of the model is based on "correctly classified" and "incorrectly classified". The predictive performance of classification models range between 0% and 100%, and a value close to 100% shows perfect performance [27].

The results from model validation (i.e. prediction of the test data set using the trained NN model) are summarised and presented in Table 2. The overall predictive accuracy of the NN model is 93.75 percent.

Table 2. Formatting sections, subsections and subsubsections Prediction results for all for the logistic regression model

Observed	Predicted				Accuracy (%)
	A	B	C	D	
A	5	0	0	0	100.00
B	1	8	1	0	80.00
C	0	0	14	1	93.33
D	0	0	0	18	100.00
				Overall	93.75

5.2 Sensitivity Analysis

Compared to regression, the NN model does not provide outputs which contain coefficients for each variable. This outcome makes it difficult to interpret the importance of each independent variable included in the final NN model. Hence, little is known about the contribution of each independent variable to the prediction of the outcome variable (i.e. rental value). This is the main reason AI models are called black-box models [28]. Sensitivity analysis was proposed in Cortez and Embrechts [29] as an approach for visualising the relative importance of variables included in AI models, such as NN. Figure 1 shows the relative importance of the independent variables used in the development of the NN model.

The RI value ranges between .0 and .25, where a .0 value indicates that the attribute does not affect the rental value, while .25 connotes a highly significant contribution to the rental value of residential properties. As can be seen from Figure 1, DFCS, Security.S, Rooms and Security are the independent variables which have a significant impact on the rental value of residential properties. Surprisingly, water has the least effect on rental value.

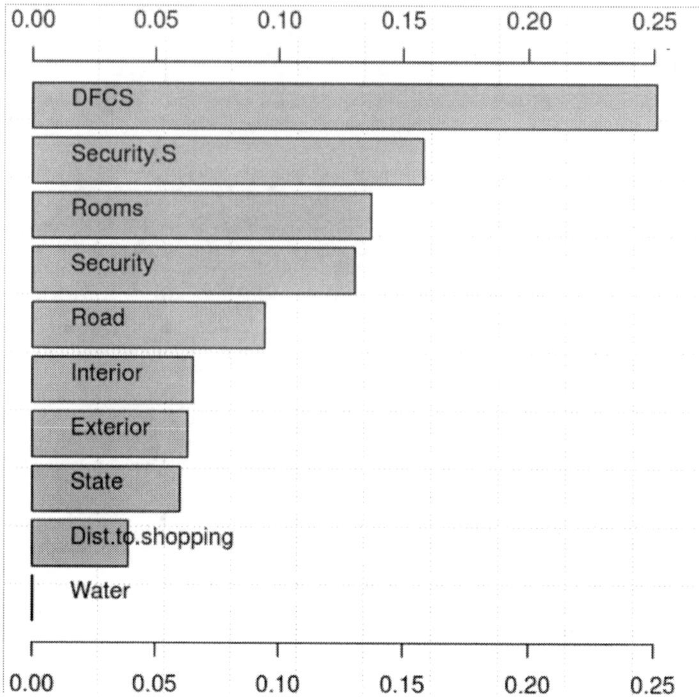

Fig. 1. The relative importance of independent variables

5.3 Discussion of Findings

Very little was found in the literature on the effect of tourist site on the rental value of residential properties. The present study was designed to address this gap in the literature by modelling and forecasting of the rental value of residential properties. The most exciting finding was that proximity to tourist site has a significant impact on the rental value of residential properties located within the study area. The predictive accuracy of the developed NN model is 93.75 percent. The finding of the present study also demonstrates the efficacy of using NN model for forecasting of the rental value of residential properties. Distance from the cultural site, the presence of security operatives, number of rooms and perceived sense of security around the location of the building are good predictors of the rental value of residential properties. Contrary to expectations, it was revealed that availability of pipe-borne water has no impact on the rental value of residential properties.

The results of this study will now be compared to the findings of previous work. These findings confirm that attributes of a residential property (see Table 1) are useful for predicting its value. For example, Abidoye and Chan [8] found that property attributes are good predictors of property value. Similar findings were also reported in Lam et al. [30]; McGreal et al. [9]; and Li and Li [4], among others. The findings observed in this study mirror those reported in previous studies focused on evaluating the efficacy of using AI models for forecasting of property value. The outcome shows that the relationship between the attributes of a residential property and its value is non-linear. The predictive performance of the NN model could be attributed to its ability to capture the non-linear relationship between property value and its attributes.

On the overall, the NN model provides a reliable forecast of the rental value of residential properties. This study has shown that proximity to a tourist site and the presence of security operatives are the two most important attributes affecting the rental value of residential properties. This study contributes to the existing knowledge in the field of property economics in two ways. First, it has provided evidence showing the influence of tourist sites on the rental value of residential properties. Second, this, to our (i.e. authors) knowledge, is the first study to apply classification models to the prediction of the rental value of residential properties in the context of developing countries, such as Nigeria. While the findings of the present study are promising, it must be acknowledged that not all predictors of rental value are captured in the developed model. The developed NN model can be used as a decision support tool for the prediction of the rental value of residential properties.

6 Conclusion

The study, reported in this paper, set out to develop a model for predicting the rental value of residential properties. Also, the outcome provides an answer to the question "does proximity to tourist site have an impact on the rental value of a residential property?" Three main findings emanate from the outcomes of this research. First, the attributes of a residential property are good predictors of its value. Second, the distance between a residential property and a tourist site has an impact on its rental value. Finally, the neural network model is excellent for forecasting of the rental value of residential properties.

The outcome of this investigation clearly shows that proximity to tourist site has an impact on the rental value of residential properties. Also, it is evident that the attributes of a residential property emerged as reliable predictors of its rental value. In general, the evidence from this study suggests that location is the most important variable that influences the rental value of a residential property. The present study contributes to the existing knowledge in the field of property economics by providing insights into the impact of tourist sites on the value of residential properties.

The findings presented in this paper are subject to certain limitations. First, the data set available for modelling is small. The lack of quantitative data remains a challenge faced by researchers in the field of construction economics and property economics. Second, the findings are based on the modelling approach. Third, the data collected is limited to a particular section of Nigeria. Despite these limitations, the use of the hold-out sample (i.e. training and test data set) ensure that the developed NN model is robust and reliable. This is similar to the approach used in previous studies (such as Abidoye and Chan [8]; Lam et al., [6]). The findings of the current study offer insight into the relationship between attributes of residential properties and its value. Further research is needed to establish whether proximity to a tourist site has an impact on the sale value of residential properties. Also, it would be interesting to assess the impact of tourist site on the value of commercial properties. These findings imply that the location and attributes of residential property should be taken into account when making a decision relating to the investment.

Reference

1. Y.H. Chiang, L. Tao, F.K.W. Wong, Causal relationship between construction activities, employment and GDP: The case of Hong Kong, *Habitat International* **46**:1-12 (2015)
2. R.E. Saks, Job creation and housing construction: Constraints on metropolitan area employment growth, *Journal of Urban Economics* **64**(1):178-195 (2008)
3. H. Jiang, X.H. Jin, C. Liu, The effects of the late 2000s global financial crisis on Australia's construction demand, *Construction Economics and Building* **13**(3):65-79 (2013)
4. H. Li, V. Li, Forecasting house rental levels: Analytical rent model versus neural network, *Journal of Urban Planning and Development* **122**(4):118-127 (1996)

5. A. Hepşen, M. Vatansever, Forecasting future trends in Dubai housing market by using Box-Jenkins autoregressive integrated moving average, *International Journal of Housing Markets and Analysis* **4**(3):210-223 (2011)
6. K.C. Lam, C.Y. Yu, C.K. Lam, Support vector machine and entropy based decision support system for property valuation, *Journal of Property Research* **26**(3):213-233 (2009)
7. S. Bond, J. Hopkins, The Impact of Transmission Lines on Residential Property Values: Results of a Case Study in a Suburb of Wellington, NZ. *Pacific Rim Property Research Journal*, **6**(2):52-60 (2000)
8. R.B. Abidoye, A.P.C. Chan, Modeling property values in Nigeria using artificial neural network, *Journal of Property Research* **34**(1):1-18 (2017)
9. S. McGreal, A. Adair, D. McBurney, D. Patterson, Neural networks: the prediction of residential values, *Journal of Property Valuation and Investment* **16**(1):57-70 (1998)
10. N. Nghiep, C. Al, Predicting housing value: A comparison of multiple regression analysis and artificial neural networks, *Journal of Real Estate Research* **22**(3):313-336 (2001)
11. H. Mallick, M.K. Mahalik, Factors determining regional housing prices: evidence from major cities in India, *Journal of Property Research* **32**(2):123-146 (2015)
12. R.B. Abidoye, A.P.C. Chan, A survey of property valuation approaches in Nigeria, *Property Management* **34**(5):364-380 (2016)
13. G. Shmueli, O.R. Koppius, Predictive analytics in information systems research, *MIS Quarterly* **35**(3):553-572 (2011)
14. R.B. Abidoye, A.P.C. Chan, Improving property valuation accuracy: a comparison of hedonic pricing model and artificial neural network, *Pacific Rim Property Research Journal* **24**(1):71-83 (2018)
15. Olatunji, The impact of oil price regimes on construction cost in Nigeria, *Construction Management and Economics* **28**(7):747-759 (2010)
16. K@kumu, Construction statistics review for Kenya, *Construction Management and Economics* **25**(3):315-326 (2007)
17. Olaleye, Property market nature and the choice of property portfolio diversification strategies: The Nigeria experience, *International Journal of Strategic Property Management* **12**:35–51 (2008)
18. K.M. Woosnam, K.D. Aleshinloye, N. Maruyama, Solidarity at the Osun Osogbo Sacred Grove: A UNESCO world heritage site, *Tourism Planning and Development* **13**(3):274-291 (2016)
19. P. Cortez, A. Cerdeira, F. Almeida, T. Matos, J. Reis, Modeling wine preferences by data mining from physicochemical properties, *Decision Support Systems*, **47**(4):547-553 (2009)
20. Oshodi, O.A. Ejohwomu, I.O. Famakin, P. Cortez, Comparing univariate techniques for tender price index forecasting: Box-Jenkins and neural network model, *Construction Economics and Building* **17**(3):109-123 (2017)
21. J. Tinoco, A. Gomes Correia, P. Cortez, Jet grouting column diameter prediction based on a data-driven approach, *European Journal of Environmental and Civil Engineering* 1-21 (2016)
22. M.S. El-Abbasy, A. Senouci, T. Zayed, F. Mirahadi, L. Parvizsedghy, Artificial neural network models for predicting condition of offshore oil and gas pipelines, *Automation in Construction* **45**:50-65 (2014)
23. T. Hastie, R. Tibshirani, J. Friedman, *The Elements of Statistical Learning: Data Mining, Inference, and Prediction* (2nd ed.), New York: Springer-Verlag (2008)
24. R Core Team., *R: A language and environment for statistical computing*. Vienna, Austria: R Foundation for Statistical Computing (2015)

25. P. Cortez, Data mining with neural networks and support vector machines using the R/rminer tool. In: P. Perner, ed. *Proceedings of the 10th Industrial Conference on Data Mining - Advances in Data Mining: Applications and Theoretical Aspects, July 2010, Berlin, Germany*. Berlin: Springer 572–583 (2010)
26. G. Zhang, B.E. Patuwo, M.Y. Hu, Forecasting with artificial neural networks: The state of the art, *International Journal of Forecasting* **14**:35–62 (1998)
27. P. Cortez, *A tutorial on the rminer R package for data mining tasks*. Teaching Report, Department of Information Systems, ALGORITMI Research Centre, Engineering School, University of Minho, Guimaraes, Portugal (2015)
28. S. Dreiseitl, L. Ohno-Machado, Logistic regression and artificial neural network classification models: a methodology review, *Journal of Biomedical Informatics*, **35**(5-6):352-359 (2002)
29. P. Cortez, M.J. Embrechts, Using sensitivity analysis and visualization techniques to open black box data mining models, *Information Sciences* **225**:1-17 (2013)
30. K.C. Lam, C.Y. Yu, K.Y. Lam, An artificial neural network and entropy model for residential property price forecasting in Hong Kong, *Journal of Property Research* **25**(4):321-342 (2008)

Identifying Barriers of Sustainable Construction: A Nigerian Case Study

Ohiomah Ifije[1*], and *Clinton* Aigbavboa[1]

[1]Department of Construction Management & Quantity Surveying, University of Johannesburg, Johannesburg, 2028, South Africa

Abstract. Sustainable development has become an important part of the lives and aspect of enterprises operations globally. There is a global trend to enhance sustainable practices in all sectors and most especially the construction sectors, this study discusses the factors that best prevent the implementation of sustainable construction in the Nigeria construction industry. The study further explores and determines the reliability of how sustainability should be measured in the Nigeria construction industry. The study used both primary and secondary data to meet the set objective. The primary data were gathered through the use of a questionnaire distributed to construction professionals, contractors and clients. Indicative findings arising from the study revealed that; Building regulations and financial incentives are found to be the main drivers of sustainable construction in Nigeria and Lack of client demand and awareness and a general perception that adopting sustainable construction is expensive. The research concluded by recommending that government help with building policies to help push construction firms towards sustainable construction and also awareness campaigns should be carried out so that clients would demand and be aware of the benefits of sustainable construction

Keywords: sustainability, barriers, construction, Nigeria

1 Introduction

The construction industry is a very important division for sustainable development because of the impact environmentally and socio-economically. The industry influences in four ways the socio-economic development [1].

The construction industry builds facilities such as roads, buildings and production facility amongst others. Due to a high demand in infrastructural development in developing countries, the contribution of the construction industry to emerging nations is very significant in terms that it supports the economic, social development which turns to wealth, social equality and increases living standard [2]. In developing countries, the construction industry

* Corresponding author: ifije93@gmail.com

contributes a high percentage to the Gross Domestic Product than the high-income countries [2, 3]. Examples of this are seen in Brazil whereby the construction industry contributes 14% to her economy, while in the European Union it contributes 11% to its GDP [4].

In developing economies which still battle with a high unemployment rate, the construction industry employs a large number of the unemployed because construction is still labour-intensive due to low skills and knowledge due to lack of technology. The end products of construction are spread throughout the country, and it has teamed up to develop private enterprise and technology transfer to all nationals of the nation [5].

Despite all this positive of the construction industry to the economy, the impact of the construction industry cannot be ignored and it is of significant importance, for instance, the construction industry is responsible worldwide for the usage of 40% of total energy production, 40% of raw materials and 25% of timber; the use of 16% of water, generates 30-40% of solid waste and 35-40% of CO2 emissions [6, 7, 8]. Hence because of the following impact on the environment, this has led to calls by industry experts on how to lessen the effect of the activities of construction on the environment. This call leads to the concept of sustainable construction which was in line with The Brundtland report [9] on sustainable development which defines sustainable development as the meeting of the wants of the present generation short of compromising the ability of the upcoming generations to meet their wants. Sustainable Construction was defined by Agenda 21 for sustainable construction in Developing Countries (SCDC) as a complete process to restore and maintain agreement amongst the built and natural environments and create settlements that sustain human self-worth and boost economic equity [10]. This description suggests that the early methods, were associated with technical issues, thus do not guarantee a sustainable development while economic and social aspects of sustainability were not well thought-out [11, 12]. Technical problems of sustainability such as efficient use of resources such as energy and water and the reduction of the environmental effects of materials. Building components and construction technologies are vital parts of sustainable construction. In developing countries, the degree of technical issues of sustainability is very low and most at times underdeveloped. Examples of low and underdeveloped technical issues of sustainability are the aspect of building energy code which does not exist. Therefore, the success of Sustainable Construction (SC) in developing countries is thought-provoking not only because their economic and social conditions may be grim but also because the technical problems are unresolved. The success of SC may necessitate approaches different among developing countries according to the development of their individual construction industries and also their specific socio-economic condition. For this reason, the overall strategy of Agenda 21 came up with an inclusive strategy for addressing the execution of sustainable construction [10]. Still, there is a conflict at this juncture. On one hand, construction businesses need to be feasible in all areas and, on the other hand, research has shown that the notion that sustainable construction project such as buildings is more expensive than the conventional buildings [13, 14]. Hence because of this notion from literature, this study is seeking to determine the barriers that make it difficult for Nigerian construction firms to implement sustainable construction.

2 Literature review

Literature has revealed that the construction industry contributes to the economy if sustainability is pursued in the areas of sustainability of countries as well as Nigeria. As a result, the necessity to implement sustainable construction is imperative as "what we build today will provide the built environment of the future and will influence the ability of future generations to meet their need".

Several countries policies on sustainable development are developed along with global initiatives. Initiatives such as the 1992 Earth Summit (UN Conference on Environmental and

Development) deliberated on ways of accomplishing sustainable development, setting Agenda 21 as the action plan. Several developed countries have gone on to develop their various national sustainable development strategies. In order for developing to be able to develop their own sustainable development and in turn, sustainable construction strategies [15] suggested a way for attaining sustainable construction, which encompasses all stakeholders such as; government, developers, clients, buyers/end users, contractors, consultants. This route begins with awareness, interest and knowledge of SC. This situation may reduce the drive of construction firms to promote SC practices. In Nigeria, it has been found that no empirical data about what drives' construction businesses in the direction of sustainable construction.

Sustainable construction cannot be discussed without discussing the impact of sustainability on construction.

2.1 Impact of sustainability

2.1.1 Environmental impact

Creation of waste; developed nations like the UK have come to estimate that 40% of all UK waste is generated by the construction industry [16]. Due to this waste, the UK government estimate that landfill capacity would stay exceeded by 2017 [17]. In order to combat this issue of landfill, most developed countries have introduced the Landfill Tax and Aggregate Levy which has aided to minimise waste due to the increased costs related to discarding [18]. But this is not the case with developing countries so, at present, construction waste is almost left unattended to.

Energy use; in the UK it has been reported that the built environment consumes roughly 50% of the aggregate energy generated; 45% to heat, light and aerate the structures and 5% to build them. The United Kingdom government is looking to reduce energy by 60% come 2050 [17]. Even with this policy, the Royal Institute of Charted Surveyors (RICS) is of the belief that the government is not doing enough.

Water use; there has been increased consumption of water in the last 30yrs, this is shown for instance in the UK it has increased to 70%, which will culminate to 4.1 million household's consumption of water by 2016. This is as a result of an increase in populations and living standards which will have an effect on the supply of water. The worldwide construction industry is implementing techniques to conserve water in new build projects. Taking the idea of water efficiency technology such a reduced flow taps, low water flush toilets. This is done with the idea that an estimated 20% improvement is achieved in proficiency [17].

2.1.2 Economic impact

The construction sector contributes meaningfully to the GDP of any nation, the construction industry in the UK contributes about 8% GDP and over 2 million persons in the UK are hired [5], nearly 20% of most job created is connected to the sector [16, 19] discovered that the key driver to sustainable construction is the client. The debate concerning the impacts on the environment has been clearly demonstrated that the penalties of poorly managed construction instruments can have serious effects on sustainability. In order for this effect to be reduced, the increasing of client awareness must be taken seriously as it is vital in a bid to deviate from mainly financial making decision.

Value management concept has been found to deliver a good economic return, accountability with this positive impact of VM, practitioners of VM have prospects to lessen environmental and social change [19]. Construction businesses in order to enhance their standing amongst stakeholders and seek to attract investment [20].

2.1.3 Social impact

CIRIA [21] noted that the commercial and residential structures designs, as well as the performance, can affect directly the quality of life, promotion of healthy living and coming together of the community. Everybody connected with a structure can profit from added sustainable practices. Walker [22] acknowledged "Stakeholders can offer tangible value, provide valued response information on how they are affected and can co-operate in delivery of the output". Keeping and shires stated that sustainable buildings benefit from lower.

2.1.4 Design impact

The concept of optimum design was better described in the [17] states that optimum design requires optimized performance on the construction site. Studies have shown that design plays a major role in achieving sustainability whereby designers' reputations can be boosted by adding sustainable designs to their building designs. Despite the fact, they have to work off the instruction of the client. The designers have a chance to create an impact in the mind of the client, for instance, capturing the reduced running costs, enhanced corporate image and the occupant's wellbeing better off [23]. Architects play a key role as argued by [24]. Published in 1999 by the Architects Registration Board code of conduct, it was detailed that the responsibility of the architect is to the client, also in consideration to save and improve the quality of the environment as well as the natural resources.

In practice, constructors are not usually tangled in the design and decisions on how sustainable a construction project possibly will be, but good practices here can cut costs and create a green image [25]. This was further backed up by [26] who specified that the choice of construction materials has noticeable and substantial energy and emission of gas implications.

3 Methodology

This study adopted a survey method for the gathering of data for this research. The population includes professionals from the built environment within the built environment in the Nigerian construction industry; specifically, in the South-West region.

The study adopted a close-ended questionnaire founded on existing knowledge from literature. The questionnaire was designed to explore the barriers to the implementation of sustainable construction practices. The circulation of questionnaires to respondents was through mainly the google forms sent via email.

The background of the respondents was surveyed in the first section of the questionnaire, while the second portion explored the barriers to sustainable construction implementation amongst the identified construction professionals. A 5-point Likert scale was used to examine based on the level of agreement. The rating was as follows: 1=Strongly disagree; 2=Disagree; 3=Neutral; 4=Agree; 5=Strongly agree. Mean item score (MIS) and standard deviation (SD) were afterwards calculated for each of the variables and the values were used in ranking and determining their position

4 Findings

The table below shows the barriers which impede the implementation of Sustainable Construction in Nigeria.

Table 1. Barriers of Sustainable Construction

Barriers of Sustainable Construction	Standard Deviation	MIS	Ranking
Lack of customer awareness	6.00	4.00	1
Additional building Costs	6.50	4.00	1
No understanding of the benefits of sustainable construction	6.70	3.90	2
Misconception of Construction cost overrun	5.30	3.80	3
Lack of coordination cost overrun	5.20	3.70	4
Lack of public awareness	5.60	3.70	4
Deployment of resources to back technological changes	5.80	3.70	4
Initializing sustainability due to lack of building regulations	3.70	3.70	4

The table showed the variables and how they are the respondents perceived the barriers, the study hereby revealed that Lack of customer awareness (SD = 6.00, MIS = 4.00, R = 1), in addition, building costs (SD = 6.50, MIS = 4.00, R = 1) was ranked the highest as the highest barriers perceived by the professionals sampled, closely followed by No understanding on the benefits of sustainable construction (SD = 6.70, MIS = 3.90, R=2) amongst others were the construction professional's view on the barriers facing the construction industry in Nigeria hindering the implementation of sustainable construction.

These view by professionals' in the Nigerian industry is not only peculiar, but this barrier is also shared by several studies carried out across different countries that found that affordability, lack of customer awareness and demand was the three highest-ranking barriers of sustainable construction in the United Kingdom. It was further corroborated by Zhou and Lowe [27] who pointed out that sustainable construction is expensive, causing a major challenge in the embracing of sustainable construction practices in emerging nations like Nigeria. Furthermore, the finding also corresponds with the study carried out by the Agenda 21 for Sustainable Construction in Developing Countries [10], where it was revealed that the problems of sustainable construction range from deployment of resources to back technological changes.

5 Conclusions and recommendations

This research reports the barriers hampering the implementation of sustainable construction practices in the Nigerian construction industry. The information used in this investigation were obtained from both primary and secondary sources. The secondary data which is literature show that the construction sector is an important contributor to the pollution worldwide which have an effect on the ecosystem in numerous ways. On the other hand, the focal test for the sector is to play an important part in the reduction of the impacts of construction happenings on the environment. Collected works also exposed that the construction industry will play an important role in achieving the society's sustainable goals but the way to achieve sustainability is a process which is proving difficult.

Results from the empirical survey showed there is a discrepancy of views on achievement practices of sustainable construction implementation in the sector such as Lack of customer awareness being the highest rank, followed by the additional building cost ranked as next to the implementation of sustainable construction. Similarly, the professionals additionally saw sustainable construction activities as an additional cost to the ever-increasing ways of construction practices in terms of purchasing new machinery and training of staff which is true as this thought could lead to not implementing SC.

It is of importance that construction professionals in the Nigerian construction industry must seek to overcome the barriers that hinder the implementation of sustainable construction. As the long-term benefits from the implementation outweigh the present practices. it is of importance that awareness of sustainable construction must be carried out amongst the professionals, clients as this will help in the drive for the implementation of SC. Lastly; it is the responsibility of construction professionals involved with sustainable construction processes to enlighten the clients on the benefits of SC.

This study has shown that there has to be an increase in awareness for the embracing of sustainable construction practices, hence it is recommended that government and non-government agencies must help in the increase of the awareness of sustainable construction practices. Henceforth, it is also suggested that more enforced approaches and actions must be pursued aggressively to hasten up the method in forming a sustainable-driven construction industry, which is principal to building a sustainable future.

References

1. G. Ofori, *Construction in developing countries*, Construction Management and Economics, 25, 1–6 (2007)
2. V. Gomes, M.G.D. Silva, *Exploring sustainable construction: implications from Latin America*, Building Research & Information, 33, 428–440 (2005)
3. V.M. John, V. Agopyan, C. Sjostrom, *An agenda 21 for Latin American and Caribbean construbusiness. A perspective from Brazil*. [online], Available: http://www.cbcs.org.br/userfiles/bancoDeConhecimento/Agenda%2021%20for%20Latin%20American%20Construbusiness.pdf (2001)
4. V.M. John, *Recycling of wastes in construction: a contribution to the methodology for research and development*, Escola Politécnica, USp (2000)
5. D.A. Turin, *The construction industry: its economic significance and its role in development. Building economic research unit*, University College of London (1973)
6. H. Son, C. Kim, W.K. Chong, J.-S. Chou, *Implementing sustainable development in the construction industry: constructors' perspective in the US and Korea*, Sustainable Development 19(5), 337–347 (2011)
7. E. Van Bueren, J. De Jong, *Establishing sustainability: policy successes and failures*, Building Research& Information, 35, 543–556 (2007)
8. U. Berardi, *Clarifying the new interpretations of the concept of sustainable buildings,* Sustainable Cities and Society, 8, 72–78 (2013)
9. *Our common future*, WCED, World Commission on Environment and Development, UK, Oxford University Press (1987)
10. C. Du Plessis, *Agenda 21 for sustainable construction in developing countries*, CSIR report BoU/e0204, CSIr, UNep-IetC, and Pretoria (2002)

11. C. Du Plessis, *A strategic framework for sustainable construction in developing countries*, Construction Management and Economics, 25, 67–76 (2007)
12. F. Shafii, Z.A. Ali, M.Z. Othman, *Achieving sustainable construction in the developing countries of Southeast Asia*, in 6th Asia-Pacific Structural Engineering and Construction Conference, Kuala-Lumpur, Malaysia (2006)
13. J. Yudelson, *Green building through integrated design*, McGraw-Hill Companies, Inc, New York
14. I.B. Robichaud, V.S. Anantatmula, *Greening project management practices for sustainable construction*, Journal of Management in Engineering, 27, 48–57 (2011)
15. N. Zainul-Abidin, *Investigating the awareness and application of sustainable construction concept by Malaysian developers*, Habitat International 34, 421–426 (2010)
16. *Sustainable Construction (Worldwide),* Royal Institute for Chartered Surveyors, Coventry, available at: http://www.rics.org RICS (2005)
17. *Better Buildings Summit Issues Paper*, Department of Trade and Industry, HMSO, London, available at: www.dti.gov.uk/construction/sustain/betbuild.pdf, Better Buildings Summit (2003)
18. *The Organisation of Economic Co-operation and Development Environmental Performance Review – UK's Progress Report,* Department for Environment, Food and Rural Affairs, Organisation of Economic Cooperation and Development, Paris, available at: www.defra.gov.uk/environment/internat/oecd/pdf/epr-ukreport OECD (2006)
19. N.S. Abidin, C.L. Pasquire, *Delivering sustainability through value management: concept and performance overview*, Engineering, Construction and Architectural Management, 12, 168-80 (2005)
20. *Making the most of Our Built Environment*, Sustainability Construction Task Group, 2004, available at: www.dti.gov.uk/construction/sustain/making_the_most.pdf (accessed 22 March 2006)
21. *Compliance Sustainability*, Construction Industry Research and Information, Council, London, available at: www.ciria.org/complianceplus/sustainability.htm CIRIA, (2006)
22. D.H.T. Walker, *Client/customer or stakeholder focus? ISO 14000 EMS as a construction industry case study*, The TQM Magazine, 12, 18-25 (2000)
23. A. Yates, *Sustainable buildings: benefits for constructors,* Building Research Establishment (2003a)
24. D.P. Wyatt, A. Sobotka, M. Rogalska, *Towards a sustainable practice*, Facilities, 18, 76-82 (2000)
25. Yates, BRE IP13/03 Part 2 Sustainable Buildings: Benefits for Designers, BRE Centre for Sustainable Construction, Watford (2003b)
26. G. Treloar, R. Fay, B. Ilozor, P.E.D Love, *Building materials selection; greenhouse strategies for built facilities*, Facilities, 19, 139-49 (2001)
27. L. Zhou, D.J. Lowe, *Economic challenges of sustainable construction*, in Proceedings of RICS COBRA Foundation Construction and Building Research Conference, 1-2 (2003)

The Intelligent use of RFID and BIM in Prefabricated, Prefinished, Volumetric Construction Work Flow

Ernest L S Abbott[1*], and *David K H* Chua[1]

[1]Department. of Civil & Environmental Engineering. National University of Singapore, Singapore

Abstract. RFID is used in many areas of commerce, and in some areas of the construction industry. Prefabricated, prefinished volumetric construction (PPVC) is one area of the construction industry that can benefit from the use of RFID. The full benefits cannot be realised by the use of RFID alone. RFID needs to be coupled with Building Information Modelling (BIM). This paper outlines a framework of marrying the two technologies in constructing PPVC from the drawing stage to the delivery on site and then to the final installation of the unit. The benefits of this union are in material stock control, part location tracking, production scheduling and re-scheduling, among other things.

Keywords: BIM, RFID, volumetric construction, intelligent logistics, PPVC.

1 Introduction

RFID's origins can be traced to the work on RADAR during the second world war [1, 2]. In 1948 Harry Stockman seminal paper, "Communications by means of reflective power" [3], suggested what is today RFID, although he fully recognized the technical problems involved, as it was not until the 1970s that Stockman's ideas started to come to fruition [4].

Since the 1970s, RFID usage has grown to fill almost every corner and aspect of life, including agriculture and livestock, defence and security, healthcare and welfare, transportation and identification system [4]. It was as long ago as 1995 that Jaselskis et al. [5] discussed the use of RFID tags in the construction industry. Since then the technology of not only the tags but also the RFID readers have seen dramatic improvements, not just in size and ability but also in a reduction in cost. The various suggestions of Jaselskis et al. were clearly limited by the then cost of using RFID. Their proposal of tagging large objects, such as gas cylinders and Concrete Trucks for tracking truck movements on and off-site illustrates this.

RFID tags have a clear advantage over other identification systems such as Bar Codes or QR codes, as they rely upon electromagnetic fields and not a line of sight. RFID tags may be

* Coresponding author: ceeaels@nus.edu.sg

active, semi-active, passive or semi-passive. Each tag type operates at a different frequency. Active RFID tags have a battery as a power source. Passive tags do not have a power source. For ease of understanding, semi-active tags can be considered as active tags without a battery, and semi-passive tags as passive tags with a battery [6]. This is summarised in Table 1.

The passive RFID is the most common tag. The cost, depending on purchase volume, is between US$0.07 and US$0.15[†]. The passive RFID is the one used in the foregoing discussion.

Building Information Modelling or BIM has been defined in several ways. John Eynon defines BIM as "Building Information Modelling is the digital representation of physical and functional characteristics of a facility creating a shared knowledge resource for information about it and forming a reliable basis for decisions during its life cycle, from earliest conception to demolition" [7]. This is the working definition used in this paper.

Several AEC software packages support BIM. Revit, Tekla, Bentley and Archicad are just four examples of widely used packages. Tekla Structures is the AEC software package used in this paper for the design of prefabricated, prefinished, volumetric construction (PPVC).

PPVC is usually used for multilevel constructions such as medium to high-rise residential buildings. The modules are cast and assembled at a production location. All finishes, such as plumbing, sanitary ware, electrical and HAVC, are installed prior to the units being delivered and installed at a construction site. The benefits are really at the construction site level where there is a reduction in manpower compared with in-situ construction and environmentally, there is a reduction in construction noise and dust.

Błąd! Nie można odnaleźć źródła odwołania. illustrates a floor slab and three walls each cast separately. Fig. **1** illustrates the assembly of a module comprising of a floor slab and three walls. Following the necessary fitting out, the completed module is transported to site where it is installed at its predefined location.

BIM models are data-rich. RFID is used to identify each component of a module. This paper sets out a framework for marrying RFID and BIM, giving a synergy that greatly benefits its users.

Table 1. Summary of RFID Tag Types

	No Batteries	**Batteries**
Emitted Energy	Semi-Active. Tags become temporally active when they receive "power" from an RFID reader.	Active. Tags transmit a signal to be read by an RFID reader. The tag data can be read at distances of 30 meters or greater.
Reflective Energy	Passive. Tags receive "power" from an RFID reader. The data is transmitted by reflecting this power from the reader. (this is known as backscatter modulation.) Data can be read up to about 6 meters.	Semi-Passive. This is also known as battery-assisted passive (BAP). The data is read from the tag in the same way as the passive tag. The battery is used for its operating power. Data can be read at distances of more than 30 meters.

2 The Framework

The marrying of RFID technology with BIM in the area of PPVC allows a systematic approach to monitoring, managing and optimizing all aspects of the factory environment, delivery to site and installation of modules.

Fig. **2** shows an outline of the proposed framework. The Tekla BIM model, with details of PPVC units, is imported to a central database. The importation of the site installation schedule and the PPVC unit data are used to generate an optimised factory production schedule in order to effect a JIT delivery at the construction site. All material quantities, from the BIM data, allows for the minimization of stock holding costs through prudent stock control. Drawing changes, leading to part modification or scrapping, are readily tracked using the parts RFID.

Fig. 1. PPVC Module before Assembly

Fig. 1. PPVC Module after Assembly

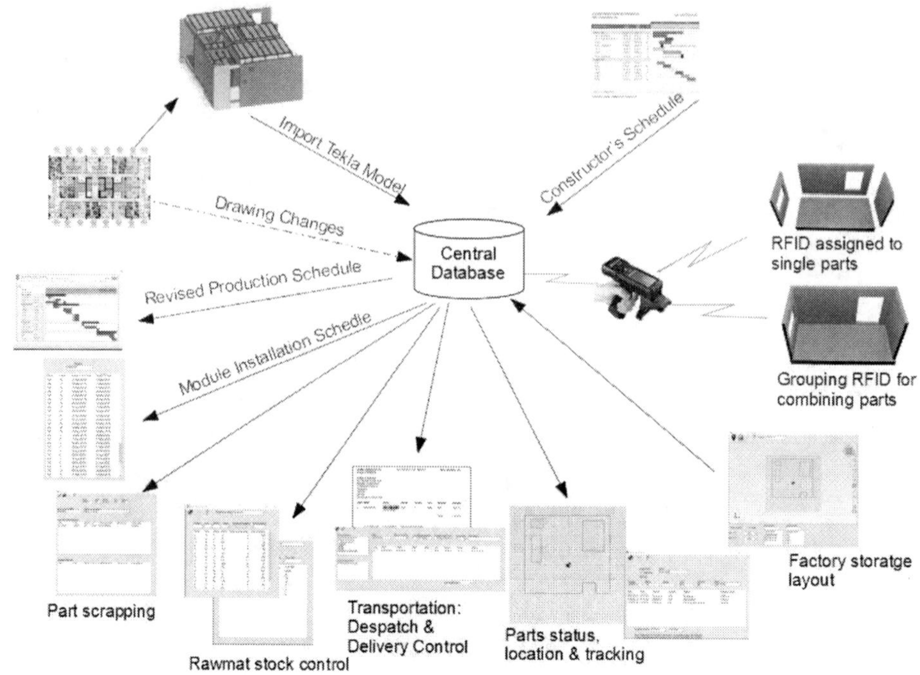

Fig. 2. Outline of Proposed Framework

3 Deriving the PPVC Module Production Schedule

The PPVC module production schedule is calculated from the broad installation schedule, which indicates an installation period for the block. The storey installation cycle is calculated as in equation (1)

$$Storey\ Installation\ Cycle = \frac{Number\ of\ Working\ Days\ in\ Installation\ Period}{Number\ of\ Storeys\ in\ Block} \quad (1)$$

The PPVC factory needs to supply the building site with modules, at the required intervals to meet the storey installation cycle.

From BIM, the number of components, walls, slabs, etc, are extracted, and a production schedule is generated. For an optimal production schedule to be generated, additional information on the factory layout pertaining to the area available for casting moulds, storing moulds, for assembling PPVC components into modules is required. Space is one metric, the other is time, i.e. the time for the various operations, e.g. fitting out the mould, pouring concrete, time to demoulding, time for curing, time for assembling into modules, time to fit out the modules ready for final installation and transportation time. Any subcontractor's information will also need to be included if one is used.

4 Extracting BIM Data

The digital model created by the designer, using propriety software, is not in a suitable format for some subsequent process. Although the model contains ample information, propriety software is not designed as a general database. To overcome this, relevant model data is extracted from the BIM and stored in a suitable form on a central database.

This paper is concerned with residential properties. The extracted database identifies modules, storey location of the module, the residential block identity, and the propriety software's unique identity of the part.

5 Module Production and RFID Tracking

Fig. 3 illustrates the schematic for RFID allocation and tracking at all stages of the production of a PPVC module. The process begins by applying an RFID tag at the point the part is moulded. (The tag is readable, provided it is more than 3mm from rebar, or any other metallic object. Any metallic object too near an RFID tag will interfere with the tag's operation.)

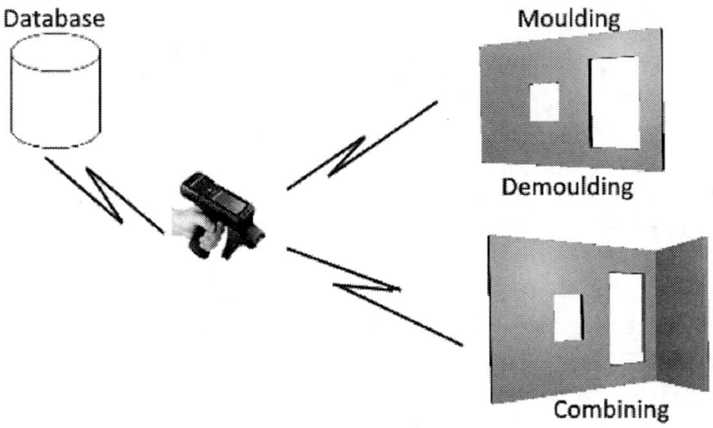

Fig. 3. RFID Tracking at All Stages of Production

Once an RFID tag is added to a part, and the computer system is notified, the part becomes trackable. The RFID reader used to read the tags, is connected, either directly or wirelessly, to a computer system, which maintains pertinent information on the status of module parts.

RFID tags are registered, in the computer system, to a specific location. This is important, particularly when more than one PPVC production site is used.

The registration of the tag is prior to using the tag on a module part. When the RFID tag is attached to a part, the RFID reader reads the tag, which links the part on the computer system to the RFID tag as well as its BIM identity. Following any change in the status of a part, the part's RFID is scanned and the status, eg moulding, demoulding, location in the factory, destination when being transported, is updated.

PPVC modules, or combined parts, but not whole modules, can be transported for a number of reasons. For example, the parts were produced at different production sites. The fitting out of the assembled module is done at a different location to the production location.

Each component part of a PPVC module has its own unique RFID tag. Parts are not necessarily assembled into a final module in one operation. Walls may be joined together before being joined to a floor slab, for example. When parts are joined, their association is recorded in the computer system. RFIDs are linked in the computer system in such a way that identifying just a single part, identifies all linked associated parts. In this way, only one part needs to be scanned for every module or group of parts to enable status updating or location identification for example.

The RFID tag is automatically linked to the BIM component. When assembling parts to compose a module, an authentication check is performed, ensuring the correct matching of mould parts to a module

6 Delivery and Site Installation

Completed and fitted out PPVC modules are transported to the construction site. This is a status change in the module and all parts that comprise the module. Using the RFID of the module (i.e. any part on the module), a despatch manifest is computer generated. Upon arrival at the delivery point, the module's RFID is read and they verified against the original delivery information.

Completed PPVC modules are delivered to the construction site. At the construction site, any part's RFID is read to identify the module and its intended installation location in the development. The installation location is obtained from the BIM model data of the development.

7 Material Stock Control

The BIM model of a residential development holds the materials used in the various parts, such as the rebar sizes and lengths and the type of concrete used. The physical measurements of panels, length, width, height and volume are also found in the BIM model. Once the BIM model has been completed, the total quantities of material required for the construction can be calculated. This value can be used as a guide to the cost of production, for example. This information combined with the PPVC production schedule gives a guide as to the periodic stock requirement.

Each PPVC production location holds stock of some material, such as sand, cement, agate and fly ash. Rebars cages and steel frames are often delivered to order. As module parts are moulded, the RFID is the key to identifying the point of moulding, the stock required to construct the prefabricated part can be depleted from the total stock held. The RFID links to a given part, whose construction quantities are calculated from the BIM data.

There are several methods of stock control. One method is using the free stock approach. This, coupled with delivery lead times of stock and minimum order quantities, facilitates a more systematic method of stock control, based on what is built. It also enables the factory to minimize their stock holding cost.

8 Scheduling and Rescheduling

Schedule disruption has many causes. Changes in design being one of them. If there is a change in a module design after the production of the module has started, this has an impact on the overall production schedule. The extent of which depends on the extent of the design change. Using the BIM model, the design change can be identified, by means of versioning. All parts that have been moulded, and their current status, are identifiable via their RFID. The impact of changes on the schedule depends on whether the module part can be modified or has to be scrapped. Modifying already moulded parts will often have a minor impact on the schedule and stock. The scrapping of whole modules can cause delays in the schedule as well as having an impact on the raw material stock.

The cost of scrapping is the material cost of the components plus the labour cost. The raw material cost is the product of the raw material content, which is from BIM, and the unit cost of the raw material, which is held on a database. The labour cost calculation depends on the method adopted by the company.

9 Case Study

The case study will not cover all the framework. It will cover the core of the framework; the extraction of BIM model data, the assignment of RFID to parts, stock control, despatch and delivery of parts/modules.

9.1 Extracting the BIM Model

Fig. 4 shows a residential unit modelled in Tekla. The residential unit consists of three modules. The modules comprise of concrete walls, reinforcement bars, pipes, steel frames and other smaller parts. Fig. 5 views the same residential unit after it has been imported into the computer system.

Fig. 4. Unit of Three Modules Viewed in Tekla

Fig. 5. Unit as Imported to Computer System

9.2 Registering RFID Tags

The registering of the RFID tags is at any point prior to their use. Fig. 6 illustrates 10 RFID tags registered to production site A. These tags will have their first use at production site A. The location of the tag changes when the part the tag is assigned to changes its location.

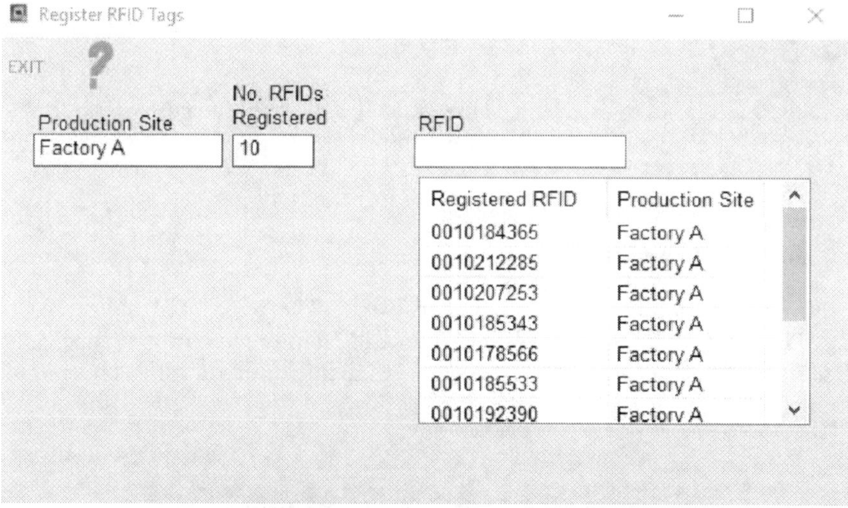

Fig. 6. RFID Tags Registered to a Production Site

9.3 Assigning RFID Tags to Parts

At part moulding time, an RFID tag is attached or embedded in the concrete. The tag is scanned. Fig. **7** shows the assignment of an RFID tag to a component wall. The cast wall's constituent parts are also shown.

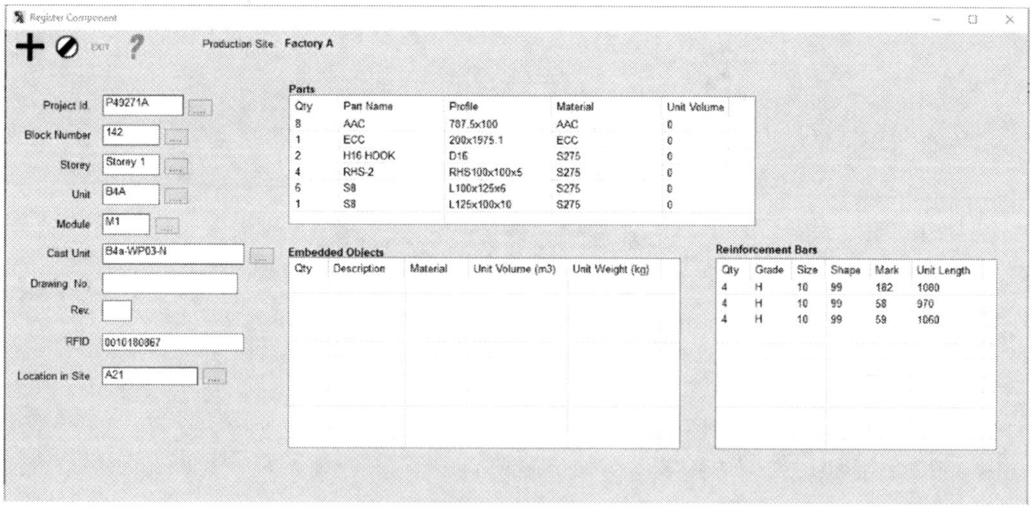

Fig. 7. RFID Assigned to a Part

9.4 Part Status

The RFID tag is assigned at moulding time. At demoulding time, the RFID tag is read and the status is changed to demoulded. The part location is also updated. Fig. **8** is the general part status change, which is used anytime there is a change in a part status. The RFID tag is scanned and the current status is displayed

When an RFID tag is assigned to a moulded part, the raw materials used in the part are automatically adjusted. Fig. **9** illustrates the current rebar stock and Fig. **10** illustrates the current raw material stock. The composition of the concrete is stored on a database. This is used, with BIM data, to calculate the quantities by which to deplete the stock.

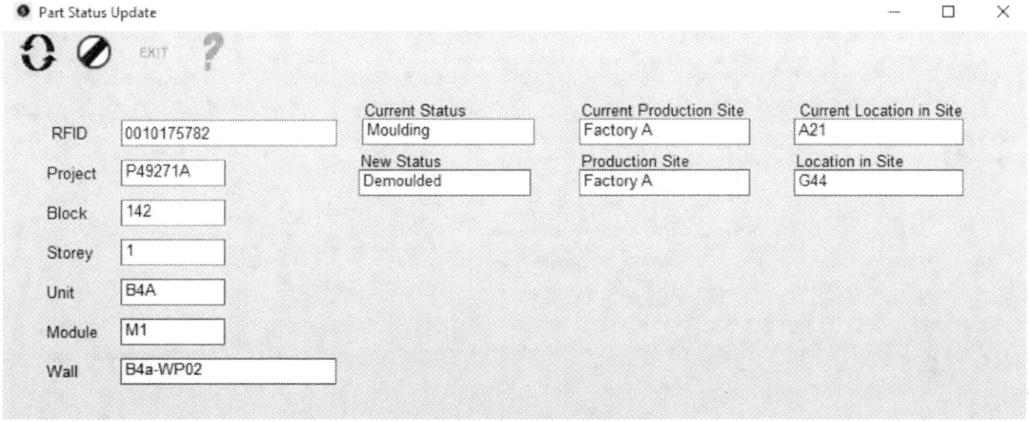

Fig. 8. Part Status Change

Stock Enquires

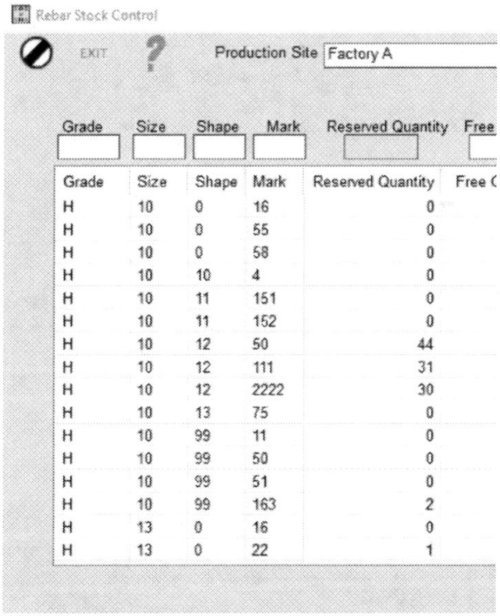

Grade	Size	Shape	Mark	Reserved Quantity	Free (
H	10	0	16	0	
H	10	0	55	0	
H	10	0	58	0	
H	10	10	4	0	
H	10	11	151	0	
H	10	11	152	0	
H	10	12	50	44	
H	10	12	111	31	
H	10	12	2222	30	
H	10	13	75	0	
H	10	99	11	0	
H	10	99	50	0	
H	10	99	51	0	
H	10	99	163	2	
H	13	0	16	0	
H	13	0	22	1	

Fig. 9. Rebar Stock Status Enquiry

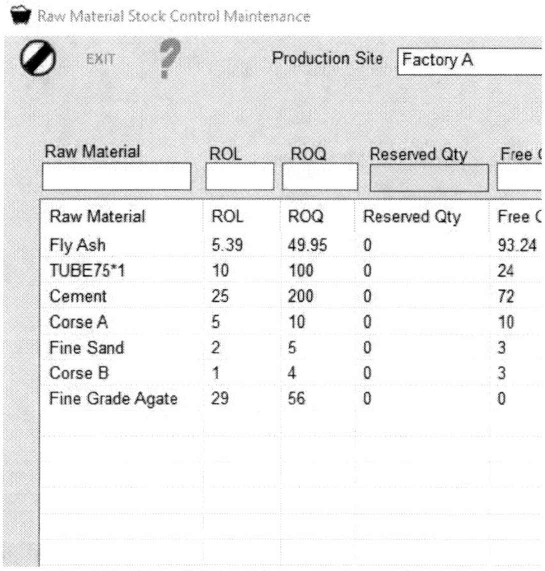

Raw Material	ROL	ROQ	Reserved Qty	Free (
Fly Ash	5.39	49.95	0	93.24
TUBE75*1	10	100	0	24
Cement	25	200	0	72
Corse A	5	10	0	10
Fine Sand	2	5	0	3
Corse B	1	4	0	3
Fine Grade Agate	29	56	0	0

Fig. 10. Raw Material Stock Status Enquiry

9.5 Parts Transportation

RFID is used to identify the parts loaded onto a lorry for transportation from one location to another. The lorry loading details are quickly produced directly from scanning the part or parts. For module parts that are joined to other module parts, the scanning of just a single RFID is sufficient to identify all joined parts. Fig. **11** illustrates the identification of parts to compose a lorry load. Once the despatch information is printed, as illustrated in Fig. **12,** the status of the parts is automatically updated to show the part is on a particular lorry. Figure 13 illustrates the arrival of a lorry load at a site. The parts' RFID is read directly, or the bar code on the despatch note is read. The part status is updated.

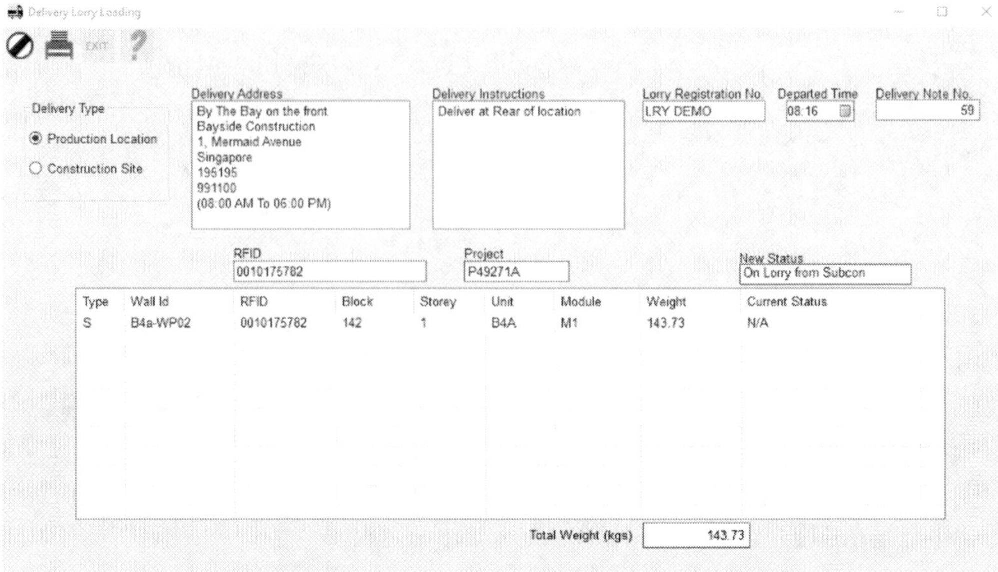

Fig. 11. Lorry Loading for Part Transportation

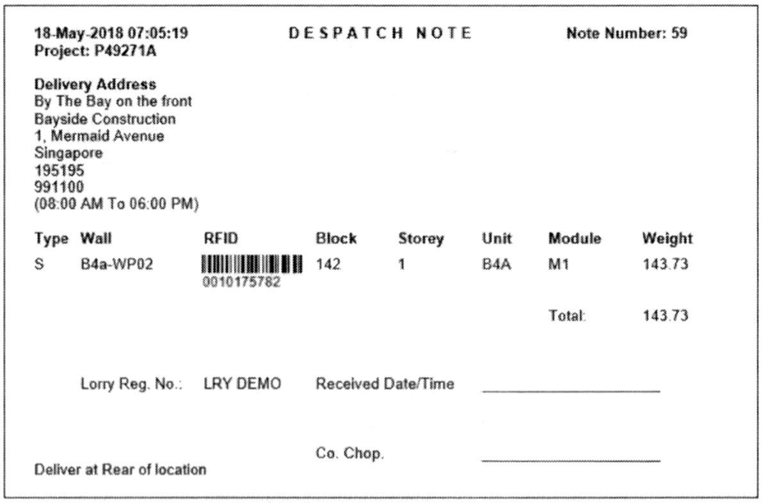

18-May-2018 07:05:19 **DESPATCH NOTE** **Note Number: 59**
Project: P49271A

Delivery Address
By The Bay on the front
Bayside Construction
1, Mermaid Avenue
Singapore
195195
991100
(08:00 AM To 06:00 PM)

Type	Wall	RFID	Block	Storey	Unit	Module	Weight
S	B4a-WP02	0010175782	142	1	B4A	M1	143.73
						Total:	143.73

Lorry Reg. No.: LRY DEMO Received Date/Time ____________________

Co. Chop. ____________________

Deliver at Rear of location

Fig. 12. Sample Despatch Note

Figure 13. Delivery to Site

10 Conclusion & Future Work

The framework outlined in this paper has shown the positive benefits of marrying together two technologies, RFID and BIM, which gives a firm foundation for the optimization of all aspect of the construction, delivery and installation of PPVC units as well as ensuring the correct part is assembled with its intended module. With component identification, at the point of production, leading to full tracking of all processes and statuses of the component, analysis of the efficiency of the production process can be readily analysed with remedial steps taken to improve workflow efficiency.

The framework outlined here has not covered all areas, due to space and time constraint. The areas omitted are the algorithms for the efficient production of the PPVC modules. There are several scenarios to consider in this respect; (i) sufficient factory capacity for continuous production by building storey, (ii) sufficient factory capacity but insufficient manpower/time for continuous production, (iii) insufficient factory space for continuous production by building storey, (iv) optimization of moulds, rather than using mould sets, i.e. all moulds for a module.

References

1. M. Roberti, The History of RFID Technology The History of RFID Technology, *Energy*, 1–3 (2005), http://www.rfidjournal.com/article/view/1338/1
2. J. Landt, The History of RFID, *IEEE Potentials* **24**(4):8–11 (2005)
3. H. Stockman, Communication by Means of Reflected Power, In *Proceedings of the IRE* **36**(10):1196-1204 (1948), doi:10.1109/JRPROC.1948.226245.
4. K. Jung, S. Lee, A Systematic Review of RFID Applications and Diffusion: Key Areas and Public Policy Issues, *Journal of Open Innovation: Technology, Market, and Complexity* **1**(1):9 (2015)
5. E. Jaselskis, M.R. Anderson, C.T. Jahren, Y. Rodriguez, S. Njos, Radio- Frequency Identification Applications in Construction Industry, *Journal of Construction Engineering and Management* **121**(2):189– 196 (1995)
6. R. Bridelall, A. Hande, Performance Metrics and Operational Parameters of RFID Systems Itle, In *RFID Systems: Research Trends and Challenges*, edited by Miodrag Bolic, David Simplot-Ryl, and Ivan Stojmenovic, 23–56, John Wiley & Sons Ltd (2010)
7. J. Eynon, *Construction Manager's BIM Handbook*, John Wiley & Sons Ltd (2016)

Acknowledgements

The authors acknowledge the financial support by the National Research Foundation (NRF) and SembCorp-NUS Corp Lab under project grant R-261-513-009-281.

Causes and Impact of Human Error in Maintenance of Mechanical Systems

Mfundo Nkosi[1*], *Kapil* Gupta[1], *and Madindwa* Mashinini[1]

[1]Department of Mechanical and Industrial Engineering Technology, University of Johannesburg, South Africa

Abstract. The concept of minimizing human error in maintenance is progressively gaining attention in various industries. The incorporation of human factors when solving engineering problems, particularly in maintenance, can no longer be ignored where high standards of performance are expected. The journey of improving maintenance performance through the reduction of human error begins with the understanding of causes and impact of human error in maintenance. This paper evaluates previous scholarly writings on human errors, to specifically establish the causes and impact of human error in maintenance. This study relies predominantly on the existing literature on human error in maintenance derived from published and unpublished research. The primary findings emerging from the research exhibit a number of key factors that cause a human error in maintenance such as poor management and supervision, organizational culture, incompetence, poorly written procedures, poor communication, time pressure, plant and environmental conditions, poor work design and many more. The literature review also revealed that human errors have a negative impact on safety, reliability, productivity and efficiency of the equipment. It was further discovered that equipment failures leading to accidents, incidents, loss of life and economic losses are the major effects of human error. Human error in mechanical systems' maintenance is a serious problem which needs adequate attention in order to develop corrective and preventive measures. This review paper serves as a basis for maintenance practitioners and interested parties to develop corrective and preventive measures for minimizing human error in the maintenance of mechanical systems.

Keywords: failure, human error, human factor, maintenance, mechanical systems

1 Introduction

Most mechanical systems require regular maintenance for best performance. However, the human error committed during the maintenance phase lead to the system's substandard

* Coresponding author: mnkosi@uj.ac.za

performance. It is during the maintenance phase where a considerable portion of human errors are committed [1]. The manifestation of human error during the maintenance phase can impact the safety and performance of equipment in a number of ways [2]. Therefore, initiatives aimed at the identification and analysis of human error in maintenance are very important, since they can lead to the development of proper strategies for the reduction of human error. The occurrence of human error is regularly considered as a threat with the probability to lead to a significant rate of accidents [3]. In the maintenance of mechanical systems, human errors stem from a number of reasons which have led some industries to develop various initiatives for addressing the issue of human error. The investigation of measures and initiatives of minimizing human error in maintenance begin with the identification and understanding of the factors responsible for human errors. Consequently, this paper examines existing scholarly writings on the causes and impact of human errors in the maintenance of mechanical systems. The error causal factors presented in Figure 1 are among many that were discovered during the literature review process. These human factors are seen as the key causal factors responsible for human error in the maintenance of mechanical systems.

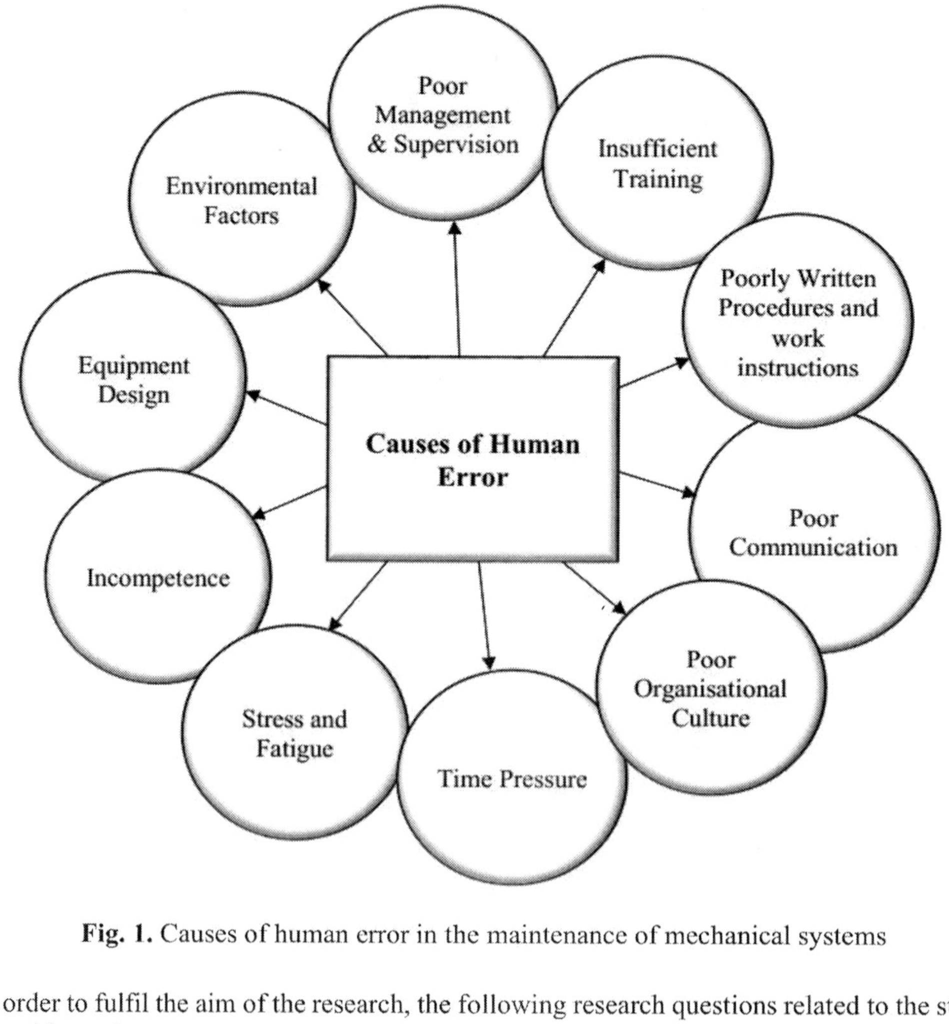

Fig. 1. Causes of human error in the maintenance of mechanical systems

In order to fulfil the aim of the research, the following research questions related to the study are addressed:

1. What are the factors responsible for the occurrence of human errors in the maintenance of mechanical systems?

2. What is the impact of human errors in the maintenance of mechanical systems and how intense is their effect?

This paper identifies the causes and impact of human error in maintenance by reviewing various scholarly writings. It begins with the introduction, follows with the literature search methodology, literature review, key literature review findings and ends with a conclusion that incorporates recommendations and proposed future work.

2 The Literature Search Methodology

The literature review research method was selected for this study. The literature review study is viewed as a "critical analysis of a segment of a published body of knowledge through summary, classification, and comparison of prior research studies, reviews of literature, and theoretical articles" [29]. Selected scholarly writings were reviewed in order to identify, evaluate and short-list the factors responsible for human error and the impact of human error in the maintenance of mechanical systems. The main was to understand the existing body of knowledge and to create a research agenda.

The study is based mainly on the analysis of the existing published and unpublished theoretical scholarly writings. The theme of this paper is predominantly a literature review concerned with human errors in maintenance of various mechanical systems. As a concept of human error in the maintenance of mechanical systems started gaining attention, a number of initiatives have been established with the aim of minimizing human errors. The establishment and improvement of initiatives aimed at reducing human error begin with the apprehension of the causes and impact of human error in the maintenance of mechanical systems. Hence, it is very crucial to analyze the causes and impact of human error. The paper follows a rigorous approach to merge, evaluate and clarify segments of findings of several research studies with specific attention to causes and impact of human error. Twenty-eight publications have been reviewed, of which twelve are aimed at aviation, seven intended for miscellaneous industries, four from a combination of chemical, oil and gas, refinery and petroleum industries and five from the amalgamation of the coal-fired and nuclear power plant, mining, electrical transmission and healthcare.

3 Human Errors in Maintenance of Mechanical Systems

There is a frequent occurrence of inadvertent human errors in the maintenance of mechanical systems. Due to the complexity of technology, it is progressively becoming hard for human operators to properly cognize the system's behaviour [4]. Hence, there is a recurrent of human errors. Human error is defined as a non-fulfilment of a stipulated task (or the execution of an unacceptable action) having a potential to disrupt planned operations and resulting in property and equipment damages [6]. Virovac et al. [5], defines human error as an inadvertent error in the execution of work which leads to sudden system damage or it can be a dormant or latent error characterized as a potential to endanger the technical system's worthiness. Based on the study by Myszewski [6], human errors are viewed as examples of the ineffectiveness of the organization. Human errors can be classified into, slips, lapses, and violations [4]. This classification is in agreement with the one put forward by Reason [7] and Siu [8]. These are slips of actions and lapses of memory both classified as distractions and loss of concentration while the violation is an intended action, especially where there is an expected reward of the violation.

The method which is easily adopted in various organizations when dealing with human error is to blame incidents or accidents on individuals performing the task and focus solutions on the mistakes of these individuals. Now, the idea of adopting the individual approach in addressing human error, organizations disregards the dormant or latent conditions within the work systems under which the workforce operate that give rise to human error [3]. It is further stated that human error should be identified as a consequence of amalgamated factors, as opposed to the root cause of an incident or accident. This paper aims to unearth the various causal factors of human error in maintenance leading to mechanical system's substandard performance, hence become a source of incidents and catastrophic accidents. It is approximated by NOPSEMA [3]; Dumitru and Boşcoianu [9]; Drury [10]; Begur and Babu [11]; Wiegmann and Shappell [12] and Pons and Dey [4] that human error is a major causal factor of between 70-80% of most equipment failures, incidents and accidents. It is about 15% - 20% of failures, incidents and accidents that are due to maintenance error [10, 11].

In the study of Dhillon and Liu [1], human error was stated as a serious problem in maintenance emanating from the operation, assembly, design, inspection, installation and maintenance phase. The errors committed in other phases of the mechanical system are inherited by the maintenance phase, and failure to identify these latent conditions during maintenance can lead to disruptive situations. There is a serious need to identify human errors, their causal factors and impact in any maintenance department. A guide developed by Health and Safety Executive [13] is based on the thought that human errors in maintenance are to a great extent predictable, hence can be identified and controlled.

4 Causes of Human Errors in Maintenance

The issue of human error in the maintenance of mechanical systems needs to be properly addressed and to do that, one needs to begin with the appropriate analysis of the causes and impact of human error. There are a number of factors during the maintenance phase that can give rise to human error when not properly identified and controlled. Causes of human errors in maintenance are the factors responsible for the manifestation of errors on the tasks performed during the maintenance phase. A number of factors tabled in a study by Dhillon and Liu [1] as a source of human error are lack of skills, insufficient training, badly written operating manuals and maintenance procedures, poorly designed equipment, usage of unsuitable tools, insufficient work layout, limited lighting in the workspace and noise levels. On the other hand, various causal factors derived from Dhillon [2] include the complexity of maintenance tasks, inadequately written maintenance procedures and obsolete maintenance manuals, the fatigue of the maintenance personnel, insufficient training and experience, under-designed work layout, inadequacy of equipment design, unsuitable tools for specified work, substandard work environment. The substandard work environment can include a poorly designed plant with insufficient accessibility of components. In a study conducted by Virovac et al. [5], communication, equipment design and fabrication, working environment, work complexity, knowledge, work organization, documentation (manuals and procedures), work planning, pressure, fatigue, insufficient personnel for work, personal problems, and distraction while doing work were identified as major error causal factors. Management commitment, casual organizational cultures, and the organization's local context enable the continued existence of human error by preventing the proper implementation of initiatives for addressing human error [14]. In the analysis of human factors as a component of the management system's holistic performance, the key human factors that impact the maintenance performance such as competence and motivation, in contrast with supervision, workload, and performance feedback were derived [15]. Lack of competence, and the inclination to disregard the established instructions, are the core causal factors of human error as per research findings of Badenhorst and Van Tonder [16]. In research by Latorella and Prabhu [17], a number of human factors responsible for the existence of human error such as time pressure, inadequate feedback, difficult ambient conditions (environmental factor) and the common erring factor of human were identified.

It was revealed that the major error causal factors are inadequate communication, complacency, insufficient knowledge, disturbances, poor teamwork, scarcity of resources, pressure, the inadequacy of awareness, insufficiency of assertiveness, fatigue, stress, norms or cultures[18]. Hobbs [19] discovered that the manifestation of human errors is related with environmental factors, inadequate communication and coordination, time pressure, maintenance procedures and documentation, lack of integration in teamwork, change of shifts and handover, organizational and team norms, fatigue, sources of stress, lack of system knowledge, equipment design and fabrication deficiencies, insufficient design for maintainability, and absent-minded. The factors such as the following: inadequacy of supervision, memory and attention issues, poor decision making and judgment, poor design, inflexibility and inadaptability, poor light in the workspace, and confined work area were revealed as the major causes of human error [20]. Alonso and Broadribb [21] discovered that organizational and team cultures, odd situations, psychological issues, procedural factors, and organizational structure, complex environments, exposure to high stress and a tendency to remain in the background are key causal factors of human errors. In the research findings of Kovacevic et al. [22], non-fulfilment of the maintenance's technical instructions, the poorly organized or coordinated training process, insufficient equipment for diagnosis, and a failure to understand the work activities are classified as the key reasons for the occurrence of human error. While Laakso et al. [23] revealed that common human errors stem from plant modifications, planning and auditing, post-installation inspection, testing programs of the start-ups and training.

Dunn [24] established a number of factors responsible for human error such as, absorbed by extra emotional or sensory demands, failure to maintain concentration or attentional focus, the decrement attentiveness, repetition of work (routine work), fatigue, time pressure, stresses emanating from physical factors, social factors, work pace and personal factors, emotional decision making or clouding better judgement, confirmation bias when diagnosing a problem, the level of motivation or arousal, morale of employees, the competence (skills, knowledge and experience) of maintenance personnel (managers, engineers, artisans, etc.,), tools availability, sufficient equipment and parts, shift changes, and sufficiency of work instructions and procedures. The research findings of Gould and Lovell [25] presented that the procedures can be both the origin and defense of human error. The substandard work environment can include a poorly designed plant with insufficient accessibility of components. By looking at these sources of human error, one can deduct that the same sources can be used as barriers or defences against human error in maintenance. Rashid [26] revealed the following main error causal factors: organizational process, documentation (manuals and procedures), maintenance personnel training, supervision, equipment design and fabrication, and resources. The substandard work environment can include a poorly designed plant with insufficient accessibility of components. By looking at these sources of human error, one can deduct that the same sources can be used as barriers or defences against human error in maintenance. It is very important to analyses the causal factors of human error in order to come up with sufficient strategies and initiatives for managing human errors in the maintenance of mechanical systems. The following event in the evolution of maintenance management is the inclusion of human factors in performance measurement [15].

5 Impact of Human Errors in Maintenance

The next step after determining the causes of human error in the maintenance of mechanical systems is to establish the impact of human errors. The impact of human errors represents the consequences or effects that are experienced when human errors occurring during the maintenance phase of mechanical systems are not properly managed, reduced and even eliminated. Dhillon [2] unveils that the impact of human error is the loss of life due to accidents and cost constraints imposed by breakdowns and accidents or incidents. On the other hand, the impact of human errors such as delays, damage to equipment, repairs and accidents were revealed [5]. It is indicated in the Health and Safety Executive [13] guide, that human error poses risks to health, the effect on safety, impairment of performance and the increased likelihood of accidents, low quality of maintenance, increased operational costs, impairment on operating life of plant and risks of occurrence of accidents.

In a study by Latorella and Prabhu [17], it was revealed that human errors have the most acute impact resulting in accidents and loss of life, delays in availability of equipment, and obstruction of productivity of equipment and efficiency of operations. It has been established that substandard maintenance due to human error has a considerable contribution to accidents and incidents [19]. During the review, accidents kept appearing as the major impact of human error, and these accidents have a negative impact on the lives of people and economic activities of the organization. Now, Krulak [20] indicates that the impact of human error includes, the untold sums of equipment and lives that paid a price for human error, the occurrence of mishaps, and enabling the odds linked to the extremity of a mishap. Human error is a common cause of many key safety incidents involving a huge loss of life [21]. In a study by Dunn [24], it is shown that there is a huge impact on maintenance quality and costs, safety and reliability equipment, and work performance. Human errors have the following impact: high social and economic cost, equipment safety, maintenance performance efficiency and effectiveness, equipment productivity, incidents and accidents and fatality [26]. Propagation of loss of lives, damage to property and environment, and disturbances on the economic state of any organization are stated as major effects of human errors [27]. It is further stated that the economic impact significantly influences the workplace, employees, society and economy. Human errors in maintenance impose the safety and economic effects [28]. These effects are very costly imposing cost constraints in the maintenance department of any organization.

6 Key Findings of the Literature Review

A number of publications were examined with the intention of establishing the causes and impact of human error in the maintenance of mechanical systems. Figure 1 below presents the classifications of reviewed scholarly writings according to industry. It can be seen that a great amount of work has been done in the aviation industry to address the issue of human error in maintenance.

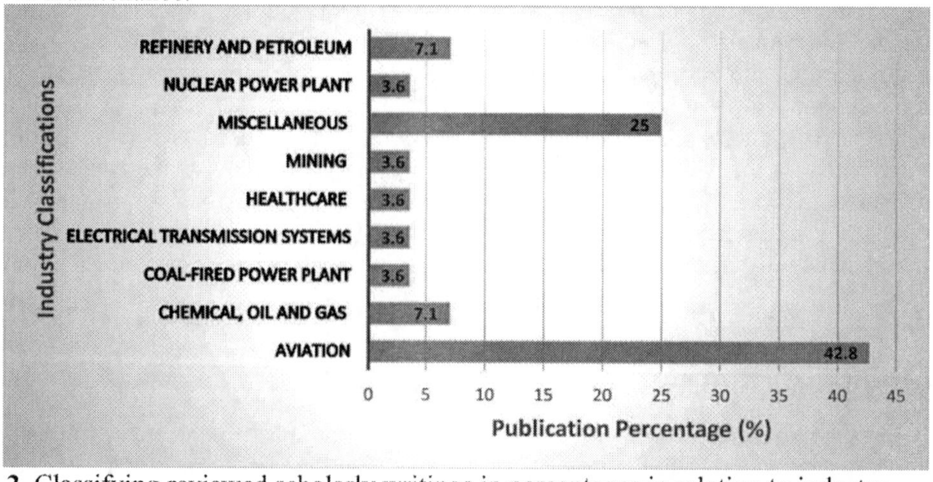

Fig. 2. Classifying reviewed scholarly writings in percentages in relation to industry

A great amount of error causal factors was discovered through the literature review and the key causal factors are presented in Table 1.

Table 1. Factors Responsible for Human Error in Maintenance

Causes	Authors
Leadership and Management Factors	
Poor management and supervision	Timmons, et al., 2014; Peach, Ellis & Visser, 2016; Krulak, 2004; Rashid, 2010
Insufficient Training	Dhillon & Liu, 2006; Dhillon, 2014); Kovacevic et al., 2016; Laakso, Pyy, & Reiman, 1998; Rashid, 2010
Work design/planning/layout	Dhillon & Liu, 2006; Peach, Ellis & Visser, 2016; B S Dhillon 2014; Dunn, 2004; Virovac, Domitrović & Bazij, 2017
Poorly written procedures, manuals and work instructions	Dhillon & Liu, 2006; Gould & Lovell, 2009; Hobbs, 2008; Dhillon, 2014; Dunn, 2004; Rashi, 2010
Poor communication and sparse feedback	Hobbs, 2008; Virovac, Domitrović & Bazij, 2017; Peach, Ellis & Visser, 2016; Laakso, Pyy, & Reiman, 1998
Time pressures	Laakso, Pyy, & Reiman, 1998; Hobbs, 2008; Dunn, 2004; Virovac, Domitrović & Bazij, 2017
Poor organizational culture	Timmons, et al., 2014; Alonso & Broadribb, 2018; Latorella & Prabhu, 2000; Rashid, 2010
Individual Factors [Cognitive Factors]	
Incompetence/Inadequate skills	Dhillon & Liu, 2006; Dunn, 2004; Peach, Ellis & Visser, 2016; Badenhorst & Van Tonder, 2004
Fatigue	Latorella & Prabhu, 2000; Hobbs, 2008; Dhillon, 2014; Dunn, 2004); Virovac, Domitrović & Bazij, 2017
Stress/Emotional demands	Dunn, 2004; Latorella & Prabhu, 2000; Hobbs, 2008; Alonso & Broadribb, 2018
Routine or repetitive work	Alonso & Broadribb, 2018; Dunn, 2004
Ignoring standard work instructions	Badenhorst & Van Tonder, 2004); Kovacevic et al., 2016; Dunn, 2004
Physical Factors	
Equipment design and construction deficiencies	Dhillon & Liu, 2006; Hobbs, 2008; Dhillon, 2014; Krulak, 2004; Rashid, 2010
Environmental Factors	
Poor work environment (e.g. lighting, noise levels and ambient conditions)	Dhillon & Liu, 2006; Krulak, 2004; Latorella & Prabhu, 2000; Dhillon & Liu, 2006

The major impact of human errors in maintenance was also discovered through the literature review, and key effects of errors are presented in Table 2.

Table 2. The Impact of Human Error in Maintenance

Impact	Authors
Incidents and Accidents	Latorella & Prabhu, 2000; Dhillon, 2014; Alonso & Broadribb, 2018; Virovac, Domitrović & Bazij, 2017; Health and Safety Executive, 2000; Rashid, 2010; Hobbs, 2008;
Loss of life	Latorella & Prabhu, 2000; Dhillon, 2014; Alonso & Broadribb, 2018; Rashid, 2010
Inefficiency, and impaired productivity of equipment	Latorella & Prabhu, 2000; Virovac, Domitrović & Bazij, 2017; Dunn, 2004; Rashid, 2010

Cost (economic loss)	Health and Safety Executive, 2000; Alkhaldi, Pathirage & Kulatunga, 2017; Dhillon 2014; Dunn, 2004); Rankin et al., 2000; Rashid, 2010
Safety/ risk to health	Rankin et al., 2000; Alonso & Broadribb, 2018; Dunn, 2004; Health and Safety Executive, 2000
Equipment damage or loss	Virovac, Domitrović & Bazij, 2017; Alkhaldi, Pathirage & Kulatunga, 2017; Krulak, 2004
Impaired maintenance quality or performance	Health and Safety Executive, 2000; Dunn, 2004; Rashid, 2010

7 Conclusion

This paper reports a review of past literature concerning human errors in the maintenance of mechanical systems. The review of the literature revealed that the causes of human errors vary from those caused by poor maintenance management (e.g. policies and procedures) and cognitive factors (stress and competence etc.,) to those that are caused by physical factors (environmental factors, component design). The literature review further revealed that there is a great negative impact of human errors in maintenance that can lead to failures and even catastrophic failures (major damage to plant and human and even lead to fatality). These failures negatively affect organizations' economic activities.

It is recommended that the errors and impact discovered in the literature review be examined in the local context of those industries that have not yet adopted human factors engineering in their maintenance policies. The training programs should be developed to assist in bringing awareness of the impact of human error at the individual and organizational level. The adoption of human factors principles in the maintenance policy and strategy development can assist the organizations to properly begin the journey of reducing and better managing human error.

The following are considered to be eligible for future research focus:

- The development of effective human error reporting systems to ensure the availability of sufficient data for the analysis and management of human error.
- Developing or improving tools for analyzing the probability of occurrence of errors in each industry to prioritize the predictive and preventive measures.
- The quantification of the impact of human error on maintenance performance and economic activities.

References

1. B.S. Dhillon, Y. Liu, Human error in maintenance: a review, *Journal of Quality in Maintenance Engineering* **12**(1):21-36 (2006)
2. B.S. Dhillon, Human Error in Maintenance: Investigative Study for the Factories of the Future, *IOP Conference Series: Materials Science and Engineering* 13 IOP Publishing (2014)
3. NOPSEMA, *Human error risk reduction to ALARP,* Perth: National Offshore Petroleum Safety and Environmental Management Authority (2015)
4. D. Pons, K. Dey, Aviation Human Error Modelled as a Production Process, *The Ergonomics Open Journal* **8**(1):1-12 (2015)
5. D. Virovac, A. Domitrovic, E. Bazijanac, the influence of human factor in aircraft maintenance, *Promet – Transport Interaction* 257-266 (2017)
6. J.M. Myszewski, Management responsibility for human errors. *The TQM Journal* **24**(4):326-337 (2012)
7. J. Reason, *Human Error,* Cambridge: Cambridge University Press (1990)

8. N. Siu, Risk Assessment for dynamic systems: an overview, *Reliability Engineering Systems Safety* 43-73 (1994)
9. I.M. Dumitru, M. Boşcoianu, human factors contribution to aviation safety, Brasov: International Conference of Scientific Paper (2015)
10. C.G. Drury, Human Factors in Aircraft Maintenance, New York: RTO AVT (2000)
11. S. H. Begur, J.A. Babu, Human Factors in Aircraft Maintenance, *International Advanced Research Journal in Science, Eng and Tech* **3**(3):14-17 (2016)
12. D.A. Wiegmann, S.A. Shappell, *A Human Error Approach to Aviation Accident Analysis,* Burlington: Ashgate (2003)
13. Health and Safety Executive, *Improving maintenance a guide to reducing human error,* UK: HSE Books (2000)
14. S. Timmons, B. Baxendale, A. Buttery, G. Miles, B. Roe, Implementing human factors in clinical practice, *Emergency Medicine Journal (EMJ)* **32**:368-372 (2014)
15. R. Peach, H. Ellis, J.K. Visser, a maintenance performance measurement framework that includes maintenance human factors: a case study from the electricity transmission industry. *South African Journal of Industrial Engineering* **27**(2):177-189 (2016)
16. F.W. Badenhorst, J. Van Tonder, Determining the factors causing human error deficiencies at a public utility company, *SA Journal of Human Resource Management* **2**(3):62-69 (2004)
17. K.A. Latorella, P.V. Prabhu, A review of human error in aviation maintenance and inspection, *International Journal of Industrial Ergonomics* 133-161 (2000)
18. B. Foyle, G. Dupont, Maintenance errors and their prevention. *International Federation of Airworthiness 48th Annual International Air Safety Seminar* 353-357, Arlington, VA: Flight Safety Foundation (1995)
19. A. Hobbs, *An Overview of Human Factors in Aviation Maintenance,* Canberra City: Australian Transport Safety Bureau (2008)
20. D.C. Krulak, Human Factors in Maintenance: Impact on Aircraft Mishap Frequency nd Severity, *Aviation, Space, and Environmental Medicine* 429-432 (2004)
21. I.J. Alonso, M. Broadribb, Human error: A myth eclipsing real causes. *American Institute of Chemical Engineers Process Saf Prog* 145-149 (2018)
22. S. Kovacevic, L. Papic, G.L. Janackovic, S. Savic, The Analysis of Human Error as Causes in the Maintenance of Machines: A Case Study in Mining Companies, *South African Journal of Industrial Engineering* 193-202 (2016)
23. K. Laakso, P. Pyy, L. Reiman, *Human Errors Related to Maintenance and Modifications.* Helsinki: Radiation and Nuclear Safety Authority (1998)
24. S. Dunn, Managing Human Error in Maintenance, *Maintenance Journal* 13-18 (2004)
25. J. Gould, S. Lovell, Human error analysis at a refinery, UK: IChemE (2009)
26. H.S. Rashid, *Human Factors Effects in Helicopter Maintenance: Proactive Monitoring and Controlling Techniques (Thesis),* England: Cranfield University (2010)
27. M. Alkhaldi, C. Pathirage, U. Kulatunga, The role of human error in accidents within the oil and gas industry in Bahrain. *13th International Postgraduate Research Conference (IPGRC): conference proceedings,* 821-834, United Kingdom: University of Salford (2017)
28. W. Rankin, R. Hibit, J. Allen, R. Sargent, Development and evaluation of the Maintenance Error Decision Aid (MEDA) process, *International Journal of Industrial Ergonomics* 261-276 (2000)
29. McKillop Library (2018), http://salve.libguides.com. Retrieved from http://salve.libguides.com: http://salve.libguides.com/c.php?g=434837

Holistic assessment of intelligent technologies: Top management's perceptions

Krzysztof Ejsmont[1]*

[1] Institute of Production Systems Organisation, Faculty of Production Engineering, Warsaw University of Technology, Poland

Abstract. Due to the beginning of the Fourth Industrial Revolution based mainly on intelligent technologies used in the production area, rational assessment of their functioning has become the subject of interest of many scientists. The main aim of the article is to present the method of intelligent technologies assessment and to determine the possibilities of its adaptation by manufacturing companies. The following methods and research approaches were used in the construction of the method: integrated method, controlling, desk research, observation of the functioning of intelligent technologies, questionnaire interview. The research procedure assumes the adoption of a three-stage assessment process (measure – module – dimension). The holistic approach adopted in the study is achieved through horizontal aggregation of obtained values of measures and modules. The method was verified for the assessment of an intelligent technological line operating in a large metallurgical company. The substantive analysis of the achieved results allowed to develop a list of recommended activities within modules that have not been assessed positively. It has also become possible to assess the implementation of strategic and operational goals realized through the use of intelligent technological line. The developed final assessment formula will help determine the effectiveness of the activities undertaken (comparative analysis).

Keywords: holistic approach, intelligent technologies, technology assessment.

1 Introduction

A number of studies have reported or suggested that Industry 4.0 is a concept characterized by the integration of intelligent machines and systems, as well as introducing changes in production processes aimed at increasing production efficiency and enabling flexible assortment exchanges. Industry 4.0 refers not only to technology but also to new forms of work and the function that workers will perform in a company [1-3]. However, it should be clearly underlined that an indispensable element of industrial development is its rational

* Corresponding author: krzysztof.ejsmont@wp.pl

and factual assessment, therefore the issue of the assessment of intelligent technologies discussed in this paper is extremely important and still actual.

Based on the review of the literature on the subject of the assessment of intelligent technologies used by manufacturing companies, there are some gaps in this area. Available publications mainly deal with issues such as the evaluation of the potential of these technologies [4] and to quality assessments of specific production processes using intelligent technologies [5]. Many publications also address the issue of assessing intelligent technologies in manufacturing companies and its impact on the development of Industry 4.0, but without proposing specific solutions (methods, models, tools) that could serve this purpose [6, 7].

After analyzing the classical methods used for technology assessment [8, 9], it can be concluded that they are characterized by certain limitations, imperfections and that do not fully take into account the specificity of intelligent technologies used in the production area. Existing methods allow for the assessment of technology only in some areas of its functioning (mainly economic and technological) and are based mainly on financial data, they reflect limitedly the specificity of the environment and management needs to be determined by the environment. Available methods do not provide the opportunity to take into consideration the complexity and new features of intelligent technologies used in the production area. After the literature review, not identified the method for assessing intelligent technologies in real-time, which would consider the implementation of operational and strategic objectives of the company.

The research problem formulated in the article is to construct a method that allows for carrying out the most comprehensive assessment of intelligent technologies in real-time.

A thesis has been also formulated, that the application of the assessment method of intelligent technologies used in the production area will allow obtaining information enabling companies to make rational decisions regarding the improvement of the functioning of intelligent technologies.

2 Method of assessment intelligent technologies

The basis for the elaboration of the solution proposed in the article was: the integrated method [10] and the controlling tool [11].

In previous publications [12-14] the author developed a model for the assessment of intelligent technologies based on a two-step approach (dimension – measure). In this paper, its development assumes creating functional modules (Table 1) within the adopted dimensions, consisting of a specific group of measures (Figure 1). The measure is understood as an indicator specifying the size, quality or value of something. It may have a quantitative or qualitative form. The module is an element of the evaluation system performing a specific function in it. It is easy to use as part of a larger whole.

In order to develop a list of measures, and then to create functional modules, it is necessary to collect key information about the research subject. In the initial phase of this process, an interview questionnaire and participant observation are recommended, which will allow the preparation of an assessment questionnaire. Its final structure will depend to a large extent on technical documentation of intelligent technology, analysis of the external and internal environment of the company as well as operational and strategic objectives implemented by the technology. The questionnaire should be completed by employees inside the company, possessing substantive and practical knowledge about intelligent technology. Thanks to this, it will be possible to determine the value of individual measures and then entire modules and dimensions. It is recommended to select both quantitative and qualitative measures, while their total number should not exceed 100. Each measure should have the most adequate method/tool to determine its value.

Table 1. Examples of functional modules

Dimension	Measures	Module	Function
Environmental	rationalization of energy use [y/n]	Energy	assessment of the level of energy consumption and determining if it is rationally used
	energy consumption [kWh]		
	adjusting level of energy consumption to the production order being carried out [y/n]		
Social	a number of accidents during the work with technology [pcs.]	Employee safety	determining whether cooperation with intelligent technology is safe for staff
	losses due to accidents [PLN]		
	level of security of handling intelligent technology [Likert 1-5]		
	risk of an accident [0-1]		
	level of employee participation in realization of the production process [%]		

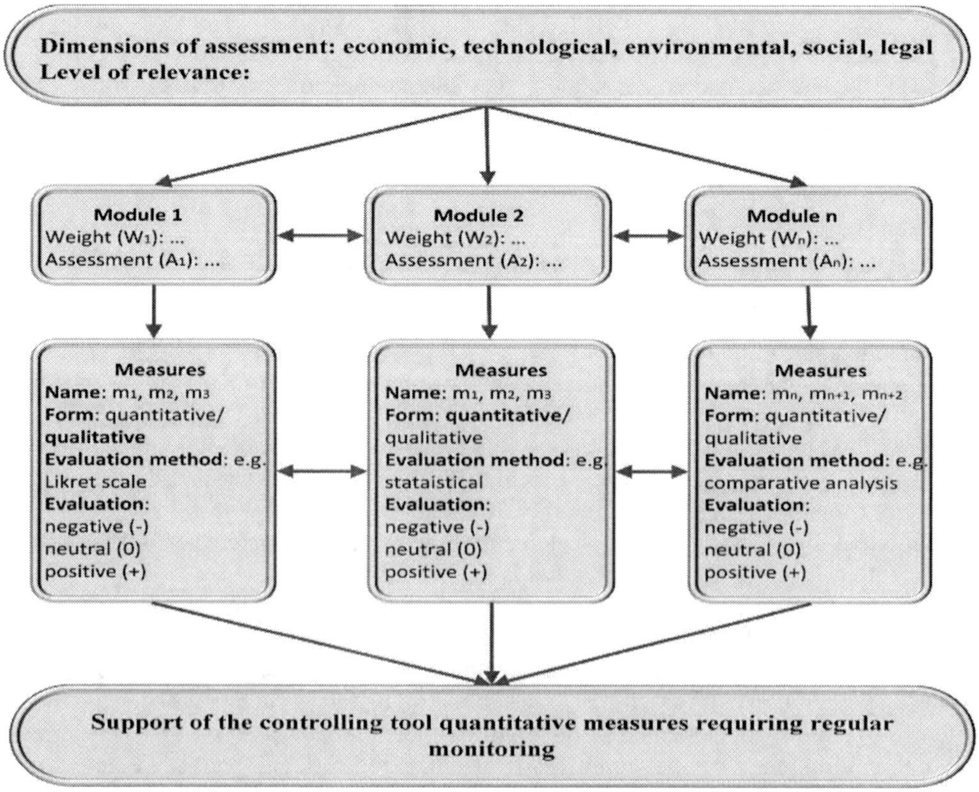

Fig. 1. Structure of the method for intelligent technologies assessment in a holistic approach

Each of the created modules should have selected (e.g. in an arbitrary manner, based on the knowledge and experience of the person/team conducting the assessment or based on the literature on intelligent technologies) specific weights (values in the range from

0 to 1, where 1 is very important). The weights can depend on many factors, such as the type, characteristics and technical specification of intelligent technology, the significance of the measures included in the module for achieving company objectives, etc. Benchmarking can also be used during selecting weights and if it is possible to analyze the processes of functioning of such intelligent technologies in other organizations. The weighting may be done by using heuristic methods or by using the available research tools (e.g. a questionnaire to be completed by the evaluation team). The final value of weight can be, for example, the arithmetic average obtained by completing the questionnaire by all members of the evaluation team.

The big advantage of assigning weights to the created modules is also the fact that if the evaluating team have decided about the slight impact of a particular module on the final result of the assessment, it is possible to disregard it by giving a weight equal to "0". Using the weight approach, it is also possible to obtain a greater objectivity of the assessment (it is useful, for example in a situation where there are differences of opinion regarding the meaning of a given module), also selection of only those modules that are particularly important from the point of view of the operational and strategic goals of the company thanks to intelligent technology.

After creating a list of measures within each of the functional modules (functions of modules should be related to the operational and strategic goals of the company), the method of determining their value should be chosen. Different methods and tools (e.g. financial, statistical, comparative analysis, etc.) can be used for this purpose.

After making a detailed analysis of each measure, determining its value and determining the evaluation (positive, neutral or negative), proceed to calculate the assessments of individual modules. Horizontal aggregation of measures takes place here. In the further stage of the assessment process, the assessments (numerator) and weights (denominator) of the individual modules within a given dimension should be summed up and multiplied by the relevance level of this dimension. In this way, a complete assessment can be obtained using the following formula 1:

$$\frac{LR_D\mathrm{E}*\sum_{i=m}^{n}A_i+LR_D\mathrm{T}*\sum_{i=m}^{n}A_i+LR_D\mathrm{En}*\sum_{i=m}^{n}A_i+LR_D\mathrm{S}*\sum_{i=m}^{n}A_i+LR_D\mathrm{L}*\sum_{i=m}^{n}A_i}{LR_D\mathrm{E}*\sum_{i=m}^{n}W_i+LR_D\mathrm{T}*\sum_{i=m}^{n}W_i+LR_D\mathrm{En}*\sum_{i=m}^{n}W_i+LR_D\mathrm{S}*\sum_{i=m}^{n}W_i+LR_D\mathrm{L}*\sum_{i=m}^{n}W_i}*100 \quad (1)$$

where:
LR_D – the level of relevance for the dimension (E – economic, T – technological, En – environmental, S – social, L – legal),
A – assessment of individual module in dimension,
W – the weight of an individual module in dimension.

Referring to modern concepts of management and technology assessments, the author postulates the pursuit of the assessment comprehensiveness (holism). However, it is not possible, when adapting the method to the conditions of a chosen company, to include all possible groups of measures in the assessment. A lot depends on the internal and external environment of the company, intelligent technology being evaluated, as well as the company's priorities regarding the achieving of operational and strategic objectives.

It is also worth noting that a given dimension may also manifest itself in an indirect way in other dimensions, which is consistent with the idea of a holistic approach. For example, in the environmental dimension, there are measures related to the emission of pollution that have a big impact on society (social dimension).

3 Results

In order to verify the method proposed by the author, it was decided to assess the intelligent technology functioning in a large Polish manufacturing company – Pruszyński Ltd. The research object that served the assessment is a line for forming profiles for steel structures (Figure 2) of the Italian company STAM S.p.A Ponzano Vento (TV). It has been designed for the production (starting from the semi-product – coils) of sheet profiles of various widths and lengths. The length of the line is 82m, it consists of several machines (straightener, punching machine, cutter, guillotine, profiler, feeder).

Fig. 2. The line for forming steel structure profiles

Functions that indicate that technology can be considered as intelligent include:

- thanks to equipping the line with sensors and devices, it is possible to collect very large amounts of data and based on carrying out analysis processes – optimization of the production processes;
- the line is able to learn from the collected data;
- energy saving as a result of the adaptation of the line to energy needs in the production of a given type of product;
- in case of any irregularities or failures, the line informs the operator (also telediagnosis option is possible), but if it is able to solve this problem by itself, it does not stop and continues production;
- working of the line takes place without human intervention (fully automatically), so it is safe – the operator is only responsible for delivering the raw material and uploading the required order data to the main computer;
- while executing the same orders (which have already taken place in the past), the line is able to independently adjust the optimal technical and operational parameters.

According to the developed method, the process of assessing intelligent technology in a particular company was carried out. For this purpose, it was necessary to thoroughly familiarize with the characteristics and technical specification of the research facility. This was possible thanks to the management of the company providing technical documentation of the intelligent production line and the author's interviews regarding its operation with a member of the top management, the main technologist and operators who work with technology on a daily basis. The author's participation in the direct observation of working technology was significant, which made it possible to understand what the entire production process looks like while using it.

After conducting an interview with a member of the top management, the collected information was sorted out, and a questionnaire for further research was prepared. The questionnaire consisted of five dimensions within which measures have been contained together with units and were grouped into functional modules. In addition, there are fields for entering weights for individual modules as well as relevance levels for the adopted dimensions. The questionnaire was completed by a member of the top management, the main technologist and two employees serving the line. Taking into account the answers contained in the questionnaires (mainly the qualitative measures), as well as the measurements made by the author, the size of the quantitative measures has become possible to analyze and evaluate them. The list of all measures with units, as well as a description of the research by which their values have been evaluated has been described in detail in the publication [15]. Synthetic results of the research are presented in Table 2.

Table 2. Research results on the assessment of intelligent technology

Dimension	Module	Weight (W)	Evaluation of measures	Assessment (A)
Economic Level of relevance: 5	Expected economical results	0.5	4 "+"	0.50
	Costs	0.3	3 "+"	0.30
	Short-term flexibility of demand	0.6	2 "+"	0.60
	Line work efficiency	1	4 "+"; 2 "0"; 2 "–"	0.63
Technological Level of relevance: 4	Line functionality	1	2 "+"; 1 "0"	0.83
	Technological modernity of the line	0.2	4 "+"; 1 "0"	0.18
	Technical and utility parameters	0.8	5 "+"; 3 "0"	0.65
Environmental Level of relevance: 1	Saving raw materials	0.5	3 "+"	0.50
	Natural environment preservation	0.5	7 "+"	0.50
	Environmental policy	1	3 "+"	1.00
Social Level of relevance: 3.5	Employees	0.5	3 "–"; 2 "0"	0.10
	Recipients of products	0.3	2 "+"; 1 "0"	0.25
	Work safety	0.3	5 "+"; 1 "0"	0.27
	Employment	0.8	3 "+"	0.80
Legal Level of relevance: 2	Compliance with legal requirements (internal and external)	1	6 "+"	1.00
	Service and warranty	0.8	3 "+"	0.80
	The legal status of technology	1	3 "+"	1.00
Total		11.1		9.91

To perform a parametric assessment for the measures evaluated positively ("+") a value of 1 was assigned, for measures evaluated negatively ("–") the value of 0, and for measures evaluated neutrally ("0") the value of 0.5. Afterwards, the measures with the values assigned to them were added together within each module and the sum was divided into the total number of measures in the module. The obtained value multiplied by the module weight is its final assessment (last column). For example, in the module "Linework efficiency" we have 4 measures evaluated positively, 2 neutral and 2 negatively. Thus, the total score is: $[(4\times1 + 2\times0.5 + 2\times0) \div 8]\times1 = 0.63$.

Due to the fact that some modules contain quantitative measures that require regular control of deviations, the way in which they were measured, analyzed and evaluated was presented in Table 3.

Based on interviews with company employees, as well as getting acquainted with the aggregate data stored in the IT system, the author was able to determine the base value of the measures. Mostly they were the arithmetic mean of the values obtained from all correctly executed production orders from the beginning of the line functionating. Similarly, acceptable deviations were determined (mainly using statistical methods). Table 3 presents the results of the evaluation for one selected production order lasting 1 hour (production of 134.71 lm trapezoidal sheet). The units of measures are given in brackets.

Table 3. Quantitative measures to regular control of deviations

Specification planned and monitored measures	**Measured value**	**Base value**	**Actual deviation**	**Acceptable deviation**	**Evaluation**
Examples	X_R	X_B	$X_R–X_B$	ΔX	A, CA, NA
Economic measures					
Delivery time [days]	8	10	-2	0	A
Work in progress [lm]	21.27	50	-28.73	20	NA
Utilization of workstations [%]	100	80	20	20	CA
Downtimes [h]	0	1.3	-1.3	0.3	A
Unit cost (per one lm of steel) [PLN]	10.22	10.22	0	0.78	A
Unit profit (per one lm of steel) [PLN]	0.92	0.92	0	0.10	A
Changeover time [min]	10	5	5	5	CA
Production added per man-hour [PLN]	123.93	230	-106.07	92	NA
Technological measures					
Tension [V]	350	400	-50	100	A
Frequency [Hz]	40	50	-10	25	A
Molding speed [m/min]	20	30	-10	15	A
Input speed [m/min.]	3	5	-2	2	CA
Acceleration [m/sec^2]	2	4	-2	2	CA
Pass speed [m/min]	25	35	-10	15	A
Pressure force [kg]	8	12	-4	6	A
The cycle of lowering and lifting sheet [sec]	0.5	0.7	-0.2	0.2	CA
Environmental measures					
The ratio of material consumption to generated waste [%]	2	3	-1	2	A
Reduction of wastes/wastage [%]	1	1	0	0.5	A

Energy consumption during using the line (on average per 1 hour of operation) [kWh]	12	15	-3	1.5	A
Noise level [dB]	80	75	5	10	A
Amount of wastes (on average per 1 hour of line working) [kg]	8.5	23.5	-15	9.4	A
Social measures					
Number of accidents (per year) during line working [pcs.]	0	0	0	1	A
Financial losses due accidents [PLN]	0	0	0	6500	A

where: A – acceptance, CA – conditional acceptance, NA – no approval.

Thanks to the controlling tool, it was possible to compare the measured values with the base values and compare these values with an acceptable deviation. This helped in the analysis and evaluation of the measures, which in turn enabled the calculation of the assessment of entire modules. According to the adopted form of evaluation of measures: "A" means a positive evaluation, "CA" – neutral, and "NA" – negative. In a brief summary, it can be stated that in the environmental and social dimensions all measures were evaluated positively, in the technological dimension, 3 measures were evaluated neutrally, and in the economic dimension, 2 measures were evaluated negatively and 2 neutrally. By regular control the value of deviations of the measures, it is possible to focus on those not evaluated positively and to develop remedial/corrective actions that may contribute to the better functioning of intelligent technology.

Using the formula 1, a complete assessment of intelligent technology has been made:

$$\frac{(5*2.09+4*1.74+1*2+3.5*1.42+2*2.8)}{(5*2.4+4*2+1*2+3.5*1.9+2*2.8)}*100 = 87{,}53\% \qquad (2)$$

The value obtained (2) can be interpreted similarly as the OEE indicator [16]. It can be an internal measurement tool used to assess the functioning of intelligent technology and help identify areas (modules) in which corrective actions are indicated. It can also contribute to improving cooperation on the operator's line – intelligent technology, as well as better adapt technology to the expectations of the society (employees, recipients, etc.).

4 Discussion

During the realization of the intelligent technology assessment process in Pruszyński Ltd. no particular difficulties were encountered. Thanks to the good cooperation of the author with the member of the top management, the main technologist and operators servicing the technology, it has become possible to obtain all the necessary data to carry out the whole research procedure. It should be emphasized strong involvement in the process of assessing workers employed in the company, as well as the evaluation team's professional approach to the tasks entrusted to it (e.g. preparation of appropriate documentation). Thanks to this, the author could obtain information interesting for him without much difficulty, as well as determine the value of particular measures. As a consequence, it became possible to develop a complete, holistic assessment of the STAM's intelligent technological line and to familiarize the persons concerned with the results obtained. The author discussed in detail the determined values of individual measures, modules and dimensions, and also indicated the areas that in his opinion, based on the conducted assessment, should be improved in the near future (e.g. employees responsible for serving technology). After a substantive discussion with the members of the evaluation team, as well as a careful analysis of the results achieved, the author recommended actions within the modules that did not achieve the maximum possible assessment.

The main practical advantages of the assessment process include primarily its speed, flexibility and no need to incur additional costs. Therefore, it has been adapted to the requirements of industrial practice, and also allows the assessment of intelligent technologies in a different time horizon.

It has also become possible to connect strategic and operational goals with the functions implemented by intelligent technology. The main strategic goals of the analyzed company were: increasing market share, acquiring new customers and expanding the offer. The operational objectives included: increasing the production volume of profiles for steel structures and increasing the unit profit (per one lm of steel). All of the above objectives were indirectly included in the developed modules. Strategic goals were included in the social dimension, in the "Recipients of products" module and in the economic dimension, in the "Expected economical results" module. Both modules have been highly assessed, so it can be concluded that Pruszyński Ltd. accomplishes the strategic goals set by it thanks to intelligent technology. In terms of operational goals, they were included in the economic dimension in the "Linework efficiency" module, which was assessed at 63%. It can, therefore, be concluded that the company should pay more attention to the execution of current orders, and strive to improve the organization of work related to the preparation of a line for the production of particularly new products (previously not manufactured).

It should also be emphasized that the economic dimension (relevance level: 5) and technological (relevance level: 4) were deemed the most important by the member of the top management and the main technologist. This confirms the classic approach to technology assessment, in which these two perspectives are considered the most important by many authors. In the case of the analyzed technology, the low significance of the environmental dimension (relevance level: 1) is fully justified, as production results in trace emissions of pollutions and the number of wastes are at a low level. Legal aspects are set at the stage of preparing the offer and their fulfilment is a condition for the purchase of technology. The social dimension is playing an increasingly important role in the methods of technology assessment, which was indirectly confirmed by the evaluation team, which defined its significance level as 3.5.

5 Conclusion

In summary, it is worth emphasizing the validity of the interdisciplinary approach in the assessment of intelligent technologies, which leads to an increase in the level of essential rationality. The need to include in the assessment of intelligent technologies many dimensions, as well as paying attention to the role which played in this process consideration of the operational and strategic objectives of the company, enabled obtaining comprehensive information on intelligent technology and contributed to improving the rationality of decisions making by Pruszyński Ltd. In addition, it is worth mentioning that the applicability of the method was also confirmed as part of the author's work in the European Project [17], whose main goal was to create a service-oriented middleware that could be used, among others, in integrated production systems. This is proof that the thesis formulated in the article is correct.

The importance of the subject matter discussed in the publication seems to be so significant from the point of view of the development of technology assessment methods that it is fully justified to continue research aimed at constructing a universal, comprehensive and coherent method of assessing intelligent technologies. To achieve this, it is advisable to conduct further research works aimed at expanding and refining the proposed method. These are the directions of future theoretical work and the continuation of cooperation with production companies interested in the obtained results. This will enable conducting empirical research as well as continuous improvement of the method through its practical verification and achieved feedback.

References

1. E. Hofmann, M. Rüsch, Industry 4.0 and the current status as well as future prospects on logistics, *Computers in Industry* **89**:23-34 (2017), https://doi.org/10.1016/j.compind.2017.04.002.
2. Y. Lu, Industry 4.0: A survey on technologies, applications and open research issues, *Journal of Industrial Information Integration* **6**:1-10 (2017), https://doi.org/10.1016/j.jii.2017.04.005.
3. F. Zezulka, Industry 4.0 – An Introduction in the phenomenon, *IFAC-Papers Online*, **49**(25):8-12 (2016), https://doi.org/10.1016/j.ifacol.2016.12.002.
4. T.U. Daim, Strategic roadmapping of robotics technologies for the power industry: A multicriteria technology assessment, *Technological Forecasting and Social Change* **121**:49-66 (2018), https://doi.org/10.1016/j.techfore.2017.06.006.
5. S.A. Kumar, Accelerated assessment of quality of compacted geomaterials with intelligent compaction technology, *Construction and Building Materials* **113**:824-834 (2016), https://doi.org/10.1016/j.conbuildmat.2016.03.117.
6. A.R. Mashhadi, S. Behdad, Ubiquitous Life Cycle Assessment (U-LCA): A Proposed Concept for Environmental and Social Impact Assessment of Industry 4.0, *Manufacturing Letters* 15B:93-96 (2018), https://doi.org/10.1016/j.mfglet.2017.12.012.
7. R.Y. Zhong, Intelligent Manufacturing in the Context of Industry 4.0: A Review, *Engineering* **3**(5):616-630 (2017), https://doi.org/10.1016/J.ENG.2017.05.015.
8. T.A. Tran, T.U. Daim, A taxonomic review of methods and tools applied in technology assessment, *Technological Forecasting and Social Change* **75**(9):1396–1405 (2008)
9. T.A. Tran, Review of Methods and Tools Applied in Technology Assessment Literature, *In*: D.F. Kocaoglu, T.R. Anderson and T.U. Daim, eds. *Proceedings Management of Converging Technologies, Portland, USA*. Portland: International Center for Management of Engineering and Technology 1651–1660 (2007)
10. S. Marciniak, *The Integrated Method of Efficiency Evaluation of Technical and Organizational Projects*, Warsaw: Warsaw University of Technology Publishing House (1989)
11. S. Marciniak, *Controlling. Theory. Application*. Warsaw: DIFIN (2008)
12. K. Ejsmont, The model of intelligent technology assessment. *In*: R. Knosala, eds. *Innovation in management and production engineering, 2016, Opole, Poland.* Opole: Publishing House of Polish Association for Production Management 2:47-58 (2016)
13. K. Ejsmont, Assessment paradigm in relation to intelligent technologies. *In*: R. Knosala, eds. *Innovation in management and production engineering, 2017, Opole, Poland.* Opole: Publishing House of Polish Association for Production Management 2:144-155 (2017)
14. K. Ejsmont, Holistic Assessment Method of Intelligent Technologies Used in Production Processes, *Procedia Engineering* **182**:189-197 (2017), https://doi.org/10.1016/j.proeng.2017.03.161.
15. K. Ejsmont, *The method of assessment intelligent technologies in a holistic approach.* Warsaw: Warsaw University of Technology Publishing House (2018)
16. H. Mansour, M. Ahmad, H. Ahmed, Potential Using of OEE in Evaluating the Operational Performance of Workover Activities, *In*: A. Azevedo, eds. *Advances*

in Sustainable and Competitive Manufacturing Systems: 23rd International Conference on Flexible Automation & Intelligent Manufacturing, Springer Science & Business Media, 877-886 (2013)

17. E-SCOP, *Embedded systems Service-based Control for Open manufacturing and Process automation* (2013-2016), Available from: https://artemis-ia.eu/project/45-escop.html [Accessed 8 May 2018]

Modelling and Simulation of a Shearcut Process Flow at a Steel Processing Company

Khelina Swate[1], *Goodwell* Muyengwa[1*], and *Yvonie N.* Mawane[1]

[1]University of Johannesburg, Department of Mechanical and Industrial Engineering Technology, Corner Siemert and Beit Streets, Doornfontein, Johannesburg, South Africa

Abstract. Modelling and simulation of industrial systems have become a conventional method for productivity improvement through optimizing design, operation, performance and troubleshooting. This paper analyses the current Shearcut process flow through modelling and simulation. A case study research was undertaken at a steel processing company that transform steel coils into sheets, plates, slits, tubes, blanks and various roofing products. Two models were created using Arena software. The models were a representation of the process flow found in the Shearcut warehouse. The first model was developed from data obtained from production records and time studies that were carried out on some of the operations. Bottleneck stations and non-value adding operations were identified. The second model was created with some improvements that included reduced non-value adding times. Results from the second model had an improved output. This paper contributes to the use of computer simulation as a tool to improve productivity.

Keywords: arena, modelling, productivity, simulation

1 Introduction

Modelling and simulation are emerging as key technologies in supporting manufacturing in the 21st century. In today's competitive global market, there have been numerous efforts to use modelling and simulation tools and techniques to improve manufacturing efficiency within the dimensions of business [1]. It has been reported that the survival of any business in today's competitive market is based on response time, production cost, market price, and flexibility of manufacturing [2]. Obviously, the manufacturing industry has to respond quickly to these changes and continuously improve manufacturing systems in order to sustain their competitiveness [3]. It is believed that there is a need for pervasive utilization of modelling and simulation for decision support in current and future manufacturing. Hence,

* Corresponding author: gmuyengwa@uj.ac.za

simulation has been adopted in manufacturing systems by a large number of industrial organisations.

Simulation is defined by Kelton et al. [4] as a broad collection of methods and applications to mimic the behaviour of real systems, usually on a computer with the appropriate software. It plays a critical role in the design of products, materials and manufacturing processes. The simulation reproduces the behaviour of a system, which assists to observe, understand and define bottlenecks of the system in order to have adjustments in time [5]. Several authors agree on the simulation potentials which includes, the ability to simulate years of the real system in a much shorter time, potentially dangerous or hypothetical systems can be studied without the physical or financial risks that may be involved in building and studying the real system, the ability to study smaller or larger versions of a system, the ability to integrate complex system components to study their interactions, the ability to study different systems in different or identical environments and everything in a simulated environment can be absolutely monitored and controlled [1, 2, 6].

According to Kelton et al. [4] modelling is the process of producing a model. It is the representation of an object or phenomena, which is utilised by the simulation to predict a future state. A model should be a close approximation to the real system and should incorporate most of its features. The purpose of a model is to enable the analyst to predict the effect of changes to the system [1].

The steel industry is one of the world's industries, which has grown tremendously. This study presents simulation modelling using arena software to improve efficiency in a steel processing company that transform steel coils into sheets, plates, slits, tubes, blanks and various roofing products. The objectives of the company are adjusted to meet the customers' requirements and accomplishing the company strategy. However, the company is faced with several challenges and the key one is to effectively manage the manufacturing system. The study focuses on the Shearcut process, which is a major bottleneck section in the manufacturing system.

2 Literature review

2.1 Arena simulation modelling

Several simulation modelling systems exist in the market and most of them are capable of planning, testing and analyzing a manufacturing system [7]. Arena modelling system is a flexible and powerful tool that allows the creation of animated models that accurately represent virtually any system [1]. Arena is built on the Siman simulation language. Simulation language is a software package that is general in nature and where model development is done by programming [8].

Arena combines the ease of use found in high-level simulators with the flexibility of simulation language and even all the way down to general-purpose procedural languages like the Microsoft Visual Basic programming system [4]. Arena also maintains its modelling flexibility by being fully hierarchical as shown in Figure 1.

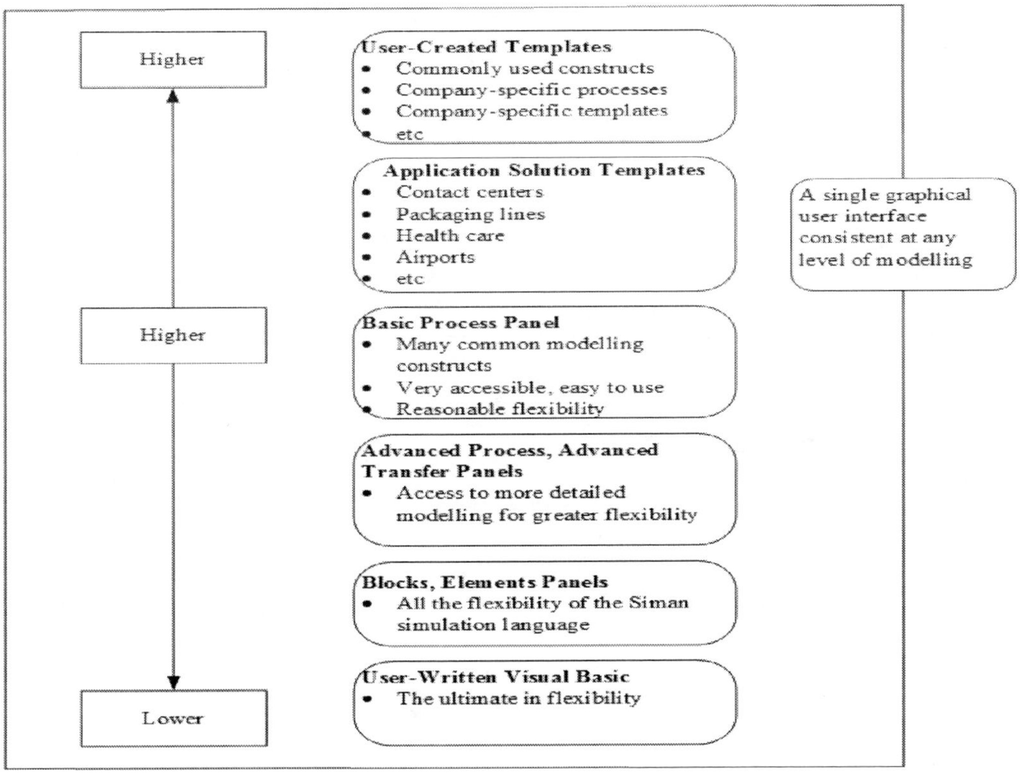

Fig. 1. Arena's Hierarchical Structure [4]

Modules in Arena are composed of Siman components. Further, Arena includes dynamic animation and also provides integrated support, including 3D graphics and business dashboards for some of the statistical design and analysis issues that are part and parcel of a good simulation study [4].

Abeya and Mulugeta [1], identified eleven steps involved in developing a simulation model, designing a simulation experiment and performing simulation analysis.

The steps are:

1) Identify the problem
2) Formulate the problem
3) Collect and process real system data
4) Formulate and develop a model
5) Validate the model
6) Document model for future use
7) Select an appropriate experimental design
8) Establish experimental conditions for runs
9) Perform simulation runs
10) Interpret and present results
11) Recommend a further course of action.

Depending on the type of simulation study and methodology used, not all steps may be required and on the other hand, additional steps may be required.

Owen and Greasley [9], carried out a literature review on the use of discrete-event simulation in modelling and simulating people's behaviour in a manufacturing set-up. Their results highlighted that the following attributes can be considered: "modelling people's decisions, availability, task performance, customer arrival rate and people movement within the studied process". They emphasized that accurate results can be obtained from models that incorporate human behaviours that included issues such as worker turnover and absenteeism. Neumann and Medbo [10], used discrete-event simulation in evaluating the operator's performance based on the operator's learning rate. However, their results were not conclusive because they lacked data on "inter-individual learning rate variability in assembly work". Kasie et al. [11], undertook a literature review on decision support systems within modelling and simulation studies. They developed a framework that incorporated artificial intelligence, decision support system database and simulation. Gopalakrishnan and Skoogh [12], carried out a simulation experiment that assessed "productivity potentials of machine criticality based maintenance". It is clear that modelling and simulation can be used in a variety of ways and can incorporate various data such as worker behaviour and machine availability in identifying areas of improvement. However, this paper focuses on the modelling and simulation of a Shearcut process in a steel manufacturing plant and does not include worker behaviour and machine availability.

2.2 Shearcut process flow

The Shearcut department studied is equipped with a computer logging system that records data. This information includes data on steel coil arriving from the mill. Information on Shearcut operating elements including value and non-value adding activities were collected manually from the Shearcut department. Figure 2, shows the Shearcut process flow.

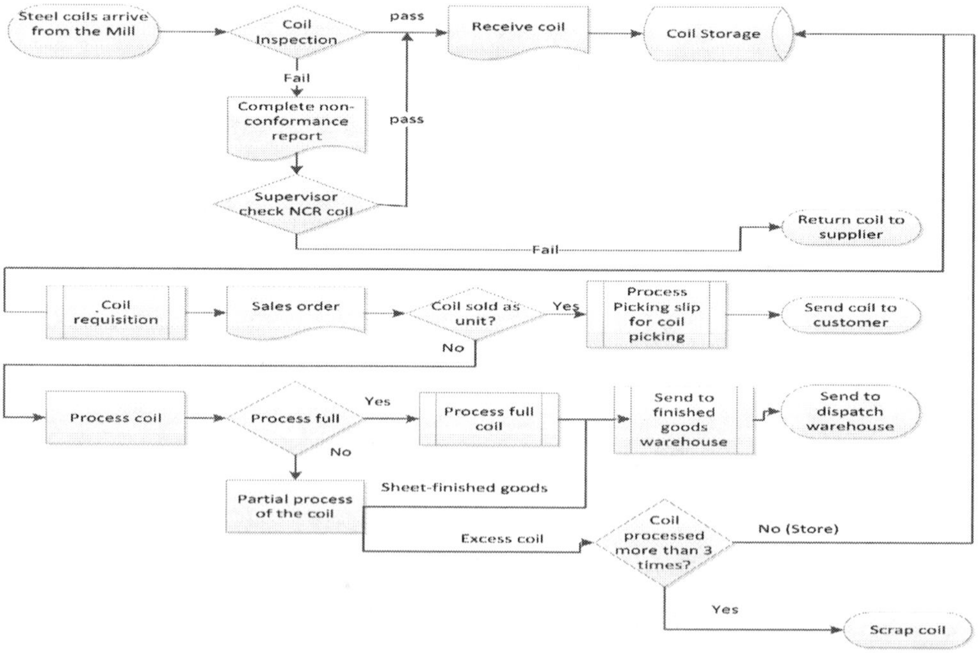

Fig. 2. Shearcut Process Flow.

3 Methodology

The major objective of this paper is to analyse and improve the current Shearcut process through modelling and simulation. The research questions for this are: To what extent can modelling and simulation be used to analyse a Sheracut process? How can modelling and simulation be used to improve productivity and resources utilization?

A case study approach was done for this paper. The standard methodology used for this study is a general computer simulation model, where two models were created using Arena software at a steel manufacturing company. Eleven tasks were identified in the Shearcut process, and these tasks are shown in Table 1. An average of ten observations was carried out on each task to improve the accuracy of the model. Input data to the model was triangulated from observations, time studies and production records. The first model was a representation of the current process. The model was first validated by experts working within the Shearcut department and these included the managers, supervisors and shop floor workers. The second validation was done through a comparison of model output results and the results from production records. The second model was an improved process, which optimized the current process. Data were collected regarding the total number of tasks, servicing time for each task, transfer of Work-in-process between stations, priorities between processes, arrival frequencies of entities or time between arrival, production output and defect rate. The parameters of the distribution used in both the current and improved model are the Triangular (TRIA) distribution, which has parameter values (Min, Mode, Max), which are the minimum time, the most likely time and the maximum time a task takes. TRIA is one of the probabilities built within the Arena software. Table 1 shows lists of the task, resources used and collected servicing time to be utilized in the first model. Table 2 shows the time durations that were used in developing the improved Shearcut process.

4 Results

The researchers obtained the processing times and the actual time is taken for all the activities that are carried out in the Shearcut processing line. All the times were standardized to Triangular (TRIA) times, which represents the minimum expected time, the most likely and the maximum expected time. These are the durations that were uploaded in the first model which represented the current Shearcut process. It is important to note that the current model was built with the average time frames obtained from the production records and skilled workers' knowledge including time studies. Included to the prototype model was also the resources involved in executing the process.

Table 1, shows Shearcut operating elements, both value-adding and non-value adding but necessary activities. Storage and picking are some of the non-value adding but are necessary to get the job done, they, however, take considerable long processing time. The prolonged times are due to factors outside the Shearcut department but can be controlled.

Table 1. Shearcut input operating elements- Current process.

Task	Resource	Service Time (mins) TRIA
Inspect coil	Overhead crane operator	(2, 2.5,5)
Receive coil	Coil logistics supervisor	(4, 5, 12)
Complete NCR	Crane operator	(1, 1.8, 2.3)
Storage	-	(120, 240,300)
Process Sales Order	Planner	(3, 7, 11)
Process picking slip	Supervisor	(2, 3, 5)
Pick coil	Picker	(20, 45, 120)
Set Machine according to the job card	Machine Operator	(5, 7, 19)
Process Full Coil	Machine	(13, 25, 45)
Process partial coil	Machine	(13, 25, 45)
Receive finished goods into finish goods warehouse	Dispatch clerk	(13, 25, 45)

Discrete event simulation was used to create the Shearcut process. Coils are delivered to the Shearcut process truck arrival station at a rate of 49 minutes (Random Exponential), a probability distribution found in Arena. The coils are routed for inspection. Normally 95% of the coils are found to be in good condition and are released to pre-storage. The inspector completes a non-conformance report (NCR) on coils found to be of poor quality (5%). The supervisor further inspects coils with NCR, and usually, 70% of these coils are approved by the supervisor for release to pre-storage. 30% of the NCR coils are returned to suppliers as defects. A process sales order is generated as per customer requirements. The sales order indicates if the coil is sold as a unit or if it needs some processing. Shop floor workers pick the sales order, the coil and go on to record if the coil is sold as a unit or not. Normally 70% of the coils are sold as a unit with 30% processed as per machine job card issued by the sales office. Of the 30% processed coils, only 605 coils get full processing into sheets and 40% coils are partially processed. Processed coils are then recorded and released to the finished goods warehouse. The partially processed coils are sent to the pre-storage. The researchers used the basic, advanced process and advanced transfer modules found in the Arena software. The Shearcut process model was animated and it was run for a replication length of 6 hours per day for 20 days, giving 7200 minutes. This was the estimated time the Shearcut process operates in a month. Simulation results from the current model gave an output of 99. Bottlenecks were identified in the storage area, coil picking time, slow overhead crane and time taken by the warehousing clerk. An Arena flowchart for the current model is shown in Appendix 1.

In the improved Shearcut process model, the following durations were reduced: storage, pick coil and receiving finished goods into the warehouse, as shown in Table 2. The research team proposed a new warehouse layout and suggested that the company purchases a new and faster overhead crane. 5S a tool and technique to properly arrange the warehouse was also introduced. This approach reduced the time taken in the storage and the picking uptime. Furthermore, on receiving finished goods there was an opportunity to reduce the time by introducing the barcoding system which can capture the coil transfer to a different warehouse by scanning the finished goods serial numbers. The process would take the clerk a constant 5 minutes instead of the current times (6, 12 and 25 minutes). The output from the improved model was 120 which gave an increase of 21.

Table 2. Shearcut input operating elements – Improved process.

Task	Resource	Service Time TRIA (mins)
Inspect coil	Overhead crane operator	(2, 2.5,5)
Receive coil	Coil logistics supervisor	(4, 5, 12)
Complete NCR	Crane operator	(1, 1.8, 2.3)
Storage	-	(60, 120,150)
Process Sales Order	Planner	(3, 7, 11)
Process picking slip	Supervisor	(2, 3, 5)
Pick coil	Picker	(10, 22.5, 60)
Set Machine according to the job card	Machine Operator	(5, 7, 18)
Process Full Coil	Machine	(13, 25, 45)
Process partial coil	Machine	(13, 25, 45)
Receive finished goods into finish goods warehouse	Dispatch clerk	(13, 25, 45)

Figure 3, shows a comparison of how the resources were seized in the two models. It can be seen from the results that in the improved model resources were seized for longer periods compared to the initial model, hence the output of the improved model is 120 an increase of 21 from an output of 99 in the current model. The increment shows that the improved process has more value-adding to the system.

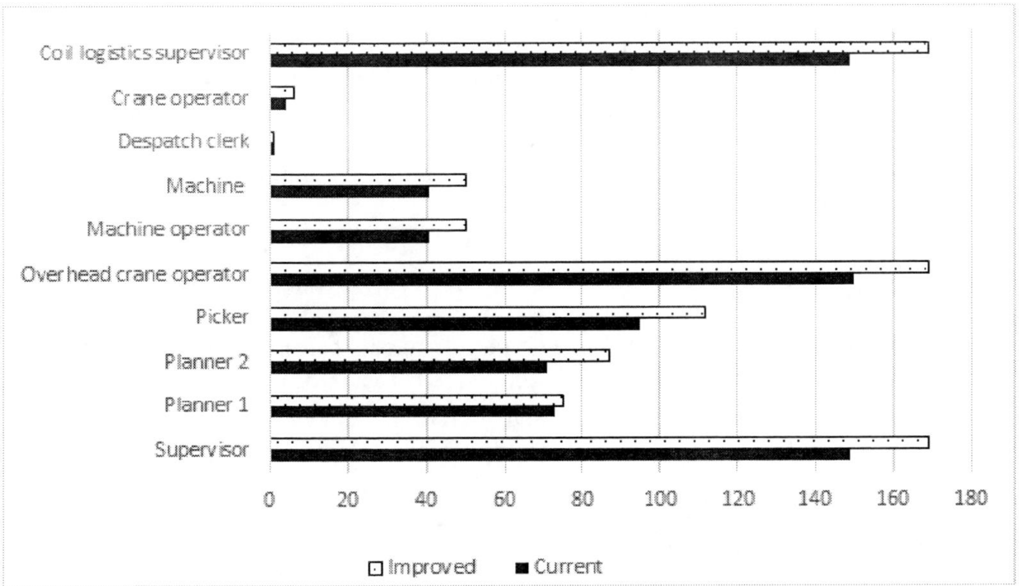

Fig. 3. Comparison of Process Value Adding (Seized Times).

Table 3 illustrates the counts of entities exiting the system. The table shows both current and improved, the figures reflect an increase except for a record of coils returned to the supplier.

Table 3. Count of entities existing in the system.

Count	Current Model	Improved Model
Record coils returned to the supplier	1.0000	0.0000
Record coils sold as a unit	94.00	112.00
Record processed coils	1.0000	1.0000
Record scrapped coil	3.0000	7.0000

5 Recommendations and future work

This research recommends that all activities that led to the improvement in the Shearcut process be considered in order to run the department efficiently and effectively. The department should use the model to track bottlenecks and their effect on the overall business. Just as reflected with the storage and picking process. Although the model and simulation practice is mostly applied for training purpose it is a good tool to use to analyse the system thus recommended for use in feasibility studies and decision analysis.

Future work will focus on connecting the simulation model with aspects of demand forecasting and human behaviour in Shearcut process. It is planned to lengthen the model with the possibility to attach explanations to processes and resources. Also, the simulation will be extended with addressing the uncertainty of the number of coils arriving at coil logistics on a daily basis.

6 Conclusion

This paper provided a basic knowledge of the Shearcut process flow. The use of Arena software to model and simulate the process made it easy to be able to manipulate what would be impossible, too expensive, or too impractical to perform on the system which it portrays. However, what the presented model does not simplify is data gathering. To recreate a realistic scenario in a simulation, it is still necessary to find out the values and numbers that are used by the simulation. For example, to map the Shearcut process flow, the sub-process within it that is the production process, the machinery runtime, duration, raw materials and all resource activities have to be gathered.

References

1. T. Abeya, N. Mulugeta, Modelling and Performance Analysis of Manufacturing Systems in Footwear Industry, Sci. Technol. Arts Res. J. **3(3)**, 132-141 (2014)
2. H. Xiaofeng, R. An, Modeling and simulation of manufacturing systems in unstable environment. London, UK, Int. J. Prod. Res. **55(3)**, 845-857 (2011)
3. P. Jondeau, M. Vonderembse, T. Ragu-Nathan, Exploring work system practices for time-based manufacturers: their impact on competitive capabilities, J. Oper. Manage. **18**, 509-529 (2000)
4. W. Kelton, R. Sadowski, N. Zupick, *Simulation with Arena,* 6th ed. (McGraw-Hill Education, New York, 2015)
5. M. Altinkilinc, *Simulation-based layout planning of a production plant*, in Proceedings of the 2004 Winter Simulation Conference (2004)
6. C. D. S. Battista, F. Giordano, R. Iannone, M. Schiraldi, *Manufacturing systems modelling and simulation software design: A reference model*, in Annals and Proceedings of DAAAM International (2011)
7. R. El-Khalil, Simulation analysis for managing and improving productivity: A case study of an automotive company, J. Manuf. Technol. Manag. **26(1)**, 36-56 (2015)
8. F. Hosseinpour, H. Hajihosseini, *Importance of simulation in manufacturing*, Int. J. Econ. Mang. Eng. **3(3)**, 229-232 (2009)
9. C. Owen, A. Greasley, Modelling people©behaviour using discrete-event-simulation: a review, Int. J. Oper. Prod. Manag. **38(5)**, 1228-1244 (2018)
10. W. Neumann, P. Medbo, Simulating operator learning during production ramp-up in parallel vs serial flow production, Int. J. Prod. Res. **55(3)**, 845-857 (2017)
11. F. M. Kasie, G. Bright, A. Walker, *Decision support systems in manufacturing: a survey and future trends*, J. Model. Manag. **12(3)**, 432-454 (2017)
12. M. Gopalakrishnan, A. Skoogh, *Machine criticality based maintenance prioritization: Identifying productivity improvement potential*, Int. J. Product. Perform. Manag. **67(4)**, 654-672 (2018)

Appendix 1: Shearcut Process model

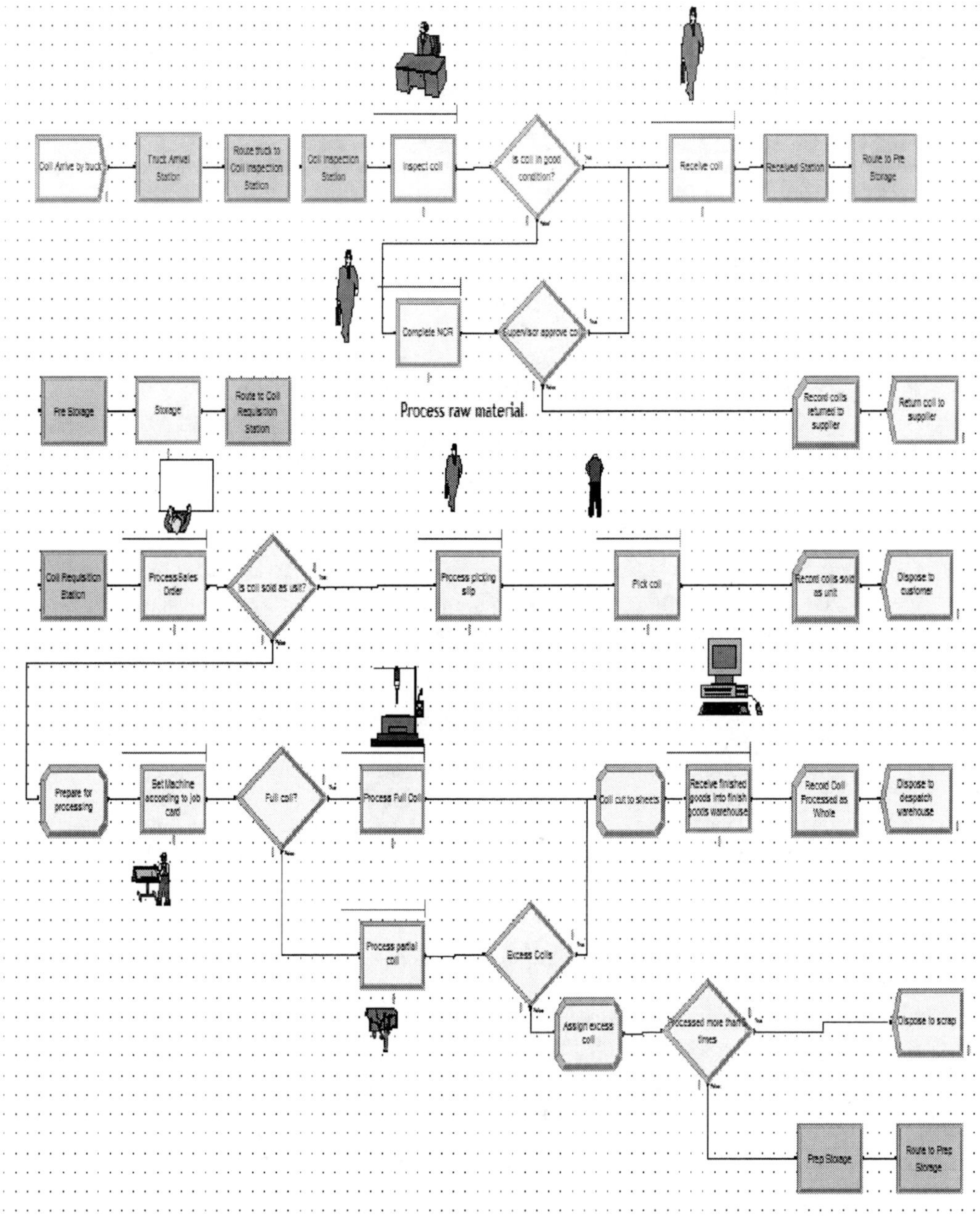

Productivity Improvement in a Vegetable Canning Manufacturing Facility

Thabiso Malatji[1], and *Goodwell* Muyengwa[1*]

[1]EDP University of Johannesburg, Department of Mechanical and Industrial Engineering Technology, Corner Siemert and Beit Streets, Doornfontein, Johannesburg

Abstract. This paper investigates current productivity levels of baked beans in a fast manufacturing consumer goods (FMCG) company. The market demand for baked beans on average has increased by 14% year on year over the past two to three years. This growth was unexpected and was unplanned for, hence equipment was utilized to maximum capacity, at times ignoring maintenance issues. The outcome of this approach was a major concern of unplanned stoppages on the production line. The canning process has manual activities such as soaking and sorting. Blanching is semi-automatic while filling and seaming are fully automated. The filling station was identified as the bottleneck station due to its slow speed (145 cans/minute) as compared to the seamer (200 cans/minute). The major objective of this study was to evaluate how the productivity of the canning process was achieved. Efforts were made to increase the output of soaking, sorting and blanching. This led to the reduced cycle time of the filler and the elimination of sources of contaminations. Industrial engineering tools such as autonomous maintenance, total productive maintenance, total quality management and some of the 20 keys were used to improve the plant's production output. This paper contributes to the theory of productivity improvement and to industry practitioners it highlights challenges faced when improving productivity.

Keywords: Automation, bottleneck, cycle time, productivity and total quality management

Introduction

In today's business environment, manufacturing organisations face challenges such as meeting delivery targets, producing quality products, creating shareholder value and improving productivity [1]. Literature suggests that some companies have successfully addressed some of these problems through the implementation of the following tools and techniques: total quality management (TQM), total productive maintenance (TPM), just in time (JIT), Kaizen, 5S, 20 keys to workplace improvement, Lean and Lean Six Sigma, [1]; [2]. Improving productivity positively impacts on revenue and profits, enhances competitiveness and maintains market share. Components that influences productivity include employees, efficient use of the equipment and standardized processes [3].

* Corresponding author: gmuyengwa@uj.ac.za

This paper analyses how a fast-moving consumer goods (FMCG) company improved its productivity. This study focuses largely on dry small white bean for baked beans manufacturing process. 80% of baked beans produced in South Africa are used in the canning industry. Canned beans are normally made ready by hydration in the water earlier before being canned in a brine of tomato sauce [4]. However, most canned beans manufacturing is largely manual. These manual processes are causes of delays on the line, with every slight stoppage affecting productivity.

The studied company will be known as Company DW, to safeguard its confidentiality. DW is the largest diversified food manufacturing company in South Africa and other African countries. The company's products cover a wide range of canning and bottled food. In the financial year of 2014, the company recorded revenue of R3.6 billion and a trading profit of R1 billion from all its operations. South Africa accounts for 85 per cent of DW group profits. The Company DW currently employs around 4800 workers throughout its South African operations.

DW has been facing some challenges in improving its productivity mainly due to a lack of adaptability to culture change in the past years. It has tried many times to implement tools to improve productivity without much success. However, the company made a new approach to improving its productivity by hiring and setting up a continuous improvement department. The department was manned mainly by Industrial Engineers who were tasked to improve productivity. The company has implemented tools like TPM, 20 Keys, TQM, and mission directed work teams.

When researchers joined this company it was realized that there was no maintenance system followed on the canning process line. Software to plan and control maintenance for all equipment in the manufacturing plants was available but it was not being used effectively. However this company was partially using a system like Pragma, and part of the 20 keys namely keys: 3 (improvement team activities); 6 (manufacturing value analysis- methods improvement); 11 (quality assurance system) 9 (maintaining equipment); 17 (efficiency control) and 19 (conserving energy and materials). This paper evaluates how Company DW implemented these tools and to what extent did these tools improve productivity.

This paper has the following objectives: to evaluate how productivity improvement was carried out on a bean canning process line. To automate and reduce cycle times on the soaking, blanching, sorting and filling stations and to eliminate the source of contaminations.

This paper answers the following research questions: To what extent does the current production practices affect productivity? What are the constraints to productivity improvement on the bean canning line? What are the current maintenance practices on the bean canning line? How did DW make use of TQM, TPM and 20 keys in improving the bean canning line?

1 Literature review

1.1 Dry Bean Value Chain

South Africa produces three types of beans, namely Red Speckled, Small White and Large White Kidney [5]. The Small White beans are used for canning. Figure 1, shows the market value chain of dry beans. Dry beans are sold to the market either as dry beans or processed canned beans. The branded canned beans are sold through well-established chain stores such as Pick'n Pay, Spar and Shoprite. The value chain diagram shows that there is potential for exports of canned beans. The potential for Company DW to expand its market share locally and venture into exports was the motivation of this study. Export earnings improve the exchange rate of the Rand.

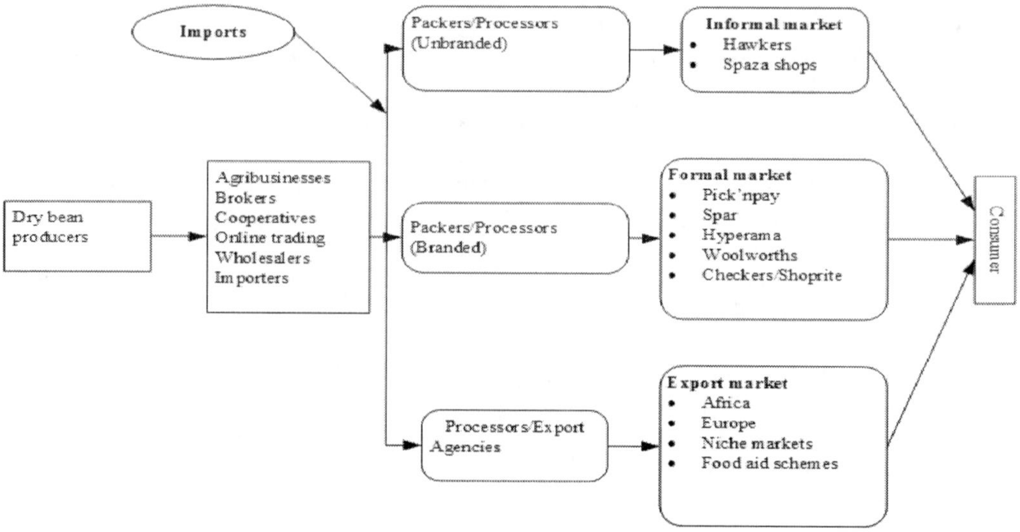

Figure 1. The market value chain of dry beans [5]

The Dry Bean Producers Organisation, [5] have indicated that bean consumption is a good source of plant proteins and beans have less salt, fat and with no cholesterol. The composition of cooked dry beans is shown in Figure 2.

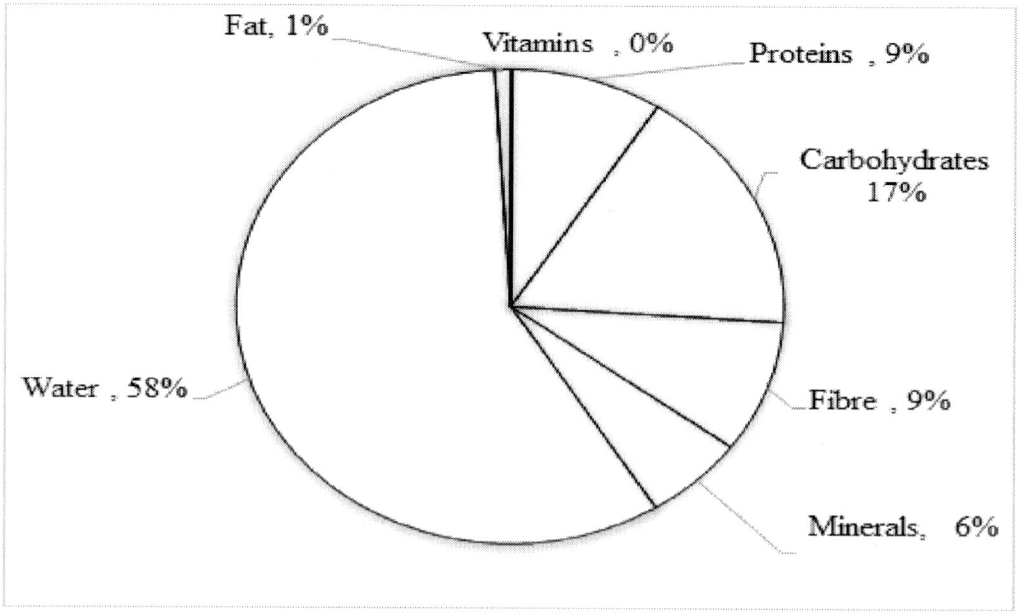

Figure 2. Composition of Cooked Dry Beans

Figure 3, shows the bean canning flow process. Targeted processes for improvement were soaking, sorting, blanching and the filling station. The filling station was identified to be a bottleneck station and the study sought to reduce the filling cycle times.

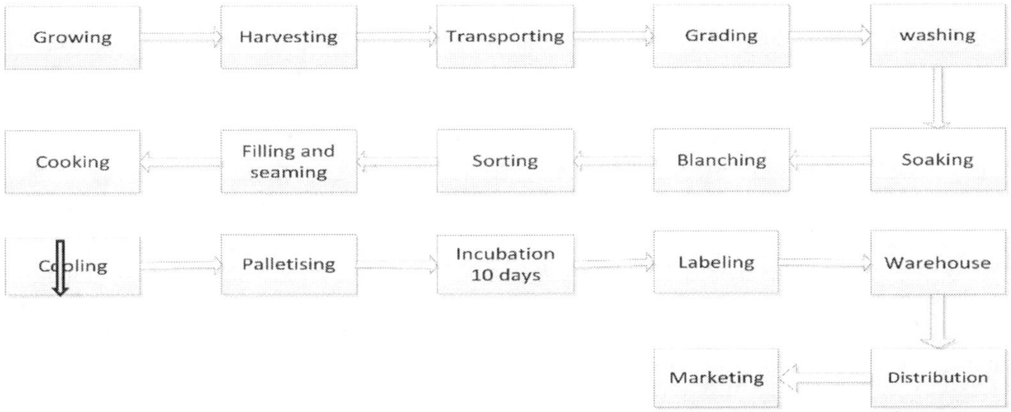

Figure 3. Bean canning flow process

Figure 4, shows that bean production increased drastically as from 2013 to 2015. This has been attributed to the demand by consumers.

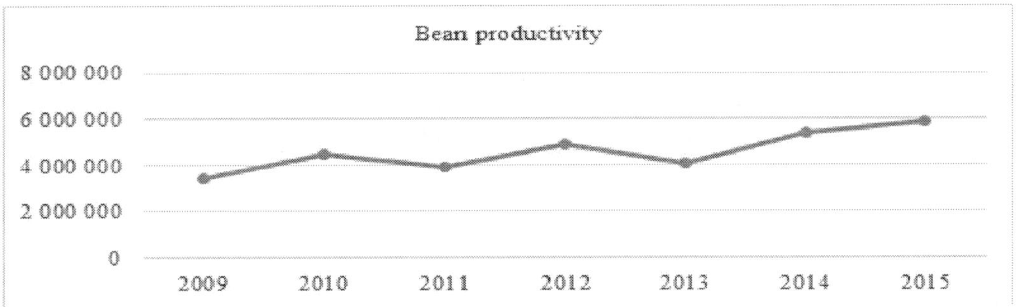

Figure 4. Bean productivity in the past seven years, [5]

Figure 5, shows an increasing gross value contribution of dry beans from the year 2005 to 2014.

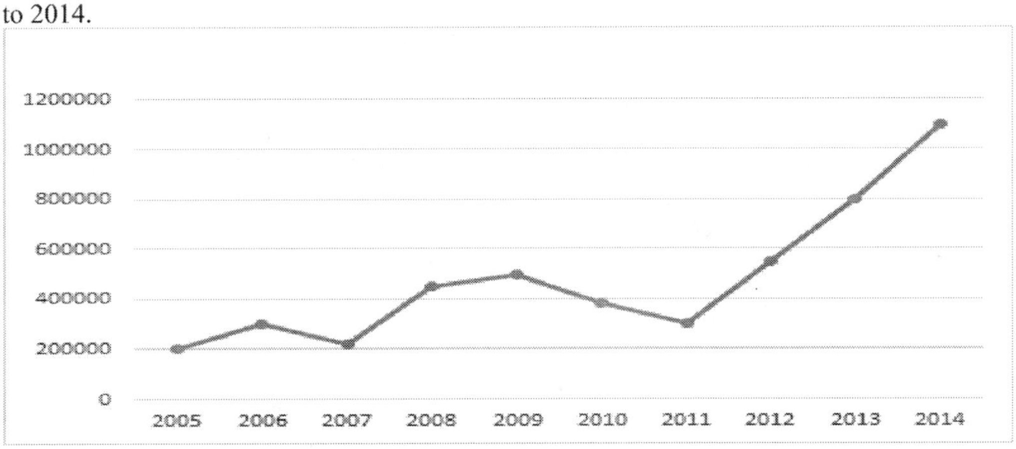

Figure 5. Gross Value of Production for Dry Beans, [5]

1.2 Productivity

Deming [6], described productivity as, "a ratio between output and input". Drucker [7], defined productivity as, "a balance between all factors of production that will give the maximum output with the smallest effort". Three productivity factors that are used when analyzing how productive a manufacturing entity is are: partial factor productivity which considers a single input in the ratio such as output/labour, output/machine, output/energy or output/capital [7]; multi-factor productivity uses more than a single factor, for example, it may consider labour and materials or at times capital [7]; and total factor productivity combines the effects of all resources used in the production to come up with an output, [7]. Productivity can be improved by reducing wastage of input resources: labour, material, machine, time, space and capital. Productivity can be improved by tools and techniques such as TQM, TPM, 20 keys, value analysis and operations research. Netland [8], highlighted 5 rules of productivity improvement and these are:

- "Deliver value for the customer,
- Get processes under control,
- Sync processes as a system,
- Shorten throughput times and
- Continuously improve".

Drucker [7], summarized the importance of productivity as an influence to the generation of wealth through higher sales due to lower cost per unit and this results in lower prices thereby improving profits for the organization. Workers can be paid more, thus improving their standard of living and productivity can be used as a vehicle to reduce poverty and unemployment. Higher productivity enhances shareholder value and improves the country's export capacity thereby generating more foreign currency.

1.3 Total Quality Management

Gunasekaran et al. [9] defined TQM as, "a management philosophy and set of techniques, procedures, involving total system approach to quality". TQM is a comprehensive method used by competitive companies to attain and maintain organisational excellence [10], and fulfilling the ever-changing demands of the customer. TQM implementation requires top management commitment, availability of resources and education and training of the workforce. This was supported by Deming [6] who presented 14 points for management to follow when implementing TQM. A brief summary of Deming's 14 points are: management must adopt a new philosophy and have a desire to improve quality of products and service; build quality into the product and avoid inspections; stop awarding business based on the price tag; improve productivity and decrease costs; train workers at the job; develop good leadership; create a conducive environment without fear; departments must work together and provide methods on how to achieve zero defects and meeting set targets. Figure 6 shows TQM implementation factors, [9], [10], [6]. This paper evaluates how TQM implementation helped productivity improvement in DW.

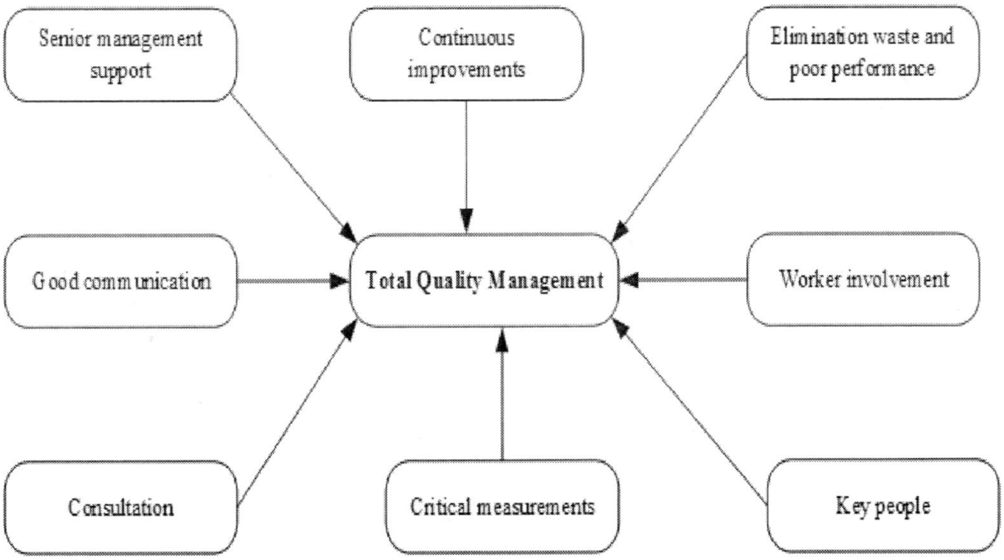

Figure 6. Total Quality Management Implementation Aspects [9], [6]

1.4 Total Productive Maintenance

Eti et al., [11], defined TPM as, "a maintenance philosophy that mitigates organisational failure". Fredriksson and Larsson [12] stated that "TPM aims at improving the efficiency and availability of equipment through the use of teamwork, zero breakdowns, zero defects and zero accidents". Rhyne [13], suggested that "TPM is the synergy between maintenance and production functions in a company aimed at improving product quality, reducing production costs, reducing waste, increases equipment availability and enhances maintenance". Nakajima, [14]; Ahuja and Khamba [3] presented 8 pillars that guides TPM implementation and these are, "autonomous maintenance, focused improvement, planned maintenance, quality maintenance, education and training, safety health and environment, office TPM and development management. Jain et al, [15] identified that TPM makes use of tools and techniques such as 5S, poka-yoke, team-based problem solving, statistical process control brainstorming, 5M, cause and effect diagrams, bottleneck analysis, Pareto analysis, reduction in waste, and simulation as tools to address TPM problems. This paper will evaluate how Company DW made use of the above tools and techniques in improving its bean canning productivity.

1.5 20 Keys to Workplace Improvement

Kobayashi [16], presented a book entitled "20 Keys to Workplace Improvement". This book is used to promote factory revolution as a total package to create synergy among the various departments in a company. The 20 keys are a methodology of implementing a practical program of revolutions in factories (PRORF), aimed at improving production. Some of the keys that are important for this study include "key 3: Improvement team activities; key 5: Quick changeover technology; key 6: Manufacturing value analysis (methods improvement); key 9: Maintaining equipment; key 11: Quality assurance system and key14: Empowering workers to make improvements". This paper will investigate how some of these keys were used by DW in improving its bean canning productivity.

2 Methodology

This study was carried out through a case study approach [17] and [18], where both qualitative and quantitative information was gathered to evaluate how Company DW improved its canned bean production. Mouton [19], stated that "Qualitative research is a correct approach which includes interviews to find information about the industry covered". Face to face interviews were conducted with senior managers, plant managers, supervisors, quality control officers and canned bean process operators. Quantitative data was gathered through close-ended questions [18], that sought to understand to what extent has DW benefited from its canned bean improvement efforts. Both qualitative and quantitative data was gathered through open-ended and close-ended questions that incorporated TQM, TPM and 20 keys' key performance indicators. The study took place from January 2015 to October 2015, but data collected and analysed was from 2012 to 2015. The questionnaire had 20 questions that sought information on the employee's understanding of productivity and implementation of TQM, TPM and 20 Keys of workplace improvement. The data were analysed through graphing techniques.

3 Research Results

A total of 32 questionnaires were distributed and on 28 usable responses were received by the researchers. The following sections present the findings of this study.

3.1 Productivity

Figure 7 summarizes the overall understanding of productivity improvement tools and benefits from the system. The overall response from all employee asked in an interview showed that DW staff understands the system. Data from interviews carried out showed that employees in the canning section had a better understanding of productivity after the company had adopted TQM, TPM and 20 keys as productivity improvement tools.

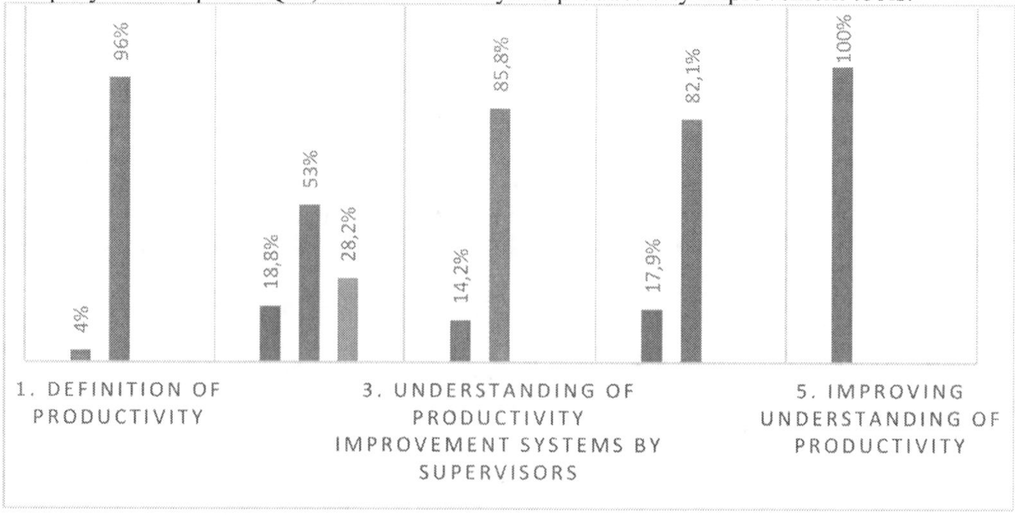

Figure 7. Employees understanding of productivity

Figure 8, shows the challenges that were pointed out by staff in the canning department. The major concern was the filling and seaming stations. The filling station was considered slow, hence it was labelled as the bottleneck station. The filling station had a cycle time of

145 cans/minute which was slow as compared to the seamer which was running at 200 cans/minute. Line preparation was also a cause of concern.

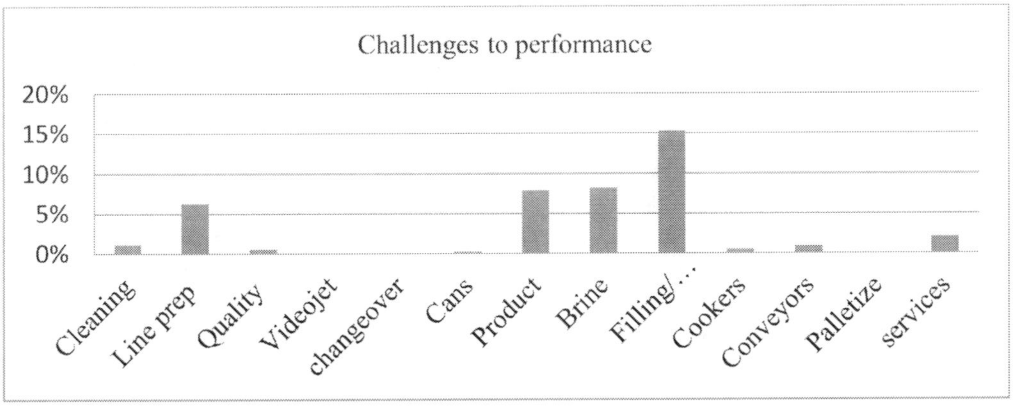

Figure 8. Challenges faced in the canning section

3.2 Total Quality Management Implementation

Senior managers of Company DW understood that TQM is a journey to excellence which cannot be achieved overnight. Their commitment to TQM implementation was witnessed by the recruitment of industrial engineers and the setting-up of a Continuous Improvement department that worked with the production personnel. Resources for training were made available, but all the training was done in-house with the industrial engineers acting as the resource personnel. Most of the production personnel were trained in the seven basic quality tools: Pareto analysis, histogram, cause and effect diagram, check sheet, scatter diagram, control charts and flow chart. The most common tools that workers were using were the histogram and the check sheet. A few of the workers understood the Pareto analysis. The continuous improvement team also used key 11 which focusses on the quality assurance system. Production operators were trained on quality issues and researchers witnessed some inspections that they were now carrying out unlike in the past. There was a reduction in defects.

3.3 Total Productive Maintenance Implementation

Maintenance personnel had a planned maintenance system that was not effectively used. The team worked on breakdown calls and attended to major breakdowns on weekends to gain overtime. The company had a committee that led to the TPM implementation. The senior production manager was in charge of that team and it included TPM Coordinators that worked together with the continuous improvement team. Maintenance strategies, policies and procedures were formulated and adopted. Autonomous maintenance was taught to employees and it followed the 7 steps of Nakajima [14]. However, during the initial phase of training employees demanded extra pay for extra duties. The intervention of top management solved the problem. Workers on the canned bean production line were now responsible for cleaning and inspection of the line. Breakdowns and time to repair were reduced as shown in figure 9. There was a noticeable improvement in Overall Equipment Effectiveness (OEE). Before TPM implementation OEE was around 53%. OEE is calculated from Availability (A) x Product Efficiency (E) x Quality rate (Q), Jain et al., (2014). Therefore OEE = A*E*Q. After TPM implementation the OEE = 0.89*0.9*0.9 = 72%. The mean time to repair (MTTR) has improved as shown in figure 9. There was a noticeable improvement in safety and cleanliness on the canning process line.

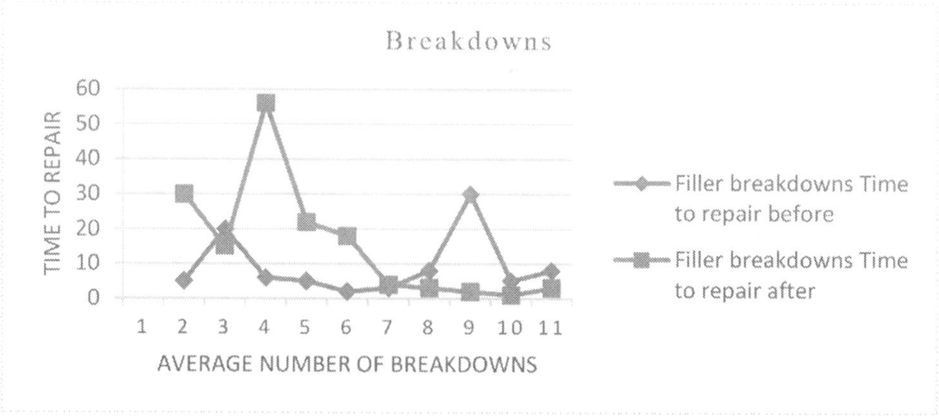

Figure 9. Time to Repair breakdowns

3.4 Automation

The company invested in new equipment, the new Lyco and Tegra machines which replaced the manual sorting and soaking. It used to take 6 hours for soaking beans before preparing for the filling. The Lyco machine takes 1hour and 30minutes to soak and release to filling station, this system improved the cycle time. The Tegra sorter was set by colour and size configuration of the bean, using pneumatics to remove all defects from the batch. New capital equipment improved productivity. A scan track was also introduced just before the cooker, to assure the quality of the product in the cans, checking if the can is over or underfilled. This instrument improved quality.

4 Discussion and Conclusions

The implementation of TQM and TPM is an ongoing process. The company has done well on the canning production line. The investment of new equipment and their efforts in implementing TQM and TPM has yielded some positive results. The researchers observed that workers were involved and communication had improved. Senior management support was clear and this gave workers confidence. The continuous improvement team developed standard operating procedures (SOPs) and they managed to eliminate non-value adding activities. TQM and TPM brought in both tangible and intangible benefits. Tangible benefits were a reduction in defects, reduced stoppages, and improved set-up times. Intangible benefits were enhanced worker morale, a cleaner environment and the general confidence of employees. Employees had a higher level of job satisfaction through their recognized involvement and contribution of new ideas.

This paper concludes that TQM, TPM and 20 keys are tools that when implemented properly can improve a company's production. However only one company was evaluated, hence these results cannot be generalized.

References

1. L.W. Hooi, T.Y. Leong, Total productive maintenance and manufacturing performance improvement, *Journal of Quality in Maintenance Engineering* **23(1)**, 2-21 (2017)
2. M. Gopalakrishnan, A. Skoogh, Machine criticality based maintenance prioritization: Identifying productivity improvement potential. *International Journal of Productivity and Performance Management* **67(4)**, 654-672 (2018)
3. I.P.S. Ahuja, J.S. Khamba, Total productive maintenance: literature review and directions, *International Journal of Quality and Reliability Management* **15(3)**, 241-756 (2008)
4. N.P. Mahalik, A.N. Nambiar, Trends in food packaging and manufacturing, *Trends in Food Science & Technology* **21(3)**,117-128 (2010)
5. *South Africa Depart of Agriculture, Forestry and Fisheries* (2015), http:www.nda.agric.za
6. W.E. Deming, *Quality, Productivity and Competitive Position,* Massachusetts Institute of Technology, Boston, MA (1982)
7. P. Drucker, The new productivity challenge, *Harvard Business Review* **69(6)**, 69-79 (1991)
8. T. Netland, *Five rules of productivity improvement* (2017), http://better-operations .com/2017/03/06/productivity-improvement-five-rules/
9. A. Gunasekaran, S.K. Goyal, T. Martikainen, P. Yli-Olli, Total quality management: a new perspective for improving quality and productivity, *International Journal of Quality and Reliability Management* **15(8/9)**, 947-968 (1998)
10. J.S. Oakland, *Total Quality Management: The route to improving performance*, Butterworth-Heinemann, Oxford-UK (1998)
11. M.C. Eti, S.O.T. Ogaji, and S.D. Probert, Implementing total productive maintenance in Nigerian manufacturing industries, *Applied Energy* **79**, 385-401 (2004)
12. G. Fredriksson, H. Larson, *An analysis of maintenance strategies and development of a model for strategy formulation*, Master Thesis, Chalmers University of Technology, Sweden (2012)
13. D.M. Rhyne, Total plant performance advantages through total productive maintenance, *Conference proceedings. APICS*, Birmingham, 683-692 (1990)
14. S. Nakajima, TPM Development Programme: Implementing Total Productive Maintenance, *Productivity Press,* Cambridge, MA (1989)
15. A. Jain, R. Bhatti, H. Singh, Total productive maintenance (TPM): a proposed model for Indian SMEs, *International Journal of Mechanical and Production Engineering Research and Development* **4(1)**, 1-22 (2014)
16. I. Kobayashi, *20 Keys to Workplace Improvement*, Productivity Press, Portland, Oregon (1994)
17. R. Yin, *Case Study Research: deesign and methods.* 4th ed. s.l.:Thousand OAKS: Sage (2009)
18. J. Creswell, V.L.P. Clark, *Designing and Conducting Mixed Methods Research.* 2nd ed. London: Sage (2011)
19. J. Mouton, *How to succeed in your master's and doctoral studies: A South African guide and resource book*, Van Schaik, Cape Town (2012)

Tension between Productivity and Respect for People in Construction

Lesiba George Mollo[1*], *Fidelis* Emuze[1], and *Nicholus* Sishuba[1]

[1]Central University of Technology, Bloemfontein, South Africa

Abstract. Productivity in the construction industry is declining in real-time. The decline in productivity is a source of worry for practitioners and researchers. The purpose of this paper is to ascertain major factors influencing productivity in relation to the notion of respects for people (RFP) in construction. The reviewed literature influences the semi-structured questionnaire used to survey construction professionals in Johannesburg, South Africa. The results reaffirm the tension productivity increment and the enhancement of RfP as both ideas appear to be moving in opposite directions on a typical construction site. It was discovered that respect for workers on a construction site is a major concern. The paper argues that ethical reasoning affects productivity. Therefore, an appropriate management system is required to improve the workers©perception of productivity and RfP working on construction sites.

Keywords: Construction, Productivity, Respect, Working Conditions

1 Introduction

The economist, contractors, and organized labour argued that to remain competitive in the industry, one needs to produce more for each money spend on projects and that every worker at a job site must contribute to improving productivity [1]. According to Abdel-Wahab and Vogl [2], the productivity of the construction industry is a key driver of the economic growth in any country. In construction, productivity is influenced by people, although the use of technology and machinery have moderating effects on specific projects [3]. In fact, Crawford and Vogl [4] state that construction productivity does not move in tandem with technological change, not with factor replacement, where cost and equipment may be replaced for labour.

In brief, low productivity is a source of anxiety for stakeholders in the construction sector [5] because it is declining in real-time for several decades [6]. The decline of productivity is a source of worry for professionals and researchers worldwide and the phenomenon is increasing unemployment rate in developing country like South Africa [7]. There are numerous factors contributing to the decline of productivity in the construction industry. For

* Corresponding author: lmollo@cut.ac.za

example, in South Africa, productivity has been worsening due to labour unrest, leading to a negative impact on the cost and quality of the product as well as the livelihood and moral of the workers [7]. The industrial factors causing productivity to decline are connected to behaviours towards people working in the construction industry.

Respect for people (RFP) is described as a method designed to create organizational culture and climate in which improvements to the work method and procedures are being made every day, by every single member of the organizations in every area of the organization within the workplace [8](47). The concept of RfP in the industry relates to the improvements of working conditions and that they are judged purely in relation to their contribution to efficiency and profitability rather than in term of moral imperatives or fairness of the organizations [9]. Therefore, the aim of this study was to ascertain major factors influencing productivity in relation to the notion of respects for people (RFP) in construction.

2 Productivity in the construction industry

To understand the term productivity, production function, in general, should be understood. The term production is defined as a network of processes and operations used in the industry [10]. Process in the industry represents a flow of material in time and space, resulting in the transformation from raw material to the semi-processed component to finished product. Operation in the industry represents the work performed to accomplish this transformation, the interaction and flow of equipment and operators in time and space [10]. Secondly, stakeholders need to understand the factors affecting productivity 'ask why productivity is declining?" [2].

According to Li and Liu [6], the term productivity has been described as a technical concept which refers to a ratio of the input to real output as a measure of the efficiency of projects. The ratio of the input in the construction industry includes labour, materials, equipment, energy, and capital, and while, the output includes; the quantity, and labour productivity of the construction projects [11]. Productivity in the construction industry refers to making use of production resources, operators that do not waste imports, for example, increasing growth rates while decreasing the use of resources [3]. According to Arditi and Mochtar [11] productivity is not only influenced by labour, but also by other factors such as materials, equipment, construction methods, and site management. However, the impact of labour productivity is the main factor in the industry. For example, the Department of Labour in South Africa reported that in 2013 the industry lost about R6.7 billion ($527 166 787.00), due to the participation of workers in wages, bonus, and other compensation strikes or protest [7].

The productivity in the sector is measured by contractors, project consultants and the clients. For example, labour productivity is measured by contractors in the bidding stage of the project and it is monitoring the daily activities at a job site. The total productivity is used by the project consultants for specific programme planning and by the clients for conceptual cost and period, estimating on individual projects [11]. The best way to comprehend productivity improvement in the construction industry is to understand the construction procedures as a visual complete system. For example, to define the management practices of the projects (i.e. scheduling, planning, data collection, job analysis, and control), material, timelines of the projects (i.e. proper procurement, scheduling, and site layout), and labour effectiveness of the projects (motivation, job safety, environmental factors, and physical limitations) [1].

3 The impact of working conditions on construction sites

According to Abrey and Smallwood [12], poor working conditions in the construction industry are part of the problems causing poor quality of work, which lead to the decline of productivity and overall performance at the job site. In the construction industry, working conditions are linked directly to construction productivity and workers' performance on-site projects [13]. There are numerous factors causing poor working conditions in the construction industry. These factors include noise, irritant or sensitising materials, dust, fumes and gases, and other hazardous materials such as asbestos [12]. These factors affect workers negatively, and often management fails to address them, which end up resulting in poor working conditions at the job site [14]. The outcomes of poor working conditions do not only reduce productivity but also raise questions about respect for safety and safe practice at job sites [1]

4 Research Methodology

Several authors have investigated the impact of productivity in the industry [1-3, 5, 7, 11]. The authors flagged a range of causal factors in their publications. The causal factors were conceptualised with the notion of RfP to produce a semi-structured survey questionnaire for this study. For example, three principle productivity factors include, site management, working conditions and construction workers' morale and satisfaction.

An expedited literature review discovered factors affecting the productivity of the construction industry. The identified factors were discussed with the construction practitioners working on project sites in Johannesburg, a city in South Africa. The research design of this study adopted a quantitative research approach as explained by Creswell [15]. For a collection of the data, survey research of 20 questionnaires was distributed among construction professionals made up of a client, project consultants, and a contractor. However, only 17 responses were received, resulting in 85%. The questionnaire consisted of questions relating to the demographics of the respondents, open-ended questions, and five-point Likert scale type questions. The five-point Likert scale questions were ranking major factors influencing productivity and respect for people in construction and the ranking factors were designed according to a scale between 1 and 5 [15]. The scale was represented as: 1 = strongly disagree (SD), 2 = disagree (D), 3 = neutral (N), 4 = agree (A), and 5 = strongly agree (SA). The results in the form of the mean score (MS) were used to rank the factors. Most responses were from contractors at 82% (14 out of 17), project consultants at 12% (2 out of 17), and clients at 6% (1 out of 17). The gender of the respondents of this study shows that 52.9% were male and 47.1% were female. In terms of years of experience in the construction industry, 41% of the respondents have 0 > 5 years, 35% have 5 > 10 years, 18% have 10 > 15 years, 0% have 15 > 20 years, and 6% have 20 > years of experience.

5 Results, Analysis and Interpretation

Table 1 indicates the ranking of nine factors causing poor productivity on construction sites. The site management is the principal factor of this listed nine factors, this is because these factors are all addressing the impact of site management on construction sites. The ranking of this factor is in terms of percentage responses to a scale of 1 = strongly disagree (SD) to 5 = strongly agree (SA), and the MS ranking between a minimum value of 1.00 and maximum value of 5. 00 [15]. The MS ranking in representing a minimum MS > 2.00 and a maximum MS 5.00. It is discovered that the highest-ranked factor causing poor productivity in the site management of the projects is in MS 4.24, and there are two factors having the same MS 4.24, namely poor management style and unrealistic deadline. It is notable that poor management style and unrealistic deadline have the same MS 4.24, but their scale ranking was differentiated with the standard deviation rule. For example, both factors scored 0 in the scale 1 and the statistical results start to differ from scale 3 to 5 in scale 3, poor management style > 5.00 and unrealistic deadline > 11.00, and in scale 5, poor management style > 29.00 and unrealistic deadline > 35.00. It is not surprising that these two factors ranked the highest, as it is explained that most of the small, and medium-sized construction business do not undertake detailed site activity planning because of a lack of skilled people and finance [16].

The lowest-ranked factor (9th) is at MS 2.94 namely; accommodation of the workers. The 3rd ranked factors at MS 4.00 is the designed construction method. The training and skills development factor ranked 4th at MS 3.88, the management of material supply factor ranked 5th at MS 3.76, the availability of resources factor ranked 6th at MS 3.41, the distance and location of site factor ranked 7th at MS 3.06, and the language barrier factor ranked 8th at MS 3.00. It is very important for management or supervisors of the projects to address this site management factor to improve productivity since these factors affect the job site of the project. This statement is supported by Valverde-Gascueña et al., [16] that it is widely proven that the most important factors affecting poor productivity in the construction industry can be influenced and improved through jobsite management effort.

Table 1. The site management

Factors affecting productivity	**Response (%)** SD.......SA					**MS**	**Rank**
	1	**2**	**3**	**4**	**5**		
Poor management style	0.0	0.0	5.9	64.7	29.4	4.24	1
Unrealistic deadline	0.0	0.0	11.8	52.9	35.3	4.24	2
Designed construction methods	0.0	0.0	23.5	52.9	23.5	4.00	3
Training and Skill development	0.0	0.0	23.5	64.7	11.8	3.88	4
Management of material supply	5.9	0.0	29.4	41.2	23.5	3.76	5
Availability of resources	5.9	6.0	35.3	47.1	5.9	3.41	6
Distance and location of sites	5.9	12.0	58.8	17.6	5.9	3.06	7
Language barriers	11.8	24.0	17.6	47.1	0.0	3.00	8
Accommodation of the workers	0.0	29.0	47.1	23.5	0.0	2.94	9

Table 2 indicates the ranking of the five factors causing poor productivity on construction sites. Working conditions are the principal factor of the listed five factors, as explained in the literature that poor working conditions in construction are part of the problems causing poor quality of work, which lead to the decline of productivity and overall performance at the job site [12]. The statistical ranking of the factors in Table 2 highlights a minimum MS > 3.00 and a maximum MS 5.00. The analysed survey responses show that the highest (1st) ranked factor is lack of supervision at MS 4.06. The 2nd ranked factor is poor safety condition at MS 3.71. The 3rd ranked factor is poor housekeeping, and the 4th ranked factor is a hostile work environment at MS 3.59. The lowest (5th) ranked factor is workers fatigues at MS 3.47. This principle factor of working condition is extremely significant to improve the productivity and respect of the workers on construction sites. According to Lee et al. [17], working conditions have a substantial influence on the workers' quality of life, and workers spend more than a half of their working hours at a project site. Therefore, the working conditions influence the life of the workers, this might be the reason why the respondents did not rate the scale of 1 (SD) in all the five factors.

Table 2. Working conditions

Factors affecting productivity	Response (%) SD.............................SA					MS	Rank
	1	2	3	4	5		
Lack of supervision	0.0	0.0	23.5	47.1	29.4	4.06	1
Poor safety conditions	0.0	5.9	23.5	64.7	5.9	3.71	2
Poor housekeeping	0.0	11.8	23.5	52.9	11.8	3.65	3
Hostile work environment	0.0	17.6	11.8	64.7	5.9	3.59	4
Workers fatigue	0.0	5.9	58.8	17.6	17.6	3.47	5

Table 3. Construction workers morale and satisfaction

Factors affecting productivity	Response (%) SD....................................SA					MS	Rank
	1	2	3	4	5		
Industrial strikes or protest	0.0	5.9	11.8	47.1	35.3	4,.12	1
Racism	0.0	5.9	23.5	47.1	23.5	3.88	2
Workers absence	0.0	0.0	35.3	52.9	11.8	3.76	3
Gender equality	0.0	5.9	41.2	29.4	23.5	3.71	4
Xenophobia or cultural	0.0	11.8	35.3	29.4	23.5	3.65	5
Staff turnover (change of jobs)	6.0	11.8	11.8	64.7	5.9	3.53	6
Disciplinary procedures	6.0	17.6	5.9	70.6	0.0	3.41	7

Table 3 indicates the ranking of seven factors which influences construction workers morale and satisfaction negatively. The scale of the ranking was in terms of percentage responses to a scale of 1 (SD) to 5 (SA), and MS ranking between a minimum value of 1.00

and maximum value of 5. 00. These seven-construction workers morale and satisfaction factors could cause low productivity as explained in the literature [5, 7]. It is notable that the highest-ranked factor is at MS 4.12 and the lowest is in MS 3. 41. The highest-ranked factor is the industrial strikes or protests ranked at MS 4.12, the 2nd ranked factor is racism at MS 3.88, the 3rd ranked factor is workers' absence at MS 3.76. The 4th ranked factor is gender equality at MS 3.71, the 5th ranked factor is xenophobia or cultural tribalism at MS 3.65, the 6th ranked factor is staff turnover, and the 7th lowest-ranked factor is disciplinary procedures at MS 3.41. It is no surprise that industrial strikes or protest ranked 1st due to the statement issued by CIDB [7] that labour productivity in South African industry has been worsening due to labour unrest, leading to a negative impact on the cost and quality of the product as well as the livelihood and more of the workers. Furthermore, Thomas and Sudhakumar [5] states that labour strikes are a critical factor causing labour productivity to decline in the construction industry

6 Conclusions

The study explored 21 factors which are categorized into three principle productivity factors, the site management principle factor, working conditions principle factor, and construction workers' morale and satisfaction principle factor. Among the 21 factors explored, poor management style, unrealistic deadline industrial strikes or protest, and lack of supervision were identified as the most critical factors impacting productivity. Designed construction method, training and skill development, racism, worker's absence, management of material supply, and poor safety conditions were the other major factors identified in the survey. Based on the survey results, poor management style and unrealistic deadline (the site management principle factor) are the most ranked factors in MS 4.24. The second-highest ranked factor is industrial strikes or protest (construction workers morale and satisfaction principle factor) at MS 4.12. It can be concluded that these three factors influence RfP on one hand and productivity on the other. Also, they discredit the adopted management system in the South African construction industry. Therefore, these factors must be addressed to eradicate low productivity on construction sites. The research findings show the need to improve respect towards construction worker on construction sites. This resonates with the CIDB [7], who contends that productivity is a major issue in South Africa. This research has identified the three principal factors impacting productivity in the construction industry, and the findings will assist contractors in setting strategies to improve productivity. Therefore, it is recommended that the scope of this study should be extended to other cities in South Africa as it is limited to one city with little data. Also, an appropriate management system is required to improve the workers' perception of productivity and respect for themselves and others on a project site.

Reference

1. S.P. Dozzi, S.M. AbouRizk, Productivity in construction, Ontario, Canada: National Research Council Canada (1993)
2. M. Abdel-Wahab, B. Vogl, Trends of productivity growth in the construction industry across Europe, US and Japan, *Construction Management and Economics* **29**:635-644 (2011)
3. T. Snyman, J. Smallwood, Improving Productivity in the Business of Construction, *Procedia Engineering* **182**:651-657 (2017)
4. P. Crawford, B. Vogl, Measuring productivity in the construction industry, *Building Research & Information* **34**(3):208-219 (2006)

5. A.V. Thomas and J. Sudhakumar, Factors Influencing Construction Labour Productivity: An Indian Case Study, *Journal of Construction in Developing Countries* **19**(1):53-68 (2014)
6. Y. Li, C. Liu, Malmquist indices of total factor productivity changes in the Australian construction industry, *Construction Management and Economics* **28**(9):933-945 (2010)
7. CIDB, *Labour & Work Conditions in the South African Construction Industry: Status and Recommendations*, Pretoria, South Africa: Construction Industry Development Board (CIDB) (2015)
8. S. Korb, "Respect for People" and Lean Construction: Has the Boat Been? In C. A. Pasquire (Ed.), *In Proc. 24th Annual Conference of the International Group for Lean Construction*, Boston, MA, USA: International Group for Lean Construction, 43-52 (2016)
9. K. Ness, The discourse of 'Respect for People' in UK construction, Construction *Management and Economics* **28**(5):481-493 (2010)
10. S. Shingo, A Study of the Toyota Production System from an Industrial Engineering Viewpoint, (A. Dillon, Trans.) London and New York: CRC Press (2005)
11. D. Arditi, K. Mochtar, Trends in productivity improvement in the US construction industry, *Construction Management & Economics* **18**(1):15-27 (2000)
12. M. Abrey, J.J. Smallwood, The effects of unsatisfactory working conditions on productivity in the construction industry, *Procedia Engineering* **85**:3-9 (2014)
13. Loera, G. Espinosa, C. Enríquez, J. Rodriguez, Productivity in Construction and Industrial Maintenance, *Procedia Engineering*, **63**:947-955 (2013)
14. G. Robles, A. Stifi, J.L. Ponz-Tienda, S. Gentes, Labor Productivity in the Construction Industry Factors Influencing the Spanish Construction Labor Productivity, *International Journal of Civil and Environmental Engineering* **8**(10):1061-1070 (2014)
15. J.W. Creswell, *Research Design: Qualitative, Quantitative, & Mixed Methods Approaches* (4 ed.). California: SAGE Publications (2014)
16. N. Valverde-Gascueña, E. Navarro-Astor, J. Fuentes-del-Burgo, J.P. Ruiz-Fernandez, Factors that affect the productivity of construction projects in small and medium companies. In C. a. Egbu (Ed.), *Procs 27th Annual ARCOM Conference*, Bristol, UK: Association of Researchers in Construction Management 879-888 (2011)
17. B.P. Lee, The relationship between working condition factors and well-being, *Annals of Occupational and Environmental Medicine*, 26-34 (2014)

An Investigation of Mixed Reality Technology for Onsite Construction Assembly

Austin DaValle[1], and *Salman* Azhar[1*]

[1]McWhorter School of Building Science, Auburn University, Auburn, USA

Abstract. The construction industry often falls short of other industries in terms of innovation; overall productivity within the construction industry has remained nearly flat for fifty years. As such, the industry is frequently exploring new technologies with the potential to increase its work efficiency as well as productivity. Mixed Reality (MR), which allows for the blending of real and virtual worlds, is one such technology that has a capability to improve productivity. The aim of this research study is to test MR's potential as an onsite assembly tool in construction. The study more specifically determined if holographic BIM models, spatially anchored in 1:1 ratio over active construction sites, could provide trades' sufficient information to assemble and install their work without using paper plans. A controlled experiment was designed to test if the electrical and plumbing components of a mock-bathroom could be installed only with MR. A total of 5 sub-groups, each consisting of two participants, took part in this experiment and the time is taken by each sub-group (i.e. the MR group) to complete the assembly was recorded. This was then compared with the time taken by a similar number of sub-groups (i.e. the Control group) to complete the same assembly using paper plans only. The analysis indicates that on average the MR group took approximately 9% less time as compared to the Control group. Qualitative analysis via a post-exercise questionnaire found several technological limitations that the MR must overcome before it sees widespread implementation as a tool for guiding construction assembly. The post-exercise questionnaire also gathered participants' perceptions about MR potential in construction. This paper highlights the benefits and limitations of the MR technology in construction along with recommendations for improvement as well as future research.

Keywords: assembly, HoloLens, productivity, mixed reality, visualization

1 Introduction

The Construction industry is frequently subject to claims of inefficiency. Studies focusing on construction efficiency have documented 25 to 50 percent waste in coordinating labor and in managing, moving, and installing materials [1]. This might not come as a surprise to most in the field; in 2016 the World Economic Forum claimed that overall productivity in the Engineering and Construction (E&C) sector has remained nearly flat for 50 years [2]. In an industry that accounts for about 6% of global GDP, that seemingly stagnant pace

* Corresponding author: salman@auburn.edu

of innovation permeates further than the industry itself. Society as a whole could benefit economically, socially, and environmentally if the construction industry caught up to other industry sectors. Many studies in the last 10 years have focused on what the construction industry can do to pick up the pace [3, 4].

Building Information Modeling (BIM) is a glimmering exception to the traditionally bleak outlook on E&C innovation. The use of BIM in construction projects has increased significantly in recent years. According to research by McGraw-Hill Construction, the percentage of companies using BIM jumped from 17% in 2007, to 49% in 2009, to 71% in 2012 [5]. In 2018, that number is likely even higher. If this is, in fact, the case, the statement could be made that most construction companies develop and use some form of digital 3D models of their projects. If inefficiency stems from failing to make the best use of accessible resources, and a resource accessible to most AEC entities is BIM, it would be imprudent not to explore ways in which entities can achieve more from their BIM models. Mixed Reality (MR) technology has the potential to offer construction professionals more out of their BIM Models [6].

Mixed Reality (MR), as defined by Paul Milgram in 1994, is the merging of real and virtual worlds somewhere along the "Virtuality Continuum" (see Figure 1) [7]. It essentially allows for digital objects to exist and interact with real objects in real-time. Similar to basic computing in the 60s, MR has traditionally been reserved for entities holding both specialized equipment and personnel. However, recent advancements in this field, such as the Microsoft HoloLens, have simplified MR hardware to the point where almost anyone can take advantage; no specialized knowledge is necessary to perform most tasks. More so, applications such as SketchUp Viewer® and 3D Viewer® have made it exceptionally simple to transform BIM models into holograms [6]. With almost no additional effort, these holographic BIM models can be scaled, moved, and further manipulated to meet the user's needs. Models can even be placed in 1:1 ratios, allowing the user to walk through and view their holographic BIM models in the same way as a person walking through a constructed building. These features open the door to countless additional ways in which entities can further utilize their BIM models via MR, one of which is guiding construction assembly.

Numerous prior research studies support MR as a tool capable of aiding assembly. Richardson et al. [8] conducted a between-subjects experiment, comparing assembly effectiveness between traditional model-based instructions (MBI), the same MBI on a moveable tablet, and AR work instructions. He found that users completed the assembly in 33% less time while using the AR work instructions. Chryssolouris et al. [9] evaluated the use of AR assembly instructions in manufacturing and found that they contributed to reduced product development times and cost savings while simultaneously improving first-time quality and market response time. An experiment conducted by Chalhoub et al. [10] showed that MR can be effective for communicating design for electrical prefabrication.

Though MR has been proven useful for assembly, much of the existing research is theory-based and largely detached from the settings and scopes of work that would be experienced in real construction. The aim of this research study is to implement MR technology for construction assembly with two specific objectives, (1) to test MR's ability to communicate design details to installers for onsite assembly; and (2) to compare assembly efficiencies using MR and traditional paper plans. The research also investigated the technological limitations that MR needs to overcome in order to see its widespread adoption in the construction industry. This study is limited to the use of Microsoft (MS) HoloLens as an MR platform for construction components assembly. The following sections highlight the experiment setup, data analysis and its interpretation, followed by conclusions and recommendations for future research.

2 Mixed Reality (MR) Applications for Construction

2.1 Defining Mixed Reality

Figure 1 explains various forms of real and digital environments using a virtuality continuum developed by Milgram [7]. At one extreme, on the left, is the case in which nothing is known about the remote world being displayed. This describes the real world as it is seen with one's own eyes, absent any virtual computer-generated images. The other extreme, on the right, refers to a world that the user perceives as completely virtual. This is essentially a world in which the user is 100% immersed in a virtual environment. In between "Real Environment" and "Virtual Environment" are the three terms which the continuum was created to define: augmented virtuality, augmented reality, and mixed reality. Mixed Reality (MR), sometimes referred to as hybrid reality, is the merging of real and virtual worlds to produce new environments and visualizations where physical and digital objects co-exist and interact in real-time. Mixed reality takes place not only in the physical world or the virtual world, but is a mix of reality and virtual reality, encompassing both augmented reality and augmented virtuality via immersive technology [11].

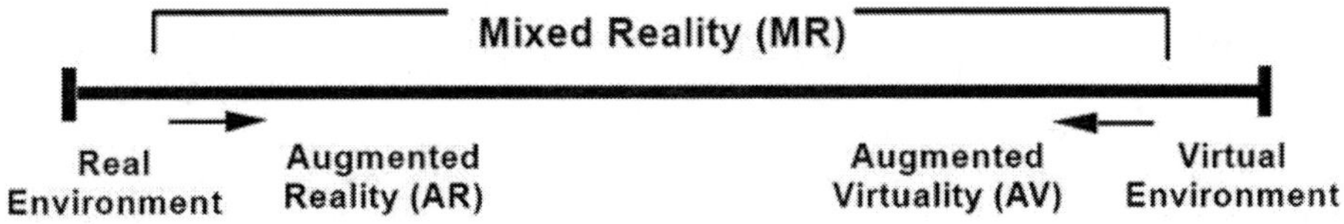

Fig. 1. Milgram's Virtuality Continuum [7]

Currently, not many companies use the term "mixed reality" to market their hardware; rather, they use the more specific term "augmented reality". The most well-known device that does market itself as MR is Microsoft HoloLens.

2.2 Microsoft HoloLens

The MS HoloLens is a self-contained head-mounted display, depicted below in Figure 2. Specialized components such as a HoloLens Processing Unit (HPU) and advanced sensors enable holographic computing. This enables HoloLens users to engage with digital content and interact with holograms in the world around them [12].

Advanced sensors within the HoloLens continuously capture data pertaining to the user's activity and the surrounding environment. They can see, map, and understand the physical places, spaces, and objects around the user. The device understands gestures and maps the world around the user, all in real-time. In addition, the HoloLens has a see-through holographic high-definition lens and an advanced optical projection system. These enable the HoloLens to generate multi-dimensional full-colour images with very low latency, allowing the user to see holograms in their own world. The headband is designed to distribute the weight around the crown of the user's head, saving the ears and nose from undue pressure. Though the HoloLens has more computing power than the average laptop, it is passively cooled without fans. Lack of wires and external cameras, as well as the lack of phone or PC connection requirements, allows the user to move freely [12].

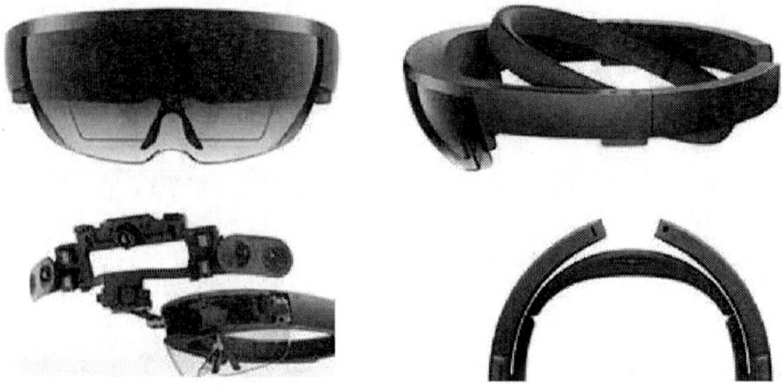

Fig. 2. Microsoft HoloLens [12]

2.3 Mixed Reality (MR) Applications in Design and Construction

MR technology has long been explored as a potential asset to the design and construction industries. In 2011, Dunston and Wang published a hierarchical taxonomy of AEC operations for MR applications. They found that MR-based technology is suitable for information-intensive tasks, which in the AEC industry, often deal with the information translation usually between a paper-based source and the work. In these tasks, MR can augment a human's ability to access information and documentation in the course of performing the work and enhance the individual's decision-making ability [13]. Table 1 outlines various applications of MR in the design and construction industries.

Table 1. MR Applications in Design and Construction

Application Area	Description/Example
Progress Monitoring	To overlay the as-planned building model of a structure over the actual as-built structure to determine the percent completion of the project.
Onsite Clash Detections	To allow trades to perform clash detections on the construction site itself by integrating holographic models with real objects.
Information Overlay	To superimpose useful information onto real objects in the surrounding environment or to add comments to their surrounding real environment.

Several designs and/or construction-related Apps are available in the Microsoft store to use with the HoloLens. Some of the most useful Apps are:

- SketchUp Viewer for HoloLens: SketchUp Viewer allows users to quickly and easily import a SketchUp model to the HoloLens for visualization as a hologram.
- ARchitect: ARchitect offers a sample home for a walkthrough. A unique feature in this app allows the user to see how the home looks in varying sun-lit conditions.
- BIM Holoview: BIM Holoview projects 3D Revit and Navisworks models into the physical world as holograms.
- HoloLive 3D: HoloLive 3D allows users to bring BIM models from native design software and place them in the real world. This app provides advanced measuring, scaling, and other tools that allow for a highly immersive experience.

3 Research Design and Methodology

A mixed-methods research design, consisting of quantitative and qualitative measures, was employed to carry out this research study. Figure 3 outlines the research methodology.

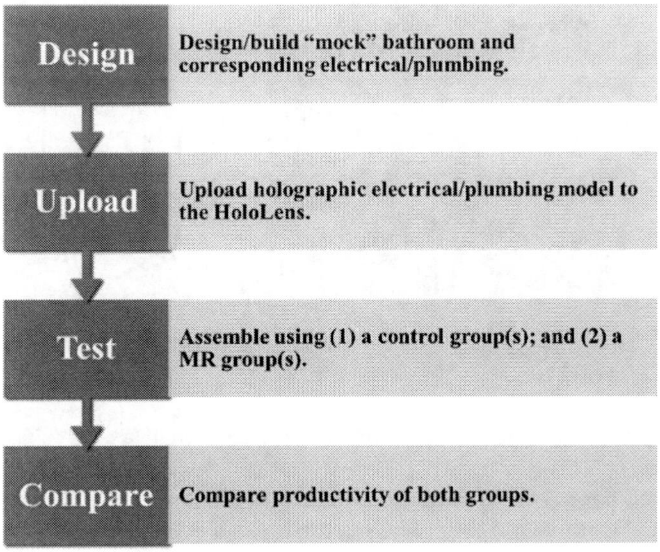

Fig. 3. Outline of Research Methodology

For quantitative data collection, a "between-groups" experimental design was employed through the creation of an exercise entitled "Electrical and Plumbing (E&P) Assembly Exercise". The E&P Assembly Exercise was created to determine the time taken by 2-member groups to install electrical and plumbing components into a mock-bathroom using "MR" and "Paper plans". The exercise required the installation of 85 components, most of which consisted of pre-cut PVC conduit and fittings. Participants were required to lay the plumbing and electrical components into their proper positions inside of a preassembled 5'x10' mock-bathroom. Each of the 85 components was labelled to guide the installation. Figure 4 shows the mock-bathroom as well as E&P assembly model.

The participants were divided into two main groups namely the "MR group" and the "Control group". Each group consisted of 2 persons. Participants of both groups were selected by convenience and were limited to willing student volunteers enrolled at Auburn University's McWhorter School of Building Science. There were a total of 5 MR sub-groups and 5 Control sub-groups. The MR sub-groups used the holographic model to install all components in place whereas the Control sub-groups used traditional paper plans. All sub-groups were filmed, monitored, and timed through their completion of the exercise. Additionally, participants were given a pre-exercise questionnaire to collect demographics and a post-exercise questionnaire (for MR group only) to collect qualitative data on their perceptions of the MR technology and/or HoloLens.

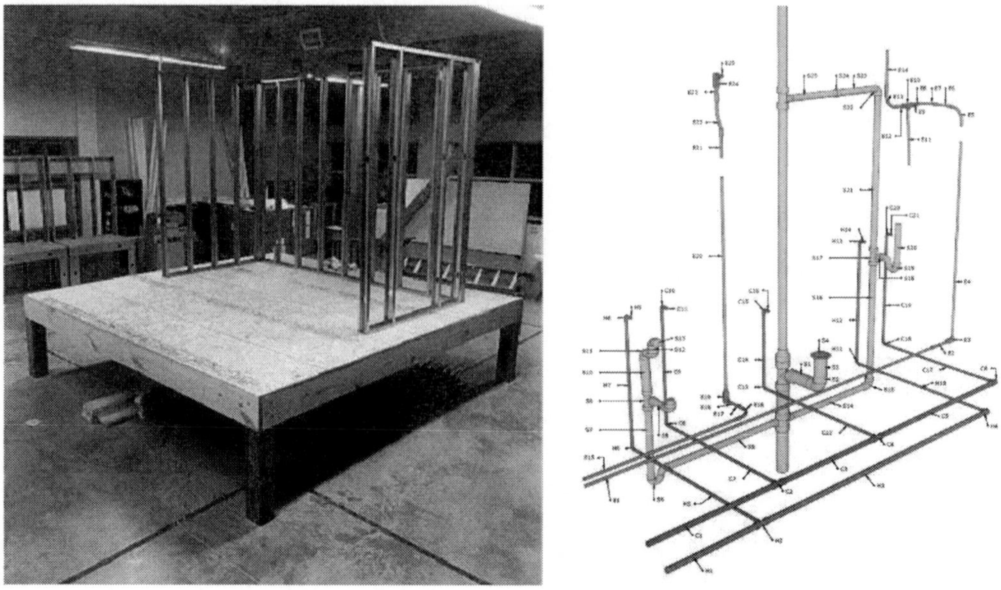

Fig. 4. Mock-bathroom and Electrical & Plumbing Assembly Model

As mentioned above, the quantitative data was gathered by measuring the sub-groups' completion times of the assembly. The exercise timer was turned on promptly at the start of each group and turned off directly upon completion when participants placed the last remaining piece into its appropriate position. This data was later used to compare the efficiency between the two groups. An additional timer, nicknamed the "discrepancy timer", was kept in addition to the primary timer. The purpose of this time was to measure any uncontrollable errors experienced by the participants. An example of a discrepancy would be if a participant found they were missing a piece required for assembly. Prior to beginning the activity, participants were instructed to promptly inform the instructor upon experiencing any uncontrollable error; in such cases, the discrepancy timer would then run from the moment the error was noted to the moment the error was resolved. Discrepancies were predicted to be much more common in the MR group, as pilot testers experienced problems such as the device turning off, the application closing, or the E&P model jumping out of place. These times were recorded in addition to the total time it took the groups to complete the exercise. Figure 5 shows an MR group completing the assembly.

Fig. 5. An MR Sub-group Completing the Electrical & Plumbing Assembly

4 Results and Discussion

4.1 Pre-Exercise Questionnaire

A pre-exercise questionnaire was given to all test sub-groups prior to commencing the exercise. A total of 6 questions were designed to collect demographic and relevant prior experience data from the participants. Table 2 shows the summarized information collected through this questionnaire. The results indicate that all sub-groups have more or less the same composition and possess very similar construction and/or E&P assembly experience. Hence it is reasonable to compare quantitative and qualitative data collected from all sub-groups.

Table 2. Pre-Exercise Questionnaire Results

Measure	Control Groups (n=10)	MR Groups (n=10)
Group composition	92% undergraduate students, 8% graduate students	100% undergraduate students
Gender	89% male, 11% female	92% male, 8% female
Age	18-24 years: 77%; 25-34 years: 23%	18-24 years: 100%
Prior construction experience	Internship: 65%; 1-2 years full-time: 15%; No: 20%	Internship: 70%; 1-2 years full-time: 30%
Prior E&P assembly experience	No: 78%; Some: 22%	No: 23%; Little: 46%; Some: 31%
Prior experience with HoloLens	No: 100%	No: 100%

4.2 Experimental Data

The E&P assembly completion times for all subgroups are reported in Table 3. The description of the recorded times is as follows:

T_1: Assembly time in minutes
T_2: Discrepancy time in minutes
T: Net time taken to complete the assembly (in minutes) = $T_1 - T_2$

Table 3. Assembly Completion Times

Sub-group #	Control Group (minutes)			MR Group (minutes)		
	T_1	T_2	T	T_1	T_2	T
1	18.52	0.00	18.52	20.44	0.00	20.44
2	21.53	0.00	21.53	22.26	2.46	19.40
3	19.36	0.00	19.36	22.24	0.00	22.24
4	31.35	0.00	31.35	21.15	0.51	20.24
5	25.05	1.58	23.47	27.36	7.34	20.02
Net Average Assembly Time			22.51			20.47

A comparison of the net average assembly time for both main groups indicates that the MR group took approximately 9% less time to complete the assembly as compared to the control group. The 9% improvement in productivity, though small, is significant because it shows that the MR technology has the potential to boost work efficiency and productivity of the construction trades. Due to the small data size, it was decided not to perform any inferential statistical tests on the collected data.

4.3 Post-Exercise Questionnaire

The purpose of the post-exercise questionnaire was to gauge the participant's perception of MR technology in construction. As such, it was only administered to the MR sub-groups. The results of the post-exercise questionnaire are summarized in Table 4.

Table 4. Post-Exercise Questionnaire Results

Measure	Response (n =10)
Effectiveness of HoloLens for MEP components assembly	- Extremely effective: 77% - Very Effective: 23%
Perception of whether the HoloLens or paper plans would be more effective if asked to complete the exercise again	- HoloLens: 100% - Paper plans: 0%
Any problems experienced	- The model moved out of position: 73% - The model was not bright enough: 27% - Application stopped/crashed: 27% - HoloLens physically uncomfortable: 9% - Other technical issues: 18%
The learning curve associated with using HoloLens	- No learning curve: 31% - Small learning curve: 62%

Based on the analysis of the post-exercise questionnaire, the following conclusions can be drawn:

1. MR in general, and HoloLens in particular, are found to be an effective tool for communicating design details to electrical and plumbing installers or other construction trades. Seventy-seven percent (77%) of participants found it to be "extremely effective" and the remaining 23% found it to be "very effective". No participants reported that the HoloLens was moderately or slightly effective, or not at all effective.
2. If asked to complete the same exercise over again, 100% of participants predicted they would be more effective using the MS HoloLens rather than paper plans.
3. Two-thirds of participants felt there was some degree of the learning curve associated with using the HoloLens, whereas the remaining one-third felt that no learning curve was required and the HoloLens was immediately effective in practice.

The following technological limitations of the HoloLens were recorded:

Spatial anchoring: Spatial anchoring refers to the HoloLens's ability to lock a hologram to a designated location in the real world. Seventy-three percent (73%) of participants reported that the model moved out of position. This makes the improvement of spatial anchoring technology one of the most prominent needs for the HoloLens. Without sufficient spatial anchoring, the Microsoft HoloLens loses the ability to depict assemblies in their accurate position to installers.

Model brightness: Approximately 27% of participants claimed that at some point or another, the model was not bright enough to see. In one instance, the discrepancy timer was even initiated due to the participants' inability to see the model. After reviewing the film of the groups who experienced problems with model brightness, it was found that all cases occurred on days that were exceptionally sunny, with bright light coming through the windows. As construction assembly predominantly takes place outdoors, the HoloLens needs to improve upon its ability to display holograms in direct sunlight.

Application reliability: The HoloLens turning off by itself or application crashing was reported by 27% of participants. Amongst the discrepancies, the timer was initiated twice because there was an error with the application and it had to be restarted. In these instances, the SketchUp model flipped upside down as the result of a glitch. As the HoloLens is new, and developers are still getting used to developing MR applications, this limitation is not surprising. But for implementation of MR into construction assembly tasks to occur on a large scale, these applications need to become more reliable.

5 Conclusions and Recommendations

This research demonstrates that MR technology can successfully communicate design details for construction assembly, specifically validating that the MS HoloLens is a tool capable of guiding electrical and plumbing component installation. Additionally, the elaborate nature of the Electrical and Plumbing Assembly exercise used in this research serves a strong proof of concept for construction assembly via MR. A 9% productivity gain is promising for a new technology that is still in its infancy. A number of technological improvements are required if MR is to see widespread adoption for assembly purposes. The most prominent need for improvement is spatial anchoring technology, as successful assembly would require the model to hold its position without jumping out of place. This is especially true in the realm of construction, where installation of components frequently requires accuracy to be within 1/16 of an inch from perfect. Other shortcomings the HoloLens must overcome before widespread adoption are occluded visuals in sun-lit conditions, as well as the inability to wear a hardhat with the HoloLens.

This study is a pilot test of MR technology and has several limitations which must be improved in future studies. One of these limitations is the small sample size, prohibiting inferential statistical testing from being carried out. One of the greatest advantages MR provides is its ability to display information at the exact spot it is required; in construction assembly, this equates to a reduction in time spent thinking about component layout, as the installer would automatically know the exact spot where the components are to be assembled. But in this research, the holes in the walls and subfloor, through which the components were installed, were pre-drilled for participants. This method took away the greatest advantage of the HoloLens, as the pre-drilled holes allowed the control groups to have a very good idea of the layout. In a scenario where the assemblers had to drill their own holes, the control groups using paper plans would not have this advantage, and they would have to spend additional time measuring out the intended layout. We predict this would work heavily in favour of the groups using MR. In addition, the 85-parts required to be assembled by the exercise were labelled in somewhat of sequential order. For example, C1, C2, C3, C4, and C5 all had to be installed in order. Although not all areas of the assembly were labelled in a sequential order that was straightforward, a better way to design the exercise would have been to label the parts completely non-sequentially. Similar to the pre-drilled hole bias, sequential part labelling took away one of the main advantages of MR for assembly.

For future research, the following measures are recommended: (1) Test MR technology against other forms of design visualization such as the 3D BIM models; (2) Expand groups' to non-construction students (i.e. novice users) as well as professionals to determine how each group is benefited from this technology; (3) Synchronize two or more HoloLenses so that all group members can see the exact same hologram; and (4) Try out more Apps to compare their effectiveness in relation to SketchUp App.

References

1. G. Tulacz, T. Armistead, Large corporations are attempting to meet the industry halfway on issues of staff shortages and risk, *Engineering News Record* (2007), Available at: https://www.enr.com/articles/29331-large-corporations-are-attempting-to-meet-the-industry-halfway-on-issues-of-staff-shortages-and-risk?v=preview [Accessed Dec. 18, 2017].
2. World Economic Forum, Shaping the future of construction (2016), Available at: https://www.weforum.org/projects/future-of-construction [Accessed Dec. 18, 2017]
3. A.A. Javed, W. Pan, L. Chen, W. Zhan, A systemic exploration of drivers for and constraints on construction productivity enhancement, *Built Environment Project and Asset Management* (2018)
4. E. Allmon, C.T. Haas, J.D. Borcherding, P.M. Goodrum, US construction labor productivity trends, 1970–1998, *Journal of construction engineering and management*, **126**(2):97-104 (2000)
5. Contractors Center Point, Use of BIM dramatically increases (2012), Available at: http://www.contractorscenterpoint.com/2012/11/use-of-bim-dramatically-increases.html [Accessed Dec. 18, 2017].
6. T. Blackmon, S. Azhar, Applications of augmented/mixed reality head mounted displays in the construction industry. *Proceedings of the 54th ASC Annual International Conference*, Minneapolis, MN, 18-21 (2018)
7. P. Milgram, K. Fumio, A Taxonomy of Mixed Reality Visual Displays. *IEICE Transactions on Information and Systems* (1994), Available at: http://citeseerx.ist.psu.edu/viewdoc/download?doi=10.1.1.102.4646&rep=rep1&type=pdf [Accessed Dec. 18, 2017].
8. T. Richardson, S. Gilbert, J. Holub, F. Thompson, A. MacAllister, R. Radkowski, E. Winer, Davies, P., and Terry, S., Fusing self-reported and sensor data from mixed reality training *I/ITSEC* (2017), Available at: http://lib.dr.iastate.edu/cgi/viewcontent.cgi?article=1178&context=me_conf [Accessed Dec. 18, 2017].
9. G. Chryssolouris, D. Mavrikios, N. Papakostas, D. Mourtzis, G. Michalos, K. Georgoulias, Digital manufacturing: history, perspectives, and outlook, *Proceedings of the Institution of Mechanical Engineers, Part B: Journal of Engineering Manufacture* **223**(5):451–462 (2009)
10. J. Chalhoub, S. Ayer, Mixed reality for electrical prefabrication tasks, *Computing in Civil Engineering 2017: Smart Safety, Sustainability, and Resilience* (2017)
11. B. Signer, T.J. Curtin, Tangible holograms: Towards mobile physical augmentation of virtual objects, Technical Report, WISE-2017-01 (2017)
12. Microsoft, Microsoft HoloLens (2018), Available at: https://www.microsoft.com/en-us/HoloLens. [Accessed on Feb. 17, 2018].
13. P. Dunston, X. Wang, A hierarchical taxonomy of AEC operations for mixed reality applications, *Journal of Information Technology in Construction* **16**:433-444 (2011)

Pavement Deterioration Rate and Maintenance Cost for Low-Volume Roads

Turki I. Al-Suleiman (Obaidat)[1], *Subhi M.* Bazlamit[1], *Mahmoud* Azzama[1], *Hesham S.* Ahmad[1*]
[1] Al-Zaytoonah University of Jordan, Department of Civil and Infrastructure Engineering, P.O. Box: 130, Amman 11733, Jordan

Abstract. Allocated budgets for maintenance of road networks are normally limited. Therefore, not all roads receive the required attention they deserve in a timely manner. These roads are left to deteriorate until the next maintenance round. The cost associated with delayed maintenance is significantly excessive. A Pavement Maintenance Management System (PMMS) can be a useful tool for evaluation, prioritization of Maintenance and Rehabilitation (M&R) projects, and determination of funding requirements and allocations. The pavement condition is normally indexed using a parameter called Pavement Condition Index (PCI) which represents an overall assessment of surface defects by type, severity and extent. Periodic collections of PCI over time for different sections within the roadway network provide an approach to monitor changes in pavement serviceability over time and can produce useful data to predict and evaluate required maintenance solutions and their associated cost. The researchers intend to use available data collected over the span of a year and a half on sections within the roadway network at the campus of Al-Zaytoonah University of Jordan (ZUJ) to study the relation between the maintenance cost and the pavement deterioration rate. This study may incorporate variables such as pavement age, traffic volumes, maintenance history and pavement condition assessment results. The available records of PCI will be analyzed and the findings will be clearly presented. The practical inclusion of the findings within the current PMMS used at the university will also be detailed.

Keywords: condition, deterioration, maintenance, pavements, serviceability

1 Introduction

The aim of PMMS is the achievement of better and smoother roads at a reasonable cost. According to Shahin and Walther [1] and Shahin [2], the maintenance at early stages of pavement deterioration proved to produce large saving before the start of the costly decline in pavement condition. Therefore, funding is normally allocated in the most efficient and

* Corresponding author: h.ahmad@zuj.edu.jo

economic manner to allow engineering pavement managers to employ an efficient decision-making process. Good pavement management systems require the collection of substantial amounts of road condition data over time. This can be used in the development of pavement deterioration models. The monitoring of pavement deterioration over time is the backbone of a pavement management system and is used to determine several fundamentals, including the rate of asset degradation at the project and network levels. Furthermore, it aids in the evaluation of remaining life and in the scheduling of future maintenance.

In this particular project, the pavement condition was evaluated using on a number of occasions where each section was evaluated for the surface defects including various types of flexible pavement failures such as cracking and other surface defects [3]. In addition, deterioration can lead to a reduction in ride quality as reported by some researchers [4]. Others have developed composite pavement condition indices based on pavement surface condition and ride quality [5]. In this project, the pavement condition was evaluated using the Pavement Condition Index (PCI) as developed by Shahin and Walther [1] and Shahin [2].

In the paved area of this study, traffic loading is not the leading contributor to pavement failures. Weather-related factors such as climate cycles of temperature and precipitation are the leading causes of distresses such as longitudinal and transverse cracking. Researchers have noted that pavement performance has shown that with the exception of longitudinal and wheel track cracking formation, the roughness of the road increases with additional precipitation [6]. Pavements experience thermal cracking due to compressive and tensile stress when the temperature fluctuates. Smith et al. [7] showed a dependence between temperature and pavement deterioration, where a rise in temperature leads to the development of rutting and propagation of cracking in the pavement. In some areas, thawing during the spring may result in deformation of pavement leading to fatigue and wheel path cracking [8]. In addition, some researchers suggest that snowstorms and floods can worsen road conditions by generating failure and cracking [9].

2 Literature Review

Some researchers have studied the relation between maintenance cost and pavement deterioration rate for roads.

George et al. [10] developed equations for predicting pavement deterioration. The authors employed over a 2-years period of historical information that includes structural information, traffic volume and pavement condition data. The studied areas (paved areas with asphalt surfacing) were classified into three groups including flexible pavements with no overlay, flexible pavements with one or more overlay(s), and composite pavements. In all the three equations developed for the three classifications, age of the pavement was found to be the most significant variable to predict road serviceability among other variables of traffic volume and weight, and the structural makeup of the pavement.

Shahin et al. [11] studied the economic effect of different M&R strategies. The different strategies were applied to pavement sections in a studied paved network. The results showed the economic effectiveness of asphalt overlay compared with other strategies. MicroPAVER pavement management system was used in this study to produce deterioration curves and work planning techniques for the different M&R strategies.

Tinni [12] has argued that the estimation of pavement maintenance costs for long periods of time mostly comes with inaccurate end results. His paper has demonstrated the inaccuracy of the used methodology in Australia. The research concluded that a way to reach a reasonable accuracy is to carry out a detailed historical long term cost study for different pavements, which is rarely to be applied. The researcher also concluded that with a time period of over 20 years, the total maintenance cost of concrete pavement is at least 19 times less than for flexible pavements with the same traffic volume.

Babashamsi et al. [13] have analyzed current methods used for Life-Cycle Cost Analysis (LCCA). LCCA is an economic analysis process used to evaluate the cost-efficiency of alternatives in order to obtain optimum pavement life-cycle costs. LCCA takes into consideration the total economic worth by analyzing the initial cost and discounted future cost including maintenance, use, reconstruction, rehabilitation, restoring, and resurfacing costs, over the life of the project segment. Another study on LCCA by Wang Z. and Wang H [14] aimed at developing LCCA model to evaluate the impact of pavement preservation on agency cost (M&R work) and Vehicle Operating Cost (VOC), and estimating the optimal time of pavement preservation treatment. The study used long-term data of the International Roughness Index (IRI), a parameter for evaluating the functional condition of the pavement. It was found that the optimal timing to apply preservation treatment depends on the type of treatment, the existing condition before the treatment (or pavement age), and the effect of treatment on pavement performance deterioration. The results also showed that the cost benefits in VOC are greater than the benefit in agency cost, while the optimal timing calculated based on VOC is always earlier than the optimal timing calculated based on agency cost.

Previous studies have investigated the relation between maintenance cost and pavement condition. However, this study concentrates on the relation between maintenance cost and pavement deterioration when the paved road subjected to low-volume vehicles, and the deterioration of pavement is caused mainly by the weather.

3 Objective and Scope

The aim of this research is to develop formulas that relate maintenance cost with pavement deterioration rate for low-volume roads. This formula will depend on data collection and analysis from the road network in Al-Zaytoonah University of Jordan (ZUJ). A Pavement Maintenance Management System (PMMS) for the road network in ZUJ was previously developed and presented in research papers [15].

This research incorporated the following stages:

- Developing a database inventory for the road network at ZUJ based on a Geographic Information System (GIS) map. This inventory includes the engineering properties for each section in the road network.
- Conducting the first-round evaluation to the pavement condition following the procedures that depend on calculating PCI for each road section developed by Shahin and Walther (1990), and by using PAVER system software developed by the U.S. Army Corps of Engineering.
- Based on the results of pavement condition evaluation, priorities of the areas that need Maintenance and Rehabilitation (M&R) were decided. After this, the required work of M&R was decided and the required quantities and budget were estimated.
- Conducting the second round of evaluation to the pavement condition and using PAVER system to estimate the reduction on PCI for each road section.
- Studying the relation between the maintenance cost and the pavement deterioration rate and developing calculation equations by conducting regression analysis.

4 Process

The first step in establishing a PMMS for the paved network in the area of the study was to prepare an inventory that organizes the paved areas for M&R management using the method presented by Shahin and Walther [1] and Shahin [2]. The paved network in ZUJ was divided into four branches. Only the results for one branch named Ring Road (RINGR) consisting of 46 sections will be used for the purpose of this paper. For practical objectives, sections were classified to identify areas with relatively consistent characteristics, such as dimensions, surface condition, traffic type and volume, and construction history. It should be noted that the pavement thickness and composition, the traffic type and volume for the different sections in the studied branch are relatively consistent.

The second step is to conduct a field inspection to evaluate the current condition of the different paved sections using Pavement Condition Index (PCI) method [1, 2].]This method uses a scale of 100 points to rate the condition of each road section that can be presented in seven pavement condition classifications as shown in Figure 1.

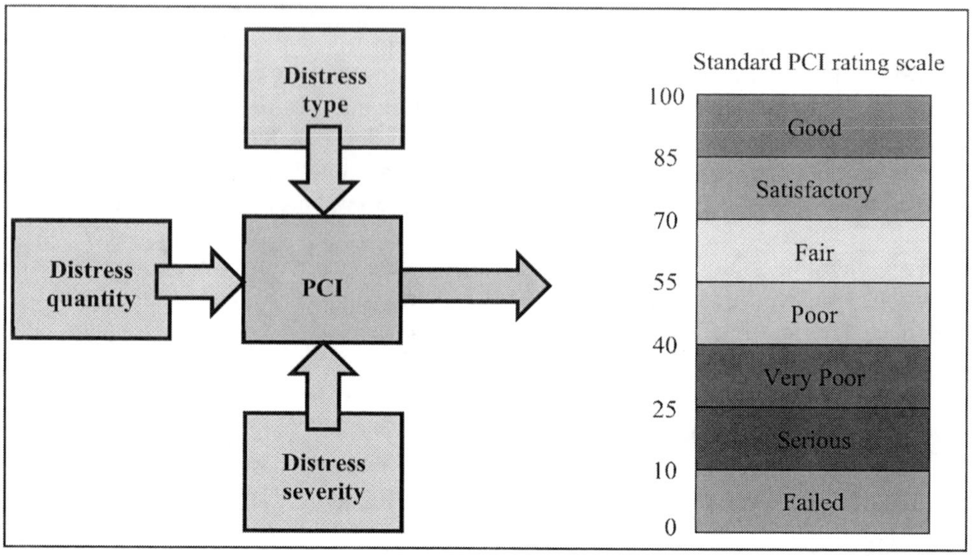

Fig. 1. Rating scale used for Pavement Condition Index (PCI) method (Source: Shahin (2005))

In this study, two cycles of field inspections were conducted with a time period of 1 year. Between the first cycle and the second, M&R project was implemented on some of the poor, very poor, serious and failed sections in ZUJ road network. The areas that need M&R were decided regarding the pavement condition evaluation, the location importance and the available budget. Hence, the number of PCI high rated sections has increased in 2018 compared with what was in 2017, while the number of low rated sections has decreased, as shown in Figure 2.

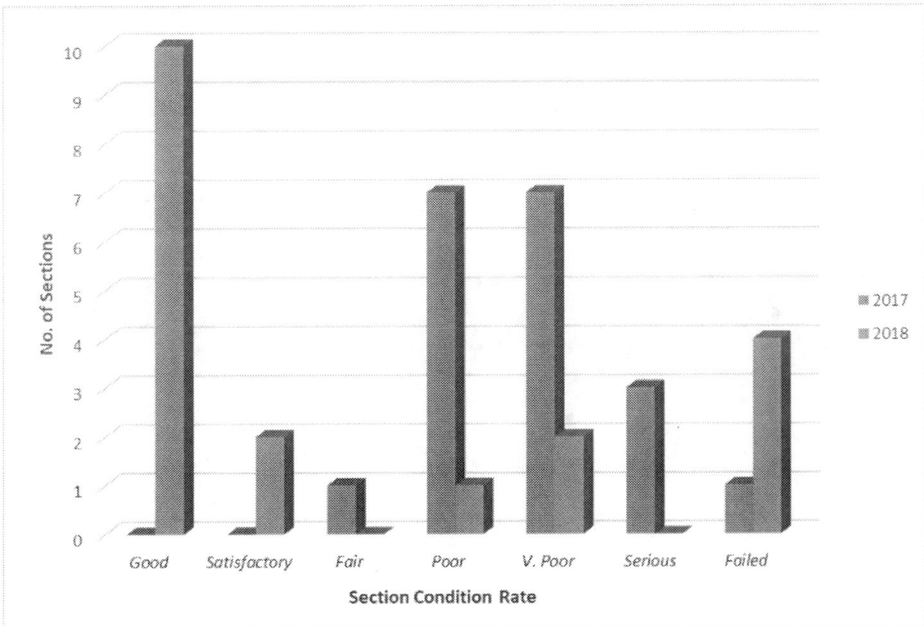

Fig. 2. Comparison of Pavement Condition between 2017 and 2018

The results of the field inspections and the calculations of PCI values for the two cycles of the years 2017 and 2018 were conducted by using Paver 7 software. Figure 3 shows the PCI results for the road section where no M&R works have executed, while Figure 4 shows the results for the maintained sections. The 100 points scale and the seven colour-coded layers for the pavement conditions were used in the two figures.

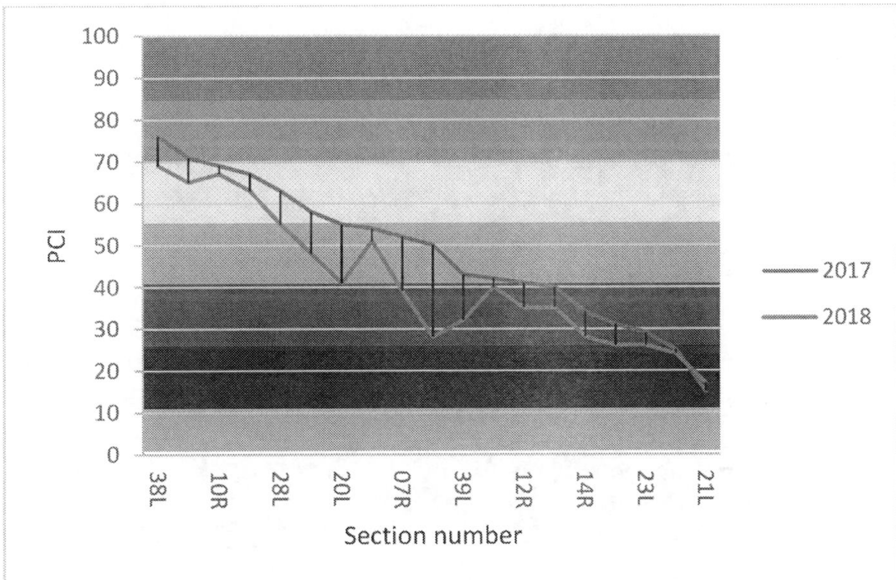

Fig. 3. PCI Results for Road Sections with no M&R Works

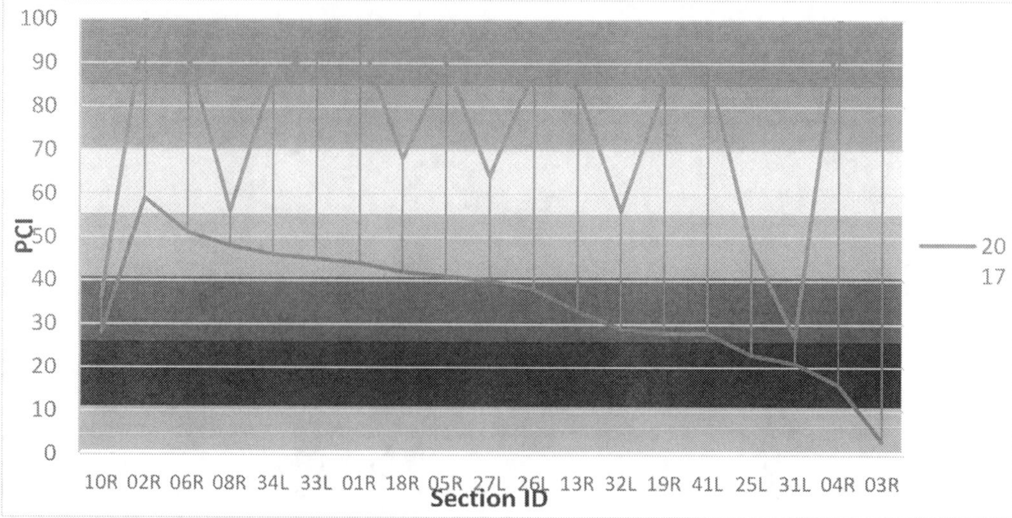

Fig. 4. PCI Results for Road Sections with M&R Works

5 Results

The aim of this study is to develop a relation between the maintenance cost and deterioration rate. To fulfil this aim, the paved areas subjected to maintenance and repair were classified into three groups regarding their condition evaluation prior to the M&R implementation. The three groups include Poor, very poor, and failed and serious pavement condition ratings to reflect the quantity, severity and type of distresses in the road sections prior to the M&R project implementation. The type of repairs used for the defected areas depended on the type and severity of each defect. Figure 4 represents examples of repair types may be used for certain conditions of pavement.

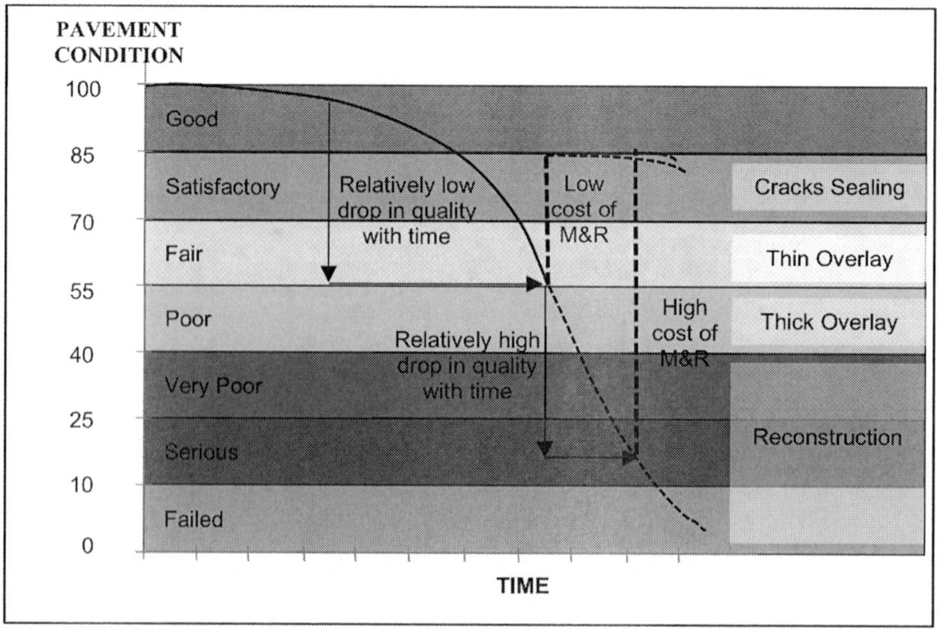

Fig. 5. Examples of repair types may be used with PCI evaluation

The sections subjected to M&R applications were used to study the relation between improvement or change in the pavement condition (ΔPCI) and maintenance cost. The relations were studied for the whole ratings as well as for the classified groups of pavement, as shown in Figure 6.

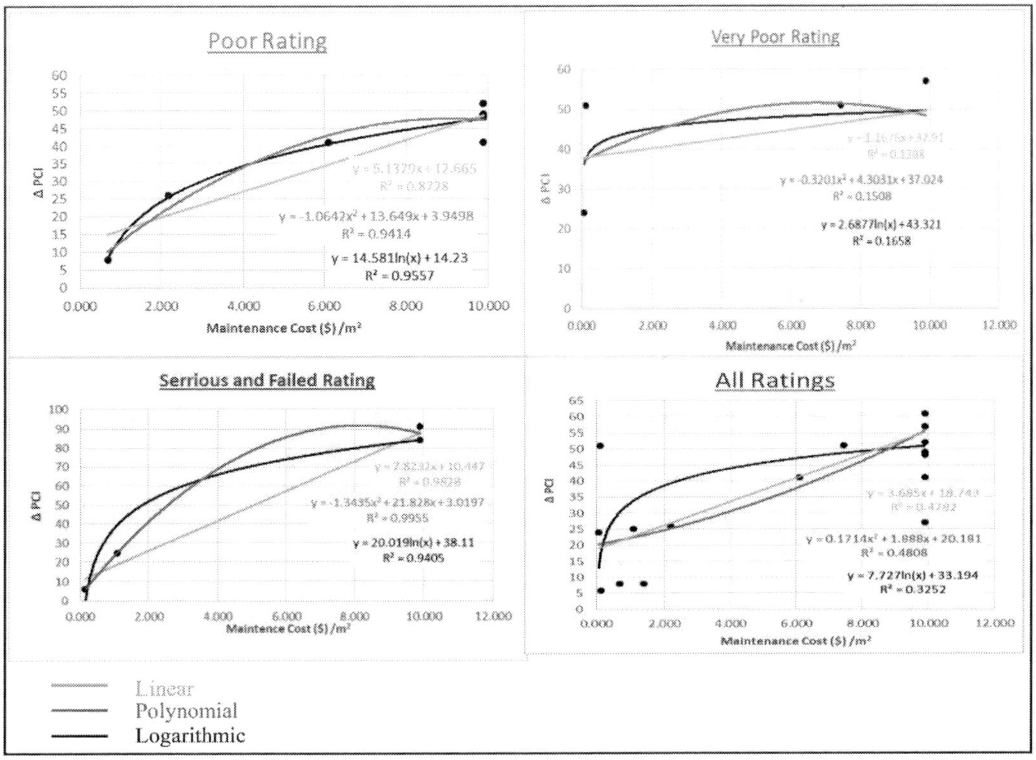

Fig. 6. Relation of ΔPCI and maintenance cost

As shown in Figure 6, regression analysis was conducted by using three types of relations including linear, polynomial and logarithmic equations. The analysis was conducted and presented for the results of the whole maintained sections as well as for the separated groups of poorly rated sections, very poor rated sections, and serious and failed sections. The results were summarized in Table 1. Also, the detailed calculations for ΔPCI and maintenance cost per meter square are shown in Tables 2 and 3.

Table 1. Formulas developed to relate maintenance cost and deterioration rate of paved areas

Rating	# of sec.	Linear		Polynomial		Logarithmic	
		Equation	R^2	Equation	R^2	Equation	R^2
Poor	7	ΔPCI = 5.1379	0.8728	ΔPCI = -1.0642(Mc)^2	0.9414	ΔPCI = 14.581	0.9557
Very Poor	7	ΔPCI = 1.1676	0.1288	ΔPCI = -0.3201(Mc)^2	0.1508	ΔPCI = 2.6877	0.1658

Rating	# of sec.	Linear		Polynomial		Logarithmic	
		Equation	R^2	Equation	R^2	Equation	R^2
Failed &	4	ΔPCI = 7.8232	0.9828	ΔPCI = - $1.3435(Mc)^2$	0.9955	ΔPCI = 20.019	0.9405
All Ratings	18	ΔPCI = 3.685 Mc +18.743	0.4782	ΔPCI = $0.1714(Mc)^2$ +1.888	0.4808	ΔPCI = 7.727 ln(Mc)	0.3252

Mc = Maintenon cost per square meter in U.S Dollar ($).

Table 2. Detailed Calculations for Sections after Maintenance

Section ID	Area (m^2)	PCI Before	PCI After	ΔPCI	Maintenance Cost ($)	Maintenance Cost ($)/ m^2
10R	180	28	36	8	175	1.373
02R	300	59	100	41	2100	9.887
06R	994.2	51	92	41	6959	9.887
08R	370.3	48	56	8	175	0.667
34L	570.2	46	87	41	2458	6.090
33L	197	45	93	48	1379	9.887
01R	465.3	44	96	52	3257	9.887
18R	919.5	42	68	26	1414	2.172
05R	174.8	41	90	49	1224	9.887
27L	2701	40	64	24	140	0.073
26L	1183.4	38	89	51	98	0.117
13R	829.6	33	84	51	4368	7.437
32L	818	29	56	27	5726	9.887
19R	301	28	85	57	2107	9.887
41L	301	28	89	61	2107	9.887
25L	495	23	48	25	378	1.079
31L	359	21	27	6	35	0.138
04R	174.8	16	100	84	1224	9.887
03R	95.7	3	94	91	670	9.887

Table 3. Detailed Calculations for Sections without Maintenance

Section ID	Area(m2)	PCI Before	PCI After	ΔPCI	Maintenance Cost ($)	Maintenance Cost ($)/ m^2
38L	506	76	69	-7	0	0
09R	1411.6	71	65	-6	0	0
10R	711.9	69	67	-2	0	0
16R	1387.3	67	63	-4	0	0
28L	279	63	55	-8	0	0
17R	191.8	58	48	-10	0	0
20L	583.4	55	41	-14	0	0
35L	292.5	54	51	-3	0	0
07R	1750	52	39	-13	0	0
15R	184.6	50	28	-22	0	0
39L	286.3	43	32	-11	0	0
40L	588.5	42	40	-2	0	0
12R	234	41	35	-6	0	0
11R	174.2	40	35	-5	0	0
14R	184.6	34	28	-6	0	0
24L	162	31	26	-5	0	0
23L	304.25	29	26	-3	0	0
29L	300	25	24	-1	0	0
21L	147.2	15	17	2	0	0

The results indicated the reliance of maintenance cost on the condition evaluation of pavement prior to the M&R projects execution. Linear regression proved to appropriately represent the relation between the cost of maintenance and the rate of deterioration. The results of R^2 calculations indicated a high level of reliability and validity of the equations. The equations can be used as a prediction model for estimating the cost of required maintenance for paved areas with low traffic volume. In future studies, it is recommended to conduct comparative studies to study the effect of the traffic volume and the structure of pavement for broader areas of pavement. This requires conducting more tests and collecting more data during a longer period of the road network life-cycle.

6 Conclusion

The developed equations can be used as a prediction model to estimate the required cost for maintaining paved areas depending on information about pavement condition, rate of deterioration and the area for each evaluated section. Values of R^2 refers that the equations are representing the results in a good manner, and so the equations can be used for cost prediction.

Conduction more iterations of PCI evaluation during the coming years and after M&R projects will help to improve the prediction equations. In the future development of this study, it is recommended to use modern tools and methods for more effective evaluation of the conditions of paved areas, such as using image processing, remote sensing and ground-penetrating radar techniques. Improvement of pavement condition valuation and setting for M&R work will aim at making the required procedures become more robust.

References

1. M.Y. Shahin, J.A. Walther, *Pavement Maintenance Management for Roads and Streets Using the PAVER System. 1st ed.*, US Army Corps of Engineering (1990)
2. M.Y. Shahin, *Pavement Management for Airports, Roads, and Parking Lots. 2nd ed.* Springer Science and Business Media, LLC (2005)
3. K. Patel, B. Prajapati, N. Kanojia, S.J. Chauhan,. Literature Review on Types of Flexible Pavement Failures, *International Journal for Scientific Research & Development*|, 5(2):145-147 (2017)
4. V.L. Ng, *A study of deterioration in ride quality on Ohio's highways*, Thesis (M.S.), University of Toledo, Ohio, United States (2015), http://utdr.utoledo.edu/theses-dissertations/1861
5. F. Reza, K. Boriboonsomsin, S.M. Bazlamit, *Development of a Composite Pavement Performance Index ST/SS/05-001*, Ohio Department of Transportation, Columbus, Ohio, United States (2005)
6. W. Li, L. Mills, S., McNeil, *The Implications of Climate Change on Pavement Performance and Design*, University Transportation Center, University of Delaware, Newark, DE (2011)
7. J.T. Smith, S.L. Tighe, J.C. Andrey, B. Mills, Temperature and Precipitation Sensitivity Analysis on Pavement Performance, *Transportation Research Circular, Surface Transportation Weather and Snow Removal and Ice Control Technology*, 558-571 (2008)
8. N. Jackson, J. Puccinelli, Long-Term Pavement Performance (LTPP) Data Analysis Support: National Pooled Fund Study TPF-5(013): Effects of Multiple Freeze Cycles and Deep Frost Penetration on Pavement Performance and Cost, Nichols Consulting Engineers, Reno, Nevada, United States (2006)
9. S.S. Shamsabadi, Y.S.H. Tari, R. Birken, M. Wang, Deterioration Forecasting in Flexible Pavements due to Floods and Snow Storms, 7th European Workshop on Structural Health Monitoring, July 8-11, 2014 La Cité, Nantes, France (2014)
10. K.P. George, A.S. Rajagopal, L.K. Lim, Models for Predicting Pavement Deterioration, *Transportation Research Record: Journal of the Transportation Research Board*, 1215, 1-7 (1989)
11. M.Y. Shahin, C. Stock, L. Beckberger, Comparing Pavement Performance and Its Effect on Maintenance and Rehabilitation Cost, 3rd International Conference on Managing Pavements, 237-245 (1994)
12. A. Tinni, Comparison of Maintenance Costs of Heavy Duty Pavements, Tinni Management Consulting, Eesti Betooniühing, March (2013)
13. P. Babashamsi, N. Yusoff, H. Ceylan, N. Nor, H. Jenatabadi, Evaluation of pavement life cycle cost analysis: Review and analysis, *International Journal of Pavement Research and Technology*, 9 : 241–254 (2016)

14. Z. Wang, H. Wang, Life-cycle cost analysis of optimal timing of pavement preservation, *Frontiers of Structural and Civil Engineering*, 11(1) : 17-26 (2017)
15. T.I.A. Obaidat, Z.M. Hamici, S.M. Bazlamit, H.S. Ahmad, Assessment of the Effect of Alligator Cracking on Pavement Condition Using WSN-Image Processing, Lecture Notes in Mechanical Engineering/ 8th International Conference on Engineering, Project, and Product Management (EPPM 2017) : 265-274(2018)

Time and Cost Performance of Fixed Price Building Contracts in Tertiary Institutions in Nigeria

Joshua S. Mangvwat[1*], *Duga J.* Ewuga[1], *Yohanna D.* Izam[2]

[1]Department of Quantity Surveying, University of Jos-Nigeria
[2]Department of Building, University of Jos-Nigeria

Abstract. This qualitative and quantitative study evaluates the time and cost performance of fixed-price contracts in Tertiary Institutions projects in Plateau State, funded as intervention projects from the Tertiary Education Trust Fund. Literature review gives the background on the types and forms of contracts. Questionnaires, interviews and records from projects are tools that were used in collecting the relevant data. Sixty-two professionals consisting of 12 Architects, 8 Builders, 12 Engineers, 22 Quantity Surveyors and 8 Estate Surveyors randomly selected responded to issues of time and cost challenges. Records were purposively obtained from Twenty-Three projects studied. Regression Analysis was used to predict the time and cost performance. Results show a cost increase of $14, 423.59 for every one-month increase in time. Interviews revealed all 23 projects suffered time overruns with only 5 overrunning in cost. Specifications of 18 projects were found to be changed in order to satisfy the client's budget objective of the firm price. The research recommends that to enhance time and cost performance, designs must be fully completed before biding. Alternatively, the entire procurement system which favours the fixed price arrangement should be overhauled to accommodate other options.

Keywords: Fixed Price, Time, Cost, Performance, Building Contract

1 Introduction

Due to the complexity of construction projects and the high demand from construction clients, various forms of building contracts are employed by the parties involved to deliver the project successfully [1]. Bennett [2] explained that the procurement method and type of project determine the choice of the contract to be used. Procurement of construction projects is the network of relationships amongst the various parties involved in the delivery of a project. This relationship is formalised by entering into a legal contract [1]. The contracts, therefore, have to be tailored towards the construction client's needs and objectives. The latter revolves around the triumvirate of

- Cost (initial expected cost, capital cost and maintenance cost),

- Time (time required for design and construction, securing timely planning approvals, timely completion etc.) and
- Quality (expected in terms of design flexibility to changes, technical specification, functionality and aesthetics/workmanship) [1, 3, 4].

Other factors that determine the type of procurement method and contracts to be used are the size, type and complexity of the project because the performance of a construction project is related to the method of procurement used in its delivery [5]. Also, the level of participation of the client mostly influences the success or failure of a project [4, 6, 7]. The client's influence can be exerted through deciding the type of contract strategy to be used which guides the decision on the form of payment. These contract strategies can be either priced-based or cost-based. The priced-based are lump-sum or re-measurement contracts with prices being submitted by the contractor in their bid while the cost-based are cost-reimbursable or target cost where the actual cost incurred by the contractor is reimbursed with a fee added to cover for overheads and profit [8]. Potts [8] further explained that the allocation of risks to the parties involved in the contract is also a factor that determines the choice of the payment system.

The procurement of public projects in Nigeria is conducted mainly through the traditional procurement system, using mostly price-based contract strategy. Olatunji [9] observes that public projects in Nigeria awarded based on the lowest price has led to contractors bidding with ridiculous rates while delivering very low-quality work and workmanship. He further observed that from the projects studied, only 44% were completed within budget and only about 5% these were delivered within the actual completion time [9]. Also, Adedokun et al. [10] reveal that educational projects in Nigeria are mostly procured through the open competitive tendering method. They explained that using this method of tendering is influenced by the need for obtaining high quality, accountability, price competition, and speedy execution. However, Olanrewaju and Anavhe [11] observe that construction projects in Nigeria have suffered from a lot of claims; some of the major sources of the claims include late payment, delayed approval of change order and delay cost which was noted to be extremely influential while the least influential were storage charges, loss of productivity, and costs of preparing claims. They found that major claim factors are behavioural rather than technical issues [11].

With the amount of investment made on infrastructure projects in Nigeria, especially in higher educational institutions through the Tertiary Education Trust Fund (TETFUND) funding there is the need for a better understanding of the performance of these projects in meeting the client's objectives. In addition, it is necessary to understand how the price based (lump-sum/fixed contract) system of the contract has helped in meeting the client's needs and objectives and also to identify areas of necessary improvement to ensure that such projects meet the client's objectives.

2 Literature Review

Background of TETFUND and procurement/contract strategies in use in construction is reviewed.

2.1 Background on Tetfund

The Tertiary Education Trust Fund (TETFUND) was set up to administer and disburse education tax collections to Federal and State tertiary educational institutions in Nigeria. The main source of income available to the Fund is the 2% education tax paid from the assessable profit of companies registered in Nigeria. The Board of Trustees (BOT) of the Fund is statutorily charged with the responsibility of administering, managing and disbursements of these funds to beneficiaries in the public tertiary educational institutions under established guidelines. The Act that set up the fund prescribes the distribution of the funds in the ratio 2:1:1 respectively to Universities, Polytechnics and Colleges of Education (COE). TETFUND has been responsible for over 60% of the infrastructure development in public tertiary institutions in Nigeria. This translates to One Trillion Naira expenditure (about $2.78 Billion) within a period of five years. Based on the 2016 allocation alone, 181 tertiary institutions comprising 74 universities, 50 polytechnics and 57 colleges of education benefitted from the particular fund [12, 13].

2.2 Procurement systems and Construction Contracts

Procurement of construction projects is the outcome of a chain of relationships amongst the various parties involved in the delivery of a project [1]. Different procurement methods use different types of contract. For example, The Joint Contract Tribunal (JCT) [14] identified the fixed-price contract as one of three types of the contract under the traditional procurement methods. It describes a fixed price contract as an arrangement where the contract sum is determined before the beginning of construction work. The contractor undertakes a defined task in return for an agreed amount of money. Furthermore, Rodriguez [15] opined that in a fixed price contract, the owner has essentially assigned all the risk to the contractor, who in turn charges a higher percentage of the cost as a safety net should any unforeseen circumstance arise.

In theory, the different contractual arrangements have a different effect on the time, cost, and quality as well as in the allocation of the risks among parties involved. These are the most important parameters, which are critical to building project performance [16]. According to the Construction Industry Institute, the main difference with respect to a fixed-price contract is the risk factor. This is because risk has a significant impact on construction project performance. How risks are shared between the parties is to a large extent governed by the procurement option and the content of the related contract document and forms [17].

In comparing the tender sums and final costs of construction projects in Nigeria awarded using due process procedures from 2003 - 2007, Olatunji [9] found that all the projects awarded were based on the lowest price. He observed that apart from the fact that it weakens competition, as some contractors are still found bidding with very ridiculous rates, low quality of workmanship and project's poor performance in its entire life are probable features of many of these projects. He further found that although 44 per cent of the construction projects were completed within budget, only 5 per cent were delivered within time. Also, Shwarka and Anigbogu [18] in examining the impact of public procurement options on building projects performance in Nigeria based on the impact of traditional and design and build methods found that there is no significant difference between the two in terms of quality but that there is a significant difference in duration and cost.

3 Methodology

This research adopted the strategy of a case study in a survey [19]. Data is collected using a combination of library/desk search, questionnaire and personal interviews. Project files are examined and interview questions are developed to enable this. A list of time, cost and variation variables were drawn from literature and from discussion with the parties involved in the projects. An interview guide was prepared based on the compiled list after a pilot study. The piloting improved the wording and increase the reliability of the questions asked. These were structured into the questionnaire we have used. Respondents were required to rate the frequency and severity of each of the factors using a 5 - point Likert scale. The primary data

was collected from the contract documents, progress reports, and minutes of monthly site meetings, correspondences as well as available site records.
The research focused on TETFund sponsored projects in tertiary institutions in Plateau state. The target population consists of three groups, namely contractors, consultants'/client's representative and construction professionals because of their expertise and experience in the projects studied.

Data collected are presented and analysed using descriptive statistics and Regression Analysis to predict the time and cost performance. Also, Analysis of Variance (ANOVA) was used to carry out a simultaneous comparison of several population means; to determine whether or not variation in sets of data produce a different outcome. The method is used in this research to test a significant difference between the mean responses on time and cost performance of all the projects studied. It is a useful technique in modern statistical methods which enables the total variation in a set of data to be reduced to components associated with possible sources of variability whose relative impact needs to be accessed [20]. The variation between samples and within a sample are the possible sources of variability and for each source of variability, the sum of squares is computed using the degrees of freedom.

A total of 29 building projects were contracted and completed within the period 2005 to 2014 under the TETFund intervention programme in the three tertiary institutions selected for the study. Records were available on 23 of these projects representing 79% of the total number. Since the total population of professionals that participated in these projects could not be ascertained due to the mobility of labour and lack of accurate personnel records, especially in the contractor and consultant organizations, the research purposively targeted 75 respondents; 25 each from the 3 institutions. The purpose is to obtain an equal representation from each institution cutting across professionals who actively participated in the projects. For the interview, 5 of the 7 respondents with over 21years working experience were selected on the assumption that they are known as professionals on TETFund projects.

4 Presentation and Discussion of Results

A total of 62 out of 75 questionnaires were returned as valid, giving a response rate of 82.6%. Table 1 shows the background of respondents comprising Quantity Surveyors (35.5%), Architects (19.4%) and 12.9% Engineers, Builders and Estate Valuers each. This depicts a cumulative of 87.1%, with a predominance of professionals commonly found on construction sites during the survey. However, a cumulative of 51.6% have experiences spanning over 10 years; an indication that the majority are reasonably experienced to contribute to the study.

Table 1. Background of Respondents

Profession	Frequency	% of Response	Experience	Frequency	% of Response	Organization	Frequency	% of Response
Architect	12	19.4	1 – 5 years	8	12.9	Contracting	18	29.0
Builder	8	12.9	6 – 10 years	20	32.3	Consultancy	22	35.5
Engineer	12	19.4	11 – 15 years	10	16.1	Government	22	35.5
Quantity Surveyor	22	35.5	16 – 20 years	8	12.9			
Others	8	12.9	Over 21years	14	22.6	Total	62	100.0
Total	62	100.0	Total	60	96.8			
			Missing	2	3.2			
			Total	**62**	**100.0**			

SOURCE: Field Survey, 2015

4.1 Factors That Promote Choice of Fixed Price Contract

Among factors that influence the choice of the traditional procurement route presented in Table 2, firmness of cost was rated highest with 58.1% response rate as a "very important" factor. This is followed by early completion with 54.8%; quality expectation with 45.2% and risk reduction with 32.3%. Hence the requirement for the firmness of cost and adherence to the time schedule for early completion are important factors that influenced the choice of a fixed price contract.

Table 2. Factors that influence the choice of the procurement system

Factors	Rating	Frequency	Percentage	Cumulative Percentage
	Not important	8	12.9	12.9
Quality expectation	Important	26	41.9	54.8
	Very important	28	45.2	100
	Total	**62**	**100**	
	Not important	4	6.5	6.5
Firmness of cost	Important	22	35.5	51.6
	Very important	36	58.1	100
	Total	**62**	**100**	
Early completion	Not important	4	6.5	6.5
	Important	24	38.7	45.2
	Very important	34	54.8	100
	Total	62	100	
	Not important	6	9.7	9.7
Risk reduction	Important	36	58.1	67.7
	Very important	20	32.3	100
	Total	**62**	**100**	

SOURCE: Field Survey, 2015

4.2 Time–Cost Performance

The differences in time and cost data of the projects studied were collected from three different institutions. A total of 23 projects were involved. Figure 1 and Figure 2 are a graphical representation of the time and cost relationship of these projects.

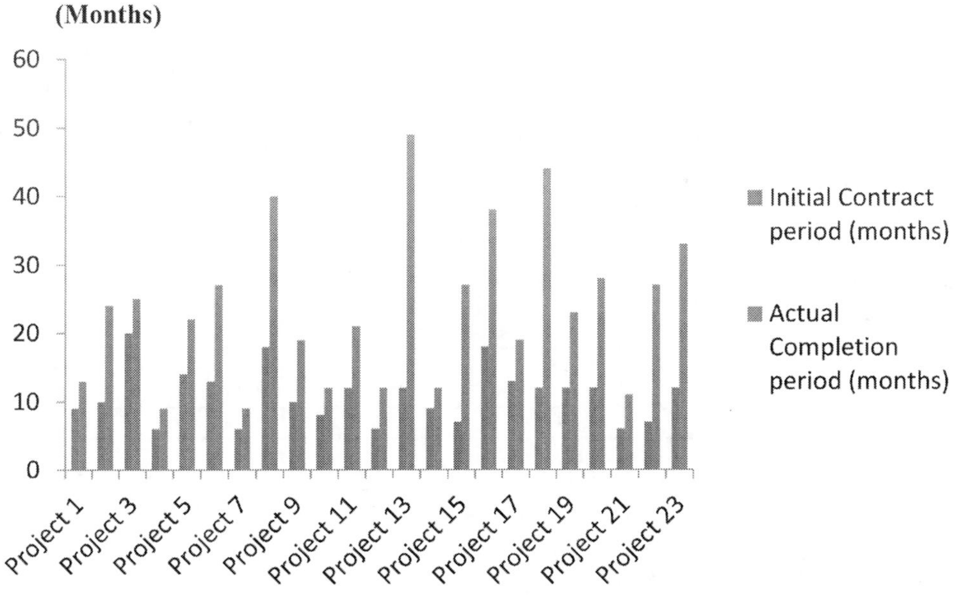

Fig.1. Initial and actual completion period (Naira)

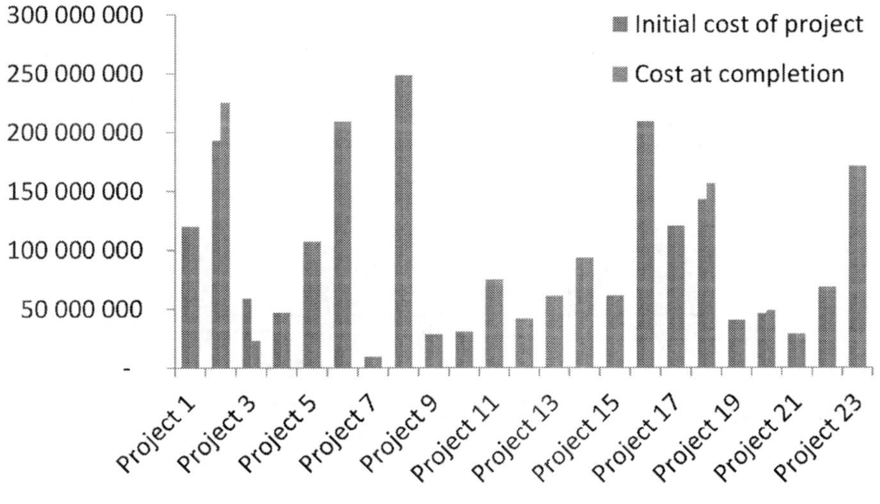

Fig. 2. Initial and actual cost of the project (Naira)

4.3 Results and Discussions

Results of the analysis are presented in Tables 3, 4 and 5.

Linear regression was used to assess the ability of initial and actual time to predict the actual cost. Preliminary analysis was conducted to ensure there is no violation of the normality, linearity, multi co-linearity and homoscedasticity. The initial and actual time was entered as independent variables while the final cost was entered as the dependent variable. The total variance explained by the model as a whole was 59.79%, degree of freedom F (2.10) = 2.78, P-value > 0.05, R= 0.597, R-square = 0.225.

From the model summary in Table 3, This is an overall measure of the strength of association and does not reflect the extent to which any particular independent variable is associated with the dependent variable. Finally, the variables were not statistically significant.

The implication of these to decision-makers, as shown in Table 5 is that when all other variables are held constant; there is an ₦5, 192,491.09 (currently equivalent to $14,423.59) unit increases in the actual cost for every unit increase in months in actual time. This is however insignificant as shown on the **t** and **Sig**. columns. Interpreting these statistics with respect to the projects studied shows that the cost increase emanated from 5 out of 23 projects. This explains the reason for the insignificance as 18 of the projects which did not have a cost increase despite the time overrun.

Table 3. Model Summary

Model	R	R Square	Adjusted R Square	Std. Error of the Estimate
1	.597[a]	.357	.228	70845434.285

a. Predictors: (Constant), Actual Time, Initial Time

Table 4. ANOVA

Model	Sum of Squares	Df	Mean Square	F	Sig.
Regression	27857091313126228.000	2	13928545656563110.000	2.775	.110[b]
Residual	50190755589642976.000	10	5019075558964298.000		
Total	78047846902769216.000	12			

a. Dependent Variable: Actual Cost
b. Predictors: (Constant), Actual Time, Initial Time

Table 5. Coefficients of Actual Cost

Model	Unstandardized B	Coefficients Std. Error	Standardized Coefficients Beta	T	Sig.
(Constant)	32947133.123	65933111.008		.500	.628
Initial Time	-3464037.680	6464861.182	-.171	-.536	.604
Actual Time	5192491.092	2419787.654	.686	2.146	.057

a. Dependent Variable: Actual Cost

The outcome of the interviews shows that although time and cost overruns were experienced, these were accommodated within the contingencies cost of the projects and also because of the firmness of the contract, material specifications and scope of work were changed. This further supports earlier studies of the significant relationship between time and cost. The participants further explained that where the scope of the work was not changed but due to delay in payments and honouring of architects certificates; these have led to increasing the running cost of the project. Other factors identified were inadequate design information which leads to discrepancies in the bill(s) of quantities, and also inadequate time provided for detailed design and other contract documents all of which contribute significantly to the delay and poor performance of the project.

5 Conclusion

In conclusion, this study was able to establish and build to the existing body of knowledge by identifying the key factors that promote the use of fixed-price/lump sum contract on TETFUND projects in Nigeria. The firmness of the cost is the major factor for adopting this type of contract. While out of the 23 projects studied, 5 suffered from cost-overrun and all the 23 suffered from time overrun. What this study indicates is that there is a trade-off in the quality of the project while trying to meet the cost target. This trade-off will eventually lead to the higher maintenance cost of the facility. Furthermore, the study found out that in the evaluation of time and cost performance of building projects executed through a fixed-price contract, the practice that allows time to overrun without adequate allowance in the cost element of buildings, and yet expecting to have a building as specified in the design, scope and quality is unrealistic.

Therefore, the study suggests that for effective use of the fixed-price contract, there is a need for team collaboration and detailed identification of the client's priority and objectives (cost, quality and time). On the alternative, the study recommends that public institutions can take advantage of the experience of project teams by adopting other alternative procurement methods that provide some level of flexibility and also gaining from the design and construction expertise of teams.

References

1. S.A. Lupton, S. Cox, H. Clamp, *Which Contract? Choosing the appropriate building contract*: RIBA Publishing Enterprises, (2007)
2. F.L. Bennett, *The management of construction: A project lifecycle approach*: Routledge (2007)
3. P.E.D. Love, M. Skitmore, G. Earl, Selecting a suitable procurement method for a building project, *Construction Management & Economics* **16**(2):221-233 (1998)
4. J. Masterman, *An introduction to building procurement systems*: Routledge (2003)
5. A. Ghadamsi, N. Braimah, *The influence of procurement methods on project performance: A conceptual framework* (2012)
6. D. Boyd, E. Chinyio, *Understanding the construction client*: John Wiley & Sons (2008)
7. S.T. Kometa, P.O. Olomolaiye, F.C. Harris, A review of client-generated risks to project consultants, *International Journal of Project Management* **14**(5):273-279 (1996)
8. K.F. Potts, *Construction cost management: Learning from case studies*. Oxon: Taylor & Francis (2008)
9. O.A. Olatunji, A comparative analysis of tender sums and final costs of public construction and supply projects in Nigeria, *Journal of Financial Management of Property and Construction* **13**(1):60-79 (2008)

10. O.A. Adedokun, O.T. Ibironke, S.O. Babatunde, Assessment of competitive tendering methods of procuring educational building projects in Nigeria. *Journal of Facilities Management,* **11**(1):81-94 (2013)
11. A.A. Olanrewaju, P.J. Anavhe, Perceived claim sources in the Nigerian construction industry, *Built Environment Project and Asset Management* **4**(3):281-295 (2014)
12. E. Uwandu, TETFund responsible for 60% infrastructure development in public tertiary institutions – Bafa, (2017), https://www.vanguardngr.com>news
13. J. Agbakuru, TETFund releases ₦1Trn to Varsities, Polytechnic in 5years, (2017), https://www.vanguardngr.com>news
14. JCT, Deciding on the appropriate JCT contract. Practice note. Published in August 2006 by Sweet & Maxwell Limited (2006), retrieved from www.jctcontracts.com
15. J. Rodriguez, *Lump Sum: What Is A Lump Sum? Lump Sum Construction Contract*, (2013), http://www.about.com guide. Accessed on May 7, 2013
16. K.K. Chitkara, Project management - planning, scheduling and controlling, New Delhi: Tata McGraw Hill (2005)
17. Y.D. Izam, Construction Estimating and Procurement Issues: A monograph of the Department of Building, University of Jos, Nigeria (2014)
18. S. M. Shwarka, N.A. Anigbogu, The impact of public procurement options on building projects performance in Nigeria, *The Professional Builder* **3**(2):46 – 54 (2012)
19. R.K. Yin, *Case study research design and methods*(3rd ed.) California: Sage Publications (2003)
20. D.C. Howell, *Statistical methods for psychology*, Wadsworth Group: CA (2002)

Appendix – Research Questionnaire

SECTION I: GENERAL BACKGROUND OF RESPONDENT

Kindly fill the information below (Tick).

1. Type of your organization (a) Contractor (b)Consultancy (c) Government
2. What is your profession? (a) Architect (b) Builder (c) Engineer (d) Quantity Surveyor (e) Others; kindly specify.................
3. Your years of working Experience
   (a) 1 – 5 years (b) 6 – 10 years (c) 11 – 15 years (d) 16 – 20 years (e) Above 21years
4. In which of these institutions have you supervised or executed building projects ***(multiple answers are accepted)***
   (a) University (b)Polytechnic/College of Agric (c) College of Education (d) Others; kindly specify.....................................
5. From the list provided below, tick the type of project you were involved with in the box that follows: ***(multiple answers are accepted)***
   (a) Residential (b) Lecture theatre (c) Multipurpose block
   (c) Laboratory/workshop (e) Others; kindly specify.....................................

SECTION II: NATURE AND PERFORMANCE OF PROJECT EXECUTED

6. Which of these procurement systems was used for the project? ***(multiple answers are accepted)***
   (a) Separated/traditional system (b) Management oriented system
   (c) Design and Build system (d) Discretionary/Partnering system

Kindly indicate your level of **"agreement"** or **"disagreement"** by ticking in the box that corresponds to each factor to answer questions (7) to (12)

7. Rate the following factors with respect to how they affect the choice of procurement system, type and form of contract

Rating → / ↓ Factors	Very significant	Significant	Uncertain	Less significant	Not significant
Quality expectation					
Firmness of Cost					
Early completion					
Risk reduction					

8. In the light of your past/present experience, how have the following elements ***of fixed price contract*** affect contract performance?

Rating → / ↓ Elements	Very significant	Significant	Uncertain	Less significant	Not significant
Completeness of Design					
Frequency of Change Orders					
Extent of Cost Variation					
Extent of Delay					

Adequacy of Tendering Time					
Integrity of Award Process					

SECTION III: CHALLENGES IN PROJECT EXECUTION

9. How critical were the following factors in your project execution?

Rating → / Factors ↓	Very critical	Critical	Uncertain	Less critical	Not critical
Design inadequacies					
Additional requirement of the client					
Compliance with new government legislation					
Discrepancy in contract drawings or bill of quantities					
Non-availability of contract specified materials/goods					
Substitution of materials, goods and workmanship specified in the contract					

SECTION IV: PROBLEMS AND PROSPECTS OF FIXED PRICE CONTRACT

10. Rate the significance of the following **problems** associated with fixed price contract in project delivery.

Rating → / ↓ Problems	Very significant	Significant	Uncertain	Less Significant	Not Significant
Changes are difficult to assess /costly to implement					
Lower financial risk to employer					
Need to complete design before bidding					
Contractors not adhering to quantities/specification					
Hard to build relationship as each project is unique					
Bidding can be expensive and lengthy					
Delays in honouring Architect's certificate					
Project/Environmental related problems					
Consultant related problems					

11. Rate the significance of the following **prospects** associated with fixed price contract in project delivery.

Rating → / **↓ Prospects**	**Very significant**	**Significant**	**Uncertain**	**Less Significant**	**Not Significant**
Lower financial risk to Employer					
Minimum owner supervision					
Higher incentive for Contractor					
Contractor selection is relatively easy					

12. From a strategic point of view, rate the factors that would **improve** the fixed price contract system

Rating → / **↓ Factors**	**Very significant**	**Significant**	**Uncertain**	**Less Significant**	**Not Significant**
Adequate design and specifications					
Stable conditions (Government policies)					
Effective competition when bidding					
Minimum scope changes (adequacy of brief)					
Sufficient time to bid and award project					

13. Please proffer other factors that you feel can improve project delivery through fixed price contract system.

A critical perspective on Integrated Project Delivery (IPD) applied in a Norwegian public hospital project

Bo Terje Kalsaas[1*], *Una Obiose* Kriston Nwajei[1], and *Christine* Bydall[1]

[1]Department of Engineering Sciences, University of Agder, Jon Lilletunsvei 9., Grimstad, Norway

Abstract. Does the IPD concept deliver as required and expected, and if not, how can that be explained? This paper is a critical realist inspired methodology based on a combination of the inductive and deductive approaches used in case study research. IPD is based on relational contracting between multiple parties, in this case between the Owner, Contractor, MEP subcontractors and a group of Consulting engineers who share control of the project. At the core of the concept is shared risk and opportunities among the parties in the IPD contract. Our theoretical perspectives are based mainly on the Principal-Agent theory (PA), Transaction Cost theory (TC), and its related incentives. This paper reports on a study of the development of an existing public hospital that is constructing first a psychiatry and then a somatic building. The data collection in the paper is mainly in connection with the construction of the psychiatry building in 2018. Our findings show that IPD represents a game-changer in the behaviours and the organizing of AEC (Architect-Engineer-Construction) projects, ex-post IPD-contract. We identify examples of swapping occurring that require deep collaboration, which stems from changes in the commercial incentives. However, different individual incentives coupled with accompanying mindsets and opportunistic behaviour are still part of everyday life and are linked to people© past experiences, which can be understood as contextual conditions. In addition, the decision-making processes were not effective and characterized by revisiting previous decisions.

Keywords: AEC-industry, alignment of interests, commercial and individual incentives, IPD, public procurement

1 Introduction

Many challenges have been registered in construction (AEC) projects within what one designates conventional project delivery models, Design-Bid-Build (DBB) or Design-Build (DB). There are challenges that are especially related to the delivery of quality and customer value, and the industry is characterized by relatively low-profit margins.

* Corresponding author: bo.t.kalsaas@uia.no

There are challenges that are especially related to a high level of conflict, limited innovation and that the industry is characterized by relatively low-profit margins [1]. It is also been argued that the industry has lower productivity growth than other industries [1]. The DB form appears to be replacing DBB as the preferred project delivery model. This is very common within the Norwegian construction (industry) and can be seen in the transition from DBB to DB regarding the construction of infrastructure projects [2].

Projects are usually carried out by many companies that specialize in branches of design, and different fields of construction, all having their own business model. In order to align commercial interests and goals, one needs a shared business model for the whole project. Furthermore, there is a trend for construction projects to become more technical in relation to automation and technology (e.g. smart buildings), which means that projects increase in complexity and require more collaboration to solve interdependencies.

In Norway, there are changes in the choice of project delivery model. There is a debate surrounding traditional models as they are characterized as models that often lead to conflict and dispute. One example of this is a meeting[†] where it was argued from a lawyer's point of view that the Norwegian Standard (NS) for contracts regarding DBB and DB has few common incentives and is more a cause for problems than solving problems.

In the Lean Construction (LC) environment in the US, there has been interest in a type of delivery model denoted Integrated Project Delivery (IPD) which is characterized as a game-changer [3]. Thus, multiple party contracts are introduced with risk and opportunity sharing, which is expected to change the direction of the parties' incentives in relation to working together without any hidden agendas by the alignment of their interests. The theoretical foundation lies within the LC-triangle [4, 5] which looks at the importance of fine-tuning the parties in relation to commercial interests, organization and production. **Our research interest is to contribute by critically highlighting the potential that lies within IPD in improving project execution**. We will do this by studying an IPD-project located in Norway, the Tønsberg project, which is in the process of building new psychiatric and somatic wards. The data in the study is mainly collected from the creation of the psychiatric building which is built before the somatic part. The paper builds upon and is the development of a master thesis by Nwajei and Bydall [6].

In the next section, the methodology used will be described and then we will examine the theoretical aspects related to understanding behaviour in construction projects. The IPD concept is further explained, including how incentives change. Three propositions have been developed that are further substantiated then an empirical analysis is carried out of the propositions and finalized with a conclusion.

2 The IPD concept

Integrated Project Delivery (IPD) according to Lahdenperä [7] has been an emerging method from North America that originated from Japan, labelled as "gentlemanly principles". This concept has its origins in Lean and the Toyota Production Systems (TPS) where adversarial supplier relationships were transformed into cooperative relationships[‡].

IPD is considered to have started in 2005 with the aim of aligning the commercial incentives of project participants in the AEC industry [8-9]. In the US, the Lean Construction environment tried to address the challenges in the construction industry, by defining an integrated process. The result of this was the five "big ideas" summarized as - collaboration; relationships; networks of commitments; optimization; and, the pairing of learning with action [3]. Several projects adopted IPD and put it into practice [9].

† Seminar at DLA Piper, March 13th, 2018

‡ Further information can be found in cases of Jaguar and Nippondenso and the Sutter Health project [3].

It was not until 2014 that the IPD-principles were defined as continuous involvement of the owner, key designers and contractors from early design through to project completion: shared risk and reward; joint project control; limited liability; and, a multi-party agreement or equal interlocking agreements. Without building on those principles, projects could not really be described as IPD (op cit.). The IPD concept consists of collaboration and coordination which can be realised by the solution of fusing the core organizations under a single agreement- integrated to work together and share ideas [10].

In an IPD, collaboration occurs early, whereby the constructors are present from the onset. They are part of the team and the team are not just focused on their own speciality. Knowledge and expertise are no longer hoarded [11]. The group make progress together, as they are aware of risks and rewards, not just their own but for others. IPD has been described as a game-changer in the way projects have been delivered. In the US, projects using all these principles have been successful, as no litigation has ensued as a result [11].

Do et al. [8] also argues that there is a close connection between IPD and the Target Value Design (TVD) concept [12], which was introduced in 2004. The American Institute of Architects [13] describes TVD as a unique way of creating value within budgeted constraints by designing to a financial target, using several iterations, rather than estimating a pre-decided detailed design. Designing to targets allows changes to occur, that normally would be regarded as an extra cost. Through combining IPD and TVD the commercial incentives are aligned towards the project's goals which are reflected in achieving customer value. It is no longer about completing unilateral contributions at the least cost. Thus, the commercial incentives move to re-aligning the thinking of participants from short term objectives to optimization and improvement of the whole product. In this paper, we study the impact of IPD in different aspects of collaboration in relation to the preservation of the parties' interests in the Tønsberg project.

3 Method

This research deals with a single project and the most obvious research approach to choose is case study methodology. In this instance our first approach was to look to [14] concerning critical realism (theoretically informed) case studies, then supplement this with Yin [15] using the case study method.

In line with critical realism thinking, we seek to identify mechanisms that have the potential to produce certain results, which we entitle propositions [15]. Incentives are something that motivates people into action, and that might affect behaviour and choices by making one alternative preferable than another. We consider incentives as a structure that together with mechanisms can lead to certain outcomes, given certain conditions [14]. Conditions can be identified through contextual analysis. It is a part of our method to compare our findings with incentives in traditional project delivery models. We focus on commercial incentives where rewards can come in the form of financial gains, but also on the internal and individual incentives which might be in the form of satisfaction or pleasure in the action or activity one has performed [16].

Qualitative data collection was done through conducting fourteen interviews, of which five are with the client, five with the main contractor (design management and production) of which one is an electro subcontractor and four are with the project consultants (design management). In addition, quantitative data were collected from 18 survey participants. 10 of those participants were from the client, 7 were from the main contractor and 1 was a subcontractor. The data were mainly gathered from the the psychiatry building in 2018.

4 Theoretical perspectives

When analysing relationships between companies and organizations in construction projects, it is relevant to first think of the principal-agent theory [17], that analyses the contractual challenges confronting business partners under conditions of information asymmetry, which is a typical situation at the beginning of a buyer-supplier relationship. Information asymmetry has the potential to lead to opportunism, defined as self-interest seeking with guile [18]. Schauwecker [19] in [20], lists the following types of opportunistic behaviours by suppliers: unpunctual delivery, quality deficits, poor service, overcharged prices for spares and additions, limited commitment to problem-solving, and the manipulation of markets through the bribing of purchasers. Moreover, opportunism can include cheating, breach of contract, stealing, distortion of data, dishonesty, false threats and promises, misrepresentation, and withholding information [18, 21-23]. However, when we examine the AEC-industry in a Norwegian context, we recognize again several aspects, such as late delivery, overcharged prices for addenda and quality deficits. According to Lai et al. [24], opportunism represents purely selfish behaviour, whereby one ignores the consequences for the other actors.

Related to bounded rationality, a contract may only include the conditions that the principal is able to predict in advance, which in turn gives rise to an incomplete contract, and the agent gets the possibility to act opportunistically after the contract is signed [25]. The risk of opportunism is, to a large extent, the driving force behind contractual control mechanisms in business relationships [26].

A challenge for the buyer is to realise an important potential capacity of transactions, that supplier commitment and trust may evolve over time. An important distinction can be made between before (ex-ante) and after (ex-post) contractual conclusion, and it is here that Steinle et al. [20] expands on agency theory by showing that not only do ex-post forms of opportunism but also ex-ante forms can lead to moral hazard which can be understood as opportunistic behaviour after contracting.

Opportunism is also a central aspect in transaction cost theory [18], which in relation to principal-agent theory is since humans have bounded rationality and are seeking self-interest. This means that if individuals are presented with the opportunity to maximize their utility, they will behave opportunistically, which leads to a rise in transaction costs. A central difference between these two theories is that agency theory has an ex-ante contractual focus i.e. alignment of interests, while transaction cost theory addresses ex-post governance structure [27]. Transaction cost theory focuses more on minimising ex-post transaction costs, while principal-agent theory aims at minimizing these same costs, but with an ex-ante alignment of incentives [28].

We understand opportunism explained earlier in principal-agent theory and transaction cost theory as opportunism based on commercial incentives. When [8] discuss the challenges in misalignment of commercial incentives on IPD and TVD projects, they are discussing the same phenomenon, even though they do not use our theoretical basis. They base their article on experiences from six IPD projects and a practical brainstorming of ideas of potential misalignments, which in our understanding is found in opportunistic behaviour based on various commercial interests. Opportunistic behaviour, however, is a broader term that is not only related to commercial incentives which we will elaborate below.

Luo [29] and Masten [30] distinguish between strong and weak opportunism, where strong opportunism violates unwritten but understood relational norms. Relational norms can be understood as "expectations about behaviour that at least partially is shared by a group of decisions makers" (Steinle et al. [19] p. 127).

Muris [31] operates with a different distinction, subtle and blatant opportunism. While subtle is difficult to detect and could be masked as legitimate conduct, blatant is defined as an obvious attempt to act opportunistically. Uncertainty occurs in a lot in AEC-projects and is furthermore a driver for opportunistic behaviour [18].

In theory and practice, however, the mechanisms of governance and incentives to regulate inter-organizational behaviour do not find universal support. Several scholars have criticised the theoretical grounds for opportunistic behaviour in business relationships. In his vast examination of contracts, Macneil [32] distinguishes between transactional and relational contracts, where the latter puts more emphasis on trust rather than monitoring mechanisms. IPD is an example of relational contracting.

5 The Case

The Tønsberg project (TP) is the first to introduce an Integrated Project Delivery (IPD) model in a Norwegian context [33, 34]. TP is in the seventh stage of a renewal process of the Hospital in Vestfold- Tønsberg, which started in 2015 and is planned to finish in 2021. The remaining stages consist of two new buildings; psychiatry (which is studied) and somatic. Handover dates for these buildings are in 2019 and 2021, respectively. The Tønsberg project has an estimated price of ca. 2.7 billion NOK. The project organization consists of three parties; The Hospital in Vestfold (SiV) representatives, entrepreneur organization (Skanska UK & Norway) and an alliance of consultants (CURA). The owner procured the consultants and the contractor alliances in parallel. The owner considered DB as a starting point with the strategy of later transforming DB to IPD. That is why the owner procured consultants individually to avoid traditional DB relationships between the contractors and the consultants. During the competitive procurement process, there were ten bids from consultant groups and three from contractor alliances. The owner had developed a sketch project as part of the basis for the competition. When evaluating the different bids, the owner weighted 20 per cent on price, 40 per cent on task understanding and how they intended to conduct an IPD and the last 40 per cent was on competence.

The consulting alliance selected is an amalgamation of six companies, under the group name CURA. The contractor alliance is made up of the main contractor and three technical subcontractors. Contractors and consultants signed a Memorandum of Understanding, as a document attachment to the DB contract, which showed a joint intention to use IPD as the project delivery model. The consultant group was contracted based on an hourly rate, while the contractor had a price per square meter and a mark-up.

With guidance from an American attorney (and one attorney representing each party), they set up an IPD contract customized to conform to Norwegian laws on public procurement, which was adapted according to the EU regulations on the same topic. The project's goals given by the owner were to build fifty per cent faster by using a high degree of industrialisation and prefabrication, to be ten per cent cheaper and improve customer quality better than similarly comparable projects. In addition, to apply IPD as a procurement strategy to reach the goals, advanced BIM and lean construction methods were introduced for design and production management.

5.1 The IPD arrangement in the Tønsberg project

The Tønsberg project has a compensation model for the parties involved in the IPD, a simplified version is illustrated in Figure 1. This figure shows four different scenarios (each represented by a column), where the top line represents the owner's cost, the lower line the target cost and the difference between owner's and target cost represent the profit in the left column. The first scenario and point of departure illustrate the profit when the project reaches the target cost. Scenario two shows what happens if they go over the target cost; they eat into their profit. If they can lower their target cost (e.g. coming up with better solutions), then the owner's cost goes down as well, and they increase the profit as illustrated in scenario three. The worst case is represented in the fourth column. That is the case where the owner's cost is exceeded, and the actors will have to give up their profit, however, the owner covers the additional cost. Risks and opportunities (reward) lie in the target cost segment.

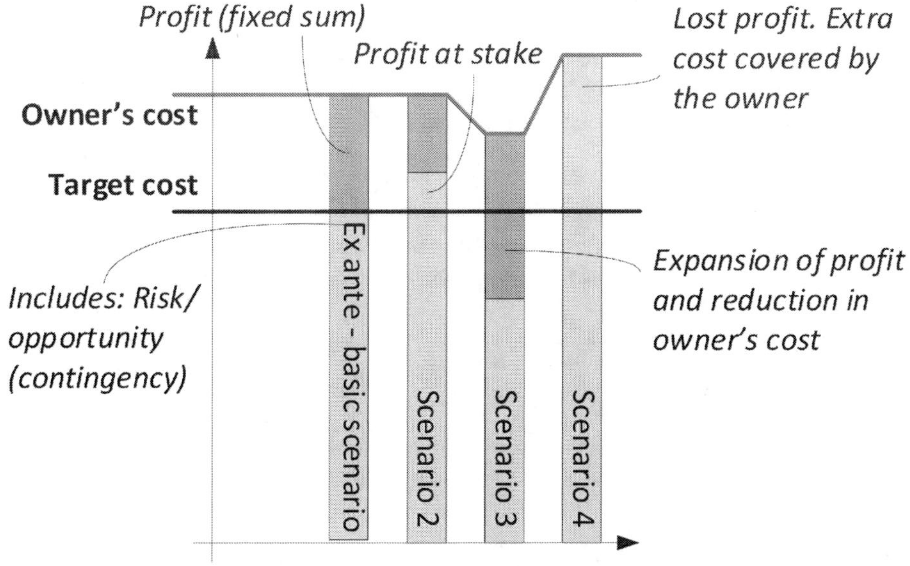

Figure 1. Illustration of the compensation model for IPD in the Tønsberg project [34]

Comparing the IPD arrangement in the Tønsberg project to the literature on IPD, there are similarities that confirm that this project is an IPD project. Firstly, when looking at the project principles, the Tønsberg project is consistent with four of the five principles stated in the latest version of the AiA guide [10]. The project applies interlocking contracts, joint decision making, shared risk and reward and continuous involvement from the owner. However, the project does not have limited liability among project participants instead it limits the use of compensation clauses in the contract for delays and changes [35]. Secondly, the use of mirrored interlocking contracts and the formation of the players is consistent with AiA guide [13] whereby projects should have IPD key and IPD supporting players. However, the conversion from a Design-Build (DB) to an IPD is unstipulated in the literature except for Ashcraft [36] in the owner's guide whereby he explains the challenges participants have felt going over from a DB to an IPD.

5.2 Theoretical analysis and propositions

Based on the description of the IPD approach in the Tønsberg project and the theoretical perspectives discussed earlier the following research question was formulated: **Is IPD a game-changer that leads to alignment of incentives and interests?** We answer the research question by testing whether we can verify it using three propositions [15], cf. Table 1. The mechanisms identified in the right-hand column are built on the thinking around economic incentives, cf. the theoretical perspectives. Mechanisms have the potential to produce what we denote as propositions. Different conditions, however, may cause the result not to be confirmed. The effort has been made to define such conditions in the contextual analysis.

Shared risk and reward mean that even though people are self-seeking-interest creatures in behaviour, the economic incentives are designed to work in such a way that no one wins if good ideas are held back to increase sales later, as all are sharing the profit. On the contrary, tactically holding back ideas could lead to lost opportunities. The incentives work in such a way that it becomes rationally best to think of what is best for the project, which is in stark contrast to sub-optimization and risk aversion. In terms of Principle Agent (PA), the IPD arrangement aligns the incentives and the interests of the IPD-involved parties where important sources of opportunistic behaviour and moral hazard is supposed to be removed. The same theoretical analysis can be applied to proposition 2, where a deepened form of collaboration occurs to include swapping of work tasks. However, there is expected to be space for ex-ante opportunism in the process of identifying the target price (Figure 1).

Table 1. Propositions and mechanisms for the study (ex-post IPD-contract)

No	Proposition	Mechanism/commercial incentives
1	IPD provides less scope for sub-optimization and opportunistic behaviour between companies in the value chain	Share risk and opportunities. Thus no one has the commercial incentive to hold back good suggestions or engage in risk aversion
2	IPD provides better conditions for unified solutions (swapping) than traditional contracts	Same mechanism as in the first proposition, but where the mechanism takes the collaboration a step further
3	IPD safeguards quality and customer value in a better way than alternative implementation models while maintaining constructability	The owner is involved in the management of the project at the same level as the IPD-contractors and the consultants

For proposition 3, the owner's participation is aligned with the other IPD partners which provide the opportunity to follow up on short and long-term interests (i.e. a building that is fit for its purpose in terms of design, operation, maintenance and energy consumption). The counterproductive incentives have disappeared from a DB whereby the owner has the incentive to lean back and avoid taking unwanted risks. In addition, the contractor has the incentives to not involve the owner in decisions related to quality and customer value. Yet in a DBB, the owner has the incentive to design and engineer a good product, but instances arise where the contractor can be opportunistic because he is not responsible for integrating design and production. Below we first address the process ex-ante contract before the propositions that belong to ex-post IPD-contract.

5.3 Empirical analysis

Ex-ante IPD-contract

In the predesign phase, it was worked on the basis of a DB-contract in parallel with the development of the IPD-contract for the execution phase. A learning point for the client is that the IPD-contract should be ready before contracting. Another central contextual issue for the project is that the target cost had to be reduced by 25% at the end of the predesign phase, otherwise the client would have terminated the project. The cost reduction was achieved by optimizing the project and by tough negotiations, according to the client. At this point, the focus was on target cost, less on target value delivery.

As addressed in theory it's found to be the difference between ex-ante contract and ex-post contract in the project. Data indicates that openness and trust have improved after the IPD-contract was signed. Moreover, is Target Value Delivery more in focus? The client, however, does accept some extra cost to smooth the system, which means that the target price increase. A learning point is moreover to put more weight on-boarding to the project from the client's part.

Proposition 1

The data shows that the Tønsberg project has removed several sources of opportunistic behaviour by establishing a common business model for the actors through the alignment of commercial incentives. As in projects organized as DB and IPD, the challenges are similar concerning the owner's decision-making, for example, delaying of decisions caused by the exposure to pressure from strong user groups. As a result of the delays, challenges have occurred in the choice of technical solutions which is not characterized as "blatant", but rather a "subtle" form of opportunism. The argument for a more expensive and better facility can perhaps be interpreted as being driven by commercial incentives. We can assume that they want to do what they think is best for their own work situation and for the owner, and so they have chosen to fight hard for these purposes.

This form of opportunism can also be seen in the different mindsets that exist between the designers and contractors, i.e. individual incentives and subtle opportunism in relation to a level of quality and cost, referring to the description of individual incentives in the method chapter. This problem is partially people dependant and forms a culture where decision-making is a rematch in discussions. In that context, it can be argued that designers search for the best possible solution while contractors focus on achieving the least possible costs. What we experience can also be based on old behaviours of thinking and acting found in traditional project delivery models where there is mistrust between the different discipline's intentions. The data confirms that the main contractor is reverting in his thinking back to a DB when it comes to the operations on site. The data also shows that the main contractor finds it frustrating not being able to control the designers as they would in a DB model.

A structural feature of the IPD is that the owner gets more leeway to demand work which might be difficult to identify from the participant's point of view as inclusive work or additional work. A representative from the consultant alliance explains the problem as: "*The customer wants something evaluated and then you spend two days, then you show him, and he says; its good but it's too expensive, I do not want it! Now you have lost two days considering alternative solutions, scenarios and materials. You can claim compensation but it's difficult, while in a DB you would demand payment before taking this type of job*".

However, this was not the case from the perspective of a respondent for the owner, who claims that resources are always set aside for calculation of alternative solutions in any form of project delivery model.

Some participants point out in the interviews that the psychiatry building has been a learning arena, and now they know each other, it is the belief that the somatic building will go much better.

Proposition 2

Swapping is a deepening of the collaboration between the actors, which is made possible by the commercial incentives of the IPD model, and the data confirms it took place. However, to make this work it is important that the actors understand the rationale behind IPD. Swapping is an example that the participating organizations have broken down important dividing lines between them and taken the variety of business models and replaced it by one common model addressing optimization of the project.

Proposition 3

IPD has several aspects that are beneficial in safeguarding customer value through the fact that the owner is an equal partner throughout the implementation phase of the project. It requires a professional and proactive owner. The data indicates that the owner's building organization is not very much involved in making design decisions. However, this must be investigated further, as some part of the design work is very important for customer value.

The project is time-compressed regarding the psychiatry building, even though there are no penalties for late delivery, but the contractors and designers choose to go for an aggressive time schedule. An aggressive time schedule may be a risk in relation to enough involvement in the choice of solutions. Lack of penalties also has the potential to be beneficial in obtaining customer value, as carelessness and shortcuts in the end phases of construction projects can be avoided.

A critical activity from the owner's side is to define quality to a reasonable extent when calculating out the cost in order to reduce the extent of change requests, which may be stressful for collaboration when safeguarding customer value.

The data also shows that there was unanimous consensus about the challenging decision-making process which was characterized by many rounds of discussions involving slow and delayed decision making. A representative for the consultants describes it this way: "*We have unclear lines as to who is making decisions, therefore we can we spend a lot of time discussing solutions, then someone else will say, no*". Furthermore, informants for the technical consultants describe joint decision making as: *"we are too many participants in the project meeting to handle details"*. In addition, respondents also gave examples of waste in the process as: "*a decision is made orally; however, it is difficult to follow up because of an unclear organizational structure*". Another example was: *"Normally we go through several rounds to get to the solution with the contractor but once we get the nod, then it's okay. But here there will be a new round afterwards. It's the biggest challenge here I've seen"*. One respondent claimed that in a DB it is often very clear what to deliver: "*either based on function or a half-described product*", however, in IPD *"it is challenging, you do not know where that list is"*.

Another statement, associated with power, addresses that there are: "*different views, many more parties, many people, many who have opinions. It's a flat organization where the strongest party wins, and everyone has their good arguments*". From a theoretical perspective, a flat organization means less hierarchy, and then we can expect less formal power and influence in that structure, however, individuals with a strong will can exert influence on that basis.

6 Conclusions

In the study, we have asked the question of whether IPD is a game-changer when it comes to an alignment of incentives and interests? The short answer is, yes when it comes to ex-post the IPD-contract, and less so the contract ex-ante. We find it important to distinguish between different types of incentives and interests because we find that what we perceive as commercial incentives have changed radically. Perhaps the best example of this practice is the swapping of resources across different budgets to achieve improved buildability and reduced cost. We are generally talking about a common business model for the Tønsberg project, and the alignment of commercial incentives work to some extent.

An exception may be found in the negotiations that occur between the constructors and the owner on the level of quality should be the basis for selecting solutions that support the budgeted target cost, where solutions are not always carefully specified. However, in relation to collaboration, the Tønsberg project exemplifies the potential of IPD as a framework for deeper collaboration in complex construction projects.

The project owner benefits from the IPD model by having a hand also on the steering wheel to ensure his short-term and long-term value-creating interests. In addition, the constructors have a good opportunity in the project to obtain an acceptable and predictable return. The model is also a game-changer when it comes to the distribution of power in the implementation phase compared to traditional DB projects. In the studied IPD-project, the main contractor must share power on equal terms with the owner, the designers and the MEP subcontractors. In addition, IPD gives better possibilities for communication as its commercial incentives encourage dialogue.

We see in the concept (structure) and in the underlying data that there may be a danger that the project owner pushes the designers and constructors too much regarding the economy in the project and with constantly demanding changes that can deteriorate the social environment and erode profits. If the IPD concept should work optimally, the owner must see his responsibility here. The data also shows that individual incentives and opportunistic behaviour play a role in forming mutual distrust between the contractors and the designers. This mistrust is often based on a different mindset and tensions in the trade-off between costs and well-designed technical and architectural solutions.

Based on our data, IPD provides at the least equally strong incentives to develop good constructible solutions which can be found in DB models. There is often a strong focus in the project to stay within, or preferably undergo, the target cost, to secure profits. Here the discussion is focused on the price of components, materials and designs of the simplest possible solutions. However, there is space for opportunistic behaviour from the contractors if quality has not been defined by the owner in the cost estimate. Nevertheless, the owner may choose higher quality solutions than those set out in the cost estimate if he makes more funds available.

Our research shows that the decision-making process was a challenge in the project, and this can be linked to the predominantly flat organisational structure stated by the informants who argue that many more people than usual are required to participate in the decision-making process. This has led to many rounds of discussions, which has particularly stressed the designers who argue that they must go through many more design iterations than they would normally be used to. Moreover, too many decisions have been sent up to the top management team, while the guiding principles state that decisions should be taken at the lowest possible level. The explanation given for these challenges was that mandates given had been unclear.

Like in traditional organized projects late client decisions were an issue and late delivery of drawings, but on the other hand, the designers argued that production started too early. These are issues we can relate to contextual factors. Contextual is also the stress imposed to the organisation that they in addition to the radical new IPD-contract they also had to adapt to new ways of working. Many new lean constructions inspired planning and management methods were introduced, and it was an aim to replace 2D-drawings with BIM and 3D. The reversed scheduling used in the Last Planner System collapsed during the construction of the psychiatry building, and 2D-drawings had to be used.

Furthermore, despite these factors, everyone was in unanimous agreement that productivity would increase in the design and construction of the somatic building. The reasoning for this unanimity was that the psychiatry building is seen as a learning arena, now that the players are familiar with each other and the decision-making process is becoming more efficient.

In relation to the methodology used, the approach in the use of critical realism has been fruitful with its distinction between structures, mechanisms and contexts. As we have stated earlier structures here are specifically the commercial incentives of the IPD. Furthermore, the nuances between different types of incentives are important in explaining and understanding the data collected. Commercial incentives are very important, however, there are also individual incentives and different mindsets that strongly affect the contextual environment.

7 Future research

In future research, there is a need to address IPD as a framework for innovation and learning. Important is also to study more closely the processes of identifying target prices in projects. To improve the validity of this case, research should also acquire more data that address other experiences from subcontractors and user groups. There is also a need for more information from actors who are outside the risk pool. In addition, more data needs to be collected from the survey and focus needs to be on providing an updated data set from the construction of the Somatic building, scheduled to be finished in 2021.

Acknowledgements

Thank you to the contract manager Bjørn Varegg who gave us access to study the Tønsberg project, and to him and all the others at the project from the client, the Cura Group, Skanska and MPE-contractors who openly have shared their experiences and perspectives. Also, thank you to Nye Veier AS who have contributed to financing our costs.

References

1. O.J. Klakegg, Byggenæring og gjennomføringsmodeller - ramme for verdiskapning. In B. T. Kalsaas (Ed.), *Lean construction : forstå og forbedre prosjektbasert produksjon* 417-449, Bergen: Fagbokforlaget (2017)
2. B.T. Kalsaas, G. Hannås, G. Frislie, J. Skaar, Transformation from design-bid-build to design-build contracts in road construction, *Proceedings of IGLC 18* 10 (2018)
3. W.A. Lichtig, Sutter health: Developing a contracting model to support lean project delivery. *Lean construction journal* **2**(1):105-112 (2005)
4. G. Ballard, *Should Project budgets be based on worth or cost.* Paper presented at the International conference of the international group for lean construction (2012)
5. G.A. Howell, *Meeting of DBIA Northern California. A presentation of "where LCI and DBIA agree and where we differ"*. Oakland, CA (2011)
6. U.O.K. Nwajei, C. Bydall, *Integrated project delivery (IPD) in Norwegian construction projects. Sharing of risk and opportunities aiming at better cooperation and project achievement.* (Industrial Economics and Technology Management Masters), University of Agder, Grimstad, Norway (2018)
7. P. Lahdenperä, Making sense of the multi-party contractual arrangements of project partnering, project alliancing and integrated project delivery, *Construction Management and Economics* **30**(1):57-79 (2012).
8. D. Do, G. Ballard, & I. D. Tommelein (2015). An analysis of potential misalignments of commercial incentives in Integrated Project Delivery and Target Value Design. In Proceedings of the 23rd Conference of the International Group for Lean Construction (pp. 277-286)
9. O. Matthews, G.A. Howell, Integrated project delivery an example of relational contracting, *Lean construction journal* **2**(1):46-61 (2005)

10. American Institute of Architects, Integrated Project Delivery – An Updated Working Definition. In AIA National and AIA California Council Sacramento, CA, 18 (2014)
11. R. Ghassemi, B. Becerik-Gerber, Transitioning to Integrated Project Delivery: Potential barriers and lessons learned, *Lean Construction Journal* (2011)
12. G. Ballard, P. Reiser, *The St. Olaf College Fieldhouse Project: A Case Study in Designing to Target Cost, In:, Bertelsen, S. & Formoso, C.T,.* Paper presented at the 12th annual conference of the International Group for Lean construction, Denmark, 3-5 (2004)
13. American Institute of Architects, Integrated Project Delivery: A Guide. In American Institute of Architects National and AIA California Council Sacramento, CA, 62 (2007)
14. A. Sayer, *Method in social science: a realist approach* (2nd ed.). London: Routledge (1992)
15. R.K. Yin, *Case study research:design and methods* (3rd ed.). Thousand Oaks, California: Sage Publications (2003)
16. D.G. Reinertsen, *Managing the design factory: a product developer's toolkit.* New York, USA: Free Press (1997)
17. K.M. Eisenhardt, Agency theory: An assessment and review. Academy of management review 14(1):57-74 (1989)
18. O.E. Williamson, Transaction-cost economics: the governance of contractual relations. The journal of Law and Economics 22(2):233-261 (1979)
19. P. Schauwecker, (2012). Opportunismus im Exportgeschäft [Opportunism in the export business]. München: Oldenbourg.
20. C. Steinle, H. Schiele, T. Ernst, Information asymmetries as antecedents of opportunism in buyer-supplier relationships: Testing principal-agent theory, *Journal of business-to-business marketing* **21**(2):123-140 (2014)
21. E. Anderson, Transaction costs as determinants of opportunism in integrated and independent sales forces, *Journal of Economic Behavior & Organization* **9**(3):247-264 (1988)
22. G. John, An empirical investigation of some antecedents of opportunism in a marketing channel, *Journal of marketing Research* 278-289 (1984)
23. K.H. Wathne, J.B. Heide, Opportunism in interfirm relationships: Forms, outcomes, and solutions, *Journal of marketing* **64**(4):36-51 (2000)
24. C.S. Lai, S.S. Liu, C.F. Yang, H.W. Lin, H.W. Tsai, Governance mechanisms of opportunism: Integrating from transaction cost analysis and relational exchange theory. *台灣管理學刊, 5*(1):1-23 (2005)
25. A. Rindfleisch, J.B. Heide, Transaction cost analysis: Past, present, and future applications. *The Journal of Marketing* 30-54 (1997)
26. O.E. Williamson, *The Economic Institutions of Capitalism: Firms, Markets, and Relational Contracting* (1985)
27. O.E. Williamson, Corporate finance and corporate governance, *The journal of finance* **43**(3):567-591 (1988)
28. M. Bergen, S. Dutta, O.C. Walker Jr, Agency relationships in marketing: A review of the implications and applications of agency and related theories. *The Journal of Marketing* 1-24 (1992)

29. Y. Luo, Opportunism in inter-firm exchanges in emerging markets, *Management and Organization Review* **2**(1):121-147 (2006)
30. S.E. Masten, Equity, opportunism, and the design of contractual relations, *Journal of Institutional and Theoretical Economics (JITE)/Zeitschrift für die gesamte Staatswissenschaft* **144**(1):180-195 (1988)
31. T.J. Muris, Opportunistic behavior and the law of contracts. *Minn. L. Rev.,* **65**:521 (1981)
32. I.R. Macneil, Contracts: adjustment of long-term economic relations under classical, neoclassical, and relational contract law, *Nw. UL Rev.,* **72**:854 (1977)
33. A.R. Aslesen, R. Nordheim, B. Varegg, O. Lædre, *IPD in Norway.* Paper presented at the 26th Annual Conference of the International Group for Lean Construction, Chennai, India (2018)
34. Tønsbergprosjektet, Integrated Project Delivery (IPD)- Presentation of SiV and the Tønsberg project (2017)
35. E.S. Jon Gresseth, *Overview comparison of risk - IPD and NS 8405*. Memorandum (2016)
36. H. Ashcraft, Integrated project delivery: The owner's perspective. *San Francisco: Hanson Bridgett LLP* (2013)

Future Preparedness and Futures Literacy Needs in Large Enterprises: A Regional Pilot Study

Lukasz Nazarko[1*]

[1] Faculty of Engineering Management, Bialystok University of Technology, Wiejska 45A, 15-351 Bialystok, Poland

Abstract. Future preparedness in enterprises is seen as an important factor affecting their performance and long-term survival. Different organisations present various approaches to reflecting on alternative future visions of their businesses. They are also characterised by different styles of translating those reflections into action with the aim of achieving a desirable version of their future. The paper presents the results of research which aimed at exploring how large Polish, mostly industrial, enterprises reflect on their long-term future. It also attempts to answer the question on the need for fostering futures literacy in Polish business milieu. The research fills in the gap in the study of future orientation of the Polish enterprises and it may be a starting point for the more in-depth qualitative and quantitative investigations. The study has been carried out on a sample of large enterprises in Podlaskie Voivodship, Poland.

Keywords: future preparedness, future orientation, foresight, industry, enterprise

1 Introduction

The ability to properly analyse signals and trends has paramount importance for competitiveness and survival of companies. Looking into the long term future of a business (5 years and more) is becoming increasingly difficult as the economic, social, technological and political systems are becoming more complex and dynamic.

This paper present selected results of a study of large enterprises in Podlaskie Voivodship, Poland. The research concerning change management, relations with labour market institutions, organisational culture and future orientation. This work focuses on the last aspect of the research: future orientation and future preparedness of large enterprises in the Podlaskie region.

In this paper, future preparedness is understood as a combination of the following elements:

* Corresponding author: l.nazarko@pb.edu.pl

- Foresight competencies of managers [1-3]
- Foresight maturity of the enterprise [4,5]
- Coherent strategic orientation (often expressed in a form of a document)

The research design aimed at shedding some light of the three above mentioned aspects of future preparedness.

2 Methods and Data

The study covered 34,5% of large companies in Podlaskie Voivodship (29 out of 84) [6]. The questioned entities represented industry (20 enterprises), construction (2 enterprises), transportation (3 enterprises), commerce (2 enterprises) and other sectors (2). The respondents were either owners/CEOs of the enterprises or represented companies' high-level management. 17 of them were men, 12 were women. The age distribution of the respondents is illustrated in Fig. 1.

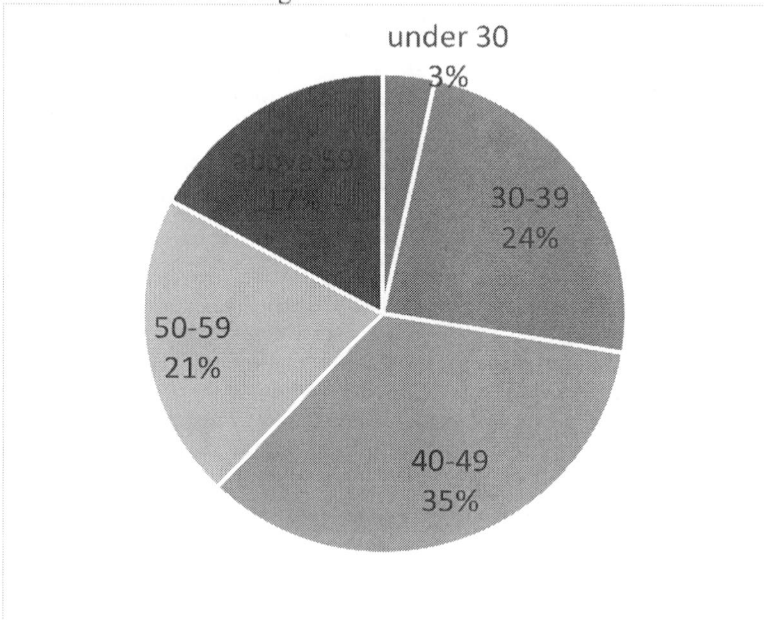

Fig. 1. Age distribution of the respondents.

The research tool consisted of a questionnaire filled in by the respondents. This paper analyses the answers given to the following questions:

1. Does the enterprise have a strategic document? (possible answers: yes; no). If yes, what is its time horizon?
2. Who is responsible for the exploration and understanding of the changes emerging in the enterprise's environment? (possible answers: Chairman/CEO/Board; assigned staff; external entities; other)
3. Has there been an event in the past when an unexpected change had a significant impact on the functioning of the enterprise? (possible answers: yes; rather yes; hard to say; rather no; no)
4. From today's perspective, would that change could have been foreseen? (possible answers: yes; rather yes; hard to say; rather no; no)
5. From today's perspective, was the enterprise able to prepare for that change? (possible answers: yes; rather yes; hard to say; rather no; no)

6. Has there been an event in the past when the enterprise gained an advantage over competitors thanks to a better/faster exploration of the incoming change in the enterprise's environment? (possible answers: yes; rather yes; hard to say; rather no; no)
7. Is there a need in your enterprise to train the employees in the field of exploring the changes emerging in the enterprise's environment and in responding to those changes? (possible answers: yes; rather yes; hard to say; rather no; no)

3 Methods and Data

The first question that probed the enterprise's attitude towards long term future was the question related to the existence (or non-existence) of a formal strategy laid down in an official corporate document. It turned out that 79% of studied companies had such a document. The most common time horizon of those strategies was 5 years (11 cases), the maximum horizon was 10 years (2 cases), the minimum horizon was 1 year.

The second question related to the issue of a foresight culture in the studied enterprise. Its aim was to verify who in the company is engaged forward-looking thinking and in the analysis of the identified trends. Most of the questioned enterprises (79%) pointed at the CEOs and Board of Directors as the sole actors responsible for the exploration and understanding of the changes emerging in the enterprise's environment. In two cases the CEO/Board of Directors were supported in this task by additional staff. In three cases it was only assigned staff that took charge of the future-oriented reflection in the company. None of the respondents used external services (e.g. professional foresight consultants) to support them in improving their future resilience.

Another two questions related to the actual utility of foresight exercises in business. Respondents were asked whether they had encountered unexpected events that had a significant impact on the functioning of their enterprise and, if yes, whether – from today's perspective – would change could have been foreseen and prepared for. The answers to the first part of the question are presented in Fig. 2.

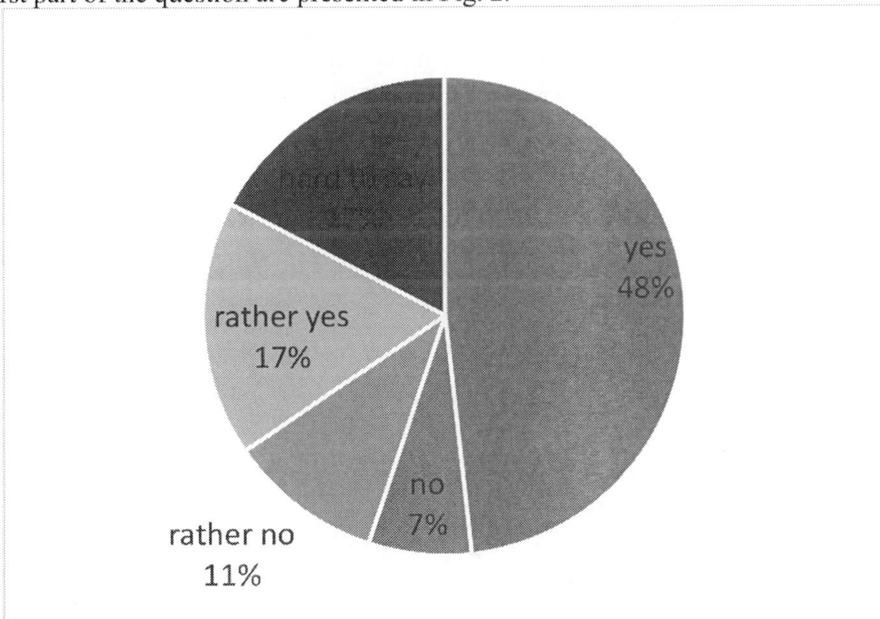

Fig. 2. Answers to the question "Has there been an event in the past when an unexpected change had a significant impact on the functioning of the enterprise?

The answers given to that questions are mixed, however, 65% of company leaders confessed they had indeed been in the past surprised by new developments in the environment of their business. More than a quarter does not have a clear opinion on that matter. 18% of the respondents claim that such events had not occurred.

Among those who feel they had been surprised in the past, some respondents (32 %) claim that the surprising and impactful event could have been anticipated. 42% of the interviewed business leaders claim that nothing could have been done anyway to anticipate the emerging situation. Details of the answers to that question are presented in Fig. 3.

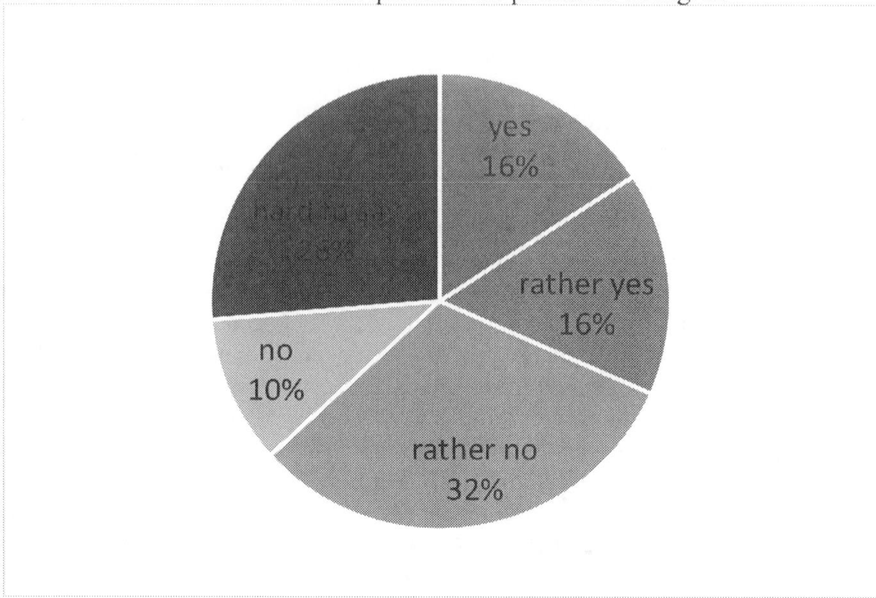

Fig. 3. Answers to question “From today’s perspective, would that change could have been foreseen?”

Another linked question concerned the issue of the future resilience of the enterprises i.e. their ability to prepare and respond to the incoming change. The managers responded to the question whether they felt that their company had been able to prepare for the incoming change had it noticed and understood it early enough. Fig. 4 is an illustration of the respondents' opinion on that.

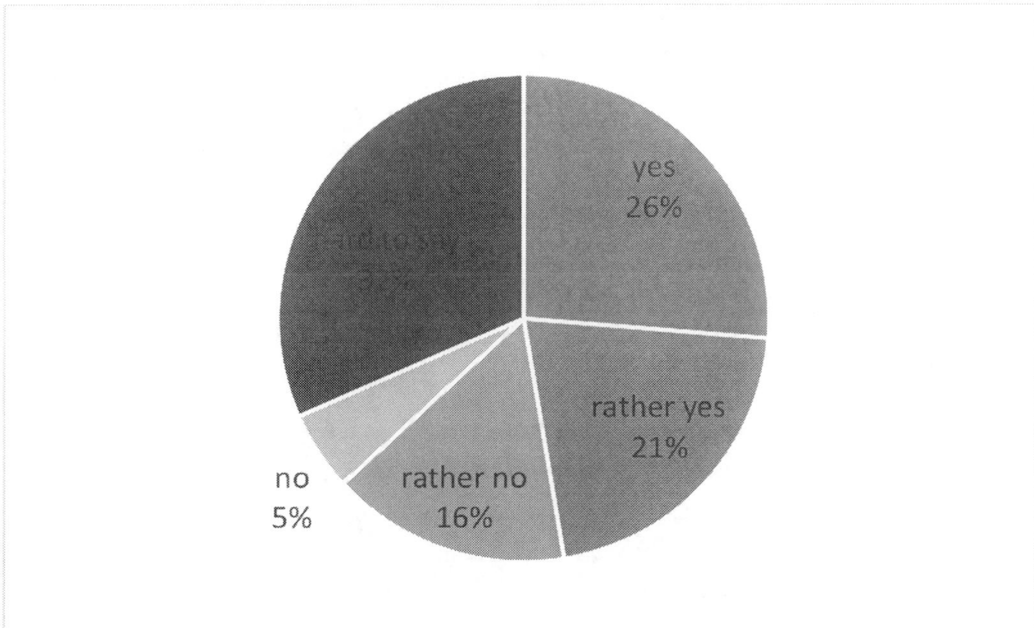

Fig.4. Answers to question "From today's perspective, was the enterprise able to prepare for that change?"

Almost half of the respondents were convinced that their enterprise had been indeed able to do something to prepare for the incoming change. 21% claim there was nothing they could do anyway. One-third of the questioned managers didn't have a clear opinion on that issue.

Next question aimed at verifying enterprises' foresight capabilities against their market success [7-10]. Respondents were asked if there had been an event in the past when the enterprise gained an advantage over competitors thanks to a better/faster exploration of the incoming change in the enterprise's environment. The answers are presented in Fig. 5.

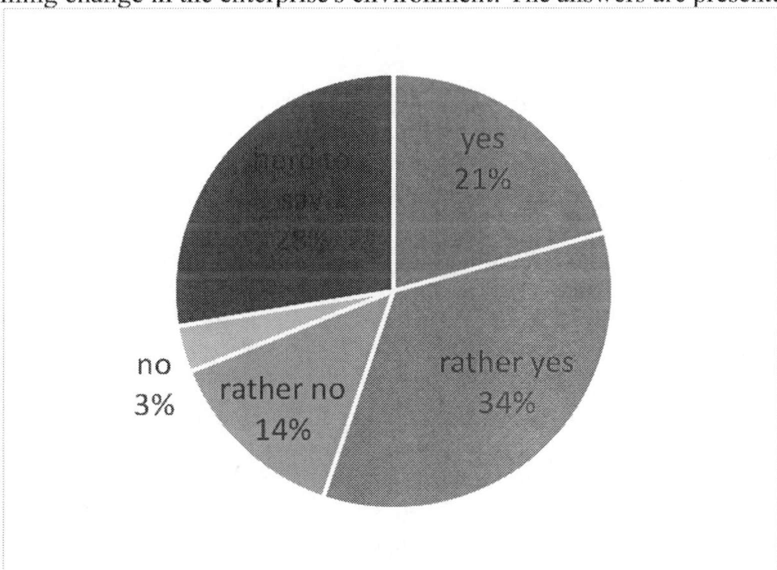

Fig. 5. Answers to the question "Has there been an event in the past when the enterprise gained an advantage over competitors thanks to a better/faster exploration of the incoming change in the enterprise's environment?"

More than half of the respondents believe that better foresight capabilities of their companies gave them a considerable market handicap. Only 17% of the interviewed business leaders don't subscribe to that statement.

In the final question, the issue of developing foresight competencies in the enterprises was raised. The respondents were asked if they saw the need for increasing the knowledge of foresight methodology and practical foresight skills in their companies [11]. The results are presented in Fig. 6.

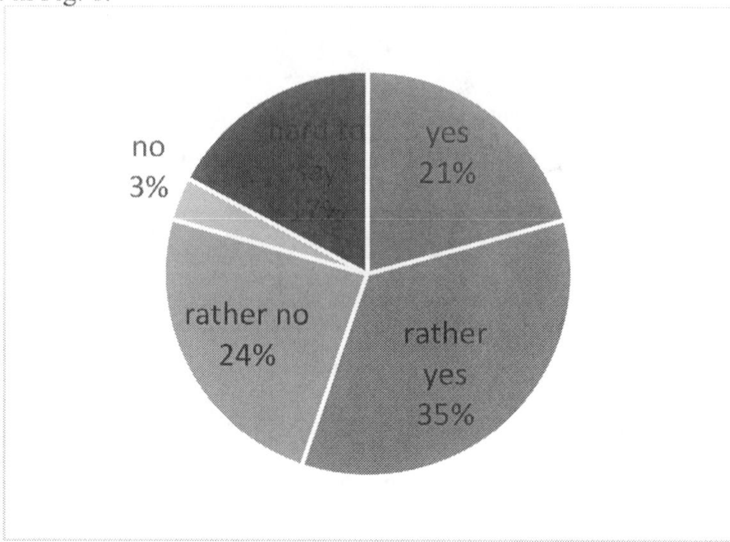

Fig. 6. Answers to question "Is there a need in your enterprise to train the employees in the field of exploring the changes emerging in the enterprise's environment and in responding to those changes?"

Again, more than half of the respondents were keen on engaging their employees in systematic training increasing their futures literacy. About a quarter of the respondents didn't see such needs in their companies.

4 Conclusions

The study covered about one-third of large enterprises in the Podlaskie region, hence its results may be treated as a good indication of prevailing trends in that population. The research allowed to understand better the level of future preparedness of the selected group of companies. The growing body of research [12] suggest the usefulness and effectiveness of foresight tools in the strategic management of companies of different sizes. It seems that the foresight potential is not fully appreciated and utilised among large companies in Podlaskie Voivodship.

Directions of future research are multiple. There is a clear need to map the foresight competencies and needs of enterprises on different levels and in different dimensions. Research on both regional and country-wide scale may shed light on differences between the level of foresight competencies among enterprises located in regions of different socio-economic development levels and different business cultures. That, in turn, could lead to interesting comparative international studies.

References

1. M. Amsteus, Managerial foresight: Measurement scale and estimation, *Foresight* **13**(1): 58–76 (2011)
2. S. Kinkel, B. Schemmann, and R. Lichtner, Critical Competencies for the Innovativeness of Value Creation Champions: Identifying Challenges and Work-integrated Solutions, *Procedia Manufacturing* **9**: 323–330 (2017)
3. A. Kononiuk, A. Sacio-Szymańska, and A. Gáspár, How do companies envisage the future? Functional foresight approaches, *Engineering Management in Production and Services* **9**(4): 21-33 (2017)
4. R. Rohrbeck, Corporate Foresight: Towards a Maturity Model for the Future Orientation of a Firm (Physica-Verlag HD, 2010)
5. Ł. Nazarko, Cele i funkcje badań foresightowych w małych i średnich przedsiębiorstwach, Studia Ekonomiczne. *Zeszyty Naukowe Uniwersytetu Ekonomicznego w Katowicach* **229**: 121-132 (2015)
6. Statistics Poland, http://www.stat.gov.pl
7. R. Rohrbeck, and M.E. Kum, Corporate Foresight and its Impact on Firm Performance: A Longitudinal Analysis, *Technological Forecasting and Social Change* **129**: 105-116 (2018)
8. J. Ejdys, and Ł. Nazarko, Foresight gospodarczy - instrumentem orientacji na przyszłość, *Prace Naukowe Uniwersytetu Ekonomicznego we Wrocławiu* **340**: 651-664 (2014)
9. J. Nazarko, and E. Chodakowska, Measuring productivity of construction industry in Europe with Data Envelopment Analysis, *Procedia Engineering* **122**: 204-212 (2015)
10. J. Nazarko, and E. Chodakowska, Labour Efficiency In Construction Industry In Europe Based On Frontier Methods: Data Envelopment Analysis And Stochastic Frontier Analysis, *Journal Of Civil Engineering And Management* **23**(6): 787-795 (2017)
11. A. Kononiuk, A.E. Gudanowska, and K. Dębkowska, The Application of Cluster Analysis in the Selection of Key Competences of Future-Oriented Entrepreneurs, CID Conference 2019 – International Scientific Conference on Collaborative Innovation Development, Poland, Bialystok, Poland, 10-11 June 2019
12. J. Nazarko, J. Ejdys, K. Halicka, A. Magruk, L. Nazarko, A. Skorek, Application of Enhanced SWOT Analysis in the Future-oriented Public Management of Technology, *Procedia Engineering* **182**: 482-490 (2017)

AUTHOR INDEX

EDP Sciences – Web of Conferences
17, Avenue du Hoggar
Parc d'Activité de Courtabouf
BP 112
F-91944 Les Ulis Cedex A
France

ISBN 978-1-7138-0887-9

9 781713 808879

CURRAN ASSOCIATES INC.
proceedings.com